PROTOCOLS FOR
PERINATAL
NURSING PRACTICE

PROTOCOLS FOR
PERINATAL
NURSING PRACTICE

ROSANNE HARRIGAN PEREZ

R.N., C.P.N.A., Ed.D.

Associate Professor of Nursing and
Chairman, Maternity/Pediatric Nursing,
Indiana University Medical Center, Indianapolis, Indiana

with 105 illustrations

The C. V. Mosby Company

ST. LOUIS • TORONTO • LONDON   1981

A TRADITION OF PUBLISHING EXCELLENCE

Editor: Alison Miller
Manuscript editor: Judi Wolken
Design: Diane Beasley
Production: Jeanne Gulledge

The C.V. Mosby Company
11830 Westline Industrial Drive, St. Louis, Missouri 63141

Library of Congress Cataloging in Publication Data

Main entry under title:

Protocols for perinatal nursing practice.

  Bibliography: p.
  Includes index.
    1. Obstetrical nursing.   2.   Pregnancy, Complications
of.   3.   Infants (Newborn)—Care and hygiene.   4.   Infants
(Newborn)—Diseases—Nursing.   I.   Perez, Rosanne
Harrigan. [DNLM: 1. Obstetrical nursing.   2. Perina-
tology—Nursing texts.   WY 157 P438p]
RG951.P76   610.73′678   80-27539
ISBN 0-8016-3805-4

GW/VH/VH 9 8 7 6 5 4 3 2   01/B/075

Contributors

SHELIA K. ADAMS, R.N., M.S.N.

Doctoral Student, Indiana University School of Nursing, Indianapolis, Indiana

PAULA BIBEAU, R.N., M.S.N.

Obstetrical-Gynecological Nurse Practitioner, Metro Health Plan, Indianapolis, Indiana

PATRICIA J. BLAKE, R.N., M.S.N.

Associate Professor, Indiana University School of Nursing, Indianapolis, Indiana

KATHLEEN BUCHHEIT, R.N., M.S.N.

Midwifery Student, University of South Carolina, Charleston, South Carolina

MARLYS CONNALLON, R.N., M.S.N.

Faculty, DePauw University, Greencastle, Indiana

LORRAINE DAYTON, R.N., M.S.N.

Major, U.S. Army, Former Perinatal Graduate Student, Indiana University School of Nursing, Indianapolis, Indiana

NANCY S. EDWARDS, R.N., M.S.N.

Graduate Student, Indiana University School of Nursing, Indianapolis, Indiana

ELIZABETH GALE, R.N., M.S.N.

Doctoral Student, Indiana University School of Nursing, Indianapolis, Indiana

DIANE IRENE GORGAL, R.N., M.S.N.

Lecturer, Indiana University School of Nursing, Indianapolis, Indiana

BEVERLY KELLER, R.N., M.S.N., C.N.M.

Former Perinatal Graduate Student, Indiana University School of Nursing, Indianapolis, Indiana

PAMELA K. MANUEL LEMONS, R.N., M.S.N.

Instructor, Indiana University School of Nursing, Indianapolis, Indiana

CAROL LEYKAUF, R.N., M.S.N.

Instructor, Indiana University School of Nursing, Indianapolis, Indiana

KATHY MARTIN, R.N., B.S.N.

Neonatal Nurse, James Whitcomb Riley Children's Hospital; Graduate Student, Indiana University School of Nursing, Indianapolis, Indiana

KAY McWHIRTER, R.N., M.S.N.

Perinatal Graduate Student, Indiana University School of Nursing, Indianapolis, Indiana

CAROL MILLAY, R.N., M.S.N.

Newborn Unit Manager, St. Vincent Hospital and Health Care Center, Indianapolis, Indiana

ROSANNE HARRIGAN PEREZ, R.N., C.P.N.A., Ed.D.

Associate Professor of Nursing and Chairman, Maternity/Pediatric Nursing, Indiana University Medical Center, Indianapolis, Indiana

JOY PRICE, R.N., M.S.N.

Former Perinatal Graduate Student, Indiana University School of Nursing, Indianapolis, Indiana

MINERVA RATLIFF, R.N., M.S.N.

Former Perinatal Graduate Student, Indiana University School of Nursing, Indianapolis, Indiana

DELIA BELL ROBINSON, R.N., M.S.N.

Former Perinatal Graduate Student, Indiana University School of Nursing, Indianapolis, Indiana

ANNA SCHMIDT, R.N., Ph.D.

Assistant Professor, Indiana University
School of Nursing, Indianapolis, Indiana

PATTIANN YOST SCHMITT, R.N., M.S.N.

Unit Manager, Parkview Hospital, Ft. Wayne, Indiana

RICHARD L. SCHREINER, M.D.

Associate Professor and Director, Neonatal/Perinatal
Medicine, Indiana University School of Medicine,
Indianapolis, Indiana

**SHERYL CODDINGTON SHIPMAN, R.N.,
C.P.N.A., M.S.N.**

Neonatal Follow-up Clinic, Methodist Hospital,
Indianapolis, Indiana

NAN SMITH, R.N., B.S.N.

Graduate Student, Ohio State University,
Columbus, Ohio

DENNIS C. STEVENS, M.D.

Assistant Professor, Pediatric and Adolescent Medicine,
Section of Neonatal Biology, University of South Dakota
School of Medicine, Vermillion, South Dakota

SUSAN M. TUCKER, R.N., M.S.N.

Assistant Director of Nursing, Kaiser-Permanente
Medical Center Hospital, Panorama City, California

SARA WHEELER, R.N., M.S.N.

Assistant Professor, University of Wyoming
School of Nursing, Laramie, Wyoming

JERRI WILLIAMS, R.N., M.S.N.

Community Health Nurse, Bureau of Community Health
Nursing, Health and Hospital Corporation of
Marion County, Indianapolis, Indiana

Preface

In recent years perinatal nursing has emerged as an area of specialization in nursing practice. Its evolution is rooted in the recognition of common ground between maternity nursing and pediatric nursing. The cause of this conceptual synthesis is the recognition of overlapping interest in nursing care, research, skills, and overall goals.

Conceptually, perinatal patients include the mother-father unit, the fetus, and the newborn infant. To meet the needs of these patients a complexity of skills and facilities is required. At the present time no single book exists containing essential theoretical considerations and guidelines for nursing practice. However, the state of the art is evolving.

This book is the best of the efforts of graduate students in perinatal nursing and their faculty to organize the concepts of two distinct disciplines into a unified whole with concrete direction for nursing practice. Each chapter considers a particular perinatal nursing problem, a review of current literature related to the problem, and a protocol for nursing practice including diagnostic, therapeutic, and educational components. Each component is supported with theoretical rationale.

The protocols evolved from a consideration of available biophysiological, psychosocial, cultural, and ethical-legal data in concert with the findings from a nursing audit of the practice of the art at this time. Direction is provided for the planning of individualized nursing care by the establishment of a framework for nursing action to be adapted by the clinician to a particular situation.

Thus, we believe the book will fill a variety of functions specific to the needs of those professionals involved in perinatal nursing care. To the *perinatal clinician* it offers a scientific basis for the application of the multidisciplined theoretical perspective. To the *student* it offers direction and an opportunity for evaluation of progress. To the *perinatal patient* it offers a structure for the assurance of quality care. Finally, to *nursing* it offers an advanced skill framework for a complex neophyte area of nursing practice.

This book reflects the growth of a discipline—a becoming. Perinatal nursing practice has evolved as a specialized area of study as evidenced by the establishment of a major in perinatal nursing in the master's program at Indiana University in 1979. The contents of this book are the result of this evolutionary process. The concept of protocols to define perinatal nursing practice began as a seed planted in the minds of a group of extraordinarily talented and motivated students. My direction served to nurture and refine the original products of their efforts. All my students are reflected in this work. They are perinatal practitioners, and this is the refinement of their art.

I thank Dr. Frances Cleary, who brought me to perinatal nursing and who allowed me to develop the program. This book would have never been completed without the assistance and commitment of Mrs. Dorothy Pock, who is not only a typist but also an editorial colleague.

My fellow faculty members have contributed essential content in their own areas of expertise. Thus the text reflects the multidisciplinary evolution of a concept. It is a beginning that we all hope to nurture.

Rosanne Harrigan Perez

Contents

PROTOCOLS FOR PERINATAL NURSING PRACTICE

SECTION ONE

INTRODUCTION

Chapter 1

The perinatal nurse

Rosanne Harrigan Perez

During the past two decades, significant advances in perinatal health care services (the care of the pregnant woman and her family, fetus, and newborn) have occurred. Scientific knowledge and technological advances have contributed to the reduction of perinatal mortality rates, especially in relation to the high-risk mother and neonate.

A high-risk pregnancy is one in which the fetus has a significantly increased chance of death, either before or after birth, and/or a greater incidence of later disability. The mother may have a serious health problem, obstetrical disorder, poor social environment, or a biological handicap, all potentially damaging to perinatal health. The progress in perinatal medicine has not only decreased mortality but also is responsible for the remarkable "health quality" of the survivors.[5]

Owing to advanced knowledge and technology, neonatal intensive care units are expanding into perinatal centers that care for high-risk mothers as well as high-risk babies. Dr. Sheldon B. Korones, Professor of Pediatrics, University of Tennessee, College of Medicine, Director of Newborn Care, City of Memphis Hospital, says, "Modern advanced methods for caring for high-risk infants require not only proper facilities and equipment but, most of all, dedicated, well-trained personnel—especially nurses." Responsibility for care of the mother during the perinatal period is believed to be a health team responsibility.[6] The prepared nurse working collaboratively with the physician has an essential role to play in this emerging field of health care.[1]

The concept of perinatal health includes prevention of risk and promotion of health, beginning with the pregnant mother and continuing throughout fetal life to the newborn period and early infancy. This has great implications for intact families and community well-being.

At this time, perinatal intensive care is primarily available at large medical centers. Perinatal health care providers have attempted to regionalize services so that they are available to all consumers who need them.[7] In the spring of 1978, the federal government gave support to the development of a nationwide network of health systems agencies. These guidelines mandate that obstetrical and neonatal intensive care services be planned and implemented on a nationwide basis.[9] This created a new demand for perinatal nurses who are not only skilled clinicians but administrators and educators as well.[3]

Nursing has responded to this newly organized body of medical science by beginning to prepare students and practitioners to function in these practice roles.[8] The related nursing corollaries have just begun to evolve.

The beginning of a multidisciplined approach to the provision of perinatal services was evidenced by the development of short-term continuing educational programs and graduate programs to prepare the perinatal nurse. The graduate program at Indiana University is a collaborative endeavor utilizing the expertise of nutrition, medicine, nursing, education, and psychology. Thiede, in 1975, stated that there was "a need to develop common goals and obtain agreement on the priority in reaching these goals."[10] He felt a colleague relationship was necessary between physicians and nurses but could only result from "a gradual increase in the number of physicians and nurses working together."[10] This approach requires the acquisition of new skills, the merging of knowledge and concepts, and the evolution of new roles.

The protocols presented in this volume include many functions for which special training is needed. It should be noted that this specialized training and demonstration of competence in these areas is a requirement for the practice of these functions. The following guidelines provide a division of perinatal nursing practice into categories of expertise. The perinatal nurse may be qualified to function in all or one of these areas.

I. Nursery
  A. These tasks may be performed by a registered nurse.*
    1. Suction with mucous trap.
    2. Initiate oxygen and adjust concentration.
    3. Initiate blood studies, including complete blood count, hematocrit, bilirubin, blood sugar, electrolytes, and blood gases.
    4. Do Dextrostix when indicated.
    5. Initiate cardiac and respiratory monitoring with mechanical appliances.
    6. Culture drainage.
    7. Bag breathing for infants.
    8. Isolate when appropriate.
  B. These tasks may be performed with additional training.
    1. Initiate peripheral intravenous fluids.
    2. Assess for need of x-ray examinations.
    3. Pass nasogastric tubes and administer feedings.
    4. Start blood and administer intravenous medications as ordered.
    5. Suction endotracheal tubes.
  C. These tasks may be performed with special educational preparation.
    1. Initial physical assessment of the newborn.
    2. Intubation of infants with follow-up x-ray examinations.
    3. Radial blood gas sampling.
    4. Chest tube placement.
    5. Umbilical catheterization.
    6. Suprapubic tap.
    7. Neonatal transport.
    8. Resuscitation.
    9. Manage the care of infants according to written protocols.

II. Intrapartum
  A. These tasks may be performed by a licensed registered nurse.*
    1. Admit and assess the status of labor clients.
      a. Evaluate maternal risk factors (blood pressure, age, and so forth).
      b. Evaluate fetal risk factors (fetal heart rate, gestational age, and so forth).
      c. Vaginal and/or rectal examination.
      d. Nitrazine paper test for ruptured membranes.
      e. Order and draw blood as appropriate.
  B. These tasks may be performed with additional training.
    1. Administer intravenous fluids (insertion of extra catheters and angiocatheters).
    2. Prescribe and administer medications according to protocol of facility.
    3. Assess newborn and resuscitate if necessary.
    4. Order and draw blood as indicated.
  C. These tasks may be performed with special training.
    1. Apply fetal scalp electrodes.
    2. Obtain fetal scalp blood for pH determination.
    3. Administer and monitor oxytocin challenge test.
    4. Monitor oxytocin-induced or augmented labor.
    5. Conduct controlled spontaneous delivery with episiotomy, if indicated, in absence of physician.
    6. Manage third stage of labor, including medications as indicated, in absence of physician.

III. Postpartum
  A. These tasks may be performed by a licensed registered nurse.*
    1. Admit and assess the physiological status of the newly delivered mother. (Assessment is continous from delivery until dismissal.)
    2. Administer ordered therapeutic agents as indicated and utilize physical means to provide comfort.
    3. Plan and organize educational programs for mothers including
      a. Postpartum hygiene.
      b. Care of infant.
      c. Role of parents.
      d. Family planning including methods of contraception.
      e. Discharge planning.

---

*These tasks may be performed by a licensed registered nurse after demonstrated competency.

*These tasks may be performed by a licensed registered nurse after demonstrated competency.

f. Health supervision of both mother and infant.

B. These tasks may be performed with additional training.
  1. Assess clients for pre- and/or postdelivery medical complications; develop appropriate nursing interventions for complications.
  2. Start oxygen.
  3. Start IV fluids.
  4. Administer oxytocin according to protocol of the health agency.
  5. Order type and crossmatch for blood if needed.
  6. Insert oral airway if needed for shock or seizures.

IV. Office
A. These tasks may be performed by a licensed registered nurse.*
  1. Gynecological examinations and treatment.
    a. Initiate pregnancy test.
    b. Obtain gonococcus smear and venereal disease–syphilis test.
    c. Family planning.
      (1) Prescribe contraceptives, according to approved medical protocol, and follow through with prescription.
      (2) Instruct and counsel in the use of jellies, condoms, rhythm methods, and temperature graphs; prescribe oral contraceptives; and insert diaphragm.
    d. Vaginal discharges—inspect and treat according to medical protocol.
    e. Remove abdominal sutures.
    f. Human sexuality counseling according to medical protocol.
  2. Annual examinations.
    a. Perform breast examination and instruct in self-breast examination.
  3. Initiate routine prenatal workup.
    a. Check fetal heart.
    b. Estimate date of confinement.
    c. Determine uterine growth (fundal height).
    d. Order routine laboratory work—complete blood count, blood type and Rh determination, venereal disease–syphilis test, sickle cell determination, and rubella titer.
    4. Routine prenatal workup (until 37 weeks' gestation).
B. These tasks may be performed with reemphasis on training.
  1. Hospital visits.

a. Assist parents to identify growth and development and establish health regime for new family members.
b. Explore various referral agencies as indicated.

C. These tasks may be performed with special training.
  1. Annual examinations.
    a. Pelvic examinations—rectal, vaginal, bimanual.
    b. Obtain Papanicolaou smear test.
    c. Physical assessment.
  2. Gynecological examinations and treatment.
    a. Insert intrauterine devices.
    b. Infertility workup.
      (1) Initial history.
      (2) Counseling.
      (3) Laboratory work as specified by physician.
    c. Cryosurgery and treatment as ordered and follow-ups.
    d. Diagnose and treat herpes and condyloma.
  3. Initiate routine prenatal workup.
    a. Pelvic measurement and assessment.
  4. Six-week postpartum checkup.

DEVELOPMENT OF THE PERINATAL NURSE

Technology and science dominate perinatal care and are considered vital to the achievement of quality outcomes. Still, with technology in place and scientific measures having proved their worth, the results are not satisfactory.

The fault is not necessarily with the technology or the science, per se, but with the fact that these disciplines are not balanced with responsiveness and humanness. Discontent evolves from the conflict between the dichotomy arising from being directed by technology and making decisions to promote patient well-being to meet the needs of the family irrespective of our feelings and attempting to make decisions compatible with our own value systems.

Significant time and energy are spent during the early developmental phase in mastering the requisite content and applying attendant clinical skills. This occurs during the nursing educational program, as well as the first 4 to 6 months of the employment experience in the perinatal health care setting. To master technology, philosophy, emotion, and values are perceived as distractions, and thus they are left to loom on the horizon without consideration.

---

*These tasks may be performed by a licensed registered nurse after demonstrated competency.

Specialization, mechanization, and technical sophistication are essential before one can go beyond this level of interaction and clarify values. During this period, there is a lack of personal nurse-patient interaction. Nurse-machine interaction predominates. Facts are sought as the basis for the direction of practice. Aspirations are not identified. Yet this area of practice is endowed with multiple dilemmas and topics of controversy without solutions, which are acceptable to all segments of society. The direction for practice sought does not exist.

During the second phase of development, an introduction to the ethics of neonatal care should take place, during which standards of behavior necessary to protect the well-being of the patients are discussed. Law relevant to this area of practice must be discussed. Finally, an opportunity should be provided for the nurse to clarify her personal values.

Personal values stem from, but may be inconsistent with, societal values. Every society has multiple, simultaneously interacting, value systems that result in the occurrence of social issues. The perinatal health care setting is a subsystem unto itself and may reflect societal values or be in conflict with them. In large medical centers, as personnel change the value system in the subsystem may change producing an ethical climate for nursing that is without consistency.

Technology can be a utopia that expands human potential or a dystopia that dehumanizes and alienates us from our nature. Its role is dependent on our perception of its place in the care provision system. The first-level employee will allow technology to act as an autonomous force rather than a means. The utopian-dystopian conceptualization is an oversimplification. We must use technology as a means and determine the manner in which it can best influence the achievement of our ends or goals. Yet we must define such ends, or the results are undeniable and in conflict with our nature; we are directed without directing and incapable in influencing our being in process or that of others. Deterministic philosophy would overtake us with its inherent pessimism.

There are three developmental roles nurses can take on in the perinatal care setting. These roles occur in a sequential progression and are essential to nurses' growth and well-being. All have philosophical and emotional conditions that require further study and recognition by leadership personnel as well as colleagues in other developmental phases. They are (1) technician, (2) surrogate parent, and (3) contracted clinician.

The technician

During the technician phase, the perinatal nurse is acquiring the skills necessary to provide both the diagnostic and therapeutic aspects of perinatal care. In recent years, the technological advances in these areas have provided not only the need for extensive orientation programs where these skills can be learned but also the need for intermittent in-service programs where new skills can be learned and existing skills can be refined. Thus one must not only achieve the developmental tasks associated with this stage but continue to work through these tasks again at later stages of development. The majority of technical skills must be acquired early in the intensive care setting. The major thrust then of this developmental phase is the acquisition of technical competency.

Initially, the nurse is consumed by learning procedures and acquiring knowledge regarding monitoring equipment and assessment techniques. Practice is dictated by the competencies of the machines that must be mastered in order to practice safely and effectively. Once these basic skills have been incorporated into practice, they can begin to be adapted to meet the individual needs of patients. These skills are not learned in the basic nursing program be it an associate of science, diploma, or bachelor's program. As one begins to adapt these skills to the individual needs of patients and in essence determine the capabilities of the machine, the developmental tasks associated with this stage have been accomplished. A great deal of learning has taken place, new competencies have been acquired, and the nurse is ready to confront another developmental task.

The surrogate parent

During the surrogate parent stage, the perinatal nurse is acquiring the skills necessary to plan and provide individualized patient care. Progression through this stage is essential, yet problematic. In this stage of development the nurses' orientation is to the individual patient. The ability to deal effectively with families and other members of the health care team is limited. Nurses believe that their values and knowledge are the correct standard of practice in this stage because the focus on one's own position difficulties is experienced in integrating the needs and values of others into the patient care plan. Nurses tend to tell parents, other nurses, physicians, and other members of the health care team what to do. Little time is spent identifying the values of others, mutually planning, and collaboratively acting. In fact, during this stage these actions may indeed be beyond the scope of practice expected of the perinatal nurse. There are some similarities between this stage and Erickson's stage of autonomy vs shame and doubt. Nurses need to develop a sense of autonomy. They essentially do this by taking on the parent role and acting out their perceived rights and responsibilities vested therein.

The phenomenon of burnout occurs in this stage because frequently expectations of the practitioner are unrealistic, and inadequate supports are provided. Leadership personnel must recognize the unique needs of this level practitioner and provide appropriate staff development programs, including experiential learning experiences in developing human potentials and values clarification. Since conflicts frequently arise during this period, negativism can flourish; if unrealistic expectations exist, nurses tend to leave the perinatal health care setting before completing the last stage of the growth and developmental process.

The contracted clinician

The last developmental stage is that of contracted clinician. In this stage the nurses have not only evolved a knowledge of self and identified their own values, but they have also evolved the expertise to identify the value systems of others. They can develop care plans that reflect input from consumers as well as health care providers on the multidisciplinary team. In fact, this is the first time they can really interact as members of a team, where roles are assigned based on patient needs and provider competencies rather than stereotypes. In addition, the nurse is comfortable communicating limitations. This clinician can clearly define what the health care consumer values, wants, and is willing to pay for. There is a sharing of belief systems but no need to

impose. Collaborative relationships with other health care providers occur, and patient care can be optimal. This is also the stage where nursing research questions arise and practical theoretical frameworks can evolve. It is a stage of development we need to await patiently. Expecting its occurrence too early in the developmental progression leads to frustration by both staff and leadership personnel.

Each of these developmental stages requires specific educational programs. We should not expect philosophy to be meaningful to the technician or skills to interest the surrogate parent. Nurses are adult learners whose developmental stage will determine the content they believe essential to meaningfully carrying out their practice. Each group requires a different supervisory approach and educational programs. Each should have a different role in delivery of care. This whole topic demands further systematic study and provokes many questions regarding the primary nursing model frequently utilized in the perinatal setting, which requires a similar level of development from each primary nurse. The following is a description of high-risk perinatal nursing practice according to the ANA Council of High-Risk Perinatal Nurses*:

Scope of practice

High-risk perinatal nursing practice includes, but is not limited to, the following:

1. *Assessment.* Assessing the psychosocial and physiological status of the high-risk child-bearing family by differentiating levels of perinatal risk; by initiating and utilizing multiple sources and assessment tools for data collection, such as histories, physical examinations, and appropriate laboratory data; and by interpreting data that leads to nursing diagnoses.

2. *Plan of care.* Establishing an appropriate plan of intervention with the high-risk perinatal family based on nursing diagnoses by collaborating with the family and other health care providers; by differentiating immediate and long-term health care goals with the family; and by determining and coordinating the plan of action to meet these identified goals.

3. *Intervention.* Implementing the interventions with the high-risk perinatal family that are based on the plan of care including initiating technical procedures and therapeutic regimes; maintaining a thera-

---

*Reprinted with permission of the ANA.

peutic environment; intervening in life-threatening situations; teaching, counseling, and facilitating family development; preventing further complications; and promoting optimum health development of the high risk perinatal family.

4. *Evaluation.* Evaluating the plan of care of the high-risk perinatal family by evaluating the interventions; evaluating the effects of the interventions on the family; evaluating the family's progress toward the identified goals; and initiating changes in the plan of care based on new data and resources and on the environment.

Comprehensive high-risk perinatal nursing care is provided in the interdependent clinical practice areas of maternal-fetal care and maternal-neonatal care.

Nursing practice in the high-risk maternal-fetal area is primarily focused on restorative care for the maternal-fetal unit, with the goal of improving the outcome for the high-risk childbearing family. This care is integrated into the continuum of care needed by the high-risk childbearing family and is extended into the maternal-neonatal areas.

Nursing practice in the high-risk maternal-neonatal area is primarily focused on either restorative care for the mother who becomes or remains at high risk after the birth of the infant, or restorative care for the neonate born with threats to his or her immediate or long-term transition and adaptation to extra-uterine life. Nursing practice within the maternal-neonatal area is a continuation of care initiated during maternal-fetal care and includes supportive care for the family during the fourth trimester, with the goal of facilitating neonatal development and family integration.

The maternal-fetal and maternal-neonatal areas in high-risk perinatal nursing practice are not discrete; they comprise a dynamic system of care throughout the continuum of childbearing events.

Professional responsibilities

In addition to the obligations common to all nurses, the obligations of nurses practicing in the high-risk perinatal area include:

1. Maintaining their knowledge and skills in order to practice according to the standards of practice established by ANA;
2. Establishing and maintaining current practice through evaluation, education, and research;
3. Assuming accountability and responsibility to the high-risk perinatal family for nursing practice and continuity of care;
4. Initiating and participating in interdisciplinary collaboration;
5. Identifying those factors that interfere with the effective practice of nursing and implementing strategies for change;
6. Participating in the recognition of professional achievement in high-risk perinatal nursing;
7. Promoting awareness of and participating in the initiation of necessary legislative changes at local, state, and national levels that affect the high-risk perinatal population;
8. Serving professional and consumer groups as a resource for high-risk perinatal nursing practice.[2]

Today nursing is changing with, as well as promoting, changes in societal health. Perinatal care providers are in a unique position in this regard since the care they provide has a significant perinatal nursing impact on the beginning family. Roles will continue to evolve; may we be flexible, systematic, and cogent in making our practice decisions along the way.

REFERENCES

1. Aladjem, S., and Brown, A.: Perinatal intensive care, St. Louis, 1977, The C. V. Mosby Co.
2. American Nurses' Association: A statement on the scope of high risk perinatal nursing practice, Kansas City, 1980, The Association.
3. Behrman, R. E., editor: Neonatal-perinatal medicine, ed. 2. St. Louis, 1977, The C. V. Mosby Co.
4. Butnarescu, G. F.: Perinatal nursing, vol. 1, New York, 1978, John Wiley & Sons, Inc.
5. Butnarescu, G. F., Tillotson, D. M., and Villarreal, P. P.: Perinatal nursing. Vol. 2: Reproductive risk, New York, 1980, John Wiley & Sons, Inc.
6. Erikson, M. L.: Assessment and management of development changes in children, St. Louis, 1976, The C. V. Mosby Co.
7. Perez, R., and Burks, R.: Transporting high risk infants, J. Emerg. Nurs. July/August, p. 14, 1978.
8. Telega, D. H.: Certification in maternal/gynecological/neonatal nursing, J. Obstet. Gynecol. Nurse 7(5):29, 1978.
9. The Robert Wood Johnson Foundation: Regionalized perinatal services, Special Report, No. 2, 1978.
10. Thiede, H. A.: The collaborative roles of the physician and nurse in obstetrical practice, J. Obstet. Gynecol. Nurse 4(6):40, 1975.

Chapter 2

Quality assurance

Anna Schmidt

Quality assurance, as a means for monitoring and improving nursing care, has been receiving increasing attention since the 1972 amendment to the Social Security Act mandated Professional Standards Review Organizations (PSRO's). With the passage of this legislation, there began an era of consumer awareness and involvement in health care, increased governmental control of health care, and an even greater concern of professionals for the need to systematically assess and improve health care.

Although not specifically mandated by law to do so, nurses took it upon themselves, as professionals, to develop standards of practice, implement systems of peer review, and devise means to continually evaluate nursing care and its benefits to the patient. In 1973 the American Nurses' Association (ANA) published the *ANA Standards of Practice*[1] in an effort to provide a framework for assuring quality care. Specialty standards soon followed to provide practice guidelines for the many specialty areas. Lang's[9] quality assurance model was adopted by the ANA as the organization's official model for quality assurance. The ANA sought and received a federal grant to develop and test model sets of criteria for populations for which PSRO's were responsible.[2] All these activities combined to truly launch nurses full scale into the world of quality assurance. The literature abounds with articles addressing quality assurance from every angle, and many national meetings and workshops have been held to discuss nurses' involvement in quality assurance activities.

Perinatal nurses, like many other specialty groups, have also become more active in quality assurance in the past several years. For example, the March of Dimes Birth Defects Foundation[8] recently sponsored a national perinatal conference to address, among other topics, quality assurance in perinatal outreach programs. A similar workshop was held in the spring of 1980. The March of Dimes Birth Defects Foundation has, over the past few years, developed, tested, and marketed self-instructional modules, some of which have dealt with the high-risk mother and baby. These modules are to be used for educational purposes by nursing staff who, as a result of their quality assurance programs or other assessments, need to update knowledge or skills. Improvement through staff education is also a part of quality assurance. The Arizona State Nurses' Association[4] has published a set of perinatal nursing standards that may well lead the way to adoption of a set of national perinatal specialty standards to serve as a model for perinatal nursing practice. These are but a few of the quality assurance activities in which nurses have been involved since the early 1970's.

PURPOSE

The purposes of this chapter are twofold: (1) to impress on the reader the need for continuing and expanding the kinds of activities just mentioned and (2) to demonstrate the interrelationship among a quality assurance model, perinatal nursing protocols, and techniques for development of criteria. At the conclusion of this chapter, the reader should be cognizant of the way in which the nurse can use the ANA model in a perinatal setting and how that model incorporates standards, criteria, and audit to improve nursing practice. In fact, the ANA model is itself a protocol for quality assurance.

THE ANA MODEL

The ANA model has been chosen for use in this chapter for several reasons (Fig. 2-1). First, this model has been adopted by the ANA as its official quality assurance model. Second, the ANA model is familiar to most nurses and should not require detailed explanation. Third, the ANA model is based on the assumptions that a scientific knowledge base for nursing practice is necessary, that criteria should be based on standards of practice to assure quality care, and that continued evaluation of care is essential for good practice.[2] Last, the ANA model for quality assurance is predicated on the concept of peer review, which is consistent with the PSRO legislation and with the Arizona State Nurses' Association's perinatal standards. One should note that, although the ANA model will be used for demonstrative purposes, the ideas and methodology for criteria development presented here are equally applicable to the Joint Commission on the Accreditation of Hospitals[12] audit procedure.

The steps in the ANA model are as follows. Initially, values must be identified and articulated. These values include personal values, professional values, values of other health team members, values of the patient, and societal values. Values guide professional practice both directly and indirectly. They dictate how we as nurses allocate our time, and they direct the allocation of funds as well. In a statement that accompanies the Arizona perinatal standards, several values are stated. These include accountability for professional practice, self- and peer evaluation, continued professional growth through education, modification of practice to meet patients' needs, and excellence of practice. These values are, in part, the impetus for the development of the perinatal standards.

On perusing the Arizona standards on the opposite page it is most evident that the standards do indeed reflect the values that were presented in the preceding paragraph. Standard I states that "Perinatal nursing practice is characterized by the continual questioning of the assumptions upon which practice is based, retaining those which are valid and searching for and using new knowledge." The assessment factors further explicate those values. Standards II through VI reflect the constant concern for use of a sound knowledge base, continual evaluation of practice, and collaboration with others for the best possible health care.

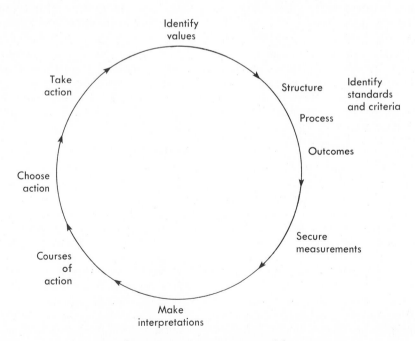

Fig. 2-1. Quality assurance model.

ARIZONA STATE NURSES' ASSOCIATION *PERINATAL NURSING STANDARDS**

STANDARD I

Perinatal nursing practice is characterized by the continual questioning of the assumptions upon which practice is based, retaining those which are valid and searching for and using new knowledge.

Assessment factors

Therefore, in practice, the perinatal nurse:
1. Assumes the responsibility for maintaining competence in practice through continuing education courses, professional journals, regional resources, peer collaboration, and research.
2. Utilizes basic knowledge and principles while continuously expanding and improving nursing practice by utilizing new theories, knowledges, research skills and techniques developed in perinatology and perinatal nursing.
3. Evaluates practice and makes changes as needed.
4. Shares experience, new knowledge and approaches to patient care with colleagues and others in the community.

STANDARD IV

The plan of nursing care includes priorities and the prescribed nursing approaches or measures to achieve the goals derived from the nursing diagnoses.

Assessment factors

Therefore, in practice, the perinatal nurse:
1. Initiates nursing measures specific to the maternal-fetal or medical/obstetrical problem
    1.1 Plans and provides physical support measures to manage, prevent or control maternal disease
    1.2 Performs medical antepartum maternal-fetal evaluation procedures that are delegated nursing responsibility at that facility
    1.3 Assesses need for fetal monitoring and recommends use and/or initiates fetal monitoring
    1.4 Initiates appropriate treatment when abnormal fetal heart rate–uterine contraction (FHR-US) patterns are identified
    1.5 Intervenes to initiate treatment of maternal obstetrical or medical emergencies in the antepartum or intrapartum period
2. Initiates nursing measures in the postpartum period
    2.1 Continues assessment and nursing intervention of previously identified or potential medical/obstetrical problem
3. Initiates nursing measures specific to the neonatal problem
    3.1 Assists in resuscitation and stabilization of the neonate
    3.2 Evaluates need for and performs laboratory screening procedures
    3.3 Evaluates need for and performs such technical procedures necessary in the care of the sick neonate
    3.4 Continuously incorporates principles of thermal regulation in providing care of the neonate
    3.5 Initiates emergency treatment as indicated

*From Arizona State Nurses' Association: Perinatal nursing standards, Phoenix, 1977, Arizona State Nurses' Association.

Continued.

ARIZONA STATE NURSES' ASSOCIATION
PERINATAL NURSING STANDARDS—cont'd

STANDARD IV—cont'd

Assessment factors—cont'd

4. Provides for mother/family participation in planning nursing care of mother or sick neonate
    4.1 Incorporates appropriate explanations and health education into the care of the high risk mother and family
        4.11 Helps the mother/family in recognizing and understanding current health status
        4.12 Keeps the mother/family informed about
            4.121 Current health status
            4.122 Changes in health status
            4.123 Total health care plan
            4.124 Nursing care plan
            4.125 Roles of health care personnel
            4.126 Health care resources
    4.2 Provides mother/family with the information needed to make decisions and choices about health care services
        4.21 Establishes health goals with mother/family in order to maximize physical and functional capabilities
        4.22 Works with mother/family in initiating changes in delivery of health services and/or initiating or developing new services
    4.3 Intervenes to assist the mother/family to solve their concurrent problems
    4.4 Intervenes to assist in meeting the special emotional needs of the high risk mother and her family
        4.41 Assists the high risk mother/family in mobilizing strengths in order to meet the demands of stress
        4.42 Establishes a relationship with the high risk mother/family directed toward helping the mother/family develop and utilize strengths
        4.43 Conveys an attitude of acceptance, understanding and concern with recognition for worth of the individual
        4.44 Gives support through
            4.441 Attentive and responsive listening
            4.442 Realistic reassurances
            4.443 Anticipatory guidance
        4.45 Assists the mother/parent to establish a positive relationship with the neonate which is conducive to an optimal parent and child relationship
        4.46 Helps mother/family to identify future problems and use problem solving techniques
5. Collaborates with other health professionals in planning care for mother/neonate/family
    5.1 Interprets patient needs to other health professionals
    5.2 Coordinates care and initiates referrals of mother/family/newborn to other health professionals
        5.21 Utilizes local and regional resources and services which can best identify needs
        5.22 Gives sufficient information to referring agency
6. Works with other health personnel to develop comprehensive health care services
    6.1 Interprets nursing needs to patients and other health professionals
    6.2 Modifies health care to reconcile health care regime with cultural variations

ARIZONA STATE NURSES' ASSOCIATION
PERINATAL NURSING STANDARDS—cont'd

STANDARD V

The plan of nursing care contains a nursing history. The care plan expresses assessment of the patient/family, defines health care goals and nursing actions. This process is recorded, communicated and accessible.

Assessment factors

Therefore, in practice, the perinatal nurse:
1. Initiates a permanent and retrievable nursing care record which is continuously revised
   1.1 The record is available throughout the patients' experience in the health care system
2. Records systematically a history, assessment, interpretation, plan, intervention and evaluation
3. Develops a maternal nursing care plan to include
   3.1 Data on the physical, emotional, cultural and socio-economic status of mother/family
   3.2 Data from maternal-fetal studies
   3.3 Defined therapeutic medical/nursing/social care goals for mother/fetus/family
   3.4 Proposed nursing actions for meeting health care needs and goals
       3.41 Teaching, explanations and supportive measures
       3.42 Definitions of roles of health care team members
       3.43 Collaboration with health care team members
       3.44 Referrals to other health care personnel and resources
   3.5 Reassessments and revisions of health care priorities for mother/fetus, mother/infant and family
   3.6 Nursing actions taken to assist mother/fetus, mother/infant and family
   3.7 Evaluation of effectiveness of nursing actions
   3.8 Transfer or discharge summary
       3.81 Summary of pregnancy, childbirth and postpartum experience
       3.82 Summary of nursing interventions
       3.83 Referrals and communication to other health care personnel
       3.84 Interconceptive counseling
       3.85 Immediate and long term plans for follow-up care
4. Develops a neonatal nursing care plan to include
   4.1 Summary of maternal high risk factors and mother's pregnancy experience
   4.2 Emotional, psychological, cultural and socio-economic status of the parents
   4.3 Data on the physical status of the neonate
   4.4 Defined therapeutic medical/nursing/social care goals for neonate and family
   4.5 Proposed nursing actions for meeting health care needs and goals
       4.51 Parental teaching and supportive measures
       4.52 Roles of health team members
       4.53 Referrals to other health care personnel and resources
   4.6 Reassessments and revisions of health care priorities and goals for neonate and family
   4.7 Nursing actions taken to assist neonate and family
   4.8 Evaluation of effectiveness of nursing actions
   4.9 Transfer or discharge summary
       4.91 Assessment of the family's ability to care for the infant at home
       4.92 Summary of nursing interventions
       4.93 Referrals and communication to other health care personnel
       4.94 Immediate and long term plans for follow-up health care

These values, in conjunction with the available scientific data, are then used in the next step of the quality assurance process—that of development or adoption of standards and criteria. As stated previously, it is obvious that the Arizona nurses clearly articulated their values and beliefs prior to generating the perinatal standards. The perinatal standards, consistent with the ANA[2] definition of standard, are statements of excellence, "something used by general agreement to determine whether a thing is as it should be." This definition of the term "standard" is different than the JCAH definition of standard. JCAH[12] operationalizes the term "standard" by indicating 100% or 0% for each criterion. This tells the reader whether a criterion is to be met by all patients (100%) or by no patients (0%), as in the case of complication criteria. The standards represent that to which we strive in professional practice. Standards may be developed locally by each institution, or the agency may choose to adopt standards that have already been developed elsewhere.

Measurable standards

The standards themselves are not measurable. One cannot measure the actual care provided and determine whether a standard has been met. This leads one to the next component of this step in the quality assurance model, the development of criteria. Criteria are the measurable statements against which actual care is compared.[2] Criteria represent the link between standards and actual patient care. By determining whether criteria have been met, one can indirectly determine whether the standard itself has also been met. However, one should note that this is only true when criteria are developed from standards. Without such a close association between standard and criteria, one would never be certain whether the standard, or level of excellence, had been met.

There are three types of criteria that have been identified and are commonly used to evaluate care. These are structure, process, and outcome.[7] Only process and outcome—the nursing intervention and the measurable change in the patient, respectively— will be addressed here. Both process and outcome criteria may be used to conduct a nursing audit.

The *Perinatal Nursing Standards* developed by the Arizona State Nurses' Association[4] provide the kind of framework that should be used when developing criteria for a nursing audit. As stated in Deets and Schmidt,[5] use of such a framework eliminates or reduces several common problems. Criteria that are developed are more likely to reflect all facets of the care that is provided. Therefore, no component is overlooked. Agencies that adopt standards that have already been developed need not expend their resources to create new standards and can put that effort into criteria development, audit, and other phases of their quality assurance programs. In addition, should a multitude of agencies adopt the same standards, these standards are more likely to be scrutinized and updated in accordance with scientific and technological advances. Such standardization of care would be helpful in comparing care among agencies and across various parts of the country in an effort to determine whether regional differences exist.

This attitude is supported by the Arizona standards as expressed in standard I, which states that "Perinatal nursing practice is characterized by the continual questioning of the assumptions upon which practice is based, retaining those which are valid and searching for and using new knowledge."[4] These standards will be used to demonstrate the development of both process and outcome criteria.

The strategy that is followed in criteria development is that which was generated by Deets and Schmidt[5] for development of process and outcome criteria based on standards. Although not addressed in detail here, the sample criteria presented were also developed using guidelines for writing measurable criteria.[10]

Assessment factors and process criteria

The development of process criteria will be addressed first. The Arizona standards, like those developed by ANA, are process oriented; they are geared to the nursing interventions that are a part of the nursing process. Process criteria, as stated previously, are simply measurable statements of nursing interventions. They are equivalent to a nursing protocol in that both are a series of statements that, when followed, are indicative of good nursing care. A set of process criteria developed for a specific patient population could be said to constitute a nursing protocol. Process criteria, or the nursing protocol, should be based on standards of practice and scientific data.

Table 2-1. Standard and assessment factors (Perinatal Standard IV: The plan of nursing care includes priorities and the prescribed nursing approaches or measures to achieve the goals derived from the nursing diagnoses.)*

Assessment factors	Process criteria
1. Initiates nursing measures specific to the maternal-fetal or medical/obstetrical problem	
1.1 Plans and provides physical support measures to manage, prevent, or control maternal disease	The mother's physical status is assessed at each clinic visit
1.2 Performs medical antepartum maternal-fetal evaluation procedures that are delegated nursing responsibility at that facility	Amniotic fluid is checked for meconium staining
4. Provides for mother/family participation in planning nursing care of mother or sick neonate	
4.11 Helps the mother/family in recognizing and understanding current health status	The nurse explains to the mother why the mother is considered high risk
4.12 Keeps the mother/family informed about	The mother is kept informed about all aspects of her care
4.121 Current health status	
4.122 Changes in health status	
4.123 Total health care plan	
4.124 Nursing care plan	
4.125 Roles of health care personnel	
4.126 Health care resources	

*From Arizona State Nurses' Association: Perinatal nursing standards, Phoenix, 1977, Arizona State Nurses' Association.

Each standard contains at least one component of the nursing process. For example, standard IV states that "The plan of nursing care includes priorities and the prescribed nursing approaches or measures to achieve the goals derived from the nursing diagnosis"[4] (Table 2-1). The ideas contained in standard IV are that nursing measures are identified and prioritized in accordance with the nursing goals and diagnoses. The assessment factors for this standard provide content that can then be used to develop process criteria. Assessment factor 1.1 states that the nurse must intervene to manage, prevent, or control maternal disease. This assessment factor can be translated into a measurable process criterion by identifying specific nursing actions that, if enacted, would meet assessment factor 1.1 of standard IV. Not only would the resulting process criterion, "The mother's physical status is assessed at each clinic visit," be appropriate for the majority of clients in a prenatal clinic, but with slight rewording the criterion could also be adopted for use in a physician's office or a home health setting. Sharing of criteria among agencies or individuals decreases the time required for criteria development and may actually stimulate new ideas for better criteria.

Assessment factor 1.2 directs the nurse to the necessary evaluation procedures for both mother and fetus. It should be noted that this assessment factor is qualified by the phrase "that are delegated nursing responsibility at that facility." Only those activities that are nursing responsibilities should be included as audit criteria. This requires the nurse to differentiate among those activities that are considered a medical responsibility, a nursing responsibility, or a responsibility of some other department. As stated in "Responsibility for Audit Criteria,"[11] this can generally be accomplished by a review of the institution's policies and the state practice acts. The sample process criterion developed for this assessment factor, "Amniotic fluid is checked for meconium staining," would most likely be a nursing responsibility in the majority of hospitals.

Many assessment factors are related to the educational and psychosocial needs of the client. For example, factor 4.11, "Helps the mother/family in recognizing and understanding current health status," results in the following process criterion: "The nurse explains to the mother why the mother is considered high risk." A second criterion might be written to include family members as well.

In some instances an assessment factor may include multiple concerns such as in assessment factor 4.12, which states that the mother/family should be kept current on all aspects of care. It may not be necessary to write individual process criteria for each subsection. Rather a more general criterion may suffice. For example, ''The mother is kept informed about all aspects of her care'' summarizes the main concern. If it would be desirable to write a set of comprehensive criteria, including all possible interventions, one might choose to write a criterion for each subsection.

The process criteria should be developed in light of the resources that are available for meeting those criteria. For the perinatal nurse who is employed in a rural area with few resources it may be unrealistic to expect a process criterion that states, ''Initiates contact with a home health service for postpartum visits.'' In the absence of such support services, it may be far more realistic to develop a criterion that states, ''Assists the mother in identifying a resource person to telephone for problems postdischarge.''

The process criteria that have been developed from the assessment factors of the Arizona State Nurses' Association standards reflect the diagnostic and therapeutic portions of what is commonly called a protocol. The educational component of the protocol results in process criteria whose content reflects the patient's educational needs. These criteria would be developed in the same manner as the diagnostic and therapeutic criteria. The educational component of the protocol that relates to the educational needs of the staff will be addressed later in this chapter as a separate component of the quality assurance process.

The process criteria that are developed for use as a protocol and in the nursing audit can be used to create outcome criteria to measure the effectiveness of the nursing intervention. Deets and Schmidt[6] presented a plan for doing just that—developing outcome criteria based on standards with the process criteria serving as an intermediary. Outcome criteria are also an integral part of nursing audit, and thus quality assurance. The primary rationale for use of outcome criteria is that nurses seem more likely to agree on the desired results of care than on which intervention is most likely to produce those results. In addition, there are often no data to support that one intervention is better than another.

Using Deets and Schmidt's[6] methodology, the first step in developing outcome criteria is the generation of process criteria from the standard's assessment factors (Table 2-2). Standard V is used to demonstrate. Assessment factor 3.7 indicates that the effectiveness of nursing actions relative to the maternal care plan must be evaluated. First, a process criterion is generated. That criterion is then used to identify ways in which the patient (in this case mother or family members) participates as the nurse is intervening. The process criterion, ''The nurse validates the patient's knowledge of care of the newborn,'' results in several ways in which the patient may participate while this process criterion is being met by the nurse. For example, the patient may give feedback to the nurse on her teaching, request additional information on the subject being taught, or ask questions as the nurse presents the content. One must then take these behaviors, determine which are most appropriate, and translate those selected into measurable outcome criteria. The following outcome criteria would most likely be appropriate outcomes for many target populations and represent measures of the effectiveness of the nurse's actions. The patient ''correctly demonstrates formula preparation''; the patient ''correctly demonstrates weighing the newborn''; the patient ''states in her own words why the infant was considered high risk'' are all criteria that come from the patient's participation in the nursing process. Additional examples of the methodology for development of outcome criteria are also presented in Table 2-2.

The securing of measures is the third phase of the ANA quality assurance model. One way in which one can secure measures of actual nursing practice is to conduct a nursing audit. There are two types of nursing audit, concurrent and retrospective. The concurrent audit is a review of patient records while the patient is still receiving care and the records are still open. A retrospective audit is one in which the records are closed and the patient has been discharged from the health care system. Although there are other means of securing measures, such as direct observation and patient interviews, the audit has proved to be the most commonly used method. The primary advantage of the audit technique is that records are generally accessible and record reviews are less expensive than other techniques of data col-

Table 2-2. Standard and assessment factors (Perinatal Standard V: The plan of nursing care contains a nursing history. The care plan expresses assessment of the patient/family, defines health care goals and nursing actions. This process is recorded, communicated, and accessible.)*

Assessment factors	Process criteria	Patient participation	Outcome criteria
3. Develops a maternal nursing care plan to include	The nurse validates the patient's knowledge of care of the newborn	Gives the nurse feedback on her teaching	Correctly demonstrates formula preparation
3.7 Evaluation of effectiveness of nursing actions		Requests additional information Asks questions regarding the content being taught	Correctly demonstrates weighing of newborn States in her own words why infant was considered high risk
3.84 Interconceptive counseling	The nurse teaches the patient about contraceptive methods	Asks questions about different methods States feelings about contraception Indicates preferences for type of contraceptive Reads literature given by nurse	Selects a method of contraception Correctly demonstrates use of contraceptive device States side effect of contraceptive
4. Develops a neonatal nursing care plan to include	The nurse meets with the family to develop nursing goals for the neonate and family	Family discusses goals with the nurse	Family states goals in own words
4.4 Defined therapeutic medical/nursing/social care goals for the neonate and family		Family offers additional goals Asks for explanation of goals	Family indicates agreement with goals Family states strategies for meeting each goal
4.94 Immediate and long-term plans for follow-up health care	The nurse develops a plan for follow-up health care	Indicates feelings about follow-up health care Makes suggestions for follow-up health care plan Consults with family members about care plan	Puts dates for follow-up care on calendar States agreement with follow-up care plan States in own words why follow-up care is important

*From Arizona State Nurses' Association: Perinatal nursing standards, Phoenix, 1977, Arizona State Nurses' Association.

lection. The greatest disadvantage of the audit, whether concurrent or retrospective, is the lack of complete, clear charting. Poor documentation can cause the audit to be meaningless if data are not available in the record.

After the data are collected, they must be interpreted. This is a crucial phase and should involve nurses who are knowledgeable about the patient population being audited. During this phase, decisions are made about the criteria that were not met to determine whether the nursing care was unsatisfactory or whether there is good rationale for the criteria not being met.

Based on the interpretation of data, the staff must then identify alternative actions to eliminate deficiencies and to improve care. This phase corresponds with the educational component of the nursing protocol. For example, it may be that staff need updating on the use of pain relieving drugs during labor and delivery. There are several ways in which this may be accomplished—through formal inservice, self-study, or continuing education programs. An alternative is chosen from among the many identified and the action is implemented.

The quality assurance process has now come full cycle. Following the implementation of the chosen action, one should allow sufficient time to pass and then reaudit to determine whether the action taken was effective. Through this continual cycle of monitoring and taking action the quality of care will be kept at a high level and will meet the profession's standards.

REFERENCES

1. American Nurses' Association: ANA standards of practice, Kansas City, Mo., 1973, The Association.
2. American Nurses' Association: Development of model sets of criteria for screening quality, appropriateness, and necessity of nursing care in settings for which PSRO's have responsibility: results of study design, Project Report, Kansas City, Mo., 1975, The Association.
3. American Nurses' Association: Guidelines for review of nursing care at the local level, Kansas City, Mo., 1975, The Association.
4. Arizona State Nurses' Association: Perinatal nursing standards, Phoenix, 1977, The Association.
5. Deets, C., and Schmidt, A.: Process criteria based on standards, AORN J. **26**(4):685, 1977.
6. Deets, C., and Schmidt, A.: Outcome criteria based on standards, AORN J. **26**(4):685, 1977.
7. Donabedian, A.: Some basic issues in evaluating the quality of health care. In Issues in evaluation research, Kansas City, Mo., 1975, American Nurses' Association.
8. Duxbury, M., Graven, S., Redman, R., and Sommers, J., editors: Proceedings of the conference on outreach programs: their integral parts and processes, White Plains, N.Y., 1978, The March of Dimes Birth Defects Foundation.
9. Lang, N. M.: A model of quality assurance in nursing, Unpublished doctoral dissertation, 1974, Marquette University.
10. Schmidt, A., and Deets, C.: Writing measurable nursing audit criteria, AORN J. **26**(3):495, 1977.
11. Schmidt, A., and Deets, C.: Responsibility for audit criteria, AORN J. **27**(4):495, 1978.
12. Smith, A. P., editor: PEP workbook for nurses, Joint Commission on the Accreditation of Hospitals, 1975.

SECTION TWO

PRENATAL PROTOCOLS

Chapter 3

Care of the prenatal patient

Sara Wheeler, Paula Bibeau, and Rosanne Harrigan Perez

Early and regular antepartal care is a key factor in potentiating a positive outcome for a pregnant woman and her unborn child. The purpose of this chapter is to provide a theoretical foundation in the physiological and psychosocial adaptations a pregnant woman makes in her 9-month journey to motherhood. The nursing process will be utilized to enable the reader to understand the development of nursing protocols in providing nursing care and management of the pregnant woman.

PHYSIOLOGICAL ADAPTATIONS

The physiological adaptations that occur are the result of hormonal and mechanical interactions between the pregnant woman and her developing embryo-fetus.

Cardiovascular system

The maternal cardiovascular system undergoes remarkable change during pregnancy. The blood volume increases rapidly, with 75% to 80% of the increase occurring by the midpoint of pregnancy to provide for the needs of the enlarging uterus, breast, and placenta. The magnitude of the increase varies from 40% to 90%, depending on the size of the fetus and the size of the individual.[14] The increased blood volume results from an expanded plasma volume and from an enlarged volume of erythrocytes, which is accomplished by an accelerated production of erythrocytes rather than by prolongation of their life span.[15]

The need for an increase in blood volume is explained by the following three factors:

1. A decrease of the intrinsic vascular tone, which appears to be due to a direct hormonal (primarily estrogens) effect on the vessel walls

2. An increased vascular capacity of the uterus and size of the intravascular compartments

3. During the second and third trimesters, a low-resistance shunt in the uteroplacental circulation[14]

The increased blood volume reaches its plateau at 32 to 34 weeks' gestation.[13]

The cardiac output increases 25% to 50% by the end of the first trimester, with an additional 10% increase by the end of the second trimester.[14] The basal heart rate increases by 10 to 15 beats/min. The mean arterial blood pressure reaches its lowest point during the second trimester owing to a significant fall in total peripheral resistance. Uteroplacental circulation acts as a low-resistance shunt, which accounts for part of the reduced peripheral resistance.[14,15] During the third trimester, the arterial blood pressure returns to a normal level or slightly rises.[6] The cardiac output in late pregnancy is higher in the lateral recumbent position than in the supine position. The inferior vena cava is compressed by the enlarged uterus, increasing the venous pressure 20 to 30 mm Hg and impeding venous flow to the heart. To some extent this also occurs in a quiet standing position during late pregnancy.[14,15] The pooling of blood in the legs and thighs may cause hypotension or fainting, frequently referred to as the "supine hypotension syndrome." Edema of the legs and an increased tendency to develop varicosities are related to the pooling of blood in the extremities.

During the antepartum period, 800 mg of iron is needed to meet the fixed iron demands of the fetus and placenta and to allow for optimal expansion of the maternal hemoglobin mass. An addition of 450 ml of red blood cells containing 500 mg of iron results from accelerated erythropoiesis. The fetus will incorporate 300 mg of iron into its body stores. The amount of iron needed for the increase in maternal red blood cell volume and hemoglobin mass cannot be mobilized from the body stores of most women; therefore, exogenous iron must be made available. The amount of iron absorbed from the diet in combination with mobilized stores fails to supply sufficient iron to meet the demand of pregnancy even though absorption of iron through the gastrointestinal tract increases during pregnancy. For these reasons supplemental iron is recommended.[14,15]

The coagulation system undergoes many changes during pregnancy; some of these changes are as follows:

1. Fibrinogen levels increase by 50%, contributing to a marked increase in the blood sedimentation rate.
2. The platelet count shows a mild to modest increase.
3. Platelet adhesiveness decreases.
4. Plasminogen concentration increases.
5. The fibrinolytic activity of the system decreases

The overall coagulability of the blood is reduced from 12 to 8 minutes, and there is a reduction in the fibrinolysis time. This has not led to an increased incidence of thrombosis, however.[14]

Other hematological changes during pregnancy include an elevated reticulocyte count, a modest elevation of leukocytes, and an increase of the iron-binding capacity. It is important to remember these factors when evaluating hematological studies of the prenatal patient. [13-15]

Common complaints relating to the cardiovascular system. A common complaint beginning in the first trimester and lasting into the second trimester is recurrent headaches. These headaches are due to the body becoming adjusted to the increased blood volume. Emotional strain may contribute to the headaches. Persistent headaches must be reported to the physician for further evaluation.

The pain and discomfort of hemorrhoids begins in early pregnancy for many women and lasts throughout their pregnancies. Constipation, sitting for long periods, and the increasing pressure of the enlarging uterus contribute to and worsen the hemorrhoids.

During the second and third trimesters, syncope (light-headedness and fainting), resulting from the pooling of blood in the extremities, may occur. Varicosities tend to develop because of the in-

creased venous pressure of the enlarging uterus. Women who are obese, have poor muscle tone, do not exercise, or are multipara tend to have an increased problem with varicosities. Some women have an inherent weakness in the walls of the superficial veins that contributes to varicosities. Another complaint frequently heard during the late second and third trimesters is that of edema in the lower extremities. This edema is due to a decreased venous return of blood and gravity (that is, standing for long periods of time).[6]

Anemia: a maladaptation of the cardiovascular system. Anemia is the most common hematological problem of pregnancy. The red blood cell volume increases by 15% to 25% but lags behind the plasma volume, which may increase by 40%, resulting in a decrease in the hematocrit and hemoglobin. This is frequently termed "hemodilution of pregnancy."[6,14]

Anemia may be caused by an inadequate production of red blood cells, premature destruction of red blood cells, or from blood loss. The prime focus of this discussion will be anemia caused by an inadequate production of red blood cells, which may result from a lack of iron, folic acid, or vitamin B_{12}; lack of hormonal stimulus; or damage to bone marrow.

Iron deficiency accounts for 77% of the anemias in women who enter pregnancy with a precarious iron balance.[21] Each patient population should have its own definition of "anemia." The changes in hematological values seen with iron deficiency include:

1. Decrease in hemoglobin
2. Decrease in the mean corpuscular hemoglobin (MCH)
3. Decrease in the mean corpuscular hemoglobin concentration (MCHC)
4. Low serum iron (60 μg/100 mg) and iron-binding capacity (300 μg/100 mg).

An iron-binding capacity measures transferrin, the iron-binding transport protein. A meaningful use of the preceding figures is to present the serum iron and the iron-binding capacity as a ratio. If the serum iron is less than 16% of the iron-binding capacity, a diagnosis of iron deficiency is made.[13] If a mild anemia is suspected, a simple way to diagnose iron deficiency is to administer iron orally; within 2 weeks a hemoglobin response is exhibited by an increased reticulocyte count. It is important that baseline data be established.[13]

To the pregnant woman, iron supplementation is necessary to supply a sufficient amount of iron for absorption. Three methods of treatment for iron-deficiency may be utilized. Oral iron preparations, such as ferrous sulfate, are usually well tolerated. The iron is absorbed best if taken with orange juice on an empty stomach. Mild nausea, indigestion, constipation, or diarrhea may be decreased or prevented if the dosage is started small and increased progressively until the full dosage is attained in 10 to 14 days.[6]

Parenteral iron is no substitute for oral supplements. Parenteral iron is preferable if an intolerance to oral iron exists, the patient refuses to take iron orally, oral iron is not absorbed, massive replacement is needed, or the patient is unreliable. An iron-dextran complex containing 50 mg of elemental iron per milliliter of dextran is given by deep intramuscular injection in the upper outer quadrant of the buttock. A ''Z-track'' technique is necessary to prevent staining.[6]

The reticuloendothelial system takes up the iron preparation, which subsequently splits off for utilization. The dosage given is calculated to provide enough iron to restore the hemoglobin to normal as well as to provide iron for storage. When the amount of iron exceeds the binding capacity of transferrin, toxicity occurs. The symptoms of toxicity include flushing, palpitations, feeling of warmth, back pain, nausea, vascular collapse, and even death.[13]

An intravenous technique for giving parenteral iron may be considered if the patient has a small muscle mass, impaired muscle absorption, tendency to develop hematomas, or is unreliable. Observation for toxicity and careful technique must be used. Blood transfusion using packed red blood cells may be considered with a hemoglobin value of less than 9 gm/dl.[13]

Urinary system

Changes in both structure and function take place in the urinary tract during normal pregnancy. The kidney increases slightly in size during pregnancy. With the increased amount of circulating blood, the renal plasma flow and the glomerular filtration rate (GFR) are elevated.[14,15] The hormone placental lactogen is thought to cause these changes, although the precise mechanism is unknown.

With the increased renal plasma flow and glomerular filtration rate, the load of substance presented to the renal tubules for reabsorption also increases. Amino acids and water-soluble vitamins are lost in pregnant women to a greater extent than in nonpregnant women.[15] The amount of filtered glucose is increased by half, and the ability of the kidney to reabsorb glucose is frequently not increased. This is referred to as a lowered renal threshold for glucose, and although glycosuria is common during pregnancy, the possibility of diabetes mellitus cannot be ignored.

The sodium and water excretion in pregnancy is difficult to analyze. The reabsorption of sodium, chloride, and water tends to be increased by steroid hormones from the placenta and adrenal cortex. The renin-angiotensin-aldosterone system is affected by pregnancy (if unfamiliar with this system, see Fig. 3-1).[9] There is an increase in the renin activity and the angiotensin concentrations. Despite this, the blood pressure response to angiotensin is reduced.

The bladder has few significant changes before the fourth month. With increased uterine size, the bladder is elevated and some thickening of the posterior aspect of the bladder occurs owing to hyperemia and hyperplasia of the muscles. Toward the end of pregnancy with engagement the entire base of the bladder is pushed forward and upward. In addition, pressure from the presenting part impairs the drainage of blood and lymph from the bladder, resulting in a delayed flow time that contributes to an increased susceptibility to infection.[14,15]

Common complaints relating to the urinary system. Frequency of urination is a complaint during the first and third trimesters of pregnancy. During the first trimester, frequency is caused by the enlarging uterus rising out of the pelvic cavity. The uterus compresses the bladder against the pelvic bones and reduces its capacity. After engagement occurs in the third trimester, the uterus compresses the bladder causing the same effect.

Nocturia is a common complaint during the third trimester. Fluid tends to accumulate in the lower extremities during the day. The horizontal position during rest favors kidney function and decreases the compression of the ureters, resulting in an increased amount of urine production.[6]

Urinary tract infection: a maladaptation of the urinary tract system. Infections of the urinary tract system are common during pregnancy largely because of the ureteral dilatation and urinary stasis.[14] *Escherichia coli* is the most common type of organ-

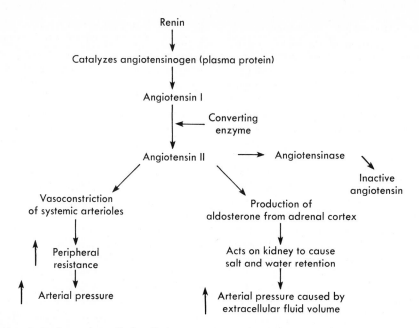

Fig. 3-1. Juxtaglomerular cells in afferent arterioles stimulated by renal ischemia (caused by decreased renal blood flow).

ism causing infection and has been found to multiply more rapidly in the urine of pregnant women.[12]

Cystitis is an inflammation of the bladder caused by bacterial infection without involvement of the upper urinary tract. It is characterized by dysuria, burning, urgency, and frequency. Associated findings include an abnormal number of leukocytes, bacteria, and red blood cells; occasionally gross hematuria is found.[15]

Asymptomatic bacteriuria is a syndrome characterized by actively multiplying bacteria with the absence of symptoms of a urinary infection. The incidence of asymptomatic bacteriuria varies from 2% to 12%, depending on parity, race, and socioeconomic status.[12,15] There is an increased incidence in black multiparas with sickle cell trait,[15] and an association exists between asymptomatic bacteriuria and low hemoglobin levels.[12] Bacteriuria has been related to premature labor and some cases of intrauterine growth retardation.[1,12]

Acute pyelonephritis is a result of bacterial infection that extends upward from the bladder or through the blood vessels and lymphatics. The incidence of acute pyelonephritis is approximately 2% and occurs generally in late pregnancy. Signs and symptoms include a temperature greater than 100° F, shaking, chills, tenderness to palpation in the region of the kidneys, anorexia, nausea, or vomiting.[15]

The diagnosis of bacteriuria is made with a clean-catch specimen of greater than 100,000 colonies of the same organism per milliliter of urine.[27] Some authorities recommend getting two consecutive clean-voided specimens within 48 hours. Urine must not be allowed to stand at room temperature for more than 30 minutes since it is an excellent culture medium. Many clinics do microscopical examinations for bacteriuria, and seldom do false negative results occur. A positive urine culture occurs with more than 20 bacteria per high dry field. There is a poor correlation between pyuria and asymptomatic bacteriuria.

Treatment of urinary tract infections begins with screening all patients. If the cultures are positive for pathogenic bacteria, sulfonamides, ampicillin, or nitrofurantoin are the drugs of choice, depending on the sensitivity of the organism. Nitrofurantoin used late in pregnancy may cause hemolytic anemia in the newborn. Sulfonamides should be withheld the last 2 to 3 weeks of pregnancy, since their use increases the risk of hyperbilirubinemia and kernicterus in the newborn. Short-term treatment for 7 to 10 days is more effective than continuous treatment. Those patients with recurrent infections may require suppressive treatment after the appropriate cultures and sensitivities have been obtained.[12]

Patients with acute pyelonephritis should be hospitalized to observe for signs of bacterial shock. Urinary output, blood pressure, and creatinine levels in plasma should be monitored.[15] Intravenous antimicrobials should be utilized for at least 48 hours; when the patient is afebrile, an oral medication may be substituted. Repeat cultures and sensitivities are mandatory. During the postpartum period, a complete urinary tract evaluation is needed in those patients with pyelonephritis to rule out renal abnormalities.[12]

Integumentary system

The hormones from adrenal and placental steroids produce changes in the integumentary system that are characterisitc of pregnancy. Estrogen and progesterone exert a melanocyte-stimulating effect that causes the line between the symphysis pubis and the umbilicus (linea nigra) and the nipple and areola to darken, and some women develop chloasma (mask of pregnancy), a pigmented area on the cheeks and forehead.[16] The changes generally occur during the first and second trimesters.[1]

Common complaints relating to the integumentary system. The increased blood circulation during pregnancy causes the fingernails and hair to grow faster, erythema (redness of the palms of the hands and soles of the feet), nosebleeds, and nasal congestion. Sebaceous and sweat glands are more active because of the increased circulation.[6] In the later months of pregnancy, reddish, slightly depressed streaks develop on the abdomen, buttocks, and breasts. These are called striae and are felt to be caused by both stretching of the skin and the effects of hormones from the adrenal cortex.[6] The striae change to a silver or brown scar tissue after pregnancy.

Vascular spiders develop as minute, red elevations of the skin that are commonly found on the face, neck, upper chest, and arms. These are thought to be secondary to high estrogen concentrations.[14,15]

Gastrointestinal system

The combination of estrogen and progesterone exerts a relaxing effect on the smooth muscles of the gastrointestinal tract, which appears to increase the absorption of nutrients from the intestinal tract.[6] During the pregnancy, the motility of the stomach is slowed, gastric secretions are reduced, and stomach emptying slows down. Because of these hormonal effects, the gums are frequently swollen, hyperemic, and may bleed easily.[14]

Common complaints relating to the gastrointestinal system. Nausea is one of the most common complaints during the first trimester of pregnancy, with peak periods occurring 60 to 100 days after conception. The physiological basis for nausea may be related to rising estrogen levels in the blood, decreased maternal blood sugar, or decreased gastric motility, although an ambivalence toward the pregnancy may be involved.

During the third trimester, heartburn and constipation are the major complaints. Heartburn occurs when the cardiac sphincter becomes slightly dilated and may be opened by the pressure of the enlarged uterus, resulting in regurgitation of acids from the stomach that irritate the mucosa causing a burning sensation. Adding to the problem, an enlargement of the opening of the diaphragm where the esophagus enters the stomach is caused by the increased movement of the diaphragm and the flaring of the rib cage. Constipation is caused by slower motility, pressure of the uterus on the lower colon, and drier stool because of increased absorption.

Pulmonary system

During pregnancy the basal respiratory rate changes little, but the volume of tidal air increases with the increased movement of the diaphragm and the expansion of the lower ribs laterally. The increased respiratory effort and an increased tidal volume lowers the blood CO_2, allowing the CO_2 from the fetus to be transferred easily to the maternal circulation.[14,15]

Common complaints relating to the pulmonary system. A common complaint expressed by pregnant woman during the late second and third trimesters is dyspnea. The symptom of dyspnea is experienced as the uterus enlarges.[6] The sensation of dyspnea may also be due to the "hyperventilation of pregnancy," with a reduced P_{CO_2} that is inappropriate. As the uterus enlarges further and presses against the diaphragm compressing the lungs, the pregnant woman may become orthopneic. Once lightening occurs or the uterus tilts forward, some of the pressure is shifted away from the lungs and she can breathe.[6]

Musculoskeletal system

Relaxin in conjunction with estrogen and progesterone is suspected as the cause of relaxation of the muscles and ligaments in the pelvic joints.[6] It is unproved, but relaxin may cause some relaxation of other ligaments and muscles. This results in increased mobility of the sacroiliac, sacrococcygeal, and pubic joints, which may alter maternal posture and cause change in gait. Progressive lordosis results from the added weight and increasing abdominal girth. The lordosis shifts the center of gravity over the lower extremities, contributing to strain on the lower back and pelvic muscles.[14,15]

Common complaints relating to the musculoskeletal system. During the second and third trimesters, the most common complaint heard is that of backache for the previously mentioned reasons. Another annoying problem is muscle cramps or spasms in the legs and feet. Some of the causes are fatigue, decreased calcium level with increased phosphorus level, and pressure on the nerves caused by the enlarging uterus.[6] During the third trimester, aching, numbness, and weakness are occasionally noted in the arms. This may be due to the marked lordosis with flexion of the neck and slumping of the shoulder girdle, which produces pressure on the ulnar and median nerves.[15] It may also result from the increased breast size and edema.

Hormonal changes during pregnancy

After conception occurs, the corpus luteum of the ovary begins to secrete increasing amounts of progesterone. Progesterone is necessary for the nidation of the fertilized ovum and maintenance of the endometrium.[6] The corpus luteum diminishes in size as the placenta grows and produces progesterone. The placenta synthesizes the following hormones: protein hormones—human chorionic gonadotropin (HCG), human placental lactogen (HPL), and thyrotropin—and steroid hormones—progesterone and estrogen in collaboration with the fetus.[9]

As the trophoblastic tissues develop, HCG is secreted and has much the same function as luteinizing hormone. Most important, HCG prevents the normal involution of the corpus luteum and causes it to secrete large quantities of estrogen and progesterone, which enlarge the endometrium and allow storage of nutrients. HCG also exerts a stimulating effect on the testes resulting in production of testosterone in male fetuses. The small secretion of testosterone during gestation helps create masculine sexual organs.[9] The physiological action of HPL seems to be promotion of growth and lactation.[2] HPL is produced solely by the placenta, and the amount rises steadily during the entire gestation.[14] HPL participates in metabolic functions by elevating free fatty acids, which provide a source of energy for maternal metabolism,[15] and diverting glucose from the maternal metabolism to the fetus.[2]

The increased estrogen levels during pregnancy cause enlargement of the uterus and breasts, growth of the breast glandular tissue, and enlargement of the female external genitalia. Progesterone plays an important role in nutrition of the early embryo and in decreasing the contractility of the gravid uterus.[9] Estrogen and progesterone together cause relaxation of smooth muscle tissue affecting the tone of the uterus, gastrointestinal tract, arteriovenous elasticity, and bladder function. These hormones also cause water retention in late pregnancy, leukocytosis, and increased respiratory function.

Relaxin is a hormone produced by the ovaries that increases relaxation of pelvic ligaments and works synergistically with estrogen and progesterone to stimulate breast growth and soften the cervix.[6,9]

Other endocrine glands. The pituitary gland enlarges during pregnancy and is not essential for maintenance of the pregnancy. The thyroid gland is enlarged during pregnancy; this is caused by hyperplasia of the glandular tissue and increased vascularity. The basal metabolic rate increases by 10% to 30% as a result of the metabolic activity of the conceptus.[15] The parathyroid gland enlarges, especially if the maternal diet is calcium deficient. Enlargement of these glands causes increased calcium absorption, thereby maintaining a normal serum calcium. There is very little morphological change in the maternal adrenal glands. An increase in the concentration of cortisol occurs, but much of it is bound to protein (transcortin). Increased amounts of aldosterone are produced by the adrenal glands as early as 15 weeks' gestation, probably because of progesterone.[14,15] If sodium intake is restricted, aldosterone secretion is further elevated. The renin-angiotensin system accounts for the marked elevation of the secretion of the aldosterone.[14]

Common complaints relating to the hormonal system. Relaxin has been felt to contribute to fatigue experienced during the first trimester.[1]

Increased vascularity owing to some hormonal effects[2] results in many complaints by the pregnant woman starting late in the first trimester. These complaints include breast tingling and tenderness, increased vaginal secretions, gums that become hyperemic and softened, and vulvar edema. During the third trimester edema is one of the common complaints.

Gestational diabetes: a hormonal and endocrine maladaptation. When a woman is pregnant, her body may react to the pregnancy in such a manner that a diabetogenic effect may exist, even in a nondiabetic woman. The maternal system provides the fetus with its major source of energy—glucose, which may produce a maternal hypoglycemic effect. Placental hormones and cortisol further affect the maternal system by exerting an anti-insulin effect, which helps create a diabetogenic effect. For example:

1. Estrogen is considered to act as an insulin antagonist.
2. Progesterone is thought to decrease the peripheral effectiveness of insulin.
3. Cortisone is felt to cause maternal hyperglycemia by increasing gluconeogenesis.
4. Human placental lactogen or HPL increases the mobilization of free fatty acids and diminishes the effect of maternal insulin.[7,11,18]

Diabetes occurs in 1% to 2% of all pregnancies, and gestational diabetes occurs in approximately 90% of those diabetic cases.[18] Gestational diabetes, or class A diabetes, refers to a disorder in carbohydrate metabolism during pregnancy that returns to normal after delivery. It is a form of latent diabetes in which the client demonstrates a normal fasting glucose level but exhibits an abnormal insulin response to the glucose load in a glucose tolerance test.

Women with class A diabetes are reported to have an increased incidence of preeclampsia, polyhydramnios, operative delivery associated with fetal macrosomia, and subsequent development of overt diabetes.[8]

Clients with a strong family history of diabetes, previous newborn with a weight over 9 pounds, unexplained stillbirth or neonatal death, and previous infants with congenital anomalies should be screened for diabetes. Other clients who should be screened are those with a previously abnormal glucose tolerance test or glucosuria when nonpregnant, those who weigh 20% more than their ideal body weight, those with unexplained hypertension or prior preeclampsia, and those with repeated infections. During the present pregnancy, indications that might become apparent and require testing are: glucosuria on two separate occasions during pregnancy, polyhydramnios, fundal height greater than expected, and postmaturity.

The client diagnosed with gestational diabetes is usually regulated with dietary control and no insulin. However, there is a small group of women with class A diabetes who develop abnormal fasting glucose levels that can be treated with strict dietary control but should be managed as women with class B diabetes because of the possibility of intrauterine and neonatal death.

PSYCHOSOCIAL ADAPTATIONS

The psychosocial adaptations a pregnant woman makes occur as a dual process of integration within herself into a pregnant/mothering role and interaction between her unborn child, significant other, nuclear and extended family, friends, and society. Factors that will influence these processes will be her physiological adaptation to her pregnancy, her desire for the pregnancy and mothering role, life situation, age, culture, relationships with others, life experiences, socioeconomic status, and so forth.

Pregnancy is a developmental phase in a woman's life in which she attains motherhood. The developmental phase of pregnancy is completed with the accomplishment of developmental tasks. The developmental tasks of pregnancy are:

1. Acceptance of the pregnancy
2. Establishing that a baby exists
3. Acceptance that the fetus is separate from herself
4. Mothering the new individual and adjusting to other role changes[4]

The tasks are not completed simultaneously but occur continuously throughout the pregnancy. The process may be accelerated in the multipara; however, previous childbearing does not indicate the tasks will be completed sooner. Each pregnancy and each child occurs under different life situations. An adolescent will progress through the tasks of pregnancy. However, if she is placing her baby for adoption, the fourth task will not be fulfilled.[20] At the present time there is no existing research to demonstrate the tasks of pregnancy in an adolescent under the age of 14. Some women will not complete any or all of the tasks before delivery, which may indicate a maladaptation of the psychosocial process of pregnancy.

In the first trimester, the woman begins to ascertain and accept the reality of her pregnancy. She seeks confirmation of the pregnancy as she constantly assesses and reassesses her body for the signs and symptoms of pregnancy. She seeks prenatal care as a validating tool and may be surprised at her ability to conceive even if the pregnancy was planned. Ambivalence is paramount during this trimester as she questions, "Why me?" "Why now?" and "Do I really want to be pregnant?" Her level of fatigue or tiredness, nausea, vomiting, soreness of breasts, and frequency of urination play an integral part in the amount of her ambivalence and expression of it. Because the only tangible signs of pregnancy to the woman are the discomforts of pregnancy and missed menstrual period(s), fantasies and dreams about the unknown, unforeseen, unfelt organisms growing within her abound as her thoughts turn inward and focus on her "self," not on the baby.[4,16,17]

The nurse's responsibility during the first trimester is to assess the meaning of the pregnancy to the woman, support the expression of positive and negative feelings toward the pregnancy, explain and validate her signs and symptoms of pregnancy with her, identify her level of anxiety with the pregnancy, and determine her support systems and/or changes in them.

In the second trimester the fetus begins to move and the physical discomforts of tiredness, nausea, and vomiting subside. The woman's anxiety is reduced as she notices the changes in her body, buys maternity clothes to accommodate the changes, and becomes more physically active. However, at times she is ambivalent about the pregnancy. As she turns inward to her "self," there is silent introspection

into reviewing the conflicts she had with her mother, deciding what must be given up in becoming a mother, and formulating her fantasy baby. She depends on her significant other to make more of the day-to-day decisions and seeks new acquaintances with pregnant women and recent new parents. Her sexual activity is somewhat improved over the first trimester; however, she shows some concern over possible injury to the fetus or miscarriage. The second trimester woman tends to increase her food intake because she wants to provide for the fetus.

The responsibility of the nurse is assessment of the pregnant woman's weight gain, physical activities, sleep, and general well-being to determine her adaptation to the second trimester. Explanation of second trimester body changes, psychosocial adaptations, and fetal development, as well as discussing mothering behaviors, is pertinent to her developmental tasks at this time. Observations should be made as to anxious behaviors, change in dress (that is, maternity clothing), noting who the mother refers to as her "significant other," and evaluating her sexual partner's response to decreased sexual activity.

The third task of pregnancy, accepting the fetus as separate from herself, probably begins in the second trimester and is not completed until the postpartum period. "It is helpful to the woman to experience labor, to watch the birth of her child, and to see and examine it immediately,"[17] thus confirming the reality of the baby that grew inside of her. To achieve the third task the pregnant woman begins to buy baby supplies, set up the nursery, tries out names for the new baby, sees her unborn child as an individual with a personality, and seeks clues as to who her baby will look like and what he/she will be like. She shows interest in attending prenatal classes, reading books about baby care, sharing with her significant other what she is feeling inside her and what she is learning about baby care, and preparing for the new baby. The becoming mother feels good about her changing body and seeks to determine how others will accept her baby, their changing roles, and how they will relate to her. She shows increased interest in children and their activities and fantasizes and dreams of babies. Her dependency needs on others are increased.

The nursing responsibilities at this time would be to determine the preparations the mother has made for her coming child and discuss her dreams and fantasies of her unborn child and what knowledge she has regarding labor, delivery, and child care. It is important for the nurse to observe the mother's grooming and dress, as well as to determine how others are responding to her dependency needs and their role changes involved with the birth of the child.

The fourth task of mothering the new child and adjusting to new roles may begin during pregnancy when the becoming mother feels warm, motherly, and protective toward her unborn child. For some women these feelings will not occur until after the child is born. For the mother who begins the fourth task during her pregnancy, this role transition period may be fraught with anxiety regarding the approaching labor, fear of harm, fear of losing control, and concerns about her coming child. Her dreams are filled with feelings about the upcoming labor, delivery, and coming child and may take on a negative aspect. Her body is a sense of frustration as its large and unwieldly state makes it difficult to continue normal tasks of living such as doing the dishes. Frequency of urination, insomnia, and shortness of breath further add to the frustration she feels, but these frustrations pave the way for her readiness for labor and delivery to occur ''now!'' She feels very dependent on others and makes plans for when she is away from home. Sexual activity is low or discontinued at this time.[4]

The nursing responsibilities at this time are to explore the woman's expectations of labor and delivery, levels of knowledge, perceptions of pain, support desired (and who will provide it), and preparations, as well as her preparations and expectations for when she goes home with her newborn. Her perceptions of how her significant other will help her during labor, delivery, and at home are discussed, and, when necessary, resources available for families in her community that she may utilize are identified.[4]

THE NURSING PROCESS IN THE ANTEPARTAL PERIOD

Before the assessment of antepartum clients is begun, it is essential to confirm that a pregnancy exists. Testing for the presence of human chorionic gonadotropin is the usual mode elected. For best results, an early morning concentrated urine specimen should be used. However, an afternoon specimen

may be used. A positive pregnancy test is usually seen 10 days after the first missed normal period or 40 days after the last normal period. False positive results may be observed if the client has proteinuria, and false negative results may be observed if the client has inadequate chorionic gonadotropin levels or has taken aspirin. The effect of marijuana on these tests is unknown, but it may have an effect. It is important to remember that a positive pregnancy test is only a presumptive sign of pregnancy.

The initial assessment of the antepartum client is usually done in two appointments. The first appointment entails history taking, initial laboratory workups, and nutritional assessment. The physical examination and other health teaching are usually scheduled in the second appointment.

The health history is an essential component in forming the basis for assessment of the client's well-being and support systems. The health history may include the following:

Family history: Hereditary diseases, cardiovascular disease, diabetes mellitus, epilepsy, blood dyscrasias, congenital anomalies, tuberculosis, mental illness or emotional problems, alcoholism, multiple pregnancies

Medical history of the client: Diabetes mellitus, epilepsy, cardiac disease, renal disease, rheumatic fever, childhood diseases, blood dyscrasias, tuberculosis, urinary tract disease, drug sensitivity, allergies, immunizations, recent viral disease, exposure to drugs or pollutants

Surgical history: Type of surgery, surgeons and hospitals where performed, diagnosis, results

Menstrual history: Age of onset, regularity, cycle, length, problems with menses

Obstetrical history: Number of pregnancies, interrupted pregnancies, abortions, premature deliveries, viable births, physical or mental problems with these infants, complications of labor and delivery, any neonatal complications, stillbirths, previous complications, any problems of infertility

Contraceptive history: Type of contraceptive used, duration of use, reason for choice, satisfaction with method, effectiveness of method, undesirable side effects

Gynecological history: Operations, infections, veneral disease, other

Sexual history: Regularity, libido, satisfaction, orgasm and/or dyspareunia

Life-style history: Attitude regarding life, self, pregnancy; smoking: how long, how much, when started; alcohol: how much, what, how often; ability to read or write and level of education; marital status; drug use: prescribed, street, over the counter, how much, how often, and

The Higgin's Intervention Method for Nutritional Rehabilitation during Pregnancy*

PROCEDURE FOR ESTIMATION OF CALORIC AND PROTEIN REQUIREMENTS

NORMAL REQUIREMENTS

The normal caloric and protein requirements for mothers 20 years of age or more are determined on the basis of ideal body weight, physical activity, and week of gestation, according to the recommendations in the Dietary Standard for Canada (1948) prepared by the Canadian Council on Nutrition. For mothers 19 years of age or less, use the Recommended Dietary Allowances (1958) prepared by the Food and Nutrition Board, National Research Council, United States. For all mothers, add 500 calories and 25 grams of protein after 20 weeks of gestation as recommended in the Canadian Standard.

ADDITIONAL CORRECTIVE ALLOWANCES

Corrective caloric and protein allowances are given in addition to the normal requirements according to the degree of UNDERWEIGHT, UNDERNUTRITION, or for special high risk conditions which may be indicative of NUTRITIONAL STRESS. A mother may have none or one or more of these conditions.

Underweight assessment and rehabilitation

Underweight. Underweight status is determined if the mother's pregravid weight is 5% or more under the weight recommended in the Table of Desirable Weights, prepared by the Metropolitan Life Insurance Company.

Underweight correction. Underweight correction should provide sufficient additional calories and protein to ensure that the mother gains during pregnancy the number of pounds she was underweight prior to conception. 20 grams of protein and 500 calories a day are added to the normal pregnancy requirements to permit a gain of one pound per week.

Undernutrition assessment and rehabilitation

Undernutrition. Undernutrition is determined if a protein deficit is found between actual dietary intake and requirement. The method used is a 24 hour recall diet history, cross-checked with a food list and family market order compared with the appropriate standard.

Undernutrition correction. Undernutrition correction is equal to the amount of protein deficit allowing 10 calories for each gram of protein added to the normal pregnancy requirements.

Nutritional stress assessment and rehabilitation

Nutritional stress. Nutritional stress is determined if any one of the following maternal conditions is present: pernicious vomiting, pregnancies spaced less than one year apart, previous poor obstetrical history, failure to gain 10 pounds by the 20th week gestation, serious emotional problems.

Nutritional stress correction. Nutritional stress correction provides for the addition of 20 grams of protein and 200 calories for each stress condition added to normal pregnancy requirements to an upper limit of 40 grams of protein and 400 calories.

*From Montreal Diet Dispensary, January 1979.

Table 3-1. Dietary food plan

Food groups	Minimum daily amount	Sources	Suggested uses
Protein			
Milk	4 glasses (1 qt) 2+ ounces ½ cup + cottage cheese	Whole, skim, low fat, powdered, evaporated, yogurt, cheese	Use beverage in cooking or milk-based desserts (ice cream, puddings, cream soups, cheese in cooked dishes, salads, or snacks)
Eggs	2	Poultry, dried	Breakfast use, chopped or sliced hard boiled eggs, in salads, custards, deviled eggs, plain or in sandwiches
Meat	2 servings (6 to 8 ounces) Liver frequently (1 to 2 times per week)	Fish, poultry, beef, pork, mixed vegetable proteins, cheese, nuts	Main dishes, sandwiches, salads, soups, snacks
Dark green leafy vegetables	1 large or 2 medium servings	Beets; collard, dandelion, mustard, or turnip greens; kale; spinach; lettuce; cabbage; broccoli	Cooked, snacks, salads
Whole grains, bread, cereals	4 or 5 servings daily	Whole grain flours, 100% bran flakes, wheateno, wheat germ, corn meal products, shredded wheat, granola	Bread, sandwiches, cereals, cooked grains with meals
Vitamin C foods			
Yellow or orange fruits and vegetables	2 servings	Whole potato, large green pepper, grapefruit half, whole orange, lemon, papaya, tomato, cantaloupe, strawberries	Snack, cooked salads, juice, soups
Vitamin A foods			
Butter, fortified margarine, oils, dark green or deep yellow vegetables or fruits	2 to 3 tablespoons with butterfat 1 to 2 plant servings	Apricots, cantaloupe, cherries, peaches, prunes, oranges, watermelon, squash, sweet potatoes, tomatoes, wax beans	In cooking foods, snacks, salads, cooked salads, stewed
Water	5 to 8 glasses	Juices, fruits, plain	With meals and between

what for; significant others: who does she see as support for her pregnancy; culture

Present pregnancy: Last normal menstrual period; determination of EDC; determination of gravida and parity; measurement of fundal height after 12 weeks' gestation; age; date of quickening; present symptoms of pregnancy: nausea, vomiting, urinary frequency, headache, leukorrhea, edema, constipation, bleeding, visual disturbances

Nutritional history: Nonpregnant weight, present weight and height, utilization of the Higgin's Intervention Method (see boxed material on p. 30) when necessary. See Table 3-1 for a dietary food plan.

Laboratory tests are important is assessing the physical well-being of the antepartum client. The following laboratory tests are usually required as part of the initial workup (see boxed material on p. 32 for normal values).

CBC—usually repeated between 29 and 32 weeks' gestation

Blood type

Rh factor—be aware of the negative client

Rubella titer

Urinalysis

Pap smear—endocervical and cervical

NORMAL VALUES*

LABORATORY VALUES FOR WOMEN

CBC
   Hgb—normal 12 to 16 mg/dl
      pregnant at term 10 to 14 mg/dl
   Hct—normal 36% to 48%
      pregnant at term 30% to 42%
   RBC—normal 4,200,000 to 5,400,000/mm^3
      pregnant—increases
   WBC—normal 5,000 to 10,000/mm^3
      pregnant 10,000 to 11,000/mm^3
   Platelets—normal 200,000 to 400,000 (not part of
      CBC)—decreases if abruption
   Reticulocyte count—0.5% to 1.5% (not part of
      CBC)

Blood type and Rh
   Be alerted to the Rh-negative client
   Antibody titers are drawn from 24 weeks on at 4-
      week intervals (range 1:1 to 1:256)

Rubella titer
   1:10 no problem
   1:10 or below vaccine should be given during
      postpartum stay

VDRL
   Nonreactive
   Weak reactive or borderline
   Reactive

Sickle cell preparation
   Reported as positive or negative
   If positive, Hgb electrophoresis is done

URINALYSIS

Observation of urine
   Normal color: light yellow
   Clear or cloudy
   Red color—indicative of presence of blood
   Brownish—hemorrhage in urinary tract

Specific gravity
   1.040—maximum specific gravity
   1.000—very dilute urine

pH
   7.0, neutral
   Urinary pH normal range 4.5 to 8.0

Protein
   Should be 0, most common is albumin

Glucose
   Should be 0, however, clinical glycosuria occurs
      most often during pregnancy (because of in-
      creased glomerular filtration rate)

Acetone
   Small amounts may occur

Epithelial cells
   Should be 0
   If present, indicates contamination by external
      sources, usually vaginal contents

RBC
   Usually 2 to 3

Casts
   Hyalin and granular casts—normal, especially af-
      ter exercise
   Cellular casts—abnormal

Bacteria
   Infection is present in clean catch midstream or
      catheterized specimen (10,000/ml)

Fasting blood sugar (FBS)
   Whole blood—90 or below
   Serum plasma—105 to 110

Two-hour postprandial (2 hr PP)
   Whole blood—145 or below
   Serum plasma—160 to 165

Glucose tolerance tests (GTT)

	Whole blood	Plasma
FBS	90-100	110
½ hr	145	+
1 hr	165	190
2 hr	140	165
3 hr	120	145

*May vary from region to region and laboratory to laboratory.

Gonococcal culture—endocervical and rectal

Sickle cell preparation

Glucose tolerance test and fasting blood sugar—if positive history

The physical examination forms the final piece of assessment of the client at her initial antepartum visit(s). The following information is gathered during the physical examination:

General survey
1. Skin color
2. Weight
3. Posture
4. Personal hygiene
5. Odors
6. State of awareness
7. Facial expression

Vital signs
1. Pulse
2. Respiratory rate
3. Blood pressure

Skin
1. Color
2. Vascularity
3. Edema
4. Turgor
5. Condition of nails
6. Moisture

Head
1. Hair
2. Face

Eyes
1. Position/alignment of eyes
2. Ocular fundi

Ears
1. Auricles
2. Canals
3. Drums
4. Auditory acuity

Nose
1. Ability to smell
2. Any deviation

Mouth/pharynx
1. Inspect lips, gums, teeth, pharynx, tongue, roof of mouth

Neck
1. Inspect/palpate nodes, trachea, thyroid

Back
1. Check for costovertebral tenderness
2. Palpate spine/muscles of back

Breasts/axillae
1. Inspect/palpate breasts for nodes
2. Check nipples
3. Palpate areola

Heart/lungs
1. Palpate/auscultate for abnormal sounds
2. Palpate pulses and correlate with heart rate

Abdomen
1. Inspect
2. Auscultate
3. Percuss
4. Palpate for masses
5. Palpate femoral pulses
6. If pregnancy is advanced, utilize Doptone to locate fetal heart rate at 12 weeks' gestation
7. Utilize fetoscope at 18 weeks' gestation
8. Measure fundal height in centimeters
9. Use Leopold's maneuvers to determine fetal lie/presentation

Genitalia
1. Inspect external genitalia
2. Speculum examination of cervix and vagina
3. Internal pelvic examination with attention to:
   a. Cervix: consistency, length, dilatation
   b. Bony architecture of pelvis
   c. Fetal presenting part
   d. Anomalies of vagina and perineum

Rectal/vaginal
1. Inspect/palpate

Problems the patient may present with initially are nausea/vomiting, fatigue, leukorrhea, hyperemic/softened gums, constipation, anemia, syncope, headaches, positive history for diabetes, and psychosocial problems, including age, unwanted pregnancy, concern over pregnancy, life-style problems, and financial concerns.

Problems that may occur after the initial visit are unsure dates, vaginal bleeding, edema, hemorrhoids, varicosities, integumentary system problems, heartburn, dyspnea, backache, muscle cramps, aching/numbness of arms, urinary tract infections, gestational diabetes, and inappropriate response to pregnancy.

After the initial appointments, the pregnant woman should be seen routinely at least once a month through the seventh month of pregnancy, bi-monthly in the eighth month, and weekly in the ninth month. Assessment of the pregnant woman's physiological progress in pregnancy includes screening of her weight, blood pressure, and urinalysis for glucose and protein, and comparing the results to the initial assessments in determining real or potential problems. Further assessment of her pregnancy would be to discuss her symptoms of pregnancy, for example, headaches; nausea and vomiting; vaginal discharge; bleeding; swelling of her feet, ankles, hands, and/or face; dizziness and fainting; constipation; heartburn; difficulty on urination or burning and frequency; or any other symptom she may be concerned about.

Assessment of fetal progress and well-being is done by determining fetal heart rate, position and activity of the fetus, and fundal height, comparing these results to normal parameters for the weeks of gestation. The normal fetal heart rate is between 120 and 160 beats/min. A primipara will probably begin to feel fetal movement somewhere between 18 to 20 weeks' gestation, and a multipara will usually feel fetal movement between 16 to 20 weeks' gestation. This information is helpful in determining the expected date of delivery. The fundal height in conjunction with the other assessments will give some indication that the fetus is growing in a normal manner. The following is the relationship of fundal height to fetal age[4]:

Linear distance (symphysis to fundus in centimeters)	Estimated fetal age (in weeks)
26.7	28
30.0	32
32.0	36
37.7	40

CONCLUSION

The objective of prenatal care is to assure that each pregnancy results in the delivery of a healthy baby from a healthy mother. Pregnancy requires many physical and psychosocial adaptations before the successful conclusion occurs. It is the responsibility of the nurse to understand these changes so that she or he may help the pregnant woman understand and offer her anticipatory guidance regarding these changes.

An essential component of the nursing process is evaluation of the nursing care and management of the client. This may be achieved by evaluating whether the goals were reached or not in terms of the results of the nursing interventions. It is not within the scope of this chapter to provide evaluation of the nursing protocols, since they have been developed through nursing and medical audits. It is, however, the responsibility of the reader when implementing the protocols to evaluate the appropriateness and effectiveness of their use.

Protocols

INITIAL PROBLEMS
Problem □ Nausea/vomiting

GOAL: To reduce the feeling of nausea and vomiting
EDUCATIONAL
1. If morning sickness occurs, offer the following suggestions:
   a. Eat some of the dry bread, cereal, or crackers that you place at your bedside before you get up in the morning.
   b. Get up slowly, avoiding sudden movements when getting out of bed.
   c. Have a window open to get rid of odors.
   Rationale: To decrease the stimuli that may cause nausea

2. If nausea occurs during the day, offer the following suggestions:
   a. Eat several small meals a day.
   b. Do not drink fluids or soups at mealtime.
   c. Do not overeat.
   d. When nauseous, eat a small amount of these foods: sugar-coated cereal without milk, ginger ale, grapefruit juice, orange juice, or grape juice.
   e. Avoid fried and highly spiced foods.
   f. If vomiting continues, notify physician.
3. If an antiemetic is prescribed by the doctor,

explain dosage, possible side effects, and when to call for problems.

   a. Bendectine—tablets, two at bedtime: may cause drowsiness; adverse symptoms include diarrhea, rash, and excessive vomiting.

   b. Tigan—capsules, 250 mg; suppository, 200 mg; may cause drowsiness; adverse reaction: rash.[6]

   Rationale: To ensure proper usage to achieve the best results

4. If vomiting continues, hospitalization may be required.

   Rationale: To prevent dehydration and electrolyte imbalances from occurring

Problem □ Fatigue

GOAL: To decrease the amount of fatigue felt

EDUCATIONAL

1. Encourage patient to rest when tired.

   Rationale: To ensure patient feels well

2. Encourage a balanced diet and vitamin supplements as ordered per physician.

   Rationale: To prevent anemia that may cause tiredness

Problem □ Leukorrhea

GOAL: To prevent vaginal infections and/or irritations to vulva

DIAGNOSTIC

1. If vaginal discharge present, do wet mount and cultures.

   Rationale: To rule out infections

EDUCATIONAL

1. Teach proper hygiene.

   a. Cleanse from front to back.

   b. Wear cotton undergarments.

   c. Avoid douching.

   Rationale: To decrease risk of infection

2. Teach patient signs of vaginal infection and notify physician if it develops.

   Rationale: To ensure prompt treatment

Problem □ Hyperemic/softened gums

GOAL: To prevent gum disease

EDUCATIONAL

1. Encourage dental evaluation (if x-ray films used, shield abdomen).

   Rationale: To assure proper dental care

2. Encourage a balanced diet.

   Rationale: To ensure adequate vitamin C intake for cell maintenance.

3. Encourage use of soft toothbrushes.

   Rationale: To prevent trauma to gums

4. Reassure mother that a pregnancy epulis, a benign vascular lesion of the gum, will regress after pregnancy, and teach her to prevent trauma to it.

   Rationale: To prevent anxiety in the mother

5. Reassure mother that pregnancy does not incite tooth decay.

   Rationale: To relieve anxiety that may be caused by old wives' tales

Problem □ Constipation

GOAL: To prevent constipation

EDUCATIONAL

1. Early in pregnancy, teach patient ways to avoid constipation.

   a. Adequate exercise

   b. Increased fluid intake

   c. Ingestion of foods containing roughage

   Rationale: To prevent the occurrence of constipation, which may lead to hemorrhoids

2. If constipation has occurred, teach patient ways to prevent it.

3. Explain how to use prescribed laxatives or stool softeners.

   Rationale: To obtain best results

4. Encourage the patient to avoid the use of mineral oil.

   Rationale: To assure that the absorption of fat-soluble vitamins A, D, E, and F is not hindered

Problem □ Anemia

GOAL: To prevent or correct anemia as defined for population caring for

DIAGNOSTIC

1. Initially draw blood for CBC and sickle cell preparation

   Rationale: To determine whether anemia or hemoglobinopathy exists (Assess diet utilizing Higgin's Intervention Method.)

2. For patients with anemia, monitor hemoglobin or hematocrit levels every 2 months during the first two trimesters and monthly thereafter. If patient is not anemic, monitor hemoglobin or hematocrit levels every trimester.

   Rationale: To detect anemia or a worsening in anemia previously established

3. If the hemoglobin value is less than 9.5 gm/dl or 30 vol%, further evaluation including a serum iron, an iron-binding capacity, a CBC, and ST/IBC ratio should be done.

   Rationale: To rule out further blood dyscrasias and ensure anemia is due to iron deficiency

EDUCATIONAL

1. Counsel patient on "balanced diet with emphasis on iron-rich food" as listed below:

   Foods containing a high amount of iron per average serving
   > Cream of wheat
   > Fortified cereals
   > Kidney
   > Liver
   > Liverwurst
   > Prune juice

   Foods containing a moderately high amount of iron per average serving
   > All-bran cereal
   > Apricots, dried
   > Baked beans
   > Beef
   > Great northern beans
   > Green peas
   > Ham
   > Lima beans
   > Malt-o-meal cereal
   > Navy beans
   > Nuts
   > Peaches, dried
   > Pork
   > Prunes
   > Turkey
   > White beans

   Foods containing a limited source of iron per average serving
   > Black-eyed peas
   > Bread, enriched
   > Chicken
   > Dandelion greens
   > Eggs
   > Macaroni and noodles, enriched
   > Mustard greens
   > Raisins
   > Spinach
   > Strawberries
   > Tomato juice
   > Turnip greens

   Rationale: To prevent further decrease in hemoglobin or other deficiencies from developing

2. Encourage patient to take dietary supplements that may include a multivitamin and/or ferrous sulfate as prescribed.

   Rationale: To provide adequate amounts of iron and vitamins for absorption to prevent deficiencies

3. Teach patient about supplements, including the following:

   a. Keep medicines out of reach of children in childproof containers.

   b. If a child ingests the medication, notify or take child to the hospital immediately with empty container.

   c. For patients on iron make sure they know their stools may turn greenish black, they may experience constipation, diarrhea, or a mild nausea, and if the iron is liquid that it may stain teeth (see theory base for further suggestions).

   Rationale: To rule out further blood dyscrasias and ensure anemia is due to iron deficiency

Problem □ Syncope

GOAL: To prevent fainting and light-headedness that might lead to physical injuries

EDUCATIONAL

1. Explain to mother the cause of syncope.
   Rationale: To ensure that mother will understand cause
2. Encourage mother to rest in a left lateral recumbent position.
   Rationale: To decrease venous pressure, which causes pooling of blood in the legs
3. Discourage rapid movement and rising.
   Rationale: To prevent supine hypotension syndrome
4. Hypoglycemia may cause fainting and light-headedness.

Problem □ Headaches

GOAL: To decrease the discomfort felt by mother and rule out pathology

THERAPEUTIC

1. Refer to physician for persistent headaches.
   Rationale: To determine cause and method of treatment

EDUCATIONAL

1. Explain physiological cause of headaches.
   Rationale: To alleviate any apprehension the mother may have
2. Assess quality, intensity, length of time, and location of the headaches.
   Rationale: To rule out pathology or headaches caused by emotional tension
3. Explain usage and side effects of medication as prescribed by physician.
   Rationale: To prevent misuse of medication

Problem □ Positive history for possible diabetes

GOALS

1. To determine if client may have diabetes
2. To discuss her history and your concern with the client

DIAGNOSTIC

1. Order an FBS and 1-hour postprandial blood sugar for the next clinic appointment.
2. Schedule an appointment early the next morning.
3. Analyze the results of the test.
   Rationale: To screen for possible diabetes and to provide an atmosphere in which the pregnant woman feels included in her health care (Learning is facilitated by proceeding from the simple to the complex, from the known to the unknown.[19])

EDUCATIONAL

1. Relate possible effects of maternal diabetes on the unborn child and the need to determine the presence of the disease.
2. Explain what tests must be performed, what is entailed in the testing procedures, and the client's responsibility. For example, client is told not to eat after midnight on the day the test is to be performed.

Problem □ Psychosocial/life-style
Age: from "child" pregnancy to "elderly" gravida

GOAL: To determine the meaning/value of the pregnancy with the pregnant woman

DIAGNOSTIC

1. Explore with the pregnant woman her feelings/needs regarding this pregnancy. For example, Is this a wanted pregnancy? What changes in her life will this pregnancy/child make? What does this pregnancy mean to her? Who knows about the pregnancy?
2. Analyze whether this is a method pregnancy.
   Rationale: To validate the reality of the pregnancy and to accept the pregnancy as real (This is the first step in acceptance of the pregnancy.)[17]

Unwanted pregnancy

GOAL: To provide initial counseling and referral so as to meet the needs of the pregnant woman in the decision-making process of pregnancy resolution

THERAPEUTIC
1. Utilize referrals in your agency or community who may better meet the needs of your client, such as, the social worker in your agency, abortion clinic, family planning agency, local Right to Life group, or adoption agencies.
   Rationale: To decide, if under 12 weeks' gestation, whether to carry the pregnancy to term or to have an abortion if this is an unwanted pregnancy (Women in the first trimester of pregnancy lack any tangible evidence of the reality of pregnancy. Pregnancy is identified as an abstract concept or fantasy, which if pleasant, can be accepted, or if unpleasant, can be accepted or rejected and terminated without involving censorship of her conscience.[10] If the pregnancy is over 12 weeks' gestation, the decision to be made over the next 28 weeks is whether to keep the baby or to place the baby for adoption. In the most optimum of situations, counseling with the pregnant woman should be done to enable her to make her own decision regarding pregnancy resolution.)

EDUCATIONAL
1. Describe the alternatives for a pregnant woman at her weeks' gestation.
2. Discuss the alternatives with the pregnant woman and her significant other when appropriate.

Concern over the signs and symptoms of pregnancy

GOAL: To provide information and education that the client can apply to herself in understanding her pregnancy

DIAGNOSTIC
1. Discuss with the client her signs and symptoms of pregnancy.
2. Assess her level of comprehension in understanding written information or verbal communication and respond appropriately to her needs.

THERAPEUTIC
1. Refer client to community services that provide information for pregnant women and their families, for example, La Leche League, Red Cross classes for expectant parents, and/or other prenatal classes.
   Rationale: According to Tarnow[19]:

   Learning styles and rates vary from one individual to another.
   Learning is facilitated when the material to be learned has relevance to the learner.
   Interpersonal relationships are important in determining the kind of social, emotional, and intellectual behavior which emerges from the learning situation.
   Learning is influenced by the learner's perception of herself and the situation she finds herself in.
   Learning is more effective when there is immediate application of what is being taught.

   The group is usually attractive to the individual and commands her loyalty if she feels her needs are being satisfied in the group, and if it helps her to achieve her personal and professional goals and objectives.[5]

EDUCATIONAL
1. Explain the physiological and psychosocial adaptations the client may make during her pregnancy.
2. Relate alternatives she may or may not try to relieve some of her symptoms of pregnancy.
3. When appropriate, provide her with pamphlets, book lists, and booklets that will help her understand her pregnancy and the special needs she has identified.

Life-style problems—smoking, excessive alcohol intake, drug abuse, overweight

GOAL: To plan with the client methods to reduce or alleviate her life-style problems that are injurious to her unborn child

DIAGNOSTIC
1. Explore with the client her perceptions or fantasies of her unborn and coming child.
2. Discuss with the client her life-style problem(s). Try to discover dependency needs, meaning/value she places on her problem, and so forth.
3. Relate the client's life-style problem and its effect on her unborn child and the child after birth.

THERAPEUTIC

1. Refer the client to community agencies that may be able to help her with her problem(s), for example, social worker, nutritionist, community mental health center, overeaters anonymous, Public Health nurses, and so forth.
   Rationale: According to Tarnow[19]:

   Learning is an active and continuous process which is manifested by growth and changes in behavior.
   Learning is dependent upon the readiness, the emotional state, the abilities, and the potential of the learner.
   Learning is facilitated when the learner has knowledge of her progress toward the goal.
   Recognition of similarities and differences between past experiences and present situations facilitates the transfer of learning.
   Learning is influenced by the learner's perception of herself and the situation she finds herself in.

The nurse must realize that the responsibility for the client's decision rests within the client herself once the situation, probable outcomes, and client's need for change have been discussed at a level the client can understand.

EDUCATIONAL

1. Provide information in the literature that is appropriate to the client's level of comprehension.
2. Utilize pictures, case studies, and/or actual clients who have or have had the same problem(s) when appropriate.

Financial concerns

GOAL: To alleviate or eliminate the client's concern regarding her financial situation

DIAGNOSTIC

1. Assess the pregnant woman's financial situation.
   Rationale: To be able to eliminate or alleviate some of the client's anxieties, which will facilitate her adaption to pregnancy (Anxiety is always present during pregnancy and is regarded as a period of increased susceptibility to crisis.[3,4])

THERAPEUTIC

1. Refer the client to appropriate agencies that provide financial support for women and children if necessary.

PROBLEMS AFTER THE INITIAL VISIT
Problem □ Unsure dates

GOAL: To establish correct dates to prevent delivery of a dysmature fetus

DIAGNOSTIC

1. Establish a correct last menstrual period.
   Rationale: To provide a starting goal, although it may be unreliable
2. Document fetal heart tones with Doptone (12 to 14 weeks' gestation) and with fetoscope (20 weeks).
   Rationale: To allow a reasonable estimation of pregnancy duration
3. Encourage the patient to record the date of quickening and let the clinic physician or nurse know.
   Rationale: To establish when to check fetal heart tones (Although subjective, quickening generally occurs 1 to 3 weeks prior to fetal heart tones with fetoscope.)
4. If possible, establish the uterine size with the physical examination during the first trimester.[27]
   Rationale: To obtain accurate uterine size (Accuracy of this clinical index decreases after the first trimester.)
5. If the patient is a poor historian or uterine size is inappropriate for date, schedule patient for ultrasonography if possible between the sixteenth and twenty-eighth week of pregnancy.
   Rationale: To determine gestational age (The most favorable time for determination of gestational age is between 16 and 28 weeks since measurement errors become more sensitive after that time.[35])
6. If patient presents with questionable postmaturity, refer to appropriate center.
   Rationale: To allow further evaluation by fetal monitoring, amniotic fluid analysis, and estriols

Problem □ Vaginal bleeding

GOAL: To determine the cause of bleeding

DIAGNOSTIC

1. Assess degree of bleeding and whether there is any cramping or tenderness when the patient calls or comes in.
   Rationale: To determine whether patient needs immediate evaluation at hospital
2. If patient presents with spotting, perform only a gentle sterile speculum examination
   Rationale: To rule out cervical polyps, infection, cervical erosion, or capillary fragility with blood vessel disruption after sexual intercourse[6]
3. If the above abnormalities are ruled out, schedule ultrasonography.
   Rationale: To locate the placenta
4. Relate sonar results to the patient as soon as possible.
   Rationale: To alleviate maternal anxiety about unknown

THERAPEUTIC

1. All patients with heavy bleeding, heavy bleeding with cramping, or abdominal tenderness in the first or second trimester and all patients with spotting in the third trimester should be sent to the hospital.
2. If placental problems are found, management in the hospital is warranted.
   Rationale: To provide continuous monitoring to prevent maternal/fetal mortality
3. If placental problems are not found by sonography, continue to follow period and degree of spotting.
   Rationale: To ensure that bleeding does not become serious
4. Encourage mother to avoid sexual intercourse.
   Rationale: To avoid trauma to cervix.
5. Reassure the mother.
   Rationale: To alleviate fears about the unknown

EDUCATIONAL

1. Instruct patient to call if there is spotting of bright red blood or bleeding.
   Rationale: To rule out pathology before it becomes detrimental to the mother or fetus

Problem □ Edema

GOAL: To prevent dependent edema

DIAGNOSTIC

1. Rule out pathology if edema occurs.
   Rationale: To rule out preeclampsia, cardiac, or renal abnormalities that may present first with edema

EDUCATIONAL

1. Teach patient ways to avoid edema.
   a. Elevate legs 30 to 60 minutes, two times daily or whenever sitting.
   b. Avoid constricting bands around legs and feet.
   c. Sleep or rest in a side-lying position.
   Rationale: To increase venous return
2. Teach mother some edema is to be expected.
   Rationale: To relieve anxiety that may be caused by edema

Problem □ Hemorrhoids

GOAL: To prevent the development or worsening of hemorrhoids

THERAPEUTIC

1. Prevent hemorrhoids by preventing constipation and decreasing obstructing venous flow to uterus.
   Rationale: To prevent necessity for treatment
2. If hemorrhoids exist:
   a. Treat constipation with high bulk diet, increased fluid intake, and stool softener.
   b. Apply topical spray or ointment.
   c. Sitz baths.
   d. Apply cold compresses.
   Rationale: To relieve discomfort of hemorrhoids

Problem □ Varicosities

GOAL: To prevent pain and discomfort caused by varicosities

THERAPEUTIC

1. Encourage firm elastic stockings or Ace bandages if varicosities exist.
   Rationale: To stimulate good muscle tone and prevent stasis in lower legs.[6]

Problem □ Integumentary system

GOAL: To prevent anxiety and promote knowledge about the skin changes during pregnancy

EDUCATIONAL

1. Reassure that skin changes such as darkening and chloasma are normal and will fade after the pregnancy ends.
   Rationale: To decrease anxiety about skin changes
2. Teach the patient about increased perspiration during pregnancy and the need for proper hygiene.
   Rationale: To help promote a good self-concept by preventing embarrassment for the patient
3. Discuss striae with the patient and how they develop.
   Rationale: To prevent shame that might be caused if the client felt she could prevent striae

Problem □ Heartburn

GOAL: To relieve the discomfort caused by heartburn

THERAPEUTIC

1. Avoid fried or greasy foods.
   Rationale: To avoid slowing down the digestive process, which results in increased heartburn
2. Advise small, frequent meals.
   Rationale: To decrease pressure in the stomach
3. Milk products as well as antacids prescribed by the physician can be used, but the importance of avoiding preparations containing sodium bicarbonate should be stressed.
   Rationale: To coat the stomach mucosa to help avoid irritation
4. Sit up after meals and elevate the chest and head at night.
   Rationale: To decrease the pressure placed on the stomach

Problem □ Dyspnea

GOAL: To avoid complications and decrease the discomfort of dyspnea

DIAGNOSTIC

1. Review medical history.
   Rationale: To determine if there are medical conditions such as rheumatic heart disease or heart problems that might lead to heart failure
2. Complete physical examination.
   Rationale: To detect signs of congestive heart failure
3. If physical examination and medical history are negative for problems, encourage patient to limit activities.
   Rationale: To help avoid dyspnea

THERAPEUTIC

1. Encourage patient to elevate her trunk and head with pillows.
   Rationale: To decrease the pressure placed on the diaphragm
2. Remind the pregnant woman that with lightening breathing will become easier.
   Rationale: To help decrease the state of anxiety

Problem □ Backache

GOAL: To relieve or prevent the discomfort caused by backache

DIAGNOSTIC

1. Rule out other problems such as urinary tract infections.
   Rationale: To prevent other problems that may worsen

EDUCATIONAL

1. Encourage good posture.
   Rationale: To provide proper body alignment
2. Teach back exercises such as pelvic tilt and pelvic rock.
   Rationale: To strengthen lower abdominal and back muscles
3. Encourage use of firm mattress and avoidance of soft chairs or couches.
   Rationale: To help align the back properly
4. Encourage usage of low-heeled shoes with proper support.
   Rationale: To prevent further strain by increasing the lordosis
5. Explain the use of heat, analgesics, and rest as ordered by the physician.
   Rationale: To ensure safe use with maximum benefit

Problem □ Muscle cramps

GOAL: To prevent or relieve the pain caused by muscle cramps

DIAGNOSTIC
1. Rule out thrombophlebitis.
    Rationale: To prevent those problems caused by thrombophlebitis

EDUCATIONAL
1. Teach patient ways to prevent muscle cramps.
    a. Exercise, especially walking.
    b. Elevation of legs when sitting.
    c. Adequate rest.
    Rationale: To prevent discomfort for the patient
2. If cramping occurs, teach patient to point toes upward and exert pressure downward on kneecap.
    Rationale: To relieve pain
3. If ordered by physician, teach patient proper dosage of calcium tablets and urge reduction of milk intake.
    Rationale: To ensure that calcium is increased and that phosphorus is reduced

Problem □ Aching, numbness, weakness of arms, shoulders, and upper back

GOAL: To relieve discomfort felt

DIAGNOSTIC
1. Rule out pathology.
    Rationale: To ensure appropriate treatment

THERAPEUTIC
1. Ensure proper posture.
    Rationale: To help align the body properly
2. Encourage adequate support of breasts.
    Rationale: To prevent strain on upper back and shoulder girdle

EDUCATIONAL
1. Teach patient to place fingers on shoulders and rotate arms.
    Rationale: To increase mobility and relieve pressure felt

Problem □ Urinary tract infection

GOAL: To prevent or minimize the effects of urinary tract infection

DIAGNOSTIC
1. Screen all prenatal patients on their initial visit and at least once each trimester with a urinalysis and urine culture.
    Rationale: To detect asymptomatic bacteriuria

THERAPEUTIC
1. If patient complains of frequency, urgency, dysuria, pain, chills, or fever, do a culture and sensitivity on a clean catch urine specimen. If available, do immediate microscopical examination of urine for pyuria and bacteria.
    Rationale: To detect urinary tract infection
2. If microscopical examination of urine is positive or culture returns positive, treat patient with medication as physician orders, avoiding sulfonamides and nitrofurantoin during the last 6 weeks of pregnancy.
    Rationale: To rid the body of the infection and attempt to avoid the neonatal effects caused by the sulfonamides and nitrofurantoin
3. Encourage patient to drink 10 to 12 8-ounce glasses of fluid daily.
    Rationale: To provide a constant flow of urine through bladder and help wash it out
4. Encourage patient to complete all medication and tell her why this is important.
    Rationale: To obtain client's compliance by helping her to understand the rationale for taking medicine
5. After completion of medication, repeat culture and sensitivity testing.
    Rationale: To ensure pathogenic organisms are eradicated

EDUCATIONAL
1. Teach patient how to get a clean catch specimen.
    Rationale: To avoid contaminated specimens
2. Teach patient ways to avoid urinary tract infections.
    a. After toileting, wipe front to back.
    b. Void when the initial sensation occurs.
    c. Drink 8 to 10 glasses of fluid daily.
    d. Notify physician or clinic as soon as any symptoms occur.
    Rationale: To prevent urinary tract infections

Problem □ Gestational diabetes

GOALS

1. To maintain client in metabolic balance during her pregnancy
2. To provide emotional support during her pregnancy
3. To plan the client's dietary control as to her dietary habits

EDUCATIONAL

1. Explain gestational diabetes to the client: what it is, how she developed it, effects on her body and her unborn child, possible outcomes, and so forth.
2. Allow the client to express her anxieties, frustrations, anger, and other responses regarding the diabetes and her pregnancy throughout the antepartum period.
3. Keep the client informed of her progress and test results.
4. Give positive support when the client is adapting positively and encouragement when she is not. Help the client to determine her own needs, problems with the diet, understanding of the risks, and to be creative within her situation.

   Rationale: According to Tarnow[19]:

   Learning is influenced by the learner's perception of herself and the situation she finds herself in.
   Learning is facilitated when the learner has knowledge of his progress toward the goal.
   Learning is facilitated when the client has the opportunity to test ideas, analyze mistakes, take risks, and be creative.

Problem □ Psychosocial responses are not appropriate to patient's trimester of pregnancy

GOALS

1. To determine patient's anxieties, fears, and/or problems she perceives during this pregnancy
2. To identify client's support systems
3. To refer client to appropriate community resources if needed

DIAGNOSTIC

1. Promote an environment conducive to facilitating communication with the client, for example, one-to-one relationship, privacy, open atmosphere.

2. Apply therapeutic communication techniques to enable the client to express herself.
3. Utilize specific questions to explore the client's anxieties, fears, and/or problems that might also reflect her psychosocial adaptation to pregnancy, for example, What preparations have you made for the baby? What fears do you have about your labor and delivery? Who helps you the most with your responsibilities at home?
4. Analyze the client's situation with her to determine health teaching needs, support systems, alternatives, and/or referrals.

THERAPEUTIC

1. Arrange for the appropriate health and/or teaching referrals.
2. Continue to collect data regarding the client's situation at subsequent appointments.

   Rationale: To facilitate communication with the client by utilizing basic principles of counseling and communication (Pregnancy is a time of increased crisis and susceptibility to crisis. Because pregnancy requires significant physiological and psychosocial adaptation on the part of the individual, it is a time in which the equilibrium can be destroyed or regained. It is essential for clients to realize another dimension of themselves, their capabilities, strengths, weaknesses,[16] and capacities to love and nurture.)

REFERENCES

1. Armstrong, M. E., et. al.: McGraw-Hill handbook of clinical nursing, New York, 1979, McGraw-Hill Book Co.
2. Butnarescu, G. F.: Perinatal nursing, vol. 1. Reproductive health, New York, 1978, John Wiley and Sons, Inc.
3. Caplan, G.: Psychological aspects of maternity care, Am. J. Public Health **47:**25, 1957.
4. Clark, A. L., and Affonso, D.: Childbearing: a nursing perspective, ed. 2, Philadelphia, 1979, F. A. Davis Co.
5. Coffey, L.: Modules for learning in nursing: Life cycle and maternity care, Philadelphia, 1975, F. A. Davis Co.
6. Dickason, E. J., and Schult, M. O.: Maternal and infant care, New York, 1975, McGraw-Hill Book Co.
7. Gabbe, S. G.: Diabetes in pregnancy: clinical controversies, Clin. Obstet. Gynecol. **21**(2):443, 1978.
8. Gabbe, S. G., et. al.: Management and outcomes of class A diabetes mellitus, Am. J. Obstet. Gynecol. **127**(5):465, 1977.
9. Guyton, A. C.: Textbook of medical physiology, Philadelphia, 1971, W. B. Saunders Co.

10. Hillman, L. M., and Pritchard, J. A.: Williams obstetrics, ed. 14, New York, 1971, Appleton-Century-Crofts.
11. Macourt, D. C.: Diabetes mellitus in pregnancy, Med. J. Aust. **1:**798, 1974.
12. Marchant, D. J.: Urinary tract infections in pregnancy, Clin. Obstet. Gynecol. **21**(3):921, 1978.
13. Messer, R. H.: Pregnancy anemias, Clin. Obstet. **17**(4):163, 1974.
14. Page, E., Villee, C., and Villee, D.: Human reproduction: the core content of obstetrics, gynecology, and perinatal medicine, ed. 2, Philadelphia, 1976, W. B. Saunders Co.
15. Pritchard, J. A., and MacDonald, P. C.: Williams obstetrics, ed. 15, New York, 1976, Appleton-Century-Crofts.
16. Rubin, R.: Cognitive style in pregnancy, Am. J. Nurs. **70:**502, 1970.
17. Rubin, R.: Maternal tasks in pregnancy, J. Adv. Nurs. Prac. **1:**367, 1976.
18. Schuler, T.: When a pregnant woman is diabetic: antepartal care, Am. J. Nurs. **79**(3):448, 1979.
19. Tarnow, K. G.: Working with adult learners, Nurse Educ. September/October, p. 34, 1979.
20. Wheeler, S. R.: Unwed middle class adolescent pregnancy: a case study approach, unpublished thesis, Indianapolis, 1977, Indiana University.
21. Worthington, B. S., Vermeersch, J., and Williams, S. R.: Nutrition in pregnancy and lactation, St. Louis, 1977, The C. V. Mosby Co.

BIBLIOGRAPHY

Adams, C. M.: Diabetes in pregnancy: a review, South Dakota J. Med. **31:**5, 1978.
Ascher, B. H.: Maternal anxiety in pregnancy and fetal homeostatis, J. Obstet. Gynecol. **7**(1): 18, 1978.
Behrman, R.: Neonatal-perinatal medicine: diseases of the fetus and infant, St. Louis, 1977, The C. V. Mosby Co.
Bjorksten, O.J.W.: Basic principles of counseling for the physician. In Kreutner, A. K., and Hollingsworth, D. R., editors: Adolescent obstetrics and gynecology, Chicago, 1978, Year Book Medical Publishers, Inc.
Brown, M. S.: A cross-cultural look at pregnancy, labor, and delivery, J. Obstet. Gynecol. **5**(5):35, 1976.
Colman, A. D., and Colman, L. L.: Pregnancy: the psychological experience, New York, 1971, Herder & Herder.
David, M. L., and Doyle, E. W.: The first trimester pregnancy, Am. J. Nurs. **76**(12):1945, 1978.
Gabbe, S. G.: Management and outcome of pregnancy in diabetes mellitus, classes B-R, Am. J. Obstet. Gynecol. **129**(7): 723, 1977.
Greenhill, J. P., and Friedman, E.: Biological principles and modern practice of obstetrics, Philadelphia, 1974, W. B. Saunders Co.
Lipkin, G. B.: Parent-child nursing: psychosocial aspects, ed. 2, St. Louis, 1978, The C. V. Mosby Co.
Newton, M.: Woman, wife, mother: meeting sexual and emotional needs during pregnancy, Fam. Health **9:**15, 1977.
Pedusen, J.: The pregnant diabetic and her newborn, ed. 2, Baltimore, 1977, The Williams & Wilkins Co.
Riebel, J. P., and Roy, Sister C.: Conceptual models for nursing practice, New York, 1974, Appleton-Century-Crofts.
Stichler, J. F., Bariden, M. S., and Rumer, E. D.: Pregnancy: emotional experience, Matern. Child. Nurs. May/June, p. 153, 1978.
Tilkian, S. M., Conover, M. B., and Tilkian, A. G.: Clinical implications of laboratory tests, ed. 2, St. Louis, 1979, The C. V. Mosby Co.
Tucker, S. M.: Fetal monitoring and fetal assessment in high-risk pregnancy, St. Louis, 1978, The C. V. Mosby Co.
Weinberg, J. S.: Body image disturbances as a factor in the crisis situation of pregnancy, J. Obstet. Gynecol. March/April, p. 18, 1978.
When a pregnant woman is diabetic: maternal and fetal care, Am. J. Nurs. **79:**448, 1979.

Chapter 4

Care of the intrauterine growth–retarded fetus

Paula Bibeau and Rosanne Harrigan Perez

Low birth weight neonates represent a significant health problem, accounting for over 200,000 live births each year.[34] Neonates can be subdivided into three categories:

1. Average size for gestational age (between tenth and ninetieth percentile on the intrauterine growth chart)
2. Small size for gestational age (below the tenth percentile on the intrauterine growth chart)
3. Large size for gestational age (above the ninetieth percentile on the intrauterine growth chart[39] (See Fig. 4-1 for Colorado Intrauterine Growth Chart.)

Approximately one third of all low birth weight infants are not premature, rather they are term infants small for their gestational age.[5] This chapter will focus on the small-for-gestational-age infant.

DEFINITION

Terms such as pseudopremature, small for dates, dysmature, fetal malnutrition syndrome, chronic fetal distress, intrauterine growth retardation (IUGR), and small-for-gestational-age (SGA) have been used to designate the fetus whose growth is retarded. Normal intrauterine growth must be delineated for a given population so no uniform definition for the small-for-gestational-age neonate can be given.[3] On the intrauterine growth curves, any neonatal birth weight on the tenth percentile or less for the gestational age is indicative of moderate intrauterine growth retardation; those weights below the third percentile or two standard devia-

tions below the mean indicate severe intrauterine growth retardation.[3,4,11,14,36]

Second only to prematurity as a cause of perinatal mortality, intrauterine growth retardation affects 1% to 2% of all pregnancies with an overall neonatal mortality rate of 3% to 6%[3,36,41] and a total perinatal mortality rate of 18% to 20%.[3,27,39]

CELLULAR GROWTH

Intrauterine development is characterized by proliferative cellular growth and differentiation.[7,12,43] Fetal growth refers to a process by which the fetus increases in size as a result of accretion dependent on transplacental growth support and the growth potential of the fetus.[11,12] Fetal growth occurs in four phases: In stage one cellular division is associated with an increase in deoxyribonucleic acid (DNA) and protein, resulting in cells of the same size and growth. The term frequently given to this process of growth caused by cellular division is hyperplasia. Stage two is characterized by hyperplasia at a slower rate owing to decelerated production of DNA and an increase in cell size. The increase in cell size caused by protein accretion at a rapid pace is called hypertrophy. During stage three DNA production ceases, resulting in growth owing to hypertrophy alone. In stage four all cell growth is completed and static. Maturity is reached.[3,7,11,12,14] During this stage enzyme systems are elaborated and all functions are integrated.[43]

The major part of gestation is devoted to cellular hyperplasia or an increase in the number of cells.

45

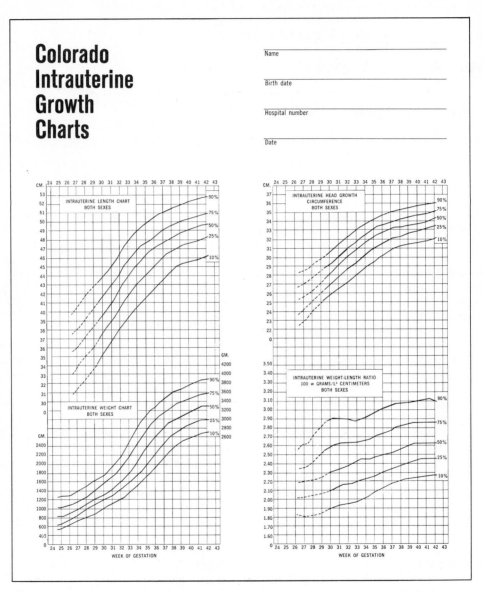

Fig. 4-1. Colorado Intrauterine Growth Chart. (From Lubchenco, L. O., et al.: Pediatrics **37**:403, 1966. Copyright American Academy of Pediatrics 1966.)

Insults during this vulnerable period may produce permanent deficiencies characterized by small organ size owing to a decreased cell number with normal cell size. The fetus is well proportioned or symmetrical and appears runted. Factors that may cause this growth retardation include genetic defects, chromosomal disarrangement, viral invasion, ionizing radiation, embryonic injury, and normal hereditary traits.[4,11,23] Growth during the latter part of pregnancy is a combination of hypertrophy and hyperplasia. An insult during this time results in small size owing to a decrease in the cell size with a normal number of cells. Any factor that compromises maternal support to the fetus such as toxemia, essential hypertension, multiple pregnancies, recurrent bleeding, and maternal malnutrition can result in a decrease of hypertrophy. This growth-retarded fetus has a long and thin look, loose skin folds, and an asymmetrical appearance.[3,4,19,23]

When a chronic compromise in the support given to the fetus exists, there is a redistribution of the cardiac output in favor of the vital organs, especially the brain. This is known as a brain-sparing effect. Other vital organs including the heart, lungs, and kidneys suffer to a lesser extent than do the liver, spleen, pancreas, and adrenal glands.[4,14,26,39]

The brain-sparing effect is maintained until 34 to 36 weeks' gestation, beyond which brain growth is compromised.[39]

Most hypertrophic growth occurs postnatally, so a neonate whose nutrition is not adequately supplied may become small for his gestational age.[3,11]

ETIOLOGY

Intrauterine growth retardation is caused by two basic mechanisms:

1. A reduction in fetal growth support provided by the mother transplacentally[11]
2. A reduction in fetal growth secondary to genetic disorders and/or infections[11]

The genetic makeup of the fetus represents an important regulator of growth.[11] The various factors affecting fetal growth potential are listed below.

I. Fetal growth potential
  A. Chromosomal abnormalities
    1. Trisomy 13, 15, 18, 21
    2. Cri du chat syndrome
    3. Turner's syndrome
    4. Fanconi's syndrome
    5. Bloom's syndrome

  B. Congenital anomalies and metabolic disease
    1. Cornelia de Lange's syndrome
    2. Osteogenesis imperfecta
    3. Dyschondroplasia
    4. Various types of dwarfism
    5. Pierre Robin syndrome
    6. Single umbilical artery
    7. Potter's syndrome
    8. Hypoplastic lung syndrome
    9. Teratoma of neck
    10. Transient diabetes
    11. Clubfeet
    12. Supernumerary digits
    13. Malformations of alimentary tract
    14. Cystic fibrosis
    15. Anencephaly
  C. Intrauterine infection (see maternal factors)
  D. Familial trait
  E. Endocrine factors
II. Fetal growth support
  A. Maternal
    1. Inadequate uterine blood flow
      a. Preeclampsia, eclampsia
      b. Chronic hypertension, renal disease
      c. Diabetes mellitus (classes, D, E, F, and R)
      d. Twins
    2. Malnutrition
    3. Possible harmful agents
      a. Tobacco
      b. Unprescribed drugs such as heroin or methadone
      c. Prescribed medication: antimetabolites, steroids, or tetracycline
      d. Alcohol
      e. Irradiation
    4. Decreased oxygen tension
      a. Anemia
      b. Cyanotic heart disease
      c. Hemoglobinopathies such as sickle cell
      d. High altitudes
    5. Intrauterine infection
      a. Viral: rubella, cytomegalovirus, hepatitis B virus, herpes simplex, varicella zoster
      b. Protozoal: toxoplasmosis
      c. Bacterial: syphilis
    6. Miscellaneous maternal factors
      a. Parity: primiparas and grand multiparity
      b. Low socioeconomic class
      c. Low prepregnancy weight, limited weight gain, weight loss in last trimester
      d. Small stature
      e. Inadequate prenatal care
      f. Age: under 15 or over 35 years of age

g. Close spacing of pregnancies
h. Previous low birth weight infant
B. Placental lesion
1. Placental failure secondary to postmaturity
2. Infarcts—gross or micro
3. Premature placental separation
4. Abnormal insertion of umbilical cord
5. Placental hemangiomas
6. Hydatidiform change
7. Avascular terminal villi
8. Thrombosis of fetal vessels
9. Multiple pregnancy*

The incidence of congenital anomalies is increased in the neonate who is small-for-dates.[13] Neonates with intrauterine growth retardation who are symmetrically small indicate an influence from the early part of pregnancy.[19,20] Runting as an immunological cause of intrauterine growth retardation may be operative in the human situation but is not well understood at present.[39]

Despite genetic variability, the characteristics of the maternal environment appear to exert a great influence on the size of the infant at birth.[9,34]

Endocrine factors have been investigated extensively but at present do not appear to have a major effect on fetal growth.[41] The growth hormones of maternal and placental origin do not reach the fetus in appreciable amounts and their roles are not well defined.[11,30] Fetal growth seems to be independent of the central nervous system and pituitary gland. This is suggested by the normal birth weight of anencephalic neonates and idiopathic hypopituitary dwarfs.[11,30]

Insulin is known to facilitate protein, fatty acid, and glycogen synthesis.[11] Some researchers indicate that insulin is the one fetal hormone that regulates the rate of growth.[30] Other researchers feel that in the normal fetus insulin has a small role. An involvement of fetal pituitary hormones is felt to be important in relation to fetal insulin production, but it is not presently understood.[11]

Thyroxine, a hormone essential for cellular and biochemical maturation of the central nervous system, does not significantly influence birth weight.[11,30] The hormones of the fetal adrenal glands do not affect birth weight as evidenced by anencephalic infants with atrophy of the adrenal cortex and normal birth weights.[30]

---

*See references 3, 4, 6, 14, 16, 33, and 39.

The second basic cause of intrauterine growth retardation is the reduction of support given to the fetus owing to inadequate uterine and placental blood flow, malnutrition, harmful agents, chronic intrauterine infection, decreased oxygen tension, and placental and miscellaneous factors. Each of these areas will be briefly discussed.

Hypertension and renal disease have the highest incidence of IUGR neonates because of vascular resistance.[6,16,19] With vascular resistance the uterine blood flow is decreased owing to vasoconstriction. The decreased blood flow provides less oxygen and nutrients to the fetus for growth.

The duration of the condition and the level of diastolic blood pressure correlate with the degree of intrauterine growth retardation. The presence or absence of organ effects such as proteinuria has an even greater prognostic significance. Severe and long-standing diabetes, resulting in vascular disease, compromises fetal growth.[6]

An increase in uterine vascular resistance may occur prior to the actual manifestation of systemic hypertension in preeclampsia. This would compromise fetal growth more than has previously been suspected.[39] The mechanism occurring is much the same as with chronic hypertension.

Intrauterine growth retardation based solely on maternal malnutrition is difficult to define and document,[26] but most physicians feel that maternal malnutrition is the leading cause of intrauterine growth retardation.[14] The nutritional status of the fetus depends on the composition of the maternal blood, the ability to transfer nutrients and oxygen across the placental membranes, and the amount of blood perfusing the placenta.[14] The role of chronic maternal malnutrition preceding conception and continuing throughout life is not well understood. The effect of malnutrition depends on both the duration and severity of the insult. Acute malnutrition results in infertility and an increase in spontaneous abortion, but there is not much of a decrease in the weight of a viable fetus.[3] Malnutrition during the first and second trimesters results in a decrease in length, weight gain, brain growth, and head circumference.

With the insult occurring in the middle or the end of the third trimester, the weight gain is impaired more than the linear growth and head circumference.[3,14] The major effects of an inadequate diet are felt to occur when the insult is imposed during the third trimester.[9,30] The possible effects of maternal malnutrition include reducing the number of cells in the placenta, increasing the protein/DNA ratio in the placenta, reducing birth weight of the infant, and reducing brain cell number at birth.[7]

Cigarette smoking is associated with a decline in birth weight, averaging between 150 to 250 gm. The weight reduction is directly proportional to the number of cigarettes smoked.[34] Several factors could be responsible for the decrease in birth weight: hypoxia caused by elevated blood carbon monoxide, placental transfer of toxic growth-inhibiting substance, chronic vascular spasm of uterine arteries, or appetite suppression of the pregnant woman.[6,14]

Intrauterine growth retardation is found in neonates whose mothers are addicted to drugs. The most common addictive drugs studied are heroin and methadone. Growth retardation in addicted mothers is probably related to erratic or inadequate nutrition because of the demands of the habit[6,39] and possibly a direct growth-inhibiting effect on the fetus. The incidence of growth retardation is less with methadone.[6]

Growth retardation is among the characteristics noted in neonates born to alcoholic mothers. Other variants noted include mental subnormality and congenital anomalies such as short palpebral fissures, ptosis, strabismus, joint anomalies, and cardiac murmurs. Whether the growth retardation is caused by inadequate nutrition and/or is a part of the fetal alcohol syndrome is not known.[3,4,6]

Decreased oxygen tension in maternal arterial blood probably results in growth retardation because of chronic fetal hypoxia. Conditions characterized by hypoxia include hemoglobinopathies, cyanotic heart disease, high altitude, and anemia.[3,6,39]

Intrauterine infection frequently causes growth retardation. These infections fall into three groups: viral, protozoal, and bacterial. The fetus may be infected by the virus either by horizontal transmission or vertical transmission. Horizontal infection occurs at or after birth and does not cause low birth weight. Vertical transmission takes place prior to delivery via the placenta,[21,30] although it is not definitely known how they cross the placenta. The pinocytotic process might be sufficient enough

to carry a few viral particles to the fetal cell.[30] The virus multiplies rapidly and impairs the metabolic activity of the cell without destroying it. There is a high incidence of chromosomal breakage resulting in poor cell division and poor growth.[14] See the outline on p. 47 for a list of viruses.

Such organisms as *Treponema pallidum* that cause syphilis may transverse the placenta under their own power.[30] Placental changes take place as the invasion of the fetus takes place. These placental abnormalities may cause the high rate of prematurity seen, but it is questionable whether inadequate nutrient transfer leading to growth retardation occurs.[3,6]

Many facts of the maternal history have been related to the growth-retarded fetus. Growth retardation of previous siblings or the mother herself is a powerful predictor.[9,11,30,34] An elevated rate of growth retardation is noted in women of lower socioeconomic groups; these women may have had poor growth owing to malnutrition in their childhood.[3,16,19] A higher rate of low birth weight infants is noted in women with low levels of education, women beyond high school (perhaps because of an older age), illegitimate births, and nonwhite populations.[34,43] The higher proportion of low birth weight infants is born to mothers under 15 and over 35 years of age.[3,34] A higher incidence of low birth weight is noted with the first birth and after the fourth birth. The interval between pregnancies is important to allow for maternal stores to be built up; therefore if the pregnancies are close together, the incidence of decreased weight is higher.[3,9,34]

A low prepregnancy weight (under 120 pounds), a weight gain less than 11 pounds, or a weight loss during pregnancy are also predictors of intrauterine growth retardation.[4,9,11,39] Short maternal stature (155 cm or less) has been correlated with low birth weight.[3,13] Some studies have not correlated fetal growth to maternal prepregnancy height, weight, or weight gain until after 33 weeks' gestation when growth retardation was correlated to weight gain.[40]

Placental size is a major determinant of fetal size.[9] Human placental cell division continues until about 34 to 36 weeks' gestation or until a fetal weight of 2400 gm has been attained.[3,7] Beyond this point a physiological uteroplacental insufficiency secondary to a normal imbalance between fetal requirements and the ability of the placenta to meet them becomes the limiting factor in fetal growth.[3,4,11] In 50% of the growth-retarded neonates the placenta is small and light in weight, and the texture of the placenta is different from a normal placenta.[16,20] Intrauterine growth retardation may result from pathological changes in the placenta,[30] but no single abnormality is common.[16] Placental conditions associated with growth retardation include:

1. Infarction, avascularity of chorionic villi, excessive deposition of fibrin in intervillous spaces, and premature placental separation, which reduces the total effective surface for maternal-fetal exchange[6,30]
2. Hemangioma of the umbilical cord or placenta, which acts as a mechanical interference with circulation
3. Parabiotic transfusion syndrome, resulting in an uncompensated arteriovenous anastomosis of placental vessels where blood is shunted from the smaller twin to the larger twin[4,28]
4. Abnormal cord insertions, which rarely result in growth retardation[4]

Maternal malnutrition limits the growth of the placenta, therefore limiting the surface available for exchange of nutrients.[7]

OBSTETRICAL MANAGEMENT

The real challenge to the obstetrical staff is the antenatal recognition of intrauterine growth retardation. Early diagnosis, intensive antepartum surveillance, and appropriate intervention will result in a decrease in fetal mortality and morbidity.[16,26]

A family and obstetrical history with maternal and paternal regulators should be obtained with emphasis on the many factors discussed earlier in this chapter.[11] The well-being of the mother should be established by physical examination, laboratory analysis, and nutritional and social assessment. At each clinical visit weight, uterine height, abdominal girth, urine analysis for sugar and protein, and reassessment of nutrition should be carefully examined. Establishing the consistency of the uterine size with the last menstrual period is an essential component of the physical examination.[6,12,27] If the mother is seen for the first time late in her pregnancy and is noted to have a smaller uterus than anticipated based on menstrual history, a diag-

nostic dilemma exists.[6] Serial clinical examinations of the uterine height help to diagnose 30% to 58% of the growth-retarded fetuses.[5,11,39] The clinical suspicion of growth retardation from lack of uterine growth can be unreliable but is the most constant of the clinical signs when done by the same examiner on successive visits.[27,39] A uterine height that shows no growth over 3 or more weeks suggests growth retardation.[40] If growth retardation is suspected, it is important to rule out hypertension, renal disease, diabetes, fetal viral infection, anomalies, maternal malnutrition, and cyanotic heart disease.[3]

Patients suspected of intrauterine growth retardation or who develop a febrile illness with a rash and lymphadenopathy should be screened for evidence of chronic infection of the TORCH group (toxoplasma, other, rubella virus, cytomegalovirus, and herpes simplex) and syphilis.[14,39]

Urinalysis should be done each trimester, since there is a correlation between urinary tract infections and low birth weight infants.[34] The rollover test and the angiotensin II infusion test may be of value in predicting patients at risk for preeclampsia and possible growth retardation at 28 to 32 weeks.[40]

If intrauterine growth retardation is diagnosed, treatment consists of (1) endeavoring to enhance blood flow to the uterus by resting in the left lateral position,[6,19] (2) attempting to correct the condition responsible for growth retardation, and (3) judicious timing of delivery based on data collected from sonography, nonstress test, oxytocin challenge test, urine estriols, human placental lactogen levels, and amniotic fluid studies.[1,19]

Sonography

Ultrasound is a method in which echoes of sound returning from the surfaces within the body are detected and analyzed. Ultrasound allows early evaluation to establish fetal age and identification of growth retardation. Measurement of the crown-rump length from the sixth to the fourteenth week of gestation is a method utilized to determine gestational age.[11] (See Table 4-1 for crown-rump measurement as determinant of fetal age.) The increase of biparietal diameter before 30 to 32 weeks' gestation is so uniform that it allows for prediction of fetal gestation with serial measurements.[11,39] All high-risk pregnancies should be scanned at 20 to 22

Table 4-1. Crown-rump measurement as a determinant of fetal age*

Menstrual maturity (weeks + days)	CRL ((mm) mean	CRL (mm) 2 SD	Menstrual maturity (weeks + days)	CRL (mm) mean	CRL (mm) 2 SD
6 + 2	7.0	3.3	10 + 0	33.0	7.2
6 + 3	6.5	1.4	10 + 1	33.8	7.6
6 + 4	7.0	4.6	10 + 2	35.2	7.3
6 + 5	6.5	4.2	10 + 3	36.0	7.9
6 + 6	10.0	2.6	10 + 4	37.3	9.7
7 + 0	9.3	2.3	10 + 5	43.4	7.7
7 + 1	10.3	8.0	10 + 6	40.1	7.1
7 + 2	11.8	5.7	11 + 0	46.7	6.1
7 + 3	12.8	4.8	11 + 1	43.6	7.2
7 + 4	13.4	6.7	11 + 2	47.5	6.2
7 + 5	15.4	3.6	11 + 3	48.8	5.9
7 + 6	15.4	4.4	11 + 4	49.0	9.5
8 + 0	17.0	4.9	11 + 5	54.0	9.8
8 + 1	19.5	5.7	11 + 6	56.2	9.5
8 + 2	19.4	6.2	12 + 0	58.3	9.4
8 + 3	20.4	5.0	12 + 1	56.8	7.2
8 + 4	21.3	3.8	12 + 2	59.4	6.6
8 + 5	20.9	2.4	12 + 3	62.6	8.6
8 + 6	23.2	3.6	12 + 4	63.5	9.5
9 + 0	25.8	6.0	12 + 5	67.7	6.7
9 + 1	25.4	4.6	12 + 6	66.5	8.2
9 + 2	26.7	4.4	13 + 0	72.5	4.2
9 + 3	27.0	2.8	13 + 1	69.7	8.5
9 + 4	32.5	4.2	13 + 2	73.0	15.1
9 + 5	30.0	10.0	13 + 3	77.0	8.5
9 + 6	31.3	5.5	13 + 4	—	—
			13 + 5	—	—
			13 + 6	76.0	5.7
			14 + 0	79.6	7.8

*This determination is a useful and sensitive indicator of gestational age. In very early pregnancy some patience is required to obtain the proper plane for measurement. From Robinson, H. P., and Fleming, J. E. E.: Br. J. Obstet. Gynaecol. **82:**702, 1975.

weeks' gestation to document gestation and provide baseline data if future scans are needed.[33]

Ultrasound has doubled the clinical detection of intrauterine growth retardation by providing reliable data on which to base diagnosis.[11,16] The biparietal diameter grows at a rate of 1.8 per week during the last 10 weeks of pregnancy.[3] Serially performed ultrasound scans during the third trimester will aid in detecting growth retardation.[3,11,33] (See Fig. 4-2 for estimation of fetal weight to biparietal diameter.) Two head growth patterns are noted in sonography. With the most common head growth pattern, the biparietal diameter will keep up until 34 to 36 weeks' gestation because of the brain-sparing effects that break down then.[39] (Because of the brain-

sparing phenomenon, there is a 21% false negative when biparietal diameter is the only criterion used.[11,19,20] These asymmetrical fetuses are more prone to perinatal asphyxia.[19,20] The second head growth pattern is symmetrical and is seen in a genetically small or deformed fetus. The symmetrically small fetus rarely experiences asphyxia and tolerates labor no differently than a normal fetus.[19,20] Total intrauterine volume (TIUV), a method using the equation for determining the volume of an ellipse, can be used to diagnose growth retardation in cases where there is brain sparing. A lack of increase in the TIUV is generally a result of growth lag of the fetal trunk and diminution of amniotic fluid volume. If the TIUV lags

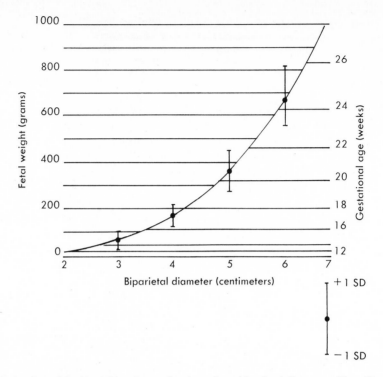

Fig. 4-2. Estimation of fetal weight and gestational age from biparietal diameter. (From Bartolucci, L.: Am. J. Obstet. Gynecol. **122:**439, 1975.)

4 weeks or more behind the biparietal diameter, the fetus is growth retarded.[19,20,39] (See Fig. 4-3 for TIUV.)

Fetuses have the capacity to maintain growth at the expense of body growth in a hostile intrauterine environment. The amount of disproportion reflects the severity of the compromise. Thus the relationship between head circumference and chest circumference is of value in assessing the degree of intrauterine growth retardation.

Ultrasound will allow for the calculation of hourly fetal urine output, which is decreased in intrauterine growth retardation. The process is time consuming, possibly harmful to the patient since she must lie on her back, and has questionable clinical efficacy.[11,20] (See Fig. 4-4 for graph on fetal urine production.) It is important to note that the value of sonography depends on the expertise of the technician performing and reading the scan.

Estriols

Estriol results from the conversion of fetal androgen precursors to estriol by the placenta with further conjugation in the maternal liver and excretion through the maternal kidney. Estriol production during pregnancy increases with gestational age, especially during the third trimester,[3,6] and is considered to correlate well with fetal size. In pregnancies complicated by chronic low estriol, the low estriol production is the result of diminished precursors combined with diminished placental conversion. (See Fig. 4-5 for examples of estriol production.)

With low estrogen values, uterine vasculature may not be adequately stimulated so that hypertrophy, which may compromise fetal growth, does not continue.[39,41] Chronic low estriols are connected with the growth-retarded infant.[3,41] It is recommended that all pregnant patients have 24-hour

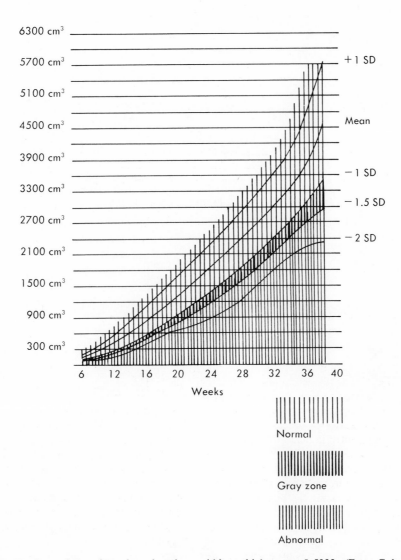

Fig. 4-3. Uterine volume: formula = length × width × thickness × 0.5233. (From Gohari, P., Berkowitz, R. L., and Hobbins, J. C.: Am. J. Obstet. Gynecol. **127:**255, 1977.)

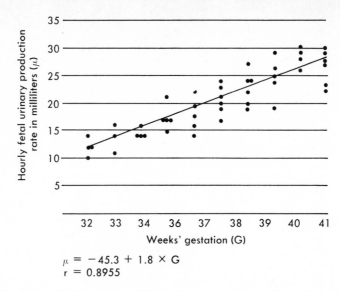

$$\mu = -45.3 + 1.8 \times G$$
$$r = 0.8955$$

Fig. 4-4. Fetal urine production rates at different times in gestation. (From Campbell, S., Wladimiroff, J. W., and Dewhurst, D. J.: Am. J. Obstet. Gynecol. **80:**680, 1973.)

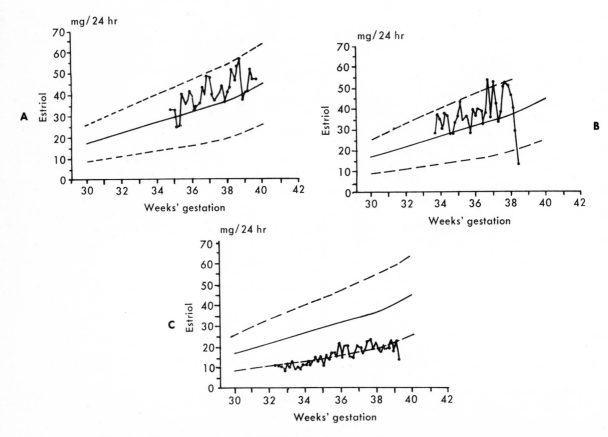

Fig. 4-5. A, Normal estriol pattern. **B,** Falling estriol pattern. Dramatic changes such as this are most often seen in diabetes. **C,** Chronically low estriol pattern. (From Avery, G.: Neonatology, pathophysiology and management of the newborn, Philadelphia, 1975, J. B. Lippincott Co.)

urine estriols monitored at 32 to 33 weeks and at 35 to 37 weeks to help identify the majority of patients with intrauterine growth retardation. The finding of normal urinary estriols does not rule out growth retardation, but it makes it unlikely that one is dealing with a severely compromised fetus[41] if the etiology of intrauterine growth retardation is vascular insufficiency. Falling estriol levels are a potentially ominous sign of fetal distress, suggesting rapid deterioration of the fetal condition.[3,38] The value of urinary estriols is increased if used in conjunction with the oxytocin challenge test.[11] The use of total plasma estrogen or plasma estriols is felt to be less satisfying than urine estriols because almost half the precursors are from the maternal adrenal glands, and they may not be sensitive to the obscure changes in the portion derived from fetal precursors.[38] In a case where renal problems may affect the urinary estriols, serum assays may be more accurate. False positives may be produced by certain drugs such as ampicillin, corticosteroids, cascara senna, and methenamine mandelate.[8]

Human placental lactogen

Human placental lactogen (HPL) is a protein hormone produced and secreted by the syncytiotrophoblast.[5,9,38] HPL levels correlate well with placental size but not with fetal size. The hormone is detected by 5 weeks' gestation and rises progressively until 34 to 36 weeks. Growth retardation may be related to a low HPL level, but not all cases of growth retardation are related to placental problems so it is expected that some cases of growth retardation would be associated with normal HPL levels.[41] Low HPL levels indicate a failing placenta and may be a sign of fetal distress but should not be depended on alone as a sign to terminate the pregnancy.[9,38]

Amniocentesis

When estriol measurement or oxytocin challenge tests do not warrant prior intervention, amniocentesis is performed at about 37 to 38 weeks' gestation to evaluate fetal maturity.[40] An error in determination of amniotic fluid constituents may be induced by blood, meconium, other particles, or prolonged exposure to light.[2] Oligohydramnios accompanies growth retardation, so aspiration of clear fluid with ease speaks against severe fetal involvement.[6]

The amniotic fluid creatinine concentration increases as the gestation advances. The increase is related to an increase in fetal muscle mass and to the improving ability of the fetal kidney to concentrate urine. A creatinine level of 2 mg% correlates well with a fetal weight of 2500 gm or a normal pregnancy at 36 weeks' gestation. A fetus may be mature but undergrown with a level of less than 2 mg%.[2,3,38] A creatinine level of greater than 2 mg does not assure lung maturity. Elevated maternal blood creatinine levels are reflected in the amniotic fluid; therefore, amniotic creatinine must be evaluated carefully.[6]

Lecithin, a phospholipid, is found to predominate in surfactant. Early in gestation the concentration of sphingomyelin is greater than lecithin until about 30 to 32 weeks when the two become equal. Lecithin increases at approximately 34 weeks, reflecting a more stable metabolic pathway for surface active lecithin production. The concentration of sphingomyelin tends to level off and fall. A lecithin to sphingomyelin (L/S) ratio greater than 2 is essential to prevent death from hyaline membrane disease and low morbidity from idiopathic respiratory distress syndrome.[3,38] (See Fig. 4-6 for L/S ratios.)

Antepartum fetal heart rate testing

Oxytocin challenge test (OCT). The oxytocin challenge test has been used as an indicator of the competence and resilience of the fetplacental unit. During this test the fetus is exposed to contractions; however, the data indicate that the test is associated with a large number of false positives. In Weingold's[42] study about one half of the fetuses born with OCT's, indicating late decelerations in fetal heart rate (positive tests), showed no indication of jeopardy during labor. Few false negative results have been associated with the test. If OCT results are negative, it is unlikely for fetal death to occur within a week following the test even in a compromised pregnancy.

The OCT is thus a measure of assessing fetal well-being. It does not provide data about intrauterine growth retardation but could be used to evaluate fetal well-being following a diagnosis of intrauterine growth retardation.

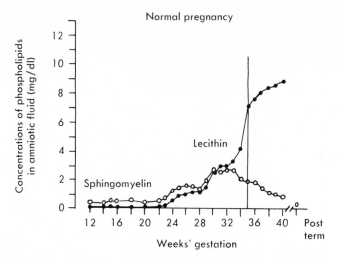

Fig. 4-6. Concentration of lecithin and sphingomyelin in amniotic fluid during gestation. (From Spellacy, W.: Management of the high-risk pregnancy, Baltimore, 1976, University Park Press.)

Nonstress test (NST). At this time several respected researchers are favoring the abandonment of the OCT in favor of the NST. Information is developing that suggests the predictive usefulness of this noninvasive method. More data are necessary before an unequivocal decision is made regarding the efficacy of the NST. Many IUGR fetuses have accelerations of fetal heart rate with fetal movement (a reactive test), but data indicate that the chances are limited that the growth-retarded fetus will die within a week of a reactive test.

At this time most institutions perform nonstress tests in all potentially compromised pregnancies and utilize only the invasive time-consuming OCT in the case of a nonreactive NST.

Delivery

Intrauterine death in the growth-retarded fetus is observed mainly during the last 2 or 3 weeks of gestation. Delivery at 37 to 38 weeks should be planned to prevent fetal death, provided earlier clinical problems do not require intervention.[33,39,40] Delivery is indicated if there is evidence of fetal jeopardy signified by decreasing estriol levels, a positive oxytocin challenge test, or meconium in the amniotic fluid at or before 34 weeks' gestation.[3,6] Delivery should also be considered if there is a persistent growth fail-

ure with evidence of fetal maturity during the last 4 weeks of gestation.[6,11] There is 10 times the risk of intrauterine death from asphyxia during labor for the fetus whose growth retardation is caused by placental or maternal factors.[14,33]

The proper method of delivery of the growth-retarded fetus is controversial. A trial of labor is advocated if close observations are made of the fetal heart rate pattern to uterine contractions.[6,33] Persistent tachycardia, bradycardia, or deceleration of the heart rate require prompt intervention.[33] Fetal scalp blood sampling is another technique for the diagnosis of fetal distress, especially if it is associated with abnormal fetal heart patterns.[3,38] Acidosis is an indicator of fetal asphyxia,[11] which will become more severe as labor progresses. Factors that must be considered when evaluating fetal distress with a fetal scalp blood pH include the acid-base state of the mother, possible edema, caput formation, and vasoconstriction of the skin overlying the presenting part. The problems with using fetal scalp blood sampling are the intermittency of the method and the need to repeat the procedure[3] if the value is low or if abnormal fetal heart rate patterns continue. The main complications of the procedure are infection with abscess formation and hemorrhage from the incision.[3,10]

Labor should be terminated with delivery by cesarean section if abnormal fetal heart rate patterns persist or if the fetal blood pH is 7.25 or less on two to three serial samples.[3,6,10] The prompt delivery of the growth-retarded fetus in distress will result in a high rate of planned and emergency cesarean sections.[11,39] If the fetus has tolerated labor, the question arises as to whether the birth should be spontaneous or forceps should be used. It is doubtful that the use of forceps will help prevent trauma, but a liberal episiotomy is advocated to shorten the second stage of labor and prevent possible injury to the fetal head.[33]

In the fetus with growth retardation, there is hyperviscosity caused by chronic hypoxia.[11] It is recommended that the cord be clamped 30 seconds after delivery and not stripped.[29]

The type of anesthesia and analgesia to be used should be carefully considered. A conduction anesthesia such as nitrous oxide or methoxyflurane with the addition of a pudendal or local block for delivery is recommended to avoid the depressant effect of narcotics[1,33] and the hypotension that decreases uteroplacental blood flow frequently caused by regional anesthetics. The hand-held inhalers with methoxyflurane can be used for labor.[38]

Because of the increased incidence of asphyxia neonatorum, meconium aspiration syndrome, postpartum hypoglycemia, and other problems, two physicians and/or nurses experienced in neonatal resuscitation and first-hour care must be in attendance at the delivery.[11,37]

NEONATAL MANAGEMENT

The diagnosis of intrauterine growth retardation can be confirmed by physical examination of the neonate at birth and examination of the neurological tone and reflexes at 24 hours of age unless the neonate is depressed or sick.[11,23,39] Classification of the neonate's gestational age and birth weight will determine whether growth retardation has taken place and can serve as a predictive tool for morbidity and mortality.[23,26] Neonates tend to perform neurologically in accordance with their age rather than weight unless they have been depressed or asphyxiated.[5] Neurologically the growth-retarded neonate has a loud cry, strong suck that is coordinated, good head control, and maximal recoil.[11] (See the neurological assessment tool in Fig. 4-7, *B*.)

CHARACTERISTICS

The physical characteristics of the growth-retarded neonate are as follows:

Body tissue: Thin, loose, dry skin, poor development or loss of subcutaneous tissue; and decreased muscle mass
Head: Large in proportion to rest of body, sparse hair with poor texture, wide skull sutures, secondary failure of bone growth without increased intracranial pressure, "old man-like" facies, worried eyes—open and looking around or fixed
Torso: Breast nodules depend on gestational age and degree of growth retardation, scaphoid abdomen, yellow thin umbilical cord that dries rapidly, mature genitalia
Extremities: Transverse foot creases[3,4,11,14,23] (See physical assessment tool in Fig. 4-7, *A*.)

The physiological maturity of fetal organs is affected little by growth retardation, and development occurs according to gestational age. In pregnancies with chronic distress an acceleration of pulmonary surfactant maturation is noted.[3] High hemoglobin concentrations and hematocrit levels are due to the chronic hypoxia in utero, which may stimulate erythropoiesis leading to an increased rate of red blood cell production.[3,14,29] Hypoxia in utero may result in the redistribution of the blood volume within the placental-fetal circuit, with a transfer of blood from the placenta to the fetus by an unknown mechanism.[29]

Epiphyseal ossification may be delayed in appearance by 2 weeks and is of little value in distinguishing the growth-retarded neonate from a premature neonate.[3]

The neonate who is growth retarded loses little weight and begins to gain weight rapidly. There is a phase of accelerated growth from delivery to 3 months, but the growth spurt is not maintained[3,25] and a permanent deficit in growth may persist.[3]

Poor glucose control is seen in the growth-retarded neonate. Immediately after delivery or a load of intravenous glucose, hyperglycemia may occur.[3] It is speculated that the hyperglycemia is the result of a persistent endogenous hepatic glucose production or decreased utilization of glucose peripherally.[32] More commonly, hypoglycemia is seen within the first 48 to 72 hours of life. The high incidence of hypoglycemia is due primarily to the lack of liver glycogen stores, increased utilization of glucose, an inefficient gluconeogenetic mechanism secondary to reduced hepatic and adrenocortical function, an

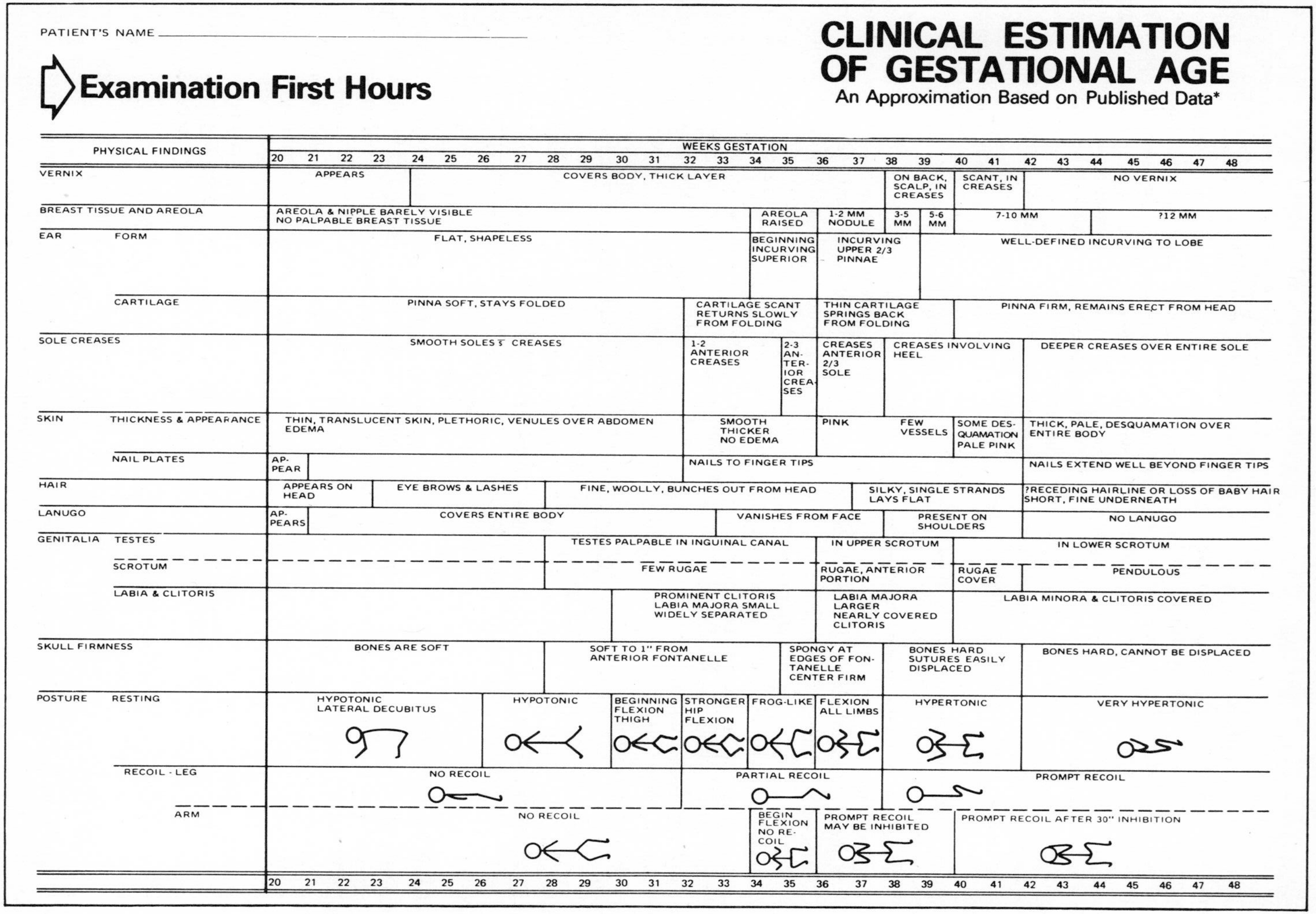

Fig. 4-7. Clinical estimation of gestational age—an approximation based on published data. **A,** Physical examination first hours.

Confirmatory Neurologic Examination to be Done After 24 Hours

Mead Johnson LABORATORIES

Fig. 4-7, cont'd. B, Confirmatory neurological examinations to be done after 24 hours. (Reproduced, with permission, from Kemp, C. H., Silver, H. K., and O'Brien, D., editors: Current pediatric diagnosis and treatment, ed. 6. Copyright 1980 by Lange Medical Publications, Los Altos, Calif. Adapted from Lubchenco, L. O.: Pediatr. Clin. North Am. **17:**125, 1970.)

insufficient intake of glucose, and a relative hyperinsulinism.[3,14,29] Blood glucose levels should be monitored every 2 to 3 hours during the first 12 hours and if stable every 6 hours until 48 to 72 hours of age. Early feedings or intravenous fluid (dextrose in water) should be started immediately to prevent hypoglycemia.[4,27,29,36]

A growth-retarded neonate has a greater oxygen consumption per kilogram of body weight than a premature neonate. The increased metabolism is related to the large percentage of body weight contributed by visceral organs that require more oxygen per kilogram.[36] The neonate has poor glycogen and fat stores, so it is important to provide adequate calories, decrease calorie expenditure, and minimize oxygen consumption by maintaining a thermoneutral environment.[14] Besides an increased metabolic rate, inefficient temperature control is related to an increased heat loss because of decreased subcutaneous fat and illness.[3,29]

Hypocalcemia is not usually increased with the intrauterine growth—retarded neonate. Neonatal hypocalcemia is related to the presence of asphyxia.[3,29] The diagnosis is based on a serum calcium level of 7 to 8 mg/dl (depending on individual laboratories). The treatment of hypocalcemia consists of administering oral calcium or calcium gluconate intravenously. With the presence of hypocalcemia, hypomagnesemia may also be present. Routine magnesium levels are hampered by the large quantities of plasma required. Hypomagnesemia is seldom present when serum calcium levels are normal.[29] Treatment consists of intramuscular administration of magnesium sulfate followed by oral magnesium.[14]

There may be an abnormal placental transfer of immunoglobulins with a decrease of serum gamma globulin levels, although these depressed levels are questionable. Elevated gamma globulins are seen in growth-retarded neonates with intrauterine infection.[3]

The growth-retarded neonate may reveal a metabolic acidosis secondary to chronic hypoxemia shortly after birth. If adequate oxygenation is established immediately after delivery, adjustment occurs in a short time with a compensatory respiratory alkalosis and hyperventilation. Alkali therapy should be given with caution only after adequate ventilation

has been established to avoid overcorrection and possible hypocalcemia.[14]

COMPLICATIONS

The complications of intrauterine growth retardation fall within four categories:
1. Those related to fetal factors
2. Those secondary to fetal distress and perinatal asphyxia
3. Those abnormalities in substrate transfer and aberrations in hormonal control
4. Miscellaneous group

Fetal factors leading to complications include congenital malformations. Growth-retarded neonates with a normal placenta for their gestational age have a high incidence of major congenital anomalies. The neonate should be followed for the detection of hidden cardiovascular and genitourinary anomalies.[5,29] Other complications owing to fetal causes include congenital infections and chromosomal malformations.[29]

Complications resulting from perinatal asphyxia include asphyxia neonatorum, meconium aspiration syndrome, persistent fetal circulation, hyperviscosity, postasphyxia encephalopathy, pulmonary hemorrhage, and renal complications.[4,11,29,36] Postasphyxia encephalopathy is a nonspecific clinical term used to describe various central nervous system symptoms ranging from cerebral edema to forms of intracranial hemorrhage. The renal complications from asphyxia include inappropriate ADH secretion and renal ischemia associated with hypotension.[5,11,29]

Abnormalities in substrate transfer and aberrations in hormonal control include hypoglycemia, hypercalcemia, metabolic acidosis, and hypocalcemia (this is thought to be more related to asphyxia). In the miscellaneous group temperature control, abnormalities in coagulation, and bleeding profiles are included.[3,11,29]

PROGNOSIS

The physical growth and development of the growth-retarded neonate depends on several factors: the cause, the severity and duration of insult, the extent of intrapartum asphyxia, the immediate care after delivery, and the diagnosis and management of various neonatal disorders.[11,29] Delivery in institutions prepared to offer intrapartal and neonatal care has a profound effect on outcome.[16] Long-term outcomes are not known. Some neonates remain undersized[25,36]; others have complete catch-up growth. The best predictor of later growth is the first 12 months of life.[36] Major neurological abnormalities are not encountered, but minimal cerebral dysfunction is present in 25% of the cases.[36,39] If the growth retardation is due to an infection, psychomotor retardation will occur; if it is caused by a chromosomal abnormality, there is a poor prognosis for a normal life.[14]

SUMMARY

Intrauterine growth retardation is a deterrent ". . . to the achievement of the goals that all infants not only will be live born and survive, but will suffer neither physical or psychological impairment as the consequence of a hostile antepartum, intrapartum, or postpartum environment."[33] Growth retardation is caused by two basic mechanisms: a reduction in fetal growth potential or a reduction in fetal growth support. Antenatal recognition is made in only 33% of the cases, resulting in possible fetal death or mor-

bidity for those not recognized because of a hostile environment. The care of the patient who is suspected of having a growth-retarded fetus should be a tertiary setting where current methods of assessment are utilized to their fullest potential. The use of sonography, estriols, amniocentesis, and stressed and nonstressed testing as assessment tools can decrease the morbidity and mortality of the fetus, but the results must be analyzed and interpreted carefully.

Delivery at 37 to 38 weeks' gestation should be planned provided earlier clinical problems do not require intervention. The growth-retarded fetus should be allowed a trial of labor with close observation and delivery by cesarean section if fetal distress occurs.

Growth-retarded neonates require specialized care to manage their special problems and to provide them with the adequate environment so they may grow. The future prognosis for the neonate is not known, but skilled care antenatally, intrapartally, and postpartally decreases the incidence of morbidity and mortality.

Protocols

Problem □ Antenatal recognition and care of intrauterine growth-retarded pregnancy

GOAL: To maintain the pregnancy as long as possible without jeopardizing the fetus

Rationale: To ensure maximal fetal growth and maturation without compromising the fetal status

DIAGNOSTIC

1. Complete a family and medical history.
   Rationale: To predict growth retardation by factors that might be elicited during the history
2. Draw following laboratory studies per physician order.
   a. VDRL (repeat at 34 weeks' gestation)
   b. Rubella titer

   c. CBC, Hct
   d. Blood type/Rh factor
   e. TORCH screen
   f. Urinalysis, urine culture, and sensitivity each trimester
   Rationale To rule out any abnormal values that may present problems
3. Complete a physical examination to determine uterine size or any physical problems.
   Rationale: To determine if uterine size is equal to dates and if any physical problems will complicate the pregnancy
   a. If uterine size is incongruent with dates, perform ultrasound.
      Rationale: To obtain accurate dating of pregnancy during first and second trimester

b. If pregnancy is considered "high risk," perform ultrasound at 20 weeks.
  Rationale: To document date of pregnancy and provide a baseline for future data collection
c. Collect 24-hour urine at 32 to 33 weeks and 35 to 37 weeks.
  Rationale: To help identify patients with fetoplacental unit dysfunction

4. A nutritional assessment should be completed.
  Rationale: To evaluate daily dietary pattern and, if deficient, to help improve maternal malnutrition to prevent decreased birth weight caused by inadequate nutrients

5. Complete a social history.
  Rationale: To help predict growth retardation by assessing social factors

6. If data collection indicates a pregnancy at risk for growth retardation, examine weight, uterine height, and abdominal girth every 2 to 3 weeks and do a nutritional reassessment.[22]
  Rationale: To assess frequently so deviations are recognized early in the pregnancy
  a. Ultrasound at 20 and 28 weeks.
    Rationale: To determine if there is an increase in biparietal diameter

7. If a growth-retarded fetus is suspected by small uterine size or abdominal girth or inadequate weight gain do the following.
  a. Ultrasound at first suspicion and repeat 2 weeks later.
    Rationale: See references 3, 6, 19, 20, and 39
  b. Do a nonstressed test after 32 weeks and repeat weekly thereafter.
    Rationale: To assure fetal well-being[3]
  c. Collect 24-hour urine estriols two times a week.
    Rationale: To observe for subnormal or falling levels, indicating fetal compromise and a failing placenta[3,4,38,40,41]
  d. If estriols are subnormal or falling or there is a nonreactive nonstressed test, perform an oxytocin challenge test (OCT).
    Rationale: To assess uteroplacental reserve and determine fetal reaction to further stress[1]
  e. If OCT is negative with subnormal or falling estriol:

(1) Monitor estriols daily.
  Rationale: To observe for further deterioration
(2) Repeat NST if further deterioration of estriols or in 1 week.
  Rationale: To reassess fetal reaction to stress of further reduction of uteroplacental reserve
f. If OCT is positive or at 34 weeks, gestation, perform amniocentesis.
  (1) If results indicate fetal maturity, deliver.
    Rationale: To prevent fetal death from a hostile intrauterine environment[3,6,41]
  (2) If results are negative for fetal maturity:
    (a) If OCT is positive with subnormal or falling estriols, consider steroid administration prior to delivery or deliver.
      Rationale: To accelerate lung maturity and prevent respiratory distress[1,41] (The risk of fetal prematurity versus the risk of fetal death must be decided.)
    (b) If 37 weeks with a negative OCT, continue to monitor estriols and repeat amniocentesis in 1 week.
      Rationale: To assure fetal maturity without risking fetal death (See Fig. 4-18 for flowchart.)

THERAPEUTIC

1. Inform health care personnel of any factors that may predispose the patient to intrauterine growth retardation.
  Rationale: To ensure frequent and accurate assessment of patient

2. Inform physician of any abnormal physical examination or laboratory values.
  Rationale: To assess whether further laboratory examinations or procedures may be indicated

3. If growth retardation is suspected or confirmed, place patient on limited activity and 2 to 3 periods of 2 hours lying in a lateral recumbent position[6] or complete bed rest.
  Rationale: To increase uterine blood flow

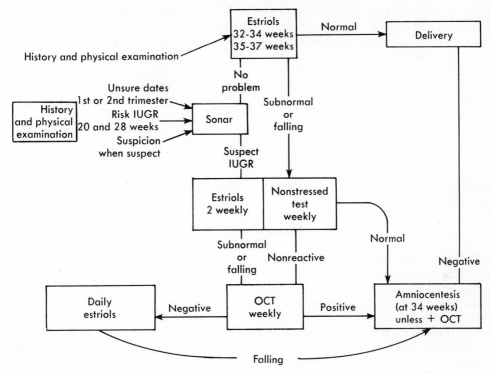

Fig. 4-8. Diagnostic factors related to the assessment of the intrauterine growth–retarded fetus.

4. Hospitalize if diagnosis of intrauterine growth retardation is made.
   Rationale: To provide continuous assessment since the risk of fetal death is high
5. Be supportive of mother and family.
   Rationale: To help patient understand and accept dangers to fetus since she may feel fine
6. Prepare for delivery.
   Rationale: To ensure readiness should an early delivery be required

EDUCATIONAL

1. Provide an in-service educational program for health care personnel concerning intrauterine growth retardation.
   Rationale: To provide current and accurate information about the cause, treatment, and prognosis to those involved with the patient so information given to the patient is consistent
2. Provide patient and significant other with in-

formation about IUGR, the procedures, their value, and purpose within her cognitive level.
   Rationale: To decrease anxiety and fear so mother and supportive other may cope with the various situations and will comply with treatment regime as well as recognize the positive prognosis if adequate therapy is provided
3. Encourage good nutrition by providing counseling, pamphlets, and praising good food habits.
   Rationale: To increase knowledge of good nutrition and reinforce former knowledge

Problem □ Assessing the growth-retarded fetus during labor

GOAL: To recognize fetal distress and manage antepartally
Rationale: To recognize fetal distress and intervene to decrease the morbidity and mortality of the growth-retarded fetus during labor

DIAGNOSTIC

1. Institute fetal monitoring on arrival.
   Rationale: To detect any aberrations in fetal heart rate patterns

2. Perform fetal scalp blood sampling if abnormal fetal heart patterns persist.
   Rationale: To check for acidosis, which is an indicator of fetal asphyxia

3. Provide a sample of maternal blood with fetal blood sample.
   Rationale: To assess maternal acid-base status, which affects the fetus

4. If fetal pH is less than 7.25, repeat immediately.
   Rationale: To determine need for immediate delivery if blood pH is 7.25 or less on two to three serial samples

5. Check amniotic fluid for presence of meconium.
   Rationale: To determine whether there is fetal asphyxia as indicated by meconium in the amniotic fluid in a cephalic presentation

6. Review maternal history, laboratory values, and physical examination.
   Rationale: To gain knowledge of prenatal course so that a plan of care can be developed and to have knowledge of maternal problems and attitudes

THERAPEUTIC

1. Inform physician of any abnormal fetal heart patterns.
   Rationale: To determine whether prompt medical intervention may be indicated

2. If abnormal fetal heart patterns present:
   a. Deliver oxygen by mask to the mother at 7 to 8 liters.
      Rationale: To provide high maternal levels of oxygen so fetal oxygen levels will be increased
   b. Place mother on her side.
      Rationale: To displace the uterus off the vena cava, therefore increasing uterine circulation by preventing supine hypotension syndrome

3. With fetal scalp blood sampling:
   a. Use sterile technique.
      Rationale: To prevent infection of the fetus and mother
   b. Collect sample within 1 minute.
      Rationale: To be considered accurate value sample must be collected within 1 minute[10]
   c. Site of incision should be compressed with dry cotton swab and observed.
      Rationale: To prevent hemorrhage[10]

4. Prepare delivery room for vaginal delivery and cesarean section.
   Rationale: To decrease fetal morbidity or mortality immediate delivery is required in the presence of persistent abnormal fetal heart patterns and/or low fetal pH's

5. Be sure delivery room temperature is as high as possible.
   Rationale: To avoid danger of cold stress

6. Reassure the mother and her significant other.
   Rationale: To minimize frightening experience of labor and delivery with fetal problems

7. Support maternal efforts to use psychoprophylactic methods.
   Rationale: To prevent or decrease the use of analgesia and anesthesia, which might have a depressant effect on an already compromised fetus

8. Notify nursery of a possible intrauterine growth–retarded fetus.
   Rationale: To have two people, either physicians and/or nurses, trained in resuscitation and first hour care and equipment available for a possibly distressed neonate

EDUCATIONAL

1. Provide in-service educational programs and supervised experience for labor room nursing personnel concerning the management of the laboring woman, with special emphasis on fetal heart monitoring, fetal scalp blood sampling, and psychoprophylactic techniques.
   Rationale: To provide nurses with knowledge so accurate assessments can be made and appropriate intervention taken

2. Provide the patient with an explanation of each procedure.
   Rationale: To decrease anxiety and fear so the mother and her significant others may cope with the situation

3. Teach and/or reinforce breathing techniques and relaxation.
   Rationale: To help decrease the anxiety, ten-

sion, and pain felt by the mother through psychoprophylactic techniques, resulting in decreased use of analgesia and anesthesia

Problem □ Immediate care of intrauterine growth–retarded neonate

GOAL: To prevent problems associated with growth retardation

DIAGNOSTIC

1. An Apgar score must be evaluated at 1 and 5 minutes.
   Rationale: To provide a quick assessment of neonatal status at birth
2. Observe for meconium-stained fluid, skin, or nails.
   Rationale: To assess for possible meconium aspiration
3. Perform a complete physical examination.
   Rationale: To rule out congenital anomalies and estimate gestational age
4. Observe for the signs of respiratory distress.
   Rationale: To prevent further asphyxia that may be causing the respiratory distress symptoms as well as an amniotic fluid aspiration or possible pneumothorax

THERAPEUTIC

1. Have two people available in the delivery room who are trained in resuscitation and first hour care.
   Rationale: To prevent neonatal morbidity or mortality, resuscitation, which requires two people, may be imperative[37] (Fig. 4-9)
2. Suction the nares and pharynx gently prior to delivery of the shoulders; if cesarean section, suction nares and pharynx prior to first breath.
   Rationale: To prevent or reduce the incidence and severity of meconium aspiration
3. Clamp umbilical cord within the first 30 seconds of life, preferably with the first cry.
   Rationale: To decrease the possibility of hyperviscosity from placental transfusion and permit the decrease in pulmonary vascular resistance to occur, thereby permitting blood to fill the previously unfilled pulmonary vascular bed
4. Dry the neonate and place under a radiant warmer with the head down.
   Rationale: To keep neonate warm, thereby preventing additional stress

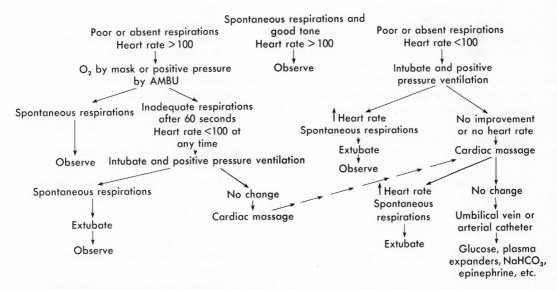

Fig. 4-9. Resuscitation outline. Delivery—quick assessment. (From Schreiner, R.: Management of neonatal problems, Indianapolis, 1977, Department of Pediatrics, Indiana University.)

5. Resuscitate neonate as indicated in Fig. 4-9.
   Rationale: To help establish cardiopulmonary status of neonate
6. Monitor vital signs including blood pressure, apical pulse, and respiratory rate.
   Rationale: To provide information about the neonate's status
7. Monitor arterial blood gases as indicated.
   Rationale: To assess oxygenation and acid-base status of neonate to determine if further intervention is needed
8. Do a Dextrostix test when heart rate and respiration are stable; transfer to special care nursery.
   Rationale: To continue to observe the neonate for complications requiring additional support
9. Allow mother and significant other to see and touch neonate as long as possible prior to transfer.
   Rationale: To encourage the bonding process to begin
10. Encourage significant other to accompany neonate to special care nursery.
    Rationale: To allow the significant other to act as a link between the mother and neonate and report current information and allay the mother's fears[24]
11. Provide emotional support to the mother and her significant other.
    Rationale: To decrease anxiety levels and reduce fears of an unknown situation

EDUCATIONAL

1. Provide in-service educational programs for nursery and delivery room personnel with emphasis on resuscitation, thermoregulation, respiratory distress syndrome, and family-infant bonding.
   Rationale: To provide nurses with knowledge needed to make accurate assessments and to take appropriate interventions
2. Provide the family unit with information about the neonate and his or her problems.
   Rationale: To decrease anxiety and fear about the neonate's ability to survive so he or she can be accepted

Problem □ Nursery care of the growth-retarded neonate

GOAL: To prevent problems associated with adjustment of the growth-retarded neonate
   Rationale: To prevent neonatal morbidity and mortality caused by problems common to the growth-retarded neonate

DIAGNOSTIC

1. Obtain a prenatal and intrapartum history of the mother and neonate.
   Rationale: To have a knowledge of prior conditions and treatment and to help predict possible causes of retardation
2. Perform physical and neurological examinations of the neonate at appropriate times.
   Rationale: To detect abnormalities and determine an estimated gestational age
3. Continuously:
   a. Assess thermoneutral regulation by temperature.
   b. Assess cardiac function by heart rate and blood pressure.
   c. Assess respiratory function by rate, breath sounds, and any signs of retracting or grunting.
   d. Assess gastrointestinal function by bowel sounds, absorption of feedings, and stooling pattern.
   e. Assess renal function by specific gravity of urine, output, hematuria, proteinuria, or glycosuria.
   Rationale: To assess for physiological adjustments and signs of complications
4. The following blood work should be done:
   a. Serum electrolytes, calcium, BUN.
   b. CBC, platelets, and hematocrit with total serum protein.
   c. TORCH screen.
   d. Blood cultures.
   e. Serum IgM levels on cord blood.
   f. Dextrostix test every hour times four, followed by every 4 hours for 24 hours; then every 8 hours until 72 hours of age unless symptomatic; if Dextrostix test is less than 45 mg%, send blood glucose to laboratory immediately.
   g. Arterial blood gases as necessary or with signs of respiratory distress or oxygen changes.

Rationale: To determine the physiological adaptation of the neonate to extrauterine life and rule out an infection

5. Other laboratory studies:
    a. Urine bacterial and viral cultures
    b. Spinal fluid studies
    c. Throat bacterial and viral cultures
    d. Fecal bacterial and viral cultures
    e. Stomach contents for cultures
    Rationale: To rule out infections
6. Assess parental performance with the neonate.
    Rationale: To detect problems in parent-neonate relations and to help the family cope with and accept their feelings of guilt, anger, frustration, and sorrow, so that they may move to a stage of acceptance of the neonate
7. Observe for signs of central nervous system aberrations.
    Rationale: To observe for aberrations that may be caused by asphyxia, sepsis, or hypoglycemia[5]
8. Observe for signs of hypoglycemia, which are related to a malfunctioning central nervous system (jitteriness, tremors, lethargy, high-pitched cry, poor suck, cyanosis, limpness or seizure activity).
    Rationale: To prevent hypoglycemia in the growth-retarded neonate who has decreased stores of glycogen and increased metabolic needs[14]
9. Observe signs and symptoms of respiratory distress.
    Rationale: To minimize chance of asphyxia

THERAPEUTIC

1. Nutritional support:
    a. If the neonate is in good condition, start oral $D_{10}W$ no later than 4 hours of age or earlier advancing to full strength, 24 calorie, and 27 calorie as tolerated; supplemental intravenous fluids should be given to fulfill fluid requirements of 80 to 120 calories/kg/day.[3,4,14,17,36]
    Rationale: To maintain blood sugar levels and promote growth
    b. If the neonate's condition is questionable, start D_{10} immediately.
    Rationale: To prevent hypoglycemia

2. Maintain thermoneutral environment.
    Rationale: To decrease the calories used for heat production, which would slow the rate of growth[14]
3. If growth retardation is due to congenital infection, utilize appropriate isolation procedures.
    Rationale: To prevent the spread of infection to personnel, other neonates, and family members
4. Facilitate family-infant bonding by:
    a. Encourage early visits and touching.
    Rationale: To allay the family's fantasies, which are worse than the actual situation[24]
    b. Allow the family to assume care.
    Rationale: To foster bonding by having the family assume caretaking activities; the more the neonate becomes theirs, their fear of the neonate not surviving decreases[24]
    c. Discuss the neonate's condition at a level parents understand; be prepared to reexplain.
    Rationale: To allow the family to understand the neonate's condition and be better able to deal with the anxiety and stress of the situation (Many times parents do not hear because of stress and the environment.)
    d. Have an optimistic but realistic attitude.
    Rationale: To help the family members bond to the neonate. If personnel display pessimistic attitudes, family members will not bond to the neonate so the death or morbidity will not "hurt.")
5. Allow the family members to express their concerns about the neonate and be accepting of their expressions.
    Rationale: To help the family cope with and accept their feelings of guilt, anger, frustration, and sorrow so that they may move to a stage of acceptance of the neonate
6. Begin discharge planning early.
    Rationale: To begin to prepare the family for the neonate's discharge, to provide time for locating resources that may be needed at home, and to provide continuity of care with other agencies

7. Maintain follow-up programs.

   Rationale: To evaluate developmental (physical, psychological, and sociological) progress

EDUCATIONAL

1. Provide in-service educational programs and supervised experience for the nursery personnel concerning the care of the high-risk neonate.

   Rationale: To provide nurses with adequate knowledge so high-risk neonates and their families will be properly assessed and managed

2. Provide the family with explanations of procedures, equipment, and treatment regimes.

   Rationale: To decrease anxiety and fear because they do not understand the purpose

3. Teach parents about the newborn, his or her care and needs.

   Rationale: To help the family realize the neonate is an individual and provide them with knowledge necessary for care

REFERENCES

1. Aladjem, S., and Brown, A. K.: Perinatal intensive care, St. Louis, 1977, The C. V. Mosby Co.
2. Andrews, B.: Amniotic fluid studies to determine maturity, Pediatr. Clin. North Am. 17(1):49, 1970.
3. Avery, G.: Neonatology, pathophysiology and management of the newborn, Philadelphia, 1975, J. B. Lippincott Co.
4. Babson, S., Pernoll, M., and Benda, G.: Diagnosis and management of the fetus and neonate at risk: a guide for team care, ed. 4, St. Louis, 1979, The C. V. Mosby Co.
5. Battaglia, F. C.: Intrauterine growth retardation, Am. J. Obstet. Gynecol. 106(7): 1103, 1970.
6. Behrman, R.: Neonatal-perinatal medicine, ed. 2, St. Louis, 1977, The C. V. Mosby Co.
7. Brasel, J. A., and Winick, M.: Maternal nutrition and prenatal growth, Arch. Dis. Child. 47:479, 1972.
8. Burosh, P.: Serial estriol determinations in high risk pregnancies: implications for primary care, J. Obstet. Gynecol. Nurs. 5(3):34, 1976.
9. Cheek, D., Graystone, J., and Neall, M.: Factors controlling fetal growth, Clin. Obstet. Gynecol. 20(4):925, 1977.
10. Cohen, H.: Biochemical monitoring by fetal blood sampling, Clin. Anesth. 10(2):71, 1973.
11. Cook, N.: Intrauterine and extrauterine recognition and management of deviant fetal growth, Pediatr. Clin. North Am. 24(1):431, 1977.
12. Dorland's Illustrated Medical Dictionary, ed. 25, Philadelphia, 1974, W. B. Saunders Co.
13. Drillien, C. M.: The small-for-date infant: etiology and prognosis, Pediatr. Clin. North Am. 17(1):9, 1970.
14. Evans, H., and Glass, L.: Perinatal medicine, New York, 1976, Harper & Row, Publishers.
15. Freeman, R., and Cetrulo, C. L.: Bioelectric evaluation in intrauterine growth retardation, Clin. Obstet. Gynecol. 20(4):979, 1977.
16. Frigoletto, F. D., and Rothchild, S. B.: Altered fetal growth: an overview, Clin. Obstet. Gynecol. 20:4, 1977.
17. Gresham, E.: Nutritional problems of the premature infant. In Schreiner, R., editor: Management of neonatal problems, Indianapolis, 1977, Department of Pediatrics, Indiana University.
18. Guyton, A.: Textbook of medical physiology, Philadelphia, 1971, W. B. Saunders Co.
19. Hobbins, J., and Berkowitz, R.: Ultrasonography in the diagnosis of intrauterine growth retardation, Clin. Obstet. Gynecol. 20(24):957, 1977.
20. Hobbins, J. C., and Winsberg, F.: Ultrasonography in obstetrics and gynecology, Baltimore, 1977, The Williams & Wilkins Co.
21. Isler, C.: Infection: constant threat to perinatal life, RN 38(8):23, 1975.
22. Kaltreider, F., and Johnson, J.: Patients at risk of low-birth-weight delivery, Am. J. Obstet. Gynecol. 124(3):251, 1976.
23. Keener, P.: Assessment of gestational age. In Schreiner, R., editor: Management of neonatal problems, Indianapolis, 1977, Department of Pediatrics, Indiana University.
24. Klaus, M., and Kennell, J.: Maternal-infant bonding, St. Louis, 1976, The C. V. Mosby Co.
25. Low, J. A., et al.: Intrauterine growth retardation: a preliminary report of long-term morbidity, Perinatol. Neonatol. Pediatr. Nutr. Curr. 4(2):3, 1978.
26. Lubchenco, L. O.: Assessment of gestational age and development at birth, Pediatr. Clin. North Am. 17(1):125, 1976.
27. Mann, L., Tejani, N., and Weiss, R.: Antenatal diagnosis and management of the small-for-gestational age fetus, Am. J. Obstet. Gynecol. 120(7):995, 1974.
28. Moore, K.: Before we are born, Philadelphia, 1974, W. B. Saunders Co.
29. Oh, W.: Considerations in neonates with intrauterine growth retardation, Clin. Obstet. Gynecol. 20(4):991, 1977.
30. Page, E. W., Villee, C. A., and Villee, D. B.: Human reproduction, ed. 2, Philadelphia, 1976, W. B. Saunders Co.
31. Petrie, R., and Pollak, K.: Intrapartum fetal monitoring by fetal blood sampling, J. Obstet. Gynecol. Nurs. 5(5):525, 1976.
32. Pollak, A., Cowett, R. M., Schwatz, R., and Oh, W.: Glucose disposal in low birth weight infants during steady-state hyperglycemia: effects of exogenous insulin administration, Perinatol. Neonatol. Pediatr. Nutr. Curr. 4(2):35, 1978.
33. Pritchard, J. A., and MacDonald, P. C.: Williams obstetrics, ed. 15, New York, 1976, Appleton-Century-Crofts.
34. Reed, D. M., and Stanley, F. J., editors: The epidemiology of prematurity, Baltimore, 1977, Urban & Schwarzenberg, Inc.
35. Robinson, L.: Psychological aspects of the care of hospitalized patients, Philadelphia, 1972, F. A. Davis Co.

36. Schaffer, A. J., and Avery, M. E.: Diseases of the newborn, Philadelphia, 1977, W. B. Saunders Co.
37. Schreiner, R.: Techniques of resuscitation. In Schreiner, R., editor: Management of neonatal problems, Indianapolis, 1977, Department of Pediatrics, Indiana University.
38. Spellacy, W.: Management of the high-risk pregnancy, Baltimore, 1976, University Park Press.
39. Tejani, N., and Mann, L. I.: Diagnosis and management of the small-for gestational age fetus, Clin. Obstet. Gynecol. **20**(4):943, 1977.
40. Tejani, N., Mann, L., and Weiss, R.: Antenatal diagnosis and management of the small-for-gestational-age fetus, Obstet. Gynecol. **47**(1):31, 1976.
41. Tulchinsky, D.: Endocrine evaluation in the diagnosis of intrauterine growth retardation, Clin. Obstet. Gynecol. **20**(4):969, 1977.
42. Weingold, A. B., DeJesus, T. P. S., and O'Keefe, J.: Oxytocin challenge test, Am. J. Obstet. Gynecol. **123**:466, 1975.
43. Worthington, B. S., Vermeersch, J., and Williams, S. R.: Nutrition in pregnancy and lactation, St. Louis, 1977, The C. V. Mosby Co.

Chapter 5

Care of the pregnant patient with diabetes

Kay McWhirter and Rosanne Harrigan Perez

Diabetes mellitus associated with pregnancy is a significant factor contributing to perinatal loss and morbidity.[39] Diabetes (overt and gestational) is reported to complicate between 2% and 3% of all pregnancies, with a perinatal mortality rate four to five times higher than the "normal" pregnancy.[31,32,39]

The understanding and management of the pregnant patient with diabetes have been enhanced in recent years by the acceptance of White's and Pederson's classification of diabetic women, the new and improved methods of screening and identifying the pregnant patient with diabetes, the rigid control of maternal glucose levels by appropriate dietary and/or insulin regulation, and the new diagnostic tests developed to assess fetal maturity and possible fetal distress.[20,21,39]

The ability to reduce the perinatal mortality and morbidity rates for pregnant patients with diabetes exists today.[39] When modern maternal and fetal diagnostic tests are used and interpreted correctly along with good clinical management of the pregnant patient with diabetes and modern neonatal intensive care units are available for infants who have problems, the perinatal mortality rate and the quality of life will improve.[3]

A general understanding of diabetes is necessary before one can understand pregnancies that are complicated by diabetes or diabetes that is complicated by a pregnancy. This chapter will present a general discussion concerning what diabetes is and how it affects normal metabolism. It will also present a detailed review of the literature on the effects that pregnancy and diabetes have on one another and the general management of a pregnancy that is complicated by diabetes.

AN OVERVIEW OF DIABETES MELLITUS
Physiology of the pancreas

The pancreas is both an exocrine and endocrine gland that lies posterior but inferior to the liver and stomach.[55] The exocrine function is carried out by cells within the walls of the tubular and acinar units of the pancreas; these cells secrete enzymes that help in the digestion of proteins, carbohydrates, and fats.[55]

The islets of Langerhans control the endocrine functions of the pancreas. These islets are differentiated into alpha and beta cells and secrete glucagon and insulin, respectively. These hormones, glucagon and insulin, both play a vital role in carbohydrate metabolism.[55] Insulin, produced by the beta cells, acts as a hypoglycemic agent by promoting glucose passage into the muscle and adipose tissue, thus lowering the blood glucose concentration.[12,13,55] Under normal body conditions the concentration of glucose in the blood that perfuses the pancreas is the most important determinant of the rate of insulin secretion.[25,26] Glucagon, produced by the alpha cells of the islets of Langerhans, acts as a hyperglycemic agent by promoting the conversion of glycogen to glucose within the liver, thereby increasing the blood glucose concentrations.[55]

Normal carbohydrate metabolism

Carbohydrates are considered the body's preferred fuel as well as its most immediate source of energy.[55] Carbohydrate metabolism involves (1) the active transport of glucose into the cell and the release of energy (involving glycolysis and the Krebs cycle); (2) the storage of the glucose, as glycogen or fat, that is not immediately needed for energy; (3) the conversion of glycogen back to glucose; and (4) the conversion of fats and proteins to glucose or glycogen whenever the energy is needed and there is a lack of readily available glucose and/or glycogen (glyconeogenesis).[55] When there is a lack of available carbohydrates, the body will obtain the needed energy by converting first fats and then proteins to glucose.[25,55]

DIABETES MELLITUS

Diabetes mellitus results from a disparity between the amount of insulin needed by the body and the amount of metabolically effective insulin available in the body.[61] Insulin must be present for glucose to get into the body cells to be used for energy. In diabetes there is an insulin deficiency that results in disorders of carbohydrate metabolism, thus finally resulting in protein and fat metabolism disorders.[55,60,61] Current literature describes diabetes as a chronic hereditary disorder characterized by hyperglycemia and glucosuria with long-term degenerative changes noted in the vascular system of the body.[22,38]

The exact cause of diabetes mellitus is not known, but it develops whenever there is a persistent insulin deficiency in the body.[38,55] The insulin deficiency may be due to (1) beta cell damage; (2) insulin inactivation by circulating antibodies or insulin antagonists; and/or (3) the body's increased need for insulin in such conditions as stress, obesity, and pregnancy.[55,61]

Diabetes mellitus ordinarily appears as one of two recognized clinical pictures: the juvenile type or the adult-onset type.[61] Juvenile diabetes usually occurs during childhood or puberty with an abrupt onset. Most often there is an absolute deficiency of insulin, requiring daily insulin injections and careful planning and regulation of diet and exercise programs.[55] Adult-onset diabetes usually occurs after the age of 40, with the onset being gradual. There is a relative insulin deficiency, and oftentimes insulin injections are not needed. Seventy percent of the adult-onset cases of diabetes can be controlled with diet and/or oral hypoglycemic agents.[41,55]

Pathophysiology for diabetic symptoms

Insulin directly controls the rate of carbohydrate metabolism and thereby indirectly affects fat and protein metabolism.[55] Therefore an insulin deficiency, whatever its cause may be, yields a chain of unwanted/unhealthy events in the body.[55] When an insulin deficiency exists, glucose cannot get into the cells so the "preferred" energy is not available, thus causing the body to obtain its needed energy from the oxidation of fats and proteins. The breakdown of fat tissue and muscle in organ protein causes a generalized tissue-wasting, which results in a negative nitrogen balance and ketosis.[12,55]

Glucose that is unable to get into the body cells because of the lack of insulin causes the blood glucose levels to rise far above their normal limits.[12,55] Because of this hyperglycemia, cellular water is lost into the blood resulting in cellular dehydration.[55] As the blood sugar levels continue to rise, glucosuria results. Because of the high osmotic pull of glucose within the urine, the kidney tubules are unable to reabsorb water causing extracellular dehydration.[12,55] Eventually as a result of these abnormalities, the four cardinal symptoms of diabetes are manifested: polyuria, polydipsia, polyphagia, and weight loss.[12,55] In addition to these symptoms, metabolic acidosis and hyperlipemia may be present.[55] Hyperlipemia along with hyperglycemia can result in vascular lesions in the peripheral arteries (and their branches) and the coronary arteries. Nephropathy, retinopathy, or blindness may result from the degenerative vascular changes associated with diabetes.[12,55] Patients with diabetes are prone to infection (because of hyperglycemia) and have retarded healing processes (because of vascular lesions and decreased circulation).

Classification of diabetes

The development of abnormal carbohydrate metabolism has been classified as (1) prediabetes, (2) latent chemical diabetes, (3) chemical diabetes, and (4) overt diabetes.[11,44,60]

Prediabetes is a condition that is present at the moment of conception, thus it has a genetic predisposition.[60] The usual tests for glucose impairment show no abnormalities in the prediabetic phase.[60]

Latent chemical diabetes, also called subclinical

diabetes, is a definite diabetic state but not very overt in nature.[11] Usually, a patient with latent chemical diabetes has a normal glucose tolerance test until the body is under some form of stress, such as pregnancy or infection.[11,44]

Chemical diabetes is an abnormal response in a person after a glucose load occurs. This state exists in the absence of stress, and the person's fasting blood glucose levels are normal.[11,44,60]

Overt diabetes exists when the four cardinal symptoms are present with varying severity.[11,44,60]

Predisposing factors to diabetes mellitus

Four major areas that are delineated in the literature as predisposing factors to diabetes include the following.

1. *Persons with a family history of diabetes:* The mode of genetic transmission is not really known, but many investigators accept the autosomal recessive hypothesis and have shown an increased family history of the disease among patients with diabetes.[45,74,81]

2. *Obesity:* In obesity the levels of circulating insulin are high,[48] and the secretion of insulin in response to glucose is abnormally high in relation to the level of blood glucose.[77] The level of insulin secretion was found to correlate with the degree of obesity and the size of the fat cells in adipose tissue,[8] while weight reduction reduces the insulin level.[49] Obesity predisposes persons to diabetes because there are increased demands placed on the pancreas to produce the needed insulin, and eventually beta cell exhaustion occurs.[81]

3. *Persons who are over the age of 40:* Once a person becomes 65 he or she has a 50% chance of having diabetes before his or her death.[81]

4. *Women:* Women, especially multiparas, are more prone to diabetes than men.[73,81]

Carbohydrate metabolism in the fasting nonpregnant state

In the fasting nonpregnant state glucose homeostasis is dependent on a balance between the production and use of glucose.[84-86] To meet the body's energy needs in the fasting state the liver produces glucose by the breakdown of glycogen or through gluconeogenesis.[25,26] A fall in insulin level is the major hormonal signal regulating the production of glucose by the liver, but small amounts of circulating glucagon and glucose precursors (for example, alanine) are also necessary to ensure hepatic glucose production.[25,26]

Carbohydrate metabolism in the fasting pregnant state

Pregnancy affects metabolism in the fasting state because of the depletion of glucose and amino acids from the maternal-to-fetal circulation.[25,26] It is important to remember that the energy requirements of the fetus are supplied primarily by glucose, and the fetus obtains its glucose from the maternal circulation by facilitative diffusion.[25,26,58,66] Fetal blood glucose levels are 10 to 20 mg/dl below that of the maternal circulation.[25,58] The placenta is not permeable to maternal insulin, thus fetal glucose utilization is independent of maternal insulin levels.[8] As early as the twelfth week after conception, fetal insulin can be detected and stimulated in response to increased availability of blood glucose and by aminogenic activity.[36,64]

Amino acids are actively transported across the placenta to be used in protein synthesis and may also be catabolized and used as energy.[26,27,37] Regardless of how these amino acids are used, their transfer to the fetus from the maternal circulation results in maternal hypoaminoacidemia.[26,27] Because the amino acids are precursors for gluconeogenesis by the maternal liver in the fasting state, the fetus causes a depletion of glucose as well as its precursors from the mother.[26,27]

The fetus is a glucose consumer whose use of glucose is not dependent on maternal insulin levels. Besides taking glucose from the maternal circulation, the fetus draws amino acids from the maternal circulation. As a result of the fetus' need for glucose, the mother is found to have hyperketonemia, hypoaminoacidemia, and hypoglycemia. As a consequence of the lower maternal glucose levels, the maternal insulin levels also fall, resulting in further starvation ketosis.[26,27] The maternal hypoglycemia is pronounced further by the fetal use of the maternal gluconeogenic precursors.[25] The overall effect to the mother is an exaggerated response to starvation.

Carbohydrate metabolism in the nonpregnant fed state

The major nutrients in a person's diet consist of carbohydrates, fats, and proteins and are metabolized or stored in the liver, adipose tissues, and/or muscle.[25,26] Insulin is the primary mechanism regulating tissue uptake of nutrients.[25,26] Following the ingestion of carbohydrates, the plasma insulin levels may increase as much as 10 times their normal amount. It is because of this hyperinsulinemia state that glucose is taken up by a variety of body tissues and is stored in the liver as glycogen or converted to fatty acids and triglycerides. Because of this storage of glucose, the blood glucose level remains fairly constant throughout the day, even between meals.[87]

Carbohydrate metabolism in the pregnant fed state

Hyperinsulinemia, hyperglycemia, hypertriglyceridemia, and decreased sensitivity to insulin are the metabolic responses to feeding during pregnancy.[26,27] A change in the responsiveness of the beta cells of the pancreas (beta cell hyperplasia) is the reason for the hyperinsulinemia manifested during pregnancy.[26,27,31]

Even though high blood insulin levels are present during pregnancy, the blood glucose response to administration of a carbohydrate load is higher than that of a nonpregnant state.[65] Some studies have shown that a high elevation in blood glucose levels following administration of carbohydrates is due to the failure of the liver to take up and store the excessive glucose.[25,26] Despite the decrease in the liver and tissue responsiveness to insulin in normal pregnancy, the range of glucose values are actually less than in nonpregnant subjects. The maintenance of glucose homeostasis is achieved by a compensatory increase in plasma insulin.[66,89]

The decreased tissue responsiveness to insulin along with the effects of pregnancy in unmasking diabetes and increasing insulin requirements in already manifested diabetes make up the basis for calling the effects of pregnancy "diabetogenic."[25,26] Some of the factors that may be responsible for the diabetogenic effects of pregnancy are the hormones that are produced by the fetoplacental unit. These include human placental lactogen (HPL), estrogen, and progesterones.[10,25,26,90]

Human placental lactogen (HPL), also known as chorionic growth hormone or human chorionic somatotropin (HCS), is a polypeptide hormone produced by the syncytiotrophoblast.[66] HPL is secreted directly into the maternal circulation with only trace amounts appearing in the fetal circulation.[66] Immunologically and chemically, HPL is similar to growth hormone but is present in much greater amounts.[76] Human placental lactogen has luteotropic and lactogenic activity as well as an insulin antagonist action.[76] HPL alters carbohydrate metabolism by decreasing the maternal insulin effectiveness, and it has lipolytic abilities that cause an increase in mobilization of free fatty acids from peripheral fat deposits.[76] Human placental lactogen reduces the maternal use of glucose and protein, thereby increasing the availability of these fuels for the fetus.[9] HPL secretion is regulated mostly by the total placental mass, but recent studies indicate that maternal starvation and insulin hypoglycemia have also caused HPL levels to rise.[33]

Other insulin antagonists produced in greater amounts during pregnancy are cortisol, estrogens, and progesterone.[26,27,47] The maternal insulin secretion also increases during pregnancy, especially in the second and third trimesters owing to the increasing amount of insulin antagonists in the maternal blood.[60]

Nondiabetic patients resist the diabetogenic effects of pregnancy by their ability to increase insulin secretion.[9] If the maternal pancreas cannot keep up with the demand for more insulin, carbohydrate intolerance and gestational diabetes develop.[53] In borderline diabetes, overt diabetes requiring treatment may result with pregnancy. In patients with preexisting insulin-dependent diabetes the insulin dosages are usually decreased the first half of the pregnancy but increased the latter half of the pregnancy.[9]

SUMMARY OF THE METABOLIC CHANGES DURING PREGNANCY

The fetoplacental unit produces significant changes in the maternal metabolism including the hypoglycemic effect, the diabetogenic effect, and the renal handling of glucose.[82]

The maternal glucose level during pregnancy is lower than the nonpregnant state and continues to show a gradual decline as the pregnancy advances toward term.[57] This decline is due to the fetus' total dependence on maternal glucose for its energy.[3,4,15] Glucose unlike insulin reaches the fetus by facilitated diffusion through the placenta, resulting in fetal blood glucose levels only 10% to 20% lower than the maternal levels.[66] Page has estimated that the rate of glucose utilization per unit body weight in an average term infant is three to four times higher than that of an adult's basal rate. Several clinical implications can be deduced from this so-called hypoglycemic effect of pregnancy.[82]

First, the normal range for fasting glucose levels during pregnancy is lower than that in a nonpregnant state.[82] A fasting blood glucose concentration of 90 mg/dl is generally considered to be the upper normal limits for a pregnant woman.[25-27]

Second, because of the continual demand by the fetus for glucose, the mother experiences a state of accelerated starvation.[72] Further complicating this state is the hypoaminoacidemia.[82] Amino acids are actively being transported across the placenta, thus depleting the maternal availability of the precursors for gluconeogenesis.[82] When the maternal glucose intake is limited, the mother responds with fat mobilization, thus increasing free fatty acids in the blood resulting in ketone bodies and finally ketonemia.[82] Pregnant women are more prone to develop starvation ketonemia because of these reasons than nonpregnant women. Because maternal ketonemia is associated with fetal problems ranging from fetal death to abnormal neuropsychological development, starvation should be avoided.[16] It is important to remember this because weight reduction along with caloric restrictions should be avoided during pregnancy.[82]

Third, in the early part of pregnancy insulin-dependent diabetic patients may require a decrease in their insulin dosage.[67,68] The hypoglycemic effects of pregnancy exist throughout a pregnancy but become less noticeable because of the diabetogenic effects in the second half of pregnancy.[25,26] With the rising amount of placental hormones there is also an increasing sensitivity to insulin in the maternal body.[25,26] After there is ingestion of any form of carbohydrates by the pregnant woman, her circulating insulin level rapidly increases (to maintain normal glucose levels) in much greater amounts than in the nonpregnant woman.[80,82] Thus, there is a hyperinsulinemia following glucose ingestion throughout the last part of a woman's pregnancy.[82] A decrease in insulin effectiveness may result in glucose tolerance even though the circulatory blood glucose levels may be within the normal range.[82] Persons with limited B-cell function may be able to cope with the demands for insulin in the nonpregnant state but become diabetic as a result of the insulin antagonist factors associated with increasing gestational age.[20,21,51] Exogenous insulin requirements are frequently increased during the latter half of pregnancy to help the person compensate for all the diabetogenic effects of pregnancy.

Pregnancy predisposes a person to the development of glucosuria, but there is a great deal of variation in glucose excretion rates even within the same person.[18,54,82] There is no correlation shown between the degree of glucosuria and the plasma glucose level during pregnancy.[82] Therefore, glucosuria by itself is a poor indicator of diabetic control. Daily insulin requirements for the pregnant diabetic patient cannot be managed on the "sliding scale" method but must be based on frequent blood glucose levels.[56,60] When glucosuria is manifested, there is a reduction in the glucose that is available for the metabolic processes, so one must assess the need to replace the loss with additional intake of carbohydrates.[82]

DIAGNOSIS AND CLASSIFICATION OF THE PREGNANT PATIENT WITH DIABETES

Today there are two general classifications of diabetes in pregnancy: those developed by White and those developed by Pedersen.[67,91,92]

White showed in her studies that perinatal mortality was strongly correlated with the duration of diabetes in the mother and was worsened when microangiopathy was present.[89] One can deduct from her findings that the initial step in managing the patient is to assess her classification.[9] Class A patients usually have asymptomatic chemical diabetes with abnormal glucose tolerance test during pregnancy and only slightly abnormal or even normal fasting blood sugar levels.[9,89] These patients

Table 5-1. Classification of the pregnant patient with diabetes*

Class	Diabetes		Need	Angiopathy
	Onset	Duration		
A (gestational)	Any	Any	−	−
B (pregestational)	Over 20 yr	Less than 10 yr	+	−
C (pregestational)	10-19 yr	10-19 yr	+	−
D (pregestational)	Before 10 yr	More than 20 yr	+	Benign retinopathy (retinitis) and calcification in leg muscles
E (pregestational)	Any	Any	+	Calcified pelvic vessels
F (pregestational)	Any	Any	+	Calcified pelvic vessels; nephropathy, and retinopathy
R (pregestational)	Any	Any	+	Malignant retinopathy

*Modified from Gugliucci, C. L., et al.: Am. J. Obstet. Gynecol. **125**(4):437, 1976.

are only treated with diet. If insulin is required for management, the patient is classified as a class B or higher.[9,89] Class B consists of those persons who had the disease after 20 and less than 10 years before the pregnancy. Class C are those with an onset age of the disease between 10 to 19 years and a duration of 10 to 19 years. Class D refers to the longer duration (20 years) with onset before age 10. Benign retinopathy may be present. Class E are those patients with calcified pelvic vessels regardless of age of onset and duration. Class F are those patients who have calcified pelvic vessels plus retinopathy and nephropathy. White's prognostic factors depend on certain conditions that are present before pregnancy, such as insulin dependency, age of onset, and duration, as well as vascular, ocular, or renal involvement[89] (Table 5-1).

The classification of pregnant diabetic patients developed by Pedersen is based on events that occur during pregnancy and have a high correlation with poor fetal outcome.[67,68] These prognostically bad signs in pregnancy (PBSP) include preeclampsia, ketoacidosis, pyelonephritis with fever, negligence in following the diabetic treatment plan, and late enrollment for prenatal care.[67,68]

Fetal survival rate in White's classification varied from 100% in class A to 0% in class F, and in Pederson's classification the survival rate was 68.5% when one or more of the PBSP's were present and 92% when they were absent.[67,68] A combination of the two classification scales applied to each individual mother will be the most accurate assessment of fetal prognosis.[5]

Tests for detection of diabetes mellitus

The detection of diabetes is more complicated during pregnancy than in the nonpregnant state.[72] In the nonpregnant person the four classic symptoms of polyuria, polydipsia, polyphagia, and weight loss have a high correlation with the presence of diabetes mellitus. In the pregnant person these symptoms may be a result of normal gestational changes rather than carbohydrate problems.[72] For example, polyuria may be confused with an increase in urinary frequency caused by the enlarging uterus and pressure on the bladder by the fetus, and polyphagia could be confused with an increase in appetite following the first trimester nausea and vomiting episodes. Alterations in renal function resulting in glucosuria without hyperglycemia, ketonuria following caloric reduction, and normal changes in fasting and postprandial blood sugar levels make laboratory confirmation of diabetes more difficult during pregnancy.[40] A pregnant insulin-dependent diabetic is hard to manage because of these factors.[17]

Clinical clues to the diagnosis of diabetes include a family history of diabetes; a medical history of obesity and/or glucosuria; an obstetrical history of unexplained abortions, stillbirths, prematurity, high parity, previous macrosomia, or congenital abnormalities; and elevated results on random blood glucose tests.[55,59]

When screening pregnant women for diabetes, complete glucose tolerance testing needs to be done when any of the preceding clinical criteria exist (thus classifying the person as a potential diabetic patient).[40,65]

The establishment of normal values of laboratory tests, especially during pregnancy, is very controversial.[88] Therefore it is essential that each institution have guidelines distributed to the staff members as to the "within normal range" values that are used at that institution so that correct interpretation and thus better patient management can be obtained.

Specific tests for diabetes during pregnancy

Glucosuria. Glucosuria during pregnancy has been a frequent finding, reaching its peak in the third trimester.[54] There have been no correlations of glucosuria in pregnancy with high blood sugar concentrations, glucose tolerance test results, pregnancy outcome, and/or the appearance of overt diabetes.[72,79] Davison and associates[18,19] explained that benign glucosuria during pregnancy is caused by an increase in the renal blood flow and glomerular filtration rate, thus causing perfusion of usually inactive nephrons that have defective tubes with a fixed limit for glucose absorption; the loss of glucose is through these defective units. Routine examination for urine sugar throughout pregnancy is a simple screening procedure for the detection of patients that *could be* in a prediabetic state and thus require further assessment. Some of the common methods to test for glucosuria include the Clinistix, Tes-Tape, and Clinitest. The Clinistix and Tes-Tape are very sensitive, with over 98% true positive results, but the specificity is low since only 79% negative specimens are identified.[59] The Clinitest is less sensitive but more specific, providing 96% of the negative urine to be identified.[59]

If a patient shows any of the factors associated with a prediabetic state (family history, and so forth), a glucose tolerance test should be performed

to further assess that client's needs. As a clinician, one must remember that glucosuria in a pregnant diabetic patient does not *necessarily* mean a "loss of control" but should be used only as an objective clue for further investigation.

Acetonuria. During pregnancy because of the energy needs of the fetus, any maternal caloric restriction may result in a shift to nonglucose (fat and proteins) energy sources with abnormalities resulting in ketonuria.[72] Freinkel and associates[29,30] have described pregnancy as an accelerated starvation syndrome. Felig[25,26] showed that after an overnight fast ketone levels in pregnant women were elevated. This type of starvation ketosis may appear in nonglucosuric pregnant women without any diabetic stigmata.[72] It can be deduced that testing for acetonuria in pregnant women who are to have a glucose tolerance test (after fasting) may be an indication that the fasting state was observed prior to administration of the test.

Fasting blood sugar. The fasting blood sugar (FBS) is an indicator for carbohydrate status in the pregnant patient. FBS levels are less variable than postprandial blood sugar levels, and they are also less variable than most glucose tolerance tests.[72] The upper limits for "FBS normals" for pregnant women are 10% lower than found in the nonpregnant state.[65,72,78] This lower glucose level is due to the maternal hyperinsulinemia.[72] O'Sullivan[65] has set the upper limits of normal as 90 mg/dl when venous blood glucose is measured in the fasting state. If plasma levels are used, the values need to be increased by 14%.[56] An elevated FBS helps to establish the diagnosis of overt diabetes, but one must be sure that the elevation is both valid and persistent and not an error in interpretation of results from laboratory variability in what is "normal" or even caused by the patient's nonadherence to the fasting state.[72]

Postprandial blood sugars. The use of 1-, 2-, and 3-hr postprandial blood sugar levels is helpful in screening pregnant women for further need of a full glucose tolerance test. In pregnant women the test values require "pregnancy-calibrated" standards.[72] The accepted upper limit normal values were proposed by O'Sullivan[65] when using whole blood; these upper limit normal values are: 1 hr, 165 mg/dl; 2 hr, 145 mg/dl; and 3 hr, 125 mg/dl.

Clients who show any abnormal postprandial blood glucose levels need to be further assessed by a full glucose tolerance test.

Glucose tolerance testing. Diabetes is mainly a disorder of pancreatic insulin production diagnosed on the basis of maternal glucose levels in response to a glucose load.[1,2] Therefore, glucose tolerance tests would be a means of assessment of pancreatic function.

The glucose tolerance tests (GTT's) are primarily used to screen prediabetic patients and other suspected persons to distinguish positive screens or class A diabetes from negative screens. This test is usually not required for patients with overt diabetes.[72] The importance of glucose tolerance testing is based on the belief that early diagnosis and appropriate management of diabetes contribute to improved fetal outcome.[24,26,83,85]

Although glucose tolerance testing can be done by administration of either an intravenous or oral glucose load, the oral test is preferred by most and will be the one discussed in this chapter.[5] Also, the oral glucose tolerance test is the most sensitive and practical test to detect latent and/or asymptomatic diabetes.[5]

Oral glucose tolerance tests (OGTT's) are based on the theory that when an oral glucose load is given in a fasting state with an adequate nutritional background, an individual will absorb this load from the gastrointestinal tract, creating a time-related increase in the blood sugar level.[72,78] This hyperglycemia in turn stimulates the release of insulin, and the blood sugar is lowered to its "normal" level over a 2- to 3-hr period.[72]

This test consists of a fasting blood sugar and a 2- and 3-hr postprandial blood sugar following the ingestion of 100 gm of carbohydrates.[65] O'Sullivan and associates[65] have shown that the criteria for interpretation of gestational glucose tolerance tests differ from those in the nonpregnant state, with high blood glucose levels normally at the 2- and 3-hr postprandial testing times.

One standard for the upper limits of a normal glucose tolerance test is: fasting, 90 mg/dl; 1 hr, 165 mg/dl; 2 hr, 145 mg/dl; 3 hr, 125 mg/dl.[65] These values are for whole blood; if plasma is used, the values should be increased by 15%.[65] For a pregnant person to be said to have an abnormal (positive) oral glucose tolerance test, O'Sullivan[65] suggested that two or more blood values be at or above the upper limits that he suggests in the preceding. Follow-up of patients with positive tests by this criteria has revealed a subsequent development of persistent diabetes in over 20% of these patients. O'Sullivan and associates[65] also showed that pregnant persons with positive OGTT's are high perinatal risks and should be followed very closely.

EFFECTS OF PREGNANCY ON DIABETIC COMPLICATIONS

Infections and neuropathies are common among any diabetic patient, but they usually become more noticeable during pregnancy.[83,89]

Infections of the vagina and the urinary tract are most commonly seen in a pregnancy that is complicated by any stage (A to R) of diabetes.[89] Pedersen showed that 6% of the pregnant patients with diabetes that he studied had clinical evidence of urinary tract infections (UTI's).[67]

Macourt[57] states that asymptomatic bacilluria in diabetic pregnancies are three times that of the general pregnant population. One can deduce that frequent screening for urinary tract infection is essential for pregnant patients with diabetes. Diagnosis of UTI's is based on clinical symptoms such as dysuria, low back (flank) pain, frequency, fever, and urine cultures. Usually urinary tract infections will respond to appropriate antimicrobial therapy. Follow-up cultures should be mandatory to be sure of the eradication of the infection following treatment.

Vaginal infections are also common during pregnancy complicated by diabetes. The most common cause of these infections is *Candida albicans*.[82] Diagnosis can be made by the presence of *Candida albicans* on wet mounts made with vaginal discharge. If *Candida* is present, treatment consists usually of vaginal suppositories or cream of nystatin or miconazole nitrate (Monistat) for 7 days. Usually following treatment there is a remission, but recurrences are common and repeated therapy may be needed throughout the pregnancy.[82]

The neuropathies in diabetic pregnancies are usually the sensory type and respond to simple analgesics.[89] Retinopathy may manifest itself during pregnancy or could be intensified during pregnancy, thus requiring close follow-up by a trained professional during the course of a diabetic pregnancy.[89]

ADVERSE EFFECTS OF DIABETES ON PREGNANCY

There are many adverse effects of diabetes on pregnancy. Early spontaneous abortions or missed abortions occur in 10% of pregnant diabetic patients.[60,89] The spontaneous abortion rates increase as White's classification increases from A to R.[89]

Hydramnios of some degree occurs in almost all pregnant diabetic patients.[90] White[90] found a higher incidence of hydramnios in class A and B patients. Some authors have commented on the class association of hydramnios and congenital anomalies, especially those of the fetus' upper gastrointestinal tract.[60] Polyhydramnios is defined as 2000 ml or more of amniotic fluid and can be found in 25% of pregnant diabetic patients.[72] Some of the maternal complications that may result from polyhydramnios include respiratory distress, premature rupture of membranes, premature labor, and postpartum hemorrhage.[82] Any amount of hydramnios can make clinical estimation of fetal weight and attempts at auscultation of fetal heart tones very difficult, thereby complicating the assessment phase for the timing of the delivery.[72]

The likelihood of preeclampsia/eclampsia is increased fourfold in a pregnant diabetic patient.[82] This increase has been noted even when there is no evidence of preexisting vascular disease.[63] Hypertensive problems are common disorders in the pregnant diabetic patient even though the exact cause is not known. Hypertension is easy to diagnose, and it should be followed very closely so that proper treatment can be instituted when needed.

Anemia may be a problem in any pregnancy but usually it is more severe in diabetic pregnancies (especially those with renal complications).[22] Frequent hematocrit or hemoglobin determinations should be performed. If anemia does exist, one must further determine what type of anemia is present before management can be initiated. If the anemia is diagnosed as "an iron deficiency anemia," oral administration of iron may be satisfactory, but some patients may need parenteral administration of iron or even transfusions of red cells.[22]

Fetal intrauterine death is a "classical accident"

in pregnant women with diabetes.[89,90] The most common time for its occurrence is after 36 weeks' gestation.[90] The maternal causes of intrauterine death have been associated with ketoacidosis, preeclampsia, and/or maternal vascular disease,[22,90] while fetal causes have been associated with congenital anomalies, renal vein thrombosis, and placental abnormalities.[90]

TIMING OF DELIVERY: EVALUATION OF THE FETOPLACENTAL UNIT AND FETAL MATURITY

Obstetrical complications are rare up to 34 weeks' gestation, but the risk of intrauterine death and other obstetrical complications are increased considerably in the last 4 weeks' gestation.[69] The exact cause of this phenomenon is not clear.[69] It may be due to hyperglycemia.

The optimal time of delivery is when the uterine environment is not "too" hazardous and when the fetus is at an age where it can survive without serious complications outside the uterus. There are other assessment techniques now.[26,83] Delivery of a diabetic mother at 36 weeks' gestation had been a general rule of thumb based on studies showing that perinatal mortality is 19% between 32 and 34 weeks, 11% at 36 weeks, and 26% between 37 and 40 weeks' gestation.[34] Thus, delivery was at 36 weeks when the perinatal mortality rates were at their lowest level. Delivering at this time should not be a rigid rule.[83] Each individual case is different, and the clinician must base the time of delivery on that patient's fetoplacental status, fetal maturity, and the severity (class A to F) as well as the degree of control of her diabetes.[83]

Some of the common assessment methods used to determine gestational age and fetal maturity include menstrual history, uterine size at initial and subsequent examinations, date of quickening (the date when fetal heart tones were first heard), phosphatidylglycerol (PG) with the lecithin-sphingomyelin ratios (L/S), serial estriols, nonstress tests (NST), oxytocin challenge tests (OCT), and ultrasound.[70,83,89] Deterioration of the fetus' health status can be followed by the methods just listed as well as by a change in fetal movement (an increase or decrease), a change in fetal heart rate patterns, an abrupt decrease in insulin requirements by the mother, and the acute onset of polyhydramnios.[83]

Determinations of maternal blood and/or urine estriols are common methods used to evaluate the fetoplacental unit.[7] Serial estriols have been determined helpful in managing pregnancies complicated by preeclampsia or hypertensive disorders, but their value in the management of the pregnant diabetic patient is questioned by many.[52,75,83]

Twenty-four hour urine estriol excretion in diabetic pregnant patients is in the same range as that found in the normal pregnancy.[46,82] To date no studies have shown a correlation between the severity of diabetes and the level of urinary estriols.[83] If one decides to follow estriol levels in the pregnant diabetic patient, it should be started at 32 weeks' gestation since before this time estriols are of little value.[46] Estriols need to be followed daily because 60% of the patients with impending problems may be missed if the test is performed less frequently.[46] Urinary estriol determination can be influenced by many things, such as maternal renal function, certain drugs, and incomplete urinary collection.[83] Daily excretion may vary from 10% to 30% or the assays may differ as much as 10%.[7] Because of these reasons, the estriol levels should not be used as a single determination of fetal well-being.

The nonstress test (NST) assesses the integrity of the reflex mechanisms that control heart rate. The status of the fetal CNS is also reflected. The response of the fetus to spontaneous contractions and fetal movement is observed. There are essentially no contraindications to this test since no oxytocin or intravenous infusions are utilized. The time required for the test is less than that needed for a stress test, and hospitalization is not required.

In addition, the NST is thought to be the best monitor of fetal physiological integrity. Fetal heart rate and beat-to-beat variability are monitored in relationship to fetal movement. A reactive pattern in which the baseline heart rate is between 120 and 150 beats/min and baseline variability is 10 beats/min or greater with at least two fetal movements accompanied by fetal heart rate acclerations of 15 beats/min during a 20-minute period is highly predictive of fetal survival for at least 1 week.

The oxytocin challenge test (OCT) can be used to detect impending fetal compromise in the pregnant diabetic patient.[28] An oxytocin infusion is given to induce contractions, and the fetal heart rate is monitored in response to the uterine contractions.[82,83] Some authors have stated that a negative OCT may indicate the fetus is safe for a period of 1 week after the test, but this has not been demonstrated in diabetic pregnancies.[82] Therefore, OCT testing should be done two times a week after 34 weeks' gestation to decrease the incidence of fetal death.[71,82]

A change of fetal heart rate of more than 16 beats/min after 3 minutes of maternal exercise (maternal exercise test) may indicate possible fetal distress and thus is another way to assess the fetoplacental unit. This test lacks standardization and hence has questionable validity in its use especially during a diabetic pregnancy.[72]

Ultrasound has become an important method of investigating the pregnant uterus; it has become very useful in gestational age assessment, thus very helpful in assessing for the time of delivery in a diabetic pregnancy.[14,62] Ultrasound can be used as a tool for assessing the fetal age and maturity in the pregnant diabetic patient between 16 and 28 weeks' gestation.[62] The correlation between the biparietal diameter and fetal weight is a commonly used index to establish the gestational age of the fetus.[82]

One of the most serious neonatal complications associated with an infant of a diabetic mother is prematurity, and this in itself increases the incidence of respiratory distress syndrome (RDS).[6,82] The severity of this syndrome is related to the lung maturity of the fetus and can be assessed by lecithin-sphingomyelin (L/S) ratios in the amniotic fluid.[82] The phosphatidylglycerol (PG) ratio, a "lung stabilizer," is more specific than the L/S ratio and a good predictor of whether the neonate will develop RDS secondary to decreased surfactant.[93] Serial L/S and PG ratios need to be performed in the pregnant diabetic patient from 35 weeks' gestation on, and if the L/S ratio begins to decline or fails to rise and PG is present, an early delivery should be considered.[93]

CONTROL OF DIABETES DURING PREGNANCY

For most pregnant patients with diabetes a larger insulin dosage is required as pregnancy progresses and the control of their diabetes is more difficult.[23] The pregnant diabetic patient generally requires two-thirds more insulin during her pregnancy than she does in her nonpregnant state.[89,90]

Tolerance for carbohydrates usually improves during the first trimester for the diabetic patient, thus requiring the lowering of her insulin dosage.[10,89] These improvements may be due to the growing fetus and its requirements for glucose from its mother. This drains the maternal glucose supply creating a state of accelerated starvation.[24,25] Also, during this time the diabetogenic effects of pregnancy have not come into full play, thus decreasing the insulin requirements.

Generally, there is a rapid size increase of the placenta at 20 weeks' gestation (second trimester), which increases insulin antagonists. Many pregnant women with diabetes will need an increase in their insulin requirements during this time, occasionally three to four times their nonpregnancy dosages.

In the third trimester there is a further intensification of diabetes and a lowering of the renal threshold for glucose exists.[24-26] The glomerular filtration rate reaches its maximum during this time, thus explaining the disproportionately excessive glucosuria compared with a lesser degree of hyperglycemia.[25,27] The intensification of diabetes in the insulin-dependent diabetic patient is caused by the maximum amounts of diabetogenic hormones being secreted by the placenta during this time.[83]

Careful monitoring of blood glucose levels is necessary during labor and delivery as well as in the postpartum period in *any* diabetic. Short-acting insulin should be used if needed during this time.[89] One must remember that the removal of the placenta decreases the insulin antagonists and thus the insulin requirements drop. During the first few postpartum days glucosuria may be present and insulin requirements need to be based on the blood glucose levels and not the sliding scale urine method. Hypoglycemia is a hazard during the postpartum period, and maternal glucose levels should be followed closely.[72] Frequently, no insulin is required by the diabetic patient during the first 3 days following her delivery, but if insulin is needed, it is likely that only one half or less of the prepregnancy dosages will be required.[10]

The critical factor in a pregnant diabetic patient concerning her perinatal outcome is how well her diabetes is controlled.[35] What constitutes "good control" is widely debated.[35] The studies of Gillmer and associates[35] showed that the mean plasma glucose levels remained below 100 mg/dl except 1 hour following a meal in "normal" pregnancies. They also found that a constancy of maternal plasma glucose levels provided the fetus with an equally constant glucose concentration, thus decreasing problems that are associated with widely fluctuating glucose levels. This provides the "professional caregiver" with a rational goal for the management of both gestational and overt diabetes associated with pregnancy.

Reliable assessment of diabetic control can be based only on glucose and ketone measurements in both the blood and urine.[72] Usually when ketonuria is present without glucosuria, it indicates starvation ketosis, but when ketonuria is accompanied by a significant degree of glucosuria, it is an indication of diabetic ketoacidosis.[72] In starvation ketosis ketonuria is present without hyperglycemia, but in diabetic ketoacidosis both ketonuria and hyperglycemia are present.[72] The treatment of starvation ketosis consists of ingestion of carbohydrates and an assessment of diet caloric intake, while diabetic ketoacidosis requires treatment with insulin and correction of any blood electrolyte problems.[72]

Diet alone may be used to control diabetes during pregnancy, or both diet and insulin may be required depending on the severity of each individual's disease.[82]

The goal of dietary therapy is to allow a normal weight gain (20 to 30 pounds) while avoiding protein restrictions, hyperglycemia, hypoglycemia, and ketonuria.[72] The classic formula of 15 calories/pound or 30 calories/kilogram of body weight may be used for patients weighing up to 250 pounds.[72] This would allow for a range of 2400 to 3400 kcal/day for persons under 250 pounds, but more than 3500 kcal/day for patients over 250 pounds. Obese patients need a lower total caloric intake, and their needs must be determined by their weight, their weight gain, and the presence of acetone in their urine.[72] The need distribution of calories in pregnancy consists of (1) 20% to 40% carbohydrates, (2) 30% to 40% fats, and (3) 20% proteins.[72]

Oral hypoglycemic agents are never used during pregnancy because (1) they cross the placenta and are associated with fetal hypoglycemia, thrombocytopenia, and hyperbilirubinemia[50]; (2) they do not control diabetes during pregnancy; (3) there has been an increase in perinatal mortality when they were used during pregnancy[42,43]; and (4) congenital anomalies have been reported following their use.[72]

When insulin becomes necessary in managing the pregnant diabetic patient, the health care provider must know the various preparations and actions of each insulin to prescribe the right insulin and dosage for each patient. The most commonly used insulin preparations during pregnancy are regular, NPH, and the lente series.[82] The dosage of insulin must be regulated according to blood sugar levels and *not* on the presence of glucosuria. After the initial evaluation and following of blood sugar, usually biweekly fasting and 2-hour postprandial blood glucose concentrations are adequate for control of insulin dosages.[82] It is important that each case be evaluated as needed and *not* based only on a biweekly rule.

In conclusion one can see that the overall management of a pregnant diabetic patient is directly related to how her pregnancy affects her glucose tolerance, how it alters her insulin metabolism and utilization, and how it increases her tendency toward ketosis. One can deduct (from the fact that multiple body systems are affected and altered by a pregnancy that is complicated by diabetes) that the multidisciplinary team approach would be the best method for the management of the pregnant diabetic patient. Members of this team would ideally consist of an obstetrician/perinatologist, an internist, a neonatologist, a nutritionist, and a perinatal nurse clinician, thereby having the expertise for "total care" of each pregnant diabetic patient.

Protocols

Problem □ Early detection and management of pregnancies that are or possibly will be complicated by diabetes

GOAL: To identify early and manage properly the pregnant diabetic patient

Rationale: To detect early and manage properly all overt or potential diabetes so that the maternal mortality rates will decrease and fetal salvage will improve

DIAGNOSTIC

1. Identify the potential or overt diabetic early by a thorough medical history.

   Rationale: To obtain clues through a thorough medical history as to those patients who are potentially at risk of developing diabetes as their pregnancy advances because of a family history of diabetes, prior unexplained stillbirths or neonatal deaths, unexplained abortions or missed abortions, a history of obesity, previous macrosomia, or infants with congenital abnormalities. (Much baseline data can be obtained, especially from the overt diabetic patient, from the medical history including such things

   as how well the patient's diabetes is controlled; the duration of the disease; treatment methods used in its control; identifying existing sequelae from the disease; and problems, treatment, and outcome of previous pregnancies that were complicated with diabetes.)

2. A thorough physical examination should be done early in pregnancy.

   Rationale: To obtain baseline data so that any deviations can be assessed as the pregnancy advances

3. Gestational age assessment should be done at the initial visit by all methods available.

   Rationale: To determine gestational age and thus fetal maturity as it is of prime importance in determining the time of delivery for a diabetic patient as White's classification scale increases from A to R

4. Test for glucosuria at each visit.

   Rationale: To screen patients who are or will become diabetic during their pregnancy

5. Test for ketonuria at each visit.

Rationale: To detect a presence of ketones in the urine, which either means inadequate diabetic control or inadequate caloric intake and thus further follow-up

6. Fasting and 1-hr postprandial (following ingestion of 50 gm of carbohydrates) blood sugars should be done.

   Rationale: To provide a method of screening potential diabetics and also to provide a way to assess the degree of control an overt diabetic patient has obtained

7. Oral glucose tolerance tests should be done on patients who are not known to have diabetes but who exhibit an abnormal result on the fasting and/or postprandial blood sugar.

   Rationale: To establish a diagnosis of diabetes

8. Funduscopic examinations should be routinely performed by a highly trained professional.

   Rationale: To detect retinopathy, which may be revealed or intensified causing vision to be impaired or lost during pregnancy

9. Evaluation of renal function by urinalysis, urine cultures, and possibly a 24-hr urine collection for total protein and creatine clearance should be done.

   Rationale: To detect urinary tract infection in pregnant diabetic patients, since as the severity of diabetes increases, renal function may become impaired

10. Measure baseline vital signs and then check vital signs frequently.

    Rationale: To provide a basis on which to assess changes in vital signs especially the blood pressure (Hypertensive disorders are more common in diabetic pregnancies as the pregnancy advances).

THERAPEUTIC

1. The patient should be hospitalized for the initial evaluation and beginning management.

   Rationale: To require hospitalization for control depending on the severity of the patient's disease

2. Institute an appropriate dietary plan.

   Rationale: To assure that each diet is individualized for each patient no matter what class (White's) her diabetes and to assure that adequate calories are consumed to prevent mobilization of body fat stores with resulting ketonuria and ketonemia, which increase the chances of poor maternal and/or fetal outcome

3. Regulate insulin dosages.

   Rationale: To assure against insulin overdose since in early pregnancy the need for exogenous insulin may decrease

4. Instruct the patient in the use of a glucose oxidase–impregnated finger stick so that she can assess her blood glucose levels at home.

   Rationale: To enable the patient to assess her blood glucose levels at home since she cannot use the sliding scale urine method to regulate or assess her insulin dosages because of the changing renal glucose threshold during pregnancy

5. Arrange for frequent antenatal visits based on each patient's individual needs.

   Rationale: To provide close supervision since the control of diabetes during pregnancy can be difficult

6. Frequently check the patient's hematocrit.

   Rationale: To detect iron deficiency anemia to which the pregnant diabetic patient is predisposed

7. Provide the patient with an opportunity to ask questions or "just talk" about her pregnancy and how diabetes has affected it from a physiological as well as a psychological viewpoint.

   Rationale: To help the patient cope with the special physiological and psychological problems caused by the impact of diabetes on pregnancy and vice versa

EDUCATIONAL

1. Provide information to the patient and her significant others concerning diabetes and pregnancy.

   Rationale: To obtain a successful outcome of the pregnancy through patient knowledge and understanding of her disease

2. Provide explanation to the patient concerning the medical approaches chosen for her.

   Rationale: To encourage the patient to participate in her care, thereby increasing the chances of a favorable outcome

3. Discuss with the patient possible danger signs

and how she is to deal with them if they should arise.

Rationale: To make patients aware of possible problems and their symptoms so that they can take corrective action to prevent serious sequelae from developing since they are under actual medical supervision very little and have complete care of themselves most of the time

4. Provide dietary education for all patients.

   Rationale: To ensure proper dietary management, which is essential in all classes of diabetes

5. If insulin is needed, the patient and/or her significant others must know and understand insulin usage and learn how to properly administer insulin.

   Rationale: To decrease the patient's fears and to assure that the insulin is given properly and that the dosage is correct

6. Provide patient education for any procedure that the patient must perform at home in her daily management of her diabetes.

   Rationale: To help the patient become more accountable to both herself and her medical care providers, and to ensure that she is an active participant in her care, which will significantly influence her pregnancy outcome

7. Provide in-service education for the staff working with the diabetic patient.

   Rationale: To provide optimal care to the patients

Problem □ Management of the pregnant patient with diabetes as her pregnancy advances

GOAL: To provide rigid control of maternal blood glucose concentrations

Rationale: To decrease or possibly prevent problems from occurring to the mother and/or fetus

DIAGNOSTIC

1. Frequent fasting blood glucose and 2-hr postprandial levels should be taken.

   Rationale: To determine insulin requirements (which may be markedly elevated during this time) so that insulin adjustments can be made

2. Frequent physical examinations with special emphasis on the cardiovascular and renal systems should be done.

   Rationale: To detect early any problems developing in the cardiovascular and renal systems

3. Test for ketonuria at each visit.

   Rationale: To detect for the presence of ketones in the urine, which could mean inadequate diabetic control or inadequate caloric intake, both requiring further assessment

4. Frequent blood pressure measurements should be taken.

   Rationale: To detect developing hypertensive disorders, which may increase as the pregnancy progresses

5. Frequent fundal height assessment should be done.

   Rationale: To check for excessive or retarded fundal growth, which could indicate fetal and/or maternal problems and indicate ultrasound

6. Urinalysis should be done frequently.

   Rationale: To detect urinary infections, which increase as the pregnancy approaches term

THERAPEUTIC

1. Encourage antenatal visits.

   Rationale: To provide supervised management of the pregnant diabetic patient

2. Treat any infections that might develop in the appropriate manner.

   Rationale: To prevent any serious complications and to decrease the patient's discomfort associated with the infection

3. Hospitalize.

   Rationale: To maintain adequate control of the diabetes in the more advanced classes as the pregnancy advances

EDUCATIONAL

1. Reinforce patient education concerning the reason for changes in management as her pregnancy advances.

   Rationale: To increase the patient's knowledge of her situation and to lessen fears and apprehensions she may have owing to the changes that are made in her treatment plan

Problem □ When to deliver the pregnant diabetic patient

GOAL: To ensure an uncomplicated delivery at term with the avoidance of neonatal problems

Rationale: To improve maternal and neonatal outcomes

DIAGNOSTIC

1. Utilize all methods available to test for fetoplacental function and fetal maturity from 34 weeks' gestation.

   Rationale: To improve perinatal outcome through the use of all available methods and objective clinical judgment

THERAPEUTIC

1. Encourage patients to express their feelings about the tests that are performed.

   Rationale: To help decrease anxiety that the patient may have and give the professional a way to assess ''where she is at'' during that particular time

2. Watch for objective signs of maternal and/or fetal problems.

   Rationale: To identify impending problems early to minimize the chances of fetal and/or maternal complications

EDUCATIONAL

1. Provide the patient with an explanation (at her level of understanding) of all procedures and medical treatments that she receives.

   Rationale: To decrease the patient's anxiety level and thereby allow her to better cope with the situation at hand

2. Provide staff education as to the methods of performing fetoplacental function tests and fetal maturity analysis along with the laboratory values that are considered to be normal at their institution.

   Rationale: To allow for the many different methods of assessing fetal maturity and fetoplacental function as well as differences in evaluating and interpreting their results

Problem □ The management of the diabetic patient during labor and the postpartum period

GOAL: To have an uneventful delivery and postpartum period with blood glucose levels being maintained within the normal range

Rationale: To improve maternal and neonatal outcomes

DIAGNOSTIC

1. Frequent blood glucose determinations should be made during labor.

   Rationale: To prevent reactive hypoglycemia in the infant (There is an increase in body glucose needs during labor and delivery and less insulin is required. Once the placenta is delivered, the insulin antagonists drop markedly, thus reducing insulin requirements. Usually during labor patients are placed on a 5% or 10% glucose solution intravenously and the possibility exists that the maternal blood glucose will become elevated, and this could cause a reactive hypoglycemia in the infant.)

2. Frequent blood sugar levels should be taken during the postpartum period.

   Rationale: To detect great variations of blood glucose levels during the postpartum period when the diabetic patient becomes very sensitive to insulin

THERAPEUTIC

1. Adjust insulin requirements as needed.

   Rationale: To prevent hypoglycemia and its complications

2. Check frequently for ketonuria.

   Rationale: To prevent starvation ketosis and provide a means for assessing the degree of diabetic control

3. Encourage breast-feeding if desired by the patient.

   Rationale: To promote action as an antidiabetogenic factor, increase nutritional requirements, retard weight gain, and effect an overall improvement in many mothers

EDUCATIONAL

1. Explain in terms the patient can understand the reasons for close monitoring of her glucose during labor and her postpartum period.

   Rationale: To provide the patient with an understanding of her condition and to decrease fears and anxiety that can be caused by the frequent changes that may be needed in her medical management

REFERENCES

1. Abell, D. A., Beischer, P. A., Papas, A. J., and Willis, M. M.: The association between abnormal glucose tolerance and estriol excretion in pregnancy, Am. J. Obstet. Gynecol. **124:**388, 1976.
2. Abell, D. A., et al.: Routine testing for gestational diabetes, pregnancy hypoglycemia and fetal growth retardation, and results of treatment, J. Perinat. Med. **4:**197, 1976.
3. Ayromlooi, J., et al.: Modern management of the diabetic pregnancy, Obstet. Gynecol. **49**(2):137, 1977.
4. Baird, J. D.: Some aspects of carbohydrate metabolism in pregnancy with special reference to energy metabolism and hormonal status of the infant of the diabetic woman and the diabetogenic effect of pregnancy, J. Endocrinol. **44:**139, 1969.
5. Baker, D. P., Hutchinson, J. R., and Vaughn, D. L.: Comparison of standard oral and rapid intravenous glucose tolerance test in pregnancy, Obstet. Gynecol. **31**(4):475, 1968.
6. Behrman, R., editor: Neonatal-perinatal medicine, ed. 2, St. Louis, 1977, The C. V. Mosby Co.
7. Beischer, N. A., and Brown, J. B.: Current status of estrogen assays in obstetrics and gynecology. Part 2: estrogen assays in late pregnancy, Obstet. Gynecol. Surv. **27:**303, 1972.
8. Bjorntorp, P., et al.: Insulin secretion in relation to adipose tissue in men, Diabetes **20:**65, 1971.
9. Boeham, F. H., et al.: Coordinated metabolic and obstetric management of diabetic pregnancy, South. Med. J. **71**(1): 37, 1978.
10. Brown, Z. A.: Diabetes in pregnancy, Fam. Commun. Health **1**(3):43, 1978.
11. Brudenell, M., and Beard, R.: Diabetes in pregnancy, Clin. Endocrinol. Metabol. **1**(3):673, 1972.
12. Cahill, G. F.: Physiology of insulin in man, Diabetes **20:** 785, 1971.
13. Cahill, G. F., et al.: Hormonal-fuel interrelationships during fasting, J. Clin. Invest. **45:**1751, 1966.
14. Campbell, S.: The assessment of fetal development by diagnostic ultrasound, Clin. Perinatol. **1**(2):507, 1974.
15. Carrington, E.: Diabetes in pregnancy, Clin. Obstet. Gynecol. **16:**28, 1973.
16. Churchill, J. A., et al.: Neuropsychological defects in children of diabetic mothers, Am. J. Obstet., 1967.
17. Cranley, M., and Frazien, S.: Preventive intensive care of the diabetic mother and her fetus, Nurs. Clin. North Am. **8:**489, 1973.
18. Davison, J. M., and Hytten, F. E.: Renal handling of glucose in pregnancy. In Sutherland, H. W., and Stowers, J. M., editors: Carbohydrate metabolism in pregnancy and the newborn, Edinburgh, 1975, Churchill Livingstone.
19. Davison, J. M., and O'Cheyne, G. A.: History of the measurement of glucose in urine: a cautionary tale, Med. Hist. **18:**194, 1974.
20. Delaney, J. J., and Ptacek, J.: Three decades experience with diabetic pregnancies, Am. J. Obstet. Gynecol. **106**(4): 550, 1970.
21. Delaney, J. J., et al.: Management of the pregnant diabetic, Acta Diabetol. Lat. **8:**1, 1971.
22. Driscoll, J. J., and Gillespie, L.: Obstetrical consideration in diabetes in pregnancy, Med. Clin. North Am. **49:**1025, 1965.
23. Exon, P. D., Dixon, K., and Malens, J. M.: Insulin antibodies in diabetic pregnancy, Lancet **2:**126, 1974.
24. Fajans, S. S.: Identification of chemical diabetes: the definition of chemical diabetes, Metabolism **22:**11, 1973.
25. Felig, P.: Body fuel metabolism and diabetes mellitus in pregnancy, Med. Clin. North Am. **61**(1):43, 1977.
26. Felig, P.: Maternal and fetal fuel homeostasis in human pregnancy, Am. J. Clin. Nutr. **26:**998, 1973.
27. Felig, P., and Lynch, V.: Starvation in human pregnancy: hypoglycemia, hypoinsulinemia, and hyperketonemia, Science **170**(3961):990, 1970.
28. Freeman, R. K.: The use of the oxytocin challenge test for antepartum clinical evaluation of uteroplacental respiratory function, Am. J. Obstet. Gynecol. **121:**481, 1975.
29. Freinkel, N.: Effects of the conceptus on maternal metabolism during pregnancy. In Leibel, B. S., and Wrenshall, G. A., editors: On the nature and treatment of diabetes, 1965, Excerpta Medica Foundation.
30. Freinkel, N., and Goodner, C.: Insulin metabolism and pregnancy, Arch. Intern. Med. **109:**235, 1962.
31. Gabbe, S. G., et al.: Management and outcome of class A diabetes mellitus, Am. J. Obstet. Gynecol. **127:**465, 1974.
32. Gabbe, S. G., et al.: Management and outcome of pregnancy in diabetes mellitus, classes B to R, Am. J. Obstet. Gynecol. **129**(7):723, 1977.
33. Gaspard, V. J., et al.: The control of human placental lactogen secretion and its interrelation with glucose and lipid metabolism in pregnancy. In Camerini-Davalos, R. A., and Cole, H. S., editors: Early diabetes in early life, New York, 1975, Academic Press, Inc.
34. Gellis, S. S., and Hsia, D. Y.: The infant of the diabetic mother, Am. J. Dis. Child. **97:**1, 1959.
35. Gillmer, M. D., et al.: Carbohydrate metabolism in pregnancy. Part II: relation between glucose tolerance and glucose metabolism in the newborn, Br. Med. J. **3:**402, 1975.
36. Grasso, S., et al.: Serum insulin response to glucose and amino acids in the premature infant, Lancet **2:**755, 1968.
37. Gresham, E. L.: Production and excretion of urea by the fetal lamb, Pediatrics **50:**372, 1972.
38. Gugliucci, C. L., et al.: Intensive care of the pregnant diabetic, Am. J. Obstet. Gynecol. **125**(4):435, 1976.
39. Gyves, M. T., et al.: A modern approach to management of pregnant diabetics: a two-year analysis of perinatal outcomes, Am. J. Obstet. Gynecol. **126**(6):606, 1977.
40. Hadden, D. R.: Glucose tolerance test in pregnancy. In

Sutherland, H. W., and Stowers, J. M., editors: Carbohydrate metabolism in pregnancy and the newborn, Edinburgh, 1975, Churchill Livingstone.

41. Haunz, E. A.: Diabetes mellitus. In Conn, H. F., editor: Current therapy, Philadelphia, 1973, W. B. Saunders Co.

42. Jackson, W. P.: Is pregnancy diabetogenic, Lancet 2:1369, 1961.

43. Jackson, W. P., et al.: Tolbutamide and chlorpropamide during pregnancy in human diabetics, Diabetes 17(Suppl.): 98, 1962.

44. Jensen, M., Benson, R., and Bobak, I., editors: Maternity Care, St. Louis, 1977, The C. V. Mosby Co.

45. Joslin, E. P., et al.: The treatment of diabetes mellitus, ed. 10, Philadelphia, 1959, Lea and Febiger.

46. Kahn, C. B., White, P., and Younger, D.: Laboratory assessment of diabetes pregnancy, Diabetes 21:31, 1972.

47. Kaplan, S. L., et al.: Serum chorionic growth hormone—prolactin; serum pituitary growth hormone in mother and fetus at term, J. Clin. Endocrinol. 25:1370, 1965.

48. Karam, J. H., Grodsky, G. M., and Forsham, P. H.: Excessive insulin response to glucose in obese subjects as measured by immunochemical assay, Diabetes 12:197, 1964.

49. Karam, H. H., et al.: Critical factors in excessive serum insulin response to glucose: obesity in maturity-onset diabetes and growth hormone in acromegaly, Lancet 1:286, 1965.

50. Kemball, M. L., et al.: Neonatal hypoglycemia in infants of diabetic mothers given sulphonylurea drugs in pregnancy, Arch. Dis. Child. 45:696, 1970.

51. Kieval, J.: Gestational diabetes: diagnosis and management, J. Reprod. Med. 4:70, 1975.

52. Klopper, A.: Assessment of fetoplacental function by hormone assay, Am. J. Obstet. Gynecol. 107:807, 1970.

53. Kuhl, C., and Holst, J. J.: Plasma glucagon and the insulin:glucagon ratio in gestational diabetes, Diabetes 25:168, 1976.

54. Lind, T., and Hytten, F. E.: The excretion of glucose during normal pregnancy, Br. J. Obstet. Gynecol. 79:961, 1972.

55. Luckmann, J., and Sorensen, K.: Medical-surgical nursing, Philadelphia, 1974, W. B. Saunders Co.

56. Macafee, C. A., and Beischer, N. A.: The relative value of the standard indications for performing a glucose tolerance test in pregnancy, Med. J. Aust. 1:911, 1974.

57. MacDonald, H. N., et al.: Serial observations of glucose tolerance in pregnancy and the early puerperium, J. Obstet. Gynaecol. Br. Commonwealth 78:489, 1971.

58. Macourt, D. C.: Diabetes mellitus in pregnancy, Med. J. Aust. 1:797, 1974.

59. Malins, J. M.: Diabetes in the population, Clin. Endocrinol. Metabol. 1(3):645, 1972.

60. Marble, A.: Current concepts of diabetes. In Marble, A., et al.: Joslin's diabetes mellitus, ed. 11, Philadelphia, 1971, Lea and Febiger.

61. Martin, M.: Diabetes mellitus: current concepts, Am. J. Nurs. 66(3):511, 1966.

62. Murata, Y., and Martin, C.: Growth of biparietal diameter of the fetal head in diabetic pregnancy, Am. J. Obstet. Gynecol. 115:252, 1973.

63. Oakley, N. W.: The evolution of the management of diabetic pregnancy, Postgrad. Med. 45(J-Suppl.):802, 1969.

64. Obsenshain, S. C., et al.: Human fetal insulin response to sustained maternal hyperglycemia, N. Engl. J. Med. 288: 566, 1970.

65. O'Sullivan, J. B., et al.: Criteria for the oral glucose tolerance test in pregnancy, Diabetes 13:278, 1964.

66. Page, E. W.: Human fetal nutrition and growth, Am. J. Obstet. Gynecol. 104(3):378, 1969.

67. Pedersen, J.: The pregnant diabetic and her newborn: problems and management, Copenhagen, 1967, Munksgaard.

68. Pedersen, J., Molsted-Pedersen, L., and Anderson, B.: Assessor of fetal perinatal mortality in diabetic pregnancy: analysis of 1332 pregnancies in the copenhagen series, Diabetes 23:302, 1974.

69. Peel, J.: Progress in the knowledge and management of the pregnant diabetic patient, Am. J. Obstet. Gynecol. 83:847, 1962.

70. Persson, B.: Treatment of diabetic pregnancy, Israel J. Med. Sci. 11(6):609, 1975.

71. Persson, B., and Tunell, N.: Metabolic control in diabetic pregnancy, Am. J. Obstet. Gynecol. 122(6):737, 1975.

72. Posner, N. A., et al.: The outcome of pregnancy in class A diabetes mellitus, Am. J. Obstet. Gynecol. 111:886, 1973.

73. Pyke, D. A., and Please, N. W.: Obesity, parity, and diabetes, J. Endocrinol. 15:26, 1957.

74. Rimoin, D.: Inheritance in diabetes mellitus, Med. Clin. North Am. 55(4):807, 1971.

75. Rivlin, M. E., et al.: Value of estriol estimation in the management of diabetic pregnancy, Am. J. Obstet. Gynecol. 106:875, 1970.

76. Samaan, N. A., et al.: Metabolic effects of placental lactogen in man, J. Clin. Endocrinol. Metabol. 28:485, 1968.

77. Seltzer, H. S., et al.: The role of adipose cell size and adipose tissue insulin sensitivity in the carbohydrate intolerance of human obesity, J. Clin. Invest. 47:153, 1967.

78. Silverstone, F. A., Solomons, E., and Rubricius, J.: The rapid glucose tolerance test in pregnancy, J. Clin. Invest. 40:2180, 1961.

79. Solomons, E., Silverstone, F. A., and Posner, N. A.: Obstetric factors suggesting diabetes evaluated by the rapid intravenous glucose tolerance test, Obstet. Gynecol. 22:50, 1963.

80. Spellacy, W. N., and Cohn, J. E.: Human placental lactogen level and daily insulin requirements in patients with diabetes mellitus complicating pregnancy, Obstet. Gynecol. 42:330, 1973.

81. Spencer, R. T.: Patient care in endocrine problems, Philadelphia, 1973, W. B. Saunders Co.

82. Tsai, A.: Perinatal management of the diabetic patient. In Aladjem, S., and Brown, A., editors: Perinatal intensive care, St. Louis, 1977, The C. V. Mosby Co.

83. Tyson, J. E.: Obstetrical management of the pregnant diabetic, Med. Clin. North Am. 55:961, 1971.

84. Tyson, J. E., and Felig, P.: Medical aspects of diabetes in pregnancy and the diabetogenic effects of oral contraceptives, Med. Clin. North Am. 55:947, 1971.

85. Tyson, J. E., and Hock, R. A.: Gestational and pregestational diabetes: an approach to therapy, Am. J. Obstet. Gynecol. 125(7):1009, 1976.

86. Unger, R. H.: Alpha and beta cell interrelationships in health and disease, Metabolism 23:581, 1974.

87. Victor, A.: Normal blood sugar variation during pregnancy, Acta Obstet. Gynecol. Scand. **53**:37, 1974.

88. West, K. M.: Substantial differences in diagnostic criteria used by diabetes experts, Diabetes **24**:641, 1975.

89. White, P.: Diabetes mellitus in pregnancy, Clin. Perinatol. **1**(2):331, 1974.

90. White, P.: Pregnancy and diabetes, medical aspects, Med. Clin. North Am. **49**:1015, 1965.

91. White, P.: Pregnancy in diabetes. In Marble, A., editor: Joslin's diabetes mellitus, ed. 11, Philadelphia, 1971, Lea and Febiger.

92. White, P.: Pregnancy complicating diabetes, Am. J. Med. **7**:609, 1949.

93. Whitfield, C. R., and Sproule, W. B.: The amniotic fluid lecithin:sphingomylin area ratio in pregnancies complicated by diabetes, J. Obstet. Gynaecol. Br. Commonwealth **80**:918, 1973.

94. Williams, J. W.: The clinical significance of glycosuria in pregnant women, Am. J. Med. Sci. **137**:1, 1909.

95. Wilson, R. B., and Morrison, M. G.: Optimal time of delivery of the diabetic patient, Clin. Obstet. Gynecol. **5**(2):419, 1962.

96. Yeast, J. D., et al.: The use of continuous insulin infusion for the peripartum management of pregnant diabetic women, Am. J. Obstet. Gynecol. **131**(8):861, 1978.

BIBLIOGRAPHY

Archimant, G., Belizan, J. M., Ross, N. A., and Althobe, O.: Glucose concentration in amniotic fluid: its possible significance in diabetic pregnancy, Am. J. Obstet. Gynecol. **119**:596, 1974.

Bates, G. W.: Management of gestational diabetes, Postgrad. Med. **55**:55, 1974.

Bennink, H. J., and Schreurs, W. H.: Improvement of oral glucose tolerance in gestational diabetes by pyridoxine, Br. Med. J. **3**:13, 1975.

Bleicher, S., O'Sullivan, J., and Freinkel, A.: Carbohydrate metabolism in pregnancy, N. Engl. J. Med. **271**:886, 1964.

Booth, M., and Elgarf, T. A.: Plasma progesterone concentration during the third trimester of diabetic pregnancy, Br. J. Obstet. Gynecol. **81**:768, 1974.

Brearly, B. F.: The management of pregnancy in diabetes mellitus, Practitioner **215**:644, 1975.

Burt, R.: Insulin resistance in pregnancy, Obstet. Gynecol. **25**:43, 1965.

Chen, W., Palar, A., and Triconi, V.: Screening for diabetes in a prenatal clinic, Obstet. Gynecol. **40**:567, 1972.

Dawes, G. S., and Shelley, H. J.: Physiological aspects of carbohydrate metabolism in the fetus and newborn. In Dickens, F., editor: Carbohydrate metabolism and its disorders, London, 1968, Academic Press, Inc.

DeAlvarez, R. R.: Toxemia of pregnancy in the diabetic, Clin. Obstet. Gynecol. **5**:393, 1962.

Essex, N., et al.: Diabetic pregnancy, Br. Med. J. **4**:89, 1973.

Felig, P., et al.: Amino acid metabolism during starvation in human pregnancy, J. Clin. Invest. **51**:1195, 1972.

Gabbe, S. G., Mestman, J., and Hibbard, T.: Maternal mortality in diabetes mellitus, Obstet. Gynecol. **48**(5):549, 1976.

Gabbe, S. G., et al.: Maternal mortality in diabetes mellitus, Obstet. Gynecol. **48**(5):549, 1976.

Garnet, J.: Pregnancy in women with diabetes, Am. J. Nurs. **69**:1900, 1969.

Graves, W. K., Neff, R., and Mark, P.: Altered glucose metabolism in pregnancy: its determination and fetal outcome, Am. J. Obstet. Gynecol. **98**:602, 1967.

Green, J. W.: Diabetes mellitus in pregnancy, Obstet. Gynecol. **46**(6):724, 1976.

Greene, J. W., and Beargie, R. A.: The use of urinary estriol excretion studies in the assessment of the high-risk pregnancy, Pediatr. Clin. North Am. **17**:610, 1968.

Gross, M: Effects of pregnancy on carbohydrate metabolism, Clin. Obstet. Gynecol. **5**:482, 1962.

Hellman, L. M., and Pritchard, J. A.: William's Obstetrics, ed. 14, New York, 1971, Appleton-Century-Crofts.

Jones, C. J., and Fox, H.: Placental changes in gestational diabetes, Obstet. Gynecol. **48**(3):274, 1976.

Kall, L.: What is diabetes? Med. Clin. North Am. **49**:893, 1965.

Karlsson, K., and Kjellmer, I.: The outcome of diabetic pregnancies in relationship to the mother's blood sugar level, Am. J. Obstet. Gynecol. **112**:213, 1972.

Khojandi, M., Tsai, Y. M., and Tyson, J. E.: Gestational diabetes: the dilemma of delivery, Obstet. Gynecol. **43**:1, 1974.

Lev-Ray, A., and Goldman, J. A.: Brittle diabetes in pregnancy, Diabetes **26**:926, 1977.

Lind, T.: Prediabetes during pregnancy, Perinatal Care, Summer, 1977.

Linzey, E. M.: Controlling diabetes with continuous insulin infusion, Contemp. OB/GYN **12**:43, 1978.

LoBue, C., and Goodlin, R.: Treatment of fetal distress during diabetic keto-acidosis, J. Reprod. Med. **20**(2):101, 1978.

Lockwood, G. F., and Newman, R. L.: Estriol determinations in gestational diabetes, Obstet. Gynecol. **44**(5):642, 1974.

Maugh, T. H.: Hormone receptors: new clues to the cause of diabetes, Science **193**:220, 1976.

Medovy, H.: Outlook for the infant of the diabetic mother, J. Pediatr. **76**:988, 1970.

Merimee, J., and Rabin, D.: A survey of growth hormone secretion and action, Metabolism **22**:1235, 1973.

Niejadlik, D. C.: The glucose tolerance test: an evaluation, Postgrad. Med. **55**:73, 1974.

Notelovitz, M., and James, S.: Growth hormone secretion in insulin-independent pregnant diabetics, Obstet. Gynecol. **47**(4):449, 1976.

Oakley, N. W., Beard, R. W., and Turner, R. C.: Effect of sustained maternal hyperglycemia on the fetus in normal and diabetic pregnancies, Br. Med. J. **7**:466, 1972.

O'Sullivan, J. B.: Gestational diabetes: unsuspected asymptomatic diabetes in pregnancy, N. Engl. J. Med. **264**:1082, 1961.

O'Sullivan, J. B., et al.: The potential diabetic and her treatment in pregnancy, Obstet. Gynecol. **27**:683, 1966.

O'Sullivan, J. B., et al.: Screening criteria for high risk gestational diabetic patient, Am. J. Obstet. Gynecol. **116**(7):895, 1973.

O'Sullivan, J. B., et al.: Gestational diabetes and perinatal mortality rate, Am. J. Obstet. Gynecol. **116**:901, 1973.

Reis, R. A., et al.: The management of the pregnant diabetic woman and her newborn infant, Obstet. Gynecol. **46**(6):663, 1975.

Reis, R. A., et al.: Pregnancy in the diabetic woman, Am. J. Obstet. Gynecol. **46**(6):679, 1975.

Samaan, N. A., Gallagher, H. S., McRoberts, W. A., and Holt, B.: Differential evaluation of the feto placental unit in patients with diabetes, Am. J. Obstet. Gynecol. **120**:825, 1974.

Scheff, D., et al.: Neonatal thrombocytopenia and congenital malformation associated with administration of tolbutamide to the mother, J. Pediatr. **77**:457, 1970.

Shannon, J. A., and Fisher, S.: The renal tubular reabsorption of glucose in the normal dog, Am. J. Physiol. **122**:765, 1938.

Shea, M. A., Garrison, D. L., and Tom, S. K.: Diabetes in pregnancy, Am. J. Obstet. Gynecol. **111**:801, 1971.

Sheldon, J., and Coleman, J.: Remission of diabetes mellitus during pregnancy, Br. Med. J. **1**:55, 1974.

Smith, B. T., et al.: Insulin antagonism of cortisol action of lecithin synthesis by cultured fetal lung cells, J. Pediatr. **87**(6):953, 1975.

Smith, H. W., et al.: The measurement of the tubular excretory mass, effective blood flow and filtration rate in the normal kidney, J. Clin. Invest. **17**:263, 1938.

Spellacy, W. N.: Diabetes mellitus complicating pregnancy, Mod. Med. **37**:91, 1969.

Spellacy, W., and Goetz, F.: Plasma insulin in normal late pregnancy, N. Engl. J. Med. **268**:988, 1963.

Spellacy, W. N., et al.: Vitamin B_6 treatment of gestational diabetes mellitus, Am. J. Obstet. Gynecol. **127**:599, 1977.

Stallone, L. A., and Ziel, H. K.: Management of gestational diabetes, Am. J. Obstet. Gynecol. **119**:1091, 1974.

Chapter 6

Care of the patient with hyperbilirubinemia

Paula Bibeau and Rosanne Harrigan Perez

Bilirubin is a breakdown product of heme, which comes from the degradation of erythrocytes and from other heme pigments.[8] Hyperbilirubinemia can be defined as an increase in the serum bilirubin characterized by jaundice. There are two types of bilirubin: unconjugated (indirect acting) and conjugated (direct acting). Unconjugated hyperbilirubinemia is an increase in the indirect serum bilirubin greater than 1 to 1.5 mg/dl (normal is less than 0.8 mg/dl) and is the most common in the neonate. Conjugated hyperbilirubinemia is an increase in the direct serum bilirubin greater than 1.5 to 2 mg/dl when this accounts for more than 10% of the total serum bilirubin. Conjugated hyperbilirubinemia is less common in the neonate and often denotes a serious derangement of hepatic function.[4] In 50% of the full-term neonates and 80% of preterm neonates displaying jaundice, it becomes necessary to distinguish between normal physiology and pathology.

This chapter will cover fetal and neonatal bilirubin physiology, causes, agents affecting bilirubin-albumin binding, complications, and various treatments followed by a suggested protocol. This chapter will not deal with conjugated hyperbilirubinemia.

FETAL BILIRUBIN METABOLISM

Bilirubin appears in the amniotic fluid at 12 weeks' gestation and disappears at 36 to 37 weeks' gestation.[10] The fetus produces approximately 1000 mg of unconjugated bilirubin during the 40-week gestational period; this is thought to be due to the shortened life span of the red blood cells.[7] The immature fetal liver allows most of the bilirubin to remain unconjugated and transferred freely across the placenta and excreted by the maternal liver.[10] The higher concentration of albumin in the maternal circulation favors clearance and transport of unconjugated bilirubin away from the placenta.[15]

Normally the bilirubin levels of amniotic fluid, measured as optical density difference (ΔOD), decrease to 0 at 36 to 37 weeks. One study had a rise in the ΔOD in 30% of the cases after a ΔOD of 0. It is felt that the increase in volume of amniotic fluid with a resulting dilution of bilirubin levels may be responsible for the decrease; also the maturation of enzymes, especially glucuronyl transferase, helps exclude unconjugated bilirubin in amniotic fluid.[1] Increasing levels of bilirubin in amniotic fluid indicated the presence of hemolytic disease.[11]

It is not known how unconjugated bilirubin gets into amniotic fluid, but some of the suggested routes follow:

1. Tracheobronchial secretions
2. Excretions via the mucosa of the upper gastrointestinal tract
3. Transfer directly across placenta from maternal circulation
4. Diffusion across umbilical cord or amniotic membranes
5. Diffusion across fetal skin
6. Fetal urine (unlikely)
7. Fetal meconium[4,10]

NEONATAL BILIRUBIN METABOLISM

In the neonate 75% or less of the bilirubin comes from the destruction of circulating red blood cells.[10,17] The remaining bilirubin is derived from heme proteins such as myoglobin, peroxidase, catalase, and cytochromes. Other sources include the

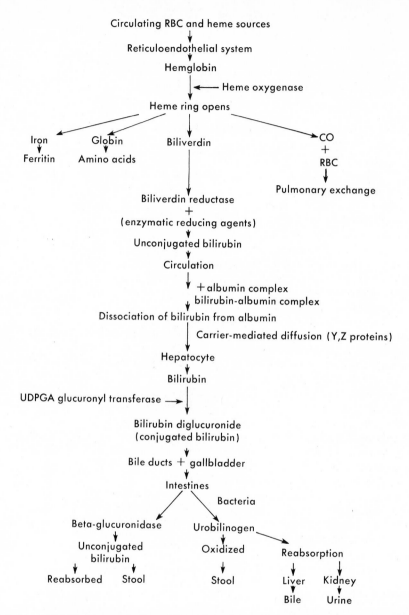

Fig. 6-1. Neonatal bilirubin metabolism. (Data adapted from Behrman, R. E.: Neonatal-perinatal medicine, St. Louis, 1977, The C. V. Mosby Co.; Evans, H. E., and Glass, L.: Perinatal medicine, New York, 1976, Harper & Row, Publishers, Inc.; Klaus, M., and Fanaroff, A. A.: Care of the high-risk neonate, Philadelphia, 1973, W. B. Saunders Co.; and Seligmon, J.: Pediatr. Clin. North Am. **24**(3):509, 1977.)

direct synthesis of bilirubin from porphyrins and the destruction of immature red blood cell precursors either in the bone marrow or soon after release.[7,10,14]

The conversion of heme from the red blood cells and other sources to bilirubin takes place within the reticuloendothelial system, but the extent of participation of various organs such as the liver, spleen, and bone marrow is not known.[9,10] An enzyme, microsomal heme oxygenase, catalyzes the oxidation of heme (within the reticuloendothelial system), resulting in iron, globin, biliverdin, and carbon monoxide.[10] The enzyme biliverdin reductase helps convert the biliverdin to unconjugated bilirubin.[17] The unconjugated bilirubin leaves the reticuloendothelial system and becomes bound to albumin in the plasma.[10] The bilirubin-albumin complex must dissociate before the unconjugated bilirubin can be accepted by the liver. The transfer of bilirubin from the extracellular fluid into the hepatic cytosol is influenced by the following:

1. Level of unconjugated bilirubin in plasma
2. Rate at which bilirubin can be conjugated in the hepatocyte
3. Rate of excretion of conjugated bilirubin
4. Amount of available Y and Z proteins
5. Blood flow to liver
   a. Ductus venosus remains patent during first week therefore shunting the blood around the liver
   b. Some question about gastric distention decreasing portal blood flow
   c. Decreases owing to asphyxia, a patent ductus arteriosus and/or a pyloric stenosis
6. Concentration gradients across cell membranes[10,14,15,17]

The two hepatic proteins transfer unconjugated bilirubin across the hepatic membrane. The Y protein (ligandin) has been demonstrated deficient in the perinatal period and is the major acceptor of unconjugated bilirubin. The Z protein is less important but will bind some unconjugated bilirubin. The Z protein is present in adult levels in late fetal life[4,7,10,15] (Fig. 6-1). Glucose serves as a precursor of uridine diphospho-glucuronic acid (UDPGA). The glucuronic acid from the UDPGA is mediated by the enzyme, UDP-glucuronyl transferase to the bilirubin resulting in conjugated bilirubin. This reaction is associated with the endoplasmic reticulum of the hepatocyte (see below).[4,7]

1. Glucose-1-phosphate + uridine triphosphate
$$\xrightarrow{\text{uridyl transferase}} \text{uridine diphosphoglucose (UDPG)} + \text{pyrophosphate}$$
2. UDPG + diphosphopyridine nucleotide
$$\xrightarrow{\text{UDPG dehydrogenase}} \text{UDP-glucuronic acid (UDPGA)} + \text{diphosphopyridine nucleotide hydrogenase}$$
3. Unconjugated bilirubin + UDPGA
$$\xrightarrow{\text{glucuronyl transferase}} \text{bilirubin diglucuronide}^{4,7}$$

There is conflicting evidence about the deficiency of UDP-glucuronyl transferase in the newborn. Unconjugated bilirubin may stimulate glucuronyl transferase activity and induce its own action, resulting in glucuronic acid. Glucuronic acid reacts resulting in conjugated bilirubin, which is excreted from the hepatocyte by an energy-dependent process.[10] Conjugated bilirubin is secreted into the bile canaliculus through bile ducts to the gallbladder and intestine. In the intestines the bacterial flora reduces the bilirubin to urobilinogens, 75% of which are reabsorbed by the ileum with the remainder being excreted in stool.[7,9]

ETIOLOGIES

Listed in the following outline are five areas felt to be the causes of unconjugated hyperbilirubinemia.

I. Overproduction of bilirubin
  A. Physiological jaundice
  B. Hemolytic anemia
    1. Membrane defects
      a. Spherocytosis
      b. Elliptocytosis
    2. Enzyme defects
      a. Pyruvate kinase
      b. Glucose-6-phosphate dehydrogenase
    3. Hemoglobin defects such as sickle cell anemia
    4. Acquired erythrocyte defect
      a. Isoimmunization
        (1) Rh, ABO, minor groups
      b. Drugs
      c. Infection
  C. Extravascular blood
    1. Petechiae
    2. Hematoma

3. Pulmonary, cerebral, or other internal hemorrhage
4. Hemangioma
  D. Polycythemia
    1. Placental hypertransfusion
      a. Twin-to-twin
      b. Maternofetal
      c. Delayed cord clamping
    2. Placental insufficiency
      a. Small-for-gestational-age infants
      b. Postmaturity
      c. Toxemia of pregnancy
    3. Endocrine
      a. Maternal diabetes
      b. Congenital adrenal hyperplasia
      c. Neonatal thyrotoxicosis
    4. Miscellaneous
      a. Down's syndrome
      b. Beckwith's syndrome
  E. Increased enterohepatic circulation
    1. Swallowed blood
    2. Pyloric stenosis
    3. Intestinal atresia or stenosis including annular pancreas
    4. Meconium ileus or meconium plug syndrome
    5. Hirschsprung's disease
    6. Hypoperistalis-paralytic ileus
  F. Infection (congenital, neonatal)
    1. Bacterial
    2. Viral
    3. Protozoal
II. Hepatic uptake impairment
  Animal studies suggest that jaundice may result from defective bilirubin uptake by the liver, but there are no data from neonatal studies to show this.
III. Deficient conjugation of bilirubin
  A. Reductions in glucuronyl transferase
    1. Autosomal recessive (Crigler-Najjar syndrome)
    2. Autosomal dominant (glucuronyl transferase deficiency, type II)
  B. Acquired defects
    1. Breast-feeding unconjugated hyperbilirubinemia
    2. Transient familial neonatal hyperbilirubinemia
    3. Pyloric stenosis, although questionable
    4. Drugs
      a. Novobiocin
      b. Pregnanediol
IV. Exaggerated neonatal jaundice with undefined mechanism
  A. Maternal diabetes
  B. Hypothyroidism in neonate
  C. Galactosemia

V. Miscellaneous causes
  A. Oxytocin-induced delivery
  B. Hypoglycemia
  C. Particular races such as Greeks, Italians, Indians, Japanese
  D. Poor illumination of nursery
  E. Idiopathic indirect hyperbilirubinemia[2-4,9,12,14,17]

This list is by no means complete or agreed on by all professions. We would like to elaborate on several areas.

Physiological jaundice

Physiological jaundice can be divided into two phases. In the full-term neonate, phase I is considered to be a rise of the serum bilirubin from 2 mg/dl in the cord blood to 6 mg/dl between 60 and 72 hours of age followed by a rapid decline to 2 mg/dl by the fifth day. In the preterm neonate this increase is more severe (10 to 12 mg/dl) and is delayed until the fifth day; a decline may not be seen until the second week of life. Postmature neonates will generally have less than a 2.5 mg increase. Phase II consists of a 5- to 10-day period when the serum bilirubin decreases to 1 mg or less.[4,7,10]

Physiological jaundice is attributed to the following mechanisms:

1. Increased bilirubin load owing to
  a. An increase in the red blood cell volume
  b. A decrease in the red blood cell life span
  c. An increase in the enterohepatic circulation
2. Defective uptake of bilirubin from plasma (decreased Y protein)
3. Defective bilirubin conjugation owing to decreased activity of glucuronyl transferase
4. Changes in the hepatic blood supply during transition from fetal to neonatal life[2,9,10,13]

Broad-spectrum antibiotics

In sick neonates broad-spectrum antibiotics that suppress intestinal flora delay the formation of urobilinogen and further increase enterohepatic uptake.[14] Enterohepatic circulation is enhanced by (1) the lack of bacterial flora to convert conjugated bilirubin to urobilinogens; (2) an increase in beta glucuronidase, an enzyme active in the intestinal mucosa that hydrolyzes the conjugated bilirubin to free pigment; (3) delayed feeding; (4) decreased intestinal motility; and (5) retaining meconium.[17]

Hemolytic disease

In hemolytic disease there is an increase in the hemolysis of red blood cells. An antibody is formed in the mother against an antigen present in the fetal red blood cell. This antibody crosses the placenta and enters the fetal circulation, causing the destruction of fetal and, after birth, neonatal red blood cells. Small placental leaks facilitate the passage of red blood cells into the maternal circulation; at delivery a large volume of fetal red blood cells may enter the maternal system. Rh incompatibilities account for 93% of the hemolytic disease and are the most severe. The mother is Rh negative and the father is Rh positive. A first pregnancy is usually not affected unless the mother has had a previous transfusion with Rh-positive blood.

Of the neonates born to mothers with type O blood, 20% to 25% have type A or B cells; 10% of these cases result in hemolytic disease. ABO incompatibilities are less severe than Rh incompatibilities; they do not increase in severity with each pregnancy and are seen in 50% of the first pregnancies.[7]

Blood extravasation

In blood extravasation, bilirubin formation occurs when macrophages move in and degrade the hemoglobin of the phagocytized red blood cells.[14]

Neonatal sepsis

In neonatal sepsis, the hemolysin elaborated by bacteria reduces red blood cell survival. The sepsis may further prevent erythrocyte replacement by bone marrow depression and cause stasis at the bile canaliculus of the hepatocyte, resulting in an increased indirect and direct bilirubin with anemia.[9]

Breast milk jaundice

Breast milk jaundice may be due to a substance in the milk that inhibits the hepatic enzyme, glucuronyl transferase. Substances suggested are 5-pregnanediol, long-chain free fatty acids, and environmental chemicals.[4,15] In breast milk jaundice the serum unconjugated bilirubin levels are at 10 to 27 mg/dl by 10 to 15 days of life without hemolysis or other illness. Interruption of breast-feeding for 2 to 14 days results in a prompt decline. Resumption of breast-feeding leads to an increase of 1 to 3 mg/dl. Failure of the serum bilirubin levels to decrease indicates other causes requiring further studies.[4]

Oxytocin administration

The risk of hyperbilirubinemia developing was greater after oxytocin administration than in groups with spontaneous labor or the use of an amniotomy.[6,12] The incidence of hyperbilirubinemia is related to the amount of oxytocin given and the duration of usage.[15] The reason for the hyperbilirubinemia is not known.

BILIRUBIN-ALBUMIN BINDING

Once unconjugated bilirubin is bound to albumin in the plasma, it cannot diffuse across the cell membrane.[14] One gram of albumin will bind 16 mg of unconjugated bilirubin at a pH of 7.40. The first binding site of the albumin is a strong one, while the second bond is much weaker.[7] The decreased ability of albumin to bind bilirubin is affected by a reduction in the available albumin; this reduction is caused by substances that displace or compete with bilirubin for binding, blood pH, and asphyxia.[3,10] The free fatty acids:albumin molar ratio must increase to a 5:1 ratio before displacement of bilirubin takes place.[15] An outline listing agents affecting bilirubin-albumin binding follows:

I. Reduces albumin pool
   A. Prematurity
   B. Hypoproteinemia
II. Agents binding and displacing bilirubin
   A. Endogenous anions
      1. Hematin
      2. Free fatty acids
      3. Bile acids
   B. Exogenous anions
      1. Salicylates
      2. Sulfonamides
      3. Oxacillin
      4. Novobiocin
      5. Sodium benzoate (found in caffeine and injectable diazepam [Valium])
      6. Cephalothin
      7. Furosemide
      8. Conjugated bilirubin
      9. Heparin
III. Blood pH
   A. Respiratory acidosis
   B. Metabolic acidosis
IV. Asphyxia[3,7,9-11]

COMPLICATIONS

Bilirubin encephalopathy or kernicterus results from the staining and deposit of unconjugated bilirubin within neurons, possibly causing necrosis.[4,7] Unconjugated bilirubin, which is lipid soluble, passes into the lipid moieties of the cell membranes and into the subcellular organelles (mitochondria) where it interferes with vital metabolic activities.[4,14] Areas of the brain most affected are the globus pallidus, hypocampus, basal ganglia, and the cerebellular nuclei.[7,9] Extraneural lesions exhibited by necrosis, intracellular crystals of bilirubin, and staining are found in the renal tubular cells, intestinal mucosa, and pancreatic cells.[4] The following factors increase the likelihood of kernicterus: hypoxia, hyperosmolality, hypoglycemia, hemolysis, bacterial infections, factors decreasing albumin-bilirubin binding (see outline on p. 93), and the male sex.[4,5,7,10] The risk of neurological impairment correlates well with the duration of serum bilirubin exceeding 15 mg/dl.[3] Kernicterus may occur at lower levels of bilirubin, especially in the sick premature infant. The increase in the total body bilirubin may not be reflected by an increase in the serum bilirubin levels because the excess pigment diffuses into the extravascular space and possibly the brain.[3,10]

Kernicterus can be divided into four phases. Phase I is characterized by hypotonia, vomiting, lethargy, high-pitched cry, poor sucking reflex, and a decreased Moro's reaction with incomplete flexion of the extremities. Phase II is exhibited by spasticity, opisthotonos, and hyperpyrexia. In Phase III there is a diminution or disappearance of spasticity, setting sun eyes, and convulsions. Seventy-five percent of these infants will succumb with a gastric, pulmonary, and/or central nervous system hemorrhage. In phase IV the survivors are characterized by athetoid cerebral palsy, sensory and perceptual deafness, mental retardation, dental enamel dysplasia, loss of vertical gaze, and visual motor incoordination. Survivors with less severe bilirubin encephalopathy have decreased short-term memories and abstract reasoning abilities and shortened attention spans.[2,3,7,9] Problems with hydrops will not be discussed.

TREATMENT

The best management for hyperbilirubinemia is prevention by giving RhoGAM to Rh-negative mothers delivering Rh-positive infants and after abortion where infant blood type is not known and the termination of premature labors if medically feasible. If prevention is not possible, support must be given to the neonate by providing a thermoneutral environment and preventing hypoglycemia by early feeding.

The three methods of treating hyperbilirubinemia are removal of bilirubin by exchange transfusion, acceleration of normal physiological process, and providing an alternate pathway for degradation of bilirubin.[7,10]

Exchange transfusions are used to correct anemia, stop the hemolytic process in a neonate with erythroblastosis fetalis, treat potential or actual hyperbilirubinemia, or rid the body of a toxic substance.[10] One percent of all neonates born require exchange transfusions, and less than 1% will die from the exchange.[9] A two-volume blood exchange will replace 85% of the circulating red blood cells and should reduce the serum bilirubin by 50%.[4] As the exchange proceeds, bilirubin from the extravascular space is drawn into the free plasma by the bilirubin-free albumin.[10] Provided there is no evidence of anemia or cardiac failure, the administration of albumin 1 hour prior to an exchange will result in the removal of approximately 40% more bilirubin by increasing the movement of bilirubin from the extravascular compartment.[9,10]

The anticoagulant used in the blood is important. Blood with acid citrate dextrose (ACD blood) will elevate the plasma glucose, sodium, and potassium while decreasing the pH, chloride, and bicarbonate. The total calcium in the blood is normal, but it does not contain ionized calcium; therefore calcium gluconate may be required. If the blood is 5 days old, it has a decreased ability to transport oxygen. It is important to watch for a rebound hypoglycemia after the use of ACD blood. Blood with heparin will obviate the need to give calcium and help the pH remain normal, but hypoglycemia may occur during the exchange. Heparinized blood is also associated with an increase in fatty acid concentration, which competes with albumin for binding with unconjugated bilirubin. Since heparin interferes with coagulation, protamine should be administered.[4,7,9,10] The complications of exchange transfusions are listed in the following outline:

1. Vascular
   a. Embolization with air or clots
   b. Thrombosis
   c. Necrotizing enterocolitis
   d. Uncontrollable hemorrhage
2. Cardiac
   a. Arrhythmia
   b. Volume overload with heart failure
   c. Arrest
3. Electrolytes
   a. Hyperkalemia
   b. Hypernatremia
   c. Hypocalcemia
   d. Acute hypercalcemia
   e. Acidosis-alkosis
4. Coagulation
   a. Overheparinization
   b. Thrombocytopenia
5. Infection
   a. Bacteremia
   b. Serum hepatitis
6. Miscellaneous
   a. Mechanical injury to donor cells
   b. Perforation
   c. Hypothermia
   d. Hypoglycemia[4,9]

Phenobarbital, diethylnicotinamide, and ethanol are felt to accelerate the maturation of the enzyme system and increase bilirubin metabolism.[17] Phenobarbital is the most widely used and studied. It is capable of stimulating and maturing the glucuronyl transferase system, increasing the rate at which the Y-binding protein appears, causing proliferation of the endoplasmic reticulum system, eliminating certain competing steroid hormones that delay maturation, and increasing bilirubin excretion.[10,18] Phenobarbital is most effective when given prenatally the last month of gestation.[15] Other effects of phenobarbital are:

1. Lethargy
   a. Decreased suck
   b. Decreased intake of milk
2. Respiratory depression
3. Alters metabolism and/or excretion of drugs and vitamin D, decreasing their effectiveness

4. Prevents normal psychosexual brain imprinting by testosterone (theoretical)
5. May depress vitamin K–dependent factors
6. Makes liver more susceptible to hepatotoxic drugs
7. May alter steroid metabolism[10,15]

Agar feeding has been used to block the enterohepatic circulation of bilirubin by stabilizing the meconium in a solution in the lumen of the small intestine. Studies are still needed to determine its effectiveness.[7,13]

An alternative pathway for metabolism is photodecomposition, a process where unconjugated bilirubin not bound to albumin absorbs light energy and transfers this energy to oxygen to form singlet oxygen. The singlet oxygen aids in the oxidation of bilirubin. Oxygen is an important part of photodecomposition, so anoxia and carotene production (decreases the amount of singlet oxygen) may decrease the rate of bilirubin destruction.[4,10,15] Phototherapy may affect bilirubin metabolism by altering albumin binding sites, altering either the pigment or the hepatocyte membrane so it becomes freely permeable, stimulating a variety of mitochrondrial enzymes, and affecting the excretory mechanism of the liver (questionable).[5,7,10]

The energy output by the light source rather than the light intensity determines how effective the light will be in lowering bilirubin levels. The daylight lamps have only 60% of the output of the blue lights.[10] However, the blue lights are hard on personnel's eyes and give the infant an ashen, cyanotic cold look.[16] A peak or slight decrease in bilirubin concentration is seen within 12 to 24 hours after phototherapy begins.[7] Phototherapy is contraindicated in congenital erythropoietic porphyria and high direct bilirubin levels.[3] The effects of phototherapy are as follows:

1. Insensible water loss caused by vasodilatation increased
2. Increases number of loose stools
3. Rash
4. Lethargy with decreased eagerness to feed
5. Changes red blood cells
   a. Decreases potassium
   b. Decreases ATP activity
   c. Increases hemolysis
6. Bronze baby

7. Damages photoreceptors of retina
8. Increases rate of platelet turnover
9. Priapism
10. Decreases growth rate in later childhood/delayed onset of puberty (not well documented)
11. Decreases ability of albumin to bind to bilirubin
12. Questionable effect on biological rhythms
13. Increases body temperature
14. Obscures diagnosis of other problems[3,5,7,10,15,16]

Protocols*

Problem □ Kernicterus or bilirubin encephalopathy

GOAL: To prevent bilirubin encephalopathy or kernicterus in the neonate

DIAGNOSTIC
1. Initial studies
   a. Maternal blood
      (1) Indirect Coombs' test
      (2) Blood type/Rh
      (3) VDRL
   b. Infant's blood
      (1) Direct Coombs' test
      (2) Blood type/Rh
      (3) Indirect/direct serum bilirubin
      (4) Hemoglobin-hematocrit
      (5) Reticulocyte count
      (6) Peripheral blood smear (platelets, RBC, WBC)
      (7) Serum protein (albumin, globins)
      (8) Protein-binding ability if available
      (9) Blood pH
      (10) Blood glucose or Dextrostix
   c. Review medications, feeding, and stooling history.
   d. Urinalysis for protein, cells, and reducing substances is done.
   e. If sepsis is suspected, cerebrospinal fluid, urine cultures, and a TORCH screen are done.
   f. Review maternal history and previous problems of jaundice in siblings.
   g. Physical examination is performed, including degree of jaundice, liver size, neurological examination, weight, and vital signs, including blood pressure.[4,9,11,15]

   h. Repeat direct Coombs' test if significant jaundice continues.
   i. Studies for hepatocellular disease should be undertaken if an elevation of direct-reacting bilirubin exists.
2. Daily laboratory tests
   a. Infant's blood
      (1) Total bilirubin levels with total protein are measured every 12 hours or more frequently if indicated.
      (2) CBC with reticulocyte count is done.
      (3) Fractionated bilirubin is measured daily or when indicated.
      (4) Glucose levels are measured every 4 to 6 hours or more frequently if indicated.
   b. Monitor and record intake.
   c. Monitor and record stooling record.
   d. Physical examination is performed, including neurological assessment.[4,7]
   e. If under phototherapy:
      (1) Monitor temperature every 4 to 6 hours.
      (2) Monitor weight and hydration status.
      (3) Platelet count should be done.
      (4) Monitor oxygenation of tissues.
      (5) Parental consent should be obtained since all effects are not known.
   f. Completion of phototherapy
      (1) Infant's blood
         (a) Bilirubin/hematocrit at 12, 24, and 48 hours after discontinuing therapy
         (b) Platelet count with CBC at 24 and 48 hours
      (2) Monitor temperature every 4 hours
      (3) Intake/output

---

*Since this institution does not use phenobarbital to treat hyperbilirubinemia, it is not included in this protocol.

(4) During follow-up monitor growth and development (If a referral, notify home physician of the use of phototherapy and suggest the importance of following growth and development since not all effects are known.)[4,7,11]

3. Exchange transfusion
   a. Prior to exchange
      (1) Send type and cross match of infant's blood; if incompatible a sample of maternal blood should be sent for cross matching.
      (2) Fractionated bilirubin on infant's blood should be checked.
      (3) Send hematocrit, electrolytes, and calcium on exchange blood.
      (4) Blood glucose or Dextrostix done
      (5) Check vital signs.
      (6) Obtain permission for exchange.
   b. During exchange
      (1) Save first 10 ml withdrawn for fractionated bilirubin electrolytes, calcium, hemoglobin, hematocrit, and total protein.
      (2) Monitor vital signs continuously. Central venous pressures should be measured after every 100 ml of blood exchanged to prevent overload if mean blood pressures are not continuously taken.
      (3) Color and blanching of feet, legs, and buttocks should be observed.
      (4) Save the last 10 ml withdrawn from the infant for fractionated bilirubin, CBC, platelets, electrolytes, calcium, hematocrit, total protein, and type and cross match.
   c. After exchange
      (1) Monitor vital signs and blood pressure every 15 minutes times four, if stable every 30 minutes times four, and if stable every 4 hours.
      (2) Blood glucose of Dextrostix done immediately after, at 1 hour, and at 2 hours after exchange.[1,9]

THERAPEUTIC
1. Routinely
   a. Pending the results of the laboratory tests and the present clinical picture:
      (1) If no jaundice and no history of increased serum bilirubin, wait for laboratory results.
      (2) If known incompatibility with experienced problems in utero, prepare to exchange.
      (3) If jaundice is evident and infant is premature, institute phototherapy.
      (4) If full-term infant with a history of increasing serum bilirubin levels, start phototherapy.
      (5) If full-term infant with clinical jaundice but no increased serum bilirubin levels, wait for result.
   b. Supportive
      (1) Provide a thermoneutral environment to prevent an increase in free fatty acids.
      (2) Early feeding should be done, if medically possible, to lessen enterohepatic reabsorption of bilirubin and prevent hypoglycemia.
      (3) Maintain an intravenous infusion if not feeding to provide glucose for UDPGA and prevent hypoglycemia, which will increase the number of fatty acids.
      (4) Prevent unnecessary stress since this may also increase the number of fatty acids.[7]
   c. Provide care normally given to a neonate and his family
2. Phototherapy
   a. Unless the direct bilirubin is greater than 50% of the total bilirubin, phototherapy should be instituted when the total serum bilirubin is between:
      (1) 5 to 9 mg/dl in the first 24 hours of life
      (2) 10 to 14 mg/dl from 24 to 48 hours of age
      (3) 15 to 19 mg/dl after 49 hours of age[7,11]
   b. Supportive
      (1) Shield the neonate's eyes from the bright light to prevent retinal damage.
      (2) Change mask daily and take off once a shift so a developing conjunctivitis is not missed and possible infection is prevented.
      (3) Remove clothing and turn frequently to provide the maximum amount of ex-

posed surface since photodecomposition takes place in the cutaneous capillaries and to prevent skin breakdown.

(4) Accurately record loose stools so fluid loss may be estimated.

(5) Skin care should be done to prevent breakdown, especially of the diaper area and the bony prominences, and to prevent infection.[7]

(6) Check to see that there is a Plexiglas shield between the light and the infant to filter out the ultraviolet radiation that may be hazardous to the infant and produce erythema.[11]

c. Discontinue phototherapy when the direct bilirubin is greater than 50% of the total bilirubin or when the total serum bilirubin is:

(1) Below 9 mg/dl in the full-term neonate

(2) Below 6 mg/dl in the premature infant

3. Exchange transfusions

a. Unless the direct bilirubin is greater than 50%, an exchange transfusion should take place when:

(1) There is a total serum bilirubin of 10 or greater in the presence of hemolysis on the first day of life[7]

(2) Total serum bilirubin reaches the following levels compared with weight:

Net (gm)	Uncomplicated (mg)	Complicated (mg)
Less than 1250	13	10
1250-1499	15	13
1500-1999	17	15
2000-2499	18	17
2500 and up	20	18

A complicated course includes asphyxia, acidosis, hypothermia, hypoalbuminemia, sepsis, hemolysis, and hypoglycemia.[5]

b. Supportive

(1) Prior to exchange

(a) Administer albumin if ordered at the appropriate time and watch blood pressure and heart rate as it is given.

(b) Restrain infant with soft gauze and safety pins or other suitable restraints to prevent moving.

(c) Prepare umbilicus with Ioprep for at least 2 minutes and cover with Ioprep-soaked gauze prior to placement of venous line to help decrease the chance of infection.

(d) Aspirate stomach contents and stop continuous feedings to prevent aspiration.

(e) Provide an adequate heat source to prevent hypothermia; also provide a heat source for the blood to prevent cold stress.

(f) Prepare equipment necessary for resuscitation.

(g) Check blood slip with actual blood to make sure it is the correct blood.[7]

(2) During exchange transfusion

(a) Accurately record blood in and out so the neonate is not overloaded or left hypovolemic.

(b) Exchange in aliquots not to exceed 10% of the total blood volume.[4]

(c) Gently rotate blood every 15 to 20 minutes to mix cells and plasma.

(d) Be aware of the complications and their manifestations. (See p. 95.)

(3) After exchange transfusion

(a) Watch umbilicus for bleeding to prevent hemorrhage.

(b) Continue to be aware of complications and their symptoms. (See p. 95.)

(c) Remove restraints and reposition neonate.

(d) Return to preexchange orders as directed by the physician.

EDUCATIONAL

1. Nursing

a. A knowledge of the following areas is necessary: bilirubin metabolism; causes of increased bilirubin levels; expected time of onset; symptoms of an increased bilirubin level and kernicterus; methods of treatment with their side effects; importance of monitoring bilirubin levels, glucose levels, and oxygen levels; and watching for sepsis.

b. Encourage parents to ask questions about hyperbilirubinemia and explain to the nurse what has been said so they can give accurate information to their spouses and family.

c. If an exchange becomes necessary, support the parents by making sure their questions are answered before permission is given, allow them to remain with the baby as much as possible, and as soon as the exchange is over allow the parents to visit or call so they know the infant is all right.

d. If bilirubin encephalopathy or kernicterus is present or thought to exist, be honest with the parents. Encourage the physician to be totally honest with the parents about the chances of survival and future problems. Give the support given to any parent with an ill or dying baby.

e. Make social service and public health referrals where appropriate and start helping the parents make future plans.

2. Parents

a. Explain the following to the parents: what bilirubin and jaundice are, the mechanism most suspected of causing the increase in this infant, the methods of checking for the increased bilirubin, and possible methods of treatment.

b. If phototherapy is instituted, explain how we think it works and why we undress the infants and cover their eyes. Encourage touching of the infant and, as much as possible, remove the mask so eye-to-eye contact can be made to help parent-infant bonding.[9]

c. If an exchange transfusion becomes necessary, explain the purpose, method, and the possibility of a second or third exchange.

d. If the infant has kernicterus, explain to the parents with the physician what has happened. Explain to the parents that it is normal to grieve over the loss of a perfect baby or over the loss of the baby if he or she dies. Prepare them for some of the future emotions they will feel. If the infant has

died, stay with the family allowing them time with him or her if it is wished and accept their feelings. Let them know that we will be in contact with them in a few days and that they may call any time.

e. Explain the importance of follow-up care since we do not know all the side effects of treatment and the importance of follow-up in health prevention.

f. Encourage parents to keep health records on their child so if it becomes necessary to seek another physician or if emergencies arise they can provide accurate and adequate information.

3. Charting: *SOAP*ing provides the most concise and accurate method of charting. An example of material needed in each section follows:

S: Maternal and paternal interview

O: Physical examination, time of onset of jaundice, maternal and neonatal histories, laboratory data

A: Hyperbilirubinemia caused by
1. Incompatibility
2. Liver immaturity
3. Breast milk and so forth

P: 1. Method of treatment
2. Further laboratory data
3. Observation of symptoms
4. Parental support
5. Supportive management normally given

If nurses do not use a SOAPing format, it is important that color, location of jaundice, times of serum bilirubin levels, activity and feeding history, intake and output, unusual activities, time that phototherapy is started and stopped, the use of eye patches, and turning are recorded. Care plans should be contained within nursing notes. This list is by no means complete.

4. Referral must be made to a secondary or tertiary center when the hospital caring for the infant cannot provide the following:

a. Unable to do fractionated bilirubin or other diagnostic tests around the clock in an infant with a rising bilirubin

b. Bilirubin is from 5 to 9 mg/dl the first day

c. ABO/Rh incompatibilities (If mother is

sensitized, she should be referred prior to birth to a tertiary center.)

d. Unable to treat

e. Increasing direct bilirubin

f. Jaundice lasting longer than 1 week in a full-term neonate or 2 weeks in a preterm infant[4,11]

REFERENCES

1. Aladjem, S., and Brown, A.: Perinatal intensive care, St. Louis, 1977, The C. V. Mosby Co.
2. Amanullah, A.: Neonatal jaundice, Am. J. Dis. Child. **130:** 1274, 1976.
3. Bauer, C., and Horiguchi, T.: Nonhemolytic hyperbilirubinemia in full-term infants, Pediatr. Ann. **5**(2):89, 1976.
4. Behrman, R. E.: Neonatal-perinatal medicine, ed. 2, St. Louis, 1977, The C. V. Mosby Co.
5. Behrman, R. E., and Hsia, D. Y.: Summary of a symposium on phototherapy for hyperbilirubinemia, J. Pediatr. **75**(4): 718, 1976.
6. Chew, W. C.: Neonatal hyperbilirubinaemia: a comparison between prostaglandin E_2 and oxytocin induction, Br. Med. J. **2**(6088):679, 1977.
7. Evans, H. E., and Glass, L.: Perinatal medicine, New York, 1976, Harper & Row, Publishers, Inc.
8. Friel, J. P., editor: Dorland's illustrated medical dictionary, ed. 25, Philadelphia, 1974, W. B. Saunders Co.
9. Klaus, M., and Fanaroff, A. A.: Care of the high-risk neonate, Philadelphia, 1973, W. B. Saunders Co.
10. Maisels, M. J.: Bilirubin: on understanding and influencing its metabolism in the newborn infant, Pediatr. Clin. North Am. **19**(2):447, 1972.
11. Maisels, M. J.: Neonatal hyperbilirubinemia. In Schreiner, R., editor: Management of neonatal problems, Indianapolis, 1977, Department of Pediatrics, Indiana University Medical School.
12. Oski, F.: Oxytocin and neonatal hyperbilirubinemia, Am. J. Dis. Child. **129:**1139, 1975.
13. Poland, R., and Odell, G.: Physiologic jaundice: the enterohepatic circulation of bilirubin, N. Engl. J. Med. **284**(1):1, 1971.
14. Schmid, R.: Bilirubin metabolism in man, N. Engl. J. Med. **287**(14):703, 1972.
15. Seligman, J.: Recent and changing concepts of hyperbilirubinemia in the newborn, Pediatr. Clin. North Am. **24**(3): 509, 1977.
16. Stern, L.: The control of hyperbilirubinemia in the newborn, Clin. Obstet. Gynecol. **14**(3):855, 1971.
17. Thaler, M. M.: Perinatal bilirubin metabolism, Adv. Pediatr. **19:**215, 1972.
18. Thomas, C.: Phenobarbital prophylaxis of neonatal hyperbilirubinemia, Obstet. Gynecol. **50**(5):607, 1977.

Chapter 7

Obstetrical hemorrhage emergency care

Kathleen Buchheit and Joy Price

PHYSIOLOGY OF COAGULATION

There are many cardiovascular changes that take place during pregnancy that are thought to be hormonally mediated. Most of these changes begin to take place during the first trimester.

The plasma volume increases by approximately 1000 ml, and the red cell mass increases by approximately 300 ml. The total blood volume exhibits an average increase of around 1300 ml. Plasma volume, red cell mass, and total blood volume increases occur early in pregnancy but are demonstrated at their greatest near the end of the second trimester and the beginning of the third trimester. These increases may serve as protective mechanisms to counteract blood loss at delivery.[23,24,30]

As mentioned, increases in plasma volume, red cell mass, and total blood volume are thought to be the results of hormonal effects on the vascular system. It is theorized that the following may also contribute to these increases: decreased vascular tone (a resultant hormonal effect), increased vascular capacity of the uterus, and the presence of a low-resistance shunt in the uteroplacental circulation (similar to the results of an arteriovenous shunt).[23,24]

During pregnancy there is also an increase in cardiac output. This is due, in part, to an increase in the resting heart rate by 10 to 15 beats/min, but it is principally due to an increase in stroke volume. The augmented cardiac output increases measurably during the first trimester but increases only slightly more during the second and third trimesters. It is important to note here that cardiac output in late

pregnancy is appreciably higher when the woman is sitting than when she is supine. In the supine position venous return to the heart is frequently obstructed by the enlarged uterus and its contents.[23,24,30]

During labor cardiac output increases 15% with each contraction, causing an increase in blood flow, a slight increase in arterial blood flow, and a slight increase in arterial blood pressure. Finally, after delivery cardiac output increases by as much as 1 unit, which occurs when the uterus contracts firmly and pushes blood from the placenta into the maternal system (referred to as autotransfusion effect). It is believed that this is a counteraction to the external blood loss (which averages approximately 300 to 500 ml) that occurs before and after delivery of the placenta.[23,24,30]

There are also changes in several blood coagulation factors during pregnancy, but before discussing these we will first review the normal coagulation process. "Hemostasis is the process which retains the blood within the vascular system."[4] For this to occur certain requirements must be met: "(1) blood vessels and extravascular tissues must be normal; (2) platelets must be normal in quantity and quality; and (3) clotting factors in plasma and serum must be present in adequate quantity."[5]

Coagulation is a complex process, owing in part to the many theories regarding the specific chemical reactions that are involved in the clotting process. This complexity is augmented by the number of different names given to the coagulation factors. To avoid confusion the names given to these factors by the International Committee on Nomenclature of Blood Clotting Factors will be used here.[4,5]

Factor	Name
I	Fibrinogen
II	Prothrombin
III	Tissue thromboplastin
IV	Calcium
V	Proaccelerin, labile factor
VI	Stable factor, proconvertin
VII	Antihemophilic globulin (AHG)
VIII	Plasma thromboplastin component
IX	Stuart-Prower factor
X	Plasma thromboplastin antecedent
XI	Hageman factor
XII	Finbrinase, fibrin stabilizing factor

When injury to a blood vessel occurs, almost immediately there is a decrease in blood flow as a result of vasoconstriction. This vasoconstriction may be due in part to the release of serotonin by the platelets that come in contact with the injured vessel. Adenosine diphosphate (ADP), which is also released by the platelets and the injured vessel, causes the platelets to adhere to one another over the site of the injured tissue. This platelet clumping forms a plug in an effort to stop the bleeding. Finally, the clotting factors present in the blood interact causing the plug to form a permanent clot.[4,5]

The coagulation process involves two systems: the extrinsic system and the intrinsic system. The extrinsic system is a rapid process that relies on factor III, which it receives from the injured cells and tissues. The intrinsic system is a less rapid process that relies on coagulation proteins that are normally found in their inactive forms in the circulating blood. It is necessary to mention here that both the extrinsic and intrinsic systems are probably both activated by tissue thromboplastin at the same time and are both involved in activating factor X.[4,5]

Based on some theories, the clotting factors appear to interact in the following manner[4,5,10]:

1. Injury activates factor XII → Factor XIIa*
2. XIIa + XI → XIa
3. XIa + IX + Calcium ions → IXa

---

*a means active form.

4. IXa + VIII + Calcium ions + Phospholipids → VIIIa
5. VIIIa + X → Xa
6. Xa + Prothrombin + Calcium ions → Thrombin
7. Thrombin + Fibronogen → Fibrin

This final product is an insoluble fibrin clot. The fibrin strands forming the clot begin to contract. This process is called clot retraction. As these strands shorten, they pull the blood vessel wall together, thus diminishing its diameter and acting as a plug.[4,5,10]

Pregnancy brings about an increase in several blood coagulation factors. These factors are: fibrinogen, prothrombin, and factors VII, VIII, IX, and X. Factor II is increased only slightly. Researchers disagree as to whether or not these increases heighten the possibility of spontaneous thrombosis or disseminated intravascular coagulation (DIC). It is theorized that a decrease in factors XI and XII may counteract these possibilities. Also, the presence of antiplasmins in the placenta may represent the body's protection against postpartum hemorrhage. Finally, one must keep in mind that although there are increased levels of certain factors leading to what some researchers refer to as a "hypercoagulable" state, these potential hazards (DIC or thrombosis) do not automatically occur. Something must first trigger the mechanism. Such triggering mechanisms include: abruptio placentae, infection, eclampsia, or vascular insult.[5,11,23,24]

During labor there are, again, marked changes in the clotting and fibrinolytic systems. There is an indication of activation of the clotting system owing to a shortened partial thromboplastin time. An elevation of factor VII occurs along with an increase in platelets. Fibrin split products (anticoagulants) may also appear in the blood. At separation of the placenta there is a rise in factors V and VII and a decrease in the fibrinogen level. Within 24 hours, these factors usually return to normal.[5,11]

PATHOPHYSIOLOGY OF HEMORRHAGE

Hemorrhage is an often discussed entity in medical and nursing literature, but it is actually rarely defined. Hemorrhage as succintly defined by Miller[19] is "the escape of blood from a vessel that is incident to a mechanical defect in the vascular or cardiac wall."

Causes

The causes of hemorrhage are multiple. They include injury, infection, ulceration of the blood vessel wall, arteriosclerosis (brittle arterial wall), purpura (small hemorrhages in the skin and mucosa), leukemia (platelet formation suppression), overdose of anticoagulants, avitaminosis K (deficiency of prothrombin formation), scurvy or avitaminosis C (fragile vessel walls), many toxins, anoxia, anatomical lesions, ruptured surgical lesions, and trauma.[19,28]

Chronic blood loss

Ordinarily the body is able to compensate for even large amounts of blood lost over an extended period. The deficiency here is mainly one of red cell mass. The bone marrow increases activity to replace the shed erythrocytes. This is known as a compensatory hyperplasia. Eventually, the body can no longer keep up this pace. The decreased red cell mass results in anemia.[15,19] If this anemia becomes severe enough, tissues will become hypoxic.

Acute blood loss

Whereas the problem of chronic blood loss is one of anemia, the problem of acute blood loss is essentially that of decreased blood volume. The body is far less tolerant of hypovolemia. A sudden 20% reduction of volume in a previously healthy individual may cause serious consequences.[15] A sudden loss of 30% or more is generally fatal.[19] Actually, individuals will respond to hemorrhage based on multiple factors, including their state of health, amount of blood loss, rapidity of blood loss, the precipitating cause, organs involved, and so forth.

The physiological responses of internal and external hemorrhage are similar. However, internal hemorrhage will often impinge on such vital organs as the cranial cavity or pericardium. The interference with such vital functions will have consequences far out of proportion to the actual volume of blood lost.[15]

COMPENSATORY MECHANISMS

To stabilize circulation the body immediately sets into play certain compensatory mechanisms with the onset of hemorrhage. If the loss is not excessive and is immediately controlled, these mechanisms are ordinarily sufficient to return the blood pressure to at least a near normal range. This assures perfusion of vital tissues. A good example is the donation of 250 to 500 ml of blood: Arterial blood pressure is ordinarily disturbed only momentarily, if at all. Body fluid stores will be replenished over the next few hours. Proteins, blood cells, and other blood constituents will be somewhat slower.[18]

If a large amount of blood is lost suddenly, the following mechanisms are set into action.

Arterial blood pressure

Hemorrhage sets a low circulating blood volume into motion. This results in lowered venous pressure. Stroke volume will be lowered with a subsequent lowered cardiac output. Finally, the arterial blood pressure is reduced.[8,12,15,17,19]

Reflex response

The *baroreceptors* (or pressoreceptors) detect the presence of a reduction of the mean arterial pressure as well as a reduction of pulse pressure. These receptors supply sensory information to the cardiovascular system. The proximal aorta and the area of the carotid sinus are the major areas for these stretch receptors. (Other areas wherein the receptors are found include the great veins, atria, and pulmonary artery.) These receptors are undifferentiated terminal nerve fibers that branch into the adventitial and medial layer of the vessel wall. An increase in arterial pressure stretches these fibers, and as a result there is an increase in the number of actively firing receptors. Finally, fibers terminate in the cardiovascular center in the medulla. These receptors become inactive as pressure falls. The cardiac inhibitory center will no longer send vagal stimulation to the heart with this loss of normal reflex inhibition from the carotid baroreceptors. This then allows the cardiovascular center to increase sympathetic nervous system activity and so permits the pressor area to increase the impulse of vasoconstriction. There is a generalized increase in peripheral resistance. Myocardial contractility may be strengthened with a corresponding increase in stroke volume. Heart rate also increases. The end result is increased cardiac output and peripheral resistance. Arterial pressure is returned to normal.[8,12,18,19,21]

Special *chemoreceptors* are located in the carotid sinus and aortic arch. Sympathetic activity is augmented by these facilitatory impulses, which are stimulated by a decrease in local blood flow with a resulting tissue hypoxia. These impulses respond to alterations in pH, Pa_{O_2}, and Pa_{CO_2}. The receptors of these sensory nerve fibers connect with respiratory and cardiovascular centers, resulting in increased pulmonary ventilation. An increase in peripheral resistance occurs to a lesser extent. Anoxia and asphyxia again increase the activity of the sympathetic nervous system, resulting in vasoconstriction.[15,19]

Sympathetic activity

The cardiovascular system responds to an increased sympathetic activity in the following manner: (1) Arteriolar constriction occurs foremost in the skin and then to a somewhat lesser degree in the skeletal muscles, splanchnic areas, and kidneys. Therefore these organs have a limited capillary flow. The vessels of the brain and heart offer little resistance. Coronary arterioles may even dilate, assuring blood perfusion to these vital organs. This of course is at the expense of the other tissues. This peripheral resistance helps to retain blood in the arterial system. (2) Vasoconstriction tends to squeeze stored blood into active circulation. (3) Heart rate and force of contractions increase. This results in a more complete emptying of the heart. Some of the blood normally stored as end systolic ventricular volume is also put into active circulation. Such mobilization of stored and reserve blood has been called autotransfusion.[8,15,18]

This compensatory mechanism lasts only for a short time. Eventually, pathological changes occur in terms of ischemia, hyperemia, a liberation of toxic substances into the general circulation, and eventually further damage of already hypoxic organs.[15]

Transfer of interstitial fluid into intravascular compartment

Hypovolemia and the constriction of resistance vessels result in a reduced capillary filtration. This change leads to a rapid net movement of interstitial fluid into the vascular compartment. Mobilization of 800 to 900 ml can occur rapidly. There is a corresponding shift of electrolytes with the fluid. This reabsorption mechanism tends to restore circulatory volume. However, there still remains a deficiency of blood cells and plasma proteins. The blood cells

and plasma protein remaining become diluted in the fluid-expanded vascular compartment. The loss of blood cells means there is a lessened oxygen-carrying capacity of the blood; this takes about 6 weeks to fully restore. The bone marrow begins to synthesize erythrocytes almost immediately, but time is required to reach a normal and mature amount of cells. If there is normal hepatic function, plasma protein concentration will be rapidly synthesized and restored. This whole reabsorption process has been called autoinfusion.[15,18,19]

It needs to be noted that there is a limit on the potential for this reabsorption from the interstitial space. The dilution of plasma protein and the corresponding reduction in oncotic pressure is the primary reason.[18]

Renal function: ADH and aldosterone

As mentioned previously, the kidneys are affected by the vasoconstriction caused by the sympathetic stimulation. This may be to the point of a severe or total reduction of glomerular filtration. The body is trying to conserve water and electrolytes in order to restore volume.[15,18]

The body reacts to the hypovolemia with an increased secretion of antidiuretic hormone (ADH) or vasopressin from the posterior pituitary gland. The thirst mechanism also serves to increase secretion of ADH. The primary effect is to reabsorb water by the renal tubules.[15,18]

The mineralocorticoid *aldosterone* secreted by the adrenal medulla also responds to hypovolemia. Its most important mechanism is that of the renin-angiotensin system. The changes in the afferent arteriole of the renal nephron stimulate the juxtaglomerular cells in the vessel wall to secrete renin. This renal hormone eventually results in the formation of the polypeptide angiotensin. It acts as a vasopressor and also stimulates the release of aldosterone. As a result of this complex pathway, aldosterone enhances the sodium-potassium exchange in the distal convoluted tubules. This induces sodium retention. The resulting hypertonicity still further stimulates secretion of ADH. Thus the retained water increases the extracellular fluid volume.[15,18]

When severe enough, glomerular filtration will eventually be compromised. Severe renal ischemia eventually leads to renal damage and complete renal failure.[8,15,18]

Epinephrine and norepinephrine

The adrenal medulla also secretes the catecholamines epinephrine and norepinephrine to reinforce the vasoconstrictive activity of the sympathetic stimulation. Epinephrine seems to increase peripheral arteriolar constriction and cardiac output and augment the blood's coagulability. Norepinephrine has as its primary function vasoconstriction of the peripheral vessels. Both of these catecholamines also serve certain metabolic functions, which include a breakdown of liver glycogen, an increase of blood glucose, and protein catabolism. All this serves to help with synthesis of plasma protein and blood cells.[18,19]

Signs and symptoms as result of compensatory mechanism

Cutaneous vasoconstriction results in pallor, cyanosis, and coolness. The skin will have a grayish color owing to blood stasis in the capillaries. Sympathetic stimulation causes tachycardia, a decreased pulse pressure, and increased diaphoresis. Chemoreceptor stimulation responds to the decreased arterial pressure with a corresponding increased respiratory effort. Dehydration is exhibited in the poor skin turgor and sunken features. Other factors include thirst, dry mouth, and oliguria. These are all results of the body's attempt to conserve fluid. There may also be apprehension owing to the increase of catecholamines stimulating the reticular formation, which helps to control cortical activities. The response may also be one of lethargy and apathy, as well as lapses into periods of unconsciousness probably caused by cerebral ischemia and acidosis.[8,15,19]

Resulting hemorrhagic shock

As long as the condition of severe hemorrhage can be reversed, this is called primary or reversible shock. When early and adequate measures are either not taken or the body does not respond, secondary or irreversible shock ensues. This is a tremendous disparity between circulating blood volume and vascular bed capacity.[6,15]

The sequence of events can be summarized in the following fashion: Blood volume continues to fall. Severe vasoconstriction impedes adequate excretion of metabolites. Eventually, this stimulates vasodilatation of the metarterioles and the precapillary sphincters. Local histamine liberation very likely causes this dilatation. Postcapillary resistance stays for a much longer time. Blood pools as a result of dilated precapillary sphincters; this increases capillary hydrostatic pressure, which decreases or even reverses the fluid from the extravascular to vascular space. Venous return to the heart is decreased. Cardiac output and blood pressure further drop. Coronary artery flow is further compromised by a lowered diastolic pressure. Hypoxia and decompensation of the heart result.[6]

Eventually, the postcapillary venules are also unresponsive to sympathetic stimulation, and the capillary and venule spaces open. Blood continues to pool. Hypoxia is causing final tissue damage and necrosis. There will be total unresponsiveness to blood replacement, ventilation, drugs, or surgery. The end result is cardiorespiratory failure.[6]

ANTENATAL (EARLY) HEMORRHAGE
Abortion

Abortion is the termination of pregnancy before the fetus has attained a stage of viability. A gestation of 20 weeks or approximately 500 gm weight is commonly accepted as the upper limit for abortion. As many as 20% of women will bleed during early pregnancy. About half of these will terminate spontaneously. Generally, the cause is a chromosomal or embryonic defect that is incompatible with life. Other than this, bleeding is often attributed to problems of placental development.

Threatened abortion. With a threatened abortion, there is slight bleeding that may persist for several weeks, and slight uterine cramping may occur. There is no evidence of tissue passed. The cervical os remains closed. Uterine size is compatible with dates. Bed rest for about 48 hours is commonly employed as a means to try to abate the bleeding problem. Actually, little can be done to halt the bleeding if it is going to persist.

Inevitable abortion. In an inevitable abortion the cervical os dilates and bleeding may increase. The amniotic sac is likely to rupture. Uterine cramping will ordinarily become increasingly stronger. The uterine size is still compatible with dates at this point, and tissue passage is still unlikely to be present. Yet progression to abortion is almost certain to occur.

Incomplete abortion. With an incomplete abortion, there is passage of some tissue. The cervical os

Table 7-1. Symptoms of abortion by type

Type	Bleeding	Contractions	Uterine size	Cervical os	Expulsion	Prognosis
Threatened	Slight	Slight	Compatible with dates	Closed	—	Variable with therapy
Inevitable	Moderate	Moderate	Compatible with dates	Dilated	—	Poor
Incomplete	Heavy	Strong	Compatible with dates	Open	Tissue	Poor
Complete	Diminished	Stop	Decreases to normal prepregnancy state	Open/closed	Fetus	Poor
Missed	Initially absent/absent delayed severe	None	Slowly decreases over months	Closed	—	Negative

remains open following tissue passage. Bleeding and cramping persist and are more severe. The more advanced the pregnancy, the more severe the symptoms.

Complete abortion. In a complete abortion all tissue of the fetus and placenta is passed. The earlier the gestational age, the more likely the complete products of conception will be passed together. Cramping stops and bleeding greatly diminishes since the placenta has been passed, and constriction of uterine muscle fibers is facilitated. The cervical os will be closed.

Missed abortion. In a missed abortion the fetus dies but the products of conception are retained for as long as several weeks. All symptoms of pregnancy ordinarily abate except amenorrhea. The fetus undergoes marked degenerative changes. After prolonged retention of about 2 months or longer, consumptive coagulopathy may occur. This quite naturally leads to severe hemorrhagic problems.

Septic (criminal) abortion. States have various guidelines for therapeutic abortions. Illegal abortions are done outside the guidelines of the law. Severe infection is sometimes the consequence because of the crude methods utilized. Bleeding may be a consequence too, owing to perforation of the uterus and retained fragments.[23,24,26,31]

Elective (voluntary) abortion. Elective abortion is the direct interruption of pregnancy that is done within the guidelines of the law. In 1973 the United States Supreme Court legalized abortions. Prior to this time, abortions would only be allowed in extreme cases of maternal disease and possibly for instances of fetal disease (Table 7-1).

Ectopic pregnancy

In an ectopic pregnancy the products of conception are implanted outside the uterine fundal cavity. This includes interstitial and cervical sites that are still uterine. Tubal, ovarian, and abdominal sites constitute the extrauterine sites. Ectopic sites within the fallopian tubes will account for 90% of these pregnancies. The reported incidences of ectopic pregnancy are from 1 in 80 to 1 in 250. It is the third most common cause of maternal death in the United States as given in 1975 statistics.

There are many things that impede the normal transport of the ovum. Prior inflammatory disease will be found at least microscopically in about one third of the situations. It is believed that this is more common since the advent of antibiotics. Prior to this time, at least theoretically, tubes would seal and subsequently the women would be sterile.

Nidation is poor within the tubes. Soon the trophoblast will penetrate an artery or arteriole. Ordinarily these attachments will be severed and hemorrhage occurs. The fetus may die and be reabsorbed or be aborted. Again, the reabsorption process would be a potential situation for ensuing consumptive coagulopathy.

Symptoms and findings depend largely on the type of ectopic pregnancy. There may be an early period with lesser symptoms followed by vaginal spotting, episodes of abdominal pain, and the development of a pelvic mass. Eventually, some form of the classic picture takes place. Women frequently are first seen with a stabbing unilateral lower abdominal pain. Vertigo and fainting are common. A lying down position allows free intraperitoneal blood to rise to the diaphragm and irritate the phrenic nerve, thus creating the referred shoulder pain. Signs of shock are evident. A pelvic examination produces great pain, and a boggy and tender mass is found in the adnexa. Culdocentesis with the procurement of blood is helpful in formulating a diagnosis. If there is any doubt at all, laparoscopy needs to be employed. Another lesion may in fact be the precipitating cause in 10% to 20% of the cases. Whatever the cause, surgery is imperative to control the hemorrhage.[23,24,26,31]

Hydatidiform mole

Hydatidaform mole is a developmental anomaly of the placenta. It is ordinarily a benign neoplasm but has the definite potential for developing into a malignancy. The chorionic villi degenerate and become transparent vesicles. These appear as clusters of grapes. Usually there is no accompanying fetus. Incidence in the United States is one is 2000 pregnancies.

Pregnancy ordinarily progresses in the beginning at least until a month after conception when the fetoplacental circulation is established. The uterus is out of proportion to the determined gestational age. Bleeding is by far the most outstanding feature. Anemia is very common. Passage of the vesicles establishes the diagnosis. Evacuation or even a hysterectomy may need to be employed.[23,24,26,31]

Invasive mole

An invasive mole or *chorioadenoma destruens* is the same as the hydatidiform mole, except it invades the myometrium and may metastasize to distant organs.[23]

Local lesions

Bleeding may result from lower or extragenital sites and could stimulate an abortion. Lower genital tract causes would include erosions, carcinoma, and trauma of the cervix; trauma, ulcerations, severe moniliasis, varicosities, and carcinoma of the vagina; trauma, varicosities, and carcinoma of the vulva. Extragenital sites include urinary tract lesions, hemorrhoids, and rectal lesions. These local lesions may cause problems throughout pregnancy.[31]

ANTEPARTUM (LATE) HEMORRHAGE
Placenta previa

Definition. Placenta previa is the implantation of the placenta in the lower segment of the uterus. (It should implant in the body of the uterus.) The placenta is located near or on the cervical os such that the encroachment of a fully dilated cervix will result in placental separation and hemorrhage.*

The following are commonly accepted classifications of placenta previa:

1. Total, central, or complete: the internal os is completely covered by the placenta.
2. Partial: a portion of the cervical os is covered by placenta.
3. Marginal or low-lying: the edge of the placenta reaches the margin of the cervical os.

It needs to be emphasized that the degree of previa depends on cervical dilatation. For example, a low-lying placenta may become a partial previa as dilatation exposes an edge of the placenta.[1,2,16,25]

Incidence. Placenta previa occurs in about 1 in 200 deliveries.[2,7,13,25] Multiparas will account for 80% of the cases.[57] The effect of age seems to be more the determining factor than parity. Incidence is three times as high in women over 35 years of age compared to 25-year-olds, regardless of parity.[1,7,25] Recurrence is about 12 times the general incidence.[1] Implantation of the placenta on the anterior wall is twice as frequent with a previa.[13]

Etiology. The precise cause of placenta previa is not known. Page[23] suggests that at the stage of chorion frondosum, the vascular development of the decidua in the uterine fundus is deficient for various reasons. Thus, lower segment attachment is preferred. This is supported by the fact that the maternal portion of the placenta is considerably larger with a previa and cord insertion is more often marginal or velamentous. Some studies have actually documented deficiency in fundal decidual development.[23] Implicated predisposing factors are: faulty implantation, previous uterine scarring (especially of the lower segment and involving the endometrium), tumors distorting the contour of the uterus, endometritis (especially after a previous pregnancy), repeated pregnancies in a short interval, multiparity, advancing age, and large placentas.[1,7,20,25]

---

*See references 1, 2, 13, 16, 23, 25, and 29.

The large placenta may be the result of fetal erythroblastosis or multiple fetuses for example. These could eventually become a previa situation.[24] When implantation occurs in the lower segment, the placenta will often be larger owing to poor vascularization, and the placenta will often extend near the cervical os.[13] If the placenta implants in a poorly vascularized portion of the upper segment, it will again enlarge because of ischemia and migrate to the lower segment. A large placenta is frequently thin and may have additional cotyledons in the form of succenturiate lobe formation. Marginal cord insertion frequently occurs. One rare additional factor to consider for implantation in the lower segment is that there is significantly less endometrium. This is a predisposing factor for abnormal adherence to the wall *(placenta accreta).* [19]

Clinical characteristics. The most characteristic feature of placenta previa is painless hemorrhage, which usually does not appear until the early third trimester.* Bleeding would ordinarily not take place earlier, since in the latter part of pregnancy the process of effacement (retraction of the internal os) occurs. This parallels the increase in uterine motility as term approaches. Consequently, there is a peak of activity at the time of labor.[23] Bleeding from torn uterine attachments is augmented by the inability of the stretched myometrial fibers of the lower segment to compress as should normally occur after delivery of the placenta.[25]

The first episode of bleeding is generally without warning and frequently occurs during sleep. This is rarely fatal.[7,16,24] Recurrence is unpredictable.[1,16,24] The bleeding is generally bright red and mostly external. The uterus will most likely remain soft.[2,20] Transverse or oblique fetal lie is frequent because placental placement hinders engagement of the presenting part.[13] Coagulation defects are rarely a problem.[25]

Approximately 90% of women with a previa will have a significant hemorrhage. Hypovolemic shock will occur with 10% to 25% of these women, but these are generally those with a more complicated previa. Patients with the more severe forms tend to bleed earlier and more profusely, and 50% of these

---

*See references 1, 2, 7, 13, 16, 19, and 23.

will bleed prior to 30 weeks.[1,7] It is imperative to assume previa until proved otherwise.

Diagnosis

Direct clinical examination. Diagnosis is established with a direct pelvic examination. Passing the finger through the cervix and palpating the placenta will confirm this. Such a procedure is only permissible in the operating room where a double setup is used. The obstetrical team should be ready for a vaginal delivery or an emergency cesarean section in case of hemorrhage owing to placenta previa.

There is little improvement in neonatal mortality after 37 weeks' gestation. In such cases, the pelvic examination may be promptly utilized.[25]

Roentgenography and isotope localization. Several radiological techniques have been used to localize the placenta. These include (1) soft tissue x-ray-films, (2) radioactive isotope injection, (3) amniography with contrast material injected into the amniotic sac, and (4) retrograde arteriography. These are not without their potential hazards and are not always completely reliable.[2,25]

Ultrasound placentography. Currently, ultrasound supersedes all other methods of diagnosing placenta previa. It is safe in that it does not involve any radiation hazards, and it is a simple technique. Above all, there is great accuracy reported, as high as 97% during the last trimester.[1,2,7,25]

Management

Expectant. If bleeding stops when the patient is less than 36 weeks pregnant, the baby is less than 2500 gm, and the woman is not in labor, waiting is a reasonable course of action. This is for the sole purpose of improving perinatal mortality and morbidity rates. This is controversial since some feel the potential results of another hemorrhage far outweigh the hazards of a premature delivery, especially now with the advent of neonatal intensive care units.[2,7]

If expectant management is chosen, the following guidelines are generally followed:

1. The patient is hospitalized and, as a more accepted practice, remains hospitalized for the duration of the pregnancy.

2. The patient will be confined to bed rest for at at least 72 hours in an effort to use the fetal body as a tamponade.[13]

3. Ultrasound will help to confirm the diagnosis.

4. Pelvic or rectal examinations must be deferred.
5. A large bore needle is inserted during active bleeding. Intravenous fluids are started.
6. Typing and crossmatching are done for at least two units of blood and kept available. Transfusion will be given for hemoglobin levels below 10 gm/dl.
7. The patient is allowed to ambulate on day three if bleeding has stopped, even with a positive diagnosis. If bleeding continues, the patient is confined to bed and transfused.
8. Amniocentesis determines fetal maturity.
9. Fetal heart tones are assessed, preferably with a fetal heart monitor during the active phase of bleeding. Following this, fetal heart tones are assessed at least every 4 hours with a fetoscope or Doptone.
10. Social Service referral is indicated owing to the long-term nature of this situation.
11. If the patient insists on going home, she must be told of all potential dangers. She must stay in bed as much as possible and be closely supervised. Douching and coitus are forbidden. Blood should be kept available in the hospital for use if an emergency admission is necessary.[7]

If bleeding continues, or if the baby is mature, or if there is not room for expectant management, the baby needs to be delivered.

Double setup. The double setup method was mentioned under the section concerning diagnosis. The purpose is for the sole confirmation of a placenta previa.[1] A careful speculum examination should first be done, as the cause of bleeding may be cervicitis. If bleeding is profuse, the double setup should be omitted.[7] The use of a double setup to confirm a previa seems to be becoming less practiced since ultrasound is so highly accurate.

Cesarean section delivery. The cesarean section is the more accepted method of delivery in practically all cases. It allows immediate delivery, and the uterus can promptly contract to halt bleeding. It also forestalls potential lacerations. Ordinarily, a low transverse incision can be made, especially if the placenta is posterior and the fetus has a cephalic presentation. A vertical incision is safer for the anterior previa.

Vaginal delivery. A vaginal delivery would possibly be the chosen method for a small, marginal previa.[7] The rationale is to exert pressure on the placenta and contract the bleeding vessels. Rupture of the membranes is now the only commonly employed method for exerting pressure.[25] Also, the presenting part should be low and bleeding contained or minimal for this type of delivery.[13]

Prognosis. Cesarean section and transfusion for placenta previa was suggested as early as 1927, and this has markedly reduced the maternal mortality rate. Since 1945, expectant treatment has been advocated, but this has remained controversial regarding improvement.[25] Considering adequate prenatal care, maternal mortality rates have been reduced to less than 1%. Morbidity remains at about 20%.[7,13]

Fetal mortality is about 20% and has not changed appreciably over the past 20 years. Part of this mortality is a result of prematurity, intrauterine hypoxia, and developmental anomalies. This apparent plateau of infant mortality is the reason many feel earlier deliveries should be advocated.[7]

There seems to be no relationship between fetal death and the number of hemorrhagic episodes.[7,13] In many cases the first episode may occur when the fetus has a good chance of survival. This supports the feeling that immediate cesarean section should be done after 35 weeks' gestation.[7]

Abruptio placentae (premature separation)

Definition. Abruptio placentae is the separation of the normally situated placenta from its uterine site of implantation after 20 weeks' gestation and before delivery of the fetus. There is resultant apparent or concealed retroplacental bleeding.*

The following are commonly accepted classifications and are graded by severity:

Grade 0: This is diagnosed only after delivery. A small retroplacental clot is seen. Usually the patient is asymptomatic.
Grade 1: There is external bleeding. There may be uterine tetany and tenderness. There will be no signs of maternal shock or fetal distress.
Grade 2: External bleeding may or may not be present.

---

*See references 1, 2, 7, 13, 16, 19, and 24.

Uterine tetany and tenderness is present. There is still no shock. The fetus shows signs of distress.

Grade 3: There does not have to be external bleeding. Uterine tetany is marked. There is shock and fetal death. Usually a coagulation problem ensues.[3]

Incidence. There is great variation in the reported incidence of abruptio placentae, often owing to variations of diagnostic criteria. Prichard and MacDonald[25] report 1 in 55 to 150 deliveries, while Cavanaugh[7] reports 1 in 250 deliveries. The incidence is significantly increased with parity but not with age.[1] Multiparas account for 80% of the cases. By 36 weeks' gestation 50% of the abruptions will have occurred.[1,7] Women with a history of abortion, premature labor, antenatal hemorrhage, stillbirth, or neonatal death have about twice the incidence of the normal population. Abruption will recur in 15% to 20% of these cases.[13]

Etiology. The exact cause of abruptio placentae is unknown. There seems to be a relationship with hypertension and increased parity.[13,25] Page believes that there are degenerative changes in the small arteries that supply the intervillous spaces, and these result in thrombosis, degeneration of the decidua, and rupture of the vessel. This results in a retroplacental hematoma. Arterial pumping further separates the placenta from its decidual attachment, thus causing complete abruption.[23] Implicated predisposing factors are trauma, shortened unbilical cord, sudden uterine decompression, polyhydramnios, uterine anomaly, tumor occlusion of the inferior vena cava, and, of course, hypertension.[1,7,25]

Clinical characteristics. Mild forms of abruption are accompanied by slight uterine irritability. There may be the escape of some dark blood. In some instances the blood may be totally concealed. This whole situation may go unrecognized until after delivery.[1]

As abruption increases in severity, there may be a sudden onset of excruciating abdominal pain described as knifelike or tearing. A significant sign is uterine rigidity, and the uterus fails to relax between contractions. Uterine tenderness can be localized or generalized. Fetal heart tones are usually absent, thus indicating a dead fetus. Frequently the mother is in a state of shock and the severity may well be out of proportion to the amount of blood lost. The concealed blood enlarges the uterus.[1,13,16,25]

Complications in the clinical course

Consumptive coagulopathy. Abruptio placentae is the most common cause of consumptive coagulopathy. Overt hypofibrinogenemia (less than 150 mg/dl plasma), elevated levels of fibrinogen-fibrin degradation products, and variations in other coagulation factors occur in 30% of the cases. The major mechanism seems to be the induction of coagulation intravascularly and, to a lesser degree, retroplacentally.[25] It is believed that thromboplastin is released from the placental detachment sites and enters the circulation. This causes hypofibrinogenemia, placental deficiency, and a decrease in factors V and VIII. There is an activation of the fibrinolytic system; fibrinogen-fibrin degradation products appear.[1]

One should always consider this potential course in abruption. Signs to consider are petechiae; excessive vaginal bleeding; and bleeding from puncture sites, gums, and gastrointestinal or urinary tracts.[1]

Renal failure. Renal failure will often be seen as a result of hypovolemia causing acute tubular necrosis or bilateral renal cortical necrosis. The major etiological factor very likely is an intrarenal vasospasm. Proteinuria is also common.[1,7,25]

Uteroplacental apoplexy (Couvelaire uterus). In the more severe forms of uteroplacental apoplexy, there may be extravasation of blood into the uterine musculature and beneath the uterine serosa. This will generally contract well after delivery.[25]

Fetal-to-maternal bleeding. Fetal-to-maternal bleeding could be a problem for the Rh-negative woman and the Rh-positive fetus. The mother may become sensitized with a fetal hemorrhage into her circulation.[25]

Postpartum hemorrhage. The incidence of postpartum hemorrhage is doubled in patients having abruptio placentae. If there is an associated coagulopathy, hemorrhage is as high as eight times the general population. This is due to the increased serum fibrinogen-fibrin degradation products.[1,7]

• • •

The aforementioned complications are the more common ones. There are still others.

Diagnosis. The diagnosis of abruptio placentae is mainly assisted by the history and physical examination. Hypertension is a common predisposing factor. This plus all the other clinical characteristics previously mentioned need to be considered.[7] Assessment is also made by the following laboratory tests: clot observation, serum fibrinolysin, and anticoagulant factor. In addition, the following workup is done: complete blood count, platelet count, fibrinogen level, fibrinogen-fibrin degradation products (FDP), thrombin, prothrombin, and partial thromboplastin time.[1]

Management. If abruptio placentae is suspected, the following guidelines are generally followed:

1. Hospitalize and confine to bed rest.
2. Defer rectal and pelvic examinations.
3. Insert a large bore needle. Start intravenous fluids.
4. Watch for potential signs of shock.
5. Monitor fluid intake and urinary output.
6. See that coagulation studies are done.
7. Assess renal function (for example, spot check for proteinuria).
8. Monitor electrolytes.
9. Continually assess for any changes in uterine size.
10. Type and cross match for at least 2 units of blood and keep available. Transfusions would be given for hemoglobin levels below 10 gm/dl.
11. Rule out placenta previa with ultrasound. If it is excluded, do a speculum examination to exclude lower genital tract bleeding.[1]
12. Assess fetal heart tones preferably with a fetal heart monitor during the active phase of bleeding. Following this, assess fetal heart tones at least every 4 hours with a fetoscope or Doptone.

Expectant. Expectant management is appropriate when there is an indication of mild abruptio placentae.[1] At term, a double setup may be done to rule out placenta previa and lower genital tract bleeding. If neither is present and all else is stable, the membranes may be ruptured. At this time, a physician may elect to attach an internal fetal scalp electrode to directly monitor fetal heart tones. An oxytocin drip may be started to induce labor. Also, the presenting part should be low and bleeding contained or minimal for a vaginal approach.[13] However, cesarean section is certainly the more generally accepted practice. It is indicated when fetal distress occurs, bleeding continues, the uterus fails to relax between contractions, or labor fails to begin promptly following the abruption and fibrinogen levels decrease.[1,7]

When the abruption is more severe, it is imperative to support circulatory volume and expedite a cesarean delivery. There needs to be blood replacement, monitoring of the central venous pressure, hourly urine outputs by way of a catheter, and administration of oxygen. Amniotomy also helps to decrease myometrial extravasation of blood, chances of coagulation problems, renal involvement, and postpartum hemorrhage owing to atony.[1,7]

Management of coagulopathy defects. Additional considerations need to be undertaken in the management of coagulopathy defects as follows:

1. Give fresh blood. This has a greater supply of platelets and clotting factors.
2. Give fresh frozen plasma to support factors V and VII and approximately 2 gm fibrinogen per liter. If fibrinogen is depleted, give cryoprecipitate.
3. Give fibrinogen only if all else fails. Some feel this is adding fuel to the already existing fire.
4. Heparin is rarely used. If it is used, the patient should be delivered; coagulation replacement factors are not controlling the bleeding.
5. Remove source of thromboplastin by emptying the uterus either abdominally or vaginally.[1,7] The chosen route is based on whether the baby is alive, the state of cervix, the quality of uterine contractions, and the general condition of the patient.[7] (Exchange transfusions and hemodialysis are presently being attempted in some medical centers.)

Prognosis. Current maternal mortality from abruptio placentae is less than 1%. The earlier the case is seen, the better the prognosis.[7]

Perinatal mortality is 20% to 80%.[7] The fetus is affected by the abruption because of hypovolemia, which leads to hypoxemia. The area for fetomaternal exchange is reduced, and the tearing of the villi also contributes to bleeding.[1]

Ruptured uterus

The reported incidence of uterine rupture is about 1 in 2000 deliveries. It is the cause of about 5% of the maternal deaths in the United States and even greater in underdeveloped countries. It may occur during pregnancy or at the time of delivery. Precipitating causes include spontaneous rupture of a previous scar (for example, cesarean section, myomectomy), trauma (for example, laceration owing to instrumentation, vigorous attempts at version, injudicious use of oxytocin), and others.[7,25]

Circumvallate placenta

In circumvallate placenta a central depression on the fetal side of the placenta is surrounded by a thick grayish ring. The fetal veins tend to terminate abruptly at the margin of the ring. The incidence of hemorrhage as well as prematurity increases with this situation.[25]

Vasa praevia

When a velamentous insertion of fetal vessels transverses the cervical os prior to the fetal head, vasa praevia occurs. The rupture of vessels is more a problem for the baby than the mother.[7,25]

Diseases and accidents

Diseases and accidents may contribute to the situation of hemorrhage at any point in the pregnancy. There are numerous other causes of hemorrhage besides those already mentioned, but they occur less frequently.

INTRAPARTUM HEMORRHAGE

There are multiple reasons for intrapartum hemorrhage. These include all the antepartal indications plus some more specific to the actual time of labor and delivery.

Past obstetrical history

Always look for *high-risk* patients, which includes those with a history of hemorrhage in pregnancy, previous uterine surgery, grand multiparas, and so forth.

Present obstetrical course

Watch for uterine *inertia* by continuous assessment of uterine tone. When the uterus tires, it may fail to contract well. Contributing factors are polyhydramnios, multiple pregnancies, a large baby, and a prolonged labor. Another problem is that of *rapid* labor and delivery, and this is often true in the case of premature labor. Rapid cervical dilatation may cause lacerations and subsequent hemorrhagic problems. Other factors contributing to a potential hemorrhagic situation include difficult instrumenta-

tion procedures and deep anesthesia.[9] The following are some specific situations associated with intrapartum hemorrhage.

Inversion of the uterus

The etiology of inversion of the uterus is generally too much traction of the umbilical cord with pronounced fundal pressure. A relaxed uterus and cervix greatly contribute. The woman rapidly shows signs of shock since there is no pressure on the severed vessels. Shock must be combated with blood, oxygen, and other emergency procedures. The patient is deeply anesthetized prior to reinsertion of the uterus. If the placenta is still attached, it should be removed. The uterus must be replaced as soon as it is relaxed.[6,25]

Placenta accreta

Placenta accreta is any abnormal adherence of the placenta to the uterine wall. It is due to the partial or total absence of the decidua basalis and imperfect development of the fibrinoid layer. The villi attach to the myometrium (placenta accreta), invade the myometrium (placenta increta), or penetrate the myometrium (placenta percreta).

Blood often is a result of the placenta previa. Invasion of the myometrium may cause uterine rupture. Delivery of the placenta may be so difficult as to cause inversion. Also, fragments may remain. If it is not possible to remove all of the placenta, a hysterectomy may be the likely course.[25]

Retention of placenta

The placenta normally separates spontaneously within 10 to 20 minutes following delivery. The delay may be a result of inadequate uterine contractions and retraction. The placenta may be firmly adhered as in placenta accreta. It will have to be removed manually if not expelled spontaneously.

POSTPARTUM HEMORRHAGE

Definition. Postpartum hemorrhage is most frequently defined as loss of blood in excess of 500 ml after delivery. It is rarely a sudden massive hemorrhage but is more often a slow, continuous loss over a period of hours that can eventually lead to an enormous loss of blood. Hemorrhage within the first 24 hours is commonly referred to as primary or immediate hemorrhage; it is referred to as secondary or delayed hemorrhage when it occurs after this time.[14,22-24]

Incidence. Loss of blood is the leading cause of maternal death in the United States. Postpartum hemorrhage is the most common cause of this blood loss and accounts for one fourth of the deaths from obstetrical hemorrhage. An estimated blood loss of greater than 500 ml occurs once in every 20 to 30 cases. Hemorrhage of greater than 1000 ml occurs once in about every 75 cases.[14,22-24,27]

Etiology. The most frequent causes of postpartum hemorrhage are (1) uterine atony; (2) lacerations of the perineum, vagina, and cervix; (3) hematomas; and (4) retained placental fragments. These factors may occur singly or in combination with each other. Clotting defects can also be classified as causes, but they are much less likely to occur and will not be discussed here.[22-24]

Each of the factors just mentioned will be discussed independently as to their definition, predisposing factors (etiology), clinical characteristics, diagnosis, and management.

Uterine atony

Definition. Uterine atony (or inertia) is an inability or failure of the myometrial cells to contract and constrict vessels within muscle fibers. Consequently, the sinuses remain open at the site of placental separation and bleeding occurs.[22,24]

Incidence. Uterine atony is the cause of 90% of the cases of postpartum hemorrhage.[14,23,27]

Etiology. The following are predisposing factors of uterine atony[14,23,24]:

1. General anesthesia—the muscles become too relaxed
2. Overdistention of the uterus—results from a large fetus, multiple gestation, or hydramnios
3. Prolonged labor leading to muscle fatigue
4. Vigorous oxytocin stimulation leading to muscle fatigue
5. Grand multiparity—decreased muscle tone
6. History of previous hemorrhage from uterine atony
7. Rapid delivery—with resultant muscle trauma
8. Uterine infection

9. Hypovolemic shock
10. Premature or incomplete separation of placenta—trauma to muscle

Clinical characteristics and diagnosis. Frequently in hemorrhage owing to uterine atony, blood may not escape through the vagina but instead as much as 1000 ml or more may accumulate within the uterus. With concealed bleeding, one may see a deviation of the uterus to the side or an increase in fundal height.

Of course, the most obvious sign of uterine atony is finding a relaxed uterus when palpating the fundus through the abdominal wall. This normally occurs within the first few hours of delivery. Finally, expelled clots, without evidence of tissue, are frequently an indication of improper involution.[23,24,26]

Management. External massage of the fundus is frequently the first step in the management of uterine atony. It is important to note that massage is not indicated if there are no signs of placental separation. Constant kneading of the fundus before placental separation can lead to incomplete placental separation.

The most frequently used drugs are ergonovine (Ergotrate), methylergonovine maleate (Methergine), and oxytocin (Pitocin). These are most often used in combination with external massage.

If bleeding persists despite these procedures, the following procedures are employed:

1. Blood transfusion
2. Bimanual compression of the uterus
3. Inspection of cervix and vagina for lacerations without curettage
4. Curettage
5. Manual exploration of uterine cavity for lacerations or retained placental fragments

Finally, if all these efforts fail to stop the hemorrhage, a hysterectomy is performed.[14,23,24,26]

Lacerations

Lacerations of the perineum, vagina, and cervix are the second most frequent cause of postpartum hemorrhage.

Etiology. Factors predisposing to the occurrence of lacerations are as follows[22-24,26]:

1. Delivery of a large infant
2. Midforceps delivery
3. Forceps rotation

4. Delivery through an incompletely dilated cervix
5. Intrauterine manipulation
6. Rapid delivery

Clinical characteristics and diagnosis. Bleeding from lacerations is tentatively differentiated from uterine atony by determining the status of the fundus. If there is persistent bleeding in the presence of a firm, contracted uterus, hemorrhage is most likely a result of lacerations. Bright red arterial blood is also frequently suggestive of lacerations.[14,23,24,26]

Management. As mentioned, hemorrhage from lacerations is usually delineated from uterine atony by persistent bleeding in the presence of a firm, contracted uterus. Should this occur, inspection of the cervix, vagina, perineum, and uterus should be performed. Bleeding from lacerations resulting from damage to vessels is usually stopped by ligating the vessels with sutures.[14,23,24,26]

Hematomas

Definition. Hematomas are most often a result of damage to a blood vessel without laceration of the superficial tissues. They may be present in the vulvar area, vagina, or retroperitoneally.

Etiology. Trauma is most often the predisposing factor in hematomas and may occur with the following:

1. Normal pressure from the presenting part against the pelvic structures during labor
2. Forceps manipulation
3. An excess of external fundal pressure
4. Paracervical or pudendal anesthesia[14,22,25]

Clinical characteristics and diagnosis. Signs and symptoms of a vulvar hematoma include increasing perineal pain and the appearance of a discolored tumor. The vaginal hematoma usually exhibits increasing pelvic pain with symptoms of pressure and inability to void. Finally, retroperitoneal hematoma is less easy to detect. If the bleeding is massive, rupture into the intraperitoneal area may occur and possibly cause death. Rupture of this hematoma into the vagina can lead to infection and even sepsis. If bleeding is slight to moderate, the hematoma may be absorbed spontaneously.[22,24]

Management. With increasing pain and evidence of enlarging hematoma, the area should be incised and evacuated. If there is severe hypovolemia,

blood transfusion should be considered. Broad-spectrum antibiotics are frequently given.

If a retroperitoneal hematoma is suspected or found, the woman is transfused and laparotomy is performed to aspirate the hematoma.[14,23,24,26]

Retained placental fragments

Retention of placental fragments is an infrequent cause of immediate postpartum hemorrhage, but it is a frequent cause of late bleeding in which profuse bleeding occurs suddenly a week or more after delivery. These separated fragments may undergo necrosis with deposition of fibrin and become a placental polyp. This polyp may interfere with proper uterine contraction or involution and therefore can cause hemorrhage.

Etiology. Retention of fragments can occur as a result of an abnormally adherent placenta such as placenta accreta or can occur as a result of a succenturiate lobe (an accessory lobe developed at a distance from the main placenta.[14,22,24,26,27]

Clinical characteristics and diagnosis. As mentioned previously, retention of placental fragments most often occurs as late postpartum bleeding. It may occur near the end of the first week or thereafter, and bleeding may be heavy. Expelled clots should be examined for tissue since this will be an indication that placental fragments have been retained.[14,22,24,26,27]

Management. Inspection of the placenta at delivery frequently leads to the finding of retained fragments. In the event that they are not found at this time and there is persistent late or secondary postpartum bleeding, treatment includes blood transfusion (if blood loss has been heavy) and uterine curettage.[14,22,24,27]

Prognosis of postpartum hemorrhage

The woman's response to hemorrhage depends on her own blood volume, the bulk of her pregnancy-induced hypervolemia, and her degree of anemia at the time of delivery. Any problems among these factors reduce the body's ability to compensate.

Frequently, postpartum hemorrhage causes only moderate alterations in pulse and blood pressure until large amounts of blood have been lost. When the blood pressure drops, one must be careful not to interpret the woman who has been hypertensive as normotensive.

Once large volumes of blood have been lost, shock ensues. The following signs and symptoms occur: rapid and thready pulse; cold, clammy skin; chills; disturbed vision; restlessness; and extreme thirst. With further hemorrhage, vascular collapse may occur and death may ensue.[23,24,26]

The following elements are of great importance to the outcome of postpartum hemorrhage[22,24]:

1. Close attention to all postpartum patients
2. A competent blood bank
3. Quick action by all members of the health team

Finally, it is important to discuss here an uncommon but serious outcome of postpartum hemorrhage. On rare occasions, early or primary postpartum hemorrhage is followed by partial or complete necrosis of the anterior pituitary portal vessels. The cause for this is uncertain. This condition is referred to as Sheehan's syndrome. The following occurrences are the result of this syndrome: absence of initiation of lactation, atrophy of the breast, amenorrhea, loss of pubic and axillary hair, super-involution of the uterus, hypothyroidism, and adrenocortical insufficiency. The hemorrhage occurs early (at or immediately following delivery), and the severity of the hemorrhage does not always correlate with the occurrence of this syndrome.[14,22,24]

CONCLUSION

Hemorrhage remains a leading cause of obstetrical emergency. Professional nurses need to be aware of women at risk for hemorrhage and those exhibiting signs and symptoms of the various hemorrhage problems. These particular areas of focus and concern for nurses include the following:

1. Prevent hemorrhage where possible.
2. Provide nursing care for the patient with hemorrhage. Be sure to include the family.
3. Patient education is essential.

Prompt early recognition and institution of care will serve to decrease complications of obstetrical hemorrhage. This is a definite nursing challenge.

Protocols

Problem □ Placenta previa

GOAL: To be aware of predisposing factors and the early recognition of signs and symptoms indicating placenta previa
Rationale: To detect and manage hemorrhage owing to placenta previa and thereby decrease the incidence of maternal and fetal mortality and mobidity

DIAGNOSTIC

1. Be cognizant of implicated predisposing factors (for example, previous uterine scarring, tumors, endometritis, repeated pregnancies in short interval, multiparity, advancing age, and large placenta).
   Rationale: To institute prompt care in an effort to decrease maternal and fetal mortality and morbidity
2. Review present prenatal history (for example, EDC and history of spotting).
   Rationale: To facilitate early recognition of placenta previa
3. Observe and assess external blood loss (for example, number of pads used and amount of saturation, color, and consistency of blood).
   Rationale: To check that the bleeding is bright and external
4. Assess pain if present. (Be aware of contractions in the event the patient is in labor.)
   Rationale: To distinguish placenta previa, which is most often characterized by painless vaginal bleeding
5. If patient is in labor, assess uterine relaxation between contractions.
   Rationale: To assure that uterus remains relaxed between contractions
6. Localization of placenta is important. (Ultrasonography is most frequently used.)

Rationale: To aid confirmation of the diagnosis of placenta previa

7. The following blood work should be drawn: CBC, Rh, type and cross match, and coagulation studies.
   Rationale: To assess need to transfuse patient if hemoglobin below 10 gm

8. Monitor maternal vital signs.
   Rationale: To be alert for signs of shock

9. Amniocentesis may be indicated.
   Rationale: To assess fetal maturity in the event that delivery is indicated

10. Assess fetal heart tones via fetal monitor during the active phase of bleeding. Following this, assess the fetal heart tones at least every 4 hours with a fetoscope or Doptone.
    Rationale: To assess fetal well-being

11. Prepare patient for double setup if indicated. (This is now a lesser practice since ultrasound is so accurate.)
    Rationale: To directly confirm placenta previa

THERAPEUTIC

1. Confine the patient to bed.
   Rationale: To allow the fetal body to act as a tamponade

2. Pelvic or rectal examinations must be deferred.
   Rationale: To avoid further bleeding

3. Insert a large bore needle during active bleeding. Start intravenous fluids.
   Rationale: To provide precautionary measures in the event that hypovolemia occurs

4. Institute expectant management for early pregnancy, nonlabor, and cessation of bleeding.
   Rationale: To improve perinatal mortality and morbidity

5. Prepare for cesarean section (for example, consent form, Foley catheterization, abdominoperineal preparation).
   Rationale: To provide for immediate delivery of fetus, so that uterus can promptly contract to control bleeding and forestall potential lacerations

6. a. Prepare for vaginal delivery.
   Rationale: To provide for delivery when there is a marginal placenta, the presenting part is low or engaged, and there is minimal bleeding

   b. Possible amniotomy is done.
      Rationale: To exert pressure on vessels in an attempt to stop bleeding.

7. Alert pediatrician and nursery of possible delivery.
   Rationale: To keep perinatal team informed

8. Support patient and family (for example, encourage verbalization of concerns and questions and explain procedures).
   Rationale: To help relieve the patient's and family's anxiety and allow them to be a part of their own care

EDUCATIONAL

1. All pregnant women need to be alerted to the danger of bleeding and any other unusual occurrence. In the event that these occur, (for example, spotting, active bleeding, cramping) they should be reported immediately to the physician.
   Rationale: To decrease incidence of mortality and morbidity by early detection of bleeding

2. Give an explanation of all procedures and treatments.
   Rationale: To assist the patient in her understanding of *why* all procedures and treatments are done and their importance to her and her baby

Problem □ Abruptio placentae

GOAL: To be aware of predisposing factors and the early recognition of signs and symptoms of hemorrhage indicating abruptio placentae

Rationale: To decrease the incidence of maternal and fetal mortality and morbidity through early detection and management of hemorrhage caused by abruptio placentae

DIAGNOSTIC

1. Be cognizant of implicated predisposing factors (for example, trauma, sudden uterine decompression, polyhydramnios, uterine anomaly or tumor, multiparity, and hypertension).
   Rationale: To promptly institute care in an effort to decrease maternal and fetal mortality and morbidity through early recognition

2. Review present prenatal history (for example, EDC, Rh, history of spotting).
   Rationale: To facilitate early recognition of

abruptio placentae (It is important to note mother's blood type and Rh factor since mother can be sensitized in the event that a fetal-to-maternal hemorrhage occurs.)

3. Observe and assess external blood loss (for example, number of pads used and amount of saturation, color, and consistency of blood).
   Rationale: To detect the escape of dark blood (in some instances, bleeding may be totally concealed. Excessive concealed blood can alter uterine size.)

4. Assess pain, if present. (Be aware of contractions in the event the patient is in labor.)
   Rationale: To assess for slight uterine irritability accompanying mild forms or a sudden onset of excruciating abdominal pain described as knifelike or tearing as abruption increases in severity

5. If patient is in labor, assess uterine relaxation between contractions.
   Rationale: To detect whether there is uterine rigidity or the uterus fails to relax between contractions (Uterine tenderness can be localized or generalized.)

6. a. Localization of placenta. (Ultrasonography is most frequently used.)
      Rationale: To rule out placenta previa
   b. If placenta previa is ruled out, do speculum examination.
      Rationale: To exclude lower genital tract bleeding

7. The following studies should be done:
   a. CBC, Rh, and type and cross match.
      Rationale: To assess need to transfuse patient if hemoglobin is below 10 gm
   b. Coagulation studies.
      Rationale: To detect consumptive coagulopathy, which is most commonly caused by abruptio placentae
   c. Monitor electrolytes.
      Rationale: To indicate altered body chemistry
   d. Renal function studies (for example, proteinuria spot check, BUN).
      Rationale: To assess for hypovolemia where intrarenal vasospasm has occurred

8. a. Monitor maternal vital signs.
      Rationale: To be alert for signs of shock

   b. If shock occurs, the following should be done:
      1. Monitor central venous pressure.
         Rationale: To indicate hypovolemia
      2. Measure hourly urine output by way of a catheter.
         Rationale: To indicate renal function

9. Amniocentesis may be indicated.
   Rationale: To assess fetal maturity in the event that delivery is indicated

10. Assess fetal heart tones via fetal monitor during the active phase of bleeding. Following this, assess the fetal heart tones at least every 4 hours with a fetoscope or Doptone.
    Rationale: To assess fetal well-being

11. Assess any unusual bleeding (for example, petechiae, excessive vaginal bleeding from puncture site, gums, gastrointestinal or urinary tracts).
    Rationale: To detect consumptive coagulopathy

THERAPEUTIC

1. Confine the patient to bed.
   Rationale: To observe patient

2. Pelvic or rectal examinations must be deferred.
   Rationale: To avoid activating further bleeding

3. Insert a large bore intravenous needle during active bleeding. Start intravenous fluids.
   Rationale: To be prepared in the event that hypovolemia occurs

4. Expectant management is appropriate when there is an indication of mild abruptio (controversial).
   Rationale: To improve perinatal mortality and morbidity

5. Prepare for cesarean section (for example, consent form, Foley catherization, abdominoperineal preparation).
   Rationale: To facilitate immediate delivery of distressed fetus and remove the source of hemorrhage

6. a. Prepare for vaginal delivery.
      Rationale: To institute vaginal delivery if the presenting part is low or engaged and bleeding is believed to be minimal.

   b. Amniotomy may be done.

Rationale: To exert pressure on vessels in an attempt to stop bleeding

7. Encourage side-lying position (especially left) during labor.

Rationale: To remove obstructing pressure on vena cava and facilitate blood return to right heart

8. Alert pediatrician and nursery of possible delivery.

Rationale: To keep perinatal team informed

9. Support patient and family (for example, encourage verbalization of concerns and questions, explain procedures).

Rationale: To help relieve patient's and family's anxiety and allow them to be a part of their own care.

10. Management of coagulopathy defects:

a. Give fresh blood.

Rationale: To supply platelets and clotting factors

b. Give fresh frozen plasma.

Rationale: To support factors V and VII and fibrinogen

c. Give cryoprecipitate.

Rationale: To replace depleted fibrinogen

d. Give fibrinogen.

Rationale: To be done only as a last resort as it adds fuel to the fire

e. Give heparin (rarely used).

Rationale: To control bleeding after patient is delivered

f. Deliver patient.

Rationale: To remove source of thromboplastin

EDUCATIONAL

1. All pregnant women need to be alerted to the danger of bleeding and any other unusual occurrence. In the event that these occur (for example, spotting, active bleeding, cramping), they should be reported immediately to the physician.

Rationale: To decrease incidence of mortality and morbidity through early detection of bleeding

2. Give an explanation of all procedures and treatments.

Rationale: To assist the patient in her understanding of *why* all procedures and treat-ments are done and their importance to her and her baby

Problem □ Postpartum hemorrhage

GOAL: To be aware of predisposing factors and the early recognition of signs and symptoms of postpartum hemorrhage

Rationale: To decrease the incidence of maternal mortality and morbidity through early detection and management of postpartum hemorrhage

DIAGNOSTIC

1. Be cognizant of implicated predisposing factors (for example, general anesthesia, overdistention of the uterus, prolonged labor, vigorous oxytocin stimulation, grand multiparity, previous history of postpartal hemorrhage, uterine infection, abruption, rapid delivery, problems with placental separation or extraction, vigorous instrumentation and other trauma of the birth canal).

Rationale: To promptly institute care in an effort to decrease maternal mortality and morbidity through early recognition

2. Assess postpartum blood loss (for example, pad count, saturation, color, and consistency).

Rationale: To keep track of blood loss to avoid hypovolemia and shock conditions. (Bright red arterial blood is most often suggestive of lacerations. Dark blood and clots could be indicative of a hematoma, uterine atony, or retained placental fragments.)

3. Assess any clots or tissue.

Rationale: To detect improper involution from expelled clots without evidence of tissue (If tissue is present, this is usually indicative of retained placental fragments.)

4. Assess location, duration, and kind of pain if present.

Rationale: To detect hematoma which is most often characterized by increased perineal or pelvic pain as a result of continued concealed bleeding

5. Assess uterine tone.

Rationale: To detect a relaxed uterus (the most obvious sign of uterine atony) when palpating the fundus through the abdominal wall (This normally occurs in the immediate postpartum period.)

6. Assess uterine position.

   Rationale: To detect a deviation to the side or an increase in height of fundus indicative of concealed blood in the uterus

7. Monitor maternal vital signs.

   Rationale: To be alert for signs of shock.

8. Assess voiding pattern.

   Rationale: To detect inability of uterus to contract owing to bladder distention or a hematoma against the urethra, resulting in an inability to void

9. The following blood work should be done: CBC, type and cross match.

   Rationale: To assess need to transfuse patient if hemoglobin is below 10 gm

THERAPEUTIC

1. Continue intravenous fluids.

   Rationale: To support circulatory volume and provide a means for blood transfusion

2. Maintain a contracted uterus through external massage, oxytoxic drugs, and bimanual compression of the uterus by the physician if all else fails.

   Rationale: To control hemorrhage

3. Support patient and family (for example, encourage verbalization of concerns and questions and explain procedures).

   Rationale: To help relieve patient's and family's anxiety and allow them to be a part of their own care

EDUCATIONAL

1. Give an explanation of all procedures and treatments.

   Rationale: To assist the patient in her understanding of *why* all procedures and treatments are done and their importance to her

2. Inform mother to report any increased bleeding or clots.

   Rationale: To detect hemorrhagic problems

3. Inform mother of the following normal occurrences

   a. Individual variations of lochia are normal.

   b. Decreased uterine tone in multiparas can account for an increased flow.

   c. Breast-feeding and increased activity can cause increased flow.

   d. Warm tub baths can cause vasodilatation and therefore increased lochia.

REFERENCES

1. Abdul-Karim, R. W., and Chevli, R. N.: Antepartum hemorrhage and shock, Clin. Obstet. Gynecol. **19:**533, 1976.
2. Affonso, D. D., and Danforth, D.: Complications arising during pregnancy. In Clark, A. L., and Affonso, D. D., editors: Childbearing: a nursing perspective, Philadelphia, 1976, F. A. Davis Co.
3. Benson, R. C.: Handbook of obstetrics and gynecology, Los Altos, Calif., 1974, Lange Medical Publications, p. 137.
4. Brown, B. A.: Hematology—principles and procedure, Philadelphia, 1976, Lea & Febiger, p. 113.
5. Cavanagh, D.: Clotting disorders in pregnancy. In Cavanagh, D., Woods, R. E., and O'Connor, T., editors: Obstetrical emergencies, ed. 2, New York, 1978, Harper & Row, Publishers, Inc., p. 7.
6. Cavanagh, D.: Shock. In Cavanagh, D., Woods, R. E., and O'Connor, T., editors: Obstetrical emergencies, ed. 2, New York, 1978, Harper & Row, Publishers, Inc., p. 25.
7. Cavanagh, R., and Woods, R. E.: Hemorrhage in late pregnancy. In Cavanagh, D., Woods, R. E., and O'Connor, T., editors: Obstetrical emergencies, ed. 2, New York, 1978, Harper & Row, Publishers, Inc., p. 177.
8. Ganong, W. F.: Review of medical physiology, ed. 7, Los Altos, Calif., 1975, Lange Medical Publications, p. 465.
9. Grandin, D., Hemorrhage in pregnancy. In Barber, J. R., and Graber, E. A., editors: Quick reference to OB-GYN procedures, Philadelphia, 1969, J. B. Lippincott Co., p. 131.
10. Grollmand, S.: The human body—its structure and physiology, ed. 4, New York, 1978, Macmillan Publishing Co. Inc., p. 302.
11. Howie, R. W.: Thromboembolism, Clin. Obstet. Gynecol. **4:**397, 1977.
12. Jacob, S. W., et al.: Structure and function in man, ed. 4, Philadelphia, 1978, W. B. Saunders Co., p. 376.
13. Jenson, M. D., Benson, R. C., and Bobak, I. M.: Maternity care—the nurse and the family, St. Louis, 1977, The C. V. Mosby Co., p. 223.
14. Kelly, J. V.: Postpartum hemorrhage, Clinic. Obstet. Gynecol. **19:**595, 1976.
15. Kelman, G. R.: Applied cardiovascular physiology, ed. 2, Boston, 1977, Butterworth (Publishers) Inc., p. 128.
16. Kilker, R. C., and Wilkerson, B.: Nursing care in placenta previa and abruptio placenta, Nurs. Clin. North Am. **8:**479, 1973.
17. Langley, L. L., et al.: Dynamic anatomy and physiology, ed. 4, New York, 1974, McGraw-Hill Book Co., p. 493.
18. Little, R. C.: Physiology of the heart and circulation, Chicago, 1977, Year Book Medical Publishers, Inc., p. 161.
19. Miller, F. N.: Peery and Miller's pathology: a dynamic introduction to medicine and surgery, ed. 3, Boston, 1978, Little, Brown and Co., p. 30.
20. Miller, M. A., and Brooten, D. A.: The childbearing family: a nursing perspective, Boston, 1977, Little, Brown and Co., p. 230.
21. Naeya, R., et al.: Abruptio placenta and perinatal death: A prospective study. Am. J. Obstet. Gynecol. **128:**740, 1977.
22. O'Connor, T., and Cavanagh, D.: Postpartum emergencies. In Cavanagh, D., Wood, R. E., and O'Connor, T., editors:

Obstetrical emergencies, ed. 2, New York, 1978, Harper & Row, Publishers, Inc., p. 293.

23. Page, E. W., et al.: Human reproduction—the core content of obstetrics, gynecology and perinatal medicine, ed. 2, Philadelphia, 1976, W. B. Saunders Co., p. 205.

24. Pritchard, J. A.: Haematologic problems associated with delivery, placental abruption, retained dead fetus and amniotic fluid embolism, Clin. Haematol. **2**:563, 1973.

25. Pritchard, J. A., and MacDonald, P. C.: Williams obstetrics, ed. 15, New York, 1976, Appleton-Century-Crofts, p. 398.

26. Reeder, S., et al.: Maternity nursing, ed. 13, Philadelphia, 1976, J. B. Lippincott Co., p. 12.

27. Rome, R.: Secondary postpartum haemorrhage, Br. J. Obstet. Gynaecol. **82**:289, 1975.

28. Sahud, M. A.: Why patients bleed, Emergency Med. **6**:231, 1974.

29. Symonds, E. M.: Management of patients with placenta praevia, Nurs. Times **74**:453, 1978.

30. Willoughby, M. L.: Haematological disorders, Clin. Obstet. Gynaecology **4**:371, 1977.

31. Woods, R. E., and Cavanagh, D.: Hemorrhage in early pregnancy. In Cavanagh, D., Woods, R. E., and O'Connor, T., editors: Obstetric emergencies, ed. 2, New York, 1978, Harper & Row, Publishers, Inc.

BIBLIOGRAPHY

Affonso, D. D.: Complications of labor and delivery. In Clark, A. L., and Affonso, D. D., editors: Childbearing: a nursing perspective, Philadelphia, 1976, F. A. Davis Co.

Avila, S., and Blinik, G.: Emergency management of vaginal bleeding, J. Emerg. Nurs. **1**:16, 1975.

Beller, F. K., and Uszynski, M.: DIC in pregnancy, Clin. Obstet. Gynecol. **17**:250, 1974.

Bennett, B., and Douglas, A. S.: Blood coagulation mechanism, Clin. Haematol. **2**:3, 1973.

Bonnar, J.: Blood coagulations and fibrinolysis in obstetrics, Clin. Haematol. **2**:213, 1973.

Brenner, W. E., et al.: Characteristics of patients with placenta previa and results of expectant management, Am. J. Obstet. Gynecol. **132**:180, 1978.

Cocklin, M. M.: DIC in the pregnant patient, J. Obstet. Gynecol. Nurs. **3**:29, 1974

DeTornyay, R., et al.: Nursing decisions: experience in clinical problem solving: Mrs. J.—an occurence of placenta previa, RN **39**:43, 1976.

Douglas, C. P.: Rupture of the uterus, Nurs. Times **73**:240, 1977.

Eagle, M.: Septicaemia proceeding to DIC, Nurs. Times **74**:17, 1978.

Evaluating high-risk pregnancies, Briefs **40**:25, 1976.

Galloway, K. G.: High risk pregnancy: the uncertainty and stress of high risk pregnancy, part I, Matern. Child Nurs. J. **1**:294, 1976.

Greenhalf, J. O.: Concealed accidental antepartum haemorrhage, Nurs. Times **71**:382, 1975.

Gustafson, J., et al.: Placenta previa and abruptio placentae, Acta Obstet. Gynecol. Scand. **53**:235, 1974.

Jones, M. B.: Antepartum assessment in high risk pregnancy, J. Obstet. Gynecol. Nurs. **4**:23, 1975.

Kitchen, J. D., et al.: Puerperal inversion of the uterus, Am. J. Obstet. Gynecol. **123**:51, 1975.

Lange, R. D., and Synesius, R.: Blood volume changes during normal pregnancy, Clin. Haematol. **2**:433, 1973.

Mickal, A., and Rye, R. H.: The value and dangers in the conservative management of placenta previa. In Reid, D. E., and Christian, C. D., editors: Controversy in obstetrics and gynecology, ed. 2, Philadelphia, 1974, W. B. Saunders Co.

Medell, L. E.: Assessment and intervention in emergency nursing, Englewood Cliffs, N.J., 1978, Prentice-Hall, p. 253.

O'Reilly, R. A.: Problems of haemorrhage and thrombosis in pregnancy, Clin. Haematol. **2**:543, 1973.

Ratnoff, O. D.: Coagulation and fibrinolysis mechanism of the fluid interphase. In Frohlich, R. D., Jr., editor: Pathophysiology—altered regulatory mechanisms in disease, ed. 2, Philadelphia, 1976, J. B. Lippincott Co., p. 621.

Richardson, D. R.: Basic circulatory physiology, Boston, 1976, Little, Brown & Co., p. 137.

Sher, G.: Pathogenesis and management of uterine inertia complicating abruptio placenta with consumption coagulopathy, Am. J. Obstet. Gynecol. **129**:164, 1977.

Stohlmann, F., Jr.: Drug-related haematological problems during pregnancy, Clin. Haematol. **2**:525, 1973.

Talbert, L. M.: Lady in pain, Emergency Med. **6**:194, 1974.

Walter, P. A.: Separation of the placenta, Nurs. Times **71**:1377, 1975.

Chapter 8

Care of the pregnant patient with a seizure disorder

Elizabeth Gale

MOTHERS WITH EPILEPSY

In the past women who had been diagnosed as having epilepsy were encouraged not to get pregnant because of the inability to control seizures and monitor the fetus during labor and delivery and because of some of the social stigmas placed on epileptic persons. Persons having epilepsy were thought to be possessed by evil spirits, to be of low intelligence, or to have special gifts. Superstitions about epilepsy are still prevalent, and it is not uncommon for epilepsy to be whispered about. Fortunately, through study, there is a greater understanding of epilepsy today. The fact that it is not a disease but only a symptom of a disease has still not alleviated the views of society as a whole. Epilepsy can be controlled in a manner similar to the way in which diabetes or heart disease is monitored; it does not have to be a long-term disability, although many believe it to be.

Women with epilepsy were often dissuaded from pursuing pregnancy and childbirth. In more recent times with better understanding of the disorder and monitoring with anticonvulsant therapy, these women have been encouraged and are getting pregnant. They are able to have their children with some attention to precautions. Women with epilepsy have found security and fulfillment in marriage and childbearing. They have been permitted, most of all, to lead normal lives.

INCIDENCE OF EPILEPSY

Since neurological disease is uncommon in youth and middle age, it is doubtful that an individual obstetrician or neurologist will have gained exten-

sive experience in the management of the pregnant patient with epilepsy throughout the course of the perinatal period. The obstetrician is more likely to care for a patient who has already been diagnosed with epilepsy than to see the onset of symptoms at the time of pregnancy.[15]

Barnes[2] reports that epilepsy occurs in approximately 0.4% (4 per 1000) of the population. In 1975, it was noted that over 1 million persons in the United States had epilepsy.[23] Hopkins[15] writes that the incidence rate (in the general population) for epilepsy is approximately 5 per 10,000 during the childbearing years. Approximately an equal number of males and females of the population are afflicted with epilepsy.[22] Whitfield[31] reports the incidence of epilepsy in the population to be 0.5% (5 in 1000). He also states that 5% of the population may have a single "epileptic attack (termed a seizure by some) at some time during their lives without being regarded as an epileptic."

The incidence of epilepsy among pregnant women is 0.15% (1.5 per 1000).[2] Jensen, Benson, and Bobak[16] write "epilepsy seriously complicates 1 of every 1000 gestations."

DEFINITION OF EPILEPSY

Epilepsy is not a disease entity in and of itself. Rather, it is a complex of symptoms, including paroxysmal attacks of unconsciousness, altered states of consciousness, tonic or clonic muscular spasms, and other abnormal behavior alterations caused by excessive or abnormal electrical impulse discharges occurring in cerebral neurons.[12] It is generally agreed that a seizure disorder is defined as epilepsy if the seizures have a tendency to recur.[23,31]

The lay term "fit" is used to describe seizures. Other terms that may be used by lay persons to describe epilepsy are spells, turns, and attacks.

Although seizures are not always accompanied by convulsions, they usually do contain elements of "temporary interruption of consciousness."[23] Another definition of epilepsy is put forth by Whitfield[31]: "intermittent or continuous disorders of awareness of consciousness (other than natural sleep) or of more limited cerebral functions, associated with changes in electrical activity of the brain." McDonald[17] writes that "an epileptic seizure is a state produced by excessive neuronal discharge within the central nervous system." Peery and Miller[22] further state that the discharge is composed of "sudden, excessive, and unruly motor neuronal discharges."

Epilepsies of known origin are called organic epilepsy. If the cause of the disorder is unknown, as it is in the majority of cases, it is termed idiopathic epilepsy.

CAUSES OF EPILEPSY

Smith and Germain[23] report that approximately four fifths of all cases of epilepsy are of unknown origin, idiopathic. The other one fifth are called symptomatic epilepsy because the seizures are indicative of some lesion in the brain, which may be a tumor, injury, or lesions that otherwise elicits seizures as a manifestation of the disease entity. Arteriosclerosis is one such disease that may cause a lesion in the brain that may cause seizures. Other causes may be severe head injuries, lack of oxygen, infections in the body of the brain, disorders of the blood chemistry, brain tumors, strokes, and diseases of the brain.[27,29] Precipitating factors of epileptic convulsions may be alkalosis in response to hyperventilation, hypoxia, hypoglycemia, and water-logging (edema).[22]

Whitfield[31] provides a succinct list of the causes of epilepsy as follows:

I. Primary (cryptogenic, idiopathic) epilepsy—no apparent cause of epilepsy in 80%
II. Secondary (symptomatic) epilepsy
    A. Intracranial causes

        1. Congenital abnormalities
        2. Brain damage
        3. Space-occupying lesions
        4. Cerebral arteriopathic disease
    B. Extracranial causes
        1. Cardiac disease
        2. Respiratory disease
        3. Renal disease
        4. Endocrine disorders
        5. Eclampsia
        6. Toxins

The causes of gestational epilepsy may be idiopathic or symptomatic. It must be emphasized that it is imperative to search for the underlying cause. Epilepsy may surface for the first time during pregnancy; thus it is termed gestational epilepsy. The patient may never have had seizures before the pregnancy, and she may not have evidence of the disorder following termination of the pregnancy. Once a seizure (or series of seizures) presents during pregnancy, an underlying disease process must be investigated. It may be that the disorder will be termed iatrogenic (of unknown etiology)[2,8]

Mirkin[19] noted that convulsive disorders frequently tend to exacerbate (increase in frequency and/or intensity) during pregnancy so that it is a serious difficulty for the epileptic mother.

Table 8-1. Conditions predisposing or preventing epileptic seizures*

Condition	Prevents seizures	Precipitates seizures
Oxygen	Rich supply	Poor supply
Acid-base equilibrium	Acidosis	Alkalosis
	Ingestion of acids or acid-forming salts	Hyperpnea—blowing off CO_2
	Breathing CO_2	
Water balance	Dehydration	Edema
Serum calcium	Increase	Decrease
Blood glucose	Normal level	Decrease (hypoglycemia)
Body temperature		Increase

*From Brobeck, J. R., editor: Best and Taylor's physiological basis of medical practice, ed. 9, Baltimore, 1973, The Williams & Wilkins Co., p. 390.

Brobeck[3] provides a summary of conditions that tend to precipitate or prevent epileptic seizures (Table 8-1).

CLASSIFICATION OF EPILEPSIES

Epilepsies are classified according to the origin of the disorder in the brain, cortex or centrencephalic; the causes (if known); the clinical features; and the electroencephalogram (EEG) findings.[31]

Several classifications of seizures have been set forth in the literature on epilepsy. A modified version of the International Classification of Seizure Types will be employed for this writing. The individual classifications are listed below.

Gastraut and Broughton[12] recognize four main groups of seizures:

1. Generalized (centrencephalic, central or diffused)
2. Unilateral; hemigeneralized or asymmetrical seizures
3. Partial: focal or local
4. Unclassified seizures

Whitfield[31] gives another classification of epilepsies:

1. Generalized epilepsies
   a. Grand mal
   b. Petit mal
   c. Myoclonic
   d. Akinetic
2. Focal epilepsies
   a. With simple symptomatology
      (1) Motor
      (2) Sensory
   b. With complex symptomatology
      (1) Temporal lobe
   c. Focal epilepsy with secondary generalization (often follows b)

Burrow and Ferris[4] provide a similar classification:

I. Generalized seizures
   A. Convulsive
      1. Tonic-clonic major motor without focal onset (grand mal)
      2. Clonic (myoclonic) generalized
   B. Nonconvulsive
      1. Brief typical absence (petit mal)
      2. Brief atypical absence
II. Focal seizures
   A. Simple
      1. Motor (brief focal only)
      2. Sensory (focal with jacksonian march)
      3. Autonomic (multifocal)
      4. Other (focal continuous—epilepsy partialis continua)
   B. Complex
      1. Psychomotor predominating
      2. Psychosensory predominating
III. Pseudoseizures (hysterical seizures)
IV. Other conditions with some features of epilepsy
   A. Narcolepsy
   B. Transient ischemic attacks
   C. Fainting
   D. Nightmares
   E. Rage attacks—dyscontrol
   F. Migraine
   G. Stokes-Adams attacks

Volle and Heron[29] provide an international classification of seizure types:

I. Partial seizure (seizures beginning locally)
   A. Partial seizures with elementary symptomatology (generally without impairment of consciousness)
      1. With motor symptoms (includes jacksonian seizures)
      2. With special sensory or somatosensory symptoms
      3. With autonomic symptoms
      4. Compound forms
   B. Partial seizures with complex symptomatology (generally with impairment of consciousness)
      1. With impairment of consciousness only
      2. With cognitive symptomatology
      3. With affective symptomatology
      4. With "psychosensory" symptomatology
      5. With "psychomotor" symptomatology
      6. Compound seizures
   C. Partial seizures secondarily generalized
II. Generalized seizures (bilaterally symmetrical and without local onset)
   A. Absences (petit mal)
   B. Bilateral massive epileptic myoclonus
   C. Infantile spasms
   D. Clonic seizures
   E. Tonic seizures
   F. Tonic-clonic seizures (grand mal)
   G. Atonic seizures
   H. Akinetic seizures
III. Unilateral seizures (or predominantly)
IV. Unclassified epileptic seizures (owing to incomplete data)

The following outline will include elements of the classifications just listed,[4,9,12,29,31] thus giving a more complete picture of the types of epilepsies.

    I. Generalized seizures: bilaterally symmetrical and without local onset
      A. Convulsive
        1. Grand mal: tonic-clonic major motor seizures without focal onset
        2. Myoclonic: generalized clonic (also known as bilateral massive epileptic myoclonus)
      B. Nonconvulsive
        1. Petit mal: brief typical absences (also known as atonic seizures)
        2. Akinetic: brief atypical absence
    II. Partial seizures: seizures beginning locally or focally
      A. Simple: partial seizures with simple symptomatology (generally without impairment of consciousness); also known as focal seizures of cortical origin
        1. Motor: brief focal only—includes jacksonian seizures
        2. Sensory: focal with jacksonian-like march
        3. Autonomic (multifocal—more than one focus)
        4. Compound forms (other—focal continuous, epilepsy partialis continua)
      B. Complex: partial seizures with complex symptomatology (generally with impairment of consciousness); also known as local seizures
        1. Impairment of consciousness only
        2. Cognitive symptomatology
        3. Affective symptomatology
        4. Psychosensory symptomatology
        5. Psychomotor symptomatology (automatisms); also known as temporal lobe epilepsy
        6. Compound forms
      C. Partial seizures secondarily generalized (focal epilepsy—often follows temporal lobe epilepsy)
    III. Unilateral seizures (or predominately); also known as hemigeneralized or asymmetrical seizures
    IV. Unclassified epileptic seizures (owing to incomplete data)

The above classification provides a cross-reference that is useful in identifying the type of seizure disorder with which a patient has been identified (diagnosed). Burrow and Ferris[4] identify hysterical seizures as pseudoseizures. Also identified are other conditions with some features of epilepsy: narcolepsy, transient ischemic attacks, fainting, nightmares, rage attacks—dyscontrol, migraine, and Stokes-Adams attacks.[4] Conditions such as hyperventilation attacks can also mimic seizures.

DESCRIPTIONS AND CLINICAL FEATURES OF THE TYPES OF SEIZURES

The response of the epileptic individual to hyperneuronal activity reflects a lower threshold than that observed for the normal individual without the disorder.

For purposes of description, the following types of epilepsy will be discussed in some detail: generalized seizures, grand mal, petit mal, myoclonic, and akinetic; and partial seizures, simple and complex.

Generalized epilepsy

Grand mal. Grand mal attacks are dramatic presentations of tonic-clonic major motor involvement. The tonic aspect is noted by the spasm and contraction of the muscles of the jaw causing it to tightly close. Previous to the onset of the convulsion, the patient may have had an aura (seen in 50% of the cases[22]) or may be tense and irritable for a few hours or a few days. The aura may be a strange taste or smell indicating the site of origin in the brain for the attack. Whitfield[31] reports that patients with primary generalized epilepsy do not experience an aura. Generalized tonus is experienced with head and neck and leg extension and flexion of the arms at the elbows and wrists. The eyes and head may turn to one side. A typical cry (not a major symptom) is caused by the force of air over the vocal cords through the closing glottis. The patient typically becomes cyanotic owing to the cessation of breathing caused by spasm in the respiratory muscles. Salivation is increased because of the stimulation of the autonomic nervous system. Fluid collects in the oropharynx, becoming a reddish mixture as the patient inadvertently bites the tongue.

Following the tonic stage, is the clonic phase—the alternating spasm and relaxation of the muscles. These may be visualized as short muscular jerks that gradually diminish in strength and frequency. The convulsion then ceases. The patient may have urinated during the attack. Following the attack, drowsiness and sleep with confusion and/or loss of memory about what happened may ensue. The patient may remain unconscious. Complaints of headaches and muscle stiffness are common. Frothiness of oral secretions may be seen as the patient resumes respiratory efforts.

Status epilepticus is a serious complication of the

grand mal attack that is rarely seen. It is usually caused by failure of the individual to take the anticonvulsant medication. Status epilepticus is visualized as one grand mal attack after another. A rise in temperature is due to muscle excitation and increased oxygen demand by the brain, causing a medical emergency. If the demands are not met, brain damage will result.[31]

Petit mal. Petit mal attacks are often the most difficult to recognize clinically. These are noted by a sudden cessation in activity. Pauses may be noted if the individual was speaking. The individual may appear to be dazed; the eyes may be vacant, staring, or blinking. Consciousness is not usually lost, so the patient does not experience a fall. The activity is resumed, often without the individual having realized that an attack was experienced. Petit mal attacks usually last 5 to 10 seconds. Whitfield[31] notes that they begin in childhood and that 50% will later develop grand mal attacks. The petit mal attacks may be seen as inattentiveness, daydreaming, lack of concentration, or even backwardness. EEG confirms the diagnosis of petit mal.

Myoclonic. Myoclonic attacks are seen as brief, sudden, muscular contractions. A sudden forward flexion of the trunk (jacknife attack) or the upward movement of the arms and flexion of the truck (salaam attack) may be seen. Nocturnal myoclonus is the term given to the sudden jerk when a person is falling asleep; it bears no relationship to epilepsy.

Akinetic. Akinetic attacks are characterized by a sudden loss of posture control and muscle tone.[31] These are sometimes called "drop" attacks because the patient may lose consciousness for a few seconds and fall. Injuries may result; if not, the person may resume activity as if nothing happened.

Partial seizures

Partial seizures are focal in origin. They are localized in the cerebral cortex of the brain. "The focus may be caused by cerebral hypoxia during birth, following a head injury or because of a space-occupying lesion."[31] The attack may remain localized or spread over the cerebral cortex. If it spreads over the corticothalamic pathways to the thalamus, a grand mal attack can be initiated.[31]

Simple. Simple motor attacks may be seen as jacksonian seizures in which there are tonic movements followed by clonic movements of the corresponding part on the opposite side, for instance, the thumb, great toe, and angle of the mouth. Clonic movements increase in intensity and spread up the arm (jacksonian march) to involve the face; then they spread down to the leg or foot. They may spread to involve one half of the body or go on to a grand mal attack.[31] Prolonged localization of the attack is known as epilepsia partialis continuas. Todd's paralysis (prolonged paralysis of affected parts) may be a result. A motor attack, in which consciousness is maintained, is also seen. The head and eyes are turned from the affected cerebral hemisphere so they are named adversive attacks.

Simple sensory attacks may spread like the jacksonian pattern, but a spreading sensation of numbness or tingling is noted in the affected parts.

Complex. Focal epilepsy with complex symptomatology involves the higher cerebral functions of memory, thought, behavior, and emotions. These may be referred to as psychomotor attacks. The majority of these attacks originate in the temporal lobe—temporal lobe epilepsies. Temporal lobe epilepsies are one of the most common of the focal epilepsies—"they account for one-third of all the epilepsies."[31] "The temporal lobes are concerned wtih taste, smell, memory storage, thinking, and emotion, via the limbic system and the autonomic nervous system: hence, the complexity of symptoms."[31]

Symptoms of temporal lobe epilepsy include an epigastric sensation that may be described as fear. It starts in the epigastrum and migrates to the throat. Associated symptoms are hallucinatory smell and taste. When the attack originates in the inner surface of the temporal lobe, movements of lip smacking and chewing are common. The inner surface of the temporal lobe forms the limbic system, which is responsible for the emotions, therefore symptoms of ecstasy or paranoia may be seen.

With progression of the attack, consciousness may become cloudy. The patient becomes confused because the level of consciousness is altered, but it is not lost. Stereotypic activity may follow such as wandering or hand rubbing. If there is persistent clouded consciousness, the term "fugue" is used. If it continues for a period of days, it is called twilight state. Whitfield[31] states that "...80% of patients with temporal lobe epilepsy proceed to grand mal attacks." This type of epileptic seizure normally lasts 30 seconds to 5 minutes. Temporal lobe seizures are part of the class of psychomotor seizures. It is useless to attempt to stop the stereotypic actions of these seizures. The attempts to help may be misinterpreted. The individuals are not aware of the actions and will not remember them afterwards. Violence or aggression is rarely seen during the attacks.

Status epilepticus, in which there are repeated and prolonged seizure attacks, sometimes for hours, develops in approximately 10% of epilepsies.[22]

DIAGNOSIS OF EPILEPSY

Epilepsy can be an easy or a difficult disorder to diagnose depending on the symptoms. Grand mal seizures that recur frequently present a typical pattern. Irregular EEG tracings confirm the diagnosis. The history of the onset of the patient's illness, the family history, and a complete neurological examination and workup are important to the diagnosis. They will assist in determining whether the seizure disorder is of idiopathic or symptomatic origin.

One single seizure is never diagnosable as epilepsy. Convulsions may be a causative symptom in a variety of problems such as high fever with severe infection. An underlying cause should always be sought before a person is diagnosed as having epilepsy.

Diagnostic procedures should include tests of the following: cerebrospinal fluid (CSF); x-ray films of the skull (may or may not be helpful), pneumoencephalograms, and arteriograms. The EEG demonstrates abnormality in 40% to 75% of the cases.[27]

Pathophysiology

In idiopathic epilepsies the pathophysiology cannot be identified. In the symptomatic epilepsies the pathophysiology is based on the underlying cause of the disorder of epilepsy.

The concept of the hyperexcitable cortex is a key to the enhanced evoked responses seen on the EEG. It is possible, however, that the response will not occur while the EEG is being recorded. There is a relationship between this concept and the use of the EEG to determine an abnormality in the cognitive process.[5]

"Psychomotor epilepsy begins and may be con-

firmed by the low-threshold limbic structures that are so involved with the processes of mood, feeling, and emotion. Perceptual distortions, particularly memory recall, emotional crises and alterations in the sense of relatedness to other persons and objects are characteristic features which can be accounted for by seizures confined to the limbic system. Focal epilepsy, petit mal and psychomotor seizures if sufficiently violent can pass into grand mal seizures by presumably invading enough neocortex or by causing generalization of seizure activity by involving the cephalic brain stem reticular formation."[11]

Persons predisposed to epilepsy experience attacks when the base level of excitability is above a certain critical threshold. Attacks do not occur as long as the degree of excitability is maintained below this threshold.[13]

The pathophysiology of epilepsy is a result of the fundamental processes of excitability of neurons and the population of neurons. The disorder may result from increased local irritability or from reduced inhibition. It is not understood why normal circuits avoid seizure activity because the possibility is always present. A seizure can be induced through chemical or electrical stimulation.

When deprived of innervation, neurons and other excitable tissues, muscles, and glands can become hyperexcitable. Normality is resumed with innervation of these tissues. Hyperexcitability is considered to be the outcome when there is any interruption in the innervation of any of these excitable tissues.

Manifestation of the epilepsy will depend on its focus. Focal epilepsy remains in one locale. Petit mal seizures probably originate in the thalamic intralaminar nuclei, which maintain consciousness. The abnormal discharge interferes with the current between the brain stem and the forebrain, which in turn causes the transient interruption in consciousness.[9,11]

Heritability

Nora and Fraser[21] emphasize that caution must be used when discussing the heritability of epilepsy. Most geneticists place epilepsy in the multifactorial inheritance pattern. Specific types of epilepsy may be heritable. The most common form of epilepsy, generalized epilepsy, may have some mendelian types of inheritance. There is some debate concerning the clinical features that may be accepted as diagnostic of epilepsy, such as seizures or abnormal EEG's. Nora and Fraser[21] report that "apart from the convulsions associated with diseases of known mendelian causation, the only category of the epilepsies for which there are reasonable reliable figures on recurrence risk is that of subcortical or centrencephalic epilepsy."[21] The problem is further complicated by the variability of the age of onset and the fact that the EEG abnormalities characteristic of this disorder may be the main indices of the disorder. These abnormalities may disappear with increasing age.

A rough guide is provided that may prove helpful in genetic counseling. "A child who has a parent or sibling with centrencephalic epilepsy has a basic risk of about 8% of being similarly affected. This is increased to 10% if the age of onset in the relative occurs before two and one-half years of age. If both a parent and a sib are affected, the risk for a sib is about 13%. The risk decreases the longer the child remains free of seizures and if the EEG is negative after five years of age."[21]

MANAGEMENT OF EPILEPSIES

The management of seizures is accomplished depending on the diagnosis of the underlying cause. If the underlying cause is a metabolic disease, an ischemic attack or heart disease, or a brain tumor, the treatment will vary accordingly. Epilepsies as a result of metabolic disease are infrequent in the adult. However, neonates often exhibit seizure symptoms as a result of a metabolic disorder. These include such problems as hypoglycemia, hypocalcemia, pyridoxine insufficiency (vitamin B_6, and hypomagnesemia.[12]

Organic causes of epilepsies are seen with such problems as lesions in the brain. If the lesions are benign, it is felt that surgical intervention should not be utilized. Surgical intervention is used for space-occupying lesions to alleviate the seizure symptoms.

The symptomatic epilepsies are treated with the medication regime best suited to alleviate the symptoms. The anticonvulsant therapeutics are helpful in the treatment of epilepsy. It has been found that certain of the anticonvulsants are specific in the control of a specified type of epilepsy. Gastraut and Broughton[12] provide a lengthy discussion of each class of drug treatments and the type of epilepsy for which it is used. Table 8-2 is provided for ease and clarification of reading.

The treatment of pregnant patients who have epilepsy or who develop gestational epilepsy must be carefully monitored. Initially, a complete neurological examination and test are imperative. Any of these pregnant patients may be using anticonvulsants as therapy for their epileptic disorder. The most commonly used anticonvulsants are phenobarbital, phenytoin (Dilantin), and primidone (Mysoline). The former two are the most common. The risk:benefit ratio must be weighed when one considers the results of some studies showing that these medications may have teratogenic effects on the fetus. It is widely accepted that patients taking phenobarbital and phenytoin have shown a higher than average rate of congenital defects, especially cleft lip and cleft palate. Phenytoin has been shown to be the more likely drug to cause the defects. However, the reports on the results are still controversial, so that no absolute conclusions can be drawn.

If a patient who has epilepsy becomes pregnant, it is not an indication for termination of the pregnancy. This may have been encouraged in the past. The woman may be told what the studies have reported, but it must be emphasized that in the majority of cases the infant is perfectly normal and healthy.

Table 8-2. Drug treatments for seizure disorders*

Class of drug	Specific for seizure disorder	Side effects
Barbiturates		
Phenobarbital (Luminal—hypnotic)	Most convulsive disorders; generalized tonic-clonic; petit mal; temporal lobe epilepsy	Drowsiness; rashes with pruritis, sometimes; edema
Sodium pentobarbital (Nembutal)	Same as above	Teratogenic effects: lower rate of birth defects than with phenytoin; possible cleft lip and palate
Mephobarbital (Mebaral, Isonal)	Reserved for use when the above drugs fail to control seizures or untoward side effects persist	Safe use in pregnancy not established; side effects are as for phenobarbital
Primidone		
Mysoline (hypnotic)	Major antiepileptic for generalized tonic-clonic attacks and for psychomotor temporal lobe and petit mal epilepsy	Stomach upsets, dizziness, drowsiness, irritability, ataxia; rarely—anorexia, rashes, or edema; few cases of megaloblastic anemia respond to folic acid therapy
Hydantoins		
Phenytoin (Dilantin—nonhypnotic)	Active against all convulsive disorders, generalized, unilateral, or partial	Drug poorly tolerated in 20% of patients; unsteady gait, blurred vision, double vision, gum hypertrophy, hirsutism Teratogenic effects: clotting defects, both vitamin K dependent; treat with vitamin before and after delivery to prevent hemorrhagic episodes in infant; treat with folic acid in mother; cleft palate and lip more commonly seen; higher dosages associated with (lower) thyroid dysfunction[25]
Mephenytoin (Mesantoin—mild hypnotic)	Generalized or partial attacks; most effective against temporal lobe epilepsy; action potentiated by phenobarbital	Rarely—blood dyscrasias, some confusion, agitation, or depression; occasional dermatitis or hematological problems; check WBC before and afterward every 3 months
Ethotoin (Peganone)	Refractory cases; antiepileptic effect is weak	Drowsiness, ataxia, diplopia
Acetylureas		
Phenacemide (Phenurone)	Mainly effective against nonconvulsive temporal lobe seizures of the psychomotor type	Liver damage, psychotic behavior, nausea, blood dyscrasias rare; blood counts and urobilinogen tests every month
Oxazolidinediones		
Trimethadione (Tridione)	Petit mal, little effect on partial seizures; when given alone, may precipitate generalized tonic-clonic seizures; use with a barbiturate	Blood dyscrasia, kidney damage, photophobia, stomach upsets Severe defects in neonate—mental retardation
Paramethadione (Paradione)	Petit mal	Mild blood dyscrasia, kidney damage, photophobia, stomach upsets Severe defects in neonate—mental retardation
Succinimides		
Ethosuximide (Zarontin)	Generalized or partial petit mal	Nausea, drowsiness, loss of appetite, rarely psychosis Three cases of bone marrow depression; blood tests must be performed
Methsuximide (Celontin)	Petit mal absences	Drowsiness, headaches

*Modified from Conn, H. F., editor: 1977 Current therapy, Philadelphia, 1977, W. B. Saunders Co., p. 716; Frederick, J.: Br. Med. J. **2**:442, 1973; Gastraut, H., and Broughton, R.: Epileptic seizures, Springfield, Ill., 1972, Charles C Thomas, Publisher, p. 3; Hollingsworth, M.: Clin. Obstet. Gynecol. **4**(2):503, 1977; and Strauss, R. G., et al: Obstet. Gynecol. **51**(6):682, 1978.

Table 8-2. Drug treatments for seizure disorders—cont'd

Class of drug	Specific for seizure disorder	Side effects
Benzodiazepines		
Chlordiazepoxide (Librium) flurazepam (Dalmane)	Antiepileptic effect	Drowsiness, ataxia
Diazepam (Valium)	Petit mal absences, generalized, myoclonic, and for status epilepticus	No serious hematological, renal, or hepatic complications have yet been described; drowsiness and ataxia with higher dosage
Mogadon	Atypical absences and temporal lobe epilepsy	None noted
Carbamazapine (Tegretol)	Generalized or partial	Drowsiness, dizziness, diplopia, nervousness, blood dyscrasias
ACTH and corticoids	Infantile spasms of West's syndrome	Serious side effects of hormonal medication are many and frequent; must be reviewed before instituting therapy
Quinicrine		
Atabrine	Typical absences that are unresponsive to anti–petit mal medication	Gastrointestinal complaints; yellowing of skin
Bromides		
K, Na, NH₃	First used to treat epilepsy, now used infrequently; effective if used with restriction of NaCl	Cutaneous reactions, drowsiness; contraindicated in renal insufficiency
Amphetamines		
Benzedrine	Ineffective as antiepileptic; treatment of narcolepsy-passovant	Irritability, instability, insomnia
Dexedrine	Used to counteract side effects of barbiturates; sometimes used for petit mal	Same as above
Caffeine	Hypnogenic effect of barbiturates lessened	Irritability
Pyridoxine (vitamin B₆)	Used for three conditions: (1) pyridoxine-deficient epilepsy—use low doses of vitamin B₆; (2) pyridoxine competition—stop intake of vitamin B₆; and (3) avitaminoses competition—stop intake of vitamin B₆	Unknown
Acetazolamide		
Diamox	Typical absences and catamenial seizures if given in days just prior to menstruation in doses of 400-1000 mg	Numbness of extremities, anorexia, vomiting, headaches, and occasional renal and bone marrow complications
Other medications	Some antiepileptic effect, but have been generally abandoned	
Ospolot		
Elipten		
Chloracon		
Posedrine		
Clonazepam (Clonopin)	Petit mal, astatic, akinetic, myoclonic	Drowsiness, dizziness, ataxia, behavior disturbances

Protocols

Problem □ Prevention

GOAL: To observe patient for problems with her epilepsy and the effects of pregnancy on her and the fetus or infant and to ascertain the type of epilepsy

Rationale: To determine the manner in which prenatal care will be provided (the effect that pregnancy will have on it)

DIAGNOSTIC

1. Define the type of seizure disorder.

   Rationale: To provide clues as to the origin of the disorder if it is symptomatic or to observe the patient more closely if it is idiopathic[4]

2. Provide for normal prenatal care.

   Rationale: Common sense

3. Ascertain the type of anticonvulsant used and the level of control achieved.

   Rationale: To determine whether it is necessary to readjust the therapeutic dose[4,30]

4. Review the maternal history of nausea and vomiting.

   Rationale: To determine whether nausea and vomiting occur concurrently with the ingestion of anticonvulsant therapy, which may cause the level of control of seizures to be altered

5. Prevent hypoxic episodes to fetoplacental unit.

   Rationale: To control the hypoxic episodes occurring with seizures that could seriously alter the oxygen content perfusing the fetoplacental unit

6. Obtain baseline family history.

   Rationale: To provide clues to the woman's chances of having additional seizure difficulties during pregnancy[28]

7. Baseline neurological examination should be done unless patient is currently being followed by a neurologist. The neurological examination should include physical subjective data, objective data from x-ray films, EEG, and blood chemistries. A problem may be encountered when trying to make a differential diagnosis between epilepsy and eclampsia. They can coexist. A past history of seizures, with absence of edema, hypertension, proteinuria, and a normal plasma uric acid, points to epilepsy.[1,16]

   Rationale: To have a baseline from which to assess data about neurological problems as they arise[4]

THERAPEUTIC

1. Obtain a blood chemistry workup at the beginning of the pregnancy if the patient is a known epileptic or if gestational epilepsy occurs.

   Rationale: To determine whether there are abnormalities specific to interrelatedness of epilepsy, anticonvulsant therapy, and pregnancy

2. Monitor blood levels of anticonvulsant therapy.

   Rationale: To prevent seizures, which may require additional anticonvulsant therapeutics, and some medications (see Table 8-2) can cause blood dyscrasia for the mother, such as folic acid deficiencies and megaloblastic anemia.[13,15,32]

3. Review maternal history in relation to seizure episodes at each visit.

   Rationale: To monitor for possible need to increase the therapy[16,32]

4. Review maternal history for stressors encountered.

   Rationale: To be aware that stressors may induce hyperexcitability of the neurons and it is possible that precipitating conditions of hypoglycemia, hypocalcemia, hyperventilation, infections, and so forth may induce seizures[27,31]

5. Monitor for normal prenatal care: weight gain, blood pressure, sugar and albumin in the urine, and infection.

   Rationale: To control these factors since any of them may have a predisposing effect on epilepsy (It is known that weight gain and/or edema are predisposing factors that may cause seizures.[3])

EDUCATIONAL

1. Provide patient with prenatal education about the effects of pregnancy on epilepsy.

   Rationale: To inform patients that most mothers do not experience difficulty with pregnancy (Hopkins[15] found that epileptic mothers who were seizure free prior to pregnancy usually remained so. It is somewhat controversial as to whether or not pregnancy causes the seizures to increase in frequency. Some reports say there is a 24% increase and some say there is 45% increase in the frequency of seizures. Aminoff[1] reported that seizures increased in about 45% and that they remained unchanged in about 50%.)

2. Provide patient with prenatal education as to the effects of anticonvulsants on the fetus.

   Rationale: To educate mothers as to the effects of anticonvulsant drugs on the fetus. (Although reports are controversial, some epileptic mothers treated with phenobarbital and phenytoin may see congenital defects in their infants. These therapies do cross the placental barrier. The most common lesions reported are cleft lip and palate, but cardiac anomalies and hypoplastic nails have been reported.[15,24] Overall, Hopkins[15] says that malformations occur in children born of mothers with epilepsy about 2½ times that of the general rate. It is not necessary to frighten these women, but they have a right to know that these things can occur. It must be remembered that epileptics who become pregnant have no reason to have a therapeutic abortion based on that reason alone.)

3. Provide the patient with an explanation of why the monitoring of blood chemistries is important.

   Rationale: To reduce the patient's anxiety, thus allowing her to cope with this added stressor (common sense)

4. Ask the patient to provide information immediately if a seizure occurs.

   Rationale: To determine whether one should look for an underlying cause or if it is a stage where additional therapy is needed (Most of the anticonvulsants do cross the placenta to the fetus.[32])

Problem □ Restoration

GOAL: To provide for additional anticonvulsant therapy and/or look for an underlying predisposing cause

DIAGNOSTIC

1. Weigh out the risks and benefits of therapy.
   Rationale: To assure that the benefits of leaving the patient on the drug outweigh the risks of her being without the therapy (Hypoxic episodes to her will not be tolerated without damage to the fetoplacental unit.)[4]

2. Observe for toxic effects of the drugs.
   Rationale: To check for signs of toxicity following delivery[12]

3. In the event of a seizure, provide for normal seizure care.
   Rationale: To prevent injuries and further deterioration and to evaluate effectiveness of drug dosage (common sense)

4. Evaluate perfusion of O_2 to fetus following a seizure.
   Rationale: To ascertain if the infant is in distress (common sense)

THERAPEUTIC

1. Monitor blood levels of anticonvulsant drug.
   Rationale: To maintain a therapeutic level in the blood to prevent seizures[6,12,25]

2. Check fetal heart rate and rhythm, fetal movements, position, and so forth.
   Rationale: To evaluate the fetoplacental unit

3. When seizures occur, readjust dosage.
   Rationale: To find the underlying cause; may indicate that a stressor is present (common sense)

EDUCATIONAL

1. Provide emotional and physical support to the mother and family.
   Rationale: To provide care and comfort to the mother, which can do much to allay fears, anxieties, and possible embarrassment (common sense)

2. Encourage the pregnant woman with epilepsy to learn about epilepsy, the cause of hers (if there is one), and the treatments.
   Rationale: To provide a basis for her to feel that motherhood for her is normal (common sense)

3. Teach the family about how to care for the mother should a seizure occur.
   Rationale: To help the husband and/or other family members to be involved in the care of the mother and bond them as a family unit (common sense)

Problem □ Promotion

GOAL: To provide a normal course of labor and a delivery that will be seizure free and conducive to the establishment of the mothering relationship and the family

DIAGNOSTIC

1. Avoid seizures during the intrapartal period.
   Rationale: To lessen the stress on the mother and infant by avoiding hypoxic episodes to both (common sense)
2. Continue assessment by monitoring the fetus and contractions.
   Rationale: To monitor for fetal distress (common sense)
3. Monitor blood levels while in labor, immediately postpartum, and several days and possibly weeks following delivery.
   Rationale: To observe for toxic side effects owing to the high dosage needed for a seizure-free pregnancy[1,15]
4. If epilepsy is poorly controlled, the need to evaluate for possible early delivery may exist.
   Rationale: To be aware that the effects of repeated seizures may outweigh the risks of allowing the pregnancy to go to term[4]

THERAPEUTIC

1. Provide for normal intrapartal and postpartal care.
   Rationale: Common sense
2. Monitor for toxic effects of anticonvulsants and readjust dosage.
   Rationale: To reduce dosage after delivery to avoid toxicity[1,15]
3. Observe infants for signs of hemorrhage.
   Rationale: To be aware that phenytoin therapy interferes with the ability of vitamin K to produce its clotting factors[15]; may administer vitamin K just prior to the delivery to the mother and to the infant after the delivery
4. Observe infant for withdrawal symptoms.
   Rationale: To watch for tremulousness, hyperexcitability, restlessness, and increased hunger, which may occur after the abrupt discontinuance of phenobarbital (Feedings and warmth may assist in alleviating of some of the symptoms.[7,18,20,26])

EDUCATIONAL

1. Provide the mother with information about what to look for as possible withdrawal symptoms.
   Rationale: To assist the mother in assessing abnormalities that may need professional medical help (She must know that symptoms may not show up for 2 to 14 days.[7])
2. Ascertain the support system of the mother.
   Rationale: To assure that mother has some assistance with infant care and housework when she returns home since she may be at a greater risk and need additional and/or prolonged assistance based on her individual case (common sense)
3. If the mother is a brittle epileptic, she may need help in feeding the infant.
   Rationale: To provide safety for both mother and baby since there is not much warning before a seizure occurs (common sense)
4. The mother should be informed about breast-feeding her infant.
   Rationale: To ensure safety for herself and the infant should she decide to breast-feed (Hopkins[15] reports that anticonvulsants are not passed through the breast milk so there is no danger to the infant in being breast-fed. Mirkin[19] showed that breast milk obtained from epileptic mothers treated with phenytoin contained very low concentrations of the drug. It does not appear to constitute a clinical hazard for the infant, and it may be very satisfactory to both mother and baby as long as the mother is safe from seizures. However, Melchoir[18] reports that there is considerable intake of phenobarbital through the breast milk. Since the infant has a slower rate of elimination of the drug, problems may be encountered with the neonate. Individual cases will need to be evaluated accordingly.)
5. Mothers with epilepsy need to be informed about their infant's overreaction to stimuli such as cold, hunger, and household noises.
   Rationale: To assist the mother in not becoming overly anxious about her baby's behavior and to encourage her to call the clinic staff for assistance if needed (Also, they need to be reassured that the problem is not likely to be permanent.[7])
6. Allay the mother's fears that the infant might be seizure prone.
   Rationale: To relieve fears that the mother may be afraid to express (common sense)

REFERENCES

1. Aminoff, M. J.: Neurological disorders and pregnancy, Am. J. Obstet. Gynecol. **132**:325, 1978.
2. Barnes, C. G.: Medical disorders of obstetric patients, ed. 4, Oxford, England, 1974, Blackwell Scientific Publications, p. 390.
3. Brobeck, J. R., editor: Best and Taylor's physiological basis of medical practice, ed. 9, Baltimore, 1973, The Williams & Wilkins Co., pp. 9-108.
4. Burrow, G. N., and Ferris, T. F.: Medical complications during pregnancy, Philadelphia, 1976, W. B. Saunders Co. p. 657.
5. Cobb, W. A., and Van Duija, H.: Contemporary clinical neurophysiology, New York, 1978, Elsevier North-Holland, Inc., p. 1.
6. Conn, H. F., editor: 1977 Current therapy, Philadelphia, 1977, W. B. Saunders Co., p. 716.
7. Desmond, M. M., et al.: Maternal barbiturate utilization and neonatal withdrawal symptomatology, J. Pediatr. **80**(2): 190, 1972.
8. Dimsdale, H.: The epileptic in relation to pregnancy, Br. Med. J. **2**:1147, 1959.
9. Eliasson, S. G., Prensky, A. L., and Hardin, W. B.: Neurological pathophysiology, ed. 2, New York, 1978, Oxford Univeristy Press, p. 3.
10. Fedrick, J.: Epilepsy and pregnancy: a report from the Oxford record linkage study, Br. Med. J. **2**:442, 1973.
11. Frohlich, E. D., editor: Pathophysiology: altered regulatory mechanisms in disease, Philadelphia, 1972, J. B. Lippincott Co., p. 569.
12. Gastraut, H., and Broughton, R.: Epileptic seizures, Springfield, Ill., 1972, Charles C Thomas, Publisher, p. 3.
13. Guyton, A. C.: Textbook of medical physiology, Philadelphia, 1971, W. B. Saunders Co., p. 713.
14. Hollingsworth, M.: Drugs and pregnancy, Clin. Obstet. Gynecol **4**(2):503, 1977.
15. Hopkins, A.: Neurological disorders, Clin. Obstet. Gynecol. **4**(2):419, 1977.
16. Jensen, M. D., Bensen, R. C., and Bobak, I. M.: Maternity care: the nurse and the family, St. Louis, 1977, The C. V. Mosby Co., p. 3.
17. McDonald, L.: Temporal lobe epilepsy, J. Neurosurg. Nurs. **8**(2):89, 1976.
18. Melchoir, J. C., Svensmark, O., and Trolle, D.: Placental transfer of phenobarbital in epileptic women and elimination in newborns, Lancet **2**(7521):860, 1967.
19. Mirkin, B. L.: Diphenylhydantoin: placental transport, fetal localization, neonatal metabolism and possible teratogenic effects, J. Pediatr. **78**(2):329, 1971.
20. Neumann, L. L., and Cohen, S. N.: The neonatal narcotic withdrawal syndrome: a therapeutic challenge, Clin. Perinatol. **2**(1):99, 1975.
21. Nora, J. J., and Fraser, F. C.: Medical genetics: principles and practice, Philadelphia, 1974, Lea & Febiger, p. 3.
22. Peery, T. M., and Miller, F. N.: Pathology: a dynamic introduction to medicine and surgery, ed. 2, Boston, 1971, Little, Brown and Co., p. 672.
23. Smith, D. W., and Germain, C. P. H.: Care of the adult patient: medical surgical nursing, ed. 4, Philadelphia, 1975, J. B. Lippincott Co., p. 390.
24. Stevenson, R. E.: The fetus and newly born infant: influences of the prenatal environment, ed. 2, St. Louis, 1977, The C. V. Mosby Co., p. 134.
25. Strauss, R. G., et al.: Epilepsy and pregnancy: serum thyroxine levels during phenytoin therapy, Obstet. Gynecol. **53**(3):344, 1979.
26. Strauss, R. G., et al.: Hematologic effects of phenytoin therapy during pregnancy, Obstet. Gynecol. **51**(6):682, 1978.
27. Thorn, G., et al.: Harrison's principles of internal medicine, ed. 8, New York, 1977, McGraw-Hill Book Co., p. 127.
28. Tsuboi, T., and Endo, S.: Incidence of seizures and EEG abnormalities among offspring of epileptic patients, Hum. Genet. **36**:173, 1977.
29. Volle, F., and Heron, P. A.: Epilepsy and you, Springfield, Ill., 1978, Charles C Thomas, Publisher, p. 3.
30. Whaley, L. F., and Wong, D. L.: Nursing care of infants and children, St. Louis, 1979, The C. V. Mosby Co. p. 229.
31. Whitfield, W.: The epilepsies, Nurs. Times, **73**:1251, 1977.
32. Zandon, M. J., and Kirkley, M.: Metabolism of diphenylhydantoin (phenytoin) during pregnancy, Br. J. Obstet. Gynecol. **86**(2):125, 1979.

BIBLIOGRAPHY

Behrman, R. E., editor: Neonatal-perinatal medicine: diseases of the fetus and infant, ed. 2, St. Louis, 1977, The C. V. Mosby Co., p. 784.
Bruya, M. A., and Bolin, R. H.: Epilepsy: a controllable disease, Am. J. Nurs. **76**(3):388, 1976.
Cooper, C. R.: Anticonvulsant drugs, Nursing '76, **6**(1):45, 1976.
Dam, M. et al.: Antiepileptic drugs: metabolism in pregnancy, Clin. Pharmacokinet. **4**:53, 1979.
Fenwick, P.: Epilepsy symposium—part 2, Nurs. Mirror **147**(5): 13, 1978.
Gestaut, H., et al.: Non-jacksonian hemiconvulsive seizures: one-sided generalized epilepsy, Epilepsia **3**:56, 1962.
Hathaway, C. E.: The bleeding newborn, Clin. Perinatol. **2**(1): 83, 1975.
Klaus, M. H., and Fanaroff, A. A.: Care of the high-risk neonate, Philadelphia, 1979, W. B. Saunders Co., p. 378.
Lander, C. M., et al.: Plasma anticonvulsant concentrations during pregnancy, Neurology **27**:128, 1977.
Leitch, C. J., and Tinker, R. V.: Primary care, Philadelphia, 1978, F. A. Davis Co., p. 497.
Ramsey, R. E., et al.: Status epilepticus in pregnancy: effect of phenytoin malabsorption on seizure control, Neurology **28**:85, 1978.
Solomon, G. E., Hilgartner, M. W., and Kutt, H.: Coagulation defects caused by diphenylhydantoin, Neurology **22**(11):1165, 1972.
Speidel, B. D., and Meadow, S. R.: Maternal epilepsy and abnormalities of the fetus and newborn, Lancet **2**:839, 1972.
Swanson, P. D.: Anticonvulsant therapy: approaches to some clinical problems, Postgrad. Med **65**(3):147, 1979.
Swift, N.: Helping patients live with seizures, Nursing '78 **8**(6): 25, 1978.
Teramo, K., et al.: Fetal heart rate during a maternal grand mal epileptic seizure, J. Perinat. Med. **7**:3, 1979.
Wolf, C. R. et al.: Anticonvulsant therapy with oral paraldehyde, Ann. Neurol. **6**(6):554, 1979.

Chapter 9

Essential hypertension and pregnancy

Minerva Ratliff

Hypertension in pregnancy is associated with increased perinatal mortality and is one of the most common complications of pregnancy.[1] The purpose of this chapter is to investigate the effects of essential hypertension in pregnancy. Essential hypertension is defined as diastolic blood pressure of more than 90 mm Hg occurring before the twentieth week of pregnancy or as hypertension that was known to be present before the onset of pregnancy.[10] In the earliest stages of essential hypertension the blood pressure elevation is usually transitory. In the female the onset of essential hypertension frequently coincides with the nonconvulsive form of toxemia of pregnancy.[20] In the absence of a specific cause the uncomplicated hypertensive state has been termed "essential" or "benign." However, because of the high incidence of maternal and fetal complications, it has been suggested the adjective "benign" should not be used in pregnancy.[18]

Chelsey[7] disagrees with the definition of essential hypertension as high blood pressure without any recognized cause. He uses the term "chronic hypertension" in recognizing that many cases classified as essential hypertension in pregnant women actually do have demonstrable, but undemonstrated, causes. In this chapter the terms "essential hypertension" and "chronic hypertension" will be used interchangeably.

Approximately 5% of all pregnancies are complicated by some form of hypertension that may be classified as follows:

1. Chronic hypertension
2. Toxemia (preeclampsia and eclampsia)
   a. Pure or specific hypertensive disease of pregnancy
   b. Superimposed on chronic hypertension
3. Chronic renal disease[18]

Essential hypertension, with or without superimposed preeclampsia, accounts for about one third of all cases of hypertension in pregnancy.[3] Evidence shows that at least 25% to 50% of the patients with so-called pure toxemia actually have unrecognized chronic hypertension that antedates pregnancy.[18] Pregnant women with elevated blood pressure have an increased fetal mortality rate and develop preeclampsia more frequently and earlier than nonhypertensive women.[19,22] In most series 70% of hypertensive pregnant women have preeclampsia or eclampsia, 25% have essential hypertension, and 5% have underlying chronic renal disease. Looked at another way, 3% to 4% of all pregnancies are complicated by hypertension caused by preeclampsia, while 1% are complicated by essential hypertension.[4] Therefore we can see that essential hypertension is not an uncommon cause of elevated blood pressure in pregnancy.

CIRCULATION AND ARTERIAL PRESSURE

Arterial pressure equals cardiac output times total peripheral resistance. Any factor that increases cardiac output or total peripheral resistance will cause an increase in mean arterial pressure. Approximately 50% of the total resistance to blood flow in the systemic circulation occurs in the arterioles, which can be constricted or dilated tremendously by nervous, humoral, or local tissue factors.[13]

It is primarily the circulatory reflexes that keep the arterial pressure from rising extremely high or falling extremely low. There are three circulatory reflexes that play major roles in arterial pressure regulation:

1. The baroreceptor reflex (operates from 60 to 200 mm Hg)
2. The chemoreceptor reflex (operates from 40 to 100 mm Hg)
3. The CNS ischemic response (operates at a pressure of 250 mm Hg)[13]

The kidneys seem to function mainly by controlling fluid volumes of the body. The output of the kidneys is highly responsive to the arterial pressure level.[13] An increase in arterial pressure causes an increase in excretion of water and salt. This increase in arterial pressure has a direct effect on the kidneys causing increased urinary output. There is an indirect effect that suppresses the aldosterone secretion. This results in an increase in sodium excretion along with water loss.

The kidneys are capable of secreting an enzyme called renin, and the renin in turn acts on the plasma proteins to cause release of a vasoconstrictor substance called angiotensin. The angiotensin in turn increases the total peripheral resistance and also increases the aldosterone secretion by the adrenal cortex.[13] This in turn acts on the kidneys to cause salt and water retention, thereby elevating the arterial pressure as a result of increasing extracellular fluid volume. The clinical importance of plasma renin determination is still controversial. Some believe that these measurements are only helpful in the diagnosis of such rare conditions as renin-producing tumors or primary aldosteronism. Others claim that plasma renin can be used as a prognostic index and as a guide to treatment in essential hypertension. The case for renin measurement rests on concepts that must be regarded as unsubstantiated.[2,17,29]

ESSENTIAL HYPERTENSION PATHOPHYSIOLOGY

The first event in the pathogenesis of essential hypertension is functional arterial constriction. This constriction may be caused by the intrinsic elaboration of a hypothetical humoral pressor substance of renal or other origin.[14] Long-term elevation of the blood pressure results in morphological changes in the vessels and increased peripheral resistance. The increased peripheral resistance causes an increased pressure in the left ventricle, which causes the left ventricle to exert more force to pump the blood into

the aorta. Over a period of time the increased work load results in hypertrophy of the left ventricle. If the load becomes excessive, there may be dilatation and eventual failure of that ventricle. Coronary atherosclerosis may also predispose to failure in these patients by producing enough myocardial ischemia to reduce left ventricular functional capacity.[2,13,14]

The earliest clinical sign observed in patients with essential hypertension is an asymptomatic and apparently uncomplicated elevation of the blood pressure.[13,17,19] The cardiac output, venous pressure, and circulatory time are not altered at first, and anatomical changes in the heart itself do not appear until years and possibly decades following the onset of sustained measurable hypertension. Progressive essential hypertension is the cause of an important form of heart disease, since approximately 75% of the patients with persistent hypertension eventually die of some cardiac complication.[13]

Generally, there are three classes of hypertension. In mild hypertension the diastolic pressure is between 90 and 115 mm Hg, and there is no or minimal target organ involvement. Moderate hypertension, diastolic pressure between 115 and 130 mm Hg, has moderate involvement of the target organs. Severe hypertension, diastolic pressure greater than 130 mm Hg, has definite target organ involvement. "Target organ" damage refers to atherosclerotic and/or hypertensive changes that result from longstanding hypertension. These include the following:

1. *Cardiac:* angina pectoris; evidence of left atrial enlargement, either with or without congestive heart failure; evidence of a myocardial infarction or ischemia
2. *CNS:* transient ischemic attacks or strokes
3. *Renal:* albuminuria (200 mg/24 hr), an early finding; azotemia, a late complication; occasionally renal failure supervenes
4. *Eye:* Keith Wagener classification of retinopathy
   a. Arteriolar narrowing
   b. Arteriolar nicking
   c. Hemorrhages, exudates
   d. Papilledema

Chronic hypertension can be divided into three distinct stages. The earliest, prehypertensive, stage may last for many years and is rarely recognized clinically because its detection depends on the observation of an exaggerated response to a cold pressor test.[13] The hypertensive patient may remain asymptomatic for 10 to 20 years.[17,20] More characteristic is the next stage, that of pure hypertension. At this time the principal finding is the presence of a persistent elevation of the blood pressure according to the criteria already defined. Specific clinical symptoms or signs are absent, and the patient often does not suspect that she has any disease. There are no pathological laboratory findings. Some patients complain of nonspecific symptoms such as headache, fatigue, insomnia, and nervousness, but their relationship to the underlying hypertension is not always clear.[13] Miller[20] suggests that these and other factors suggest that a neurogenic mechanism, acting through the autonomic nervous system, may cause spasm of the arterioles, initiating the disease.

The third stage of the disease is that of late complications and is accompanied by considerable clinical disability. As the elevation of blood pressure continues, there is an extra burden on the cardiovascular system that predisposes it to certain complications. These include hypertrophy of the left ventricle; sclerosis of the small renal arterioles, leading to reduced glomerular filtration, nitrogenous retention, and uremia; and concurrent development of atherosclerosis, especially in the coronary and cerebral arteries, leading to thrombotic occulsion or rupture with hemorrhage.

CARDIOVASCULAR CHANGES DURING PREGNANCY

There is a 30% to 35% increase in the total blood volume during pregnancy. This includes an increase in the plasma (45%) and erythrocytes (33%). It is generally believed that the hypervolemia of pregnancy serves to fill the greatly expanded vascular bed of the uterus and the expanded venous reservoir, particularly that of the lower extremities.

Cardiac output increases during pregnancy largely to meet the demands of the growing uterus and placenta. By 24 weeks' gestation the cardiac output has increased 30% to 40%. When the mother is lying on her side, there is no significant change in cardiac output, but in the supine position it may be decreased related to pressure from the heavy uterus on the vena cava.

The blood vessel tone decreases, particularly venous pressure. The peripheral vascular resistance decreases, thus arterial blood pressure decreases. The vascular arrangement of the uterus makes it act as a low-resistance network. Uterine vascular resistance in the nonpregnant state is about 10 times greater than during pregnancy.[2] The fall in vascular resistance is responsible for the decrease in the diastolic and mean arterial pressure. In a normal pregnancy there should not be an increase in the blood pressure. The systolic pressure may fall a few points, and the diastolic pressure may fall 5 points or more.[2,13]

INDIVIDUALS AT RISK

In about 90% of the cases of cardiovascular disease, no definite cause can be identified for hypertension. These cases make up the group known as primary or essential hypertension. Although the cause is not usually known, the following factors are thought to be predisposing to the development of essential hypertension[20]:

1. *Heredity:* If both parents are hypertensive, the chances are increased that the offspring will be hypertensive.
2. *Age:* The frequency of hypertension increases steadily with age, at least to the age of 50 years.
3. *Sex:* Hypertension is more common in females, perhaps owing to its relation to toxemia of pregnancy, but the malignant type is more common in males.
4. *Climate:* Hypertension is more common in temperate than in tropical climates.

DIAGNOSIS AND CLINICAL FEATURES

Hypertension is present by definition when there is a persistent blood pressure elevation of 140/90 mm Hg or greater. Another method of diagnosing essential hypertension would be a persistent elevation over the average or normal blood pressure of 30 mm Hg systolic and 15 mm Hg in the diastolic reading. These elevations should be present on two or more occasions at least 4 hours apart.

Some people are more likely to develop essential hypertension than others. They are people who have some or all of the following characteristics: 30 years of age or older, of the black race, a family history of hypertension, and a history of hypertensive pregnancy.[19]

The diagnosis of essential hypertension can be

made following measurements of basal blood pressure; medical history; physical examination, including funduscopic examination; and routine laboratory tests to rule out secondary causes.

COMPLICATIONS WITH PREGNANCY

There are certain findings during pregnancy that suggest the existence of underlying hypertensive disease. These include the following:

1. Elevation of blood pressure to previously defined levels before the twentieth week of gestation
2. Family history of hypertension—limited diagnostic significance
3. Obese individuals more often affected than thin ones
4. Various endocrine disturbances, such as diabetes mellitus
5. Patient's emotional background apparently related in an obscure way to the development of the chronic hypertensive state

The first problem with essential hypertension during pregnancy is diagnosis if the elevated blood pressure is being evaluated for the first time during pregnancy. When patients are observed during the first 20 weeks, and hypertension is present at the time of the initial observation as well as on subsequent occasions, it can be assumed that it was present before pregnancy.[21] Hydatidiform moles may also cause an increase in blood pressure before 20 weeks' gestation, so this would need to be ruled out as a cause.[6] The diagnosis is made on the basis of a documented history of sustained hypertension prior to pregnancy, with little persistence after puerperium. In practice the diagnosis is made on presumptive evidence as follows:

1. Detection of hypertension before the twentieth week of gestation, with little or no proteinuria and in the absence of hydatidiform mole or fetal hydrops
2. Retinal angiosclerosis and, far less commonly, hemorrhages and exudates
3. Definite cardiac hypertrophy
4. A history of earlier hypertensive pregnancies[6]

Chronic hypertension is more likely than preeclampsia to be the correct diagnosis in multiparas, especially in the absence of sustained proteinuria and generalized edema; exorbitant hypertension usually denotes chronic hypertension, often with superimposed preeclampsia.[6] It is uncommon for the systolic blood pressure in preeclampsia to exceed 200 mm Hg, and when it does, one should suspect that it has developed on a basis of essential hypertension.[3] When the rise in blood pressure precedes the appearance of proteinuria, essential hypertension is the more likely cause.[3]

The characteristic blood pressure pattern of normotensive women displaying a slight fall in the second trimester is also observed in a significant proportion of those with essential hypertension. In a study done in 1970, Barnes[3] examined a series of 145 patients with essential hypertension. He found a fall of 20 mm Hg or more in systolic blood pressure in 60% and a corresponding fall in diastolic pressure in 25% of the cases. It is significant that in the group of patients who showed a fall of blood pressure in the second trimester, Barnes reported a fetal loss of 4.6% as compared with 16% in those who showed no such fall.

The impact of chronic essential hypertension on pregnancy is often severe and carries with it a high perinatal morbidity and mortality rate. The maternal mortality among mothers with essential hypertension is under 1%. When death occurs, it usually follows a sudden increase in blood pressure accompanying preeclampsia or eclampsia and results from cerebral hemorrhage, acute left ventricular failure, or malignant hypertension. Death is more likely to occur in patients with established hypertensive disease than among women with only a short history of essential hypertension.[3]

There is considerable indirect evidence that in both toxemia and essential hypertension there is a reduction in the effective blood flow through the uterine wall and placenta. Dixon and associates showed that the reduction is more marked when proteinuria is present as well as hypertension.[3] Under these conditions the placenta may be small and become infarcted late in pregnancy and then the fetus may be underweight and die in utero between the thirty-sixth week and term. According to a study by Page and Christianson, high mean arterial pressures exceeding 90 mm Hg during the fifth and sixth months of pregnancy are associated with a significant increase in the frequencies of third trimester preeclampsia, intrauterine fetal growth retardation, and stillbirths.[11]

The fetal mortality rate of infants of hypertensive

women without superimposed preeclampsia is 8.5%. The incidence of fetal death and intrauterine growth retardation increases with increasing levels of maternal blood pressure.[22] The death rate for infants of hypertensive mothers with superimposed preeclampsia is 20% compared to 6% to 8% in infants of preeclamptic mothers not previously hypertensive.[11] The fact that preeclampsia develops earlier in pregnancies of hypertensive women may explain the increased fetal mortality rate. Severe preeclampsia is about seven times as common in patients with essential hypertension as it is in normotensive women, and when it develops before 32 weeks' gestation, 75% of the infants are lost.[3]

An increased incidence of "prematurity" reflected by slowed fetal growth has been documented when the maternal heart volume as estimated radiographically did not adjust to the demands of pregnancy.[8] This finding has been questioned by other investigators.[8] Bieniarz and associates demonstrated by angiography that the speed and extent of filling of the uterine arteries with contrast medium during pregnancy bear a significant relationship to fetal growth.[12]

Some of the problems associated with the small-for-gestational-age (SGA) infant include hypoglycemia, hypocalcemia, asphyxia at birth, meconium aspiration, polycythemia (hyperviscosity), pulmonary hemorrhage, increased risk of infection (impaired immune function), and others.[27] Each of these problems can lead to other problems. It is recommended that a Dextrostix and hematocrit be done on the infant on admission to the nursery, and the Dextrostix should be rechecked frequently for infants at risk. The method in *Care of the Newborn*[27] is as follows: q 1 hr × 4, q 4 hr × 5, and q 12 hr × 2. The hematocrit is rechecked q 12 hr × 2, and the infant is observed for signs of other problems. Untreated hypoglycemia may result in severe neurological deficits or death. Neurological and developmental sequelae are not as common in neonates with asymptomatic hypoglycemia as in those with symptomatic hypoglycemia.[23]

The hazards to the fetus of a mother with chronic hypertension include placental abruption, increased perinatal mortality, premature delivery, and intrauterine growth retardation. Therefore it is essential to evaluate the status of the tests that monitor fetoplacental function: serial determinations of estriol levels, human placental lactogen values, oxytocin challenge tests, and "nonstress tests." The use of ultrasound is valuable for monitoring the intrauterine growth of the fetus. Amniocentesis is done to determine the lecithin-sphingomyelin ratios in the amniotic fluid, which are helpful in assessing fetal lung maturity. Sole reliance should not be placed on any of these tests.

The concentration of estriol is markedly elevated during pregnancy. The excretion of estriol may increase by as much as 1000 times. The other estrogen concentrations increase also but not nearly as much as estriol. The disproportionate rise in estriol concentration in pregnancy as compared to the rise in estrone and 17β-estradiol is a reflection of a remarkably active 16,L-hydroxylase in the fetal adrenal glands and liver.[21] The measurement of this estrogen in urine, serum, or amniotic fluid can serve as an index of fetal well-being. To be of value, serial estriol determinations must be done. The technique for measuring urine estriol is accurate and fairly rapid, but it requires a 24-hour urine collection, which is not always convenient for pregnant women. In recent years serum estriols have been used for measurement. The studies that have been done indicate these may be valid, but there are variables to consider such as the mother's activity and the time of collection. In a high-risk pregnancy management protocol by Crane, Savage, and Arias,[9] the plasma-free estriol determination is used. They gave the following reasons as advantages over the urinary and other plasma techniques: the avoidance of 24-hour urine collections and problems with interpretation when the sample is incomplete; the results are normally available within 7 to 12 hours; glycosuria and the maternal use of drugs such as phenolphthalein-containing stool softeners, ampicillin, and methenamine (Mandelamine) have no effect on plasma-free estriol as they do with urinary determinations.

Plasma-free estriols also eliminate the problems of diurnal and postural variation seen with urinary and total or conjugated plasma techniques. Also if the mother has some renal dysfunction, this would affect the other methods. The effect of renal function on plasma-free estriol has not been thoroughly evaluated, although the lack of significant diurnal and postural variation would suggest that it is relatively independent of renal excretion.[9]

Diagnostic ultrasound is an excellent method to evaluate growth and development of the fetus. The energy levels utilized in ultrasonography are very low in intensity. These low-energy levels have no detectable effect on tissue cultures, chromosomes, infants, or mothers. In patients with a questionable EDC, ultrasound can be used for dating and for biparietal measurements on two or three occasions between 20 and 30 weeks' gestation. The fetal head growth during this time is mostly linear and rapid, about 3 mm per week. Ultrasound is used during the third trimester to monitor fetal growth that is dependent on placental support. Abnormal slowing of third trimester head growth often provides an early sign of developing placental insufficiency.

The oxytocin challenge test is used to evaluate placental respiratory function. A 10- to 15-minute baseline recording of fetal heart tones and uterine activity is obtained prior to beginning the test. A temporary stress is applied to the fetus in the form of uterine contractions. If the placental respiratory reserve is adequate, the fetal heart rate remains normal during and following the contractions. If the placental reserve is inadequate, fetal hypoxia and late deceleration of the heart rate are observed. The oxytocin challenge test is usually begun at 34 weeks' gestation, but if intrauterine growth retardation is suspected or severe maternal hypertension is present, the test may be indicated as early as 28 weeks' gestation. A negative test (three contractions in 10 minutes—FHR: normal) should be repeated at weekly intervals. If the test is positive (persistent late deceleration), the pregnancy is usually terminated if the fetus is mature. The fetus would need to continue to be monitored until delivery. An unsatisfactory test is repeated in 24 hours. Contraindications to the oxytocin challenge test include any of the following: placenta previa, abruptio placentae, previous vertical (classical) cesarean section, multiple gestation, and premature ruptured membranes.

In those mothers who are risks for the oxytocin challenge test, the nonstress test may be done. This involves monitoring the fetal heart rate and uterine activity. Oxytocin is not used. A fetus with good heart rate variability, accelerations of heart rate with fetal movement, and no late decelerations with spontaneous contractions is considered a "reactive" fetus whose prognosis for survival is excellent.[5]

Human placental lactogen is a protein hormone secreted by the placenta. The levels in serum rise throughout gestation and are indicative of placental size. The normal range for this protein is very broad. Its main use is in conjunction with other tests for placental insufficiency, unusually low values may be valuable in diagnosing placental insufficiency.

Amniocentesis is performed to examine the amniotic fluid. It is visually inspected to determine the presence of meconium and then tested for the lecithin-sphingomyelin ratio. The determination of the amniotic fluid concentration of lecithin relative to that of sphingomyelin (a phospholipid lacking surfactant properties), originally described by Gluck,[24] is the most widely used amniotic fluid surfactant test. Lecithin and sphingomyelin are present in similar concentrations until the middle of the third trimester. At this point, the level of lecithin begins to increase, whereas that of sphingomyelin remains relatively constant. By 35 weeks' gestation, on the average the lecithin-sphingomyelin ratio approximates 2:1. The risk of developing respiratory distress syndrome is relatively low with a lecithin-sphingomyelin ratio of 2:1; the lower the ratio, the greater the risk.

Factors that indicate an unfavorable prognosis for the fetus include:

1. Mother over 40 years of age with long-established hypertension
2. Failure of the blood pressure to fall by the end of the second trimester
3. Blood pressure rise in the second trimester
4. Appearance of proteinuria or sudden rise in blood pressure before the thirty-fifth week of gestation
5. Falling urinary estriol excretion during last 6 weeks of pregnancy (or serum estriol fall)
6. Failure of mother to gain weight normally
7. Initial blood pressure 180/110, especially if proteinuria is present
8. Any demonstrable decrease of renal function

Barnes[3] emphasizes that, apart from the rare complications of malignant hypertension and left ventricular failure in the mother, pregnancy is terminated in cases of essential hypertension for the sake of the infant and not the mother. The fetus is at grave risk as soon as proteinuria develops, but the mother's kidneys are not damaged permanently by the renal lesions of preeclampsia nor is the risk of permanent maternal hypertension increased by the duration of preeclampsia.[3]

When a patient with chronic hypertension becomes pregnant, many complex clinical interrelationships are involved. An especially complicated problem is the connection between hypertensive disease not specifically related to pregnancy and the hypertensive component of true pregnancy toxemia, since essential hypertension and toxemia of pregnancy are both diseases of unknown etiology.[14]

Toxemia is the most common complication of pregnancy in patients with chronic hypertension. The incidence of toxemic superimposition is unrelated to the severity of underlying chronic hypertension.[18] The perinatal mortality rises with severe chronic hypertension and the superimposition of toxemia. Landesman and Holze[6] found a 28% incidence of toxemic superimposition in both mild and severe grades of the disease. Whereas the perinatal fetal mortality in mild uncomplicated chronic hypertension was no higher than normal (2%), superimposition raised the mortality to16%. The perinatal mortality in severe, uncomplicated chronic hypertension rose to 41% with superimposition.[18]

Pregnancy is generally contraindicated in severe essential hypertension because of the tremendous incidence of complications accompanied by high morbidity and mortality rates in both mother and baby. The hypertensive mother has a significantly greater than normal chance of developing toxemia, abruptio placentae (occurs approximately 10 times more often than in normotensive women[18]), cerebral damage, retinopathy, renal insufficiency, vascular accident, and cardiac failure.

The management of a patient with hypertension in pregnancy must be determined by the individual case and presents some special problems. A large proportion of patients who start their pregnancy with a fixed mild to moderate hypertension have an uncomplicated pregnancy despite the fact that in a number of them there is a further rise in the blood pressure during the course of pregnancy. In the experience of Barnes, patients whose blood pressure does not exceed 160/100 mm Hg before and during the first 20 weeks of pregnancy have, as a rule, an excellent prognosis.[3,28]

Patients who have more severe hypertension early in pregnancy will require special medical and obstetrical care. They should have long periods of rest and delivery should be brought about as soon as the risk of fetal death in utero is greater than the risk of delivery and neonatal death. Except in mild cases where the blood pressure does not exceed 160/100 mm Hg, there is considerable risk of intrauterine death of the fetus from uteroplacental insufficiency in the last 2 weeks of pregnancy.[3]

Sodium intake has commonly been restricted during pregnancy by obstetricians. Also diuretics have been prescribed routinely by some in the presence of edema. The reasoning behind these actions was that edema was frequently associated with preeclampsia-eclampsia. More recently the observation that rigid sodium restriction or the administration of diuretic drugs to nonpregnant hypertensive patients often lowers the blood pressure has probably influenced the administration of diuretics to pregnant patients.

In pregnancy, however, not all edema is pathological. There is normally an appreciable increase in maternal extracellular fluid volume as a consequence of maternal hypervolemia. In addition, the enlarged uterus compresses the vena cava and leads to pooling of blood in the lower half of the body in all normal body positions except the lateral recumbent position. The venous compression raises dependent venous blood pressure, which promotes the accumulation of extravascular extracellular fluid in the lower half of the body. The edema so formed has been erroneously considered to be pathological and has commonly prompted both the recommendation of rigid sodium restriction and the administration of potent diuretic agents.[24] The response is generalized reduction of all the maternal and fetal extracellular fluid volume rather than just that extra fluid pooled in the lower half of the body. The more direct and more desirable treatment for such dependent edema, if troublesome, is a body position that relieves the elevated venous pressure, that is, lateral recumbency at intervals throughout the day as well as the night.[24]

It has become apparent that salt restriction has no place in the management of pregnant women with essential hypertension, particularly since some investigators have demonstrated that these women have a decreased ability to conserve sodium normally.[4] A restriction in sodium may cause a fall in the intravascular volume, resulting in a decrease in renal and uteroplacental perfusion. This may result in a paradoxical increase in blood pressure despite a decrease in intravascular volume.[8] The observation that hypertensive patients who generated larger blood volumes seemed to be protected against development of severe disease and the associated risks to the fetus may be significant in the management of these pregnancies.[8] It has been suggested that liberal ingestion of salt may be beneficial in the maintenance of good blood pressure control during pregnancy.[4] The results of a study done by Schewitz and associates that involved dietary sodium chloride in pregnant hypertensive patients indicate that there is no apparent justification for the restriction of sodium intake in pregnant hypertensive patients.[26]

There is much controversy concerning the use of antihypertensive medications during pregnancy. The following information is not complete because the effects of antihypertensive therapy are still being studied and have not been well studied previously. There is general agreement that the women who became pregnant while receiving antihypertensive medication should be continued on treatment even if pretreatment pressures did not indicate acute risk.[22]

Because too vigorous pharmacological lowering of the systemic blood pressure may impair uteroplacental perfusion, initiation of antihypertensive therapy in pregnant women is commonly deferred until the diastolic pressure exceeds 100 mm Hg in the second trimester or 110 mm Hg in the third trimester, and it should be the clinician's aim to maintain the diastolic pressure at no less than 90 mm Hg.[4] The medications selected should be those that increase or at least do not decrease uterine blood flow. Any pregnant woman who is to be started on pharmacological antihypertensive therapy should be hospitalized and monitored closely. A discussion of the mechanisms, major side effects, and specific side effects relevant to pregnancy of some of the antihypertensive agents will be examined.

Alpha-methyldopa is a potent antihypertensive agent that acts as a false neurotransmitter interfering with the transmission of sympathetic impulses. This results in a decrease in total peripheral resistance and an increased or unchanged renal blood flow. There are no reported complications to pregnancy.[22] Methyldopa also lowers cardiac output and probably lowers uteroplacental perfusion.[19] A study by Redman and associates[25] evaluated the effect of antihypertensive therapy on fetal survival (medica-

tion used was methyldopa [Aldomet]). In a controlled study of 242 hypertensive women, there were nine pregnancy losses in the control group and one fetal loss in the treated group. The birthweight and maturity of viable infants were similar in treated and control groups.

Hydralazine, a direct vasodilator, has been the drug of choice for acute hypertension in pregnancy. In human subjects cardiac output is increased, largely by reflex tachycardia, with a subsequent increase in renal blood flow and perfusion in the uteroplacental perfusion.[19,22] There are no recorded side effects unique to pregnancy.

Reserpine acts by depletion of norepinephrine from sympathetic nerve endings. There are several well-recognized side effects that are similar in pregnant and nonpregnant women. In addition, reserpine crosses the placenta, and the neonate whose mother has received reserpine may develop nasal congestion. The newborn infant is an obligate nose breather, and nasal obstruction owing to reserpine-induced congestion may be a serious side effect and fatal if unrecognized.[22]

Propranolol, a beta-adrenergic blocking agent, is used as an adjunct to antihypertensive therapy. It inhibits renin release, which may be useful in certain types of hypertension. It is frequently administered in conjunction with hydralazine. Propranolol does cross the placenta and has recently been linked with cases of multiple fetal anomalies, and it may cause neonatal respiratory depression. The combination of hydralazine and propranolol, therefore, generally should be avoided during pregnancy.[4]

Guanethidine is an antihypertensive agent reserved for patients in whom blood pressure cannot be controlled by less potent agents. It lowers blood pressure by depleting catecholamines at sympathetic nerve endings, leading to decreased cardiac output and renal blood flow. Guanethidine causes orthostatic hypotension, which is exaggerated during pregnancy. However, in patients requiring this drug, careful dosage titration and patient instruction can minimize the impact of this effect.[22]

Diazoxide lowers peripheral resistance markedly; after an initial rise in cardiac output, there is a profound fall and perfusion is dramatically decreased.[19] Diazoxide crosses the placenta and can cause fetal or neonatal hyperbilirubinemia.[17]

During pregnancy diuretic-induced volume depletion may interfere with renal and uteroplacental perfusion, which may result in a syndrome simulating worsening preeclampsia. Thiazide diuretics act by decreasing plasma volume and cardiac output initially. Later the action results from decreased total peripheral resistance. It does cross the placenta.[22] Thiazide also appears in breast milk. The hazards to the baby include fetal or neonatal jaundice, thrombocytopenia, and possibly others.[17] Thiazide diuretics have also been implicated in fatal maternal hemorrhagic pancreatitis and hyponatremia and in neonatal pancytopenia. More potent diuretics acting on the loop of Henle have an even stronger tendency to produce depletion of the extracellular fluid volume and electrolyte imbalance. Furthermore, furosemide has been reported to cause congenital abnormalities in experiments with animals. Therefore during pregnancy diuretic agents should be avoided, although administration of powerful loop diuretics may be lifesaving, for example, in the treatment of acute left ventricular failure associated with accelerated hypertension.

The last method of antepartum treatment to be discussed is therapeutic abortion. This is not usually advised or necessary, but for the following reasons it may be recommended:

1. Maternal age over 30 years with an initial blood pressure of 180/110 mm Hg
2. Evidence of hypertensive disease
   a. Cardiac enlargement
   b. Retinal changes
   c. Proteinuria
3. Previous pregnancy with preeclampsia (probable recurrence)

The mother who is seen with the previously listed symptoms has an increased risk of cerebrovascular accident, heart failure, and permanent increase in hypertension after delivery.[4] Haynes[14] comments that it should always be kept in mind that hypertensive disease is inherently progressive in nature, and there is consequently no rational indication for interruption before viability in the hope that a future pregnancy will have a better chance of being carried to term. The present pregnancy is the one to try for, since the patient's hypertensive status will in all probability be worse rather than better in any future pregnancy.

A common medication used in the management of eclampsia-preeclampsia is magnesium sulfate. It prevents or controls convulsions by blocking neuromuscular transmission and decreasing the amount of acetylcholine liberated by the motor nerve impulse. It is administered to control convulsions and not as an antihypertensive agent. As a side action, it may increase uterine blood flow.[15] Magnesium sulfate is administered parenterally and is excreted only in the urine. If the patient's urine output is less than 25 ml/hr and repeat doses of magnesium sulfate are given, the magnesium level of the blood can rise to toxic levels, completely blocking the patellar reflex or, with increasing levels, depressing the respiratory system; severe overdose can result in cardiac arrest. The antidote is calcium gluconate, which should be kept in the patient's room.

It has been known for many years that the cardiovascular system of the pregnant woman is "sensitive" to spinal anesthesia. In fact, at one time circulatory shock caused by spinal anesthesia was a major cause of maternal death, and in many obstetrical services the use of spinal anesthesia was prohibited.[2] During pregnancy the vasomotor tone of the circulatory system is controlled by markedly increased activities of the autonomic nervous system. Blockade by any means (including regional anesthesia) produces a marked fall in the arterial blood pressure along with manifestations of circulatory shock. The circulatory response to autonomic blockade, reflected by the magnitude of hypotension, increases with the progress of gestation, reaching a peak at term.[2] Further studies have shown that the hypotension that develops following autonomic blockade in the pregnant patient is related to venous pooling. A simple corrective measure is to elevate the patient's legs 90 degrees to restore pooled blood to the general circulation. When the venomotor tone is blocked by any regional anesthetic or by chemical agents, the veins are left practically without tone; their capacity is, therefore, increased so much so as to accommodate about one third of the effective circulating blood volume.[2]

Chelsey[6] and others have pointed out that the remote annual death rate of the immediate survivors of eclampsia is slightly more than twice the expected death rate. Although there is some doubt that toxemia actually produces essential hypertension in patients not predisposed to this disease, a sizable number of posteclamptic women will have residual hypertension of the essential type, and their prognosis for normal pregnancy is worse than that of the general population. If the patient has no residual signs of hypertension or albuminuria at 6 weeks, the prognosis is relatively good, and future pregnancy need not be discouraged.[4] Essential hypertension is not completely understood, but through the studies that have been done and are being done we are more able to treat effectively the problems that it presents. This is aiding further in decreasing the maternal and infant morbidity and mortality rates.

SUMMARY

A summary of some important factors in the management of hypertensive pregnant patients follows:
1. Close antenatal care
2. Hospitalization if antihypertensive medications become necessary
3. Repeated laboratory tests for fetal growth and placental function

4. Prolonged rest, side-lying position, elevation of legs
5. Delivery at 37 to 38 weeks' gestation unless clinical improvements evident
6. Following delivery, do not administer ergotamine (may use oxytocics that do not cause vasopression)

Any woman who is hypertensive during pregnancy should be watched closely. When first seen in the clinic, a number of pregnant women have a raised blood pressure that returns to normal after some rest. These patients have, on the whole, an uncomplicated pregnancy but may develop essential hypertension at a later time. There is also a well-known familial tendency to hypertension, and this has also been shown to occur in the hypertension of pregnancy.[16]

Protocols

Problem □ Pregnancy with hypertension

GOAL: To recognize deteriorating condition early, to prevent eclampsia, and to decrease perinatal morbidity and mortality
Rationale: To be aware that the hypertensive mother is at increased risk for developing complications such as preeclampsia-eclampsia

DIAGNOSTIC
1. Obtain medical history—previous history of hypertension or family history of hypertension.
   Rationale: To determine whether there is family history of hypertension since there is strong indication of hereditary influence on development of essential hypertension
2. Obtain previous history of hypertension during pregnancy.
   Rationale: To be alerted to likely recurrence with successive pregnancy
3. Perform physical examination, including retinal examination, percussion of cardiac borders, and routine laboratory tests.
   Rationale: To determine extent of hypertensive involvement

4. Determine accurate or reasonably close EDC by menstrual history, physical symptoms, fetal heart sounds, and ultrasound.
   Rationale: To distinguish between essential hypertension and toxemia and plan interventions and/or tests for appropriate time
5. At each antenatal visit check blood pressure, urine for protein, and weight.
   Rationale: To screen for toxemia, which is main complication of essential hypertension
6. Monitor vital signs, particularly blood pressure.
   a. Blood pressure greater than 200 mm Hg indicates essential or chronic hypertension.
      Rationale: To rule out preeclampsia
   b. A rise in blood pressure precedes the appearance of proteinuria.
      Rationale: To diagnose essential hypertension
   c. Blood pressure greater than 140/90 mm Hg at 20 weeks' gestation or earlier.
      Rationale: To diagnose preeclampsia, which develops earlier in patients with essential hypertension

THERAPEUTIC

1. Observe closely through biweekly visits until 28 weeks' gestation and weekly visits after 27 to 28 weeks' gestation.

   Rationale: To assess maternal and fetal progress; weekly visits after 28 weeks because condition may deteriorate more rapidly from then until delivery

2. Promote rest.

   Rationale: To improve circulating blood volume and lower blood pressure

   a. Have patient take frequent rest periods, up to 4 hours at a time. If unable to rest at home, hospitalization should be recommended.

      Rationale: To promote bed rest to lower blood pressure (Hospitalization for rest is preferred before starting antihypertensive drug therapy.)

   b. Have patient rest in side-lying position and elevate legs.

      Rationale: To decrease vena cava compression and decrease edema in lower extremities

   c. Recommend patient wear support stockings, particularly if problem with edema of lower extremities.

      Rationale: To increase venous return and blood flow to oxygenate fetus

3. Blood pressure uncontrolled by above measures may require antihypertensive medication.

   Rationale: To prevent risk of hypertensive crisis in mother that would also be detrimental to fetus

4. A mother on antihypertensive medication must be hospitalized.

   Rationale: To be able to use fetal monitor

5. Patient should follow a balanced diet and avoid excessive weight gain.

   Rationale: To avoid increasing the work load of the cardiovascular system

EDUCATIONAL

1. Explain the importance of frequent prenatal visits, the tests done, and the reasons why they are done.

   Rationale: To reduce the patient's anxiety level, which will also help lower blood pressure (An informed patient is more apt to follow the treatment plan and be cooperative.)

2. Instruct the patient about symptoms to be on the alert for during pregnancy and to notify the nurse or physician should these occur (headaches, dizziness, blurred vision, extraorbital edema).

   Rationale: To detect worsening of condition early and allow the patient to become a participator in her care

3. Instruct the mother about her disease, essential hypertension, and the importance of being checked frequently for progression of disease.

   Rationale: To prevent the complications that frequently occur through patient education

4. Provide nutrition counseling or diet instruction to maintain weight at optimal level.

   Rationale: To avoid increased cardiovascular work load and further strain on hypertensive cardiovascular system

Problem □ Developing fetus in hypertensive mother

GOAL: To prevent or lessen perinatal neonatal morbidity

Rationale: To decrease perinatal morbidity and mortality

DIAGNOSTIC

1. Establish EDC.

   Rationale: To plan treatment and/or intervention for most appropriate times.

   a. Obtain menstrual history of mother.

   b. Assess fetal movement.

   c. Listen for fetal heart sounds.

   d. Employ untrasound two to three times between 20 and 30 weeks' gestation.

      Rationale: To provide baseline for later assessment of fetal growth

2. Employ ultrasound during third trimester.

   Rationale: To detect slowing of fetal growth

3. Estriol determination should be done.

   Rationale: To give indication as to placental function (The estriol levels should progressively increase during pregnancy.)

4. Oxytocin challenge test or "nonstress" tests should begin at 34 weeks. Do at least weekly thereafter, if negative test. In serious hypertensive patients may do oxytocin challenge test as early as 28 weeks' gestation.

Rationale: To indicate placental respiratory reserve

5. Amniocentesis should be done at 34 to 35 weeks to determine lecithin-sphingomyelin ratio. Note color and consistency.

   Rationale: To provide information about fetal lung maturity (After 36 to 38 weeks' gestation, fetus is at greater risk for intrauterine death.)

6. Determine human placental lactogen levels.

   Rationale: To indicate poor placental function if values are low

THERAPEUTIC

1. Monitor blood pressure and other vital signs.

   Rationale: To establish baseline values and detect early development of superimposed toxemia

2. Base treatment on clinical condition and the tests indicating fetal well-being.

   Rationale: To provide key to safe, effective treatment

3. Deliver infant when uterine environment becomes hostile.

   Rationale: To increase infant's chance of survival; increase in intrauterine death after 38 weeks

   a. Continuously monitor uterine contractions and fetal heart rate.

      Rationale: To recognize changes and stresses that will affect labor management or delivery time via cesarean section

EDUCATIONAL

1. Explain all the tests and procedures to the mother and support person.

   Rationale: To assure that the patient is informed about her care (Many of these tests require informed consent, which means the patient must understand.)

2. Allow the mother and others concerned about the infant's and mother's condition to express their feelings.

   Rationale: To allay anxiety, which will also influence blood pressure (Begin to set up support systems in the event that more problems with the pregnancy or the baby develop.)

3. Staff-development meetings should be held for

all personnel involved with patients in the perinatal area.

Rationale: To establish data base so staff can understand some of the patient's problems and concerns and deal with them more effectively

Problem □ Delivery of infant of chronically hypertensive mother

GOAL: To recognize and treat problems common to these infants

Rationale: To recognize and treat risk factors such as gestational age, hypoglycemia and hypocalcemia, meconium staining, along with other problems, which may increase the incidence of morbidity and mortality

DIAGNOSTIC

1. Ultrasound should be done during pregnancy at the times stated earlier.

   Rationale: To detect growth-retarded infant

2. Continuously monitor fetal heart rate and uterine contractions during labor.

   Rationale: To graph fetal response to repeated stresses (contractions) and guide clinical management and to provide record for detection of fetal distress

3. Amniocentesis should be done for maturity studies; note color and consistency.

   Rationale: To determine immature fetus through lecithin-sphingomyelin ratios and to detect for meconium-stained fluid so that resuscitation team and intensive care nursery personnel can be alerted

4. Do Apgar evaluation at 1 and 5 minutes.

   Rationale: To obtain initial evaluation of newborn status

5. Have resuscitation team available in delivery room.

   Rationale: To provide safer, quicker resuscitation with trained team

THERAPEUTIC

1. Notify neonatal intensive care nursery that high-risk patient is in labor.

   Rationale: To alert them to prepare for the baby

2. Mother should be positioned in a side-lying position during labor.

   Rationale: To decrease compression of vena cava and increase circulating blood volume and oxygenation to uteroplacental blood flow

3. Administer O_2 (4 L/min) to mother if fetal heart decelerations occur. Notify physician.
   Rationale: To increase the circulating O_2 in mother's blood and to increase the baby's O_2 (The decision of how to proceed will be the physician's; may want to do further tests or cesarean section.)

4. Aspirate nose and mouth. Endotracheal suctioning is indicated if meconium is present in amniotic fluid prior to initiation of respiration.
   Rationale: To prevent aspiration pneumonia, especially since meconium is chemical irritant

5. Dry infant thoroughly and place under warmer.
   Rationale: To decrease heat loss and prevent additional problem of cold stress (Infant already has decreased reserve.)

6. Dextrostix q 1 hr × 4, q 4 hr for 24 hr (in neonatal nursery).
   Rationale: To treat hypoglycemia, which these infants are likely to develop, early

EDUCATIONAL

1. Inform mother and family about infant's condition. Provide emotional and physical support to family.
   Rationale: To help family deal with their anxiety more realistically

2. Instruct the delivery room and newborn intensive care personnel about the particular problems of these babies.
   Rationale: To provide high-quality nursing and medical care to the newborn and family

Problem □ Labor patient with essential hypertension

GOAL: To recognize deteriorating condition early and to decrease perinatal morbidity and mortality
Rationale: To assess for abruptio placentae and other problems associated with superimposed toxemia

DIAGNOSTIC

1. Review maternal history and medications during pregnancy.
   Rationale: To provide base for plan of care during labor and be alerted to possible problems with neonate

2. Continuously monitor fetal heart rate and uterine contractions
   Rationale: To be alert to change in fetal status or uterine activity, particularly late deceleration or tetanic contraction

3. Monitor patient's blood pressure every half hour minimum and other vital signs every 1 to 2 hours.
   Rationale: To check for sudden possible rise in arterial pressure

4. Do urinalysis (particularly check protein and glucose).
   Rationale: To check for preeclampsia

5. Perform neurological tests, for example, reflex checks.
   Rationale: To determine if patient is hyperreflexive and may need treatment

6. Do optical examination.
   Rationale: To check for hemorrhage and papilledema

THERAPEUTIC

1. Monitor blood pressure every 30 minutes.
   Rationale: To detect elevation of blood pressure

2. Administer IV fluids continuously during labor and delivery.
   Rationale: To provide adequate hydration (Dehydration increases blood pressure.)

3. Have a nurse with the patient continuously.
   Rationale: To observe, monitor, and chart patient's condition and to institute emergency measures should the patient become eclamptic

4. Provide quiet, restful environment.
   Rationale: To decrease stimuli that may provoke a convulsion

5. Set up safety measures (seizure precautions) in the patient's room.
   Rationale: To have medications available to shorten length of seizure
   a. Maintain adequate airway so patient can breathe.
   b. Pad side rails of bed.
      Rationale: To prevent patient from hurting self by thrashing against metal rails
   c. Place patient on side during convulsion if possible.
      Rationale: To facilitate drainage of mucus and saliva

d. Alert nursing personnel to watch for signal light.
   Rationale: To call for help if patient has a seizure
e. Note when seizure starts, where movements or stiffness starts, and progression—how long it lasts.
   Rationale: To document for physician and future reference
f. Reorient patient to environment when she awakens.
   Rationale: To reorient in unfamiliar environment after loss of consciousness
6. Assess patient's response to medication.
   Rationale: To be alert for side effects or increased effect
7. Following delivery may give oxytocin, but ergotamines should not be given.
   Rationale: To avoid ergotamine, which is a generalized vasoconstrictor

EDUCATIONAL
1. Inform patient about the labor room, the various pieces of equipment present, and the treatments or procedures done.
   Rationale: To allay anxiety and reduce blood pressure
2. Give information also to family or support person present and include them in treatment plan.
   Rationale: To make this a positive experience
3. Educate staff about care of patients with hypertension and processes involved.
   Rationale: To provide better, more effective care and decrease complications arising from essential hypertension

Problem □ Follow-up care of postpartum hypertensive women

GOAL: To prevent "target organ" damage (cardiovascular, CNS, renal, retinopathy) and to delay progress and control disease
Rationale: To limit damage to vulnerable organs with proper medical treatment

DIAGNOSTIC
1. Perform yearly physical examination including retinal examination, laboratory studies for organ involvement, vital signs recorded, weight.
   Rationale: To detect problems early and avert further complications
2. Other tests and laboratory studies to be done include:
   a. Electrocardiogram—to establish a baseline
   b. Chest x-ray film—to determine cardiac size
   c. Urinalysis, BUN, specific gravity, and protein studies—to indicate renal function

THERAPEUTIC
1. Report laboratory data and vital signs to physician if abnormal for patient.
   Rationale: To prescribe medications to control blood pressure
2. Advise patient in balanced diet appropriate for age, weight, and body build and suggest weight reduction if necessary.
   Rationale: To prevent obesity, which will reduce the risk of cardiovascular problems and decrease cardiac work load
3. Arrange for blood pressure to be checked periodically every 2 months. May have visiting nurse come to patient's home to check blood pressure if transportation is a problem.
   Rationale: To detect progression of disease early in onset

EDUCATIONAL
1. Instruct patient about medications to be taken, time to be taken, other medications to avoid, specific side effects to be alert for, and purpose of medication.
   Rationale: To increase patient's willingness to follow prescribed therapy
2. Help patient select suitable means of birth control. Oral contraceptives should not be used.
   Rationale:
   To assure consistent use of birth control method by having the woman select it herself
   To inform the patient that oral contraceptives are contraindicated in patients with hypertension, thrombophlebitis, or cerebrovascular accident
   To help the patient plan her pregnancies for the maximal benefit of the baby and least detriment to self
   To consider sterilization since this disease is progressive
3. Instruct patient about methods to assist in lowering blood pressure: rest, avoid emotional

upsets, anxiety, weight at accepted limits for height, and avoid cigarette smoking.

Rationale: To avoid increase in blood pressure

REFERENCES

1. Arias, F.: Expansion of intravascular volume and fetal outcome in patients with chronic hypertension and pregnancy, Am. J. Obstet. Gynecol. **123**(6):610, 1975.
2. Assali, N. S., and Brinkman, C. R., III: Disorders of maternal circulatory and respiratory adjustments. In Assali, N. S., editor: Pathophysiology of gestation. I: maternal disorders, New York, 1972, Academic Press, Inc., p. 270.
3. Barnes, C. G.: Medical disorders in obstetric practice, ed. 4, Oxford, England, 1974, Blackwell Scientific Publications.
4. Bear, R. A., and Erenrich, N.: Essential hypertension and pregnancy, Can. Med. Assoc. J. **118**:936, 1978.
5. Chapman, N. L.: Antepartum assessment: the oxytocin challenge test and nonstressed heart rate testing, J. Obstet. Gynecol. Nurs., September/October (Suppl.), p. 745, 1976.
6. Chelsey, L. C.: Remote prognosis after eclampsia. In Katz, A. I., et al., editors: Hypertension in pregnancy: perspectives in nephrology and hypertension, New York, 1976, John Wiley & Sons, Inc., p. 31.
7. Chelsey, L. C.: Hypertensive disorders in pregnancy, New York, 1978, Appleton-Century-Crofts, p. 524.
8. Connaughton, J. F., Kaufmann, B. E., and Soffronoff, E. C.: Intravascular volume determinations and fetal outcome in hypertensive diseases in pregnancy, Am. J. Obstet. Gynecol. **127**(1):4, 1977.
9. Crane, J. P., Savage, J. P., and Arias, F.: A high-risk pregnancy management protocol, Am. J. Obstet. Gynecol. **125**(2):227, 1976.
10. Davey, D. A., and Knutzen, V. K.: Hypertension in pregnancy and perinatal mortality, S. Afr. Med. J. **51**(19):675, 1977.
11. Friedman, E. A., and Neff, R. K.: Pregnancy hypertension: a systematic evaluation of clinical diagnostic criteria, Littleton, 1977, PSG Publishing Co., Inc.
12. Gruenwald, P.: Intrauterine growth. In Stave, U., editor: Perinatal physiology, New York, 1978, Plenum Publishing Corp. p. 1.
13. Guyton, A. C.: Textbook of medical physiology, ed. 4, Philadelphia, 1971, W. B. Saunders Co., p. 1001.
14. Haynes, D. M.: Medical complications during pregnancy, New York, 1969, McGraw-Hill Book Co., p. 676.
15. Jones, M. B.: Hypertensive disorders of pregnancy, J. Obstet. Gynecol. Nurs. **8**(2):92, 1979.
16. Mac Gillivray, I., and Campbell, D. M.: A prospective study of factors affecting intrauterine growth (with an emphasis on blood pressure and diuretics). In Katz, A. I., Lindheimer, M. D., and Zuspan, F. P., editors: Hypertension in pregnancy: perspectives in nephrology and hypertension, New York, 1976, John Wiley & Sons, Inc., p. 23.
17. McMahon, F. G.: Management of essential hypertension, Mount Kisco, N.Y., 1978, Futura Publishing Co., Inc., p. 459.
18. Mendelson, C. L.: Disease in pregnancy, Philadelphia, 1960, F. A. Davis Co., p. 371.
19. Merrell, D. A.: Hypertension in pregnancy, S. Afr. Med. J. **53**(24):985, 1978.
20. Miller, F. N., Jr.: Peery and Miller's pathology, ed. 3, Boston, 1978, Little, Brown & Co., p. 998.
21. Page, E. W.: The hypertensive disorders of pregnancy, Springfield, Ill., 1953, Charles C Thomas, Publisher.
22. Perloff, D. L., and Roberts, J. M.: Hypertension and obstetrician-gynecologist, Am. J. Obstet. Gynecol. **127**(3):316, 1977.
23. Pildes, R. S.: Metabolic and endocrine disorders. In Behrman, R. E., editor: Neonatal-perinatal medicine, St. Louis, 1977, The C. V. Mosby Co.
24. Pritchard, J. A., and Whalley, P. J.: High risk pregnancy and reproductive outcome. In Gluck, L., editor: Modern perinatal medicine, Chicago, 1974, Year Book Medical Publishers, Inc., p. 449.
25. Redman, C. W., et al.: Fetal outome in trial of antihypertensive treatment in pregnancy, Lancet **2**(7989):753, 1976.
26. Schewitz, L. J., Rodriguez, G. A., and Voyewidka, I. L.: Dietary sodium chloride in pregnant hypertensive patients: a preliminary report. In Katz, A. I., Lindheimer, M. D., and Zuspan, F. P., editors: Hypertension in pregnancy: perspectives in nephrology and hypertension, New York, 1976, John Wiley & Sons, Inc.
27. Schreiner, R. L., editor: Care of the newborn, Indianapolis, 1978, Indiana University School of Medicine, p. 198.
28. Snaith, L., and Szekely, P.: Heart disease and pregnancy, Edinburgh, 1974, Churchill Livingstone.
29. Zamit, R.: The renin-angiotension system, S. Afr. Med. J. **53**(24):974, 1978.

BIBLIOGRAPHY

Ascher, B. H.: Maternal anxiety in pregnancy and fetal homeostasis, J. Obstet. Gynecol. Neonat. Nurs. **7**:18, 1978.

Chelsey, L. C.: Disorders of the kidney, fluids, and electrolytes. In Assali, N. S., editor: Pathophysiology of gestation. I: maternal disorders, New York, 1972, Academic Press, Inc., p. 356.

Cibils, L. A.: The placenta and newborn infant in hypertensive conditions, J. Obstet. Gynecol. **118**(2):256, 1974.

Curet, L. B., and Olson, R. W.: Evaluation of a program of bed rest in the treatment of chronic hypertension in pregnancy, Obstet. Gynecol. **53**(3):336, 1979.

Datta, S., et al.: Propranolol and parturition, Obstet. Gynecol. **51**(5):577, 1978.

Finnerty, F. A., Jr.: Hypertension in pregnancy, Angiology **28**(8):535, 1977.

Mac Gillivray, I.: Blood pressure in pregnancy. In Philipp, E. E., Barnes, J., and Newton, M., editors: Scientific foundations of obstetrics and gynecology, Philadelphia, 1970, F. A. Davis Co.

Pritchard, J. A., and MacDonald, P.: Williams obstetrics, ed. 15, New York, 1976, Appleton-Century-Crofts.

Seftel, H. C.: Epidemiology of hypertension in developed and developing populations, S. Afr. Med. J. **53**(24):957, 1978.

Thomas, R. D., et al.: Abnormal sodium transport in leukocytes from patients with essential hypertension and the effect of treatment, Clin. Sci. Mol. Med. **48**(Suppl.):169s, 1975.

Chapter 10

Herpes simplex virus

Shelia K. Adams

Herpes simplex virus (HSV) belongs to a group of large DNA viruses that commonly affect humans and animals. Other herpesviruses known to cause disease in humans are cytomegalovirus, Epstein-Barr virus, and varicella zoster. Syndromes associated with HSV have been noted in the medical literature since 100 AD. From the first descriptions through 1920, the pathology and clinical picture of various forms of HSV were studied, and finally HSV was isolated. Over the next 40 years, some advances in understanding herpes were due to increasing sophistication in culturing herpes and studying the virus. Notable realizations during this period were that pronounced HSV infections occurred even in the presence of antibodies in the host's serum, that the disease could be without clinical manifestations, and that HSV cross-infection occurred in hospitals.

With the biochemical and immunological breakthroughs occurring in the late 1960's and the postulated relationship of herpes to cancer in humans, a new surge of interest in HSV has developed. It became possible to differentiate two antigenic types of HSV (HSV 1 and HSV 2). Early reports typically correlated HSV 1 with infections above the waist and HSV 2 with infections below the waist.[17] In 1974 Chang and associates[8] first described the association of genital infection with HSV 1, refuting the formal conviction that only HSV 2 infected the genital region.

Herpes infections are of epidemic proportions. It is the second most common venereal disease, surpassed in frequency only by gonorrhea. Herpes is the most frequent culprit in lesions of the female genitals and second only to syphilis as a cause of male genital lesions. Herpes infection in obstetrical patients has been linked with spontaneous abortions, stillborn infants, congenital malformations, and ominous neonatal infections. The frequently grave prognosis associated with fetal or neonatal infection and the potential for prevention make HSV a serious perinatal concern.[17]

While a variety of experimental treatments for HSV are currently under study, the most recent advances in the management of the perinatal patient center around early diagnosis and prevention of neonatal involvement. Following a brief overview of recent research contributing to the present understanding of this disease entity, a protocol aimed at education, prevention, and diagnosis will be presented at the end of this chapter.

PERINATAL INCIDENCE

Batignani[5] in Italy and Hass[13] in the United States first described neonatal infections due to HSV. One hundred and fifty-six cases were reported in the next 35 years (1934-1969). From 1970 to 1975, 155 cases were reported, which is approximately 30 cases per year. It is estimated that there are at least 120 cases per year, but many of these go unreported and/or undiagnosed. Asymptomatic neonatal HSV is thought to be rare, but in many cases the "classic" symptoms may not be apparent—the characteristic stigmata of herpes—vesicular lesions of mouth, skin, and eyes.[21]

Nahmias and Tomeh[18] reported that in 198 cases of neonatal HSV infections 62% died, 16% survived with sequelae, and 22% were without apparent sequelae. These figures are comparable to other reports that generally find a mortality and morbidity rate of 75% in diagnosed neonatal herpes. They further estimated a 50% infection rate of infants delivered vaginally or after rupture of the membranes equal to or greater than 6 hours in mothers with active genital herpes.

Herpes neonatal infections are estimated approximately once in 7500 deliveries. Its occurrence seems to vary inversely with the socioeconomic status of the population considered. Positive serological evidence of previous infections with HSV 2 has been demonstrated in 80% to 90% of women from population samples of lower socioeconomic groups. Less than half of that percentage was found in samples of private patients. Virological and cytological cervical samples yield about 1% positive findings in lower socioeconomic class gravidas and about one tenth that amount in more affluent populations. Antepartal incidence seems to increase with advancing pregnancy. Neonatal HSV is diagnosed more frequently in infants born to primigravidas. Premature infants seem to be more frequently and more seriously affected. These findings are thought to be related to defects in cell-mediated immunity.[16] While it is possible to differentiate HSV 1 and 2 infections, there does not appear to be significant clinical difference between HSV 1 and 2 in neonatal infections.[12] Herpes 2 is the organism isolated in 90% of the infants infected with HSV and in 95% of genitally infected females.[23]

CHARACTERISTICS OF THE VIRUS

The herpes virion is relatively large with a central DNA coil, shaped like a doughnut, with proteins arranged in the form of a barbell passing through the opening of the DNA formation. Protein layers (the capsid) surround this core, which is then encapsulated by a fibrous covering called the tegument. This entire particle is then covered by a membrane known as the envelope, which is a loose but impermeable coat containing at least 12 glycoproteins, lipids, and polyamines. The envelope of the virion has been implicated as the infectious unit, but this remains poorly understood. One theory is that the envelope enables the virus to endure various stresses and is important in absorbing cells. The virion is negatively charged. Herpes 1 and 2 are now readily distinguished, but their antibodies are not as easily

differentiated (particularly in individuals who have had both types of HSV). Some investigators postulate the presence of ''intermediate'' antibodies.

The wide range in the clinical spectrum of the disease and the ability of the virus to persist in its host in a dormant or subclinical (but not readily recoverable) form is puzzling. One theory that may eventually explain these phenomena and the questionable relationship of HSV to cancer is that the virus may behave in at least two ways after entering a cell: (1) it can set up a productive infection that results in viral progeny and host cell death and (2) alternately, nonproductive infection is thought to result in perpetration of the virus, survival of the host cell, and possibly RNA alterations. The ability of HSV to persist in its host and cause recurrences of symptoms remains poorly understood. It has been theorized that the virus could persist after the initial infection in nerve roots, lymphocytes, at the local site of infection, or at more distant sites.[17]

EPIDEMIOLOGY

The spread of HSV by direct contact with the lesions or oral or genital secretions of an infected person is well documented. In both types of HSV there is suggestive evidence that infrequently airborne droplets may also transmit the disease. The contaminated hands of professionals are a vehicle in nosocomial infections. Infection from the lesion or secretions of a person with active HSV can be directly or indirectly transmitted in a variety of ways.[18] Sheward[26] reports passage of HSV 1 from the lip of a father to the perineum of an infant, supposedly indirectly spread through common use of a tube of zinc oxide ointment. In 1968, Nahmias and associates[19] reported nonsexual spread of HSV 1 from the mouth to the genitals.

Reportedly, the most frequent mode by which the newborn or fetus is infected is through contact with the infected maternal genital tract during birth or via ascending infection after rupture of the membranes. Some cases reported suggest transplacental infection with maternal viremia and the possibility of ascending infection over intact membranes.[1,29]

While HSV 1 was previously considered to be spread through oral secretions or contact with the lesions and HSV 2 through sexual activity, the increased incidence of oral-genital sex is changing this pattern. In 1977, Wolontis and Jeansson[30] documented the correlation of the type of HSV with the age of the patient; they noted that HSV 1 was responsible for HSV genital infections in approximately one third of patients between 15 and 24 years of age, while it was responsible for infections in only 7% of patients over 25 years of age. Their research demonstrated that 16% of total genital HSV infections were of type 1 origin. That year Chang[7] again demonstrated that one third of young patients wtih genital herpes were infected with HSV 1, supporting the thesis that the type of HSV is not specific to location of a given body region but that lesions of either etiology occur at locations dependent on the mode and site of transmission.

PATHOLOGY

Cytological examination of scrapings from the base of herpetic vesicles frequently reveals the classic changes of multinucleated giant cells with intranuclear inclusion bodies. In disseminated disease, focal coagulative necrosis, usually without inflammatory infiltrates, is characteristic. Nuclear inclusions peripheral to the necrotic areas are usually seen.[18]

CLINICAL MANIFESTATIONS

Eight-five percent of primary HSV 2 infections in females are subclinical.[15] The usual incubation period is from 2 to 7 days. Primary infections that are symptomatic usually persist for 7 to 14 days. Both HSV 1 and 2 affect tissues of ectodermal embryonic origin.[23] Clinical primary infection with HSV 2 begins as itching and tingling pain over the site, which rapidly progresses to vesicular eruptions that rupture, forming shallow ulcers that are exquisitely painful. The labia is the most common site with the cervix and perineum frequently involved. The lesions heal without scarring if there is no secondary infection. Disseminated disease in adults is extremely rare.

Recurrent HSV infections are usually not as severe clinically. They may be precipitated by any stress, the most frequent being ultraviolet rays, fever, psychological stress, fatigue, trauma, and hormonal changes such as pregnancy and the menses.[4]

Amstey and associates[3] reported that genital HSV infections in pregnancy are more severe and persist longer. He[2] has suggested that the more pronounced severity and duration of HSV lesions in pregnant patients may be due to effects of the increased amounts of hormones (estriol, progesterone, HCG, and HPL), increased blood perfusion, and an altered immune state and/or increased infectivity of the virus owing to the hormonal changes. Present related research is inconclusive but potentially promising.

Infection of the embryo or fetus may result in spontaneous abortion, stillbirth, or congenital defects as previously mentioned. These outcomes have been reported sporadically but have not been well studied. Infection of the neonate may present in a variety of ways. Subclinical cases are believed to be much less common. Localized infections in the neonate commonly involve the eye, ranging from conjunctivitis and keratitis to chorioretinitis, sometimes resulting in blindness. Skin lesions, when present, are characteristic vesicular lesions that rapidly ulcerate and become denuded. They are often found on the presenting part but may occur anywhere. Other lesions less frequently described are red patches, erythematous macular rash, and petechiae. Occasionally lesions are present orally. Local CNS involvement with encephalitis is possible and carries a poor prognosis. Disseminated HSV involves the viscera, most frequently the adrenal glands and liver. Other common sites of dissemination are the brain, spleen, trachea, lungs, esophagus, stomach, kidneys, pancreas, heart, and bone marrow. Often external signs are absent and nonspecific constitutional signs herald the onset of a stormy and rapidly deteriorating course often ending in convulsions, shock, or disseminated intravascular coagulation. Few infants survive disseminated HSV infections.[8]

The unpredictability of the natural course of HSV 2 in the neonate is well illustrated by Gershon and associates[11] in their description in 1972 of a perinatally infected neonate with CNS and cutaneous involvement. They reported following him to 2 years of age and noted the absence of any sequelae, assessing his growth and development to be within normal limits. They note with interest that had this infant been treated with a DNA inhibitor his favorable outcome might well have been attributed to the chemotherapy.

Komorous, Wheeler, and Briggaman[14], a group of dermatologists, reported two cases of neonatal

HSV attributed to intrauterine infection. They included a review of seven similar cases and concluded that the severity of clinical findings and sequelae in neonatal HSV did not correlate well with the timing in gestation and duration of maternal infection, unlike the correlation of these variables with the effects of rubella and cytomegalovirus infections. They document a range of outcomes as spontaneous abortion, subclinical infection, severe congenital malformation, and mild disease with minimal sequela. They suggest that this wide range of effects and lack of correlation with timing, severity, and duration of HSV may indicate the relationship of outcome to imperfectly defined immune mechanisms.

DIAGNOSIS

The best aid in diagnosing HSV in the perinatal patient is a high index of suspicion; the starting point is a thorough history and physical examination. Differential diagnosis in the female presenting with vulvovaginal lesions of herpetic appearance includes trichomonas, syphilis, gonorrhea, chancroid, lymphopathia venereum, pruritus vulvae, abrasions, and leukoplakia.[23] The diagnostic procedures for excluding these entities will not be included here. HSV is an opportunistic virus and is frequently found in combination with other vaginal infections, particularly trichomoniasis, hemophilus infections, and condyloma acuminatum.[9]

Laboratory tests vary in their ability to provide information leading to an unequivocal diagnosis and in their availability. They fall into three broad categories: virology, cytology, and immunology. Histological examination is less frequently used, occasionally in biopsy and in autopsy specimens.[17]

Virological cultures can demonstrate growth of HSV virus specific to the type in as short a time as 24 to 48 hours. Aspirates from vesicular lesions most frequently give excellent and reliable results by this method. Samples from amniocentesis, scrapings from the base of an ulcerated lesion, cerebrospinal fluid, and tissue samples can also be used but with less productive results.[17] The diagnosis of HSV cannot be excluded on the basis of no growth.

Cytological examination, performed in the same manner as a routine Pap smear, can reveal characteristic cellular changes of HSV—multinucleated giant cells with intranuclear inclusions and ground glass appearance with chromatin changes. The advantages of the cytological examination are that it is quick, easy, inexpensive, and available almost anywhere.[9] These attributes make it an efficacious screening device. Some investigators claim that they can differentiate a primary from a recurrent infection based on the cellular changes identified cytologically.[22] A disadvantage is that diagnoses made by this means are presumptive and must be discriminated from other viral infections by correlation with the history and clinical picture.[17]

Immunological studies depend on the host's production of viral antibodies. With the exception of an immunofluorescent antibody study performed on a specimen collected much like a Pap smear, these are serological tests that vary by technique in their ability for specificity. Common procedures that fall into this group are cross-neutralization, complement fixation, immunofluorescence, and indirect hemagglutination. Results and their interpretation depend on the procedure used by the laboratory. In general, an initially low titer in the presence of symptoms indicates a primary infection. The titers rise as the patient convalesces and remain high indefinitely. Infections with high titers indicate recurrent infection. Specific antibody titers for HSV have proved particularly interesting in studying the course and effects of the disease in neonates.[17] Smith and Hanna[28] reported the finding that neonates born to mothers with recurrent infections had the same proportions of IgG antibodies as their mothers (transplacental immunity). This provided some feasible rationale for the earlier finding of Nahmias and associates[20] that neonates born to mothers with recurrent infections were not as often or as severely infected as those born to mothers with primary infections. Newborns with rising IgM titers 2 to 3 weeks after birth demonstrate perinatally acquired infections.[17]

Much present diagnostic research is purely of exploratory and academic value at this point, particularly that in immunology, but offers promising prospects for potential intervention. As newer therapies evolve, it may become much more important to make an early diagnosis and to differentiate a primary from a recurrent HSV infection.[6]

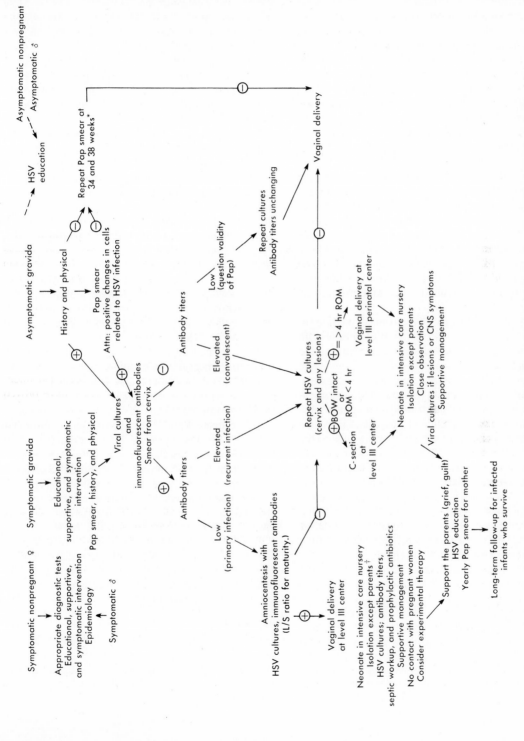

Fig. 10-1. Flowchart. * Suggested as a screening procedure, particularly in high-risk populations. † Both the mother and infant should be isolated for the duration of the hospitalization.

MANAGEMENT

As previously noted, most components of present management of perinatal HSV are directed at early diagnosis in the prenatal period (discussed above) and isolating the neonate from exposure to infection during birth and in the immediate postpartum period. Accomplishment of this latter objective has been attempted through performing abdominal deliveries of infants whose mothers are thought to be infected and who have intact membranes or recently ruptured membranes (less than 4 to 6 hours). This is still advocated although various reports and studies have not proved this to be consistently effective. It is also recommended that the newborn be isolated from any person with active HSV. Thorough handwashing by those who handle newborns is essential.

Many experimental treatments for HSV infections are currently being studied. Some reports have been promising, some have been disappointing, and many offer conflicting results. Most fall into two basic categories: immunotherapy and chemotherapy.

Immunological agents that produce passive or active immunity and those that control disease with interferon or interferon inducers are, perhaps, the most promising.

Chemotherapeutic agents, such as IDU (idoxuridine), Ara-C, and Ara-A, are being tried experimentally in systemic treatment of disseminated disease and in immunodeficient subjects. They are DNA inhibitors and are potentially quite toxic to the subjects. DNA inhibitors have been used quite successfully in ocular HSV.[17] A similar but different drug that inhibits glycoprotein synthesis, 2-DG (2-deoxy-D-glucose), is a sugar analogue used successfully in rabbits with HSV keratitis. It has generated interest because it seems less toxic than the DNA inhibitors.[24] BCG vaccination is again being studied as a preventive agent for recurrent HSV infections. A topical cream containing zinc sulfate, urea, and tannic acid is applied with ultrasound to local herpetic lesions in another form of experimental therapy.[25]

Studies of hyperthermic effects on HSV inhibition in animals suggest that there may be a future role of thermotherapy in prevention of neonatal disease. Earlier phototherapy, combined with topical vital dyes increasing the photosensitivity of HSV organisms, was advocated and used in obstetrics before falling into disfavor when implicated as possibly carcinogenic.[17]

None of the immunological or chemotherapeutical regimes just mentioned can be presently recommended for routine use in perinatal patients until well-controlled studies, demonstrating safety and effectiveness, are available.

Prevention of the spread of HSV remains the best weapon against its grave effects. Significant progress in accomplishing this goal can be realized through education of professionals and the public. Edwards[10] asserts that this is one area in which nursing can have impact independent of medicine. She suggests the need for widely based dissemination of information concerning HSV, its cause, mode of transmission, and the potential dangers of its sequelae. She further advocates that nursing "flex its muscle" in pressing for legislation that would make HSV 2 a reportable disease, noting that this is presently the case only in Massachusetts. Until better methods are developed for the prevention and treatment of HSV, health care providers must be creative in their approach to educating the public in preventive measures. Chang[7] recommends the use of condoms during intercourse with casual partners or those who have previously been infected and avoiding close contact with anyone who has suspicious lesions. Singh[27] reported that spermicidal creams were also virucidal and recommends their use to prevent spreading HSV. Detailed and specific instructions for HSV prophylaxis should be given to every gravida and every person with a present episode or history of HSV. Such instructions should be tailored to specifically match the patient's experience or lack of experience with the disease.

Based on the current knowledge of HSV presented in this chapter as a rationale, the following protocol (in the form of a detailed flow chart) is offered for prevention and management of HSV in the perinatal patient (Fig. 10-1).

REFERENCES

1. Altshuler, G.: Pathogenesis of congenital herpesvirus infection, Obstet. Gynecol. Surv. **29:**794, 1974.
2. Amstey, M. S.: Effect of pregnancy hormones on HSV and other DNA viruses, J. Obstet. Gynecol. **129:**159, 1977.

3. Amstey, M. S., Lewin, E., and Meyer, M. R.: HSV infection in the newborn, J. Obstet. Gynecol. **47:**33, 1976.
4. Anderson, F., Ushijma, R., and Larson, C.: Recurrent herpes genitalis, Obstet. Gynecol. **43:**797, 1974.
5. Batignani, A.: Conjunctive da virus erpetico in neonato, Boll. Ocul. **13:**1217, 1934.
6. Bolognese, R., et al.: Herpes virus hominis type II infections in asymptomatic pregnant women, J. Obstet. Gynecol. **48:**507, 1976.
7. Chang, T.: Genital herpes and type 1 herpes virus hominis, J.A.M.A. **238:**155, 1977.
8. Chang, T. W., Fiumara, N. J., and Weinstein, L.: Genital herpes: some clinical and laboratory observations, J.A.M.A. **229:**544, 1974.
9. Dale, R. A.: Maternal and neonatal herpes infection, J. Miss. State Med. Assoc. **27:**261, 1976.
10. Edwards, M. S.: Venereal herpes: a nursing overview, J. Obstet. Gynecol. **7:**7, 1978.
11. Gershon, A. A., Fish, I., and Brunell, P. A.: Herpes simplex infection of the newborn, Am. J. Dis. Child. **124:**739, 1972.
12. Hanshaw, J. B., and Dudgeon, J. A.: Viral disease of the fetus and newborn. In Major problems in clinical pediatrics, Philadelphia, 1978, W. B. Saunders Co., p. 153.
13. Hass, G. M.: Hepato-adrenal necrosis with intranuclear inclusion bodies: report of a case, Am. J. Pathol. **11:**127, 1935.
14. Komorous, J. M., Wheeler, C. E., and Briggaman, R. A.: Intrauterine herpes simplex infections, Arch. Dermatol. **113:**918, 1977.
15. McIndoe, W., and Churchouse, W.: Herpes simplex of the lower genital tract in the female, Aust. N.Z. J. Obstet. Gynecol. **12:**14, 1972.
16. Nahmias, A. J., Alford, C., and Korones, S.: Infection of the newborn with HSV, Adv. Pediatr. **17:**185, 1970.
17. Nahmias, A. J., and Roizman, R.: Infection with HSV 1 and 2, N. Engl. J. Med. **289:**667, 719, 781, 1973.
18. Nahmias, A. J., and Tomeh, M. O.: HSV infection, Curr. Probl. Pediatr. **4:**1, 1974.
19. Nahmias, A., et al.: Genital infection with HSV 1 and 2 in children, Pediatr. **42:**659, 1968.
20. Nahmias, A. J., et al.: Perinatal risk associated with maternal HSV infection, Am. J. Obstet. Gynecol. **110:**825, 1971.
21. Nahmias, A. J., et al.: HSV infection of the fetus and newborn, Prog. Clin. Biol. Res. **3:**63, 1975.
22. Ng, A. B. P., Reagan, J. W., and Yen, S. S.: Herpes genitalis: clinical and cytopathological experience with 256 patients, Obstet. Gynecol. **36:**645, 1970.
23. Poste, G., Hawkins, D. F., and Thomlinson, J.: Herpes virus hominus infection of the female genital tract, Obstet. Gynecol. **40:**871, 1972.
24. Ray, E. K., Halpern, B. L., Levitan, D. B., and Blough, H. A.: A new approach to viral chemotherapy. Lancet **2**(7882):680, 1974.
25. Rubin, W.: Newer agents for genital herpes simplex infections, Ob. Gyn. News. **13:**2, 1978.
26. Sheward, J. D.: Perianal herpes simplex, Lancet **1:**315, 1961.
27. Singh, B., Postic, B., and Cutter, J. C.: Virucidal effect of certain chemical contraceptives on type II HSV, Am. J. Obstet. Gynecol. **126:**422, 1976.
28. Smith, R. N., and Hanna, L.: Herpes virus infections in pregnancy: a comparison of neutralizing antibody test in mothers and their infants, Am. J. Obstet. Gynecol. **119:**314, 1974.
29. Von Herzen, J., and Benivschke, K.: Unexpected disseminated herpes simplex infection in a newborn, Obstet. Gynecol. p. 728, 1977.
30. Wolontis, S., and Jeansson, S.: Correlation of HSV Type 1 and 2 with clinical features of infection, J. Infect Dis. **135:**28, 1977.

SECTION THREE

INTRAPARTUM PROTOCOLS

Chapter 11

Fetal monitoring

Susan M. Tucker

The status of the fetus can be monitored biophysically, biochemically, and by electronic fetal heart rate monitors. Biophysical monitoring techniques include ultrasonography, radiography, amniography, amnioscopy, and fetoscopy. Biochemical monitoring techniques include urinary estriol determinations, maternal blood studies (human placental lactogen [HPL], unconjugated and plasma estriols, maternal enzymes [alkaline phosphatase, oxytocinase], Coombs' test), and amniocentesis. Fetal status is assessed by electronic fetal heart rate monitoring during the antepartum period via the nonstress and contraction stress tests and during the course of labor.

In this chapter each of these techniques will be described and protocols for their use presented. The reader should keep in mind that no single technique is an adequate indicator of fetal status and that the use of multiple parameters as well as clinical judgment is essential to the promotion of optimum perinatal health.

BIOPHYSICAL FETAL MONITORING

The biophysical monitoring techniques described in this section include ultrasonography, radiography, amniography, amnioscopy, and fetoscopy. The uses of these techniques are listed in the following outline.[11,14]

A. Ultrasonography
   1. Diagnosis of early pregnancy
   2. Measurement of biparietal diameters and crown-rump length to assess fetal gestational age*
   3. Localization of the placenta

---

*Serial measurements required.

4. Identification of multiple gestation
   5. Detection of fetal malformations
   6. Confirmation of fetal position
   7. Diagnosis of
      a. Molar pregnancy
      b. Adnexal tumors
      c. Ectopic pregnancy
      d. Fetal death
B. Radiography.
   1. Identification of fetal skeletal parts (16 weeks)
   2. Diagnosis of multiple pregnancy (second trimester)
   3. Detection of fetal malformations (third trimester)
C. Amniography
   1. Diagnosis of hydramnios, oligohydramnios, placenta previa, and the soft tissue silhouette of the fetus
   2. Identification of the fetal gastrointestinal tract owing to fetal swallowing
D. Amnioscopy
   1. Identification of meconium staining of the amniotic fluid
   2. Visualization of the presenting part after rupture of the membranes.
   3. Collection of fetal blood sample for blood gas analysis
E. Fetoscopy
   1. Visualization of portions of the fetus directly.
   2. Collection of fetal blood samples

Ultrasound

In 1958 Dr. Ian Donald of Glasgow, Scotland first used ultrasound techniques in the practice of obstetrics. This procedure utilizes sound waves that exceed the audible range for human hearing and create an echo when they traverse an object at a 90-degree angle. These echos are recorded as dots of light on a cathode-ray oscilloscope screen. The density and

159

acoustic impedance met by the beam of sound directed at tissue surfaces causes a change in the intensity and brightness of the dots. The display of dots is photographed and displayed on echograms for a permanent record following the scanning of a specific region.

To date diagnostic ultrasound has not been associated with either maternal or fetal untoward effects. Thus it can be used frequently to acquire diagnostic data without jeopardizing the fetus or the mother.

There are several methods of ultrasound utilized today in obstetrics: A mode, B mode, Doppler ultrasound, M mode, and real-time imaging. The uses of these methods of ultrasonic diagnosis follow:

A. A mode (amplitude mode)
   1. Measurement of biparietal diameters (BPD) of the fetal skull (16 to 28 weeks)
   2. Measurement of the fetal chest diameter
B. B mode (brightness mode): gray scale
   1. Display tissue texture as well organ contours
   2. Diagnosis of early pregnancy
   3. Confirmation of fetal lie, position, and presenting part
   4. Identification of multiple gestation
   5. Localization of placenta
   6. Assessment of placental volumetric growth
   7. Diagnosis of molar pregnancy
   8. Detection of anomalies such as anencephaly and hydrocephalus
   9. Diagnosis of fetal death
  10. Diagnosis of ectopic pregnancy
  11. Diagnosis of hydramnios
C. Doppler ultrasound method
   1. Monitoring fetal heart rate during pregnancy and labor
   2. Localization of the placenta
   3. Determination of the point of entry of the umbilical cord into the placenta
D. M mode (motion mode)
   1. Echocardiography
   2. Detection of cardiac anomalies
E. Real-time imaging
   1. Visualization of fetal limb movements, respiratory movements, and myocardial contractions
   2. Display fetal presentation, biparietal diameters, and placental location and amniocentesis guidance

In A mode the ultrasound penetrates the fetal skull, and the sounds reflected by the tissue interfaces are recorded as spikes on a horizontal baseline. The distance between spikes reflects the distance between the lateral cranial walls. B mode ultrasound produces a two-dimensional image. The brightness and position of the dots correspond to the echo strength and position of the tissue interfaces. Doppler ultrasound is used to detect sound from moving rather than stationary surfaces. Examination with a small ultrasound stethoscope can provide information about fetal heart sounds, pulsations of the umbilical artery in the cord, placental sounds, maternal arteries, and movement of fetal extremities. In M mode ultrasonography time is depicted on the horizontal plane, and the distance from the transducer is illustrated in the vertical plane. Prior to delivery fetal cardiography is unreliable because of positional variations. Real-time ultrasound using gray-scale and linear array imaging allows continuous cross-sectional motion pictures of internal structures. The main benefit of real time is that it takes a fraction of the time as compared with the B mode static modality, and this outweighs the slightly poorer resolution. Portable units are used in physicians' offices for cursory screening of the gravid uterus and amniocentesis guidance, and they are found with increasing frequency in the delivery suite to identify fetal presentation and placenta location.[11,14]

Protocols

Problem □ Preparation of the patient for diagnostic ultrasound

GOAL: To reduce the patient's anxiety and provide for optimal resolution in the ultrasonogram

DIAGNOSTIC

1. Determine what the patient understands about the procedure.
   Rational: To begin teaching at the patient's level of understanding

THERAPEUTIC

1. Request the patient refrain from voiding for 3 hours prior to the procedure.
   Rationale: To promote a full bladder, which serves as an anatomical landmark and improves ultrasonic resolution as well as elevates the presenting head so that a BPD measurement can be made
2. Request patient drink 1 liter or more of fluid 1 to 2 hours prior to the procedure.
   Rationale: To promote a full bladder

EDUCATIONAL

1. Explain the procedure to the patient using handouts and diagrams.
   Rationale: To provide a basis for realistic expectations and reduce anxiety
2. Provide the patient with rationale for requiring a full bladder in order to perform the procedure.
   Rationale: To prepare the patient for some discomfort caused by the pressure of the presenting part on the bladder

Problem □ Performance of ultrasound procedure

GOAL: To acquire diagnostic information and provide for maternal and fetal comfort and safety

DIAGNOSTIC

1. Verify that the patient has a full bladder.
   Rationale: To improve ultrasound resolution and help elevate the presenting head so that a BPD measurement can be made

THERAPEUTIC

1. Position the patient in a recumbent position with a pillow beneath the knees and a firm pillow beneath the buttocks.
   Rationale: To assist in elevating the presenting part (Comfort is important since the procedure lasts about 30 minutes.)
2. Mineral oil is applied to the skin surface.
   Rationale: To reduce friction and help move the transducer over the abdomen; also acts as a conductive medium for the ultrasound
3. The transducer is moved up and down over the gravid uterus every 1 to 2 cm in the longitudinal plane.
   Rationale: To assure visualization of all fetal parts in the long axis
4. The transducer carriage is moved to the side of the patient.
   Rationale: To perform transverse scanning
5. The transducer is moved transversely every 1 to 2 cm above the symphysis pubis.
   Rationale: To assure visualization of all fetal parts
6. The location of each sonogram is keyed and printed on the film. (Longitudinal sonograms are identified as to the number of centimeters to the right or left of the midline; transverse sonograms are identified as to the number of centimeters below the xiphoid process or above the symphysis pubis.)
   Rationale: To aid in interpretation
7. When the procedure is complete, assist the patient in dressing and provide an opportunity to empty the bladder.
   Rationale: To provide for safety (the possibility of supine hypotension should be considered) and promote comfort
8. The ultrasonograms should be then read by the radiologist and the findings reported to the patient's physician.
   Rationale: To ensure maximum value of the procedure

EDUCATIONAL

1. Explain to the patient that the results of the examination will be available from her physician.
   Rationale: To integrate findings into the total concept of obstetrical care
2. Share the sonogram with the patient following the presentation of findings by the physician.
   Rationale: To share with families the films of their expected infant.

Radiography

Radiological assessment for fetal size, maturity, and placental localization has generally been replaced by ultrasound. Should cephalopelvic disproportion be suspected, x-ray pelvimetry may be done prior to labor or during labor if failure of descent or arrest of descent occurs.

Amniography

Contrast medium is instilled into the amniotic fluid during amniocentesis to visualize radiographically the uterine contents. Indications for amniography include suspected hydramnios, oligohydramnios, placenta previa, and soft tissue deformities. Scalp edema can be clearly demonstrated as well as fetal swallowing, fetal attitude, and protuberance of the abdomen. Subtle neural tube defects may also be identified with amniography.

This invasive technique utilizing ionizing radiation is usually not done if ultrasonography can give comparable information.[10,14]

Amnioscopy

Direct visualization of amniotic fluid through the membranes with a cone-shaped hollow tube requires that the cervix be sufficiently dilated. This is not a widely practiced screening procedure for the presence of meconium in amniotic fluid because of the variations in clinical significance of meconium passage.

Fetoscopy

Direct visualization of the fetus via transabdominal insertion of a small caliber endoscope is currently done by only a few researchers. Diagnosis of fetal hemoglobinopathies, hemophilia, and immunodeficient diseases has been done by taking fetal blood specimens and skin biopsies. Fetal malformations have also been identified with this invasive procedure. Investigation of fetal diagnosis by fetoscopy was initiated in 1973 initially in patients about to undergo pregnancy termination. Since then it has been done on a selected number of patients as of January 1980. J. C. Hobbins and M. J. Mahoney have performed 127 fetoscopies with 99 patients continuing their pregnancies; 28 elected to terminate based on the results. Five pregnancies resulted in spontaneous abortion, which was considered a procedure-related loss. Seven pregnancies resulted in premature delivery between 28 and 35 weeks' gestation with all infants surviving. Fetal mortality rate caused by the procedure is considered to be between 5% and 6% at the present time. Further experience with diagnostic fetoscopy without termination of pregnancy and long-term follow up are necessary to provide information concerning outcomes.[11]

BIOCHEMICAL MONITORING

The biochemical monitoring techniques described in this section include urine estriol determinations, maternal blood studies, and amniotic fluid analysis. Table 11-1 presents a summary of biochemical monitoring techniques.

Urinary studies

Estrogen production increases throughout the gestational period. After the twentieth week of gestation, approximately 90% of the estrogen produced from fetal precursors is converted to estriol by the placenta, conjugated by the maternal liver, and excreted in the maternal urine. In that the production of estriol depends both on the integrity of the fetus as well as the placenta, estriol determinations are used to assess fetal well-being.

Estriol assays are utilized in high-risk pregnancies. In patients with toxemia of pregnancy estriol determinations are done to assure rising values indicating the fetus is thriving and providing a data base on which the pregnancy can be continued until the fetus is mature, whereas serial estriol determinations are used during the diabetic pregnancy to detect fetal distress and impending fetal death.

Daily urinary estriol determinations are usually done to ascertain a pattern of estriol excretion. Singular estriol measurements are of little or no value, and measurements taken at long intervals provide little data reflective of fetal well-being.

Table 11-1. Summary of biochemical monitoring techniques*

Test	Results	Significance of findings
Urine estriols	High and rising levels	General fetal well-being
	Low and falling levels	Possible fetal jeopardy
Maternal blood		
Human placental lactogen	High levels	Large diabetic fetus; multiple gestation
	Low levels	Threatened abortion; IUGR; postmaturity
Unconjugated and plasma estriol	High and rising levels	General fetal well-being
	Low and falling levels	Possible fetal jeopardy
Heat-stable alkaline phosphatase	Normally elevated during pregnancy	Poor correlation with fetal outcome
Oxytocinase	200 to 400 U at term	General fetal well-being
	Low levels	Associated with fetal death; postmaturity; IUGR
Coombs' test	Titer of 1:8 and rising	Significant Rh sensitization
Amniocentesis		
Color	Meconium	Possible hypoxia/asphyxia
Lung profile		Fetal lung maturity
L/S ratio	>2.0	
Phosphatidylglycerol (PGL)	Present	
Desaturated acetone- precipitated lecithin		
Phosphatidylinositol (PI)		
Creatinine	>2.0/100 ml	Gestational age>36 weeks
Bilirubin (ΔOD 450)	<0.015	Gestational age >36 weeks; normal pregnancy
	High levels	Fetal hemolytic disease in isoimmunized pregnancies
Lipid cells	>10%	Gestational age >35 weeks
Alpha fetoprotein	High levels after 15 weeks' gestation	Open neural tube defect
Osmolality	Decline after 20 weeks' gestation	Advancing nonspecific gestational age
Genetic disorders	Dependent on cultured cells for	
Sex-linked	karyotype and enzymatic activity	
Chromosomal		
Metabolic		

*In an effort to summarize these studies in tabular form, generalizations must be made. The reader is referred to the text for a complete description. Adapted from Tucker, S. M.: Fetal monitoring and fetal assessment in the high-risk pregnancy, St. Louis, 1978, The C. V. Mosby Co.

Protocols

Problem □ Preparation of the patient for urinary estriol determination

GOAL: To reduce anxiety and assure accurate valid results

DIAGNOSTIC

1. Determine what the patient knows about the procedure.
   Rationale: To begin teaching at the patient's level of understanding

THERAPEUTIC

1. Label the container for the 24-hour urine collection with the patient's name, other identifying data, the date, and the time of starting and completing the collection.
   Rationale: To accurately interpret the results
2. Have patient empty her bladder and discard urine.
   Rationale: To ensure that all urine collected during a period is produced during that period

EDUCATIONAL

1. Explain the entire procedure to the patient.
   a. Provide rationale explaining the need for serial determination (use visual aids).
   b. Provide rationale explaining the need for all urine collected in a 24-hour period.
   c. Reinforce the need to refrigerate the specimen.
   Rationale: To ensure the patient's compliance with the diagnostic regime
2. Provide all instructions in written form to the patient following the inital discussion.
   Rationale: To provide reference material for patient to check when questions arise later

Problem □ Acquisition of a 24-hour urine specimen for estriol determination

GOAL: To determine estriol level

DIAGNOSTIC

1. Levels of urinary creatinine are measured to ensure 24-hour collection is complete (mean value during the last month of pregnancy is 1.35 gm ± 0.14 gm SD). Creatinine excretion is relatively constant over a 24-hour period.[13]
   Rationale: To check for levels below 1.0 gm in a 24-hour urine collection, which would indicate an unreliable urine collection in the absence of renal pathology
2. Determine the estriol excretion pattern.[1,2]
   a. Normal: pattern follows a mean without falls exceeding 40% and is usually above 12 mg/24 hr.
   b. Elevated: a value consistently above the mean for a given gestational age.
   c. Falling: a value that suddenly drops 40% off the mean.
   Rationale: To assess fetal well-being through excretion pattern

THERAPEUTIC

1. Give patient a labeled container and have her place all urine voided in the 24-hour period in the container.
   Rationale: To ensure that the results of the determination are valid[3]
2. Refrigerate urine and use no preservatives.
   Rationale: To reduce excessive bacterial growth and ensure accurate analysis (Some preservatives destroy estriol.)

Maternal blood studies

As with other types of biochemical monitoring techniques, maternal blood studies are most valuable when used as a component of a total clinical assessment.

Human placental lactogen. Human placental lactogen (HPL) is produced by the syncytiotrophoblast cells of the placenta in progressively larger amounts during normal pregnancy. HPL levels may identify a pregnancy compromised by placental insufficiency as there is a correlation between HPL levels and the functional mass of the placenta. Values below 4 μg/ml after 30 weeks' gestation are considered in the "fetal danger zone" range. Fetal demise from a nonplacental cause such as prolapsed cord or fetal anomaly may occur with normal HPL levels if the placenta continues to function. HPL measurement is currently an adjunct in perinatal care, an indirect measurement of fetal growth, and helpful in monitoring fetal status in IUGR, preeclampsia, and postmaturity.[1,2,11]

Unconjugated and plasma estriol. Unconjugated (plasma free) and plasma estriol levels are similar to patterns noted following urinary assessment. The advantage of this technique in assessing estriol levels is that sample acquisition is not altered by human error in urine collection or impairment of renal function, and reductions in placental production can be noted earlier. Serial measurements are essential for accurate interpretation and parallel patterns utilized for urinary estriols.[14]

Maternal enzymes. Heat-stable alkaline phosphatase rises as pregnancy progresses. Researchers are presently investigating the relationship between both absolute and serial values and placental functional abnormalities that cause fetal hypoxia and malnutrition. Low values, high values with progressive falls, and abrupt rises and falls have all been reported to be associated with problematic fetal outcomes; however, definitive relationships are yet to be determined.

Oxytocinase levels in maternal sera have been measured in an attempt to illustrate a relationship between the presence of this amino peptidase of placental origin and fetal outcome. Low levels have been associated with fetal death, postmaturity, and intrauterine growth retardation. However, further study is indicated before the relevance of oxytocinase levels can be meaningfully interpreted.[14]

• • •

Coombs' test is used to identify Rh antibodies in pregnant and previously sensitized Rh-negative women since anti-Rh antibodies can produce hemolytic disease in the Rh-positive fetus and newborn. In this test Coombs' serum is added to a mixture of maternal serum and Rh-positive red blood cells. A positive reaction is noted if agglutination occurs. Titers of antibodies present are then determined. If the titer is greater than 1 to 8, an amniocentesis is indicated to assess the amount of bilirubin present. Serial measurements of bilirubin pigment are usually done to assess the severity of hemolytic disease.

In that the acquisition of maternal sera according to a standard procedure is all that is needed to perform these biochemical assessments no protocol will be provided.

Amniocentesis

Amniocentesis is performed for two different purposes during pregnancy: in the second trimester between 15 and 18 weeks' gestation for prenatal diagnosis of genetic and metabolic disorders and during the third trimester after 31 weeks' gestation to assess fetal maturity and distress.

An amniocentesis is the penetration of the amniotic cavity through the abdominal and uterine walls for the purpose of withdrawing some fluid for examination.

The indications for genetic amniocentesis during the second trimester are as follows:
1. Maternal age over 35 years
2. Parent or previous child with chromosome abnormality
3. Carrier state for metabolic disorder
4. A previous child with a neural tube defect
5. Elevated maternal serum α-fetoproteins (AFP)

Performing amniocentesis at this time allows for the results to be determined within the time limits for an elective abortion.[11,14]

Amniocentesis performed during the third trimester provides assessment of general well-being and fetal lung maturity.

The risk of amniocentesis to the mother or the fetus is generally accepted to be in the range of 1%. These risks include trauma to the fetus or placenta, bleeding, infection, premature labor, and Rh sensitization from fetal bleeding into the maternal circulation.[14]

Protocols

Problem □ Preparation for and performance of an amniocentesis

GOAL: To acquire amniotic fluid for chromosome and biochemical test analysis to gain data regarding fetal status, thus providing safety for the mother and fetus.

DIAGNOSTIC

1. Assess mother's and father's level of knowledge regarding the procedure.
   Rationale: To inform patients about the slight risk in the amniocentesis procedure so that they can give their informed consent
2. Auscultate the fetal heart rate prior to the procedure.
   Rationale: To establish a baseline fetal heart rate
3. Assist ultrasound technician in positioning patient for optimum visualization when procedure done under ultrasound guidance or palpate the abdomen if localization of the placenta has already occurred via ultrasound.
   Rationale: To determine fetal position

THERAPEUTIC

1. Have patient sign consent form.
   Rationale: To indicate that the patient has had an opportunity to ask questions and believes she is fully informed about the procedure (The informed consent includes the knowledge that (1) the expected risk to the mother and fetus is about 1%; (2) the fetal cell culture, and/or chromosomal analysis, and/or biochemical analysis may not be successful; (3) the procedure may need to be repeated; (4) normal results (chromosomal or biochemical) do not eliminate the possibility that the infant could have birth defects or mental retardation because of other disorders, and (5) in the case of undiagnosed twins the results reflect the status of only one twin.)
2. Have patient void.
   Rationale: To reduce risk of bladder puncture
3. Explain the procedure again and reassure the patient.
   Rationale: To reduce anxiety

4. Reassure patient the procedure will not harm the infant.
5. Prepare skin with an antiseptic solution.
6. The skin and subcutaneous tissue are infiltrated with a local anesthetic.
7. Maintain sterile field while physician:
   a. Inserts 20-gauge 3½-inch needle with stylet into the amniotic sac (A 20- to 22-gauge needle 3 to 6 inches may be used, depending on the thickness of the abdominal wall, uterine size, and puncture site.)
   b. Removes stylet awaiting a droplet of amniotic fluid
   c. Attaches a 20 ml syringe to needle
   d. Aspirates amniotic fluid (If genetic studies are anticipated, the first 5 ml of aspirate is discarded to ensure the absence of maternal cells in the specimen.)
8. Place amniotic fluid directly into taped test tubes, or amber vials may be used to protect the specimen from light.
9. Place adhesive bandage over the puncture site.
10. Turn patient to left side to counteract any supine hypotension. This will increase venous return, blood pressure, and cardiac output.

EDUCATIONAL

1. Read and discuss consent form with the patient explaining components of the procedure.
2. Have patient sign consent form.
3. Explain procedure to patient.

Problem □ Recovering the patient following amniocentesis

GOAL: To ensure stability of mother and fetus following procedure

DIAGNOSTIC

1. Assess blood pressure, pulse, respirations, and fetal heart rate at least twice in a 15-minute time interval.
   Rationale: To assure that vital signs are within normal limits
2. Palpate the uterine fundus to assess fetal and uterine activity.

Rationale: To note any hyperactivity of the fetus

EDUCATIONAL

1. Instruct patient to report any vaginal drainage, fetal hyperactivity or unusual quietness, uterine contractions, signs of infection such as fever or chills, abdominal pain, and vaginal bleeding.

Rationale: To assure fetal and maternal well-being and reinforce physician's findings

2. Answer questions factually.

Rationale: To advise the parents that the results will be integrated into the total concept of obstetrical care

---

ELECTRONIC MONITORING

The main objective of obstetrics is that every pregnancy be desired and culminate in a healthy mother and baby. The maternal mortality rate has decreased markedly in the United States over the past 30 years. There were 320 maternal deaths reported in 1978 or 9.9/100,000 live births. This contrasts with 1935 when there were 12,544 maternal deaths or 582.1/100,000 live births.[15] The decrease in maternal mortality is generally due to the improvement in medical practice with recent advances in recognition and management of high-risk pregnancy and biophysical-chemical fetal assessment tools.[10]

The perinatal mortality rate (stillbirths plus neonatal deaths within 7 days of birth) has declined by 50% in the 25 years preceding 1977 data of 15.4 perinatal deaths per 1000 live births.[15] Almost one half of all perinatal deaths are stillbirths. As the quality of care throughout pregnancy improves, there is a decline in stillbirths. Prompt recognition of medical complications in pregnancy and high-risk assessment techniques with appropriate hospitalization and care contribute to a decline in the numbers of stillbirths. There are, however, a large proportion of intrauterine fetal deaths that have no overt explanation.

Neonatal deaths occur slightly less often than stillbirths. Nearly half of all neonatal deaths occur in the first day of life. The number of deaths occurring during the first 24 hours of life is greater than that from the second month to the completion of the first year. The most important cause is low birth weight usually caused by preterm delivery. Neonatal morbidity is primarily attributed to low birth weight, which results in neurological and intellectual defects that impact on society.

Trauma is the second most common cause of neonatal death. Injuries to the central nervous system are caused by intrauterine hypoxia and traumatic injury to the brain during labor. Congenital malformations are another important cause of neonatal death.[10]

Antepartum and intrapartum risk scores are assigned in some centers in an effort to identify patients for continuous electronic fetal heart rate monitoring during labor. Other hospitals monitor all patients who are in labor and a few hospitals monitor no one. Studies have shown that patients at very high antepartum risk have almost twice the chance of a low 1-minute Apgar score compared with patients at very low antepartum risk. Patients at very high risk during the intrapartum period had nearly an eightfold increase in the incidence of low Apgar scores compared with patients at very low intrapartum risk. These findings indicate that the infant is likely to have a depressed 1-minute Apgar score when the risk is high during both the antepartum and intrapartum periods. Because a low 1-minute Apgar score is more closely related to complications that develop during labor than those from the antepartum period, continuous electronic fetal monitoring should be considered on those with intrapartum complications.[13]

Monitoring means to check on a person or thing. In this section the discussion is on electronic monitoring of fetal heart rate and uterine activity.

According to Hon,[6] labor is a stressful time for the fetus because with each uterine contraction there is reduction in the flow of oxygenated maternal blood through the placental intervillous spaces. Superimposed on the usual phenomena of uterine contractions, some fetuses are already handicapped by intrinsic fetal disease, placental disease, cord compression, maternal disease, drugs administered for analgesia and anesthesia, or maternal hypotension. Hon stresses the need to detect fetal distress during labor, and this can be achieved by continuous monitoring of the fetal heart rate and uterine contractions.[6,10]

One method of electronic monitoring is the indirect method. A tocodynamometer is placed on the maternal abdomen at the site of the uterine fundus and records uterine contractions via a pressure-sensing device. The printout displays the frequency and duration of uterine contractions. Absolute intensity of contractions cannot be assessed, but a hand placed on the uterine fundus area can palpate and distinguish between mild, moderate, and strong contractions. An ultrasound transducer is placed on the maternal abdomen at the site where the fetal heart rate is the most clear as determined by auscultation. The ultrasound transducer monitors the fetal heart rate, and the data are recorded on the permanent strip chart.

The indirect or external method can be used during both the antepartum and intrapartum periods as it is noninvasive. It is used in nonstress tests (NST) and oxytocin challenge tests to assess fetal well-being. The general disadvantages of the external mode of monitoring are as follows: excessive fetal movement can cause inaccurate fetal heart rate recordings; maternal position change usually requires adjustment of the transducer; the monitor is sensitive to external artifact; short-term variability cannot be assessed accurately because of electronic logistics that edit artifact; there is difficulty in obtaining a recording caused by both maternal obesity and gestational ages less than 34 weeks having a low voltage signal. External monitoring does not provide as accurate a measurement as internal monitoring.

The internal method of monitoring gives information on uterine activity in terms of frequency, duration, and amplitude of contractions. A small, fluid-filled plastic catheter is introduced vaginally into the uterus after the cervix is dilated 2 to 3 cm and the fetal membranes have been ruptured. The catheter is compressed during uterine contractions and the strain gauge converts the pressure into millimeters of mercury, which is recorded on the strip chart. The spiral electrode monitors the fetal electrocardiogram (FECG) from the presenting part. To apply the electrode fetal membranes must be ruptured and the

cervix must be dilated 2 to 3 cm. Also the presenting part must be accessible and identifiable. The face, fontanelles, and genitalia must be avoided. The internal method is invasive; because of the fact that the membranes must be ruptured and some cervical dilatation is present, it is limited to the intrapartum period. There is also a slight potential for uterine rupture owing to incorrect insertion of the uterine catheter as well as fetal abscesses, hemorrhage, and infection from the spiral electrode. A highly skilled clinician is required to do this procedure. Internal monitoring does provide accurate measurement compared with the external method, [10,14] and it allows the pregnant woman more freedom to change positions.

The following relates to the information that can be obtained via the fetal monitor and possible nursing interventions.

Uterine activity

During labor, contractions progress in frequency, duration, and amplitude. The frequency depends on the stage of labor or the stage of induction or augmentation. Contractions generally occur about every 3 to 5 minutes. Duration of contractions refers to the length of time a contraction lasts, which is about 30 to 60 seconds. The amplitude refers to the intensity of the contraction and usually registers between 50 to 75 mm Hg, with a resting tone between 8 and 12 mm Hg. The shape of a normal contraction on the strip chart resembles that of a bell-shaped curve. Irregularities at the acme of the contraction can be caused by increased intraabdominal pressure such as in pushing or vomiting. The contraction pattern is usually depicted at rhythmic intervals. Contractions occurring in close conjunction with each other (couplets, triplets) may indicate a physiological or a dystonic labor.

The following outline lists possible causes of abnormal contraction patterns:

I. Frequency of contraction
   A. Possible causes of decreased frequency
      1. Braxton-Hicks contractions
      2. Hypotonic labor
      3. Cephalopelvic disproportion
      4. Latent phase of labor
   B. Possible causes of increased frequency
      1. Acceleration of labor
      2. Hypertonic labor

3. Precipitous labor
4. Oxytocic hyperstimulation
5. Abruptio placentae

II. Duration of contraction
  A. Possible causes of decreased duration
    1. Braxton-Hicks contractions
    2. Latent labor
    3. Deceleration of labor
    4. Cephalopelvic disporportion
    5. Hypotonic labor pattern
  B. Possible causes of increased duration
    1. Acceleration of labor pattern
    2. Oxytocic drugs
    3. Tetanic contractions
    4. Precipitous labor
    5. Pushing activity

III. Amplitude
  A. Possible causes of decreased amplitude
    1. Hypotonic labor
    2. Cephalopelvic disproportion
    3. Malfunction of uterine catheter
  B. Possible causes of increased amplitude
    1. Acceleration of labor
    2. Hypertonic pattern
    3. Exaggerated response to oxytocic drugs
    4. Malfunction of catheter

IV. Resting tone
  A. Possible causes of decreased resting tone
    1. Equipment malfunction
    2. Oxytocic regime
  B. Possible causes of increased resting tone
    1. Equipment malfunction
    2. Oxytocic regime
    3. Tetanic contractions
    4. Abruptio placentae
    5. Overdistended uterus
    6. Hypertonic labor pattern[6]

The nurse needs to assess the relationship between frequency of contractions and fetal heart rate. Uteroplacental insufficiency may occur with marked increase in contraction pattern or increased fetal stress because of long-term nonproductive contractions.

Baseline fetal heart rate

The baseline fetal heart rate refers to the heart rate present when the patient is not in labor or between uterine contractions. The baseline fetal heart rate is usually between 120 and 160 beats/min in the normal, full-term infant. At 20 weeks the average fetal heart rate is above 160 beats/min, and that is considered normal.[9,14] Fetal tachycardia is considered to be a fetal heart rate baseline over 160 beats/min, which lasts through two contraction cycles or 5 or more minutes. Fetal bradycardia is considered to be a baseline fetal heart rate below 120 beats/min, which persists through at least two complete contraction cycles of 5 or more minutes.

Tachycardia. Tachycardia is associated with maternal fever, fetal hypoxia, fetal immaturity, fetal hypovolemia, maternal anemia, maternal hyperthyroidism, atropine-type drugs, and fetal infection. If tachycardia occurs, oxygen administration may be of some value, and discontinuance of oxytocin may increase uteroplacental blood flow. Medical personnel should be notified to further evaluate the cause. Tachycardia is an ominous sign when it occurs with late decelerations or severe variable decelerations or absence of variability (Fig. 11-1).[6,9,14]

Bradycardia. Bradycardia is associated with fetal hypoxia, drugs (propranolol, anesthetics, oxytocin),

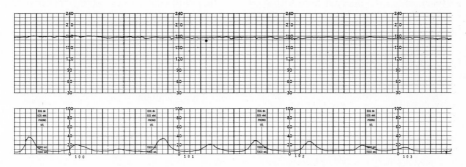

Fig. 11-1. Tachycardia with minimal variability.

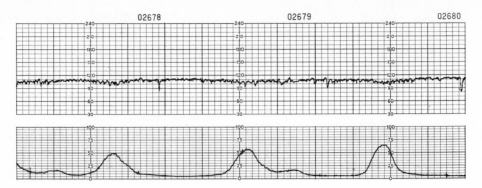

Fig. 11-2. Fetal bradycardia. (From Tucker, S. M.: Fetal monitoring and fetal assessment in high-risk pregnancy, St. Louis, 1978, The C. V. Mosby Co.)

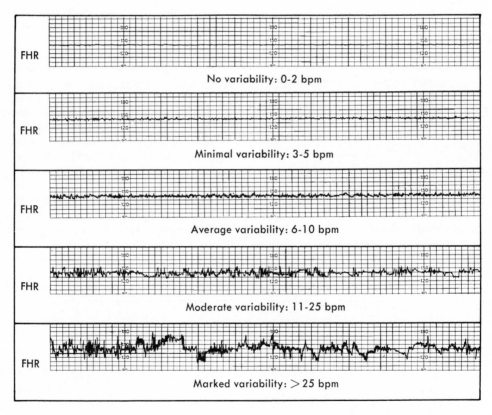

Fig. 11-3. Fetal heart rate variability. Short- and long-term variability tend to increase and decrease together. (From Tucker, S. M.: Fetal monitoring and fetal assessment in high-risk pregnancy, St. Louis, 1978, The C. V. Mosby Co.)

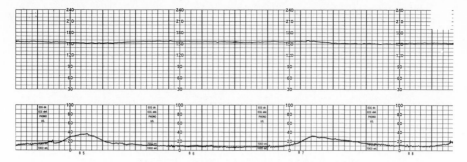

Fig. 11-4. Minimal baseline variability.

maternal hypotension, prolapse or prolonged compression of the umbilical cord, fetal cardiac arrhythmias, and idiopathic causes. Nursing measures are based on etiological factors. Moderate to severe bradycardia may lead to fetal acidosis. Administration of oxygen, discontinuing oxytocin, and placing the mother in a lateral position may be of some value (Fig. 11-2).[6,9,14]

Baseline variability. Baseline variability is the normal irregularity in fetal heart rhythm. It is described as short term when there is a variation in rate from one cardiac systole to the next. Long-term variability describes the fluctuation or oscillatory changes that occur over the course of a minute. Generally both short- and long-term variability tend to increase and decrease together (Fig. 11-3). Good variability is indicative of normal neurological control of the heart rate and a measure of fetal reserve. Decreased variability indicates some degree of central nervous system depression, and this is often associated with hypoxia. The range of short-term variability considered reassuring is between 5 and 20 beats/min. The range of fluctuations over the course of a minute in long-term variability considered reassuring is 2 to 6 oscillatory cycles per minute.

Increased baseline variability is associated with fetal stimulation. Decreased baseline variability is associated with prematurity, drugs (narcotics, tranquilizers, barbiturates), fetal hypoxia, fetal acidosis, fetal sleep, and fetal cardiac arrhythmias.

With good variability no nursing intervention is indicated. Variability above 25 beats/min should be closely observed as it may be a forerunner of hypoxia. In decreased variability nursing action is dependent on the etiology. Stimulation of the fetus is recommended as well as changing the maternal position and checking to see if the mother has received CNS depressants. If the baseline remains smooth, fetal blood sampling and/or prompt delivery should be considered (Fig. 11-4).[6,9,14]

Periodic changes in fetal heart rate

Periodic changes in fetal heart rate are short-term fetal heart rate (FHR) alterations that occur usually in relation to contractions, with the FHR returning to the baseline. There are two basic types: acceleration (FHR above the baseline) and deceleration (FHR below the baseline: early, late, and variable).

Acceleration. Acceleration is thought to be caused by stimulation of the sympathetic division of the autonomic nervous system. It may or may not be associated with contractions. Acceleration may be caused by manipulation of the fetus, spontaneous fetal movement, vaginal examination, uterine contractions, and breech presentation. Acceleration is not associated with fetal distress, but it should be observed when it is uniform and consistent as it may be a forerunner of late deceleration.

Early deceleration. Early deceleration has a smooth, curvilinear wave that mirrors the pattern of the uterine contractions (Fig. 11-5). It is usually observed between 4 and 7 cm dilatation and in the second stage as the fetal head descends through the pelvis. This pattern represents head compression as the vertex is compressed against the tissues of the birth canal and causes a vagal-like response, resulting in a decrease in fetal heart rate. At present, early deceleration is considered a benign condition if not

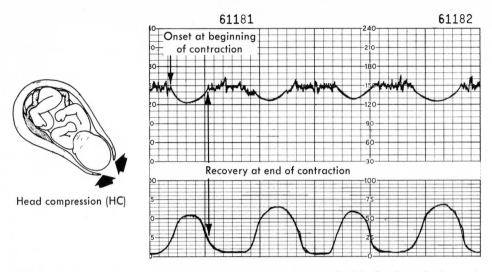

61181   61182

Onset at beginning
of contraction

Recovery at end of contraction

Head compression (HC)

Fig. 11-5. Early deceleration (head compression). (From Tucker, S. M.: Fetal monitoring and fetal assessment in high-risk pregnancy, St. Louis, 1978, The C. V. Mosby Co.)

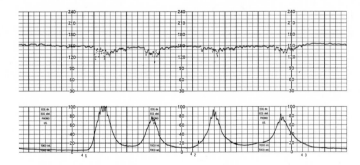

Fig. 11-6. Early decelerations.

associated with decreased variability of the baseline or a developing tachycardia (Fig. 11-6).

Early deceleration (head compression) is due to uterine contractions, vaginal examination, fundal pressure, and placement of internal mode of fetal monitoring.

Late deceleration. Late deceleration is a uniform periodic change and a mirror image of the uterine contractions beginning at the acme of the contraction with the nadir of the late deceleration occurring well after the peak of the contraction. It is associated with uteroplacental insufficiency (Fig. 11-7).

Late deceleration (uteroplacental insufficiency) is due to hyperstimulation of the uterus with oxytocin; maternal supine hypotension syndrome; toxemia; postmaturity; amnionitis; intrauterine growth retardation; maternal diabetes; placenta previa; abruptio placentae; spinal, caudal, and epidural anesthesia; maternal cardiac disease; and maternal anemia.

Nursing actions include maternal position change

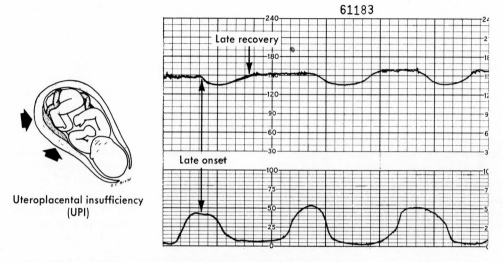

Fig. 11-7. Late decelerations (uteroplacental insufficiency). (From Tucker, S. M.: Fetal monitoring and fetal assessment in high-risk pregnancy, St. Louis, 1978, The C. V. Mosby Co.)

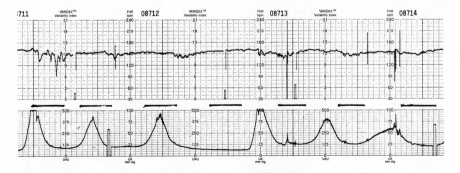

Fig. 11-8. Late decelerations.

(left lateral preferred), correction of maternal hypotension, administration of oxygen, stopping oxytocin drugs, and fetal blood sampling (for pH). If the condition remains uncorrected and variability decreases, early or immediate delivery should be considered (Fig. 11-8).[10,14]

Variable deceleration. Variable deceleration is a nonuniform periodic change in the fetal heart rate not necessarily related to uterine contractions. Variable deceleration has a jagged wave mimicking a U or V shape and is characterized by an abrupt fall in the fetal heart rate and rapid return to the baseline, sometimes with transitory acceleration, shouldering, or "overshoot." It is thought that the transient compressions of the umbilical cord promote a peripheral vagal response (Figs. 11-9 and 11-10).

Variable deceleration (cord compression) is due to maternal-fetal position compressing the cord, cord around the body or an extremity, short cord, knot in cord, and prolapsed cord.

Variable deceleration can be divided into three categories: severe (prolapse of the cord, overt or occult, should be suspected) moderate, and mild. Patterns of mild or moderate can usually be corrected by changing the maternal position. If severe, prolapse of the cord should be ruled out, oxytocin should be discontinued, and oxygen should be administered. If severe variable decelerations cannot be corrected, immediate delivery should be considered (Figs. 11-11 and 11-12).[10,14]

• • •

In electronically monitoring the fetus during labor, another parameter of assessing fetal well-being is achieved. If appropriate, interventions can be initiated in the hopes of correcting the problem. If the problem cannot be corrected and the intrauterine environment is not conducive to fetal well-being, early delivery may be indicated. Electronic monitoring also allows the medical team to prepare to immediately initiate care of a potentially compromised newborn.

Caution must be exercised in that fetal monitoring is only as good as the health professional working with the patient and the monitor (as well as the efficiency of the machine). It is but one of several tools, which together help predict the fetal condition and assist in making decisions for fetal well-being.

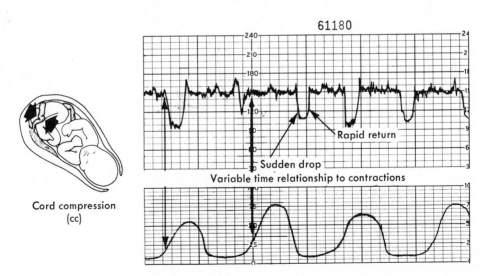

Fig. 11-9. Mild variable decelerations (cord compression). (From Tucker, S. M.: Fetal monitoring and fetal assessment in high-risk pregnancy, St. Louis, 1978, The C. V. Mosby Co.)

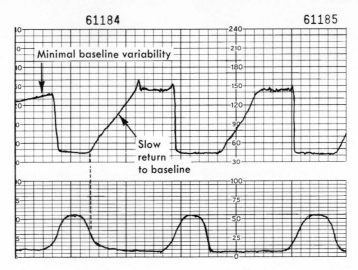

Fig. 11-10. Severe variable decelerations (cord compression). (From Tucker, S. M.: Fetal monitoring and fetal assessment in the high-risk pregnancy, St. Louis, 1978, The C. V. Mosby Co.)

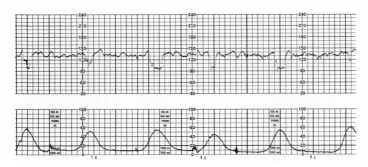

Fig. 11-11. Mild variable decelerations.

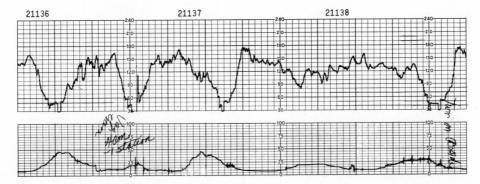

Fig. 11-12. Severe variable decelerations. (From Tucker, S. M.: Fetal monitoring and fetal assessment in high-risk pregnancy, St. Louis, 1978, The C. V. Mosby Co.)

Protocols

Problem □ Assessment of the fetal heart rate

GOAL: To determine the fetal heart rate dependent solely on the ability of the listener

EQUIPMENT
1. Fetoscope—a modified stethoscope worn on the head of the listener so that bone conduction from the skull increases audibility of fetal heart sounds (Fig. 11-13, *A*).
2. Leff stethoscope—a stethoscope with a large, weighted bell to amplify fetal heart sounds (Fig. 11-13, *B*).
3. Ultrasound stethoscope (Doppler)—amplifies sound and is useful for hard-to-hear fetal heart sounds and for allowing parents to listen to the fetal heart rate (Fig. 11-13, *C*).

THERAPEUTIC
1. Elevate head of bed so patient assumes a semi-Fowler's position.*

---

*It may be necessary to lower the head of the bed so that patient assumes a dorsal recumbent position because of difficulty in hearing fetal heart sounds.

Rationale: To reduce the potential supine hypotensive syndrome
2. Determine position and presentation of fetus through execution of Leopold's maneuvers.
Rationale: To identify quadrant where fetal heart sounds are best heard, sparing the patient the discomfort of having the entire abdomen probed in search of fetal heart sounds; accomplished between contractions causes the patient less discomfort
3. Position fetoscope on listener's head.*
4. Place the bell of the fetoscope on the abdomen and press firmly.
Rationale: To begin placement of the bell midway between the symphysis and umbilicus,

---

*Use of the Leff stethoscope only requires placement of earpieces in the listener's ears.

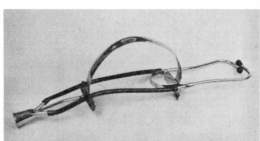

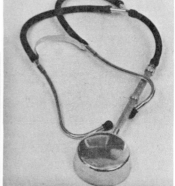

Fig. 11-13. A, DeLee-Hillis fetoscope with headpiece to provide bone conduction to enhance hearing of fetal heart tones. **B,** Leff stethoscope with large, weighted bell to amplify fetal heart tones. Frequently used in delivery rooms since the bell can be placed beneath sterile drapes. **C,** Ultrasound stethoscope that utilizes Doppler effect to count fetal heart rate. (From Zeigel, E., and Cranley, M.: Obstetric nursing, ed. 7, New York, 1978, Macmillan Publishing Co., Inc. Copyright © 1978, Macmillan Publishing Co., Inc.)

and if necessary, work from the midline to the outer aspects of the quadrant until fetal heart sounds are clearly heard

5. After placement on the abdomen, remove fingers from the bell.

   Rationale: To avoid extraneous sounds, which interfere with clarity of sound

6. Count the rate for a minimum of 60 seconds.*

   Rationale: To allow time to detect changes in volume and regularity of the fetal heart rate by listening for a full minute

7. Record according to hospital policy.

   Rationale: To recognize that guidelines for frequency of assessing and recording may vary from agency to agency and might include assessing and recording every hour during the early phase of labor, every half hour during the active phase of labor, every

5 minutes during the second stage of labor and/or after each contraction (Other than routinely, fetal heart rate should be assessed and recorded immediately after rupture of membranes, whether artificial or spontaneous; after an enema; and after the patient has been ambulatory for a period of time).

EDUCATIONAL:

1. Explain procedures and equipment to patient.

   Rationale: To increase patient's understanding and acceptance and reduce anxiety

Problem □ Assessment of the frequency, duration, and intensity of uterine contractions simultaneously with the fetal heart rate (External monitoring methods are within the scope of nursing practice.)

GOAL: To identify the fetal heart rate pattern in response to uterine contractions using the indirect method of monitoring (or external mode) (Fig. 11-14)

---

*Timing of listening in relation to contractions and duration of listening vary according to different authorities.

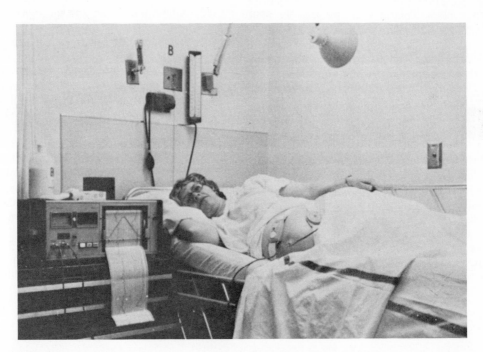

Fig. 11-14. External monitoring with patient in side-lying position. (From Tucker, S. M.: Fetal monitoring and fetal assessment in high-risk pregnancy, St. Louis, 1978, The C. V. Mosby Co.)

EQUIPMENT

1. Monitor with ultrasound transducer and tocodynamometer and connector cables.
2. Transmission gel.
3. Elastic or disposable belts

THERAPEUTIC

1. Encircle patient's abdomen with belts.
   Rationale: To reduce friction on contact with patient's skin by lightly dusting with baby powder or cornstarch if rubber belts are used
2. Elevate head of bed so that patient assumes a semi-Fowler's position.
   Rationale: To reduce the potential for supine hypotensive syndrome
3. Prepare equipment and plug the connector cable for the transducer in the appropriate receptacle of the monitor.
4. Determine presentation and position of fetus through execution of Leopold's maneuvers. A fetoscope may be used to further pinpoint where fetal heart sounds are best heard. Or turn the power on to the monitor and increase the volume control while locating the FHR with the ultrasound transducer.
   Rationale: To identify the quadrant where fetal heart sounds are best heard, sparing the patient the discomfort of having the entire abdomen probed in search of fetal heart sounds; accomplished between contractions causes the patient less discomfort
5. Apply a small amount of transmission gel to the transducer or the area of the abdomen where fetal heart sounds are best heard.
   Rationale: To enhance conduction of sound
6. Place the transducer over the transmission gel and secure in place with the appropriate belt.
7. Place the tocodynamometer on an area of the fundus where it will best pick up the pressure of the contracting uterine muscle.
   Rationale: To pick up contractions of uterine muscles, which push against a pressure-sensing device in the tocodynamometer that creates an electric signal

8. Secure the tocodynamometer in place with the appropriate belt.
   Rationale: To allow the patient freedom of movement in changing positions
9. Plug the connector cable for the tocodynamometer into the appropriate receptacle of the monitor.
10. Identify the patient's monitor strip by writing on the beginning of the graph paper the following information:

Date	Physician
Patient's name	EDC
Para Gravida	Aborta
Status of membranes	

   Rationale: To assure that monitor graph is appropriately labeled with pertinent patient information since it is a legal document and becomes part of the patient's permanent chart
11. Observe tracing for fetal heart rate and rhythm. Listen for audible heartbeat. Observe digital display when testing monitor.
12. Adjust transducer and tocodynamometer as needed.
    Rationale: To be aware that maternal position change and fetal activity may affect clarity of sound and tracings on monitor graph
13. Record notes according to hospital policy.
    Rationale: To be sure chart includes fetal heart rate baseline, variability, and periodic changes and frequency, duration, and relative intensity of contractions (Any event that occurs such as vaginal examination, administration of medications, or other procedures that might influence the fetal heart or contraction pattern should be noted on the monitor graph.)

EDUCATIONAL

1. Explain procedures and equipment to patient.
   Rationale: To increase understanding and acceptance and to reduce anxiety

Problem □ Assessment of fetal heart rate and uterine contractions simultaneously and directly through use of an electrode attached to the presenting part and fluid-filled catheter introduced into the uterine cavity, especially useful for identifying baseline fetal heart rate and actual variability (Application of the internal mode is done by a physician or a nurse who has been trained and approved in the technique according to hospital policy and protocol.)

GOALS: To obtain an accurate evaluation of fetal response to contractions, which is least distorted by environmental conditions such as the mother's movements and fetal activity; to accurately measure the intensity of contractions; and to provide data for objective evaluation of fetal status

EQUIPMENT

1. Monitor with connector cables to the strain gauge and leg plate.
2. Spiral electrode.
3. Intrauterine catheter.
4. Sterile glove(s).
5. Sterile solution—normal saline.
6. Amnihook or other appropriate instrument if membranes not previously ruptured.
7. Lubricant—water soluble.

THERAPEUTIC

1. Lower the head of the bed so that the patient assumes a dorsal recumbent position with knees flexed.
   Rationale: To allow easier access to the cervix
2. Have patient concentrate on relaxing perineal muscles during the vaginal examination.
   Rationale: To make the vaginal examination less difficult for the examiner and less uncomfortable for the patient
3. Prepare the patient for a sterile vaginal examination according to accepted hospital procedures.
   Rationale: To reduce the potential for infection by cleansing the perineal area and using sterile materials
4. Determine fetal heart rate.
   Rationale: To assess fetal well-being before procedures are begun

5. Assess dilatation, presentation, and station before membranes are ruptured.
   Rationale: To check for a closed "unripe" cervix, faulty presentation, or a fetus high in the pelvis, which are contraindications for rupturing membranes
6. If membranes are not already ruptured, the Amnihook or other instrument is introduced into the vagina and a small tear is made in the amniotic membranes.
   Rationale: To ensure that membranes are ruptured and the cervix is dilated at least 2 cm before insertion of the catheter
7. Reassess the fetal heart rate.
   Rationale: To validate fetal well-being or identify deviations in fetal heart rate pattern induced by rupture of membranes
8. Insert the sterile water–filled catheter and the catheter guide no more than 2 cm inside the cervix.
   Rationale: To assure that the catheter guide is not inserted too far because it is made of a very hard, noncompliant plastic and is potentially harmful
9. Advance the catheter through the catheter guide until the black mark on the catheter reaches the introitus.
   Rationale: To assure accurate intrauterine pressure measurement
10. Attach the free end of the catheter to the three-way stopcock and attach this to the strain gauge.
11. Turn stopcock off to the monitor and flush the intrauterine catheter with the sterile water–filled syringe connected to the stopcock.
    Rationale: To assure a continuous fluid-filled column of sterile water to the strain gauge and to remove any air bubbles in the catheter
12. Turn the stopcock off to the catheter.
    Rationale: To exclude intrauterine pressure
13. Release pressure valve on strain gauge and flush with sterile water.
    Rationale: To remove any air bubbles and assure a noninterrupted flow of water over the strain gauge.

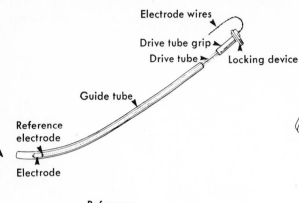

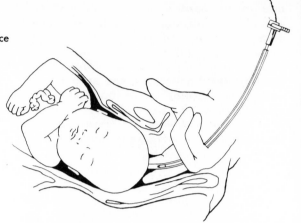

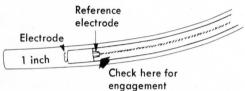

Electrode
1 inch

Check here for
engagement

Fig. 11-15. **A,** Spiral electrode. **B,** Spiral electrode attached to scalp. **C,** Attached spiral electrode with guide tube removed. (Courtesy of Corometrics Medical Systems, Inc., Wallingford, Connecticut 06492. Operators Manual 112 Fetal Monitor.)

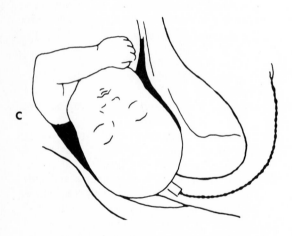

14. Remove syringe from stopcock and observe strip chart for uterine activity (UA) printout to be on the 0 line.
    Rationale: To assure that printout reads 0 when there is no pressure on the strain gauge
15. Adjust zero control device to assure that UA prints out on 0 when the strain guage is open to atmospheric pressure.
    Rationale: To assure that intensity and resting tone of uterine contractions are accurate

16. Reattach syringe to stopcock then turn stopcock off to the syringe.
    Rationale: To reconnect intrauterine catheter directly with strain gauge
17. Chart intrauterine resting tone (Fig. 11-15).
    NOTE: Never "0" when strain gauge is open to the intrauterine catheter as this falsifies actual intrauterine resting tone
18. Plug leg plate cable into monitor outlet.
19. Attach leg plate to the patient, then place ECG conductive gel on the metal surface of the leg plate.
    Rationale: To assure transmission of fetal ECG
20. Perform a sterile vaginal examination spreading two fingers on the presenting part.
    Rationale: To assure adequate location on presenting part for spiral electrode placement
21. Insert the guide tube between the fingers until the presenting part is touched.
22. Release the lock and attach the electrode by turning the drive tube clockwise.
    Rationale: To assure a good ECG signal the spiral electrode must be placed securely; maximum penetration is 1.5 mm

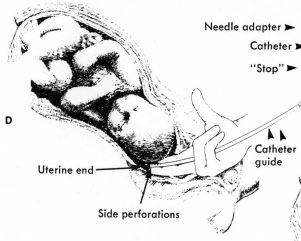

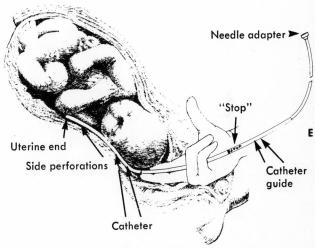

Fig. 11-15, cont'd. D, Insertion of catheter guide. **E,** Advancement of intrauterine catheter through catheter guide until stop marker reaches the introitus.

23. Remove the drive tube and discard.
24. Attach the electrode wires to the leg plate according to the manufacturer's instructions.
    Rationale: To observe that some manufacturers have color-coded wires and push posts on the leg plates that must be matched
25. Turn the power on and the recorder to 3 cm/min paper speed.
26. Evaluate fetal heart rate and rhythm. Listen for audible beep with each QRS complex. Observe digital display when testing monitor.
27. Identify the patient's monitor strip by writing the following information on the initial section of the strip chart.

Date	Physician
Patient's name	EDC
Para Gravida	Aborta
Status of membranes	

  Rationale: To assure that strip chart is appropriately labeled with pertinent patient information since it is a legal document and becomes a part of the patient permanent chart

28. Reapply ECG transmission gel to leg plate as necessary.
    Rationale: To ensure accurate and clear signal
29. Record notes according to hopsital policy.
    Rationale: To be sure chart includes FHR baseline, variability, and periodic changes and frequency, duration, intensity, and resting tone of uterine contractions (Any event that occurs such as vaginal examination, administration of medications, or other procedures that might influence the fetal heart or contraction pattern should be noted on the graph paper.)

EDUCATIONAL
1. Explain the equipment and procedures
   Rationale: To allay patient's concerns about personal discomfort and infant safety

FETAL DISTRESS

Once intrapartum monitoring is established, the strip chart must be assessed for signs of fetal distress. The following protocol should be in effect.

Protocols

Problem □ Identification and nursing intervention for "warning" FHR patterns

GOAL: To detect warning patterns early and intervene appropriately

Rationale: To correct FHR pattern and to prevent ominous signs of fetal distress through prompt identification and appropriate nursing intervention

DIAGNOSTIC
1. Observe strip chart for mild variable decelerations.
   Rationale: To identify mild umbilical cord compression

THERAPEUTIC
1. Attempt correction of pattern with change of maternal position.
   Rationale: To alter location of compressed cord and relieve this FHR pattern by repositioning mother

EDUCATIONAL
1. Explain to patient that fetus is pressing against umbilical cord and that position change may alter this relationship.
   Rationale: To ensure patient's cooperation by informing her of reason for nursing interventions

DIAGNOSTIC
1. Observe strip chart for any of the following:
   a. Progressive increase or decrease in baseline fetal heart rate
   b. Tachycardia of 160 beats/min or greater
   c. Progressive decrease in baseline variability.
   Rationale: To possibly indicate some degree of fetal hypoxia

THERAPEUTIC
1. Administer 7 to 8 L/min of oxygen per face mask.

Rationale: To increase oxygen saturation of maternal hemoglobin and subsequently correct the FHR pattern if it is caused by fetal hypoxia

EDUCATIONAL
1. Instruct the patient to breathe normally with the oxygen mask in place; explain that the fetus might benefit from added oxygen especially during contractions and that some fetus' are more sensitive than others in their response to uterine contractions.
   Rationale: To allay maternal anxiety, to elicit cooperation in breathing with an oxygen mask in place, and to individualize the care given to the fetus

Problem □ Identification and management of "ominous" FHR patterns

GOAL: To deliver a healthy noncompromised fetus

Rationale: To promptly identify and manage appropriately ominous FHR patterns, thereby decreasing or preventing perinatal morbidity and mortality

DIAGNOSTIC
1. Observe the strip chart for any of the following:
   a. Severe variable decelerations
   b. Late decelerations
   c. Absence of variability
   d. Prolonged deceleration
   e. Bradycardia
   f. Unstable heart rate
   Rationale: To be aware that the fetus is distressed with hypoxemia and acidosis, and that an unstable heart rate may be indicative of central nervous system depression

THERAPEUTIC

1. Initiate systematic interventions to identify specific cause of ominous pattern.
   a. Change maternal position
      Rationale: To rule out or confirm umbilical cord compression and to correct maternal supine hypotension syndrome
   b. Perform vaginal or speculum examination or both if severe variable decelerations are present.
      Rationale: To rule out or confirm prolapsed and compressed umbilical cord
   c. Correct maternal hypotension by elevating patient's legs.
      Rationale: To increase venous return of blood to heart in order to increase cardiac output
   d. Discontinue oxytocin if infusing.
      Rationale: To decrease uterine activity
   e. Increase rate of maintenance IV.
      Rationale: To correct hypotension by increasing intravascular fluid volume and cardiac output and to stimulate excretion of oxytocin
   f. Administer 7 to 8 L/min oxygen.
      Rationale: To increase oxygen saturation of maternal hemoglobin and subsequently decrease fetal hypoxemia
   g. Assess fetal blood pH.
      Rationale: To identify presence of acidosis and confirm fetal distress and to avoid premature or inappropriate intervention if pH is acceptable

EDUCATIONAL

1. Provide explanations to the patient, father, or labor coach regarding specific therapeutic interventions at their level of understanding, degree of receptivity, and appropriateness at the specific time.
   Rationale: To elicit cooperation of the patient, father, or labor coach. (This is of critical importance in some situations, for example, when the patient must assume the knee chest position for a prolapsed umbilical cord.)

Final intervention for fetal distress rests with the physician and may vary based on other clinical parameters including station, dilatation, presentation, position, uterine activity, and underlying maternal medical complications. Low forceps delivery may be indicated in some situations with "crash" cesarean section indicated in others.

FETAL BLOOD SAMPLING

Assessment of fetal pH can be done by fetal blood sampling. This is an important adjunct in the definitive diagnosis of fetal distress, since unnecessary cesarean sections can and have resulted based on interpretation of fetal heart rate pattern disturbance alone. Combining continuous intrapartum monitoring with fetal blood sampling may help to eliminate a significant number of cesarean sections that are now performed for suspected fetal distress.[11]

To sample fetal blood, the membranes must be ruptured and the presenting part must be accessible.

Protocols

Problem □ Collection of fetal blood sample

GOAL: To obtain a sufficient sample of fetal blood using accepted techniques to ensure an accurate pH reading

DIAGNOSTIC

1. Assist patient into lithotomy position.
   Rationale: To provide access to presenting part
2. Prepare external perineal area with an antibacterial solution.
   Rationale: To decrease potential intrauterine contamination
3. Amnioscope with attached light source is inserted by physician.
   Rationale: To assure visualization of incision site
4. Presenting part, usually fetal scalp, is cleansed with a sterile cotton swab.
   Rationale: To assure that specimen is not contaminated with amniotic fluid or mucus
5. Ethylchloride spray may be used on the selected site (optional).
   Rationale: To induce a local hyperemia
6. Silicone gel may be applied to fetal scalp via a small sterile sponge inserted through the amnioscope.

   Rationale: To promote beading of blood droplets
7. A small incision is made on the scalp. Blood droplets are collected with a heparinized glass capillary pipette.

THERAPEUTIC

1. The endoscope is maintained in place until all bleeding ceases.
   Rationale: To make it easier to find the incision site
2. A gauze sponge may be applied to the incision site with some pressure.
   Rationale: To assure hemostasis

EDUCATIONAL

1. Explain procedure to patient.
   Rationale: To allay anxiety
2. Relate importance of maintaining position and not moving during specimen collection.
   Rationale: To elicit patient cooperation and assure adequate specimen collection
3. Assist and teach breathing and relaxing techniques that patient can use during uterine contractions.
   Rationale: To assist patient in maintaining the lithotomy position during uterine contractions

ANTEPARTUM MONITORING

The desired goals of antepartum monitoring are to prevent intrauterine fetal death and avoid unnecessary premature intervention. Antepartum monitoring developed as an outgrowth of intrapartum electronic monitoring. The oxytocin challenge test (OCT)[4] was the first test used on a large scale, and as clinical experience increased it became clear that certain FHR responses seen during the OCT were also good predictors of fetal well-being. These observations led to the development of the nonstress test (NST).[12] These tests used in conjunction with other tests of fetal well-being and maturity have been useful in achieving the goals of antepartum monitoring.

Indications for both the OCT and NST are as follows:[13]

1. Diabetes mellitus
2. Chronic hypertension
3. Toxemia
4. Intrauterine growth retardation (IUGR)
5. Sickle cell disease
6. Maternal cyanotic heart disease
7. Suspected postmaturity
8. History of previous stillbirth
9. Rh sensitization
10. Meconium-stained amniotic fluid at the time of amniocentesis
11. Abnormal estriol excretion pattern
12. Hyperthyroidism in pregnancy
13. Collagen diseases
14. Elderly gravida ($\geq$40)
15. Chronic renal disease

Absolute contraindications for the OCT are rupture of membranes and previous classical cesarean section. The following are considered relative contraindications: multiple pregnancy, previous premature labor, placenta previa, polyhydramnios, and previous low transverse cesarean section.[5] There are no contraindications for the NST.

Nonstress test

The basis for the nonstress test is that the normal fetus will produce characteristic heart rate patterns. Acceleration of fetal heart rate in response to fetal movement is the desired outcome of an NST. This then allows most high-risk pregnancies to continue

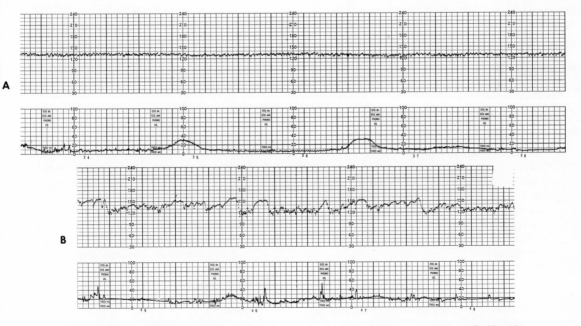

Fig. 11-16. A, Decreased variability owing to fetal sleep cycle during nonstress test. **B,** Negative nonstress test, 15 minutes later.

with the test being repeated on a weekly basis. A reactive pattern suggests fetal well-being and a subsequent good perinatal outcome.

The protocol for indirect fetal monitoring should be followed.

The fetal heart rate patterns observed during the nonstress test are classified into three categories. Generally the nonstress test is used as a screening test to identify those patients who will need additional testing (Fig. 11-16).[12]

A guide for the interpretation of the nonstress test follows[7,8,12]:

Result	Interpretation
Reactive	Two or more accelerations of FHR of 15 beats/min lasting 15 seconds or more associated with fetal movement in a 10-minute period
Nonreactive	Any tracing with either no FHR accelerations or accelerations less than 15 beats/min or lasting less than 15 seconds throughout any fetal movement during the testing period
Unsatisfactory	Quality of the FHR recording not adequate for interpretation

The clinical significance of the interpretation of the NST is as follows:

Reactive NST: As long as weekly NST's remain reactive, most high-risk pregnancies may be allowed to continue.
Nonreactive NST: Further indirect monitoring may be attempted with abdominal fetal electrocardiography in an effort to clarify FHR pattern and quantitate variability. External monitoring should continue and an OCT should be done.
Unsatisfactory: Test should be repeated in 24 hours or an OCT should be done, depending on the clinical situation.

Oxytocin challenge test

The basis for the oxytocin challenge test is that a healthy fetus can withstand a decreased oxygen supply during the physiological stress of an oxytocin-stimulated contraction, and a compromised fetus will demonstrate late decelerations that are nonreassuring and indicative of uteroplacental insufficiency.[4,5]

The following protocol specifically delineates additions to the indirect fetal monitoring protocol described earlier.

Protocol

Problem □ OCT using indirect fetal monitoring

GOAL: To detect compromised fetus
DIAGNOSTIC

1. Monitor baseline FHR and uterine activity (UA) until 10 minutes of interpretable data are obtained prior to the administration of oxytocin.
   Rationale: To provide a baseline for future comparison
2. If less than three spontaneous contractions occur within a 10-minute period and if late decelerations do not occur with intermittent spontaneous contractions, oxytocin can be initiated.

   Rationale: To be aware that stimulation of contractions may not be necessary if adequate uterine activity is present
3. Initiate an IV with a plain base solution (frequently 5% dextrose in lactated Ringer's solution).
   Rationale: To assure that the primary IV remains available to infuse rapidly in the event of uterine hyperstimulation or maternal hypotension; oxytocin must always be piggybacked
4. Piggyback an infusion of oxytocin in a similar solution by means of a constant infusion pump.
   Rationale: To allow controlled administration of exact dosage at exact rate

5. Start the oxytocin infusion at 0.5 mU/min.
   Rationale: To ensure that the amount of existing uterine activity will determine the rate of infusion
6. Observe for fetal heart rate response to contractions.
   Rationale: To indicate continuance or discontinuance of the oxytocin infusion
7. Increase infusion rate by 0.5 mU/min at 15- to 20-minute intervals until three uterine contractions of good quality in 10 minutes are observed.[4]
   Rationale: To be aware that uterine activity is usually experienced after 5 to 10 mU/min of oxytocin infusion[4]
8. Interpret the fetal heart rate pattern.

Rationale: To determine how soon or whether another OCT will be scheduled and if other methods of fetal evaluation or delivery are appropriate
9. Turn off oxytocin solution and continue monitoring fetal heart rate pattern until it returns to baseline status.
   Rationale: To continue observation of fetal response until 30 minutes has elapsed (It takes approximately 30 minutes for the body to metabolize oxytocin.)
10. Observe patient until uterine activity subsides and/or returns to preoxytocin infusion level.
    Rationale: To prevent discharge of a laboring patient (Occasionally a patient near term will go into labor after an OCT.)

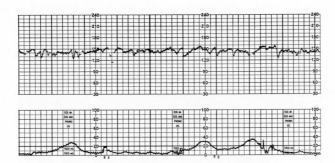

Fig. 11-17. Negative oxytocin challenge test.

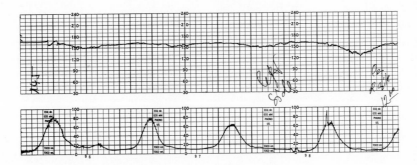

Fig. 11-18. Positive oxytocin challenge test.

A guide for the interpretation of the oxytocin challenge test follows[5,7]:

Result	Interpretation
Negative	No late decelerations with a minimum of three uterine contractions lasting 40 to 60 seconds within a 10-minute period (Fig. 11-17)
Positive	Persistent and consistent late decelerations occurring with more than half of the contractions (Fig. 11-18)
Suspicious	Late decelerations occurring with less than half the uterine contractions once an adequate contraction pattern has been established
Hyperstimulation	Late decelerations occurring with excessive uterine activity (contractions more often than every 2 minutes or lasting longer than 90 seconds) or a persistent increase in uterine tone
Unsatisfactory	Inadequate uterine contraction pattern or tracing too poor to interpret

The clinical significance of the interpretation of the OCT is as follows:

Negative OCT: Reassurance that the fetus is likely to survive labor should it occur within 1 week; more frequent testing may be indicated based on the clinical situation.

Positive OCT: Management lies between utilization of other fetal assessment tools and termination of pregnancy as the test indicates that the patient is at increased risk for perinatal morbidity and mortality. Premature intervention must be seriously considered since high false positive rates have been reported when the test was used to predict fetal-infant outcomes. All other clinical parameters should be carefully assessed including gestational age, fetal lung maturity, estriol pattern, and maternal condition.

Suspicious, hyperstimulation, unsatisfactory: NST and OCT should be repeated in 24 hours. If interpretable data cannot be achieved, other methods of fetal assessment must be used.

REFERENCES

1. Aladjem, S., editor: Obstetrical practice, St. Louis, 1980, The C. V. Mosby Co.
2. Babson, S. G., Pernoll, M. L., and Benda, G. I.: Diagnosis and management of the fetus and neonate at risk, St. Louis, 1980, The C. V. Mosby Co.
3. Clark, A., and Affonso, D.: Childbearing, a nursing perspective, ed. 2, Philadelphia, 1979, F. A. Davis Co.
4. Freeman, R. K.: The use of oxytocin challenge test for antepartum clinical evaluation of uteroplacental respiratory function, Am. J. Obstet. Gynecol. **121**:481, 1975.
5. Garite, T. J., Freeman, R. K., Hochleutner, I., and Linzey, E. M.: Oxytocin challenge test, Obstet. Gynecol. **51**(5):614, 1978.
6. Hon, E.: An introduction to fetal heart rate monitoring, Los Angeles, 1973, University of Southern California.
7. Jarrell, S. E., and Sokol, R. J.: Clinical use of stressed and non stressed monitoring techniques, Clin. Obstet. Gynecol. **22**(3):617, 1979.
8. Nochimson, D. J., et al.: The non-stress test, Obstet. Gynecol. **51**(4):419, 1978.
9. Parer, J. T.: Physiological regulation of fetal heart rate, J. Obstet. Gynecol. Nurs. **5**(5):265, 1976.
10. Pritchard, J. A., and MacDonald, P. C.: Williams obstetrics, ed. 15, New York, 1976, Appleton-Century-Crofts.
11. Queenan, J. T.: Management of high risk pregnancy, New Jersey, 1980, Medical Economics, Co.
12. Schifrin, B. S.: The contraction stress test and the non stress test. In Queenan, J. T.: Management of high risk pregnancy, New Jersey, 1980, Medical Economics Co.
13. Sokol, R. J., Stojkov, J., and Chik, L.: Maternal fetal assessment: a clinical guide to monitoring, Clin. Obstet. Gynecol. **22**(3):547, 1979.
14. Tucker, S. M.: Fetal monitoring and fetal assessment in high-risk pregnancy, St. Louis, 1978, The C. V. Mosby Co.
15. U.S. Department of H.E.W.: PHS No. 80-1232, Washington D.C., 1980, Health United States DHEW Publication.

Chapter 12

Control of pain in labor

Beverly Keller

Labor and delivery are painful processes for most women. For many first-time mothers the pain greatly exceeds their expectations and prior experience. Indeed, for many, it may be the most painful experience in their lives. However, for most women it can also be an exceptionally rewarding experience. The birth of one's baby is often one of the greatest emotional peaks in a whole lifetime.

The five major desires of women relating to labor are as follows[40]:

1. To be sustained by another human being
2. To be assured of a safe outcome for both herself and the baby
3. To have attendants accept her personal attitude toward, and behavior during, labor
4. To receive bodily care
5. To have relief from pain

Regardless of the methods used to achieve comfort during labor and delivery, the central determining factors between a happy experience and a devastating one for the new family are the interpersonal relations and interactions between the family and members of the perinatal team.[40]

CRITERIA FOR THE IDEAL METHOD OF PAIN RELIEF IN OBSTETRICS

The ideal method of pain relief in labor would ensure that:

1. The health of the mother is not endangered
2. There would be no harmful effect on the fetus or residual behavioral effects in the newborn
3. The agent has the ability to abolish or diminish pain and the memory of suffering
4. The efficiency of uterine contractions would not be decreased (prolonging labor and predisposing to postpartum hemorrhage)

5. The ability of the mother to cooperate intelligently with the staff would be maintained
6. The ability of the mother to be awake and to share important early bonding experiences would be fostered
7. No need for operative interference evolve solely because of the anesthetic
8. The method be reasonably simple to accomplish

GENERAL CONSIDERATIONS

Pain is a subjective experience. Wide variation exists in the degree of analgesia needed, from no medication or minimal doses designed to take the edge off peak contractions to the complete abolition of sensation. The experience of pain depends on the interrelationship of a great many physical, psychological, and cultural variables. All of these must be considered to obtain the best results in each individual childbirth experience.

As much as possible, the mother's and family's requests should be honored. With regard to medication, the smallest effective dose is best. Timing is crucial to effectiveness. Given too soon or in excessive doses, medications may interfere with contractions or prolong labor. Given at the appropriate time, pain is relieved *before* it becomes unbearable, and labor may be enhanced owing to relaxation of tension.

Vertebral blocks (spinal and epidural) given too soon may increase the requirement for oxytocin augmentation and increase the incidence of forceps extractions. Generally, giving a medication or block as soon as pain relief is needed in optimal doses in active labor will not interfere with progress.

Premature and compromised infants are very susceptible to narcotics and sedatives/tranquilizers. Their physiological resistance to adverse effects is minimal, and postnatal metabolism may be quite prolonged.

The quantity and quality of medical and nursing supervision determine to a great extent what methods can be used safely, as do the skill, experience, and availability of the anesthetist.

There is no doubt that childbirth education eases the experience and reduces the levels of medication required. The orientation to the hospital environment and to what can be expected in labor and delivery does much to reduce apprehension and anxiety. The relaxation techniques trained mothers learn can serve them far beyond the brief experience of childbirth.

It is good to remember that the experience a young family has with the perinatal team during childbirth often influences their attitude toward all health professionals and health care during the prime years for health promotion and disease prevention. The empathy and respect shown during this crisis period may have far-reaching effects.

THE PAIN OF PARTURITION

Before exploring approaches to the control of pain in parturition, we must first understand its source. Recent studies emphasize that the pain experience is the total effect of many interrelated physiological and psychological mechanisms. These include sensory, motivational, cognitive, and psychodynamic processes.[5] Knowledge of the anatomy, physiology, and psychology of pain in childbirth is essential.

The anatomy of pain in labor

The nerves that supply the uterus are autonomic, both sympathetic and parasympathetic. The role of the parasympathetic nerves in labor is unknown. Pain sensation in the first stage of labor is carried by the afferent sympathetic nerve fibers of the uterus, cervix, adnexa, and ligaments. These fibers pass to the region of the uterosacral ligaments and, by way of the uterine, pelvic, hypogastric, and aortic plexuses, into the spinal cord at levels T-10 through L-1, inclusively. The pain sensation is then transmitted along the spinal nerves to the brain stem, stimulating the whole central nervous system. Impulses then travel through the thalamus to the cerebral cortex.[5]

The perception of pain and the response to it are not straight-through transmissions. There is a great degree of modification along the way achieved by facilitation, inhibition, convergence, summation, divergence, and other phenomena.[5] There are mechanisms that allow distinctions among mechanical, thermal, and chemical stimuli with regard to time, location, and intensity. Involvement of the cerebral cortex brings into play all sorts of factors based on experience, conditioning, judgment, anxiety, attention, suggestion, cultural background, and emotions.[7]

In addition to the visceral pain of contractions late in the first stage and early in the second stage, pain is transmitted from the perineum via the pudendal nerve to segments S-2 through S-5.

Another anatomical factor is the relationship of the uterine muscles to their blood supply. The muscles of the uterus are in three layers. The outer layer fibers run longitudinally, the inner fibers in lateral circles, and the middle layer in a crisscross mesh. The blood vessels serving the uterine muscle run between these muscle fibers and are effectively clamped during contractions. This leads to the anoxic pain associated with strong contractions.

The physiology of pain in labor

Gentle birth of the baby is achieved by a balance between the expulsive forces (uterine contractions and auxiliary bearing down) and the resistant force of the lower uterine segment, cervix, and peritoneum. Analgesia and anesthesia may influence one or more of these forces so their physiology must be understood.

Uterine activity is the product of the intensity of contractions multiplied by their frequency. In the last month of pregnancy, the Braxton Hicks contractions (1 to 2 per 10 minutes) exercise the uterine muscles and cause progressive softening and effacement of the cervix. During the first stage of labor, expulsive forces are due solely to contractions of the uterus. Bearing down efforts at this time cause only harm. They delay cervical dilatation, hurt the patient needlessly, and force the uterus downward, stretching the supporting ligaments and predisposing to later prolapse.

Uterine contractions are considered "normal" when there is fundal dominance, a descending gradient, an intensity of 30 to 60 mm Hg, a frequency of three to five per 10-minute period, and enough time for relaxation between contractions so that the resting tone is 8 to 12 mm Hg.[6] Their function is to efface and dilate the cervix and cause progressive descent of the fetal presenting part. During this time, the pelvic floor helps in the flexion and rotation of the head (if the head is the presenting part).[3]

Pain during labor is usually related to one or more of the following factors:

1. Stretching of the cervix and lower uterine segment
2. Contraction of the uterine muscle during a period of relative ischemia and metabolic accumulation of wastes (As the uterus contracts, it uses more energy while at the same time interfering with its blood supply. The resulting ischemia and accumulation of metabolites produce pain. When uterine relaxation between contractions is insufficient to allow adequate oxygenation, severity of pain increases.)
3. Traction on the supporting ligaments (Each time the uterus contracts it moves forward and pulls on the ligaments.)
4. Pressure on the nerves adjacent to the cervix and vagina
5. Traction on the tubes, ovaries, and peritoneum
6. Pressure on the urethra, bladder, and rectum
7. Stretching of the pelvic floor and perineum
8. Skeletal muscle spasm and vasospasm in structures supplied by the same spinal cord segments that supply the uterus
9. Pressure of fetal bony parts on maternal bone and tissue (especially noticed when the fetus presents with occiput posterior)

In the first stage pain is caused primarily by stretching the cervix and contractions of the uterine muscles. In the late first stage and second stage there is additional pain owing to stretching of the vagina, vulva, and perineum. Late in the second stage there is perineal distention that causes stretching and possible tearing of fascia and other sensitive parts.[1,4,16]

During the second stage uterine contractility increases and is aided by the voluntary bearing down efforts of the mother. Bearing down consists of deep inspiration, closure of the glottis, and contraction of the diaphragm and abdominal muscles with simultaneous relaxation of the pelvic floor muscles. The bearing down reflex is stimulated when the cervix is sufficiently dilated to allow the presenting part

to descend and distend the perineum. The sensory impulses travel through the pudendal nerve to the spinal cord and thence to the brain stem, where efferent nerves send impulses to the appropriate muscles. Approximately one third of the force necessary to expel the infant must be produced by bearing down (and/or with traction by forceps).[55]

Large doses of sedatives or narcotics administered during the latent phase of the first stage may slow labor progress; whereas if given during the active phase (3 to 4 cm dilatation), they have little or no effect on progress.[43,44] Systemic arterial hypotension often causes lessened intensity and duration of contractions and interferes with rhythmicity, whereas hypertension has the opposite effect.[64] Fear, anxiety, and other emotional reactions may impair contractions, although sometimes they intensify them. Spinal and epidural blocks may produce a temporary decrease in contractility, but if the block is started in the active phase and hypotension is avoided, labor progresses normally.[32] It is thought that an epidural block may interfere occasionally with proper internal rotation of the head owing to premature relaxation of the pelvic floor, but this is debatable.[6] Spinal, epidural, and pudendal blocks all diminish or eliminate the afferent bearing down reflex but should not impair the mother's ability to contract the diaphragm and abdominal muscles, provided she has been taught how to push and the analgesia does not extend above T-10. At the same time as the mother bears down, it is important that the pelvic floor be relaxed. Tearing or overstretching these muscles weakens the pelvic floor and may cause extensive damage. This is one reason for the current widespread use of episiotomy. Childbirth education classes teach prospective mothers appropriate exercises in which they learn not only how to strengthen the muscles but also how to relax them while simultaneously pushing.

Pain is felt in the first and second stages when intrauterine pressure reaches about 25 mm Hg and in the third stage when pressure reaches 55 mm Hg. This is an estimation owing to variation in the pain threshhold of each patient.[22] During the fourth stage (stabilization after delivery of the placenta) there is residual cramping as the uterus clamps down to minimize bleeding. Very frequently this is partly the result of oxytocic drugs given after the baby is born. There is also pain from stretching and/or

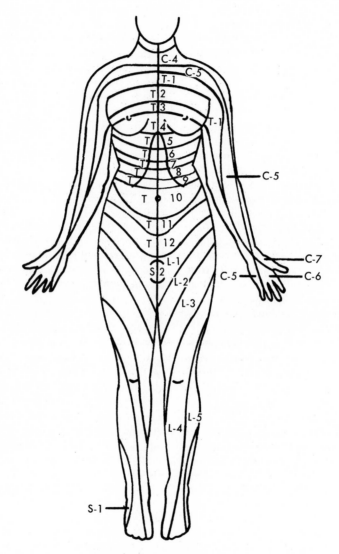

Fig. 12-1. Cutaneous dermatomes.

lacerations of the perineum aggravated by the swelling that usually occurs. This can be minimized by the immediate application of an ice pack after transfer from the delivery room. In mothers who have had cesarean sections, this is when postoperative pain begins. Often these mothers have had no preoperative sedation, and unless they received a narcotic in surgery after the delivery of the baby, the onset of postoperative pain can be rapid and severe. If a spinal or epidural block was used for analgesia, the pain may be delayed in onset.

Referred pain

There are many explanations for the phenomenon of referred pain. One logical explanation is that both the uterus and other somatic structures within the same dermatome share neurons at the spinal and thalamic levels. When stimulus from the uterus is strong enough, the neurons for corresponding muscles, ligaments, and skin are also stimulated. The brain interprets the pain as if it were arising from the referred area as well as the original site.

Thus, early labor pain is felt anteriorly in the lower abdomen below the umbilicus, laterally over the iliac crest, and posteriorly over the lower lumbar and upper sacral regions. With more intense contractions, pain is spread above the umbilical region to the upper thighs, gluteal, and midsacral areas.[20] Fig. 12-1 shows the dermatome patterns that can be used to predict not only the regions of referred pain but also the regions that will be affected by vertebral blocks.

THE PSYCHOLOGY OF PAIN IN LABOR

In addition to physiological factors, there are many psychological factors that affect the perception of pain and response to it. Depending on physical conditions, the mother's tolerance for pain may be reduced (for example, if she is exhausted or ill). The mood and attitude of the mother are important. The emotional impact of childbearing may help her to transcend or to succumb to the pain. In patients with unplanned or unwanted pregnancies, the onset of labor may signal the beginning of an unpleasant life situation leading to a heightened reaction. Expectations from suggestion, previous experience, or "old wives' tales" play an important role. An unusually difficult or easy previous labor can result in high anxiety or casual relaxation. Expectations resulting from childbirth education make the experience of labor less frightening and can alter perception and expression of pain.

Distraction raises the pain threshold since a limited number of stimuli can be processed by the brain at one time. Conditioning reflex reaction to uterine contraction also helps raise the threshold. For instance, if a mother practices relaxation in response to the Braxton Hicks contractions throughout the latter part of her pregnancy, she will automatically tend to respond with relaxation when true labor begins. Concentration on breathing and relaxation techniques or on a hypnotist's voice also reduces awareness of pain. Mothers who have been coached to tolerate pain or who ardently believe in a birth without medication are highly motivated to withhold expression of pain even if it is well perceived.

Fear, ignorance, apprehension, and anxiety all potentiate the pain experience. They not only impair emotional well-being but also activate the autonomic nervous system. High levels of sympathetic nervous system activity secondary to stress can lead to decreased uterine blood flow with subsequent fetal hypoxia.[38] It may also exacerbate incoordinate uterine activity, prolonging labor.

With regard to pain relief, the mother may fear that she will be subject to unbearable pain. On the other hand, if she accepts relief, she may worry that she will harm the baby, lose control, or reduce her "aware" participation in the birth of her child. Ideally, through prenatal education and counseling, the mother can express her ideas and fears and learn realistic expectations of labor, delivery, and the comfort measures available. This counseling should include the significant other, often the father, who will accompany the mother in labor, since his or her ideas and expectations will also greatly affect the course of labor.

The deleterious effects of pain are manifold.[7,27] In addition to emotional distress of the mother (plus the family and staff), maternal oxygen consumption increases dramatically. There is a steady increase in the concentration of free fatty acids in the blood with a concurrent increase in maternal metabolic acidosis. The hyperventilation associated with pain leads to hypocarbia and decreased cerebral and uterine blood flow.[33] Breath-holding can lead to respiratory acidosis and the buildup of toxic accumulations in the blood. Any change in maternal pH status can have detrimental effects on the fetus, causing acidosis.[17] Pain also stimulates the sympathetic aggravation of incoordinate uterine action previously mentioned. Maternal stress also causes fetal hypoxia by epinephrine-induced vasoconstriction of the uterine vessels. Epinephrine release also leads to elevated maternal glucose levels of glycogen breakdown. The concomitant increase in fetal blood and brain glucose decreases the fetal brain cell tolerance to hypoxia, predisposing to brain damage.[39]

Pain can increase cardiac output and work from 15% to 60%, and it also increases the blood pressure. Severe pain may also cause rhythm changes and decreased coronary blood flow.[68] Altered function in every organ system can result, and reflex spasm of skeletal muscles is conducive to cramps, nausea, and vomiting.[27]

Pain also aggravates the apprehension, tension, and anxiety already present. Reflexive tightening of the pelvic floor can make the birth more traumatic for the baby and preclude manipulations that may become necessary during delivery.[25,26]

The memory of pain can be buried deeply in the subconscious shortly after delivery. But it is quite possible that the experience of severe pain and discomfort can interfere with the optimal maternal-infant bonding potential that could exist were the mother not totally exhausted after delivery.

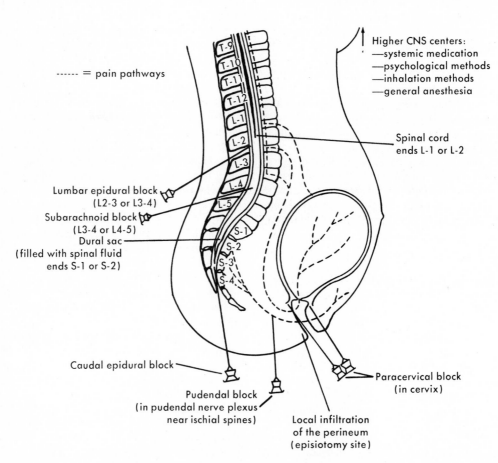

Fig. 12-2. Major route of pain impulses in the laboring woman.

Methods of pain control

There are many ways of relieving pain and discomfort. They vary according to the stage of labor, its progress, the condition of the mother and fetus, the skill and availability of the anesthetist, and the experience of the obstetrical team. Fig. 12-2 shows the major routes of pain impulses in the laboring woman and the sites of application of the various analgesic/anesthetic techniques.

First stage labor pain can be relieved by lumbar, caudal epidural, or paracervical block. Block of higher centers can be achieved to various degrees by psychological methods, systemic medications, or intermittent inhalation anesthesia.

In the second stage spinal block may be given or epidural block can be extended to include the sacral segments. Pudendal nerve block or local infiltration can achieve anesthesia of the perineum to augment any of the former methods. General anesthesia by inhalation and/or intravenous agents may be required for operative delivery procedures (for example, cesarean section, difficult forceps procedures, manual removal of the placenta). In the third and fourth stages following vaginal delivery, additional anesthesia is rarely needed unless local infiltration is required for repair of episiotomy or lacerations.

MATERNAL PHYSIOLOGICAL CHANGES PERTINENT TO ANESTHESIA

The process of pregnancy and parturition produces many physiological and anatomical changes in the mother. With regard to pain relief in labor, the changes involving blood volume, cardiovascular, respiratory, renal, and gastrointestinal function are most important. They evolve from the physiological effects of hormones, the presence of the conceptus, and the mechanical effects of the enlarging uterus.[35]

Blood volume changes

The plasma volume increases progressively from the sixth week to levels of 1000 to 1500 ml over prepregnancy volume at term. This is an increase of 40% to 50%. Red cell volume increases by 250 to 450 ml, only 20% to 35%, resulting in hemodilution, often called the physiological anemia of pregnancy. Blood viscosity decreases about 20% because of this hemodilution, reducing the resistance to flow and the force required to circulate blood.

Hypervolemia enables the circulatory needs of the conceptus to be met and fills the large venous reservoir of the uterus and lower extremities. It helps protect the mother and fetus from supine hypotensive syndrome and from potential hemorrhage at the time of delivery.

In uncomplicated deliveries approximately 500 ml of maternal blood is lost during labor and the first 3 postpartum hours. In elective cesarean section 900 to 1000 ml is lost. In spite of the loss, the hematocrit changes little. By 8 weeks postpartum, blood volumes are close to prepregnant levels.

In preeclampsia and eclampsia plasma volumes below normal pregnancy levels are seen, reducing the blood reserve. These women are especially susceptible to intrapartum shock. Because the volume deficit is primarily related to vasoconstriction rather than to reduced extracellular body water, rapid administration of intravenous fluids does not correct the problem. Indeed, rapid intravenous fluids may contribute to pulmonary edema and heart failure in preeclamptic women.

Cardiovascular changes

Cardiac output increases 30% to 40% (reflecting increased venous return) through 32 weeks' gestation and then declines to approximately 15% above prepregnant levels by term. The increased output is due to increased stroke volume during early pregnancy and later to increased heart rate (10 to 15 beats/min above normal). During labor the cardiac output progressively increases to 50% above prelabor values, and each contraction raises the output even more by expelling up to 500 ml of blood from the uterus into the general circulation. The magnitude of these changes depends on the intensity of contractions and the associated pain, anxiety, and apprehension. With the mother in a lateral position, the heart work of contractions is much less than when she is supine, owing to release of aortic and vena caval compression. In the third stage cardiac output is greatest (100% above nonpregnant levels) until delivery of the placenta reduces the blood volume, venous return, and stroke volume. By 6 to 8 weeks, the rate, output, and stroke volume approximate prepregnant levels.

Systolic blood pressure changes little during pregnancy, but diastolic pressure drops by 10 to 15 mm

Hg owing to decreased systemic vascular resistance. Lowered resistance is due primarily to the addition of the placental pool. Venous blood pressure remains normal except for the lower extremities where it is elevated because of venous obstruction by uterine pressure on the vena cava and other veins. Blood pressure in pregnancy is greatly influenced by posture. Venous obstruction is exaggerated in the supine position and greatest in the lithotomy position. In most patients this compression is offset by a compensatory increase in sympathetic tone and peripheral vasoconstriction. In 10% to 15% of patients the obstruction is so great that blood pressure cannot be maintained, resulting in supine hypotensive syndrome. This hypotension is aggravated when anesthetics that cause autonomic blockade are given, interfering with compensatory vasoconstriction.

The obstruction of the inferior vena cava causes blood to return to the heart via collateral vessels in the vertebral canal. These vessels become greatly engorged, reducing the size of the extradural and subarachnoid spaces. This requires a reduction in anesthetic doses given for epidural and spinal blocks. It also enhances systemic absorption of drugs from these spaces.

For all of these reasons, it is very important that *no* laboring woman be allowed to remain for long periods in the unmodified supine position. If the supine posture is required, the right hip can be raised by a pillow or wedge to achieve left lateral displacement of the uterus. Uterine displacement devices have been devised and may be useful during short procedures. During operative procedures a slight left down tilt of the table is sometimes used. These modifications are usually sufficient to permit satisfactory venous return, normal blood pressure, and adequate placental perfusion.

Respiratory changes

The metabolic needs of the growing fetus, placenta, and uterus increase the requirement for oxygen and the production of carbon dioxide in pregnancy. The enlarging uterus displaces the diaphragm upward in later pregnancy, but the internal volume of the thorax is unchanged. This is due to a compensatory increase in diameter along with flaring of the ribs. The nasopharynx, larynx, trachea, and bronchi become swollen and reddened owing to capillary engorgement. This may make nose breathing difficult for some women and may cause voice changes. It also tends to make endotracheal intubation (especially nasal intubation) more difficult.[4] Total pulmonary resistance is reduced by approximately 50%, mainly owing to progesterone-induced smooth muscle relaxation.

There is progressive decrease in expiratory reserve volume and residual capacity during pregnancy with concomitant increase in inspiratory capacity, tidal volume, and vital capacity. The total work of breathing is not increased primarily because of reduced pulmonary resistance.

Ventilation increases by up to 50%, and resting oxygen consumption increases approximately 20%. In labor these are further increased with varying degrees of hyperventilation in most women because of pain and excitement. Anxiety, drugs, and overzealous performance of breathing exercises also contribute to hyperventilation.

Clinically, respiratory changes have important implications. Changes in lung volumes and increased ventilatory exchange enhance transfer of oxygen and carbon dioxide between mother and fetus. On the other hand, the woman is more susceptible to rapid changes in blood gas levels during respiratory complications or anesthesia. Hypoventilation, breath-holding, or obstruction rapidly produce hypoxia, hypercarbia, and respiratory acidosis. Hyperventilation by the mother spontaneously, or by excessive positive pressure ventilation on the part of the nurse of anesthetist, can quickly cause respiratory alkalosis with decreased cerebral and possibly uterine blood flow.[6] Decreased cerebral flow may cause paresthesia, transient mental effects, and tetany, while reduced uterine circulation will produce fetal hypoxia and metabolic acidosis. Because of increased oxygen needs, excessive doses of drugs that depress maternal respiration can rapidly produce fetal asphyxia.

The enhanced ventilation of pregnancy allows rapid induction with small doses of inhalation anesthetics *and* more rapid toxicity. In spite of the dangers of overmedication, adequate analgesia is beneficial for both the mother and the fetus by reducing the respiratory drive and uterine artery vasoconstriction.

Renal changes

Renal plasma flow increases to 800 ml/min at term, and glomerular filtration rises to 180 ml/min. Tubular reabsorption of sodium is enhanced, while that of glucose and amino acids is not so efficient. Glycosuria and proteinuria may occur in normal pregnancy. Dilatation of the upper urinary tract, along with reduced tone and peristalsis of the ureter (induced by hormones), increases retention of urine and contributes to urinary tract infection. Postpartum diuresis occurring between the second and fifth days seldom exceeds 2 L/day, and glomerular-tubular balance is precisely maintained in the normal parturient. Urinary retention owing to a lax bladder, reduced muscle tone, and labor trauma occurs in about one third of all mothers.

Preeclampsia and eclampsia impair renal function. Renal plasma flow, glomerular filtration, and clearance of creatinine and uric acid are all reduced. Inability to reduce body sodium and extravascular water levels leads to oliguria or anuria, making the toxemic mother very susceptible to pulmonary edema and cardiac failure from fluid overload. Improvement usually begins by 12 hours postpartum. All these factors affect the body's capacity to clear drugs and metabolites from the system.

Gastrointestinal and liver changes

Pregnancy is associated with a decrease in gastric emptying time, gastric secretion, and gastrointestinal motility. Intragastric pressure is increased and esophageal reflux is common. Emptying time is greatly reduced, and accumulation of gas and gastric juices in the stomach is significantly increased in labor. Reduced competence of the gastroesophageal sphincter and occurrence of reverse peristalsis make the labor patient especially prone to regurgitation, vomiting, and aspiration. These effects are exacerbated by general anesthetics, narcotics, and sedatives. Women prone to heartburn in pregnancy are especially prone to these problems in labor. The administration of antacids every 2 hours in labor and prior to general anesthesia reduces the risk of chemical pneumonitis (Mendelson's syndrome) by raising the pH of gastric contents above the critical level of 2.5. Keeping labor patients NPO except for small amounts of ice chips or water along with the antacids is important.

Liver function is basically unchanged except for decreased serum cholinesterase activity (responsible for the breakdown of some drugs). This reduces, for instance, the dose of succinylcholine needed to provide paralysis for general anesthesia.

PLACENTAL TRANSFER AT TERM

The placenta has two separate and independent circulatory systems—maternal and fetal. The capability of the placenta to maintain fetal homeostasis and to determine fetal and neonatal effects of drugs given to the mother depends on (1) the uteroplacental circulation, (2) placental transfer, and (3) the fetal circulation, uptake, and excretion of drugs.

Maternal circulation

Nutrients and oxygen reach the maternal side of the placenta by the uterine and ovarian arteries. Maternal blood enters the intervillous space in fountain-like spurts that bathe the fetal villi and their capillaries. The uterus probably has no compensatory system of autoregulation, so adequate blood flow depends entirely on adequate perfusion pressure. Uterine circulation is under strong alpha-adrenergic receptor control and mild beta control. Therefore stress and subsequent norepinephrine release increase vascular resistance and decrease blood flow.

Factors that decrease perfusion pressure and blood flow are extremely important. In addition to sympathetic stimulation these include preeclampsia, renal disease, uterine hypertonus, reduced cardiac output, maternal hypotension from any source (caval occlusion, shock, hemorrhage, vertebral block), and vasopressor drugs that constrict uterine vessels.[54,57,58] During strong uterine contractions, placental blood flow is greatly reduced hindering transfer of nutrients and toxic waste products.

Placental transfer

The blood-placental barrier is composed of three tissue layers, in total about 2 to 6 μ thick. Any substance in the maternal blood must cross this barrier to reach the fetal circulation and vice versa. Placental transfer of most substances occurs primarily by simple or facilitated diffusion across concentration gradients from areas of higher concentration to areas of lower concentration. Diffusion is the mechanism of transfer for oxygen, carbon dioxide, and almost all drugs used for analgesia, anesthesia, and sedation.

Fetal circulation

There are three umbilical vessels that carry blood between the placenta and fetal systemic circulation: one umbilical vein carries arterial blood to the fetal liver and inferior vena cava, while two umbilical arteries carry venous blood from the internal iliac arteries to the placenta.

DRUG TRANSFER ACROSS THE PLACENTA

As previously stated, drugs used in obstetrical analgesia generally cross the placental barrier by simple diffusion. Fick's law defines the basic physiochemical relationships that govern simple diffusion. The relationship is stated thus:

$$\frac{Q}{t} = K \frac{A (C_m - C_f)}{D}$$

where Q/t is the rate of diffusion (quantity per unit time); A is the surface area available for transfer; C_m is the drug concentration in maternal blood; C_f is the drug concentration in the fetal blood; D is the density of the placental membrane; and K is the diffusion constant of the particular drug across the membrane. The diffusion constant is related to molecular size, configuration, lipid solubility, and so on. The placenta rarely presents an absolute barrier to the transfer of drugs; however, there are many factors that contribute to the extent and rate of trans-fer. Table 12-1 lists these factors. Among the most important are the lipid solubility of the drug and the extent of its ionization in the blood. The factors that influence placental transfer are basically the same factors that influence the transfer of substances by diffusion across the blood-brain barrier and other biological membranes. Therefore it is unlikely that the ideal nontransferable anesthetic drug will be found. If a drug is able to reach its site of action within the maternal CNS or peripheral nerves, it must possess the same characteristics that allow its placental transfer.[33]

Following is an explanation of the factors listed in Table 12-1.

Drug factors

The blood-placental barrier is a lipoprotein membrane with small pores and an electrically charged surface.

Lipid solubility. Fat-soluble substances pass easily through the membrane since they can mix readily with the lipoprotein substance.

Molecular weight. Substances with molecular weights over 600 have difficulty traversing the membrane by diffusion because of the physical disparity with the size of the pores. Most analgesic-anesthetic drugs are well below this size limit.

Degree of ionization. Ions of drugs carrying the same electrical charge as the membrane itself are repelled, whereas those with an opposite charge are attracted and bound to the membrane. This ionization makes transfer difficult—nonionized substances pass more easily.

Table 12-1. Factors influencing placental transfer and fetal distribution of drugs at term

Drug factors	Placental factors	Maternal factors	Fetal factors
Lipid solubility	Separation of maternal and	Mode of administration	Fetal liver
Molecular weight	fetal circulation	Elimination of the drug	Extensive fetal shunting
Degree of ionization	Concentration gradient	Uteroplacental blood flow	Progressive dilution of
Binding capacity to	across the membrane	Nonhomogeneity of	blood enroute to the
proteins and red cells	Placental metabolism	intervillous blood	fetal brain
Tissue binding capacity	Configuration of placental	Maternal blood volume	Enzymatic systems
Drug interaction	membranes	Maternal plasma proteins,	Immaturity of the brain
Drug metabolites		red cells, and pH	Fetal plasma proteins, red,
			cells, and pH
			Cord compression

Blood binding capacity. Drugs that bind readily to large molecules (that is, plasma proteins and red cells) pass the membrane with great difficulty again because of size limitations. Primarily only the unbound portion of the drug passes.

Tissue binding capacity. The capacity of drugs to be bound in the tissues at the site of injection (for example, the fatty epidural tissue) affects their circulating concentrations.

Drug interaction. Competition of different drugs for plasma and tissue binding sites affects how much of each drug reaches the fetus. Some bind more readily and are transferred to a lesser degree than the competing drug.

Drug metabolites. Fetal effects may be due to metabolites of drugs more than to the drug itself (for example, peak effects of meperidine [Demerol] occur long after peak blood levels are reached, indicating that the delayed effects of a metabolite in the fetus are being seen.[6]

Placental factors

Separation of maternal and fetal circulations. Separation of maternal and fetal circulations precludes instantaneous exchange.

Concentration gradients across the membrane. Substances tend to diffuse from a region of higher concentration to one of lower concentration eventually reaching equilibrium.

Placental metabolism. Placental metabolism of drugs has not yet been well defined. It appears that the placenta does have limited oxidative and reducing capacity, especially after enzyme-inducing agents are given. This could have variable effects on the fetus, since the metabolites produced may be more or less toxic than the original drug form.

Configuration of placental membranes. As gestation proceeds, there is increasing placental permeability owing to increased surface area and thinning of the membrane.

Maternal factors

Mode of administration. Given intravenously, a drug is carried around the body in bolus form for one or two circulations,[1] reaching the placenta in peak concentrations within minutes. Slow intravenous injection decreases this bolus effect, protecting the fetus. In addition, the amount of drug transferred to the fetus can be decreased by injecting it at the beginning of a contraction. By the time the bolus reaches the uterine circulation, the contraction would be at its peak, greatly limiting placental perfusion. Intramuscular injection of the same dose results in less transfer because of slow release of the drug into the circulation and lower concentration gradients.

Elimination of the drug from the maternal circulation. This is accomplished by extravasation, metabolism, and excretion.

Uteroplacental blood flow. Hypoperfusion delays transfer of drugs and their metabolites. This may be due to uterine contraction, hypotension, or uterine vasoconstriction.

Nonhomogeneity of intervillous blood. Nonhomogeneity of intervillous blood is caused by differing levels of circulation in different regions of the placenta and by different timing of discharge into the intervillous space by the maternal spiral arterioles. It means that levels vary throughout the placenta and that equilibrium of drug levels is delayed.

Maternal blood volume. Hypovolemia results in higher concentrations of drugs in the maternal blood for an equivalent dose.

Maternal plasma proteins, red cells, and pH. Maternal plasma proteins, red cells, and pH control the availability of drug-binding sites in the mother and the level of ionization that occurs, thereby controlling the amount of free drug available for transfer.

Fetal factors

Fetal liver. One third to two thirds of umbilical venous blood flows through the fetal liver before reaching the general circulation. The liver extracts a considerable amount of drugs, protecting other vital organs.

Extensive fetal shunting. About 50% of the fetal cardiac output returns to the placenta without perfusing fetal tissues via shunting through the foramen ovale and the ductus arteriosus. Thus, in each circulation the tissues are exposed to only half of the absorbed quantity of drug.

Progressive dilution of blood enroute to the fetal brain. Blood from the gastrointestinal tract and lower body dilutes umbilical vein blood before it reaches the fetal CNS, reducing and delaying depression.

Enzymatic systems. Enzymatic systems are poorly developed in the fetus and newborn inhibiting drug metabolism. Sometimes when mothers have received enzyme-inducing drugs (such as phenobarbital) for a period of time prior to delivery, the ability of the fetus to metabolize certain drugs is enhanced.[45] (This is not adequate grounds for the administration of barbiturates to the mother!)

Immaturity of the fetal brain. Brain cells and nerve fibers in the fetus are immature and incompletely myelinized, making them much more vulnerable to the effects of drugs (the protective layers of myelin are not present in adequate amounts).

Fetal plasma proteins, red cells, and pH. The fetus binds drugs much the same as the mother, but levels are different owing to the slight differences in fetal plasma proteins, red cells, and pH within the fetus. Some drugs are bound with greater affinity in the fetus, leading to higher concentrations in fetal blood than in maternal blood.

Cord compression. Cord compression occurs to some extent in many labors (sometimes positional and sometimes owing to occult occlusion by compression between the fetal presenting part and the pelvis) and temporarily reduces flow.

SYSTEMIC MEDICATION IN LABOR
Barbiturates

Drug	Common dose
Secobarbital (Seconal)	100 mg IM, PO
Pentobarbital (Nembutal	100 mg IM, PO
Phenobarbital (Luminal)	100 mg IM, PO
Pentothal sodium (Thiopental)	2.5 mg/kg—used only for induction of general anesthesia, IV

Therapeutic effects. The barbiturates are used in early labor (latent phase) for sedation and sleep with some amnesia. Tension and apprehension are replaced with indifference and lowered anxiety. Alone the barbiturates do not affect the pain threshhold, but they may reduce the amount of analgesic narcotics required when given in combination. There may be some mood elevation and release of inhibitions. Barbiturates may improve labor progress by reducing tension and sympathetic uterine spasticity. They should not be given in active labor.

Maternal side effects. Maternal side effects include lethargy, vertigo, restlessness, delirium, decreased perception of sensory stimulus, nausea/vomiting, and decreased blood pressure. Labor may be slowed if barbiturates are given in large doses.

Fetal/newborn side effects. Barbiturates are highly lipid soluble and cross the placenta readily. They can cause CNS depression, apnea, and prolonged newborn drowsiness. Metabolism and excretion are slow. Neurobehavioral effects include decreased alertness, difficult arousal, delay in establishment of adequate feeding,[30] and decreased muscle tone. On the other hand, barbiturates may reduce lactic acid buildup in the presence of fetal hypoxia by reducing metabolism in the brain. Also, increased oxygenation of the placenta may result from reduced sympathetic uterine vessel constriction in the presence of excessive maternal stress. Given early in latent labor the relaxing effect may be beneficial in a very apprehensive or exhausted mother by permitting rest and sleep.

The use of barbiturates is discouraged in active labor because of the prolonged action in the newborn and the lack of an antagonist. (The exception to this is administration of the ultrashort-acting sodium pentothal for rapid induction for surgical intervention.) Barbiturate effects are exaggerated and more serious in the premature or compromised infant and are contraindicated.

Narcotic analgesics

Drug	Common dose
Morphine sulfate	8 to 15 mg IM
Meperidine (Demerol, Pethidine)	50 to 100 mg IM; 25 to 50 mg IV
Pentazocine (Talwin)	30 to 60 mg IM
Alphaprodine (Nisentil)	20 to 40 mg IM, IV
Anileridine (Leritine)	25 to 50 mg IM; 5 to 10 mg IV *slow*

Therapeutic effects. Narcotics increase pain tolerance by about 50% and take the edge off peak contractions. They promote relaxation and may allow sleep between contractions. The relaxation may speed cervical dilatation. After a rest, increased efficiency and coordination may replace colicky uterine action. Contrary to popular belief, instead of slowing labor meperidine (Demerol) has a slightly oxytocic effect. After a brief respite, contractions resume their former level and may even improve.

Maternal side effects. Maternal side effects may include euphoria, apathy, lethargy, nausea/vomiting (especially with IV administration), mild respiratory and circulatory depression, restlessness, slowing of early labor with very large doses, transient mental impairment, and decreased gastrointestinal motility and emptying time. Giving a tranquilizer along with the narcotic potentiates its action and reduces nausea.

Fetal/newborn side effects. Narcotics easily cross the placenta, and the level of fetal/neonatal CNS depression depends on dose, route, and timing of injection.[54] This may be seen as fetal bradycardia (average decrease of 15 to 20 beats/min). Respiratory depression, acidosis, hyporeflexia, and hypotonia are greatest when delivery occurs in the second or third hour after IM administration. If delivery is within 1 hour, the baby is usually minimally depressed. The risk is greatest in prematurity or if general anesthesia becomes necessary within a few hours after administration.

Neurobehavioral effects are also dose related and include decreased ability to reduce response to nonmeaningful stimuli. Also impaired is the infant's response to spoken sounds, comforting measures, alerting stimuli, and cuddling. This may interfere with early infant-parental bonding experiences.[9,10,11]

Narcotic antagonists

Drug	Common dose
Nalorphine (Nalline) levallorphan (Lorfan)	Dose must be titered to narcotic dose given to mother
Naloxone (Narcan)	0.02 to 0.04 mg IM or IV to the newborn— comes in "neonatal Narcan" vials as well as adult vials

The narcotic antagonists are closely related to the narcotics and can reverse their effects (*not* those of barbiturates or tranquilizers). Nalorphine and levallorphan, if given in greater doses than required, cause respiratory depression instead of improvement. Naloxone is the antagonist of choice because

it will not cause CNS depression even with overdosage. It is preferable to administer the antagonist directly to the newborn via the umbilical vein or intramuscularly so as to achieve maximal newborn effect without reducing maternal analgesia. Naloxone has also been shown to reduce neurobehavioral effects of narcotics.[8,23] Improvement is seen within moments of newborn injection, provided supportive/resuscitative measures have been instituted promptly. At this time there appears to be no valid contraindication to giving naloxone (Narcan) to the newborn if it is believed that depression has been induced by narcotics.

Tranquilizers

Drug	Common dose
Phenothiazines	
Chlorpromazine (Thorazine)	25 mg IM, IV
Propiomazine (Largon)	20 to 40 mg IM, IV
Promethazine (Phenergan)	25 to 50 mg IM, IV
Promazine (Sparine)	25 mg IM, IV
Benzodiazepines	
Diazepam (Valium)	2, 5, or 10 mg IM or IV
Chlordiazepoxide (Librium)	5 to 10 mg IM, IV
Hydroxyzine (Vistaril, Atarax)	10 to 25 mg IM, IV

Therapeutic effects. Tranquilizers (ataractics) induce relaxation and potentiate the effects of narcotics. They reduce the dose of analgesics required and help eliminate nausea and vomiting. There may be mood elevation.[18] An intravenous dose of diazepam (Valium) is used by some obstetricians for brief unconsciousness during very short manipulations such as manual removal of the placenta. This is risky, however, because of the danger of aspiration during even brief periods of semiconsciousness.

Maternal side effects. Maternal side effects may include vertigo, drowsiness, hypotension unresponsive to vasopressors, light-headedness, and reduced concentration. Extrapyramidal reactions may occur with any of the phenothiazines. These include oculogyric crisis and spasm and arching of the neck and back (mimicking meningitis symptoms).

Fetal/newborn side effects. All tranquilizers cross the placenta, and they and their metabolites may remain in the bloodstream of the newborn for over a week. There may be fetal tachycardia and loss of normal beat-to-beat variability seen on fetal heart monitor tracings. There may be delayed onset or depression of respiration, hypotonia, hyporeflexia, apneic spells, hypoxia, reluctance to feed, and impaired thermoregulation.[67] Again, the effects are worse in premature infants. Learning behaviors have been thought by some to be slowed, but in the doses used, this is very debatable.

Muscle relaxants

Drug	Common dose
d-Tubocurarine (Tubarine)	6 to 9 mg IV
Suxamethonium, succinylcholine (Anectine)	2 to 3 mg/kg IV
Alcuronium (Alloferin, Toxiferene)	10 to 15 mg IV
Pancuronium (Pavulon)	0.065 mg/kg
Gallamine (Flaxedil)	2 mg/kg IV

Therapeutic effects. Following intravenous administration, rapid, brief skeletal muscle relaxation and paralysis occur owing to myoneural blocking. The muscle relaxants are used to produce relaxation of voluntary muscles prior to anesthesia and endotracheal intubation.

Maternal side effects. Maternal side effects may include bradycardia, tachycardia, and transient apnea. Respiratory failure occurs only with large doses. Bronchospasm may occur making intubation difficult. These drugs are contraindicated in hepatic, renal, pulmonary, and cardiovascular disease. The combined effects of muscle relaxants and magnesium sulfate must be considered when giving anesthesia to a preeclamptic mother who has received magnesium sulfate to preclude seizures.

Fetal/newborn side effects. These skeletal muscle relaxants have a low degree of lipid solubility and are highly ionized at normal pH levels. They pass the placenta with great difficulty. Fetal paralysis occurs only with excessively high maternal doses, and depression/hypoxia only occur if the mother is not adequately ventilated.

Belladonna alkaloids

Drug	Common dose
Atropine	0.4 to 0.6 mg IM, IV

Therapeutic effects. Atropine is used as an anticholinergic and smooth muscle antispasmodic. It is used prior to surgery to suppress salivation, bronchial mucus, and gastric secretions.

Maternal side effects. Maternal side effects include dry mouth, thirst, mydriasis, light-headedness, and tachycardia.

Fetal/newborn side effects. Rapid passage through the placenta causes tachycardia and reduced beat-to-beat variability.[21] The heightened fetal heart rate does not correct the fetal hypoxia associated with late decelerations. Care must be taken not to mistake the increased fetal heart rate for improving fetal condition when atropine is given prior to cesarean section for respiratory distress. NOTE: Hyoscine (scopolamine) has no place in modern obstetrical practice because alone it causes agitation and little pain relief. Together with narcotics, it predisposes to serious fetal and maternal depression.[1]

VERTEBRAL AND REGIONAL ANALGESIA

Regional anesthetic techniques include subarachnoid (spinal), lumbar and caudal epidural, paracervical, pudendal, and local blocks. The spinal technique makes use of the lowest dosage of local anesthetic solution. There is little evidence that fetal depression can be caused by the anesthetic itself with spinal block.

Lumbar and caudal epidural blocks require the greatest amounts of anesthetics, but infants are usually vigorous unless there have been serious maternal side effects such as hypotension. Special care must be taken with all vertebral blocks to position and move the patient carefully, owing to reduced coordination and muscular strength or paralysis of the lower extremities.

Paracervical block is the only regional technique that exposes the fetus to significant risk of overdosage. The high level of local anesthetic in fetal blood leads to cardiac depression, bradycardia, and acidosis. There is also a greater chance of direct injection of the fetus or the uterine vessels, leading to severe toxicity or death.[19]

Pudendal block and local infiltration of the perineum have limited effects and are useful only when delivery is imminent and for repair of lacerations or episiotomy.

Subarachnoid block

Subarachnoid block, also known as subdural, spinal, or saddle block, is the reversible nerve block produced by injection of local anesthetic into the dural sac. The spinal cord ends at L-1 or L-2, with the subarachnoid space continuing caudally to S-2. The spinal needle is inserted at L4-5 and is extended to T10-11 for midspinal anesthesia (literal saddle block—low spinal—is usually inadequate). It is extended to T-5 for cesarean section. Spinal block, because of its limited duration (1 to 2 hours at most), is used toward the end of labor, often in the delivery room. The addition of dextrose to the anesthetic solution makes it hyperbaric, allowing positional control over its spread. Spinal block is usually given with the patient sitting and leaning forward to spread the intervertebral spaces. The sitting position is maintained for 3 to 5 minutes after injection until the anesthetic has become fixed in the neural tissues. The block may be given in the lateral curled position usually used for lumbar puncture as long as the spinal column is kept in slight reverse Trendelenburg position to avoid spread of the block to higher segments. After 5 minutes, position change has very little effect on the level of anesthesia, so the mother can be helped to her position of comfort.

The bladder should be emptied prior to any vertebral block, and an intravenous infusion (usually of dextrose in 5% Ringer's lactate) should be running. Wide preparation of the back with antiseptic solution and strict aseptic technique is mandatory. Injection is not given during a contraction because this compresses the subarachnoid space and forces the anesthetic to spread to higher levels. For the same reason, coughing, pushing, and vomiting are to be avoided during the first 5 minutes after injection. The dose is determined by the height of the patient and the particular anesthetic agent being used. Vital signs, especially blood pressure and respirations, must be measured prior to the block and until well stabilized after administration.

Therapeutic effects. With a midspinal block, complete relief of the perineal and uterine pain, perineal muscle relaxation, and partial loss of sensation in the abdomen and thighs occurs. Spinal block allows painless forceps manipulation and manual removal of the placenta should these be indicated. Relief of pain lasts about 1 to 1½ hours, depending on the anesthetic and dose.

Maternal side effects. Effective progress of labor is halted, so the spinal block is given only with full dilatation and adequate descent of the fetus for low forceps delivery.[28] The bearing down reflex is obliterated so that forceps delivery is often required. Hypotension owing to sympathetic blockade occurs more frequently with spinal blocks than with any other block, and it tends to be more severe. Hypotension is avoided by hydration (500 to 1000 ml Ringer's lactate over 30 minutes) prior to the block. This must be done with caution to avoid overload. Lateral position (or left uterine displacement as previously described), oxygen by mask, and intravenous ephedrine, if required to restore pressure, are instituted after the block.

Postspinal headache owing to cerebrospinal fluid leakage can be severe and prolonged. However, headaches are much less common now with the use of 25-gauge (or smaller) needles and adequate hydration. Occasionally a 10 ml homologous blood patch is injected into the epidural space at the site of spinal puncture with immediate relief.[42] Adequate hydration and bed rest for 12 to 24 hours after the block are still often recommended for prevention, and abdominal binders may be helpful.

Dyspnea or respiratory arrest is possible if a large dose or spread results in a high or "total" spinal. Therefore, emergency equipment for ventilatory support must be *immediately* available.

Bladder dysfunction is frequent, and periodic catheterization may be necessary. Postpartum backache is sometimes attributed to spinal block, especially if repeated attempts have been made or if care in positioning of the patient was inadequate. Often backache occurs whether or not the patient has had a spinal block.

Temporary neurological complications such as cranial nerve palsy, paresthesia, and unilateral footdrop have occurred and are very frightening to the patient. Continual assurance that they are temporary may be needed. Rarely there may be some permanent nerve damage.

Spinal block should not be given to a patient on anticoagulant therapy or in the presence of hemorrhage, shock, infection, tumor at the site, increased intracranial pressure, history of severe headaches, or acute fetal distress.

Fetal/newborn side effects. The dose of anesthetic used for spinal block is usually insufficient to produce fetal bradycardia, respiratory depression, or altered neurological behavior in the newborn unless significant maternal hypotension or respiratory insufficiency is allowed to occur.

Epidural block

Epidural block may be caudal, lumbar, or a combination of both. They are rapidly becoming the anesthetic of choice for normal and complicated deliveries because of the superior pain relief and safety obtained.[45-47,49] For surgery they offer the advantage of little neonatal depression and minimal risk of maternal aspiration.

Lumbar epidural block

Lumbar epidural block, also known as peridural, extradural, and spinal epidural block, is a vertebral block produced by the injection of local anesthetic solution into the lumbar epidural space outside the dura. It is most often used as a continuous technique by threading a Teflon catheter through the spinal needle for a few centimeters prior to removal of the needle. Epidural injection can be used as a one-time technique if delivery is expected within an hour, although a spinal at this point would probably be easier and safer.

The fatty tissues of the epidural space absorb the anesthetic, although some is absorbed by the distended vertebral vessels into the bloodstream. The preparation and precautions used with a spinal block are also necessary with epidural procedures. A 17-gauge epidural needle is inserted into the L3-4 or L4-5 interspace with the patient in the lateral position (minimal curl needed) using a loss of resistance technique to avoid puncture of the dura. A test dose of anesthetic is injected; if there is tingling of the legs with warmth and dryness of the feet and no paralysis after 5 minutes, the needle is properly placed. The catheter is then introduced no further than 3 cm past the needle tip (to avoid diversion or kinking resulting in spotty inadequate block). The

needle is then withdrawn over the catheter, and the catheter is taped well along the back, attached to a filter, and capped until subsequent injections are needed. A full anesthetic dose based on height and drug is given. The patient is turned to the supine position with left uterine displacement, or she is turned from one side to the other to achieve a bilateral block while avoiding hypotension. The level of effect is tested by pinpricks within the various dermatome levels 15 minutes after injection. Fig. 12-3 shows appropriate sites for pinprick tests.

Small doses of low-concentration anesthetics can be given to restrict analgesia to the uterus and cervical regions, T-10 through L-1, during the first stage of labor. It is undesirable and unnecessary to block the sacral roots at this stage because it might prematurely relax the muscles of the pelvic floor, thereby possibly interfering with flexion and rotation of the fetal head.

Later, the pain caused by distention of the perineum can be relieved by extension of the block. This can be achieved by using larger doses and giving the last injection with the patient sitting up. A double catheter technique (lumbar and caudal) can allow definitive control of analgesic/anesthetic levels.

Solutions used for epidural blocks are strong enough to block pain but should not block large motor nerves. Therefore, theoretically, the mother can cooperate fully and should be capable of pushing even though the urge will be lost.

Continuous fetal heart rate and uterine contraction monitoring should be used along with frequent assessment of vital signs and blood pressure.

An epidural block can be administered as soon as the patient needs relief, although many doctors wait until 4 to 6 cm of dilatation has been achieved. Precluding excessive doses and hypotension, effects on labor are minimal. Augmentation with oxytocin may be needed. "Top-up" injections are given whenever pain returns. Aspiration of the syringe is essential prior to each injection to preclude injection of a vessel. The catheter is removed when anesthesia is no longer needed. An antiseptic may be applied to the site followed by a sterile dressing. No prolonged pressure is necessary.

Therapeutic effects. Excellent analgesia and anesthesia are achieved throughout labor and delivery without the complications of inhalation anesthesia

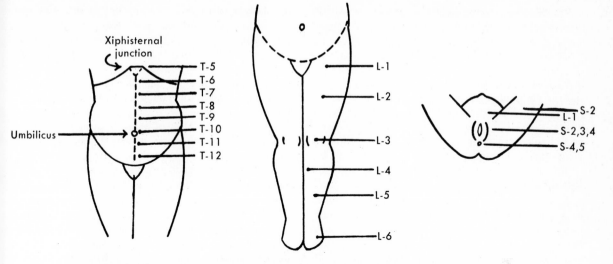

Fig. 12-3. Pinprick points for determining level of vertebral analgesia and anesthesia. Testing of abdomen should be close to midline because of slanting distribution of each dermatome. One prick is made for each appropriate level no sooner than 15 minutes after block. Normal pinprick sensation should be demonstrated to patient prior to instituting block.

or the postspinal headache sometimes associated with spinal anesthesia. The mother is alert and cooperative and relaxed for the birth of her baby. Painless operative delivery and manipulations are permitted. Epidural block also helps to smooth incoordinate uterine contractions, and it reduces maternal sympathetic vasoconstriction of the uterine vessels.

Maternal side effects. Hypotension is the cardinal complication of epidural blocks, although its incidence and severity are usually less than with spinal blocks. Prevention and treatment are the same as described for spinal hypotension.[31,56-59] Accidental intravenous injection may cause convulsions and loss of consciousness; therefore the catheter is always aspirated carefully prior to each injection. Accidental puncture of the dura by the large needle can lead to severe headache. Rarely there may be infection or backache. Loss of the urge to push can be countered by thorough teaching prior to the block. There is increased use of forceps and oxytocin with epidural blocks. Rarely a piece of catheter breaks off and is retained within the epidural space. Usually this causes no problem, although the patient

and her doctor should be aware of its presence. (For this reason, the catheter is never withdrawn through the needle during placement.)

Bladder dysfunction is not uncommon, although how much of this is related to labor and delivery trauma is not known. Toxic reactions to the relatively large quantities of local anesthetics used may occur. Total spinal block owing to inadvertent injection of large doses beneath the dura is treated with ventilatory and cardiovascular support as needed until the effect wears off. Contraindications for the use of epidural blocks are the same as those for spinal blocks.

Fetal/newborn side effects. Properly administered and monitored, lumbar epidural block has little deleterious effect on the fetus. In fact, it may reduce the severity of fetal hypoxia by increasing uterine blood flow, shortening labor, and decreasing the forces resistant to the passage of the fetus through the birth canal (a tight pelvic floor). If severe maternal hypotension occurs or intravenous injection has been made, fetal and newborn bradycardia, hypoxia, acidosis, and toxicosis may occur. Whenever a local anesthetic is administered, some reaches the fetus and causes some degree of the toxic effects that will be discussed later.[52,53]

Caudal epidural block

Caudal epidural block, also known as sacral epidural, caudal peridural, and caudal anesthesia, is a form of epidural block in which a local anesthetic is injected into the epidural space by way of the sacral hiatus. Like a lumbar epidural block, it may be used as a one-time injection or as a continuous technique via catheter placement. The caudal block may be more difficult technically because of the high incidence of variation in the sacral anatomy. However, there is very little risk of puncturing the dura. The caudal block is applied with the patient in the Sims's or semi-prone flexed position. Caudal block, owing to its anatomical placement, anesthetizes the sacral levels first, regardless of stage of labor. It requires larger doses of anesthetic solution than lumbar epidural block in order to block up to level T-10. With caudal block, perineal anesthesia is obtained rapidly without resorting to special positioning. The first signs of successful block are loss of the urge to push (if it was present), loss of the anal reflex, hypalgesia of the perineum, numbness and tingling of the toes, and dryness and warmth of the feet. These occur in 5 to 15 minutes. Gradually analgesia extends upward to include the abdomen. Caudal block should not be used when the presenting part is on the pelvic floor because of a higher risk of direct injection of the fetus. A caudal epidural may be used as part of a double catheter technique to restrict its action to the second stage. It may be extended, like the lumbar epidural block, for cesarean section.

Therapeutic effects. With caudal epidural block there is excellent relief of pain with an awake, relaxed, and cooperative mother. Perineal anesthesia is excellent.

Maternal side effects. Hypotension is the greatest risk. Generally the side effects are the same as the lumbar epidural block with the following exceptions: The incidence of one-sided or partial block is less likely than with lumbar epidural block because of the reduced chance of catheter diversion. There is higher incidence of infection owing to the proximity of the injection site to the anus. Because of higher doses, toxic reactions may be more frequent. Dural puncture is less likely so there is less risk of total spinal anesthesia and postspinal headache. Owing to premature blocking of the sacral segments, there may be more interference with flexion and rotation of the fetal head.

Contraindications for caudal block and treatment of side effects are the same as with lumbar epidural block.

Fetal/newborn side effects. The fetal/newborn side effects are the same as with lumbar epidural block, except that direct injection of the fetus is more likely and higher doses may lead to increased potential for toxicity and depression.

Paracervical block

Paracervical block is a form of nerve block in which a local anesthetic is injected into the vicinity of the cervix to block impulses from the uterine body and the cervix. It was very popular for relief of first stage labor pain until the high incidence of fetal bradycardia was recognized. Modification of the technique has improved its safety.[63] Fetal heart monitoring should be instituted (preferably by continuous technique) before the block to reveal baseline characteristics. With the patient in the lithotomy position, the perineum is prepped. There is no preparation of the vagina. The anesthetist, using aseptic technique, injects 10 to 20 ml of low concentration (1%) local anesthetic in divided doses at two to four sites around the cervix. A needle guide is used to prevent penetration of the needle more than 1 cm into the mucosa. Actually, penetration of only 2 mm is adequate and safer.[1] The dose is divided to give more uniform anesthesia and to avoid injection of high doses at any one site. Aspiration of the needle prior to each injection is essential to avoid injection of a blood vessel. The patient is turned on her side, and fetal heart rate monitoring must be continued for at least 30 minutes until the rate is back to baseline levels.

Analgesia starts in a few minutes and lasts for 1 to 2 hours, depending on the drug and dose used. It may be repeated if necessary, using the same precautions and technique. Paracervical block is ineffective during the second stage for pain originating in the perineum, and it is often supplemented with pudendal block or local infiltration near the time of delivery.

Therapeutic effects. Most mothers experience good relief of pain for 1 to 2 hours, and there is little risk of hypotension.

Maternal side effects. Failure to produce adequate analgesia is not uncommon, and its incidence varies with the skill of the anesthetist. Late first stage block is more likely to fail than one instituted early in active labor. A transient (about 20 minutes) decrease in intensity and frequency of uterine contractions may occur. Inadvertent intravascular injection or rapid absorption of the anesthetic into the bloodstream may result in mild to severe toxic reactions. Numbness of the lower extremities and sacral neuritis may occur. Maternal hypotension occurs in about 1:600 owing to compression of the vena cava.[1] Paracervical block is contraindicated in the presence of vaginal infection because of the possibility of endometritis.

Fetal/newborn side effects. Fetal bradycardia is the most common and serious complication of paracervical block.[14] It involves a decrease in the fetal heart rate below 120 beats/min for more than 1 minute and occurs in 25% or more cases. The fetal heart rate usually drops within 10 minutes of injection and takes about 10 to 20 minutes to recover. These times are very variable, and the bradycardia is often much more dramatic. The bradycardia may be caused by decreased uterine blood flow owing to aortocaval compression or constriction of the uterine vessels caused by the anesthetic itself or to added epinephrine. For this reason, epinephrine should not be added to paracervical block anesthetics in an attempt to prolong their effects.

It is more likely that bradycardia is due to the direct effect of the anesthetic on the fetus. This may be caused by direct injection of the fetus, injection into a uterine vessel, or rapid diffusion into the uterine vessels. The effect is direct myocardial depression in the fetus and may lead to acidosis with lowered Apgar scores if the bradycardia lasts more than 10 minutes. The greatest effect is seen if the baby is born within 30 minutes following the block before restoration of the baseline rate and in the presence of a premature or compromised fetus. For these reasons, paracervical block is contraindicated when prematurity is known or suspected, when the fetus is significantly compromised in any way, or when delivery is expected within 1 hour. Convulsions and death may occur if the fetus is injected directly.[13] Treatment of the bradycardia during labor consists of positioning the mother on her side and giving oxygen by mask. Usually delivery is delayed until the fetal heart rate resumes its normal level because the newborn metabolism of local anesthetics is quite prolonged. Treatment of the newborn with toxicity is explained later.

Pudendal block

Pudendal block is the transvaginal or transperineal injection of a local anesthetic solution bilaterally through the sacrospinous ligament posterior and medial to the ischial spines. The transvaginal approach makes use of a needle guard to avoid injecting the solution too deeply. Timing is important to success. Once the perineum is distended, it is too late for adequate analgesia. In primigravidas the block is made when the cervix is fully dilated and the presenting part is at +2 station. In multiparas it is given at about 7 to 8 cm dilatation. The technique is relatively simple, and it is adequate for vaginal delivery. It is often combined with earlier paracervical block. Failure of the block, often caused by timing, is not uncommon. Failure to obtain good analgesia may lead to repeated injections, which can lead to overdosage. It is not adequate analgesia for intrauterine or midforceps manipulations.

Therapeutic effects. Pudendal block can give good analgesia of the vagina and the perineum if it is properly timed and performed.

Maternal side effects. The reflex urge to bear down is lost with pudendal block. Trauma to the sciatic nerve is possible. Accidental injection of the large pudendal artery or vein, or of the fetus, may occur leading to toxic reactions. Hematomas are not uncommon, and rare puncture of the rectum may occur.

Fetal/newborn side effects. There is a low incidence of newborn toxicity unless direct injection of the fetus or a maternal blood vessel has occurred.

Local infiltration of the perineum

Local infiltration is used primarily for episiotomy and repair of lacerations. Injection can be made with care even when the presenting part is very low. The technique is simple with almost 100% success. Injection of a large amount of anesthetic solution is made into the subcutaneous tissues, muscles, and fascia. The area anesthetized is triangular, bounded by the clitoris, perianal region, and the points half-way between the anus and the tuberosities. Repeated aspiration is necessary to avoid intravascular injection. Anesthetic effect occurs within 5 minutes.

The local anesthetic drugs

The local anesthetics commonly used in obstetrics are as follows:

Drug	Common dose
Ester-linked	
Procaine	
(Novcain)	
2-Chloroprocaine	
(Nesacaine)	
Tetracaine	
(Pontocaine)	
Amide-linked	
Lidocaine	0.5%, 1.0%, 1.5%, or 2.0% so-
(Xylocaine)	lutions are used, depending on
Mepivacaine	the region of infiltration:
(Carbocaine)	epidural—10 to 15 ml
Bupivacaine	of 1% to 2%
(Marcaine)	spinal—1 to 1.5 ml
Etidocaine	paracervical—10 to 20 ml
(Duranest)	of 1%
Dibucaine	pudendal—10 to 20 ml
(Nupercaine)	of 1%
Prilocaine	
(Citanest)	

The addition of epinephrine to anesthetic solutions may be desirable for certain blocks to slow systemic absorption and prolong the action. However, this may also cause undesired uterine vasoconstriction,[13,24] especially with paracervical and pudendal blocks.

Allergic reactions to the "caine" drugs are not uncommon, and screening of patients for prior reaction in themselves or their immediate blood relatives is essential. A small patch test may be indicated prior to the institution of a full block.

Local anesthetics, when used for regional blocks (except spinal block), are rapidly absorbed into the maternal bloodstream and readily transferred to the fetus. Except with spinal block, relatively large doses are given, and this may lead to high fetal blood levels, direct myocardial depression, and neonatal depression. Highest levels of toxicity are probably seen with paracervical block, although fatal

levels can be reached by inadvertent injection of the drug into the fetus or into a maternal vessel with other techniques. The local anesthetics can cause fetal bradycardia, loss of beat-to-beat variability, and induced effects owing to maternal hypotension.

The ester-linked anesthetics are rapidly broken down by plasma cholinesterases in the mother, fetus, and possibly the placenta. Thus they are relatively short acting and may require more frequent repeat injections, leading to buildup.

The amide-linked anesthetics are broken down more slowly by liver enzymes and have a longer duration of action. Bupivacaine and etidocaine require smaller total doses, have the greatest maternal plasma binding, and are highly ionized and long acting. Thus they are often favored in obstetrics. However, like the other amide-linked types, they are very slowly broken down by the fetal liver and are contraindicated in paracervical block owing to greater fetal absorption. Prilocaine has been implicated in both maternal and fetal methemoglobinemia and is rarely used anymore.

Maternal toxicity may be signalled by palpitations, dry mouth, tinnitus, vertigo, nausea, and confusion leading into loss of consciousness, muscle twitching, and convulsions. Eventually there will be hypotension, bradycardia, respiratory depression, and cardiac and respiratory arrest. Maternal toxic reactions are treated with oxygen, intravenous diazepam, vasopressors (ephedrine), intubation, and ventilation as indicated by response. Allergic reactions are treated with antihistamines and corticosteroids if needed.

Toxic newborn reactions involve alterations in the CNS, peripheral vascular tone, and cardiac function.[59] Seizures, bradycardia, hypotonia, apnea, cyanosis, and unresponsiveness to ventilation are common indications of severe toxicity in the newborn. The seizures usually occur early, within 6 hours, as opposed to hypoxic seizures, which usually begin 12 to 24 hours after delivery. Mepivacaine has been shown to have the highest incidence of toxicity.

Significant effects of local anesthetics on early infant sensorimotor function have been reported[52] and are demonstrated by impaired muscular, visual, and neurological performance. The newborn's response decrement to repeated nonmeaningful stimuli may be impaired, and there may be lower scores on tests of muscular strength and tone, diminished rooting quality, and a less vigorous Moro reflex. Increased irritability and diminished motor maturity were also found. These effects are less prominent than those seen with the maternal systemic medications. They appear to be of short duration, but longitudinal studies are needed to rule out long-term developmental abnormalities.

Treatment of fetal local anesthetic toxicity includes appropriate supportive care and promotion of drug elimination. Prompt resuscitation, ventilation, and maintenance of normal acid-base levels may permit the infant to avoid hypoxic damage. Forced diuresis is the safest, most effective means of eliminating the drug. Intravenous infusion of 140 ml/kg/day of 5% of dextrose and water is indicated with care not to overload the infant. Exchange transfusion may help if diuresis is inadequate. Barbiturates or diazepam are given cautiously as anticonvulsants. Since the drug is attracted to the acidic stomach and tends to pool there, gastric lavage also helps eliminate the drug.[17]

INHALATION ANESTHESIA

The common agents used for inhalation analgesia and general anesthesia are:

Drug	Common dose
Inhalation agents (may be self-administered with inhalers)	
Nitrous oxide and O_2	50:50 or 33:66
Methoxyflurane (Penthrane)	0.1% to 1.5%
Trichloroethylene (Trilene)	0.5%
Inhalation agents (uterine relaxants)	
Halothane (Fluothane)	0.5%
Diethyl ether	2.0% to 5.0%
Cyclopropane	3.0% to 5.0% — highly flammable
Enflurane	
Fluroxene (Fluoromar)	1.0% to 2.0%
IV agents for induction	
Sodium pentothal	2.5 mg/kg IV
Ketamine	0.25 to 0.5 mg/kg IV

The use of inhalation anesthetics has two primary means of application: intermittent, for analgesia, and continuous, for general anesthesia. Inhalation analgesia produced by the administration of appropriate concentrations of the gaseous agents is effective, although it is not used very frequently in the United States. It is used when sedatives, narcotics, and psychoprophylaxis are no longer effective for controlling moderate to severe pain in the active phase. The inhalation agents are more potent analgesics than the narcotics in doses used. There is little metabolism or accumulation with intermittent use so that fetal effects are minimal. Uterine contractions are unimpeded, and the mother remains conscious with protective reflexes intact and full ability to push and cooperate. Usually a pudendal block is necessary to achieve perineal anesthesia during delivery. The agents most widely used for intermittent administration are nitrous oxide with oxygen; methoxyflurane, 0.35%; and trichloroethylene, 0.5%. All are safe, efficient, and pleasant. Halothane and enflurane are not used because of their low analgesic quality and their profound myometrial relaxation.

During labor the gases may be administered by the mother herself with a special hand-held apparatus, or they may be given by an anesthetist. The proper use of self-inhalers includes proper fit of the mask, application of the mask at the very beginning of each contraction (before pain is felt), and deep inhalation. When the contraction subsides, the mask is removed. In any case, if the patient begins to lose consciousness, she will drop the mask. If administered by an anesthetist, very careful observation is necessary to detect the first sign of excitement or loss of consciousness. Continued conversation with the mother helps in this respect.

Continuous general anesthesia is not usually indicated for normal vaginal delivery. It carries all the usual risks of general anesthesia plus the potential for depression of the newborn. It is usually achieved by a combination of intravenous drugs and inhalation agents and is reserved for operative procedures. Inhalation anesthesia is usually well accepted by the patient (as opposed to surgery while fully conscious), and a light plane of anesthesia can be achieved rapidly, making it a good technique for emergency procedures.

A common "balanced" IV-inhalation technique is the following:

1. Sidelying position or supine position with left uterine displacement maintained throughout
2. Antacid, 30 ml PO (sometimes preceded by gastric emptying)

3. Preoxygenation/denitrogenization for 3 to 10 minutes during preparation (IV infusion, bladder catheterization, shave, and skin preparation)
4. Atropine, 0.4 to 0.6 mg IV to decrease secretions
5. d-Tubocurarine 3 to 6 mg IV to prevent fasciculations from subsequent succinylcholine
6. Induction with a sleep dose of IV pentothal (2.5 mg/kg)
7. Cricoid pressure immediately to prevent regurgitation and aspiration
8. Succinylcholine, 80 to 100 mg for muscle relaxation
9. Immediate endotracheal intubation with cuffed ET tube
10. Maintenance with intermittent positive pressure ventilation with nitrous oxide:oxygen and small dose of halothane (0.5%), the latter needed for decreased awareness
11. Deepening of anesthesia after cord is clamped
12. Oxytocin IV drip (10 units/1000 ml) to preclude hemorrhage from an atonic uterus
13. Sublimaze or other narcotic may be given (since no premedication) to preclude severe pain on awakening
14. Full consciousness required before extubation to prevent aspiration

Maternal side effects. The chief risks of general anesthesia for the mother are aspiration of gastric contents and uterine atony with hemorrhage. Aspiration remains the most common cause of anesthetic-related maternal mortality.[51] The propensity for vomiting and regurgitation is high during pregnancy and increased during labor. The pH of gastric contents is usually quite low (less than 2.5). Gastric emptying time is also very slow, and often the mother has particulate food matter in the stomach from a meal eaten many hours before. General anesthesia eradicates the laryngeal and cough reflexes and often stimulates vomiting. Aspiration of low-pH gastric juices leads to a chemical pneumonitis known as Mendelson's syndrome, while aspiration of particulate matter leads commonly to pneumonia. Preventive measures include (1) oral antacid administration (15 to 20 ml every 2 hours during labor and 30 to 50 ml within an hour before anesthesia), (2) maintaining mothers NPO with only small amounts of ice chips or sips of water during labor, (3) decompression or emptying of the stomach prior to induction, (4) smooth induction, (5) application of cricoid pressure with induction (by an assistant), and (6) prompt endotracheal intubation maintained until the mother is fully awake after surgery.

Mendelson's syndrome is a particularly problematic type of aspiration and can rapidly lead to death. It is produced by aspiration of small amounts of highly acidic gastric fluid (pH < 2.5), resulting in fulminant chemical or allergic tracheitis and pneumonitis. The regurgitation is often silent, and attendants may be unaware that it has occurred. Very small quantities (25 ml) are sufficient to cause death. The acidic material causes intense bronchospasm followed by a congestive reaction. The patient becomes restless or agitated. Respiratory rate increases as the patient becomes tachycardic and cyanotic. Frothy pink secretions may be produced, and eventually shock and heart failure occur.

Early diagnosis and treatment are essential. Endotracheal irrigation is followed by instillation of steroids. Systemic corticosteroids are used to limit the extent of the inflammatory reaction and to reduce bronchial edema. Assisted ventilation is often needed, and antibiotics are given to preclude infection. Bronchoscopy may be done to rule out obstruction, and tracheostomy may be necessary.

The other most common complication, uterine atony with hemorrhage, is usually secondary to the use of halothane, enflurane, ether, or cyclopropane anesthetics. These agents cause profound uterine relaxation, which may be desirable for some operative maneuvers. However, after delivery the uterus is incapable of maintaining firm contraction to preclude hemorrhage. It is essential that a continuous dilute intravenous drip of oxytocin be started immediately after delivery and continued until bleeding (hemorrhagic) is unlikely to occur. Close monitoring of vaginal bleeding is vital.

Other postoperative problems caused by general anesthesia are assessed and treated with usual postoperative nursing measures, with the special consideration of providing for early maternal-infant bonding experiences.

Fetal/newborn side effects. Inhalation anesthetics rapidly cross the placenta because of high lipid solubility, low molecular weight, and rapid diffusion. Given intermittently with oxygen at analgesic levels, there is little depression of the newborn regardless of duration of labor. However, when administered in anesthetic concentrations, the degree of fetal CNS depression is proportional to the depth and duration of maternal anesthesia.

When induction to delivery time with nitrous oxide is greater than 15 minutes, the alveolar concentration of anesthetic during the first breaths is very high. This reduces the partial pressure of oxygen in the alveoli and may lead to hypoxemia and depression, even with good initial Apgar scores. Therefore oxygen by mask or blown over the face, for the first few minutes of life would be a good precaution for all newborns born under general anesthesia. The other anesthetics also produce CNS depression; however, with the light plane of anesthesia used prior to delivery, the effects are not marked. If the infant is premature or was in distress prior to delivery, the effects are additive and may require vigorous resuscitative efforts.

Neurobehavioral effects are similar to those seen with the local anesthetics but are usually more pronounced. In addition to the inhalation agents, intravenous thiopental has been shown to have neurobehavioral effects similar to the other barbiturates. Ketamine's newborn effects are not fully understood, and various reports have shown it to be safe. Again, long-term studies are needed to fully assess the effects of these agents. Ketamine is a dissociative anesthetic. It maintains maternal cardiovascular function well, benefiting the infant in that respect. But there is a high incidence of maternal dreams and hallucinations, indicating that the same effects may be occurring in the fetus.

PSYCHOLOGICAL/EDUCATIONAL METHODS OF PAIN CONTROL IN LABOR
Prepared childbirth/psychoprophylaxis

The main principles of prepared childbirth are education, training, conditioning, distraction, motivation, suggestion, and expectation.[62] The patient's understanding of pregnancy, labor, delivery, nursing the newborn, and the hospital environment is achieved by a process called "cognitive rehearsal." This reduces anxiety and increases pain tolerance.

Fear sets off a vicious cycle of skeletal muscle spasm, hypoxia, and pain.[50] Removal of apprehension interrupts the cycle and allows bearable childbirth to be possible. The great advantages of prepared childbirth are minimal fetal depression and the active participation of an awake, alert mother. Early parent-infant bonding has its optimal opportunity to develop. Training includes the following:

Practice in relaxation. Relaxation reduces anxiety, and the mind decreases awareness of pain. The mother is taught to relax all muscles, especially those of the abdomen, back, and pelvis. Tension here exacerbates pain. She practices tightening and relaxing each muscle group separately. Relaxation can be applied to all tension-producing situations and can improve sleep. It is a form of distraction, since it requires concentration. The mother is amenable to suggestion. The ability to relax the pelvic floor helps the mother, doctor, and baby during delivery. Often the mother is taught to respond to touch of a bodily part, or to a command word, with conditioned relaxation.

Muscular exercises. The purpose of the exercises is to strengthen the muscles of the back, abdomen, buttocks, and perineum as well as to limber the joints. The mother has better overall tone, well-being, and ability to push. There is often less backache, better control of bowels, and more rapid healing of episiotomy or lacerations. The exercises should be taught by a qualified person and practiced for 30 minutes twice daily.

Breathing exercises. The mother learns how to breathe properly during each stage of labor. She is taught to concentrate on breathing for distraction, pain control, and better gas exchange for herself and the baby.

The first type of breathing is regular, deep, and slow (10/min), with relaxation of the abdominal wall. The second type is rapid, shallow breathing (panting—60/min) and is used when the slower type is inadequate to control pain. With either type a complete, or clearing breath is taken at the beginning and at the end of each contraction. A complete breath consists of (1) inhaling as deeply as possible, (2) hissing or blowing the air out slowly, and (3) allowing the whole body to go limp. A premature urge to push is counteracted with shallow, rapid blowing, being careful not to hyperventilate. Effective pushing cannot be done unless the breath is held.

During the second stage, pushing breaths are used to augment contractions. The mother breathes in as deeply and quickly as possible at the onset of a contraction. Holding the breath fixes the diaphragm, while intra-abdominal pressure pushes the baby through the birth canal. Catch up breaths are taken as needed, and pushing continues for the duration of the contraction. No type of controlled breathing should be overdone as this can lead to tetany and fetal acidosis. Practice in bearing down is also learned in prenatal classes, although no force should be applied.

Conditioning. An association is developed between breathing and the painless Braxton Hicks contractions during pregnancy. When she feels a contraction, the mother places her hand on her abdomen and breathes regularly and deeply. A conditioned reflex is thus developed between contractions and breathing.

Distraction. Distraction can be achieved by (1) a dissociative process, whereby the mother concentrates on the nonpainful character of a painful stimulus (that is, muscular work as opposed to hurt), or (2) the interference strategy, whereby the mother concentrates on something other than the painful stimulus, making awareness of pain a peripheral consideration.[61] Distraction is more effective in early labor and can consist of effleurage, back pressure or massage, breathing and relaxation exercises, the use of a focal point, or conversation.

Motivation. Women may vary in their motivation to participate in "natural childbirth." The nature of the motivation and the enthusiasm of those around her can help determine the effectiveness of her efforts.

Suggestion. It is stressed that labor and delivery are usually normal physiological events. A brief explanation of cesarean section and the reasons necessitating it are given (especially since the cesarean section rate is so high today).

Expectation. The mother is taught to expect work and discomfort in labor but not pain. This can alter the patient's reaction to contractions.

· · ·

It is highly desirable that the baby's father participate in the childbirth education classes with the mother.[48] The father or significant other person provides support, encouragement, and coaching during labor. Through much practice and conditioning, the pair develops their own set of verbal cues and behaviors to use when labor comes. The nurse should observe and learn these cues early in labor so that she can effectively take over for the coach if necessary.

Reluctant women should never be compelled to participate in childbirth education classes. Also, mothers should not be told that labor will be painless. It is emphasized that pain relief will be available if it is needed, and the various methods should be explained well in advance of labor.

While group classes can provide extra motivation, it is important that no mother be placed in competition with others or be led to believe that only an analgesia-free labor is a success. This may lead to expressed or "silent" feelings of failure for mothers who request medication or who remain outwardly calm knowing inside that the pain was truly almost unbearable.

Hypnosis

Hypnosis is a temporary condition of altered consciousness that can be induced by the self or another person. A variety of effects can be produced including[2]:

1. Alterations in emotional response (increased rapport, suggestibility, and compliance)
2. Alterations in mental response (loss or improvement of memory for an event or change in reasoning and sensibility, such as paresthesia or anesthesia)
3. Alterations in autonomic function (changes in vasomotor systems or endocrine function)
4. Alterations in motor response (varied speed, strength, or nature of stimulus response)

The mother is not unconscious during hypnosis—she is awake and concentrating deeply.

Hypnosis may be safely used by any trained hypnotist who is capable of appraising the psychological status of the patient. It may be applied to any susceptible and emotionally well-adjusted patient. Techniques usually include visual concentration, suggestive conversation, or prerecorded monologues. Six or more prenatal sessions are required, usually beginning around the fifth month. In various studies, about 15% of patients could not be hypnotized, and of those who could, an average of 50% had "comfortable" labors.[12,15,37] The use of hypnosis requires special training of the hypnotist and the mother. Staff must be supportive and provide a quiet, nondistracting environment. The use of hypnotism is limited because of the less than high success rate (for the time invested). The hypnotist usually must be present for the labor and most hospital atmospheres are quite distracting. Hypnosis is contraindicated in patients with significant psychological problems or hysteria, as the condition may be worsened. For selected patients with suggestibility and training, hypnosis can be a safe, effective form of pain control, and aspects of hypnosis are incorporated into childbirth education methods.

Acupuncture

Acupuncture consists of the insertion and vibration of tiny needles into precise points along certain pain pathways specific to labor and delivery. It must be performed by a highly trained acupuncturist, and the success rate for obstetrics is very low. There is no known adverse effect in the fetus, but electric vibration of the needles may interfere with electronic fetal monitoring.

Biofeedback

Extensive studies on the use of biofeedback techniques in obstetrics have not been reported. But considering the high success achieved in training patients to control stress disorders (such as migraine, ulcerative conditions, high blood pressure, refractive pain, and anxiety),[65] it seems likely that obstetrical patients could make use of the effective relaxation techniques taught in biofeedback. The ability to control pain in a mother who learns the method should be greatly enhanced.

CONTROL OF PAIN IN COMPLICATED LABORS

Pathophysiological conditions secondary to or coexistent with pregnancy create special risks for the mother and infant. The choice of method for management of pain can be critical to the health of both. While the side effects of all drugs are more potentially harmful to the premature or compromised infant, adequate pain relief is essential to prevent further harm resulting from maternal anxiety, tension, resistance, and hyperventilation with altered cardiovascular function.

Heart disease

Labor and delivery greatly increase the work of the heart. With rheumatic heart disease, the main goal is to prevent cardiac failure. During labor the following measures are advisable[60]:

1. Hydration with a slow infusion of 5% dextrose in water
2. Relief of stress and apprehension by use of a tranquilizer early in labor
3. Complete relief of pain and abolition of the bearing down reflex with regional block
4. Oxygen administration by nasal cannula or mask
5. Close monitoring of vital signs and auscultation of the chest for signs of pulmonary edema or changed heart sounds
6. Monitoring of ECG, central venous pressure, and blood gases may be necessary
7. Proper positioning for optimal patient comfort, breathing, and placental function
8. Continuous electronic monitoring of fetal heart and uterine contractions

The continuous lumbar epidural (or caudal) block is the anesthetic of choice except in cases of severe hypo- or hypertension, hypovolemia, anemia, or severe supine hypotensive syndrome. If hypotension does occur, phenylephrine is preferred to ephedrine as a vasopressor because the former does not increase heart work.

In congenital heart disease with cyanosis and left-to-right shunt, the great risk is reversal of the shunt. For this reason, maintaining systolic blood pressure is essential. Pain must be relieved and hypoxia prevented. Systemic analgesia and tranquilization are usually followed by paracervical and ultimately pudendal block. Vertebral blocks are contraindicated.

Essential hypertension

Since the fetus is usually compromised already by reduced placental blood flow, fetal distress is common in a mother with essential hypertension. Methods of pain relief that may further reduce placental blood flow are avoided. Analgesics and hypnotics that increase neonatal depression are used sparingly.[34] Oxygen administration may reduce the chance of fetal hypoxia. Lumbar or caudal epidural anesthesia is a good way to control pain and to keep the blood pressure within bounds. It is undesirable to reduce the blood pressure significantly below pre-labor levels since these pressure may be necessary to achieve adequate placental perfusion. If hypotension occurs, raising the legs sharply and giving ephedrine can reverse the effect.

Toxemia

Toxemia of pregnancy is an acute hypertensive disease that consists of (1) widespread arteriolar spasm leading to varying degrees of tissue hypoxia, (2) retention of sodium far above normal, and (3) localized intravascular coagulation causing fibrin deposits in the vessels of various organs, especially the kidneys and placenta. Proper management of toxemic patients is complicated because of the widespread effects of the disease. Goals are (1) to avoid stress on the kidneys, heart, lungs, liver, and CNS, since they are already compromised; (2) to avoid hypoxia and hypercarbia; (3) to avoid further elevation of the blood pressure or severe hypotension; (4) to avoid a further increase in cardiac output by elimination of pain and the bearing down reflex; (5) to avoid excitement of the mother to help preclude convulsions; and (6) to avoid agents that depress the fetus and neonate.

Continuous lumbar epidural anesthesia is often best[36] in that it provides excellent pain relief, decreases cardiac output and the risk of pulmonary edema, reduces the risk of hypertensive crisis, and may increase placental blood flow allowing better oxygenation of the fetus.

Diabetes mellitus

Along with the changes in glucose tolerance and insulin requirements and the tendency toward ketosis and acidosis, the diabetic mother is prone to premature deterioration of the placenta and other medical problems. The fetus is prone to overweight and intrauterine death, especially in the last few weeks of pregnancy. Death is usually the result of uteroplacental insufficiency or maternal ketoacidosis. Elective termination of pregnancy is usually done by 38 weeks' gestation after appropriate gestational age determination. During labor and delivery, intravenous fluids are administered to prevent dehydration and ketoacidosis.[60] Pain management is aimed at avoiding aggravation of the preexisting disturbance of glucose and acid-base metabolism

and loading the fetus with large doses of drugs for degradation. It must be remembered that placental blood flow is already compromised, the fetus is probably premature, labor may be prolonged, and asphyxia may be increased because of the size of the baby. The fetus may also have a serious anomaly. Continuous caudal or lumbar epidural block is probably the best choice in most cases, and it is easily amenable to extension should cesarean section become indicated. The ester-linked anesthetics are preferable. Paracervical anesthesia is not recommended.

Obesity

Obesity contributes to illness and is often associated with hypertension, diabetes mellitus, and myocardial disease. Significant obesity (20% or more above optimal weight) usually results in chronic hypoventilation. During pregnancy added weight and abdominal growth further increase heart and respiratory work loads. There is a much higher incidence of essential hypertension and toxemia. Labor is longer and delivery is difficult, often requiring forceps. It also makes abdominal fetal assessment difficult and often leads to cesarean section owing to the large fetus. Obesity is also associated with increased perinatal morbidity and mortality.

During labor a sidelying semi-Fowler's position may be best to promote easier maternal ventilation and better uteroplacental blood flow. Problems related to anesthesia include (1) difficulties with venipuncture, (2) difficulties with external monitoring, and (3) difficulties with the location of anatomical landmarks. It is important not to aggravate hypoventilation, and an IV should be started early to avoid difficulty in finding a vein if emergency arises. Also, fluids with dextrose should be given to prevent hypoglycemia.

If it can be accomplished anatomically, a paracervical block with later pudendal or epidural block with minimal doses of anesthetics will provide good relief without respiratory depression. It is essential to avoid hypotension, which is more frequent with epidural block in obese patients.

Maternal addiction

Addiction presents the mother and baby with special problems in labor, delivery, and the newborn period. The drugs to which the mother is addicted may include alcohol, narcotics, barbiturates, amphetamines, meprobamate, and glutethimide (Doriden). Often these mothers do not seek prenatal care so there is a higher incidence of pregnancy complications along with the potential withdrawal syndrome and fetal compromise.

Abstinence syndrome usually develops from 4 to 12 hours after admission. Signs include yawning, lacrimation, rhinorrhea, sneezing, perspiration, anorexia, and tremors. Restlessness, irritability, mental depression, muscular weakness, dilated pupils, and shallow respirations follow. By this time the mother will probably indicate a strong need for the drug. Weakness, nausea, vomiting, diarrhea, and depression increase, and severe hypotension develops. This may be disastrous for the fetus. Chills, flushing, and delirium may occur, followed by a long period of sleep. This cycle may be repeated several times. Violent fetal movements may also occur owing to fetal withdrawal.

Acute withdrawal often results in hyperirritability of the uterus with premature or short labor. Perinatal mortality is about 25% and low birth weight (<2600 gm) occurs in 40% of these infants. Acute abstinence in the newborn develops rapidly and includes excessive mucus production, shrill cry, tremors, and gastrointestinal disturbances. Therapy must be given to prevent death.

If the mother is addicted at the time of labor, she is maintained on the lowest dose of the drug possible to preclude withdrawal symptoms. It may be difficult to distinguish the syndrome initially from anesthetic toxicity, vena caval obstruction, sympathetic block, and other labor phenomena. A venous cutdown may be necessary for the narcotic-addicted mother, as all other veins may effectively be lost. Regional anesthesia is best for most addicted mothers because of the minimal depression it causes. The infant should not be given narcotic antagonists, as this will only precipitate an earlier more violent withdrawal.

Hemorrhage

Placenta previa and abruptio placentae are the most frequent causes of maternal hemorrhage in labor. Placenta previa is placental implantation over the lower uterine segment and/or the cervix. It is usually first indicated by painless third trimester bleeding. Abruption is premature separation of a normally implanted placenta. Symptoms vary with the severity and location of the abruption. The patient may have no signs other than mild vaginal bleeding. If it is more severe, the mother may have a painful, tender, enlarged uterus that is firm even between contractions. She may have obvious vaginal hemorrhage or a concealed hemorrhage with hypovolemia and shock. The primary danger to the mother is hemorrhage. The dangers to the fetus are placental insufficiency and secondary effects of maternal hypovolemia and hypotension.

A double setup (for sterile speculum examination or immediate cesarean section) is used to examine the mother and to differentiate between the two. In moderate to severe cases, blood transfusions are usually begun as soon as they are available and clotting studies are begun.

Paracervical/pudendal block combined with oxygen administration is probably best if vaginal delivery is permitted because of its decreased potential for hypotension. If there is minimal bleeding, some doctors prefer epidural block; however, vertebral block is usually contraindicated whenever hemorrhage is anticipated. For a cesarean section, balanced IV/inhalation anesthesia is the method of choice. Cyclopropane is often preferred because of its support of the maternal cardiovascular system and its rapid effect. High doses of halothane are contraindicated owing to increased hemorrhage from the uterine vessels.

Fetal distress and prematurity

Fetal distress may be determined by fetal heart monitoring and blood pH determinations from the presenting part. Acute uteroplacental insufficiency produces characteristic patterns of late decelerations. The mother is managed in labor so as to keep the ominous pattern to a minimum and fetal pH greater than 7.25.[41]

Uteroplacental insufficiency is treated according to its cause. Aortocaval compression is treated by positioning for uterine displacement; maternal hypotension is treated by intravenous hydration and ephedrine; oxytocin-induced uterine hyperactivity is treated by decreased rate of drip; spontaneous hyperactivity is treated by intravenous magnesium sulfate; and excessive hyperventilation is treated by appropriate pain relief.

Cord compression leading to variable decelerations is treated by repositioning the mother. Inhalation of oxygen is helpful in both situations. If ominous fetal heart rate patterns persist for 30 minutes despite corrective measures or if the fetal pH is less than 7.2 in two consecutive samples, then termination of labor is usually achieved promptly by whatever means is necessary. Forceps vaginal delivery may be possible if dilatation is complete. Otherwise cesarean section is used. If an epidural block has been established, it can be extended. If not, balanced IV/inhalation anesthesia is indicated for speed of induction.

The premature newborn is more sensitive to the depressant effects of all drugs and has prolonged metabolic delays. Epidural block with the lowest possible doses is used for long labors, and spinal block is often sufficient for rapid deliveries. Oxygen is always indicated. Paracervical block is contraindicated.

Operative obstetrics

For elective cesarean section, unless contraindicated, continuous lumbar epidural or spinal anesthesia is the method of choice. If the mother resists surgery during which she is awake, balanced IV/inhalation anesthesia is a safe, equally effective alternative. If the mother is awake, she can enjoy the initial viewing and touching of her baby at the time of delivery.

For emergency cesarean section speed is of the essence. If an epidural block is in place, it is usually extended to T-5 for surgery. If an epidural block has not already been started, balanced IV/inhalation anesthesia is the most likely choice.

For operative vaginal deliveries, uterine and perineal relaxation may be required for safe intrauterine manipulation. In these cases, a balanced technique employing halothane, enflurane, or cyclopropane is indicated. This may be superimposed on vertebral block if it has already been started. In any case, no matter how brief the procedure, if unconsciousness

is produced, intubation is mandatory to good technique to prevent aspiration.

These methods for analgesia in complicated labors have been generalized and all require modification based on the maternal and fetal considerations in each individual case.

CONCLUSION

Medication during labor must not be regarded only as pain relief for the mother but as an aid to prompt, safe, and less traumatic birth of the child, with maximum safety for the mother. The detrimental side effects of pain are many, not the least of which is a postpartum physical and emotional reaction that may affect optimal maternal-infant bonding.

Modern techniques, judiciously employed, may well be beneficial rather than harmful. By the same token, in view of the many known acute effects and the unknown long-term effects of maternal-fetal drug transfer, the American Academy of Pediatrics has recommended that it would be advisable to avoid the use of drugs or doses that have been shown to produce significant changes in the neurobehavior of infants. The minimum effective dose of analgesic and anesthetic drugs should be administered, when indicated, for reasonable relief of maternal pain.[29] The potential benefits and side effects of maternal analgesia on both the mother and infant should be discussed with the mother and family whenever possible before labor.

Enough cannot be said for childbirth education and preparation of the mother and father or other supporter. The principles learned in prenatal classes must be enhanced by trust in the judgment and decisions of the perinatal team who are responsible for a safe delivery. With trust and conscientious effort on the part of all concerned, a safe, rewarding, and resonably comfortable childbirth experience can be provided for every family.

Protocols

Problem □ Pain and discomfort

GOAL: To provide relief of maternal discomfort without causing or exacerbating problems for the infant

Rationale: To effectively control pain in labor without increasing perinatal morbidity and mortality

DIAGNOSTIC

1. Obtain a complete medical and obstetrical history on admission. Obtain prenatal records. Check allergies and previous labor patterns.
   Rationale: To provide safe childbirth care

2. Check and record vital signs and blood pressure every hour and more often if there is a significant change in signs or symptoms.
   Rationale: To provide a good indicator of CNS and cardiovascular function

3. Monitor fetal heart tones during and after contractions every 30 minutes in the latent phase and every 5 minutes in the active phase or utilize electronic monitoring devices with backup auscultation.
   Rationale: To assess fetal status and the nature of fetal compromise

4. Observe uterine contractions for frequency, duration, and quality.
   Rationale: To maintain labor progress (Prolonged contractions, without adequate rest, do not permit adequate placental perfusion.)

5. Assess progress every 1 to 2 hours during active labor by vaginal examination.
   Rationale: To determine the nature and timing of pain relief measures (Lack of progress may be an indication of the need for intervention to enhance labor.)

6. Assess the need for pain relief, taking into acount the mother's tolerance and requests, stage of labor, progress, condition of the mother and fetus, anticipated time of delivery, and the availability of the anesthetist and staff.
   Rationale: To determine the choice of analgesic and its necessity and timing

7. Monitor vital signs and blood pressure every minute for the first 15 minutes following vertebral block, then every 5 minutes until stable after each dose of anesthetic.
   Rationale: To detect significant hypotension that can greatly reduce placental blood flow

8. Be aware of the therapeutic expectations and side effects of medications.
   Rationale: To enable the nurse to assess effectiveness of comfort measures and to anticipate complications

9. Be aware of the symptoms of overdose and adverse reactions to drugs. Consciously look for them in the mother and fetus.
   Rationale: To detect problems early enough to preclude complications for the mother and baby

10. Be aware of cutaneous dermatome patterns and be able to test the level of vertebral block.
    Rationale: To enable the nurse to detect if a block is becoming too extensive and to determine if the dose has been optimal

11. Assess hydration and bladder status frequently.
    Rationale: To assess for dehydration and water toxicity in the mother

12. Be conscienciously aware of the patient's signs and symptoms, verbalized and unspoken.
    Rationale: To detect significant symptoms (Nausea and light-headedness may indicate hypotension; palpitations, tinnitus, and vertigo may mean local anesthetic toxicity; dyspnea, restlessness, and increased respiratory rate and heart rate may indicate Mendelson's syndrome. All indicate potential threats to the mother and/or her baby.)

13. Do not leave a patient in active labor alone.
    Rationale: To detect symptoms early

14. Have equipment available for fetal blood gas sampling and analysis.
    Rationale: To indicate fetal compromise

15. Monitor the patient who is semiconscious or unconscious with exceptional care.
    Rationale: To detect silent aspiration in a patient who cannot express such feelings as dyspnea

16. Be aware of postpartum medication needs, especially with cesarean section mothers.
    Rationale: To be aware of the need for medication for severe cramping especially if oxytocic drugs have been given rapidly, and severe pain, which many cesarean section mothers may experience on regaining consciousness

17. Check frequently postpartum for fundal firmness, bleeding, bladder status, and vital signs.
    Rationale: To detect uterine atony, which can lead to hemorrhage, and a full bladder, which can displace the uterus and keep it from contracting as it should after delivery

THERAPEUTIC

1. Positioning is vital. Sim's position (the left side is best) or a variation of the supine position with elevation of the right hip to affect left uterine displacement is optimal. Sometimes other positions are necessary to relieve cord compression (determined by trial and error).
    Rationale: To avoid aortocaval compression and significant reduction of uterine blood flow

2. Have oxygen equipment working and immediately available.
    Rationale: To give oxygen by mask or endotracheal tube to the mother to increase the FIO_2 of her inspired air and allow the maximum possible amounts to reach the fetus

3. Have resuscitation equipment and emergency drugs immediately available and know how to use them.
    Rationale: To assure that precious time is not lost if emergency equipment and medications are needed.

4. Begin an intravenous infusion of 5% dextrose in Ringer's lactate (or other solution if ordered) with a large bore (18-gauge) catheter early in the active phase of labor.

Rationale: To maintain hydration of the NPO mother, and preclude ketosis and electrolyte imbalance and to provide easy access to the bloodstream for medications or blood products (The large bore needle is necessary to permit rapid fluid or blood infusion.)

5. Give oral antacids 15 to 20 ml every 2 hours in active labor and 30 to 50 ml within the hour preceding any general anesthesia.
    Rationale: To raise the gastric pH above the critical level of 2.5 and thus prevent Mendelson's syndrome and to deacidify the fluid that is often vomited or regurgitated by laboring women

6. Maintain the laboring mother NPO except for occasional ice chips or sips of water.
    Rationale: To avoid vomiting and aspiration. (Since reverse peristalsis and reflux are so common in labor, along with a much prolonged gastric emptying time, it is highly likely that anything eaten may be vomited or aspirated. Water in small amounts is rapidly absorbed from the stomach even in labor.)

7. Observe good medication technique (the right drug in the right dose by the right route to the right patient at the right time).
    Rationale: To prevent medication errors, which can be tragic for the mother and baby

8. Prior to giving any medication, consider its appropriateness with the weight of the patient, the status of labor, the maturity and size of the fetus, and the patient's allergies.
    Rationale: To reduce the incidence of errors

9. Give all intravenous medications at the beginning of a contraction if possible, over a period of a few minutes.
    Rationale: To ensure that the bolus effect is minimized and that a lesser amount of drug will be able to cross the placenta during the first few circulations

10. Do *not* give vertebral "top-up" injections during contractions.
    Rationale: To avoid causing a more than desirable spread of the anesthetic

11. Always aspirate the syringe prior to giving *any* medication.

Rationale: To know whether the needle or catheter is in the bloodstream prior to injecting anything (Extravascular injection of IV drugs can cause reduced effectiveness and tissue irritation. Intravascular injection of non-IV drugs can be dangerous, even fatal.)

12. Use filters with all intravenous medications and epidural catheters.
    Rationale: To screen out glass particles and bacteria that have been shown to be present commonly in ampules after they have been broken open

13. Use sterile technique with medications and block procedures. Anticipate traffic patterns in the room prior to setting up and opening sterile trays.
    Rationale: To avoid infection

14. Encourage bladder emptying every 2 hours and catheterize the mother as necessary if she is unable to void.
    Rationale: To avoid a distended bladder, which interferes with labor and can traumatize the urinary tract

15. Promptly treat hypotension. If it is caused by sympathetic blockade from medication:
    a. Speed up the IV infusion.
    b. Turn the mother to her left side and raise the legs.
    c. Give oxygen by mask.
    d. Give IV ephedrine if necessary.
    e. Monitor both mother and fetus closely.
    Rationale: To prevent hypotension, which can be rapidly harmful or fatal to the fetus and reduce the uterine blood supply, sparing the mother and sacrificing the child

16. Keep siderails up.
    Rationale: To prevent falls (unless the mother tries to crawl around the rails), provide a sense of security (especially on the high beds often found in labor suites), and help the mother to move herself in bed

17. Do not allow the mother to ambulate after sedation or block.
    Rationale: To avoid falls that can occur because the mother may be dizzy or have numbing or paralysis of the legs

18. Do not hold an inhalant mask for the patient.
    Rationale: To eliminate the nurse not recognizing the beginning loss of consciousness

19. Do not perform any technique or give any drug that is beyond your level of knowledge or skill.
    Rationale: To avoid jeopardizing both the mother and the baby

20. Do not allow techniques to be used that cannot be properly supervised.
    Rationale: To assure constant supervision and consequently a well cared for patient

21. Provide routine comfort measures: peace and quiet in the labor rooms, prompt change of soiled and damp linen, mouth care and ice chips, emesis basin and mouth rinse in easy reach.
    Rationale: To provide much relief of discomfort, increasing the mother's tolerance of pain and making her aware of the concern of the staff

22. Apply effleurage of the abdomen if desired by the mother, or assist her significant other in doing this.
    Rationale: To provide muscle relaxation and relief of tension

23. Apply sacral pressure, back support, or massage as desired by the mother.
    Rationale: To relieve back pain, thereby greatly enhancing the mother's ability to cope with uterine pain

24. Assist the mother with appropriate breathing techniques, relaxation exercises, and pushing when indicated if there is no other trained coach (that is, significant other).
    Rationale: To teach the mother appropriate techniques and to enlist the active involvement of another, which will help inspire her to persevere

25. Encourage the presence of the baby's father or a significant other throughout labor and delivery if possible.
    Rationale: To provide more empathy and support in a way that is meaningful to the mother (If the mother does not want a friend or family member present, this wish must also be honored.)

26. Coach the coach. Encourage with timing, pacing, and alternate methods if needed. Relieve when necessary.
    Rationale: To assist the coach to ensure maximal support to the mother
27. Maintain a flexible approach.
    Rationale: To meet the needs of the mother and family regardless of the inclination of the staff with regard to the "best" approach
28. Respect the mother and family with regard to their self-worth and needs. Never minimize their feelings or ridicule them in any way.
    Rationale: To ensure that each member of the team (including the family) is respected and feels important to the effort
29. Never mislead the family in any way; keep communication open with the perinatal team and the family.
    Rationale: To provide the highest level of care for all
30. Provide privacy; be careful of what is said near the family.
    Rationale: To avoid apprehension of the patient and family
31. Provide ventilation in the room, especially if inhalants are being used.
    Rationale: To avoid contact with stale air and gaseous anesthetics, which can affect staff as well as the patient if there is inadequate ventilation
32. Allow no smoking in the labor and delivery area.
    Rationale: To avoid danger of fire or explosion risk in the presence of inhalants and oxygen
33. Have all equipment ready for resuscitation of the newborn both in labor and delivery areas
    Rationale: To be prepared should the baby be depressed by medication or birth trauma
34. After delivery, begin an infusion of dilute synthetic oxytocin (10 U/L).
    Rationale: To help the uterus clamp down strongly to preclude extensive bleeding (A bolus causes vasodilatation, hypotension, tachycardia, and increased cardiac output, so dilute infusion is preferred. Synthetic oxytocin has less impurities.)
35. Be gentle with postpartum fundal massage.
    Rationale: To tone up a boggy uterus by gentle massage and to avoid vigorous massage, which is painful and unnecessary
36. Apply an ice pack to the perineum immediately after transfer from the delivery room.
    Rationale: To reduce potential swelling, which puts traction on any stitches and makes moving and sitting painful
37. Reassure the mother and family during any complications or side effects of medications.
    Rationale: To reduce anxiety
38. Ambulation should not be attempted after delivery until the effects of narcotics, sedation, or vertebral block have worn off.
    Rationale: To avoid a fall
39. Be especially careful with transport and positioning of patients with vertebral blocks.
    Rationale: To avoid causing a temporarily pinched nerve or cramped leg
40. Suggest pain medication if the mother is in obvious distress but resisting the need for relief (for the purpose of "natural childbirth" or fear of its effects).
    Rationale: To obviate the mother's guilt feelings, especially if she is reassured that the drug is safe and that counteractive measures are available "if anything happens"
41. Encourage early parent-infant bonding experiences within the bounds of safety and good care for the mother and baby.
    Rationale: To allow interaction between the parents and baby for at least brief periods early in life to effect later parent-child interaction

EDUCATIONAL

1. Obtain a fully informed consent prior to any treatment, medication, or block.
   Rationale: To allow the patient to make a rational decision and protect the staff legally
2. Explain all procedures fully ahead of time, and repeat the steps during the procedure.
   Rationale: To ensure the mother's cooperation with a procedure
3. Make prenatal classes available to all mothers, including a tour of the obstetrical ward and discussion of methods of pain relief.

Rationale: To ensure that the environment and comfort measures will be less threatening and more readily accepted

4. Encourage participation in psychoprophylaxis classes.

   Rationale: To enable the mother to work with her body during labor and apply the techniques to any stress-provoking life situation later

5. Report progress after examinations and explain the implications.

   Rationale: To help the parents keep their sense of purpose and help them to know that their labor is not in vain and that it won't last forever

6. Teach relaxation, breathing, and pushing techniques to the untrained mother *early* in labor. Review them with trained parents.

   Rationale: To ensure concentration and cooperation, which are greatest before pain interferes with learning and to help solidify training and facilitate communication between family and staff by "getting the signals straight" through review

7. Give instructions calmly, slowly, and simply when the patient is in active labor. Repeat patiently as often as necessary.

   Rationale: To ensure that only necessary instruction is attempted and then only between contractions in the simplest possible way

8. Encourage realistic expectations of labor, delivery, and pain relief measures.

   Rationale: To avoid disappointment and less than ideal rapport between the family and the staff

9. Inform the patient of the anticipated effects of all medications given.

   Rationale: To ensure that she will not be frightened as much by transient feelings or symptoms that accompany most drugs and can also know when to inform the nurse of *un*expected feelings

10. Encourage positive conditioning of the parents and maintain a positive attitude.

    Rationale: To help the patient and family to see the bright side of a difficult time

11. Explain that oxytocin given after delivery may cause strong cramping and that this is necessary to make sure that hemorrhage does not occur because of a weak uterus.

    Rationale: To limit fear and overreaction to the pain

12. The staff should learn each couples' individual cues and be prepared to assist or take over with the same cues should it become necessary.

    Rationale: To facilitate smooth communication during labor and help to achieve maximal response and cooperation from the mother

13. The staff should have current knowledge of the mechanisms of pain, factors affecting its experience, means of applying various forms of pain relief, effects of each method, and methods of dealing with complications.

    Rationale: To safely and effectively provide pain relief during labor

14. Promote ongoing communication between all members of the perinatal team.

    Rationale: To ensure that the staff will be more organized and provide better care

15. Educate the staff in the importance of *attitude*. There is *never* a maternal "failure" in labor and delivery. Their relationship with the family will have an effect on the family's attitudes toward health care and health care providers for many years.

    Rationale: To ensure a satisfactory experience for the new family

16. Be aware of community trends, cultural factors, and local needs.

    Rationale: To provide current approaches to meet current needs

REFERENCES

1. Abouleish, E.: Pain control in obstetrics, Philadelphia, 1977, J. B. Lippincott Co.
2. August, R.: Hypnosis in obstetrics, New York, 1961, McGraw-Hill Book Co.
3. Bonica, J. J., Principles and practice of obstetric analgesia and anesthesia, vols. 1 and 2, Philadelphia, 1969, F. A. Davis Co.
4. Bonica, J. J.: Obstetric analgesia and anesthesia, Berlin, 1972, Springer-Verlag.
5. Bonica, J. J.: Management of pain, ed. 2, Philadelphia, 1975, Lea & Febiger.
6. Bonica, J. J., editor: Obstetric analgesia-anesthesia, Clin. Obstet. Gynecol. **2:**3, 1975.
7. Bonica, J. J., and Akamatsu, T. J.: Current concepts of pain in labor and parturition, Am. J. Obstet. Gynecol. 1975.

8. Bonta, B. W., et al.: Naloxone reversal of mild neurobehavioral depression in normal newborn infants after routine obstetric analgesia, J. Pediatr. **94:**102, 1979.

9. Brazelton, T. B.: Psychophysiologic reactions in the neonate II—effects of maternal medication on the neonate and his behavior, J. Pediatr. **58:**513, 1961.

10. Brazelton, T. B.: Effect of prenatal drugs on the behavior of the neonate, Am. J. Psychiatr. **126:**1261, 1970.

11. Brazelton, T. B.: Neonatal behavioral assessment scale, Philadelphia, 1973, J. B. Lippincott Co.

12. Buxton, C. L.: A study of psychological methods for relief of childbirth pain, Philadelphia, 1962, W. B. Saunders Co.

13. Cibils, L. A.: Response of human uterine arteries to local anesthetics, Am. J. Obstet. Gynecol. **126:**202, 1976.

14. Cibils, L. A., and Santonja-Lucas, J. J.: Clinical significance of fetal heart rate patterns during labor III: effect of paracervical block anesthesia, Am. J. Obstet. Gynecol. **130:**73, 1978.

15. Chertok, L.: Psychosomatic methods in painless childbirth, New York, 1959, Pergamon Press, Inc.

16. Crawford, J. S.: Principles and practice of obstetric anaesthesia, ed. 3, Oxford, England, 1972, Blackwell Scientific Publications.

17. Davies, G. S., Fetal and neonatal physiology, Chicago, 1968, Year Book Medical Publishers, Inc.

18. Davies, J. M., and Rosen, M.: Intramuscular diazepam in labour: a double blind trial in multiparae, Br. J. Anaesth. **49:**601, 1977.

19. Dodson, W. E.: Neonatal drug intoxication: local anesthetics, Pediatr. Clin. North Am. **23:**399, 1976.

20. Eastman, N. J., and Hellman, L. M.: William's obstetrics, New York, 1971, Appleton-Century-Crofts.

21. Ettinger, B. B., and McCart, D. F.: Effects of drugs on the fetal heart rate during labor, J. Obstet. Gynecol. Nurs. September/October, (Suppl.), 1976.

22. Friedman, E. A.: Labor: clinical evaluation and management, New York, 1967, Appleton-Century-Crofts.

23. Gerhardt, T., Bancalari, E., Cohen, H., and Fernandez, R. L.: Use of naloxone to reverse narcotic respiratory depression in the newborn infant, J. Pediatr. **90:**1009, 1977.

24. Greiss, F. C., Still, J. G., and Anderson, S. G.: Effects of local anesthetic agents on the uterine vasculature and myometrium, Am. J. Obstet. Gynecol. **124:**889, 1976.

25. James, L. S.: The effect of pain relief for labor and delivery on the fetus and newborn, Anaesthesia **21:**1960.

26. James, L. S.: Physiologic adjustments at birth: effects of labor, delivery and anesthesia on the newborn, Anaesthesia **26:**501, 1965.

27. Javert, C. T., and Hardy, J. D.: Measurement of pain intensity in labor and its physiologic, neurologic, and pharmacologic implications, Am. J. Obstet. Gynecol. **60:**552, 1950.

28. Johnson, W. L., et al.: Effect of pudendal, spinal, and peridural block anesthesia on the second stage of labor, Am. J. Obstet. Gynecol. **113:**116, 1972.

29. Kitzinger, S.: Pain in childbirth, J. Med. Ethics **4:**119, 1978.

30. Kron, R. E., Sleim, M. S., and Goddard, K. E.: Newborn sucking behavior affected by obstetric sedation, Pediatrics **37:**1012, 1966.

31. Matadial, L., and Cibils, L. A.: The effect of epidural anesthesia on the uterine activity and blood pressure, Am. J. Obstet. Gynecol. **125:**846, 1975.

32. McDonald, J. S.: Obstetric anesthesia, Clin. Obstet. Gynecol. **21:**489, 1978.

33. Miller, F. C., et al.: Hyperventilation during labor, Am. J. Obstet. Gynecol. **120:**489, 1974.

34. Milunsky, A.: Management of the high risk pregnancy, Clin. Perinatol. **1:**2, 1974.

35. Moir, D. D.: Obstetrical anesthesia and analgesia, London, 1976, Baillière Tindall.

36. Moir, D. D., Rodrigues, L., and Willocks, J.: Epidural analgesia during labor in patients with preeclampsia, J. Obstet. Gynecol. Br. Commonw. **79:**465, 1977.

37. Moya, F., and James, L. S.: Medical hypnosis in obstetrics, J. A. M. A. **174:**2026, 1960.

38. Moya, F., and Smith, B. E.: Uptake, distribution, and placental transfer of drugs and anesthetics, Anaesthesia, **26:** 465, 1965.

39. Myers, R. E., and Myers, S. E.: Use of sedative, analgesic, and anesthetic drugs during labor and delivery: bane or boon? Am. J. Obstet. Gynecol. **13:**83, 1979.

40. Myles, M. F.: Textbook for midwives, ed. 8, London, 1975, Churchill Livingstone.

41. Nesbitt, R. E. L.: Symposium on perinatal medicine, Clin. Perinatol. **1:**1, 1974.

42. Ostheimer, G. W., Pulahnirik, R. J., and Shnider, S. M.: Epidural block patch for post lumbar puncture headache, Anaesthesia **41:**307, 1974.

43. Oxorn, H., and Foole, W. R.: Human labor and birth, ed. 3, New York, 1975, Appleton-Century-Crofts.

44. Page, E. W., Villee, C. A., and Villee, D. B.: Human reproduction: the core content of obstetrics, gynecology, and perinatal medicine, Philadelphia, 1972, W. B. Saunders Co.

45. Pearson, J. F., and Davies, P.: The effect of continuous epidural analgesia on the acid-base status of maternal arterial blood during the first stage of labor, J. Obstet. Gynecol. Br. Commonw. **80:**218, 1973.

46. Pearson, J. F., and Davies, P.: The effect of continuous epidural analgesia on maternal acid-base balance and arterial lactate concentration during the second stage of labor, J. Obstet. Gynecol. Br. Commonw. **80:**225, 1973.

47. Pearson, J. F., and Davies, P.: The effect of continuous lumbar epidural analgesia upon fetal acid-base status during labor, J. Obstet. Gynecol. Br. Commonw. **81:**971, 1974.

48. Phillips, C. R., and Anzalone, J. T.: Fathering: participation in labor and birth, London, 1976, Baillière Tindall.

49. Ralston, D. H., and Shnider, S. M.: The fetal and neonatal effects of regional anesthesia in obstetrics, Anaesthesia **48:** 34, 1978.

50. Read, G. D.: Natural childbirth, London, 1933, Wm. Heinemann, Ltd.

51. Roberts, R. B., and Shirley, M. A.: The obstetrician's role in reducing the risk of aspiration pneumonitis, Am. J. Obstet. Gynecol. **125:**611, 1976.

52. Scanlon, J. W., Brown, W. U., Weiss, J. B., and Alper, M. H.: Neurobehavioral responses of newborn infants after maternal epidural anesthesia, Anaesthesia **40:**121, 1974.

53. Schifrin, B. S.: Fetal heart rate patterns following epidural anesthesia and oxytocin infusion during labor, J. Obstet. Gynecol. Br. Commonw. **79:**332, 1972.

54. Shnider, S. M., and Moya, F.: Effects of meperidine on the newborn infant, Am. J. Obstet. Gynecol. **89**:1009, 1964.
55. Shnider, S. M., and Moya, F.: The Anaesthesiologist, mother, and newborn, Baltimore, 1974, The Williams & Wilkins Co.
56. Shnider, S. M., et al.: Vasopressors in obstetrics. I: correction of fetal acidosis with ephedrine during spinal hypotension, Am. J. Obstet. Gynecol. **102**:911, 1968.
57. Shnider, S. M., et al.: Vasopressors in obstetrics. II: fetal hazards of methoxamine administration during obstetric spinal anesthesia, Am. J. Obstet. Gynecol. **106**:680, 1970.
58. Shnider, S. M., et al.: Vasopressors in obstetrics. III: fetal effects of metaraminol infusion during obstetric spinal hypotension, Am. J. Obstet. Gynecol. **108**:1017, 1970.
59. Sinclair, J. C., et al.: Intoxication of the fetus by a local anesthetic, N. Engl. J. Med. **273**:1173, 1965.
60. Spellacy, W. N.: Management of the high risk pregnancy, Baltimore, 1976, University Park Press.
61. Stevens, R. J., and Heide, F.: Analgesic characteristics of prepared childbirth: techniques; attention focusing and systemic relaxation, J. Psychosom. Res. **21**:429, 1977.
62. Stone, C. I., Demchik-Stone, D. A., and Horan, J. J.: Coping with pain: a component analysis of Lamaze and cognitive behavioral procedures, J. Psychosom. Res. **21**:451, 1977.
63. Thiery, M., and Vroman, S.: Paracervical block analgesia during labor, Am. J. Obstet. Gynecol. **113**:988, 1972.
64. Vasicka, A., Hutchinson, H. T., Eng, M., and Allen, C. R.: Spinal and epidural anesthesia, fetal and uterine response to acute hypotension and hypertension, Am. J. Obstet. Gynecol. **90**:800, 1964.
65. Wickramasekera, I., editor: Biofeedback, behavior therapy, and hypnosis, potentiating the verbal control of behavior for clinicians, Chicago, 1976 Nelson-Hall Publishers.
66. Yaffe, S. J., and Catz, C. S.: Pharmacology of the perinatal period, Clin. Obste. Gynecol. **14**:722, 1971.
67. Yeh, S. Y., Paul, R. H., Cordero, L., and Hon, E. H.: A study of diazepam in labor, Obstet. Gynecol. **43**:363, 1974.
68. Zuspan, F. P., Cibils, L. A., and Pose, S. V.: Myometrial and cardiovascular responses to alterations in plasma epinephrine and norepinephrine, Am. J. Obstet. Gynecol. **84**:841, 1962.

BIBLIOGRAPHY

American Academy of Pediatrics, Committee on Drugs: Effects of medication during labor and delivery on infant outcome, Pediatrics **62**:3, 1978.
Beasley, J. M., editor: The active management of labor, Clin. Obstet. Gynecol. **2**:2, 1974.
Behrmen, R. E.: Neonatology, St. Louis, 1973, The C. V. Mosby Co.
Borgstedt, A. D., and Rosen, M. G.: Medication during labor correlated with behavior and EEG in the newborn, Am. J. Dis. Child. **115**:221, 1968.
Bowes, W. A., Brackbill, Y., Conway, E.; and Steinschneider, A. editors: The effects of obstetrical medication on the fetus and infant, Monogr. Soc. Res. Child Dev. **35**:4, 1970.
Cogan, R., Henneborn, W., and Klopfer, F.: Predictors of pain during prepared childbirth, J. Psychosom. Res. **20**:523, 1976.
Corke, B. C.: Neurobehavioral responses of the newborn: the effect of different forms of maternal analgesia, Anaesthesia **32**:539, 1977.

Crawford, J. S.: Obstetrics, analgesia, and anaesthesia, Br. J. Anaesth. **49**:19, 1977.
Drage, J. S., et al.: The Apgar score as an index of infant morbidity, Dev. Med. Child Neurol. **8**:141, 1966.
Fielding, W. L.: The childbirth challenge: commonsense vs "natural" methods, New York, 1962, The Viking Press.
Flowers, C. E., Jr.: Obstetric analgesia and anesthesia, New York, 1967, Harper & Row, Publishers.
Ghoneim, M. M., and Long, J. P.: The interaction between magnesium and other neuromuscular blocking agents, Anaesthesia **32**:23, 1970.
Grad, R. K., and Woodside, J.: Obstetrical analgesics and anesthesia: methods of relief for the patient in labor, Am. J. Nurs. **77**:242, 1977.
Hester, J. B., and Heath, M. L.: Pulmonary acid aspiration syndrome: should prophylaxis be routine? Br. J. Anaesth. **47**:630, 1975.
Hodgkinson, R., Marx, G. F., Kim, S. S., and Miclat, N.: Neonatal neurobehavioral tests following vaginal delivery under ketamine, thiopental, and extradural anesthesia, Anesth. Analg. **56**:548, 1977.
Malinowski, J. S., Burdin, C. P., Lederman, R. P., and Williams, P. S.: Nursing care of the labor patient, Philadelphia, 1978, F. A. Davis Co.
McAllister, R. G.: Obstetric anesthesia: a two-way street, J. Obstet. Gynecol. Nurs. **5**:1, 1976.
McNall, L. K., and Galeener, J. T.: Current practice in obstetric and gynecologic nursing, vol I, St. Louis, 1976, The C. V. Mosby Co.
Mozingo, J. N.: Pain in labor: a conceptual model for intervention, J. Obstet. Gynecol. Nurs. **7**:47, 1978.
Regional Anesthesia in obstetrics, Department of Nursing Services, Ross Laboratories, Columbus, Ohio, 1970.
Scanlon, J. W.: How is the baby? The Apgar score revisited, Clin. Pediatr. **12**:61, 1973.
Scanlon J. W.: Obstetric anesthesia as a neonatal risk factor in normal labor and delivery, Clin. Perinatol. **1**:465, 1974.
Scott, D. B.: Analgesia in labor, Br. J. Anaesth. **49**:11, 1977.
Scott, D. B., Owens, J. A., and Richmond, J.: Methemeglobinemia due to prilocaine, Lancet **2**:728, 1964.
Smith, B., Priore, R., and Stern, M.: The transition phase of labor, Am. J. Nurs. **73**:448, 1973.
Stechler, G.: Newborn attention affected by medication during labor, Science **144**:315, 1964.
Tronick, E., et al.: Regional obstetric anesthesia and newborn behavior effect over the first ten days of life, Pediatrics **58**:1, 1976.
Tronick, E., et al.: The infant's response to intrapment between contradicting messages in face to face interaction, J. Am. Acad. Child Psychiatr. **17**:1, 1978.
VanPetten, G. R., and Miller, R. F.: Effect of some autonomic drugs on fetal cardiovascular function, Proc. Can. Fed. Biol. Soc. **11**:31, 1968.
Werboff, J., and Kesner, R.: Learning deficits in offspring after administration of tranquilizing drugs to the mothers, Nature **197**:106, 1963.
Yaffe, S. J., and Juchau, M. R.: Perinatal pharmacology, Ann. Rev. Pharmacol. **14**:219, 1974.

Chapter 13

Meconium aspiration

Kay McWhirter and Lorraine Dayton

Meconium aspiration can cause a wide range of respiratory problems in the newborn from mild respiratory distress to respiratory failure and death.

The literature reports that the incidence of meconium staining of the amniotic fluid is present in 8% to 29% of all pregnancies.[2] There have been various theories concerning what triggers the passage of meconium, but the exact cause remains debatable.

Theoretically, there could be two ways that meconium gets into the lungs: (1) by intrauterine aspiration or (2) by aspiration that occurs during the first few breaths of life. Animal studies do not support that intrauterine aspiration occurs,[7,15,17] thus suggesting that meconium aspiration occurs at the time of birth or shortly thereafter.

Once meconium is passed, there is an increased incidence of perinatal morbidity and mortality. Even with the advanced medical management of infants who have aspirated meconium, the therapy is often prolonged and ineffective. Therefore *prevention* is the most effective form of management for these infants.

PATHOPHYSIOLOGY
Composition of meconium

Meconium, the sticky black-green fecal material in the fetal intestine, begins to appear by the end of the fourth month.[22] Meconium consists of (1) desquamated cutaneous and gastrointestinal cells, (2) lanugo, (3) vernix caseosa, (4) amniotic fluid that was swallowed by the fetus, and (5) intestinal secretions.[2,4,5,9,23]

Buchanan and Rapoport[4] found through chemical analysis that meconium is composed of 72% water. Eighty percent of its dry weight is composed primarily of carbohydrates with a few lipids. No protein was found, which these researchers attributed to the proteolytic actions of trypsin.

Pathogenic properties of meconium

Rubowits and associates[24] studied the pathogenic properties of meconium by subcutaneously or intramuscularly injecting sterile human meconium into rats. They found that inflammation resulted with local tissue necrosis and proliferation of connective tissue. These authors also found that if filtered meconium was intravenously injected into dogs, the result was hyperventilation, shock, cardiac failure, and eventual death.

Cruichshank[6] studied the responses of adult rabbits to tracheal injections of human amniotic fluid with and without meconium. The amniotic fluid alone stimulated a foreign body reaction, which consisted of infiltration of macrophages and proliferation of body giant cells. In the presence of meconium the reaction was enhanced and led to eventual alveolar collapse. The one fallacy of this study was that the meconium he used was contaminated at the time of collection. Amniotic fluid has been shown to have bactericidal properties; once it is contaminated with meconium, it becomes an optimal medium for bacterial growth.[26] Cruichshank and associates[6] found by testing the constituents of meconium that the bile salts caused the most acute inflammatory reaction, producing fetal pulmonary edema, leukocytic proliferations, and hemorrhage.

Driscoll and Smith proposed that the irritating action of meconium on the pulmonary parenchyma might initiate a chemical pneumonitis adding to the already compromised pulmonary function in infants who have aspirated meconium. This might explain the inflammatory changes that are seen and the increased incidence of pleural fluid seen on chest x-ray films in these infants.[2,10]

Complete or partial mechanical airway obstruction by the meconium particles probably plays the most important role in the pathophysiology of meconium aspiration.[2] Complete obstruction of the trachea is possible when large amounts of thick meconium are aspirated, thus resulting in rapid death from asphyxia and acute cor pulmonale.[2] With complete obstruction of the distal airways, atelectasis of the alveoli distal to the obstruction occurs.[3] The collapsed alveoli that remain perfused cause right-to-left intrapulmonary shunting of blood, which helps to explain the hypoxemia, hypercapnia, and acidosis that is commonly found in these infants.[25]

Partial airway obstruction by meconium produces a "ball-valve" effect that causes gas trapping.[2,3,26,28] Gas trapping can be understood by discussing inspiration and expiration movements around the obstruction. During inspiration the airways widen, thus the air can move around the obstruction and enter the alveoli. During expiration the airways constrict or collapse around the obstruction, causing air to remain trapped distally.[2,3] Because of this ball-valve mechanism, the lungs of these infants are very susceptible to pneumothorax or pneumomediastinum.[28]

Pathophysiology of meconium staining amniotic fluid and intrauterine aspiration

The incidence of meconium staining the amniotic fluid is 8% to 29% of all pregnancies.* The appearance of meconium during any stage of labor has long been considered a clinical sign of fetal distress.[9] Within the last few years, the traditional views of meconium as a clinical sign of fetal distress have been questioned because some infants who have been delivered through meconium-stained fluid have had no evidence of any kind of distress.[1,8,9,21]

Abramovici and associates[1] suggested that meconium passage represents a sign of temporary "compensated fetal distress," where the fetal vital organs remain well oxygenated at the expense of peripheral hypoxia. In other words, if the fetus is

delivered in a compensated state, no sign of fetal distress such as cardiac or cerebral depression, respiratory distress, or acidosis will be manifested.

Other theories of why meconium is passed in the absence of fetal distress have been formulated by Hon and Fenton and Steer.[12] Hon felt that any compression of the umbilical cord would cause a vagal response (most fully developed in term infants) that produces an increase in gastrointestinal motility, anal sphincter dilatation, and meconium passage.[2] Fenton and Steer[12] felt that meconium passage was an indication of fetal maturity and a normal physiological function of the term and postterm infant.[12]

Many maternal factors are thought to contribute to the passage of meconium before birth; these include (1) maternal age, (2) prolonged gestation, (3) breech deliveries, (4) obesity, (5) anemia, and (6) toxemia of pregnancy.[1,8,9] The fetal factors related to the passage of meconium remain debatable. Once meconium is passed, the possibility for meconium aspiration and poor fetal/infant outcomes exists.[1,8,9,17]

Theoretically, once meconium is in the amniotic fluid, there are two ways for it to get into the fetal or newborn lungs; these are (1) intrauterine aspiration or (2) aspiration that occurs during the first few breaths of life. Some animal studies do not support the premise that intrauterine aspiration occurs.[7,15,17] To date, there are insufficient published data concerning human intrauterine aspiration for it to be said that it does or does not occur. Simmons feels that in human newborns 99% of meconium aspiration occurs during the first few breaths and is an almost totally preventable phenomenon.[26]

RESPONSE OF OBSTETRICAL PERSONNEL TO MECONIUM STAINING OF THE INFANT IN THE DELIVERY ROOM

The presence of meconium staining of the amniotic fluid and fetus should alert the perinatal nurse to the possibility of several adverse conditions in the neonate. Although studies have concluded that meconium passage per se does not indicate fetal distress, the occurrence of fetal asphyxia when meconium is present enhances the potential for meconium aspiration and poor neonatal outcome.[14,21]

Meconium staining is considered an indication for continuous close monitoring of the fetus during labor for any other evidence of distress. Measure-

---

*See references 8, 9, 14, 17, and 26 to 28.

ments of pH of capillary blood may help to identify the fetus in serious distress, and continuous electrical monitoring is indicated. The labor room nurse must be alert to the possible occurrence of a pattern of type II dips—a slowing of the fetal heart rate late in the contraction phase; this pattern has most often been shown to be the consequence of fetal hypoxia.[23] If this pattern persists and if the diagnosis of fetal acidosis (pH below 7.0) is confirmed by fetal blood sampling, prompt delivery is indicated.[3,23]

The main point of several authors' discussions has been their belief that meconium aspiration and its sequelae are almost totally preventable in the delivery room if managed promptly and aggressively.[13,26] The importance of early preparation of both personnel and equipment for the meconium-stained infant cannot be overemphasized. Every delivery room must be equipped with resuscitation equipment for the newborn. Personnel must be readily available for intubation of the infant, if necessary, whenever meconium staining is present.

There is almost universal agreement that the first, and most important, step in caring for these infants is suctioning the nose and mouth with a DeLee mucus trap or bulb syringe *before* delivery of the baby's trunk stimulates gasping respirations.* The most recent literature concludes that the severity of meconium aspiration is related to the amount of aspirated meconium. Because any meconium in the trachea at the time of delivery moves rapidly into the lung periphery, clearing the pharynx and trachea of all meconium-stained amniotic fluid as soon as possible after delivery may be highly beneficial.[2] The findings of several studies indicate that infants with tracheal meconium present have a significantly decreased mortality rate and markedly shorter duration of respiratory distress if they were thoroughly suctioned at birth.[2,13,17,26,27]

Because asphyxia is often the basis for the presence of meconium in the amniotic fluid, the infant who aspirates meconium at birth is often depressed and requires some resuscitation. The nurse in the delivery room must be aware that if the infant has severe, gasping respirations, marked retractions, and poor air exchange, tracheal occlusion by a meconium plug should be suspected. In such a situation, intubation with suction applied directly to an oral endotracheal tube to extract a large, viscous

---

*See references 2, 5, 13, 23, 26, and 28.

plug unable to be cleared with a suction catheter may be lifesaving.[2,13,23]

Similarly, when a meconium-stained newborn does not immediately breathe spontaneously or shows signs of respiratory distress, rapid intubation and tracheal suctioning, either by direct suction to the endotracheal tube or a large suction catheter, must be carried out. Positive pressure ventilation of these infants with bag and mask or endotracheal tube is generally not recommended until after initial tracheal suctioning because of the possibility of forcing more meconium down the airway.[2,13,21] Even though several authors do not recommend the use of positive pressure ventilation of these infants until several suctionings have occurred to clear the bronchial tree of all possible meconium, Fox and associates[13] have made a very important point. They feel that when an infant with meconium aspiration is hypoxic or cyanotic, oxygenation is as important as adequate suctioning. Thus, they recommend that after intubation and initial tracheal suctioning have been performed, if oxygenation with positive pressure seems indicated, it should be employed to expand the lungs since its benefits outweigh the relatively small disadvantage of possibly forcing meconium down the airway.[13] If the infant is apneic or in severe respiratory distress and no means for intubation is immediately available, the delivery room nurse must be familiar with resuscitation techniques with bag and mask and provide these to the infant until intubation can be done.

Consensus generally is that any infant born with moderate to severe staining of the skin, umbilical cord, and nails, even though he is vigorous and in no immediate respiratory distress, should be placed in a head-dependent position, with his head turned to the side to collect the meconium-stained fluid in the cheek pouches, and the posterior pharynx and the buccal pouches should be quickly suctioned. For these infants, some recommend immediate intubation and suctioning[2,13]; while others recommend laryngoscopic visualization of the larynx and trachea to be followed by intubation only if meconium is present at the cords or below.[3,23,26] The stomach should also be emptied to avoid further possible aspiration of meconium containing gastric contents.[2,16,30]

Manipulation of an infant's airway by deep suctioning, laryngoscopy, or intubation has often been discouraged because of the fear of laryngospasm and reflex bradycardia.[5,13,20] But neither Carson and associates[5] nor Gregory, Gooding, and Phibbs[17] reported any untoward sequelae of the tracheal suctioning procedure of the meconium-stained infant in their work. Nevertheless, the nurse in the delivery room must continuously monitor these infants and be alert to any signs of laryngospasm manifested by an increase in respiratory distress or bradycardia.

Lavage of the tracheal tree with sterile normal saline along with thorough suctioning has also been recommended by several experts.[2,27,30] Recent research has found that many of the infants who had tracheal lavage with saline had an x-ray picture that looked like wet lung disease, and therefore it has been concluded that the tracheobronchial lavage was, in fact, increasing the infant's morbidity.[5,26]

The most controversial group of meconium-stained infants are those with no meconium-stained secretions in the mouth on initial suctioning. Gregory, Gooding, and Phibbs[17] found that 17% of infants with tracheal meconium had nonvisible meconium in their oropharynx. Because of these findings, the majority of authors now recommend that every infant with moderate to severe meconium staining should be intubated with direct tracheal suctioning in the delivery room.[13]

As in other pulmonary diseases in which gas exchange is limited, the thermal environment should be neutral to reduce oxygen consumption and to keep carbon dioxide production to a minimum.[16] A radiant heat source must be provided for these infants, and the infant should be thoroughly dried as soon as possible to decrease heat loss by evaporation. An increased oxygen environment may be necessary to prevent hypoxia.[13,16,30] The vast majority of authors recommend that infants receive 100% oxygen via face mask or endotracheal tube during the suctioning and intubation procedures.[13,27]

SIGNS AND SYMPTOMS OF MECONIUM ASPIRATION

Although the signs and symptoms of meconium aspiration may not be immediately apparent or the infant may have been successfully resuscitated in the delivery room and looked well on admission to the nursery, the overall incidence of symptomatic meconium aspiration still remains 1% to 3%.[2] The nurse must be aware of the broad spectrum of signs and symptoms that occur in these infants.

The mere presence of meconium in the trachea does not necessarily cause respiratory problems. In Gregory's work two thirds of those infants from whom meconium was recovered had no respiratory difficulties, although half had abnormal chest x-ray films.[17] However, many of the infants with minimal meconium aspiration will have tachypnea and mild cyanosis beginning shortly after birth.[2,16] Rales may or may not be heard.[16] Usually these patients have a benign clinical course with resolution of their distress by 24 to 72 hours of life.[2]

Another group of meconium-stained infants exhibited a strong respiratory effort with deep restrictions of the costal margins, loud grunting, and appreciable cyanosis after initial resuscitation.[19] Affected infants often develop progressive respiratory failure with significant hypoxemia during the first 2 to 3 days of life.[5] Many of these babies may run a course of moderate clinical respiratory distress for several days, requiring only supportive oxygen therapy. In contrast, the infant with massive meconium aspiration may be severely depressed at birth. These severely ill infants usually require a continuous high oxygen environment, repeated buffering of pH, and some form of ventilatory assistance for several days.[19] Respirations often are irregular and gasping, cyanosis is profound, and the chest is hyperexpanded as represented by a barrel-shaped chest.[2,26] Hypoxia may be out of proportion to the degree of hypercapnia. In fact, many of these babies, when seen early, will have severe hypoxia but low P_{CO_2}.[26] Hypoxemia that does not respond to ventilatory assistance is not an unusual finding in babies with severe meconium aspiration. This may be due to widespread atelectasis, which results in lung tissue that cannot be expanded even with positive pressure.[2] The hypoxemia, along with associated acidosis, has been found to be a potent stimulus to pulmonary vasoconstriction.[2] Persistent fetal circulatory patterns, demonstrated by a significant right-to-left shunt or ventilation perfusion abnormalities, are common in these severely ill babies.[2,19,26] The right-to-left shunting would explain hypoxemia and pulmonary hypoperfusion seen in these babies.[2] The high carbon dioxide tension that is seen in the arterial blood reflects the degree of right-to-left shunting as well as probable diffusion impairment within the lung. The lowered arterial pH found reflects the degree of respiratory acidosis, but this is frequently accompanied by a profound metabolic acidosis.[19]

RADIOGRAPHIC FINDINGS IN MECONIUM ASPIRATION

A characteristic radiographic picture of meconium aspiration has also been described by several authors. A chest x-ray film usually shows patchy, irregular gross densities and radiolucent densities, indicative of the inequality of aeration of various portions of the lung.[2,15,19] These areas have been described as atelectasis by many.[2,26] Simmons[26] adds that the infiltrates may appear to move within a few hours on the x-ray films, which he feels is probably due to the change in air-trapping and atelectasis that can occur over a few hours.

Even mildly symptomatic infants may have highly abnormal chest roentgenograms.[19] It has been observed that the coarse infiltrates in this group of infants often undergo substantial clearing over 12 to 24 hours.[2,17] This has been found to be well correlated with rapid improvement in the condition of the infant.[2] Gregory, Gooding, and Phibbs[17] found that a large number of the infants who developed characteristic radiographic features of meconium aspiration remained asymptomatic. All the symptomatic infants in the series had abnormal chest x-ray films, the severity of which roughly correlated with the severity of their clinical respiratory distress.

In severe cases, hyperexpansion and flattening of the diaphragms are commonly noted.[2,15,19,26] Pleural fluid has been seen frequently.[2,17] Extra-alveolar air, seen as pneumothorax or pneumomediastinum, is a frequent complication of the partial obstruction and airtrapping that occurs in these infants.[2,17,19]

TREATMENT OF INFANT WITH MECONIUM ASPIRATION IN THE NURSERY

Previous literature has described the importance of maintaining pulmonary toilet in the delivery room, but very little research has been done on maintaining this vigorous pulmonary toilet after the immediate newborn period. Zachman[30] found that meconium moves out very rapidly to the peripheral part of the lungs in animal models with meconium aspiration. Hence, he feels that intubation, suction, and lavage are probably only worthwhile if done within a short time after delivery. Gregory, Gooding, and Phibbs[17] recommend an intensive treatment protocol of meconium aspiration infants for the first 8 hours of their lives. They suggest infants be placed

in an environment of ultrasonic distilled water mist. In addition, the nursery nurses precuss and vibrate the chest and suction the nasopharynx every half hour during the first 2 hours of life and every hour for the next 6 hours. Between pulmonary physical therapy, the infants are alternated from side to side and between a 20-degree head-up and 20-degree head-down position. In most instances, Gregory's group found no meconium in the pharynx beyond 4 hours of age. Bacsik[2] purposes that if infants had tracheal meconium on initial suctioning or chest x-ray films consistent with meconium aspiration, they should receive postural drainage for the first 8 hours of life.[2] Simmons[26] agrees that pulmonary toilet is important in the management of meconium aspiration and should be started early. Every nurse working with sick newborns must learn correct procedures for postural drainage, percussion, and suctioning of a young infant. The nurse must continuously monitor the infant during these procedures, and the procedures must be promptly discontinued if any worsening of the infant's condition occurs.

If there is no response to an enriched oxygen environment, end-expiratory pressure has been found to be beneficial for these infants. The additional pressure has been shown to be equally effective whether used as constant positive airway pressure in patients breathing spontaneously or positive end-expiratory pressure in patients being ventilated mechanically.[2,26]

Most commonly, end-expiratory pressure is initiated when more than 80% oxygen is required to keep the arterial Pao_2 above 50 mm Hg.[2,17] Low to moderate amounts of end-expiratory pressure, 4 to 7 cm of water, have been recommended.[2,26] All nurses caring for these infants must be familiar enough with this equipment to recognize when a malfunction is occurring. If the equipment is malfunctioning, the infant must be immediately disconnected and his respirations assisted by bag and mask or endotracheal tube, as necessary, until a person thoroughly trained in the mechanics of the equipment is available to check the machinery.

Antibiotics have been used by many as part of the treatment of meconium aspiration. Where there is no evidence that infected material has been aspirated, the meconium itself should be considered sterile.[3] Nevertheless, the basis for this treatment method has been related to animal studies, which concluded that meconium reduced the number of bacteria necessary to cause death owing to bronchopneumonia.[30] Most authors now advocate that broad-spectrum antibiotics (such as ampicillin and gentamicin) be started after obtaining full cultures if there are signs of maternal infection at the time of delivery or if Gram stains of initial tracheal and gastric aspirates show organisms or many polymorphonuclear leukocytes.[2,16,18,30]

The use of antibiotics to prevent "secondary" superinfection has also been advocated.[3] However, the efficiency of antibiotic therapy in meconium aspiration has not been confirmed clinically.[2,3,18] Ting and Brady[27] feel that antibiotics have not altered the outcome in their babies at all. Individual protocols for antibiotic administration to these infants must be developed by each nursery.

Corticosteroids have been advocated by some to minimize possible inflammatory reaction to the chemical irritation of meconium although steroid therapy has not been studied in a controlled fashion.[2,3,30] Yeh and associates[29] indicate that hydrocortisone is not an effective therapeutic agent for meconium aspiration at all. They feel that corticosteroids may prolong the duration of oxygen requirement and respiratory distress.[2,29]

If the hypoxemia, which may be present in severe meconium aspiration, does not respond to conventional respiratory support measures, ensuring that optimal respiratory parameters are achieved, paralysis with curare has been recommended as the next step in the treatment of these infants. The dramatic rise in Pao_2, which occurs after paralyzing, may be related to an increase in chest wall compliance, diminished struggling, or the release of histamine, which is a pulmonary vasodilator in man.[2] The nurse must remember that these comatose infants must be given the meticulous care necessary to any unconscious patient. If the infant is still hypoxemic despite paralysis, persistent fetal circulation should be suspected and direct measures to reduce pulmonary vasoconstriction are required.[2]

Bronchodilators have been recommended for use by some,[19] although Zachman feels that these drugs should not be used on a routine basis since they have not been studied in meconium aspiration.[30] Tolazoline (Priscoline), a vasodilator and adrenergic blocking agent, has been used by some centers in an attempt to increase pulmonary blood flow. Simmons,[26] in Denver, states that even though his experience with tolazoline has not been successful, other centers have reported success with this drug. He does not think it should be used except as a last-ditch effort in the treatment of hypoxia secondary to meconium aspiration.

Associated metabolic acidosis, hypoglycemia, hypocalcemia, hypovolemia, and anemia should be vigorously corrected.[2] The remaining aspects of treatment in meconium aspiration are those required by any critically ill neonate, namely maintenance of adequate heat, hydration, and parenteral or oral nutrition, although in anticipation of postasphyxia cerebral edema, it is wise to place the infant on some degree of fluid restriction, particularly during the first 48 to 72 hours of life.[2]

COMPLICATIONS OF MECONIUM ASPIRATION

A pneumothorax has been observed as a complication in approximately 10% of all infants who are delivered covered with meconium[16] as the result of a partial "ball-valve" obstruction.[2] Small collections of extra-alveolar air, which are asymptomatic to the infant, require only close, careful observation. However, if the trapped air compromises ventilation or cardiac output, emergency needle aspiration and placement of a closed chest tube connected to an underwater seal are necessary.[2] Infants with this complication may appear pale and in shock because of a compromise of cardiac output. An infant with meconium aspiration should be considered at risk to develop pneumothorax; a 50 cc syringe, needle, and stopcock should be placed at the bedside so that emergency treatment may be readily available.[3]

Of particular importance to the infant with severe meconium aspiration is the sequelae of asphyxia neonatorium, which is often associated with the entity. The child should be watched carefully for evidence of, and promptly treated for, anoxic cerebral injury manifested by cerebral edema, inappropriate secretion of antidiuretic hormone, or convulsions.[2,27] The cerebral injury may require anticonvulsant medication and under circumstances of cerebral edema, an osmotic diuretic agent such as mannitol may be indicated.[3]

The postasphyxiated infant may experience excessive bleeding secondary to hypoxic hepatic damage with depression of liver-dependent clotting factors or disseminated intravascular coagulation (DIC). Treatment must be initiated rapidly to avoid life-threatening intracerebral or pulmonary hemorrhage.[2]

Hematuria, oliguria, or anuria may result from anoxic tubular or cortical renal damage, and intestinal necrosis from ischemia may cause gastrointestinal obstruction or hemorrhage.[2]

PROGNOSIS OF THE INFANT WITH MECONIUM ASPIRATION

Even with improvement in ventilation therapy and more recent developments in respiratory management, therapy is often prolonged and ineffective once meconium aspiration is established in these infants. Mortality rates as high as 28% have been reported, and neurological impairment is common in the survivors.[2,5,15] There is no long-term deficit known in pulmonary function,[3] but survivors must be carefully monitored following discharge from the nursery because of the high incidence of neurological sequelae.[11]

DISCUSSION AND SUMMARY

Meconium-stained amniotic fluid is one of the possible clinical signs of fetal jeopardy; its prompt recognition by the nurse is of value in selecting the fetus that requires continuous monitoring. By early recognition of possible fetal distress, the delivery room staff can be prepared to give direct, prompt, and aggressive treatment to the depressed infant, thereby increasing the changes for intact survival.

Prevention of respiratory failure is by far the most important aspect of caring for infants with meconium aspiration. It is the only way to avoid the numerous sequelae that may rapidly occur from hypoxemia and associated metabolic disturbances in these infants. Nurses, by early recognition and prompt treatment, caring for these infants are the first line of defense in prevention of these problems. Continuous assessment by observation, auscultation, palpation, and percussion of the infant is a direct responsibility of nurses, and they must be thoroughly trained in all of these techniques to provide quality care for these sick infants. They are with the infant constantly; thus nurses must be continuously alert to the complications that may arise in

these infants with little or no warning. The early recognition and prompt treatment of these complications, which well-trained nurses can provide, may be lifesaving to many of these infants. Every area of caring for sick infants must have detailed protocols as to the nurses' level of responsibility when emergency conditions occur.

The most controversial area of treatment for infants with meconium aspiration is the use of drugs; the protocols for these treatments must be carefully outlined by each unit and adhered to religiously by all members of the health care team. There is one drug, oxygen, that is universally used in caring for these infants. Nurses must meticulously follow the basic principles of oxygen administration for the infant with meconium aspiration as one would with any infant receiving oxygen:

1. Oxygen must be warm and humidified—no matter what route of administration is being used.
2. Management with oxygen therapy without arterial blood gas determinations is dangerous.
3. It is essential that the concentration of oxygen be measured with an oxygen analyzer at least every 2 hours.
4. Rapid changes in the oxygen supply to the infant must be avoided.
5. All orders for oxygen therapy must be written by the physician.
6. In emergency situations oxygen therapy should be initiated by the nurse in concentrations to keep the infant "just pink" and the physician should be notified as soon as possible of the change in the infant's condition.

Nurses, in their unique position in the health care team of providing the majority of the care to the sick infant, can provide essential support and guidance to the infant's family during this time of stress that no one else can. Assisting the family to establish their parenting roles with the sick infant is one of the most important tasks of nurses. It is undoubtedly true that much of this guidance and support is being done by nurses, but documentation of these important tasks is conspicuously lacking when nursing records are reviewed.

These authors found no published follow-up studies relating to the growth and development of infants who have survived treatment for meconium aspiration. Experience suggests that the outcome of these infants depends primarily on the severity of the perinatal asphyxia and the neonatal course.

Recognition of perinatal outcome associated with meconium aspiration will provide a basis for determining the risk associated with future development in these infants. These data will only become available when longitudinal follow-up is planned according to a comprehensive research design.

Even with improvement in ventilation therapy and more recent developments in respiratory management coupled with optimal quality of nursing care, therapy is often prolonged and ineffective once meconium aspiration has occurred in these infants. Even though no long-term deficit in pulmonary function has been found, the actual incidence of neurological and other sequelae has not been studied in the infant with meconium aspiration. Thus, since this disease has been shown to be preventable, the *primary goal* in treatment must be its *prevention*.

Protocols

Problem □ Presence of meconium in amniotic fluid after rupture of membranes

GOAL: To recognize early the signs or symptoms of fetal distress
Rationale: To decrease the risk of poor fetal outcome

DIAGNOSTIC

1. Amniotic fluid is checked for meconium staining by color and consistency.
   Rationale: To detect increased fetal and neonatal mortality and morbidity rates
2. Institute continuous fetal heart monitoring.
   Rationale: To determine any stress factors that may endanger fetal or infant's survival rate (Changes in fetal heart rate pattern are indicators of fetal distress.)
3. Fetal blood sampling should be done when indicated.
   Rationale: To screen for detection of fetal distress
4. Review maternal data base history at the time of admission.
   Rationale: To assess history for any possible cause or signs of fetal asphyxia

THERAPEUTIC

1. Inform a physician of any abnormalities noted in fetal heart rate monitoring.
   Rationale: To institute prompt medical management by further assessments or delivery
2. If signs of fetal distress are observed, deliver oxygen (3 to 4 liters) to the mother and place her in left lateral position.
   Rationale: To increase PO$_2$ levels in the fetus
3. Perform fetal blood sampling in a sterile manner.
   Rationale: To minimize the chances of fetal and/or maternal complications
4. Notify nursery of possible meconium-stained infant.
   Rationale: To have nursery personnel and equipment prepared for a possibly distressed infant

EDUCATIONAL

1. Provide in-service educational programs for the labor room personnel concerning the management of women whose labor is complicated by the presence of meconium-stained amniotic fluid.
   Rationale: To detect early warning signs of fetal distress and/or maternal complications
2. Provide patient with an explanation of all procedures and medical treatments that are appropriate to her educational level.
   Rationale: To decrease the patient's anxiety level, thereby enabling her to better cope with the situation at hand

Problem □ Infant being delivered through meconium-stained amniotic fluid

GOAL: To prevent meconium aspiration
Rationale: To prevent an increase in the incidence of perinatal mortality and morbidity

DIAGNOSTIC

1. Note the color and consistency of amniotic fluid.
   Rationale: To assess for the presence of meconium in the amniotic fluid
2. An Apgar score must be evaluated at 1 and 5 minutes of life.
   Rationale: To provide a quick, systematic, and reliable appraisal of the infant's condition at birth
3. Observe for any signs and symptoms of respiratory distress, such as nasal flaring, grunting, substernal retractions, cyanosis, diminished breath sounds, and the presence of rales or rhonchi on auscultation.
   Rationale: To recognize asphyxia in the neonate because the infant's life and future well-being are in jeopardy if no immediate action is taken
4. Direct visualization of the trachea and cords should be done by largynoscopic examination.
   Rationale: To assess for the presence of meconium in the trachea.

THERAPEUTIC

1. Have personnel in the delivery room who are trained in immediate management of the high-risk infant.
   Rationale: To provide high-quality care to the infant
2. Suction the infant's pharynx with a DeLee catheter, bulb syringe, or any soft suction catheter prior to delivery of the infant's shoulders. Use the same procedure at a cesarean section as soon as the nares are seen.
   Rationale: To prevent or reduce the incidence and severity of meconium aspiration
3. Dry infant completely and place in a warmer.
   Rationale: To provide a neutral thermal environment, thereby preventing any additional stress on the infant
4. Direct visualization of larynx and suctioning should be done until all meconium is removed.
   Rationale: To reduce the chance of meconium aspiration
5. If meconium is noted at or below the cords, intubation is necessary and direct suctioning to the endotracheal tube should be applied.

Rationale: To remove tracheal meconium and to decrease the severity of complications that are associated with meconium aspiration

6. Avoid any positive pressure ventilation, if possible, until the trachea is cleared of all visible meconium.
   Rationale: To avoid the possibility of forcing more meconium down the airways, thereby decreasing the infant's chances of an intact survival
7. If, after initial suctioning, the infant remains distressed, careful and immediate assessment of the infant must be done to determine what type of cardiopulmonary support is indicated.
   Rationale: To prevent complications that might jeopardize adequate tissue perfusion and oxygenation to all body cells, thereby increasing the infant's chances of an intact survival
8. Closely monitor all of infant's vital signs.
   Rationale: To provide information as to the infant's cardiopulmonary status
9. Empty gastric content by using an oral gastric or nasogastric tube.
   Rationale: To avoid further aspiration of meconium that might be found in the gastric content
10. Monitor arterial blood gases when equipment is available.
    Rationale: To provide a way to assess the effectiveness of resuscitation measures that are used and to evaluate the infant's present cardiopulmonary status
11. Based on an assessment of the infant's condition, administration of emergency drugs may be necessary.
    Rationale: To support and/or maintain adequate cardiopulmonary functioning and to correct associated metabolic disturbances that might occur in a distressed infant
12. When heart rate and respiratory status are stable, transfer the infant to an intermediate care nursery or a neonatal intensive care unit depending on the infant's condition.
    Rationale: To provide the infant with additional observation, support, and interventions that may be necessary to provide for growth and development at the optimal level possible for that infant

EDUCATIONAL

1. Provide emotional and physical support to the mother and her family.

   Rationale: To keep mother and family informed of what is being done for their infant, which helps to decrease their anxiety levels and reduces the chances of their fantasizing unrealistic danger to their infant

2. Personnel who are giving care to these infants must be trained in neonatal physiology and immediate management of high-risk infants.

   Rationale: To provide immediate quality care to the high-risk infant

Problem □ Neonatal intensive care treatment of the infant with meconium aspiration

GOAL: To maintain optimum physiological functioning of the infant and to enhance his ability to cope effectively with the pathophysiological processes of meconium aspiration

Rationale: To promote optimal physical well-being and intact survival of the infant

DIAGNOSTIC

1. Radiographic evaluation of the chest should be done.

   Rationale: To confirm the occurrence of aspiration

2. Arterial blood gases should be monitored.

   Rationale: To determine oxygenation of blood and acid-base status

3. The following blood work should be drawn:
   a. Serum electrolyte and calcium levels
   b. Blood cultures
   c. Dextrostix q 1 hr × 4, followed by q 4 hr for 24 hours, and if stable as necessary thereafter; serum glucose levels should be drawn immediately if Dextrostix is less than 45 mg%
   d. Hematocrit

   Rationale: To determine the physiological adaption to the extrauterine environment

4. Continuous assessment should be done of the following by observation, auscultation, palpation, and percussion:
   a. Respiratory status
   b. Cardiac function
   c. Renal function
   d. Central nervous system function
   e. Metabolic balance
   f. Gastrointestinal function

   Rationale: To recognize early complications that may further compromise the sick infant

5. Obtain a complete prenatal and intrapartum history of mother and infant.

   Rationale: To obtain data base as to infant's condition and treatments received prior to admission to the nursery

THERAPEUTIC

1. Promote maintenance and/or improvement of respiratory status:
   a. Provide postural drainage, percussion, and suction, as necessary, depending on assessment of lung involvement on x-ray films and auscultation.

      Rationale: To remove secretions from the bronchi, facilitated by the use of gravity, hand pressure applied to the thoracic wall, and removal of loosened secretions by suctioning

   b. Provide oxygen therapy and/or ventilatory assistance, with or without end-expiratory pressure, depending on condition of the infant

      Rationale: To promote lung inflation and gas exchange

   c. Provide a warmed (32° to 35° C) humidified environment for the infant to breathe either by humidity added directly to the isolette, and/or by bubbling the oxygen supply through warmed, sterile, distilled water.

      Rationale: To liquify secretions and soothe irritated and edematous airways

   d. Adequate hydration is essential.

      Rationale: To ensure thinned pulmonary secretions, thus aiding in their removal from the bronchial tree

   e. Observe for signs and symptoms of the occurrence of pneumothorax and/or pneumomediastium.

      Rationale: To prevent these common complications of meconium aspiration

2. Assess kidney function by measuring:
   a. Urinary output
   b. Specific gravity

c. Edema

d. Hematuria, proteinuria, and/or glycosuria

   Rationale: To assess the possibility of changes in kidney function caused by hypoxia

3. Observe for CNS complications such as signs of intracranial bleeding and/or increased intracranial pressure.

   Rationale: To prevent CNS complications associated with the hypoxia and/or administration of hypertonic drugs, such as sodium bicarbonate, in those infants with meconium aspiration

4. Observe for gastrointestinal complications such as obstruction or hemorrhage.

   Rationale: To prevent intestinal necrosis, which has been shown to occur in infants with meconium aspiration from ischemic changes resulting from asphyxia

5. Provide metabolic support by:

   a. Maintain adequate fluid, electrolyte, and caloric requirements either parentally or orally, depending on infant's condition.

      Rationale: To meet resting metabolic requirements, provide sufficient energy for physical activity, counter losses through gastrointestinal and urinary tracts, and supply constituents for growth

   b. Promote acid-base balance by maintaining optimal ventilation parameters and, if absolutely necessary, administration of sodium bicarbonate or THAM.

      Rationale: To maintain the pH within normal limits to halt the major alterations in the metabolic processes and to overcome the acidosis that steadily increases with respiratory distress

6. Maintain infant in a neutral thermal environment.

   Rationale: To decrease oxygen consumption and prevent further stress on an already compromised neonate

7. Administer drugs as indicated, which may include:

   a. Antibiotics

      Rationale: To prevent bacterial growth within the lung

   b. Corticosteroids

   Rationale: To minimize possible chemical pneumonitis because, theoretically, the acid pH of meconium may cause irritation and inflammatory changes within the lung

   c. Bronchodilators

      Rationale: To alleviate the ''ball-valve'' effect, which has been seen as occurring in meconium aspiration

   d. Curare (paralytic agent)

      Rationale: To prevent a dramatic rise in PaO_2, which occurs after paralyzing the infant and is related to an increase in chest wall compliance, diminished struggling, or the release of histamine (which is a pulmonary vasodilator in man)[2]

8. Promote the emotional and developmental needs of the neonate, his family, and the interactions between them.

   Rationale: To develop infant's sense of trust. (One cannot foster health or well-being in the infant unless the parents are both physically and emotionally healthy.)

9. Maintain follow-up evaluational programs of these infants with assessment of psychological and physiological growth and development.

   Rationale: To be on the alert for anoxic insults, which may not manifest themselves until later in childhood

EDUCATIONAL

1. Family unit:

   a. Allow time for the family unit to express their feelings about the condition of the infant and his prognosis

      Rationale: To help the parents explore their feelings and methods of coping with the family crisis

   b. Reemphasize and repeat physician's explanation of the cause, present condition, treatment, and possible prognosis of the infant.

      Rationale: To help the family unit arrive at a realistic perception of the event

   c. Encourage the family unit to visit, touch, and assist in care of the infant when appropriate. Be available to assist the family unit when they visit, and help the family unit keep in touch with the infant until his discharge.

Rationale: To facilitate early, parent-child contact to provide an optimal environment for parent-infant bonding

2. Nursing staff: Education must be provided to the nursing staff caring for sick infants by in-service education programs, provision of current pertinent literature, and/or on-the-job training.

Rationale: To provide the nurse with the tools necessary for early recognition and prompt treatment of complications in these infants and to facilitate the nurse's recognition of the needs of the family unit during this period of crisis

REFERENCES

1. Abramovici, H., Brandes, J., Fuchs, K., and Timor-Tritsch, I.: Meconium during delivery: a sign of compensated fetal distress, Am. J. Obstet. Gynecol. **118:**251, 1974.
2. Bacsik, R.: Meconium aspiration syndrome, Pediatr. Clin. North Am. **24:**463, 1977.
3. Behrman, R.: Neonatal-perinatal medicine, ed. 2, St. Louis, 1977, The C. V. Mosby Co.
4. Buchanan, D. J., and Rapoport S.: Chemical composition of normal meconium and meconium from a patient with meconium ileus, Pediatrics **9:**304, 1954.
5. Carson, B., et al.: Combined obstetrical and pediatric management of meconium staining, Pediatr. Res. **10:**459, 1976.
6. Cruickshank, A. H.: The effects of introduction of amniotic fluid into rabbit lungs, J. Pathol. Bacteriol. **61:**527, 1949.
7. Dawes, G. S., et al.: Respiratory movements and rapid eye movements during sleep in fetal lamb, J. Physiol. **220:**119, 1972.
8. Desmond, M., Moore, J., and Lindley, J.: Meconium staining of the amniotic fluid—a marker of fetal hypoxia, J. Obstet. Gynecol. **9:**91, 1957.
9. Desmond, M., et al.: Meconium staining of newborn infant, J. Pediatr. **49:**540, 1956.
10. Driscoll, S. G., and Smith, C. A.: Neonatal pulmonary disorders: meconium aspirations, Pediatr. Clin. North Am. **9:**325, 1962.
11. Evans, H., and Glass, L.: Perinatal medicine, New York, 1976, Harper & Row, Publishers.
12. Fenton, A., and Steer, G.: Fetal distress, Am. J. Obstet. Gynecol. **83:**354, 1962.
13. Fox, W., et al.: A delivery room approach to the meconium aspiration syndrome, Clin. Pediatr. **16:**325, 1977.
14. Fujikura, T., and Klionsky, B.: The significance of meconium staining, Am. J. Obstet. Gynecol. **121:**45, 1975.
15. Gooding, C. A., et al.: An experimental model for the study of meconium aspiration of the newborn, Radiology **100:**137, 1971.
16. Gould, J., et al.: Respiratory problems. In Williams, T. J.,
    editor: Handbook of neonatal respiratory care, Riverside, Calif., 1976, Bourns, Inc., p. 29.
17. Gregory, G., Gooding, C. A., and Phibbs, R. H.: Meconium aspiration in infants: a prospective study, J. Pediatr. **85:**848, 1974.
18. Herrman, W., and Moore, J.: Monitoring health care, Am. J. Obstet. Grynecol. **123:**382, 1975.
19. Kendig, E.: Disorders of the respiratory tract in children, Philadelphia, 1977, W. B. Saunders Co.
20. Klaus, F.: Care of the high-risk neonate, Philadelphia, 1973, W. B. Saunders Co.
21. Miller, F. C., et al.: Significance of meconium during labor, Am. J. Obstet. Gynecol. **122:**573, 1975.
22. Page, E., Villee, C., and Villee, D.: Human reproduction, Philadelphia, 1976, W. B. Saunders Co., p. 362.
23. Pritchard, J., and MacDonald, P.: Williams obstetrics, ed. 15, New York, 1976, Appleton-Century-Crofts.
24. Rubowits, W. H., et al.: The pathological properties of meconium, Am. J. Obstet. Gynecol. **36:**501, 1938.
25. Schaffer, A. J.: Massive aspiration syndrome. In Schaffer, A. J.: Disease of the newborn, ed. 2, Philadelphia, 1965, W. B. Saunders Co.
26. Simmons, M.: Meconium aspiration. In Schreiner, R., editor: Management of neonatal problems, Indianapolis, 1977, Department of Pediatrics, Indiana University, p. 203.
27. Ting, P., and Brady, J.: Tracheal suction in meconium aspiration, Am. J. Obstet. Gynecol. **122:**767, 1975.
28. Vidyasagar, D., and Andreou, A.: Management of meconium aspiration syndrome. In Aladjim, S., and Brown, A. K., editors: Perinatal intensive care, St. Louis, 1977, The C. V. Mosby Co., p. 413.
29. Yeh, T. F., et al.: Hydrocortisone therapy in meconium aspiration syndrome: a controlled study, J. Pediatr. **90:**140, 1977.
30. Zachman, R.: Perinatal news **5**(6):1, 1975.

BIBLIOGRAPHY

Avery, F.: The lung and its disorders in the newborn infant, ed. 3, Philadelphia, 1974, W. B. Saunders Co.

Clark, A.: Childbearing, Philadelphia, 1976, F. A. Davis Co.

Clausen, J.: Maternity nursing today, New York, 1973, McGraw-Hill Book Co.

Gluck, L., and Kulovich, M.: Respiratory distress syndrome, New York, 1973, Academic Press, Inc. p. 183.

Hellman, L., and Pritchard, J.: Williams obstetrics, ed. 14, New York, 1971, Appleton-Century-Crofts.

Hobel, C. J.: Antepartum clinical assessment of fetal distress, Am. J. Obstet. Gynecol. **110:**336, 1971.

Jensen, M. D., Benson, R. C., and Bobak, I. M.: Maternity care, St. Louis, 1977, The C. V. Mosby Co.

Korones, S.: High-risk newborn infants, ed. 3, St. Louis, 1981, The C. V. Mosby Co.

Rapoport, S., and Buckman, D. J.: The composition of meconium: isolation of blood group specific polysaccharides: abnormal composition of meconium in meconium ileus, Science **112:**150, 1950.

Ziegel, E., and Van Blarcom, C.: Obstetric nursing, ed. 6, New York, 1972, Macmillan, Inc.

SECTION FOUR

NEONATAL PROTOCOLS

Chapter 14

Normal newborn care

Sheryl Coddington Shipman and Delia Bell Robinson

The delivery of infants has long proved a rich area for dogma and controversy. Whether the cord is severed by grinding it between two magically selected stones or sterily cut according to the latest scientific rationale, those who administer care to the woman in childbirth and the new infant are frequently in agreement only about their desired outcome. Scissors under the mattress supposedly to "cut the pain," a hard slap on the baby's buttocks, or immersion into first cold and then warm water—so many techniques have waxed and waned, yet the purpose has been singular, the evolution of a healthy mother and infant. Delivery room postures and practices have made some amazing alterations in the course of history.

It is the goal of this chapter to review some currently accepted practices for normal infant care and explain the rationale that has led to their acceptance.

DELIVERY ROOM CARE
Preparation

The nurse who receives the newborn in the delivery area has made a thorough review of the mother's history prior to the infant's arrival. The object here is to prepare for any of the extensive array of neonatal problems that are secondary to maternal causes. Readiness, in sudden emergencies, often determines outcome. Therefore, those in the delivery area should be prepared to resuscitate, even when a healthy infant is anticipated.

Before the delivery, one should be confident that appropriate equipment is available and functioning. Required basic equipment includes:

Stethoscope (Forestall mislaying this essential item by having it attached by a chain to the resuscitation console.)

Suction bulb and DeLee apparatus

500 ml resuscitation bag and masks (in assorted sizes) The bag should be capable of delivering 100% O_2 and should either be filled with an aneroid manometer or pop-off valve to avoid excessive pressures.[18]

Plastic infant airways, assorted sizes

Laryngoscope with premature and newborn blades (sizes 0 and 1)

Oxygen supply, face masks

Endotracheal tubes, sizes 2.5 through 4 mm

Lines and fluids for umbilical catheterization ($D_{10}W$)

Resuscitation drugs in appropriate amounts

Overhead warmer, turned *on*

Warmed blankets and towels

Timer for Apgar scoring

Birthing

Let us suppose the birth has gone well; there has been nothing signaling possible trouble, no meconium staining of fluid, no significant alteration in the fetal heart rate, and so on. The infant has been delivered and suctioned when the head appeared on the perineum, the cord has been clamped, and cord blood and any other indicated samples have been obtained. The infant has been placed in a preheated warmer.

The warmer

There is some controversy about appropriate positioning of the infant in the warmer. Some authorities[22] suggest a 15-degree Trendelenburg position to promote draining of secretions, while others opt for a prone posture. Clearly, if there has been significant cephalopelvic disproportion and a difficult pas-

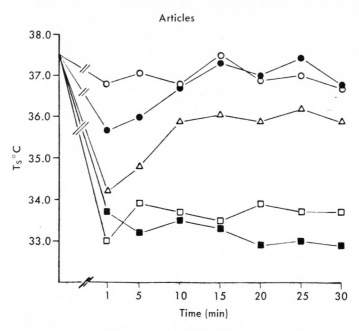

Articles

Fig. 14-1. Mean abdominal skin temperature (T_s) of each group during first 30 minutes of life. T_s is on ordinate and minutes postdelivery on abscissa. ■, Wet infants in room air; □, dry infants in room air; ●, wet infants under radiant heater; Δ, dry infants wrapped in a blanket; ○, dry infants under radiant heater. (From Dahm, L. S., and James, L.: Pediatrics **49:**509, 1972. Copyright American Academy of Pediatrics 1972.)

sage of the head or a forceps delivery, a Trendelenburg position, raising intracranial pressure, may not be ideal.[15]

Rapidly pat the infant dry with warmed linens (paying special attention to hair and scalp). Chilling predisposes the infant to acidosis.[18] The initial rapid loss of heat through convection can be significantly detrimental to an otherwise unstressed infant. Figs. 14-1 and 14-2 demonstrate the amount of chilling infants experienced in the delivery area in relation to the care received.[10]

Rapid drying in addition to an overhead warmer seems to be a useful measure in preventing an initial plummet in temperature, which often takes hours to recover. Drying the infant also provides stimulation. There is, however, yet another option that is not included in Dahm and James' study. Many women want to hold their newly born infant while in the delivery room. Keeping the baby warm often justifies a refusal when a mother requests holding her infant for more than the briefest encounter. It

has been demonstrated that a well-dried and bundled infant held in its mother's arms for up to 15 minutes remains within the acceptable temperature range.[31] With an awakening popular interest in early bonding, this and other techniques, for example, the "skin-to-skin" method where the naked infant is placed on the mother's chest and a blanket is placed over both of them, will be receiving more attention. However, these techniques require further research before they become accepted practice.

In this case, as with so many options available to us in our practice, the key is not *how* the infant is kept warm but merely the assurance that he *is* warm. Cold stress easily could provide the negative impetus for a difficult transition from birth to stabilization.

During this period, the nurse should observe the infant's color, noting cyanosis, pallor, retractions, nasal flaring, grunting, respiratory rate abnormalities, and any indication of respiratory distress. If any of these are present, the oropharynx should be

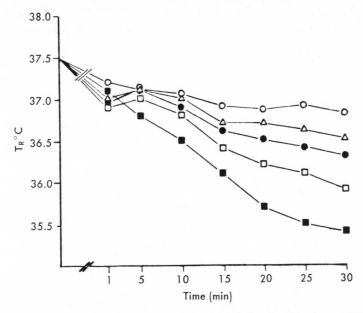

Fig. 14-2. Mean deep body temperatures (T_R) of each group during first 30 minutes of life. T_R is on ordinate and minutes postdelivery on abscissa. ■, Wet infants in room air; □, dry infants in room air; ●, wet infants under radiant heater; Δ, dry infants wrapped in a blanket; ○, dry infants under radiant heater. (From Dahm, L. S., and James, L.: Pediatrics **49:**509, 1972. Copyright American Academy of Pediatrics 1972.)

suctioned first (not more than 15 seconds) and then the nose. Suctioning the nose induces gasping, so it is wise to first suction the oropharynx.[22] The heart rate should be checked prior to suctioning, since suctioning may well induce vagal stimulation and bradycardia or apnea.

When two people are working with the baby, it is sometimes recommended that one listen to the heart with a stethoscope and indicate the rate by finger movement, while the other is suctioning or intubating the infant. In reality, the person peering down the barrel of a laryngoscope blade is not likely to be also concentrating on variations of a moving finger. One can always resort to practicality and tell the person suctioning when the rate decelerates, whereupon intubation can be interrupted and oxygen can be given until the rate returns to normal.

After suctioning, the infant should be stimulated to reinforce sensory input.[22] Vigorous or traumatic stimulation is not recommended. Painful stimuli may also stimulate the vagal reflex. Skin stimula-

tion, such as rubbing the soles of the feet, is generally adequate.

When a vigorous cough or cry is present within seconds of birth, procedures other than brief initial bulb suctioning and the stimulation of drying are generally not needed. Between assigning Apgar scores, the nurse can proceed with the more elective procedures of newborn care, although always with a watchful eye for developing problems.

Systematized by the celebrated Dr. Virginia Apgar, the Apgar scoring system is so widely used and well known that only a brief discussion should be required here (Table 14-1). Although subjective, it has proved to be a handy tool for indexing the degree of depression at 1 minute after birth and again at 5 minutes. For each of the five categories assessed, a score of 0, 1, or 2 is assigned, the total score of 10 indicating a presumably optimal condition. This would reflect an infant with a lusty cry, flexed extremities, irritable reflexes, a pink color, and a heart rate within the normal range (120 to 160

Table 14-1. The Apgar score

Sign	0	1	2
Heart rate	Absent	100 beats/min	100 beats/min
Respiratory effort	Absent	Weak cry	Strong cry
Muscle tone	Limp	Some flexion	Good flexion
Reflex irritability (feet stimulated)	No response	Some motion	Cry
Color	Blue, pale	Body pink, extremities blue	Pink

beats/min). A score of 5 or less at 5 minutes would indicate the need for immediate resuscitation if it has not already been instituted.[2]

It is valuable to obtain a rapid assessment of gestational age in the delivery area (Fig. 14-3). Assignment to a nursery is often decided by gestational age, and a large-for-gestational-age infant, unless appropriately assessed, may unwittingly be tucked in a corner in a normal nursery where he can decompensate unobserved. The method shown in Fig. 14-3, a short form of the commonly used Dubowitz[12] examination, is rapid and accurate.

A complete newborn physical examination will be given later in the nursery, but an initial physical assessment is essential in the delivery area to rule out life-threatening problems; birth trauma, both mechanical and hypoxic in origin; and various syndromes. Naturally, if an infant has a congenital problem, a better outcome can be hoped for with early identification. Twenty percent of all newborns have some abnormality, ranging from a birthmark or an extra digit to the 4% with serious congenital anomalies. About 50% will be detected before discharge from the nursery, but as indicated, earlier recognition can frequently lead to a better outcome.[36]

The first day of extrauterine life is the most perilous day we face. The common statement that more deaths occur on the first natal day than any other day of life remains true.[6] Therefore, in addition to care, a thoughtful, albeit quick, delivery room physical examination should be made.

Evaluation of respiratory status is continuous. Cyanosis or pallor, breath sounds, and respiratory quality and rate are noted. The nares are examined for patency by using a wisp of cotton or by blocking first one naris and then the other or by any number of other ways. The heart is auscultated and mur-

murs are noted. Pulses are palpated. Many life-threatening cardiopulmonary problems may be present in the first hour with beguiling subtlety. Without proper attention, the nurse can suddenly be faced with a desperately sick infant requiring transportation to a regional center, with nothing in readiness.

The abdomen should be observed for protuberances or, conversely, a sunken appearance that could indicate a diaphragmatic hernia. Auscultate the abdomen, and palpate for masses. An abdominal examination should be far more easily accomplished in the delivery room than later because the musculature should be quite relaxed and the intestines relatively free of air.[3] Therefore, take advantage of this opportunity and examine the belly carefully, including palpation of both kidneys.

Examine the hand creases, the fingers and toes, and the genitalia and check for clubfeet, spinal closure, and cleft lip and palate.

Some authorities recommend aspirating the stomach contents at this time and then instilling air while auscultating the stomach to rule out the most common type of tracheoesophageal fistulas. The same catheter can be used to check rectal patency.[3]

If there is a question in assigning gender to a newborn, the rule is, *please don't*. Tell the parents that there has been a problem in the baby's development, and although the gender is uncertain at the moment, a positive answer is forthcoming. A team should immediately be assembled to provide an answer that satisfies both the geneticist and the urogenital specialist. Beware of giving the impression that the child is a neuter, for in all probability it is genetically a "real girl" or a "real boy" and most assuredly should be raised as one or the other. Advise the family to wait before presenting their new baby with a name. Unisex names are not appropriate for

A. Variables					
Nipple formation	Nipple barely visible: no areola — 0	Well-defined nipple: areola <0.75 cm — 5	Areola stippled not raised >0.75 cm — 10	Areola raised >0.75 cm — 15	
Skin texture	Thin, gelatinous — 0	Thin and smooth — 5	Smooth, medium thickness, superficial peeling — 10	Slight thickening, superficial cracking, and peeling of hands and feet — 15	Thick and parchment like — 20
Ear form	Pinna flat and shapeless — 0	Incurving of part of edge — 8	Partial incurving of whole of upper pinna — 16	Well-defined incurving of pinna — 24	
Breast size	No breast tissue — 6	Diameter <0.5 cm — 5	Diameter 0.5-1 cm — 10	Diameter >1 cm — 15	
Plantar creases	No creases — 0	Faint red marks over anterior 1/3 — 5	Definite red marks over anterior 1/2, indentations over anterior 1/3 — 10	Indentations over anterior 1/2 — 15	Deep indentations over more than anterior 1/2 — 20
Scarf sign	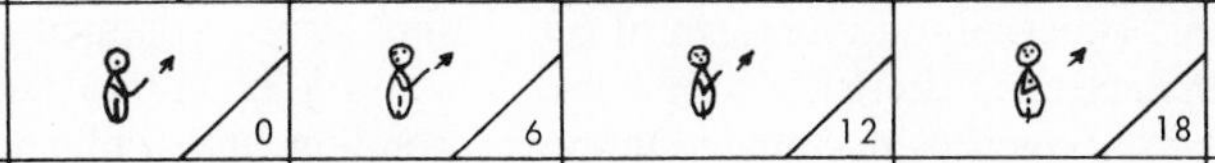 0	6	12	18	
Head lag	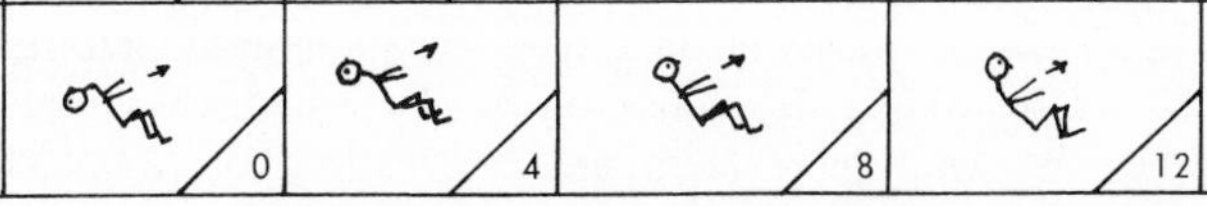 0	4	8	12	

(Row labels at left: B. — Somatic and neurological; Somatic; K = 204 days; K = 200 days)

Fig. 14-3. Variables and assigned scores in modified Dubowitz method for assessment of gestational age. *A*, Gestational age in days = 204 + total somatic score (for neurologically depressed infants). *B*, Gestational age in days = 200 + total combined somatic and neurological score (for healthy infants). (From Dubowitz, L. M. S., et al.: J. Pediatr. **77:**1, 1970.)

Table 14-2. Stages in the sleep-wake cycle

State	Characteristics
1. Regular sleep	Eyes closed, regular respiration, no movement
2. Active (REM) sleep	Eyes closed, rapid eye movements, irregular respiration, no gross movements
3. Quiet wakefulness	Eyes open, no gross movement
4. Active wakefulness	Eyes open, gross movement, no crying
5. Fussing	Eyes open or closed, crying
6. Indeterminate	Transitional

these children and should be vehemently discouraged because the initial confusion and aura of sexual nonbeing will be carried by that family through the child's name. Counseling for the parents and grandparents should be arranged to dispell any confusion concerning the child's gender.[11,14]

The newborn state of consciousness is generally one of quiet wakefulness, although the level of consciousness in the immediate postdelivery period has received little attention. It is presumed that the neonate initially retains an unresponsive autonomic nervous system for the first hour or so of life. Therefore, alterations in heart rate at this time with crying are not seen as would be expected later. The infant usually reaches a peak of activity at a median of 60 minutes of age and then sleeps. Thereafter, the baby will move through the six levels as designated in the sleep-awake cycle (Table 14-2). Variation in time spent in any given state is seemingly dependent on age, the condition of the central nervous system, and environmental influences. Extreme abnormalities in state may be noticed in the delivery area.[4]

Weights in the delivery area should depend on the condition of the infant, but in general unnecessary procedures should be deleted. The baby will have to be weighed again in the nursery to establish a baseline weight with their scales with which to compare daily weights. Therefore a delivery room weight is not absolutely necessary and is detrimental to a child who has already been chilled or stressed in any way.[22]

In the journey through the birth canal, or even after prolonged rupture of the membranes, an infant may acquire an inoculum of *Neisseria gonorrhoeae.* Highly infectious, gonococcal ophthalmia results in blindness unless vigorously treated. Silver nitrate, in single-dose containers, has proved to be a safe, inexpensive preventive measure.

Perhaps about 3% of the women have gonococcal infections at the time of delivery,[36] with 90% of that group being asymptomatic.[38] Although not all babies of infected mothers develop gonococcal ophthalmia, a 1% solution of silver nitrate instilled in each eye is 98% effective in preventing this damaging condition.[36]

Routine use of prophylactic antibiotics is no longer advised, both from fear of sensitizing the infant to the antibiotic and the possible development of resistant organisms.[16]

Formerly, the infant's eyes were rinsed after the instillation of silver nitrate, but it is now recommended by the National Society for the Prevention of Blindness (NSPB), Committee on Ophthalmia Neonatorum, that no rinse should be used. They stress that proper instillation technique is the single most crucial factor in successful prophylaxis.[5]

A single drop of the solution should be allowed to fall on the cornea. The lids should then be manipulated with the fingers to spread the solution throughout the conjunctival sac. The NSPB states "if the medication strikes the lids and lid margins only and fails to strike the cornea, the instillation should be repeated.[16] Excess solution on the lids, unless patted dry, will cause temporary skin discoloration, which should be explained to the parents.

With the current interest in optimal mother-infant bonding, the application of silver nitrate to the eyes is sometimes deferred until the baby is in the nursery. Chemical conjunctivitis and the accompanying swelling of periorbital tissues will not foster the wide awake, alert gaze that mothers find so rewarding as they meet their new infants. The NSPB does recommend that no more than 1 hour elapse after delivery without this procedure being completed,[16] but whether it occurs in the delivery room or nursery area is a matter of preference.

An intramuscular injection of 1 mg of vitamin K is routinely given in most delivery areas to correct the transient low levels of clotting factors produced by the liver. Hemorrhagic disease of the newborn is seen in 1 in 200 or 300 live births not receiving vitamin K. One injection generally is sufficient until the various systems responsible for vitamin K production, assimilation, and use are underway. The infants of mothers receiving anticonvulsant medications during pregnancy are especially prone to bleeding disorders, and one injection may not prove adequate. With these infants cord blood for laboratory prothrombin time evaluation is usually desirable prior to the administration of intravenous vitamin K.[2]

Before the mother and infant can be separated, all identification procedures must be completed. The guidelines for this routine are set down in the *Standards and Recommendations of Hospital Care of Newborn Infants.*[37] Basically, one is required to make a footprint of the infant and fingerprint of the mother on the same document. A smeared print is of no value.[2] Bracelets giving the infant's sex, date and time of birth, hospital number, and mother's name and hospital number are affixed to both the infant's wrists and ankle, and the same information is placed on the mother's wrist. These bracelets are compared periodically according to policy. Legal ramifications of failure in this area are obvious.

With identification complete, the presumably healthy newborn is free to be taken to the nursery or for a visit with the family in the recovery room. Safe transport to any area is probably best accomplished in a wheeled transport container, which allows warmth and visibility. If this type of device is used, move the baby forward foot first. Should a collision occur, the head will not be used as a battering ram. In many places transport is accomplished with the child held in the nurse's arms. The nurse's elbow should protrude protectively beyond the infant's head to ward off doorjambs and sharp objects. A bulb syringe should be carried while transporting the baby.

On arrival in the nursery, all delivery information should be given to the attending nurse. This should include antepartum history; course of labor and delivery; amount of amniotic fluid, including the amount of vernix rubbed off when drying the infant; and care given to the baby in the delivery area, including drugs used, oxygen, and any procedures done.

Through the popular press and because of widespread interest in the women's movement, birth has been considerably demystified. Rather rapidly one has seen the entry of fathers and friends into the delivery area. Birthing couches are being designed and marketed by traditionally conservative corporations making hospital equipment, signaling an end to the feet-in-the-air back-lying posture brought into com-

mon use through the voyeuristic urges of a decadent French king. Changes will be in evidence as birth and newborn care continue to adjust to new medical and popular knowledge.

NEWBORN CARE

Newborn care standards provide a structural framework to plan optimal care for the newborn infant. Guidelines to generate initial comprehensive individual care have been suggested earlier in this chapter. The newborn has been transported in a warmed incubator through the hall accompanied, most probably, by an adoring father with close relatives and/or friends. The vulnerable newborn is awaiting the challenges of (1) maintaining a physiological body temperature; (2) avoidance of contact with infectious agents, personnel, and property, (3) establishing adequate nutrition; and (4) continued respiratory maintenance.[30] As caregivers nurses have quite an obligation not only to our little client but also to the family to facilitate a new therapeutic beginning.

The American Academy of Pediatrics (AAP) publishes a manual for hospital care of newborn infants. The medical director and staff generate many nursery standards of care from this reference.[37] Nurses must familiarize themselves with these recommendations to understand the rationale for the myriad of constantly changing practices in this working environment.

Owing to the work of epidemiologists and other researchers of bacterial/viral components of newborn nurseries, we have become aware of the requirement to keep some of the neonate's potentially lethal germs at a minimum.[30,33,37] The ensuing topics support this idealism of maintaining an environment that will jeopardize the newborn the least.

Admission data

The foundation on which to build a therapeutic environment for the newborn should include a data base consisting of maternal prenatal history, labor, and newborn delivery history components. This comprehensive record should be completed, beginning in the labor and delivery areas and terminating in the nursery. Continuity of optimal health promotion begins with a thorough and meticulously compiled history. See Fig. 14-4 for a suggested maternal-infant history form.

Nurses have a unique opportunity to observe the

```
I.   Maternal

     A.   General information

          Name_____ Address_____

          _____

          Home phone _____Hospital number_____

          Room number_____Marital status M_____S_____Div_____Sep_____Wid_____

          Age_____Race_____Religion_____

          Infant:  Nursery_____ Rooming-in_____

          Feeding:  Breast_____Bottle_____

          Prenatal care:  Private _____Clinic_____Obstetrician_____

II.  Family history:  Maternal

     Diabetes_____Heart disease_____ Sickle cell_____

     Other_____

     Comments:  (include relationship)

     Family history:  Paternal

     Diabetes_____ Heart disease_____ Sickle cell_____

     Other_____

     Comments:  (include relationship)

III. Past obstetrical history:

     Para_____Prematures (less than 37 weeks)_____
     Grav_____  Low birth weight (less than 2500 gm)_____
     AB_____Fetal deaths (greater than 20 weeks)_____
     Neonatal deaths_____Congenital anomalies_____
     Comments:  (abnormalities or other relevant data)

 IV. Current pregnancy

     LMP_____EDC_____ Nonpreg wt _____ Wt now_____
     Ht_____Cigarettes/day_____ Alcohol/day_____
     Serology rubella titer _____VDRL_____
     Blood type_____Rh _____Antibodies_____
     Complications with details:  (tests, physical, meds, include weeks of
     gestation)
```

Fig. 14-4. Maternal-infant history sheet. (Data compiled from Evans, H., and Glass, L.: Perinatal medicine, New York, 1976, Harper & Row, Publishers, Inc.; Silver, H. K., Kempe, C. H., and Bruyn, H. B.: Handbook of pediatrics, ed. 12, Los Altos, Calif., 1977, Lange Medical Publications; and *Standards and Recommendations for Hospital Care of Newborn Infants,* Evanston, Ill., 1977, American Academy of Pediatrics Committee of Fetus and Newborn.)

V. Labor

Spontaneous_____Induced _____ Method
Reason if induced:

Drugs received_____ Dose _____ Route_____Time_____

Anesthesia_____ Type_____ Time_____Problems_____

First stage _____hours
Second stage_____minutes
Membranes (include time, color, odor of fluid)

SROM_____ AROM_____

Monitored

Yes_____ No _____
Internal_____ External_____
Type of pattern and fetal distress if any:

VI. Delivery

Time_____ Date _____ Presentation_____
(if multiple births)

Forceps: Low_____ Mid_____ High_____ Outlet_____

Delivery type: Vaginal_____

    C section_____ Indications _____

Apgars (include why points taken off)
        1 minute_____
        5 minute_____
Placenta wt _____Vessels: Artery_____ Vein _____
Abnormalities (infarcts, etc)

Continued.

Fig. 14-4, cont'd. Maternal-infant history sheet.

VII. Newborn:

Meconium_____ Void _____

Resuscitation measures_____

Use of O_2/amount/how administered_____

Aquamephyton: Amount_____Site_____

$AgNO_3$ (opth): Yes_____No_____

Bracelet identified and checked/by whom_____

Initial physical exam abnormalities:

ID# checked with chart: Yes_____ No_____

Wt_____ gm   Length_____cm

OFC_____ cm   Chest circumference_____cm

Temp_____ °C (axillary)

Apical pulse_____ /min Regular _____ Irregular_____

Murmur_____

Respiratory rate_____ /min Describe

B/P_____ Which extremity_____

Dextrostix_____

Color_____

Pediatrician_____ Time notified_____

Any findings:

Nurse signature _____

Fig. 14-4. cont'd. Maternal-infant history sheet.

neonate. The nurse must document visual perceptions factually. Familiarization with the newborn either through literature and/or practice is an ongoing responsibility, as the state of the art is in constant flux.

On admission the nurse should place the infant in a heated crib or under a radiant warmer. The fact that the infant has a potential for approximately four times greater heat loss than the adult should be of primary concern when administering care. Silverman, Sinclair, and Agate[35] suggest maintenance of an abdominal skin temperature (as monitored by skin probe) of 36° C to maintain a ". . . neutral thermal state. Superficial not deep thermoreceptors exert dominant influence over metabolism of the neonate." Waiting 4 to 6 hours until the temperature is stable (36° to 37° C) before bathing the neonate is essential to prevent cold stress.

The use of radiant warmers must be regulated scrupulously. When the radiant surface temperature falls by 10° C or more, there probably will be cooling of the thermal environment. Oxygen requirements may increase by 25% because of the metabolic response stimulation.[19] Clinical evidence of temperature instability may be noted by hyponatremia, hypoglycemia, lethargy, poor feeding, mottled skin, and so forth.

Gentle oral and nasal bulb suctioning should be provided for alleviation of mucus and consequent airway compromise. Babies are obligate nose breathers so the oral airway should be cleared before suctioning the nasal passages. Close observance of color, respiratory patterns, and vital signs provides valuable tools for assessing cardiorespiratory status or its changes.

Following completion of weight, Dextrostix, temperature, apical pulse rate, blood pressure, respiratory rate, color appraisal, evaluation, and maintenance of airway assessment parameters, a nursing physical examination should be done. The pediatrician by now has been notified of admission.

Nelson, Vaughan, and McKay[30] suggest two purposes of the physical examination of the newborn: "(1) To detect abnormalities, and (2) to establish baseline information for subsequent exams." This examination should be performed by the nurse and the physician as soon as possible after birth. The need for a comprehensive newborn medical examination cannot be stressed too much. "In the United States ⅔'s of the deaths in the first year of life occur in the first twenty-eight days of life."[30]

The particular comprehensiveness of the examination will vary according to the nurse's clinical assessment skills. Depending on the institution of employment, this may be a deciding factor in what the nurse wild do. Frequently in large medical centers there are externs or interns to chart the Dubowitz, Colorado Intrauterine Growth Chart, and Neonatal Mortality Risk Based on Weight and Gestational Age Curves.[12] These charts should be used as parameters in facilitating optimal health predictors for outcome.

The nurse is responsible for measurements (length, weight, head circumference, chest circumference), vital signs, initial blood pressure, Dextrostix, palpation of the abdomen, and reporting on the absence of meconium or urine passage in the first 24 hours.[13,30,34] The physical examination is so essential that the integration of it into every contact with the infant is an understatement.

An easy and useful method that has been described to evaluate blood glucose levels is the use of a Dextrostix. This treatment is generally administered on entrance to the nursery by the admitting nurse. The Dextrostix is obtained by using a 2 mm penetration lancet to prick the lateral aspect of the heel. It is an especially important part of care for premature, small-for-gestational-age babies, and infants of diabetic mothers. Glucose levels are affected by such factors as activity, thermoregulation, and metabolic states. Compromise or competition for these states may alter the blood sugar levels. Evans and Glass[13] suggest abnormality when blood glucose levels are less than 30 mg/dl (in the nursery this is done on a microsample) the first 3 days of life and 40 mg/dl thereafter for normal term infants. The nurse should order a stat blood sugar level from the laboratory if the Dextrostix is in one of these ranges, then institute treatment per nursery protocol. The physician should be notified at this time.

The important role of the nurse in the neonate's transition from intrauterine to extrauterine life cannot be overemphasized. The importance of establishing both physiological and attachment processes in the first 48 to 72 hours (usual hospital stay) can be facilitated to maximum potential by the observational, sensitive, and methodical qualities the nursery nurse should possess.

Control of infection

The newborn is in an ideal situation to host numerous pathogens because of his relatively sterile body systems. The first few days of life will colonize these systems. His caregivers must provide a safe environment with minimal threat to his vulnerable integument. This component of the chapter will focus on handwashing techniques and personnel attire.

The nursery personnel are the most importnat determinants of infection control measures.[37] Breaks in technique may cause epidemic *Staphylococcus* bouts.[33,37]

Rigid health standards must be recognized and adhered to by the individual as well as the health team. Individual criteria standards are provided by each hospital concerning colds and/or other physical variables that restrict entrance to the nursery. A general guideline includes restriction of personnel who have colds, skin infections, and gastrointestinal or mucocutaneous manifestations.[33,37] It is necessary to obtain rubella titer levels and immunizations as needed on female personnel.

Restrictions on attire, jewelry, and hair are required. Short-sleeved scrub suits or dresses should be worn by caregivers who work with the infants for most of the day. Covergowns are worn by those who come in contact with the infant for short periods of time, for example, physicians/nurses giving newborn examinations and laboratory personnel. The gown should be fastened securely to cover the clothing adequately. In the event of isolation techniques all personnel are to wear long-sleeved covergowns. The personnel must wear covergowns when leaving the nursery, for example, breaks, lunch, errands. Long hair should be restrained so that it does not touch the infant or equipment.

Facial masks worn for specific procedures should cover the nose and mouth. The nursery directors must designate the length of time one mask is worn before changing to another.

The hands require conscientious washing since they may potentially transfer disease to the infant. Stringent guidelines for technique and utmost respect for this task should convert handwashing into a ritual.

Gluck and Richardson (in Shirkey[33]) describe the ineffectiveness of the scrub versus handwashing methods in regard to reducing bacterial counts. On entrance to the nursery the arms should be exposed to the elbow. A lather of iodophor preparation (water-soluble complexes of iodine with surfactant agents) should be used for 2 minutes.[37] The fingernails should be cleaned with an orangewood or plastic stick. A 15-second wash between infant handling or contact with contaminated articles is advised thereafter.

Fundamental to compliance with handwashing technique is well-planned accessibility to materials and facilities.

Newborn bathing and umbilical cord care

Hexachlorophene (HCP) has been used as a bacteriostatic agent for more than 20 years.[29] Most literature had supported the use of HCP until its implications were presented to the Society of Toxicology by Gaines and Kimbrough in 1971.[17] The neuropathological (primarily spongiosis lesions) findings affecting the cerebellum, brain stem, and all parts of the spinal cord were significant to the alteration of HCP usage in ordinary newborn care. Consequently, on February 2, 1972, a joint statement was issued by the Federal Drug Administration (FDA) and the American Academy of Pediatrics (AAP) stating that "there is a firm basis for concern about the indiscriminate or prolonged exposure of humans to hexachlorophene."[23,24] Supported by the Gaines and Kimbrough study, the FDA and AAP recommended publically that routine body bathing with HCP be discontinued.

Literature concerning the nosocomial infection increase filled many pediatric journals after the AAP advised withdrawl of HCP; even to date, HCP usage is controversial.

A myriad of bathing and cord care techniques appear in newborn care texts and journals. The AAP[9] states that skin manipulations are performed for two reasons: "(1) for prevention of infection and (2) for aesthetic and cleansing purposes." The vulnerability of the infant's integument caused by lack of normal flora and exposure to personnel who may harbor threatening agents, presents a challenging situation to caregivers. Thus the use of the dry technique is advocated by the AAP. "The dry technique is recommended for the following reasons: (1) it subjects the infant to less heat loss by exposure; (2) it diminishes skin trauma; (3) it requires less time, and (4) it does not expose the infant to agents with known, or unknown, side effects."[9]

Hargiss and Larson[21] suggest that rising *Staphylococcus aureus* colonization rates reflect personnel technique modifications, especially poor handwashing technique.

The lack of normal skin flora compromised by two potentially open wounds, umbilical cord and circumcision, has led other institutions to give suggestions for newborn skin care. Campbell and Pitkewicz[7] at the Yale–New Haven Hospital found a 3% HCP emulsion for total body bathing followed by a thorough water rinse for a maximum of five baths effective in reducing staphylococcal infections. They further suggest that HCP should be continued in cross-infection control measures.

Light and Sutherland[28] suggest that "the use of antistaphylococcal topical agents including hexachlorophene has a profound effect on the total bacterial flora permitting an increase in colonization with gram-negative bacilli." The authors conclude that hexachlorophene bathing should be done with caution.

Johnson and Malachowski's[26] findings were not conclusive to Light and Sutherland. Their research concluded that the use of a 3% HCP solution for daily baths followed by a complete water rinse decreased the incidence of endemic staphylococcus; there was no increase in gram-negative infections.

The AAP[9] states that "there is no method of cord care which has been proven to limit colonization and disease." Review of several antimicrobial agent studies will assist the nurse in assessing his or her institution's choice.

Hardyment, Wilson, Cockcroft, and Johnson[20] found that hemolytic *Streptococcus* and *Staphylococcus aureus* grew on the umbilical cord. To remedy this potential reservoir several alternatives were considered. To decrease staphylococcal pyoderma, antibiotics were used. However, staphylococcus has been known to acquire resistance to antibiotics. The success of Jellard[25] with triple dye proved significant. There was a decrease in staphylococcal colonization from 83% to 9% in the group of infants whose cords were treated with triple dye.

Katzman[27] found an abrupt halt in hospital and pediatricians' offices' staphylococcal infection rates by the single application of triple dye 2 cm around the umbilical area.

Johnson and Malchowski[26] found that bacitracin applied to the circumcision, umbilicus, and fetal scalp electrode sites, three times a day, reduced the colonization of coagulase-positive staphylococci during an endemic period. Pildes, Ramamurthy, and Vidyasagar[32] reported that bacitracin compared favorably with HCP and triple dye.

The nurse is in a strategic position to alter the nosocomial infections in newborns. There are many factors involved in the transmission of environmental flora, and the staff should be aware of these variables. Monthly reports by the epidemiological team should be reviewed by the staff and suggestions made. A medicinal barrier should never be relied on in exchange for nursing techniques.[7]

CONCLUSION

Leaving the hospital with a healthy, normal infant is clearly not only a beginning, it is also the conclusion of much thoughtful planning and preparation. The family anticipating this child, the obstetrical physician and counselors, the delivery room personnel, and the nursery caregivers have all worked to provide this new being with the best start possible. Each aspect of care has been considered and weighed, and when found lacking in some respect, it is replaced by another.

The nurse working in this area is asked to contribute insight and skill in caring for the transitional infant, yet the nurse must also remain flexible to the frequent changes in medical knowledge that are so apparent in this field. Birth and infant care are currently areas with many opening doors. An understanding of the complexities of the neonatal system is richly increasing. Only a short time has elapsed since newborn infants were believed to be sightless, feelingless, and helpless. We now know them to be alert to their new world, taking in and studying those around them, and possibly much influenced, as we would be, by the treatment they receive. Therefore one can readily champion the move toward more humane treatment of newborn infants and combine this with the wealth of medical advances that will assure optimal health, both mentally and physically to the baby and its family.

Some of the currently accepted procedures for the care of apparently healthy neonates have been presented. Accept it as a resume of the "state of the art" and not as static fact, for this is a time of transition and change.

Protocols

Problem □ Adaptation to extrauterine life requiring rapid alterations in many systems

GOAL: To recognize early any failure to achieve transition to extrauterine life

Rationale: To detect early and manage problems in adaptation to extrauterine life, thereby leading to more favorable outcomes

DIAGNOSTIC

1. Predelivery review of maternal history and laboring patterns and procedures should be done.

   Rationale: To be prepared for any eventualities in outcome that may be foreshadowed in the prenatal history

2. Cord blood samples should be obtained as necessary.

   Rationale: To diagnose blood incompatibilities

3. Obtain Apgar scores at 1 and 5 minutes of age.

   Rationale: To provide a rapid index by which well-being is assessed

4. Observe for signs of respiratory distress, such as grunting, cyanosis, retractions, nasal flaring, diminished or unequal breath sounds, rales, and rhonchi.

   Rationale: To provide early management and better outcome

5. Monitor vital signs (temperature, blood pressure, respiratory rate).

   Rationale: To provide baseline data for adequate cardiopulmonary functioning

6. Do a rapid gestational age assessment (Dubowitz or physical signs).

   Rationale: To facilitate appropriate care

7. Rapid physical assessment should be done.

   Rationale: To rule out life-threatening anomalies that would require immediate attention

THERAPEUTIC

1. Prepare resuscitation equipment. Check that all needed supplies are available and functioning.

   Rationale: To allow for immediate response in an emergency situation

2. Place infant in open warmer that has been preheated.

   Rationale: To prevent acidosis

3. Dry infant rapidly and completely.

   Rationale: To achieve neutral thermal environment and temperature stabilization

4. Suction infant's mouth, nasopharynx, and nares gently with bulb suction. Infant has been already suctioned with the delivery of the head.

   Rationale: To prevent aspiration of mucus and provide a clear airway

5. Apply silver nitrate to the eyes (see p. 244).

   Rationale: To provide ophthalmia neonatorum prophylaxis, which has greatly decreased the incidence of gonococcal eye infection and resulting blindness

6. Give 1 mg water-soluble vitamin K, IM.

   Rationale: To prevent hemorrhagic disease of the newborn

7. Place infant in mother's arms.

   Rationale: To facilitate mother-infant bonding and a more harmonious future partnership between them.

8. Appropriately label the mother and baby with fingerprinting and/or infant footprinting and bracelets before leaving the delivery area.

   Rationale: To ensure appropriate identification as required by law before mother and baby are separated and to prevent confusion and errors

9. Transport baby to nursery area in heated isolette.

   Rationale: To ensure that baby is near facilities for continued care

EDUCATIONAL

1. Provide emotional and physical support to the mother and support person.

   Rationale: To decrease fears and anxiety by introducing the infant to the family and presenting its condition factually

Problem □ Inadequate data base to provide for optimal health maintenance

GOAL: To establish complete maternal-infant history sheet

Rationale: To provide a baseline for newborn care and consequent appropriate interventions

DIAGNOSTIC

1. The nurse will obtain the maternal-infant history sheet from the chart on the newborn's admission to the nursery.
   Rationale: To assess criteria for appropriate newborn care interventions/considerations
2. Perform a Dextrostix on admission; if less than 30 mg% visually, order stat blood sugar. Notify pediatrician immediately for further orders.
   Rationale: To ensure that the brain has glucose at all times so that its status will not be compromised
3. Assessment and observation shall be monitored continuously concerning:
   a. Color
   b. Respiratory rate and quality
   c. Heart rate, rhythm, or murmur
   d. Renal and gastrointestinal functioning (urine output, passage of meconium)
   e. Central nervous system functions (reflexive examination)
   f. Axillary temperature (and patency) on admission
   g. Axillary temperature every hour until 36.5° to 37° C then every 4 hours unless otherwise indicated
   Rationale: To recognize early failure to adapt to extrauterine life and to institute appropriate interventions to promote the physical and psychological integrity of the infant

THERAPEUTIC

1. Inform the physician of the admission of the infant to normal newborn nursery.
   Rationale: To allow early recognition of abnormalities and consequent pediatric considerations
2. The admission nurse will fill out the maternal-infant history sheet as indicated.
   Rationale: To provide a comprehensive tool for continuity of newborn care
3. Provide a neutral thermal environment.
   Rationale: To keep oxygen consumption at a minimum

EDUCATIONAL

1. All personnel responsible for newborn admissions will receive instructions on how to fill out history form through in-service or orientation tracts.
   Rationale: To promote utilization of the tool
2. Nursery personnel must understand and demonstrate knowledge of neonatal pathophysiology to recognize an infant in distress.
   Rationale: To provide comprehensive neonatal care
3. The family will become involved with their infant as soon as possible. Many nurseries have glass windows to allow visualization of the admission process.
   Rationale: To involve the family in care given to the infant
4. The parents will learn bathing, handling, feeding, and health promotion principles while in the hospital through demonstration and return demonstrations. (Some health promotion principles are: how to take a temperature and what is abnormal, a wet diaper before each feeding usually indicates adequate hydration, poor feeding in an infant who previously ate well may be an indication of illness. The pediatrician should be notified for deviations of the infant's norm.)
   Rationale: To foster a healthy newborn period

Problem □ Spread of pathogens from infant-to-infant

GOAL: To minimize the transfer of germs to the newborn
   Rationale: To realize that the newborn may serve as an ideal reservoir for many potentially pathogenic hosts

DIAGNOSTIC

1. Routine (as determined by hospital) cultures will be obtained from randomly selected nursery sites such as sinks, hands, basinetts, and linen closets to determine endemic bacterial counts.
   Rationale: To help determine compliance and effectiveness of the nursery's existing procedures
2. The employee health service will report mucocutaneous and skin (primarily seen are herpes and staphylococcus) infections of the nursery personnel to medical director, nursing director, and a responsible member of the epidemiological team of nursery.
   Rationale: To reduce incidence of neonatal morbidity

THERAPEUTIC

1. On entrance to nursery remove hand and wrist jewelry.
   Rationale: To avoid sources of infection since jewelry crevices may harbor bacteriological agents
2. Secure hair in a restrictive fashion.
   Rationale: To alleviate contamination of infant and work field
3. Wash hands, between fingers, and forearms to elbows for 2 minutes working up a sudsy lather. Clean under fingernails with plastic or an orangewood stick. Dry well with paper towels.
   Rationale: To reduce bacteria on the washed areas, thus reducing potential caregiver-to-infant germ transfer
4. Apply covergown (shortsleeved for nonisolation infants, longsleeved for isolation infants) and tie with back ties to completely conceal clothing.
   Rationale: To avoid contact with bacteriological agents in clothing (Nursery personnel may forgo covergowns if infant is not held, such as taking a temperature with infant in basinett. A covergown must be worn when personnel leave the nursery such as break, lunch, or when holding an infant.)
5. A 15-second handwash between infants is mandatory or a bactericidal hand cream may be utilized. Covergowns must also be changed.
   Rationale: To alleviate the transfer of germs from infant-to-infant

EDUCATIONAL

1. Handwashing technique will be paramount in orientation instructions.
   Rationale: To reinforce the concept that handwashing is fundamental to newborn care
2. Staff will be assisted by staff development of unit to interpret epidemiological results pertaining to the unit.
   Rationale: To aid in compliance to germ control measures

Problem □ Susceptibility of the infant to nosocomial infections

GOAL: To prevent unnecessary manipulation of the integument
Rationale: To protect the skin since the newborn has not yet established skin flora

DIAGNOSTIC

1. The skin and periumbilical regions will be observed for:
   a. Rashes
   b. Pustules
   c. Redness
   d. Localized warm areas
   e. Malodorous or suppurative cord
   Rationale: To diagnose bacterial invasion and system response early to aid in early treatment
2. Report to physician any change in temperature, feeding, activity levels, or irritability.
   Rationale: To prevent infection, which may be represented by alterations in thermoregulatory or metabolic status

THERAPEUTIC

1. Skin care should consist of the following[9]:
   a. Cleansing of the newly born infant should not occur until temperature is stabilized (usually 4 to 6 hours).
   b. Scalp and facial blood may be removed with cotton sponges soaked in sterile water. Meconium should be cleansed from the perianal region with cotton sponges soaked in sterile water.
   c. The rest of the body should remain untouched unless grossly soiled. No evidence documents that vernix caseosa is harmful.
   d. The buttocks and perianal region may be cleansed with sterile water during hospitalization. If needed, a mild soap followed by water rinse may be used.
   Rationale: To avoid embarrassment to the integument by harmful agents (Any break in the skin predisposes to infection.)
2. The cord and surrounding 2 cm may be treated with one application of triple dye. Other treatment may be antimicrobial agents (Neosporin, bacitracin), water, or alcohol for drying. Regardless of method, expose the cord to air and do not allow diaper to cover the healing umbilicus.
   Rationale: To allow the cord to dry and fall off, thereby eliminating one source of infection

EDUCATIONAL

1. The parents should be shown bath and cord care technique then requested to return the demonstration.

   Rationale: To learn by observation and doing

2. Cord clamps should be removed 24 hours after delivery.

   Rationale: To avoid infection from the clamp

3. The parents should be introduced to their infant through the use of a Brazelton examination and encouraged to provide developmental stimulation appropriate to their own infant's needs and capacities.

   Rationale: To foster optimum development through parent-infant interaction

REFERENCES

1. American Academy of Pediatrics Committee on Drugs: Effect of medication during labor and delivery on infant outcome, Pediatrics **62:**402, 1978.
2. Avery, G., editor: Neonatology: pathophysiology and management of the newborn, Philadelphia, 1975, J. B. Lippincott Co.
3. Behrman, R. E.: Neonatal-perinatal medicine, diseases of the fetus and infant, St. Louis, 1977, The C. V. Mosby Co.
4. Binzley, V.: State: overlooked factor in newborn nursing, Am. J. Nurs. **77:**102, 1977.
5. Boyce, V. (executive director of the National Society for the Prevention of Blindness): Letter to Marjorie Kochanczyk, R. N., dated December 27, 1977 quoting Dr. Phillips Thygeson. p. 2.
6. Cahill, B.: The neonatal nurse specialist—new techniques for the asymptomatic newborn, J. Obstet. Gynecol., p. 34, 1974.
7. Campbell, A. G., and Pitkewicz, J. S.: The incidence of infections in nurseries since the discontinuation of hexachlorophene bathing, Pediatrics **51:**360, 1973.
8. Committee on fetus and newborn, American Academy of Pediatrics: Hexachlorophene and skin care of newborn infants, Pediatrics **49:**625, 1972.
9. Committee on fetus and newborn: Skin care of newborns, Pediatrics **54:**682, 1974.
10. Dahm, L. S., and James, L.: Newborn temperature and calculated heat loss in the delivery, Pediatrics **49:**509, 1972.
11. Donahoe, P. K., and Hendren, W. H.: Evaluation of the newborn with ambiguous genitalia, Pediatr. Clin. North Am. **23:**361, 1976.
12. Dubowitz, L. M. S., et al.: Clinical assessment of gestational age in the newborn infant, J. Pediatr. **77:**1, 1978.
13. Evans, H., and Glass, L.: Perinatal medicine, New York, 1976, Harper & Row, Publishers.
14. Felderman, D. D.: Disorders of sexual development, N. Engl. J. Med. **277:**351, 1967.
15. Fitzpatrik, E., Reeder, S. R., and Mastroianni, L.: Maternity nursing, ed. 12, Philadelphia, 1971, J. B. Lippincott, Co.
16. Foote, F. M., et al.: Control of ophthalmia neonatorum: a statement by the National Society for the Prevention of Blindness Committee on Ophthalmia Neonatorum, The Sightsaving Review **43:**11, 1973.
17. Gaines, T. B., and Kimbrough, R. D.: Paper read at the 10th annual meeting of the Society of Toxicology, Washington, D.C., March 7-11, 1971.
18. Gluck, L.: Special problems of the newborn, Hosp. Pract. **13:**75, 1978.
19. Grausz, J. P.: The effect of environmental temperature changes on the metabolism rate of newborn babies, Acta Paediatr. Scand. **57:**98, 1968.
20. Hardyment, A. F., Wilson, R. A., Cockcroft, W., and Johnson, B.: Observations on the bacteriology and epidemiology of nursery infections, Pediatrics **25**(Suppl.):921, 1960.
21. Hargiss, C., and Larson, E.: The epidemiology of *Staphylococcus aureus* in a newborn nursery from 1970 through 1976, Pediatrics **61:**348, 1978.
22. Harper, R. G., and Yoon, L.: Handbook of neonatology, Chicago, 1974, Year Book Medical Publishers, Inc.
23. Hexachlorophene and newborns, FDA Drug Bulletin, December, 1971.
24. Hexachlorophene decisions at the FDA, Pediatrics **51:**430, 1973.
25. Jellard, J.: Umbilical cord as reservoir of infections in a maternity hospital, Br. Med. J. **1:**925, 1957.
26. Johnson, J. D., and Malchowski, N. C.: A sequential study of various modes of skin and umbilical care and the incidence of staphylococcal colonization and infection in the neonate, Pediatrics **58:**354, 1976.
27. Katzman, G.: Letter, J. Pediatr. **86:**313, 1975.
28. Light, I. J., and Sutherland, J. M.: What is the evidence that hexachlorophene is not effective? Pediatrics **51**(Suppl.):345, 1973.
29. Lockhart, J.: How toxic is hexachlorophene? Pediatrics **50:**229, 1972.
30. Nelson, W. W., Vaughan V. C., III, and McKay, R. J.: Textbook of pediatrics, ed. 10, Philadelphia, 1975, W. B. Saunders Co.
31. Phillips, C.: Neonatal heat loss in heated cribs versus mothers' arms, J. Obstet. Gynecol. Nurs. **3:**11, 1974.
32. Pildes, R. S., Ramamurthy, R. S., and Vidyasagar, D.: Effects of triple dye on staphylococcal colonization in the newborn infant, J. Pediatr. **82:**987, 1973.
33. Shirkey, H. C., editor: Pediatric therapy, ed. 6, St. Louis, 1980, The C. V. Mosby Co., pp. 355-374.
34. Silver, H. K., Kempe, C. H., and Bruyn, H. B.: Handbook of pediatrics, ed. 12, Los Altos, Calif., 1977, Lange Medical Publications, pp. 120-138.
35. Silverman, W. A., Sinclair, J. C., and Agate, F. J., Jr.: The oxygen cost of minor changes in heat balance of small newborn infants, Acta Paediatr. Scand. **55:**294, 1966.
36. Somers, A. R., et al.: Lifetime health monitoring: preventative care from birth to age one year, Patient Care **4:**168, 1979.
37. Standards and recommendations for hospital care of newborn infants, Evanston, Ill., 1977, American Academy of Pediatrics Committee on Fetus and Newborn.
38. Yasunaga, S., and Kean, E.: Effect of three ophthalmic solutions on chemical conjunctivitis in the neonate, J. Dis. Child. **131:**159, 1977.

BIBLIOGRAPHY

Abramson, H., editor: Resuscitation of the newborn infant, ed. 3, St. Louis, 1973, The C. V. Mosby Co.

Affonso, D.: The newborn's potential for interaction, J. Obstet. Gynecol. Nurs. **5:**9, 1976.

Barnett, C. R., and Leiderman, P. H.: Neonatal separation: the maternal side of deprivation, Pediatrics **45:**197, 1970.

Behrman, R. E., editor: The newborn, Pediatr. Clin. North Am. **17:**759, 1970.

Bishop, B.: A guide to assessing parenting capabilities, Am. J. Nurs. **76:**1784, 1976.

Bowlby, J.: The nature of the child's tie to his mother, Internat. J. Psychoanal. **39:**350, 1958.

Bowlby, J.: Attachment and loss, vol. 1, New York, 1969, Basic Books, Inc., Publishers.

Brazelton, T. B.: The early mother-infant adjustment, Pediatrics **32:**93, 1963.

Brazie, J., and Lubchenco, L.: The newborn infant. In Kempe, C. H., Silver, H. K., and O'Brien, D., editors: Current pediatric diagnosis and treatment, Los Altos, Calif., 1976, Lange Medical Publications.

Bruck, K.: Temperature regulation in the newborn infant, Biol. Neonatol. **3:**65, 1961.

Bruck, K., Parmallee, A. H., Jr., and Bruck, M.: Newborn temperature range and range of thermal comfort in premature infants, Biol. Neonatol. **4:**32, 1962.

Clark, A., and Affonso, D.: Infant behavior and maternal attachment; two sides of the coin, Am. J. Matern. Child Nurs. **1:**93, 1976.

Committee on infections within hospitals: Infection control in the nursery, ed. 3, Chicago, 1974, American Hospital Association, pp. 135-141.

Day, R.: Respiratory metabolism in infancy and childhood. XXVII: regulation of body temperature of premature infants, Am. J. Dis. Child. **65:**376, 1943.

Erickson, M.: Trends in assessing the newborn and his parents, Am. J. Matern. Child Nurs. **3:**99, 1978.

Follow-up on nursery streptococcal disease and its relationship to the use of hexachlorophene, Morbid. Mortal. Week. Rep. **21:**253, 1972.

Gezon, H. M.: Control of staphylococcal infection and disease in the newborn through use of hexachlorophene bathing, Pediatrics **51:**331, 1973.

Gluck, L.: A perspective on hexachlorophene, Pediatrics **51:**400, 1973.

Gollober, M.: A comment on the need for father-infant postpartal interaction, J. Obstet. Gynecol. Nurs. **5:**17, 1976.

Gray, J. D.: Prediction and prevention of child abuse, Pediatr. Res. **10:**303, 1976.

Greenfield, S.: Protocols as analogs to standing orders. In Bullough, B., editor: The law and the expanding nursing role, New York, 1975, Appleton-Century-Crofts, pp. 63-80.

Gresham, E. L.: Birth trauma, Pediatr. Clin. North Am. **22:**317, 1975.

Gutrecht, N. M., et al.: Cardiopulmonary emergencies of the newborn, Heart Lung **2:**878, 1973.

Hansfield, H. H., et al.: Neonatal gonococcal infection, J.A.M.A. **225:**697, 1973.

Hey, E. N., and Katz, G.: The range of thermal insulation in the tissues of the newborn baby, J. Physiol. **207:**667, 1971.

Investigation of hospitals' use of hexachlorophene and nursery streptococcal infections, Morbid. Mortal. Week. Rep. **21:**37, 1972.

Jacobs, A.: The incidence of birthmarks in the neonate, Obstet. Gynecol. Surv. **32:**94, 1977.

Klaus, M. H., and Kennell, J. H.: Mothers separated from their newborn infants, Pediatr. Clin. North Am. **17:**1015, 1970.

Klaus, M. H., and Kennell, J. H.: Maternal attachment, N. Engl. J. Med. **286:**460, 1972.

Klaus, M. H., and Kennell, J. H.: Maternal-infant bonding, St. Louis, 1976, The C. V. Mosby Co.

Klaus, M. H., Plumb, N., and Zueheke, S.: Mothers' behavior at first contact with baby, Pediatrics **46:**187, 1970.

Kotoyan, M.: Aspects of perinatal endocrinology, Pediatr. Clin. North Am. **24:**529, 1977.

Lubchenco, L. O.: Assessment of gestational age and development at birth, Pediatr. Clin. North Am. **17:**125, 1970.

MacIntosh, R., et al.: The incidence of congenital malformations: a survey of 5,964 pregnancies, Pediatrics **14:**505, 1954.

McCracken, G. H., Jr.: Group B streptococci: the new challenge in neonatal infections, J. Pediatr. **82:**703, 1973.

Moore, A. U.: Effects of modified care in the sheep and goat. In Newton, G., and Devine, S., editor: Early experience and behavior, Springfield, Ill., 1968, Charles C Thomas, Publishers, pp. 481-529.

Newton, N., and Newton, M.: Mothers' reactions to their newborn babies, J.A.M.A. **18:**206, 1976.

Nicolopoulos, D., et al.: Estimation of gestational age in the neonate, Am. J. Dis. Child. **130:**477, 1976.

Nurses Association of the American College of Obstetricians and Gynecologists: Obstetric, gynecologic and neonatal nursing functions and standards, Chicago, 1977, NACOG.

Nurses Association of the American College of Obstetricians and Gynecologists: Physical assessment of the neonate, NACOG Technical Bulletin, No. 2, 1978.

Oliver, T. K., Jr.: Temperature regulation and heat production in the newborn, Pediatr. Clin. North Am. **12:**765, 1965.

Penfold, K. M.: Supporting maternal love, Am. J. Nurs. **74:**464, 1974.

Roberts, F.: Perinatal nursing: care of newborns and their families, St. Louis, 1977, McGraw-Hill Book Co.

Robson, K. S.: The role of eye-to-eye contact in maternal-infant attachment, J. Child Psychiat. **8:**13, 1967.

Schreiner, R., editor: Care of the newborn, Department of Pediatrics, Indianapolis, 1978, Indiana University School of Medicine and Riley Hospital for Children.

Sinclair, J. C., Driscoll, J. M., Heird, W. C., and Winters, R. W.: Supportive management of the sick neonate, Pediatr. Clin. North Am. **17:**863, 1970.

Sloan, D.: Childbirth without separation, The Female Patient **2:**10, 1977.

Stevenson, R. E.: The fetus and newly born infant: influences of the prenatal environment, ed. 2, St. Louis, 1977, The C. V. Mosby Co.

Stortz, L. J.: Unprescribed drug products and pregnancy, J. Obstet. Gynecol. Nurs. **6:**9, 1977.

Chapter 15

Maintaining a neutral thermal environment

Rosanne Harrigan Perez

OVERVIEW

Thermoregulation is a critical determinant of neonatal survival. It is a relatively simple topic, yet many authors believe that assisting the newborn to maintain body temperature is the most significant aspect of neonatal nursing care.

Temperature control has long been associated with intact neonatal survival. In 1907 Pierre Budin[5] reported that there was a decrease in the mortality rate, from 98% to 23%, of infants weighing less than 2000 gm when an attempt was made to keep the body temperature within normal range. Budin's observations indicated that only 10% of infants survived when the temperature was maintained between 32.5° and 33.5° C (90.5° and 92.3° F). When the temperature was maintained in a normal range of 36° to 37° C (98.6° F), 77% of the infants survived.

It is interesting to note that in spite of Budin's work relatively little in-depth investigation in relation to this topic took place prior to 1958. Blackfan and Yaglo[4] studied clothed infants who were placed in an humid environment with an air temperature of 25° C (77° F) and noted that these infants appeared to do better and had a decreased mortality rate in comparison to cooler unclothed infants.

During the 1940's environmental care included high humidity; infants were unclothed, and the temperature of incubators remained unchanged. It was not until 1958 when Silverman, Fertig, and Berger[17] demonstrated that there was a decrease in mortality when additional warmth was provided that neonatal care providers critically began to investigate this issue. Keeping an infant warm had been considered essential since the time of Budin but "how warm" has only recently become an important question.

Silverman's data indicated that infant survival in warmed incubators, 31.7° C (89° F), increased as compared with survival in slightly cooler environments, 29.5° C (85° F). Infant mortality under 1000 gm (2 lb 2 oz) was reduced from 86% to 50% by providing a warmer environment. In 1959 Hillferst described the neutral thermal zone and established the fact that the newborn was a homeotherm.[11] Day, Caliguri, Kamensky, and Ehrlich[8] provided additional data to support the need for temperature management to increase survival rates of low birth weight infants.

The relationship between inadequate temperature regulation and neonatal morbidity has also been documented. In 1970 Davies and Davies[7] reported in a follow-up study that brain growth was impaired in a group of premature infants that received inadequate warmth and feeding. They also noted that spastic diplegia occurred with an increased frequency in this group of infants. Glass, Silverman, and Sinclair[10] demonstrated that there was a degree of reversible growth retardation in infants maintained at slightly cooler skin temperatures, 35° C as compared to 36° C. Thus, when one considers both the relationship between neonatal mortality and neonatal morbidity, there is little question of the importance of careful maintenance of the temperature of the newborn to neonatal survival. This is particularly true in the stressed newborn.

PHYSIOLOGICAL PROCESSES AND TEMPERATURE REGULATION IN THE NEWBORN

Humans, both neonates and adults, are homeothermic. They attempt to maintain their body temperatures within a relatively narrow range. The adult can accomplish this task effectively in a wide range of environmental temperatures, the neonate cannot. The range of environmental temperatures at which the neonate can achieve homeothermy is very narrow. The newborn's impaired ability to maintain body temperature is related to several factors, including relatively large surface area in comparison to body mass, often limited metabolic capabilities for heat production, and inadequate thermal insulation.

Mechanisms of heat production

The newborn's thermoregulatory response is limited but it is appropriate. Metabolic processes to provide heat production are initiated when the environment "cools," thus indicating that skin or central receptors are present that provide feedback that is interpreted within the central nervous system. This provides for appropriate responses elicited through neuroendocrine channels.

Newborns produce heat as a result of metabolic activity. Heat is produced in an attempt to maintain body temperature. There is an attempt to maintain temperature within a relatively narrow range. To maintain a constant body temperature there must be a balance between heat loss from body surfaces and heat production. In the neonate the maintenance of a stable body temperature, where the amount of heat lost is about equal to that being produced, is possible only within a narrow range of environmental temperature fluctuation.

Sensory systems for regulating and responding to temperature fluctuations

The primary means by which the newborn is able to maintain a stable body temperature were described by Scopes in 1975.[16] Scopes proposed that both an affector and effector arc were in the sensory system.

The affector arc is the central control system where data are collated and interpreted. The control is located in the central nervous system in the hypothalamus. This system receives data from skin and central receptors. The function of the affector arc can be affected by drugs, intracranial hemorrhage, cerebral abnormalities, asphyxia, trauma, cerebral edema, and infection.

The effector arc is the responding component of the sensory temperature control system. The primary modalities by which a newborn is able to re-

spond include vasomotor control, thermal insulation, alterations in heat production, and sweating.

Vasomotor control. The ability of the newborn to control skin perfusion by vasoconstriction or vasodilatation is well documented. This mechanism is developed even in the small preterm infant. However, this capacity may be limited in the small infant under a radiant warmer.

Thermal insulation. Thermal insulation varies directly with the white fat content of the body. Fetal fat comprises about 19% of the body weight at 24 weeks' gestation and 11% to 17% at term. Substantial amounts of fat do not accumulate until after 32 weeks' gestation. Thus the preterm infant lacks adequate body insulation to prevent rapid heat loss or to permit the body mass to act as a heat reservoir.

Heat production—shivering. Shivering is an important mechanism of heat production in the adult, but its function is limited in the neonate. Shivering does occur in the newborn in the presence of extreme cold stress, but it does not contribute substantially to heat production. Muscular activity and body movement do contribute to chemical thermogenesis.

Heat production—nonshivering. The ability to increase heat production by nonshivering mechanisms is found in cold-adapted and hibernating animals and the newborn. This mechanism appears to be the most important and consistent mechanism of heat production in both the full-term and perterm neonate. In 1966 Hull[12] documented that brown fat was the site of heat production in the human newborn mammal. The term "brown fat" evolved because of the histological features of this tissue. In comparison to white fat, brown fat contains numerous small fat vacuoles and many mitochondria. This dense mitochondrial population that contains iron-cytochrome enzymes assumes a brownish color when it is depleted of highly unsaturated fats.

Brown fat is located between the scapulae, behind the sternum, around the neck, head, heart, great vessels, kidneys, and adrenal glands, and in the axilla. It provides local heat as well as central heat, warming blood as it enters and leaves the heart. In 1975 Peckham[15] suggested that the metabolism of fatty acids in brown fat was enhanced by norepinephrine. Other researchers have proposed that adrenalin stimulates the sodium-ATP pump. This mechanism also affects fatty acid oxidation.

In the presence of cold stress, skin sensing recep-

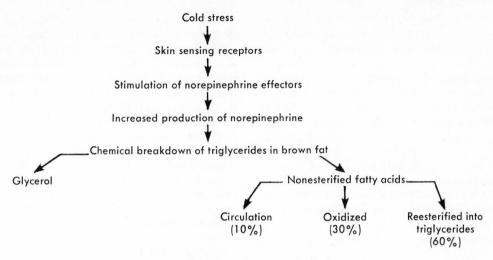

Fig. 15-1. Thermogenic process in newborn.

tors stimulate the production of norepinephrine. This causes the chemical breakdown of triglycerides in brown fat. Glycerol and nonesterified fatty acids are the by-products of this reaction. Nonesterified fatty acids are released into the circulation and oxidized or recertified into triglycerides. Those that are oxidized provide the major heat source for the newborn. This process is described in Fig. 15-1.

The overheating of an infant will result in the infant attempting to dissipate heat. Skin vessels dilate and limited sweating occurs (infants born 8 weeks prematurely have no ability to sweat according to Hey and Katz[11]); at 37 weeks' gestation sweating is still limited. In addition, in a heat-gaining environment, metabolic rate is increased, oxygen consumption is increased, the work of breathing is increased, and calorie consumption is increased.

Difficulties in heat production

Thus either overheating or underheating can produce metabolic demands that a stressed newborn is unable to accommodate because of the problems mentioned earlier in this chapter. The newborn has a relatively large surface area for weight, poor thermal insulation because of the decreased amount of subcutaneous fat, reduced amounts of brown fat, and decreased ability to produce heat. In addition, the stressed newborn probably has a calorie intake that is inadequate to deal with the metabolic de-

mands of heat production. The presence of respiratory problems, which are a frequent occurrence in the premature infant, also decreases the amount of oxygen available for thermal needs.

MECHANISMS OF HEAT LOSS IN THE NEWBORN

There are four mechanisms of heat loss that have direct application to the newborn: conduction, convection, evaporation, and radiation.

Conduction involves the loss of heat during direct contact of the infant's skin with cooler surfaces in the environment. The thermal conductivity of the surface as well as the temperature of the surface affects the amount of heat transferred.

Convection involves the flow of heat from the body surface to cooler surroundings. This mechanism of heat loss is dependent on the air temperature and movement. It is frequently not considered for its significance especially in the delivery room or cesarean section suite.

Evaporation occurs when surface moisture that is warmed by the infant's body heat comes in contact with dry air. During this process heat is carried away as the surface moisture is converted to vapor. The amount of heat loss is dependent on the environmental humidity and air speed. Evaporative heat loss is minimal in the presence of high humidity and maximal in dry environments.

Radiation involves the loss of heat to a colder environmental surface that is not in direct contact with the baby. Radiant heat loss is affected by the amount of surface exposed as well as the surface temperature of the objects. Radiant heat loss is proposed to be a major mechanism of heat transfer in the newborn. It can occur independent of the ambient air temperature in the isolette. The inside surface of an isolette wall acts as the radiant receiving surface. This wall is affected not only by the ambient air temperature in the isolette but also by room temperature. It is possible for the temperature inside an isolette wall to be markedly different from the temperature on an isolette thermometer, and neonates can radiate heat to the walls of an isolette even though the air temperature inside the isolette is sufficiently warm.

MAINTAINING A NEUTRAL THERMAL ENVIRONMENT

The neutral thermal environment is the range of thermal environment in which an infant with a normal body temperature has minimal oxygen and calorie consumption and expands the least metabolic effort. Oxygen consumption is a measure of the number of calories the infant is burning.

When a newborn becomes cold, its metabolic rate is increased to increase heat production. This means both glucose and oxygen are used more rapidly. The rate of oxygen consumption soon exceeds the rate at which it is supplied to the cells. If the supply of oxygen is inadequate, less heat is produced from each mole of glucose that is metabolized. This increases the amount of glucose that is required to produce heat and hypoglycemia may result. In addition, when the metabolism of glucose takes place in an anaerobic environment, lactic acid is produced, oxygen is not present, and metabolic acidosis can result.

If the air temperature is below the neutral thermal range, the metabolic response is increased to replace lost heat; if the air temperature is above the neutral thermal range, an increase in body temperature occurs and therefore an increase in metabolic rate. This continues until a critical point is reached at which the metabolic rate falls rapidly and the infant dies. The neutral thermal range is in contrast to the thermal range of minimal stress.

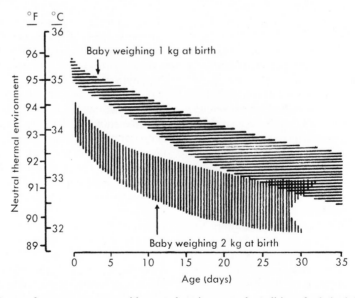

Fig. 15-2. Range of temperature to provide neutral environmental conditions for baby lying on warm mattress in draft-free surroundings of moderate humidity when mean radiant temperature is same as air temperature (From Hey, E. M., and Katz, G.: Arch. Dis. Child. **45:**328, 1970.)

Scopes[16] documented in 1975 that "there is no single environmental temperature that is appropriate for all sizes and conditions of babies." In 1970 Hey and Katz[11] described the ranges of temperature required to provide a neutral thermal environment (Fig. 15-2). The shaded area in Fig. 15-2 illustrates the average neutral temperature range for a healthy baby weighing 1 or 2 kg at birth. The "optimum" temperature is most probably the lower limit of the neutral range of this diagram. To derive the appropriate neutral air temperature for a single-walled incubator, approximately 1° C should be added to these operative temperatures. When the room temperature is less than 27° C (80° F), and 1° C should be added to these operative temperatures. Additional heat may be necessary if the room temperature deviates by more than this amount.

There are also a number of other factors that affect the appropriate selection of air temperature for a given baby. These include motor activity (seizures, and so forth), clothing, single-walled incubators, and metabolic compromise. Infants who exhibit increased motor activity or who are clothed require somewhat cooler temperatures to be in their neutral thermal zone. Infants who are in single-walled incubators or who are metabolically compromised, require higher temperatures to maintain their neutral thermal zone.

FINDING THE NEUTRAL THERMAL ENVIRONMENT

It is important for the nurse to understand the means by which an infant's temperature is taken and maintained. The usual sites for temperature assessment are the rectum, axilla, and abdominal skin.

The rectal assessment of temperature is a reasonable measurement of core temperature. However, core temperature is often normal in the presence of heat or cold stress and is therefore an inadequate measure of thermal neutrality. At the time the rectal temperature becomes abnormal, compensatory mechanisms have already failed. In addition, there is no relationship between rectal temperature and oxygen consumption.

The abdominal skin temperature is indicative of a neutral thermal environment and is usually maintained between 36.0° and 36.5° C (96.8° to 97.7° F) according to Silverman, Sinclair, and Agate.[18] A relationship exists between oxygen consumption and skin temperature. Thus, skin temperature is indicative of the neutral thermal zone. The temperature of the abdominal skin is usually measured between the xyphoid process and the umbilicus. In an environment that is too warm skin vessels dilate to dissipate heat and the skin temperature rises, and in an environment that is too cold skin blood flow decreases, vessels constrict, and the skin temperature drops.

Axillary temperatures are usually maintained between 36.0° C and 36.5° C (96.8° F and 97.7° F) according to Silverman.[17] Nursing personnel frequently measure the newborn's temperature using axillary assessment because it is a safe and easy means. Yet, there are no data available that describe the relationship between axillary temperature and rectal or core temperature. It is thought that axillary temperatures are somewhat lower than rectal temperatures. It is actually possible that axillary temperatures may be somewhat elevated during periods of cold stress because of the presence of brown fat. If this situation is suspected by the nurse, assessment of the abdominal skin temperature must be done to confirm the possibility of hypothermia. Axillary temperature assessment is thought to be a useful diagnostic tool.

CLINICAL ASPECTS AND MANAGEMENT

Servo-controlled isolettes are frequently used in an attempt to maintain a neutral thermal environment. There are advantages and disadvantages to this procedure. One must monitor both the temperature of the infant and the isolette to evaluate the infant's condition. One should record these data on a flow sheet and assess this information for trends. A single temperature measurement is not an adequate assessment of thermal protection. Nurses must also be alert to isolette and servo malfunctions because they frequently occur. Staff development programs in units that utilize servo control should include equipment problem-solving skills and assist nurses to learn to correlate infant and isolette temperatures.

If servo control is used in an environment that is low in humidity, evaporative heat loss occurs. This may result in a paradoxical body temperature decrease as the isolette temperature increases. In 1975 Belgaumakar and Scott[1,2] recommend that high humidity (77.0%) be maintained in the isolette especially when the infant is small or sick.

It has also been postulated that the frequency and severity of apnea is increased in low humidity environments. In 1975 Belgaumakar and Scott[1,2] proposed that this was due to the fluctuating humidity and the resulting effect on core temperature.

THERMAL FACTORS THAT AFFECT INSENSIBLE WATER LOSS

Insensible water loss occurring during heat loss is a factor that must be taken into consideration in managing fluid, calorie, and electrolyte imbalance in the neonate. When heat loss occurs, there is a considerable increase of insensible water loss from the respiratory tract and the skin. The ambient temperature, relative humidity, basal metabolic rate, body temperature, and activity level as well as phototherapy can also affect insensible water loss. In the small premature infant where the surface area to body weight ratio is increased, the subcutaneous fat is diminished, the epidermis is thin, and the skin-water content and permeability are increased, there is also an increased rate of insensible water loss.

Nursing measures can be implemented to reduce heat loss and insensible water loss. Incubators should be kept away from cold walls, windows, and other objects. Fanaroff, Wald, Gruber, and Klaus[9] proposed that a Plexiglass heat shield be placed over the small premature infant to assist in maintaining a neutral thermal environment and reduce water loss occurring as the result of the shield's alteration in air movement patterns leading to a decrease in diffusion of water vapor from the skin. Radiant heat loss is also reported to be diminished. Besch and associates[3] in 1971 suggested that a baby bag be used to reduce evaporative and convective heat loss. These bags are especially useful when heat is provided via radiant sources. The bags are transparent and provide for an opportunity to visualize the infant. Baum and Scopes suggested the use of a silver swaddler in 1968.[16] This method of heat loss reduction involves the use of a swaddler or the placement of a layer of nonabrasive foil on the inside of the walls of the incubator. Protection is provided for the infant against evaporative, convective, and radiant heat loss. The problem involved with the use of foil lining is that the material is opaque and observation of the infant is limited.

Marks, Friedman, and Maisels[13] in 1977 documented the fact that the use of a thermal blanket reduced insensible water loss 70%. A caloric savings of 27 kcal/kg/day was also seen in these infants. The thermal blanket is transparent and pro-

vides minimal interference with the provision of nursing care. The use of thermal blanket required a 0.3° C decrease in the mean ambient temperature to maintain the desired abdominal skin temperature by preventing heat loss to the environment. However, Darnall and Ariagno[6] noted in 1979 that O_2 consumption was not decreased.

In 1979 the Narco Air Shields isolette became available. This is a double-walled isolette that reduces radiant heat loss. It provides for excellent infant visibility and minimizes evaporative heat loss known to occur in single-walled incubators.[14] Evaporative heat loss in large preterm infants can be reduced by 23% in this type of environment, while heat loss in small premature infants can be reduced as much as 60%.

A moment should be taken here to discuss the radiant warmer versus the convection-type isolette. Insensible water loss is known to be significantly greater for infants under radiant warmers compared to those in isolettes. Williams and William documented in 1974 that a need existed to increase maintenance fluid intake for infants under radiant warmers.[16] This problem is compounded in the very small premature infant by the fact that it may be difficult to meet the increased fluid needs resulting from the use of a radiant warmer. Thus the radiant warmer is far from the environment of choice for the small premature infant.

Since small premature infants (<1250 gm) may require frequent assessment of weight, electronic balance scales that can be utilized within the isolette are recommended. This will prevent removing the infant from the controlled environment, promote maintenance of a neutral thermal range, minimize the need for the infant to increase its metabolic rate as well as oxygen consumption rate, and limit insensible water loss.

In summary, although considerable advances have occurred in the body of knowledge related to neonatal thermoregulation, there is still much to be learned. An exact prescription for the newborn's environment is not available at this time, but there are numerous interventions available to the nurse who is willing to painstakingly monitor both the infant's temperature and the temperature of the environment. Nursing measures are geared toward environmental manipulation and prevention of heat loss owing to conduction, convection, evaporation, and radiation.

Protocol

Problem □ Cold stress

GOALS

1. To prevent cold stress
2. To recognize cold stress early
3. To maintain a neutral thermal environment

Rationale: To eliminate cold stress, thereby controlling O_2 consumption and the rate of insensible water loss

DIAGNOSTIC

1. Monitor temperature, utilizing either axillary or abdominal skin probe.

   Rationale: To indicate the maintenance of a thermal neutral environment

2. Monitor isolette temperature, utilizing probe and servo control. Record data on flow sheet and be alert for trends.

   Rationale: To obtain an adequate assessment of thermal protection

3. Assess function of servo control unit.

   Rationale: To be alert for servo malfunctions, which frequently occur

Assessment of thermo control

A. Incubators
   1. Manual thermostat control
      a. The temperature in an incubator may be controlled by a thermostat. This keeps the environment at a set temperature. The nurse must adjust the thermostat according to the infant's temperature. If the axillary temperature is below 36° C, the thermostat must be turned up.
      b. Assessment: Compare the thermometer reading with the neonate's axillary temperature. Check to see that the selector switch is maintained on manual.
   2. Servo control
      a. An alternative method of temperature regulation is that of servo control. A probe (temperature sensor) is placed on the infant's skin to the left of the umbilicus. The servo control system adjusts the environmental temperature to keep the skin temperature constant. The servo control system will increase the environmental temperature anytime the skin temperature drops below a designated level. This is a desirable method of temperature regulation, but nurses must be alert for servo malfunctions. The unit is usually set to maintain the skin temperature between 36° C and 36.5° C.

      The infant is usually placed in a supine position with the probe taped securely to the skin at the left of the umbilicus. Care should be taken not to allow the infant to be on the probe as an increased temperature may be sensed and the unit will reduce the environmental temperature while the infant is indeed cold. If the probe comes off the infant, the unit will sense a lower temperature and increase the environmental temperature, possibly overheating the infant.
      b. Assessment
         (1) Check to see that the mode selector switch is on servo.
         (2) Calibrate servo meter.
         (3) Set control temperature (meter).
         (4) Check
            (a) Skin temperature reading (meter)
            (b) Hood thermometer reading (incubator)
            (c) Axillary temperature
            (d) Probe placement
         (5) Analyze O_2 concentration
         (6) Check
            (a) That power lamp is on and plugged in
            (b) Humidity control level—set to 75%
            (c) Water level in humidity resevoir and fill
            (d) To see that circulation vents are not obstructed

B. Radiant warmers
   1. Heat energy is radiant energy. It travels in waves. The radiant warmer provides a heat source from above the patient and heat radiates down onto the infant. A radiant warmer *must* be on servo control at all times. Radiant warmers are equipped with audible temperature alarms. These alarms should always be turned on. Visual and audio alarms are triggered when the infant's temperature is more than 1° F above or below the control temperature.

      The skin probe must be covered with sponge or gauze following placement to prevent it from sensing heat from the warmer.

Again, if the infant lies on the probe, the heat output will be decreased and hypothermia will occur, and if the probe comes off, the heat output will increase and hyperthermia will occur.

Older radiant warmers have the option of a rectal servo control probe. These should never be used. Rectal temperature is reflective of core temperature, and the core temperature is not altered until the infant has long experienced cold stress. In addition, complications such as infection, vagal stimulation, and rectal perforation have been documented.

Infants should never be completely covered when under a radiant warmer (for example, as during spinal taps or chest tube insertions). A covered infant will not receive heat from a radiant warmer.

Infants maintained under radiant warmers require frequent assessment of fluid volume, specific gravity, and area output/kg/hr because of increased evaporative losses.

2. Assessment
   a. Check to see that power is on.
   b. Check audible high/low temperature alarm on servo control unit.
   c. Check probe selector or meter calibration.
   d. Check set temperature.
   e. Check skin temperature read out.
   f. Check neonate's axillary temperature.
   g. Check probe placement.
   h. Reset servo control if necessary.

THERAPEUTIC
1. Dry infant in delivery room and place in preheated isolette or radiant warmer.
   Rationale: To prevent cold stress
2. Utilize isolettes rather than radiant warmers for small premature infants.
   Rationale: To decrease insensible water loss and fluid requirements, which are increased when radiant warmers are used
3. Carry out all procedures quickly, closing isolette port holes immediately after removing hands.
   Rationale: To avoid compromising the neutral thermal environment
4. If a prolonged procedure is required, place infant under preheated radiant warmer and return to isolette as soon as possible.

Rationale: To avoid compromising the neutral thermal environment
5. Monitor elastic patency in port hole shields, change at least every week.
   Rationale: To avoid an inadequate seal, which will increase air flow and compromise the neutral thermal environment
6. Avoid infant contact with cold wet surfaces, for example, work tables, x-ray plates, and so forth.
   Rationale: To prevent conductive heat loss
7. Use warm, humidified oxygen when giving directly to infant.
   Rationale: To prevent evaporative heat loss
8. Provide adequate humidity in incubator (approximately 75%).
   Rationale: To prevent insensible water loss, thus promoting thermal integrity
9. Keep incubator away from cold walls, air currents, windows, and other objects.
   Rationale: To prevent conduction and convective heat loss
10. Do not warm infant too rapidly if cold stress occurs.
    Rationale: To avoid rapid warming, which may cause apnea
11. With small infants, use Plexiglass shield, foil, or bubble paper to assist with thermo regulation.
    Rationale: To minimize heat loss
12. Maintain infant's temperature in neutral thermal range (36° to 36.5° C [97° to 97.7° F]; skin—36.5° to 37° C [97.7° to 98.5° F]).
    Rationale: To prevent cold stress (see Table 15-1)

Table 15-1. The optimal neutral thermal environment for naked infants*

Age (days)	Birth weight 1 kg	Birth weight 2 kg
1	35°-35.5° C	34°-34.6° C
5	34.5°-35° C	33°-33.8° C
10	34°-34.6° C	32.5°-33.5° C
15	33.5°-34.4° C	32.2°-33.3° C
20	33.2°-34.2° C	32.1°-33.2° C

*Modified from Hey, E. M., and Katz, G.: Arch. Dis. Child. **45:** 328, 1970.

EDUCATIONAL

1. Provide staff development programs related to:
   a. Calibration of servo control and manual temperature control units
   b. Recognition of increased fluid requirements for infants under radiant warmers
   c. Recognition that increased or decreased temperature may indicate sepsis, asphyxia, intracranial hemorrhage, or meningitis
   d. Recognition that servo control diminishes the use of temperature as a clinical sign and that a record of incubator temperature must be kept if the infant is maintained under servo control
   e. Recognition that full-term newborns in normal room temperature (25° to 27° C) should not require an incubator (The inability to regulate temperature in a full-term neonate indicates a problem. The full-term neonate utilizes recoiled posturing to assist with thermoregulation.)
   f. Recognition that cold stress of a cold air current (oxygen, room air) in a normal thermal environment even to a small body area will trigger increased oxygen consumption and increase metabolic rate

   Rationale: To ensure that nursing personnel, who are the primary managers of thermo control for the high-risk neonate, are educated in all aspects of temperature control

2. Provide an explanation to parents of all thermo control interventions utilized.

   Rationale: To decrease the parents' anxiety and prevent long-term parent-infant interactional problems

REFERENCES

1. Belgaumakar, K., and Scott, K.: Effects of low humidity on small premature infants in servocontrolled incubators, I: decreased rectal temperature, Biol. Neonate **26:**337, 1975.
2. Belgaumakar, K., and Scott, K.: Effects of low humidity on small premature infants in servocontrolled incubators, II: increased severity of apnea, Biol. Neonate **26:**348, 1975.
3. Besch, J., et al.: The transparent baby bag: a shield against heat loss, N. Engl. J. Med. **284:**121, 1971.
4. Blackfan, K., and Yaglo, C.: The premature infant: a study of the effects of atmospheric conditions on growth and development, Am. J. Dis. Child. **46:**1175, 1933.
5. Budin, P.: The nursling, London, 1907, Caxton Publishing Co.
6. Darnall, R., and Ariagno, R.: Resting oxygen consumption of premature infants covered with a plastic thermal blanket, Pediatrics **63:**547, 1979.
7. Davies, P., and Davies, J.: Very low birth weight and subsequent head growth, Lancet **2:**1216, 1970.
8. Day, R., Caliguri, L., Kamensky, C., and Ehrlich, F.: Body temperature and survival of premature infants, Pediatrics **34:** 171, 1964.
9. Fanaroff, A., Wald, M., Gruber, H., and Klaus, M.: Insensible water loss in low birth weight infants, Pediatrics **50:**236, 1972.
10. Glass, L., Silverman, W., and Sinclair, J.: Effect of the thermal environment on cold resistance and growth of small infants after the first week of life, Pediatrics **41:**1033, 1968.
11. Hey, E. M., and Katz, G.: Optimum thermal environment for naked babies, Arch. Dis. Child. **45:**328, 1970.
12. Hull, D.: Brown adipose tissue, Br. Med. Bull. **22:**92, 1966.
13. Marks, K., Friedman, Z., and Maisels, M.: A simple device for reducing insensible water loss in low birth weight infants, Pediatrics **60:**223, 1977.
14. Okken, A., Jonxis, J., Rispens, P., and Zylstra, W.: New standards for "basal" heat production and evaporative and non-evaporative heat loss in low birth weight newborn infants, Pediatr. Res. Abst. II:539, 1977.
15. Peckham, G.: Infants at high risk: thermal regulation of the neonate, Indiana, 1975, Meade Johnson and Co.
16. Scopes, J.: Thermoregulation in the newborn. In Avery, G., editor: Neonatology, pathophysiology and management of the newborn, Philadelphia, 1975, J. B. Lippincott Co., pp. 99-109.
17. Silverman, W., Fertig, J., and Berger, A.: The sequential trial of the nonthermal effect of atmospheric humidity on survival of newly born premature infants, Pediatrics **20:**477, 1957.
18. Silverman, W., Sinclair, J., and Agate, F.: The oxygen cast of minor changes in heat balance of small newborn infants, Acta Paediatr. Scand. **55:**294, 1966.

BIBLIOGRAPHY

Dailey, W., Klaus, M., and Meyer, H.: Apnea in premature infants: monitoring, incidence, heart rate changes, and effect of environmental temperature, Pediatrics **43:**510, 1969.
Darnall, R., and Ariagno, R.: Minimal oxygen consumption in infants cared for under overhead radiant warmers compared with conventional incubators, J. Pediatr. **93:**283, 1978.
Hey, E.: The relationship between environmental temperature and oxygen consumption in the newborn baby, J. Physiol. **200:**589, 1969.
Hey, E.: Thermal neutrality, Br. Med. Bull. **31:**69, 1975.
Jolly, H., Molyneux, P., and Newen, D.: A controlled study of the effect of temperature on premature babies, J. Pediatr. **60:** 889, 1962.
Klaus, M., and Fanaroff, A., editors: The physical environment in care of the high risk newborn, Philadelphia, 1973, W. B. Saunders Co., pp. 58-79.

Perlstein, P., Edwards, N., and Sutherland, J.: Apnea in premature infants and incubator-air-temperature changes, N. Engl. J. Med. **282:**461, 1970.

Rutter, N., and Null, D.: Response of term babies to a warm environment, Arch. Dis. Child. **54:**178, 1979.

Rutter, N., Brown, S., and Hull, D.: Variation in the resting oxygen consumption of small babies, Arch. Dis. Child. **53:**850, 1978.

Silverman, W.: Incubator-baby side shows, Pediatrics **64:**127, 1979.

Silverman, W., and Blanc, W.: The effect of humidity on survival of newly born premature infants, Pediatrics **20:**477, 1957.

Sulyok, E., Jequier, E., and Ryser, G.: Effect of relative humidity on thermal balance of the newborn infant, Biol. Neonate **21:**210, 1972.

Wu, P., and Hodgman, J.: Insensible water loss in preterm infants: changes with postnatal development and non-ionizing radiant energy, Pediatrics **54:**704, 1974.

Chapter 16

Necrotizing enterocolitis

Nan Smith

Necrotizing enterocolitis (NEC) has been the focus of research for many individual experts in its recognition and management for the last 5 years. The initial report of NEC is credited to Genersich in 1891.[7] His description of presenting symptoms and postmortem examinations parallel ours today. Thelander,[13] in 1939, presented a review of a similar pathological process. The operative survival of an infant with NEC was reported in 1943 by Agerty.[1] The 60's brought an accurate description of the clinical manifestations of the disease.

The widely published reports of the 70's have assumed the task of defining predisposing factors, etiology, and treatment. With this assumption, they are also faced with the question as to whether the increased diagnostic skills can be solely attributed to the increased awareness and incidence of this entity or whether they may be a direct contribution to its development. Although the etiology of necrotizing enterocolitis is unknown, current research is taking several directions. A review of this research follows, providing substantial understanding of the pathology.

Neonatal asphyxia is frequently suggested as a prime factor in the pathogenesis of necrotizing enterocolitis.[14] Asphyxia is thought to trigger a redistribution of cardiac output with reflex vasoconstriction of intestinal vasculature, bowel ischemia, and mucosal damage. Lloyd[9] popularized the concept that gastrointestinal perforation and necrotizing enterocolitis result from an asphyxial defense mechanism, selective circulatory ischemia. In response to asphyxia, blood is shunted away from the mesenteric, renal, and peripheral beds and shunted to the brain and heart, organs that do not tolerate hypoxia well. Lloyd's contention is that this mechanism occurs as a physiological reflex in diving animals and birds, and that the diving reflex functions in all mammalian life during the perinatal period as a protection against asphyxia and shock.

Necrotizing enterocolitis and experimental interruption of bowel blood flow present similar pathological findings. There are areas of submucosal edema and later hemorrhage. Villous and mucosal damage lead to necrosis and ulceration. Small vessel thrombi are minimal, inflammation is slight, and distribution of bowel necrosis is patchy.[10]

There has been speculation that patients who have recovered from acute NEC develop strictures on the basis of antibiotic suppression of bacterial flora, ischemic injury to the bowel, and resulting fibrosis.[3] Cohn previously showed that if bacterial growth in the intestinal lumen is inhibited, bowel ischemia may result in fibrosis and stricture rather than frank gangrene and perforation.

There are many conditions that may result in reduced blood flow to the bowel. Asphyxia can be defined as anoxia and carbon dioxide retention resulting from failure of respiration leading to respiratory and metabolic acidosis. Reported conditions occurring prior to the development of NEC reveal that not all of these are necessarily associated with asphyxia or even hypoxia. Among those most frequently mentioned are low Apgar score, exchange transfusions, umbilical artery and vein catheters, toxemia of pregnancy, maternal vaginal bleeding, breech deliveries, prolonged labor, neonatal anemia, and premature rupture of membranes. A more common feature among these conditions than asphyxia is inadequate tissue perfusion.[8]

Other research has lent itself to investigation of the following premise: that NEC could find its origin as the result of an immature immunological system. The inadequacy of intestinal immunity during the neonatal period undoubtedly plays an important role in the progression of the disease.[12] The delayed appearance of antibodies in secretions exposes the neonatal intestine to a period of increased permeability to sensitizing antigens and microorganisms. Ogra and Marson[11] in the studied role of immunoglobulins in the mechanism of mucosal immunity to infection feel that proliferating organisms gain access to the bowel wall and may present a pathological picture of necrotizing enterocolitis.

The following will address itself to the examination and exploration of selected aspects of the function of the newborn's gastrointestinal tract that might contribute to the development of necrotizing enterocolitis. In the newborn the total absorptive surface of the intestine may be greater than that of the older child or adult. In the premature infant the height and structure of the villi are similar to the adult.[4] The normal process of epithelial replacement is operative at term, but the rate at which migration proceeds is probably much slower than in the adult. Whether migration rate is reflective of their digestive and transport capacity is undetermined.[15] Another aspect of gut development particularly relevant to the problem of necrotizing enterocolitis is the lymphatic and vascular supply to the bowel. Disordered intestinal motility in the premature could affect emptying of the upper gut and absorptive function.

Engel[5] postulates that necrotizing enterocolitis may have an infectious etiology. His findings reveal that the mural blebs in NEC contain hydrogen, which is a product of bacterial metabolism, and the strong association between the formation of blebs and feedings may support bacterial production to which the premature infant is most susceptible.

The symptoms of necrotizing enterocolitis usually develop within the first week of life and are characterized by the onset of lethargy, temperature instability, large gastric residuals or frank vomiting, obstipation, or bloody diarrhea.

The above research is helpful in planning. The fact that there is not total agreement on etiology and that there are gaps in available knowledge does not preclude a nursing protocol for management of these infants. Lists of objectives for care of the infant with necrotizing enterocolitis, problems later in management, and prevention in very immature or seriously ill infants follow:

Objectives for care

Prevention of generalized deterioration
Prevention of dehydration and electrolyte imbalance
Observation for apnea, presence of bradycardia
Prevention of acute respiratory distress
Observation for symptoms indicating potential for surgical intervention
Relief of abdominal distention
Maintenance of fluid and electrolyte balance

Problems later in management[2]

Prolonged requirements for parenteral nutrition to allow healing of gastrointestinal tract
Frequency of short gut syndrome after significant bowel resection, often leading to gastrointestinal intolerance to feeding because of malabsorption
Strictures on healing

Prevention in very immature or seriously ill infants[2]

Caution in the introduction and rate of increase in parenteral feeding (consider temporarily substituting parenteral alimentation)
Feeding of iso-osmolar milks initially (20 cal/30 ml or less—mid-chain triglyceride [MCT] oil added to feedings will aid in caloric support)
Prevention of distention from high-volume feedings

Protocols

Problem □ Abdominal distention

GOALS

1. To recognize distention early
2. To promptly institute appropriate medical regime
3. To relieve abdominal distention (assessment of lessening abdominal distention within reasonable period of time based on clinical judgment and the amount of gastric secretions removed, lessening of tension of abdominal wall through gentle palpation, decrease in tympany noted by percussion, and decrease in measurement of abdominal circumference)

DIAGNOSTIC

1. Observe and assess abdomen through gentle palpation for hardened bowel loops, noting contour and tensity.
   Rationale: To assess for distention in the abdomen (Radiographs show small distention and strips of intramural gas and occasionally perforation. There may be air extending through the venous drainage of the small bowel into portal radicals of the liver.[6] Vomiting and abdominal distention are primary presenting signs of necrotizing enterocolitis.[6])
2. Observe for presence of visible peristaltic waves.
   Rationale: To assess for intestinal obstruction
3. Palpate liver and spleen to rule out hepatosplenomegaly. Auscultate for presence/absence/hypoactive bowel sounds. Note time of onset of abdominal distention.
   Rationale: To assess for decreased intestinal motility obstruction

THERAPEUTIC

1. If feeding, discontinue immediately, NPO.
2. Institute nasogastric suction to low intermittent suction using No. 8 feeding tube.
3. Measure and record amount and note characteristics of gastrointestinal secretions, especially blood—frank or old. Hematest all gastrointestinal secretions.
4. Monitor increase/decrease in abdominal distention by measurement with tape measure every 8 hours or mark abdomen with pencil. Report findings.

5. If oral feedings are in progress, monitor amount of stomach aspirants every 2 hours noting consistently large aspirants.
6. If NPO, change feeding tube to suction every 8 hours.

EDUCATIONAL

1. Explain all procedures to parents.
   Rationale: To reduce parental anxiety and promote maternal-infant interaction
2. Encourage participation in care.

Problem □ Vomiting

GOALS

1. To recognize and detect early potential pathological vomiting
2. To prevent dehydration and maintain fluid and electrolyte balance

DIAGNOSTIC

1. Note time of onset and associated manifestations such as abdominal distention and note characteristic vomitus.
   Rationale: To recognize the primary presenting signs of necrotizing enterocolitis
2. Hematest vomitus and observe for presence of blood—frank/old flecks—and bilious vomiting, and determine the origin of RBC's by performing an alkali denaturation test (Apt). Report findings of frank blood immediately and obtain blood pressure, hematocrit, platelets, and Apt test.
   Rationale: To distinguish between necrotizing enterocolitis and maternal blood the fetus has swallowed during delivery (Differentiation must be made from acute gastrointestinal hemorrhage.)

THERAPEUTIC

1. Institute low intermittent nasogastric suction if bilious vomitus occurs.
   Rationale: To detect obstruction distal to the ampulla of Vater (Significant abdominal distention is more likely to accompany the vomiting if the obstruction is relatively low.)
2. Provide mouth care for infant with lemon glycerin swabs every 2 to 4 hours and as necessary.

Rationale: To reduce oral irritation and tissue breakdown

EDUCATIONAL

1. Explain all procedures and describe etiology of problem.

   Rationale: To provide parent education, thereby reducing parental anxiety and promoting the parent-child relationship

Problem □ Diarrhea

GOALS

1. To prevent dehydration
2. To assure prompt recognition, maintenance of electrolyte balance, and prevention of shock and metabolic acidosis
3. To assure cessation of diarrhea and establishment of fluid and electrolyte balances
4. To maintain adequate urinary output

DIAGNOSTIC

1. Assess frequency, consistency, characteristics, and presence of blood in stools. Hematest all stools. If positive within 1 minute (?), consider significant.

   Rationale: To note diarrhea, occasionally bloody, which may be seen in necrotizing enterocolitis

2. Assess skin turgor and fontanelles for state of hydration:
   a. Dry skin
   b. Parched tongue
   c. Sunken fontanel
   d. Decreased urinary output
   e. Irritability
   f. Lethargy
   g. Specific gravity, 1008
   h. Recent weight loss, 6% body weight

   Rationale: To assess for elasticity of skin (Pinched skin returns to normal configuration when released.)

3. Report abnormal serum electrolytes and seek orders for proper solution, determine frequency, amount, and characteristics of voiding.

   Rationale: To recognize fluid and electrolyte imbalance

THERAPEUTIC

1. Administer prescribed parenteral fluids. Observe and regulate rate of flow. Check serum electrolytes, report abnormalities, and seek orders for proper solution.

EDUCATIONAL

1. Explain all procedures and encourage parents to participate in the assessment.

   Rationale: To reduce parental anxiety and promote the parent-child relationship

Problem □ Sepsis

GOALS

1. To recognize clinical manifestations promptly
2. To control sepsis
3. To reestablish stability of vital functions: TPR
4. To establish fluid and electrolyte balance and adequate urinary output

DIAGNOSTIC

1. Monitor vital signs every 4 hours, noting any abnormalities such as temperature below 36.2 consistently or persistent thermal instability. Then monitor vital signs with frequency consistent with stability.

   Rationale: To detect poor temperature control, which may be an early indicator of infection, with hypothermia seen more commonly than elevations of temperature with infection in the newborn period

2. Observe and assess for change in activity and muscle tone and record observations. Note especially lethargy.

   Rationale: To note lethargy, which may be the first presenting sign of sepsis (Hypothermia may be responsible for signs of lethargy. If the axillary temperature is subnormal in a lethargic infant, it may mean that either the lethargy is secondary to accidental cooling or that both the lethargy and hypothermia are secondary to more serious illness.)

3. Apply neonatal urine bag for specimen collection, urinary analysis, and culture and sensitivities.

   Rationale: To rule out the diagnosis of pyelonephritis, which may be an isolated infection or concomitant finding with sepsis

4. Be alert to persistent apnea and bradycardia; monitor heart rate and respirations. Treat in early stages by gentle stimulation.

   Rationale: To recognize that apnea is primarily an extension of periodic breathing in the immature infant with his decreased sensitivity to carbon dioxide and oxygen

5. Prevent dehydration and temperature irregularity that may increase frequency of apnea.

Rationale: To prevent bradycardia and cyanosis (When apnea persists beyond 10 seconds, bradycardia is likely and if respirations do not resume in another 20 seconds, cyanosis will develop, accompanied by asphyxia. Approximately 30% of infants less than 32 weeks' gestation (1750 gm) and nearly all infants of less than 30 weeks' gestation have apneic periods.)

THERAPEUTIC

1. Suction nasopharynx if cyanosis persists.
2. Administer antibiotics prescribed parenterally.
   Rationale: To promote ventilation

EDUCATIONAL

1. Explain all procedures and discuss respiration in the premature infant.
   Rationale: To reduce parental anxiety and promote the parent-child relationship

Problem □ Separation of mother and infant

GOALS

1. To optimally establish the mothering process
2. To promote the mother's participation in infant care
3. To encourage communication of information, especially when mothers do not ask for explanations
4. To permit the mother to learn how to care for her infant while he is in the hospital so that after discharge she will be competent and relaxed caring for him
5. To help the mother begin building a close affectional tie to her infant, developing a mutual interaction so that she will be attuned to her baby's special needs as he grows

DIAGNOSTIC

1. Note consistency of worrisome responses, overconfidence, over optimism, unconcern about baby's clinical state, failure to ask questions, lack of visitation, and infrequent phone calls.
   Rationale: To detect any pathology in establishment of mothering process (If a mother does not visit her child, this is a sign of pathology. The establishment of the mothering process is endangered and demands immediate attention. The answer may not always be to increase interaction between the mother and her premature infant; circumstances may require investigation of what may be blocking the mother from having the capacity to interact with her baby.)
2. Elicit concerns and question in a positive manner: "How did the baby look to you? What did you notice? How do you feel about the baby and what we just told you? What questions do you have?"

THERAPEUTIC

1. Provide mother and father with opportunity to fondle and stroke infant in isolette. Place high-back chairs at the bedside. Foster parental participation in infant care by having them change diapers, provide mouth care, position infant, and so forth.
   Rationale: To foster the appropriate types of stimulation (Stimulation should not be thought of as just providing additional or more stimulation to the premature infant. More thought should be given to the appropriate types of stimulation and its timing; in fact, many infants are bombarded with stimuli in the early home situation, when their capacity to deal with stimulus overload is less. They may even develop irritability and crying behavior because of stimulus overload.)

EDUCATIONAL

1. Provide explanation of importance of touching—improves infant's breathing, physical development, and rate of weight gain and relaxes the infant and reduces apneic episodes.
2. Encourage the mother to talk about her thoughts: "How are things going? How have you slept? How is your husband managing? How are both of you getting along?"
   Rationale: To allow the mother to verbalize her feelings and thus become attached to the newborn
3. Emphasize attainment of milestones—physical, feeding ability, weight gain, temperature control, reduction in and color of gastric secretions.
   Rationale: To avoid giving the mother a task if there is the slightest possibility that she will not succeed
4. Provide *simple* explanations of the infant's condition as is appropriate to the situation.

5. Counsel the mother about the behavioral changes she might see and how to interpret them.

    Rationale: To ensure that the mother feels she is making an important contribution to the care of her infant, thereby fostering optimal mother-infant attachment

6. Explain the cardiac monitor and apnea monitor and their *alarms,* the nasogastric tube and its purpose and function, the need for intravenous alimentation and how it functions as a substitute for bottle feeding.

    Rationale: To reduce parental anxiety and promote the parent-child relationship

REFERENCES

1. Agerty, H. A., Ziserman, A. J., and Shollenberger, C. L.: A case perforation of the ileum in a newborn infant with operation and recovery, J. Pediatr. **22:**233, 1943.
2. Babson, S., Pernoll, M., and Benda, G.: Diagnosis and management of the fetus and neonate at risk, ed. 4, St. Louis, 1980, The C. V. Mosby Co.
3. Cohn, J., editor: Intestinal antisepsis, Springfield, Ill., 1968, Charles C Thomas, Publisher.
4. Deren, J. J.: Development of intestinal function and structure, Handbook Physiol. **6:**1099, 1968.
5. Engel, R. R., Virnig, N. L., Hunt, C. E., and Leavitt, M. D.: Origin of mural gas in necrotizing enterocolitis, Pediatric Res. **7:**292, 1973.
6. Evans, H. E., and Glass, L.: Perinatal medicine, New York, 1976, Harper & Row, Publishers, Inc.
7. Genersich, A.: Bauchfellenzundung beim neugeborenen in folge von perforation des ileums, Arch. Pathol. Anat. **126:** 485, 1891.
8. Joshi, V. V., et al.: Neonatal necrotizing enterocolitis, Am. J. Dis. Child. **126:**113, 1973.
9. Lloyd, R.: The etiology of gastrointestinal perforations in the newborn, J. Pediatr. Surg. **4:**77, 1969.
10. Morson, B. C.: Histopathology of intestinal ischemia. In Boley, S. J., Schwartz, S. S., and Williams, L. F., editors: Vascular disorders of the intestine, New York, 1971, Meredith Corporation, pp. 103-110.
11. Ogra, P. L., and Karson, D. T.: The role of immunoglobulins in the mechanism of mucosal immunity to virus infections, Pediatr. Clin. North Am. **17:**385, 1970.
12. Rotherberg, R. M.: Immunoglobulin and specific antibody synthesis during the first weeks of life in premature infants, J. Pediatr. **75:**391, 1969.
13. Thelander, H. E.: Perforation of the gastrointestinal tract of the newborn infant, Am. J. Dis. Child. **58:**371, 1939.
14. Touloukian, R. J., Posch, J. W., and Spencer, R.: The Pathogenesis of ischemic gastroenterocolitis of the neonate, J. Pediatr. Surg. **2:**194, 172.
15. Younoszai, M. K.: Gastrointestinal function during infancy. In Fomon, S. J.:, editor: Infant nutrition, ed. 2, Philadelphia, 1974, W. B. Saunders Co.

BIBLIOGRAPHY

Chinn, P. L., and Leitch, C.: Child health maintenance, ed. 2., St. Louis, 1979, The C. V. Mosby Co.

Klaus, M. H., and Avory, M. B.: Care of the high-risk neonate, Philadelphia, 1973, W. B. Saunders Co.

Klaus, M. H., and Kennell, J. H.: Maternal-infant bonding, St. Louis, 1976, The C. V. Mosby Co.

Korones, S. B.: High-risk newborn infants, ed. 3, St. Louis, 1981, The C. V. Mosby Co.

Chapter 17

Diaphragmatic hernia

Kathy Martin, Jerri Williams, and Rosanne Harrigan Perez

Many advancements have been made over the past few years in both the medical and surgical management of the newborn infant at risk. Of particular importance are the improvement and specialization in the transport of the high-risk infant to tertiary care centers. Thus many infants born with diaphragmatic hernias, who would have died before these advancements, are now reaching the centers equipped to meet their highly specialized needs. Maternal transport would, of course, be the optimal procedure with respect to the mortality and morbidity rates for the newborn. However, with the specific disease entity to be discussed, the option of maternal transport over that of the newborn is inapplicable. This is due to the fact that infants with diaphragmatic hernias are usually the result of an uneventful pregnancy, labor, and delivery.[11] Not until the infant begins breathing does the situation present itself. In some instances, diaphragmatic hernia has been diagnosed through the use of amniography.[1]

The incidence of congenital diaphragmatic hernia varies greatly from setting to setting but averages about 1 in 2000 births. This frequency is certainly of enough significance to warrant the time and efforts of personnel to become aware of the special needs of these infants.

The mortality rate of an infant presenting with early symptoms is very near 100% without prompt surgical treatment. Even with optimal care, mortality can be as high as 50%.[2,24,28] Through the following discussion and presentation of a proposed protocol we hope to provide for a further increase in the skills of recognition and prompt appropriate treatment of infants with diaphragmatic hernias.

EMBRYOLOGICAL DEVELOPMENTS

There are four basic embryonic structures from which the diaphragm develops: the septum transversum, mesentery of the esophagus, pleuroperitoneal membranes, and the body wall (Fig. 17-1).

As early as the end of the third week, the septum transversum can first be identified as a mass of mesoderm cranial to the pericardial coelom. After the head fold during the fourth developmental week, this structure grows dorsally to envelop the gut, inferior vena cava, and aorta, fusing with the mesoderm ventral to the esophagus. The pleuroperitoneal membranes fuse with the dorsal aspect of the septum transversum and the dorsal mesentery of the esophagus by the eighth week. It is during this period that the majority of cases of diaphragmatic hernia develop, since this is also the period during which the gut begins to return from the umbilical cord to the abdominal cavity. The midgut tends to return to the thorax rather than the abdomen when the pleuroperitoneal canals have not yet fused. Two speculations have been made for the occurrence of this situation: either delayed closure of the canals or premature return of the gut. During the ninth to the twelfth week of development as the thoracic cavity enlarges, the tissue from the body wall forms the peripheral edges of the diaphragm. The pleural cavities extend further into the body walls forming the costal diaphragmatic recess.[7,22,24] This gives the diaphragm its dome shape. Diaphragmatic hernia is compatible with fetal life to full term, thus it is rare that it will occur in a premature infant. The prematurity results from other perinatal problems.[28]

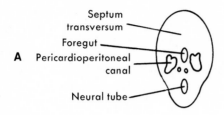

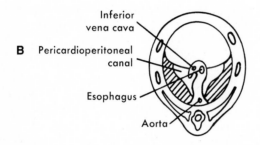

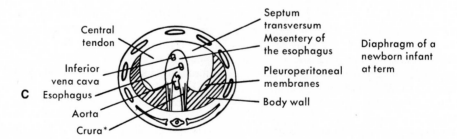

Fig. 17-1. Transverse section at various stages of development. **A,** At 4 weeks of embryological development. **B,** About the fifth week of gestation. Note the unfused pleuroperitoneal membranes. **C,** Embryological origins.* Pillars connecting the diaphragm to the spinal column. (Adapted from Moore, K.: The developing human, Philadelphia, 1973, W. B. Saunders Co.; and Osebold, W. R., and Soper, R. T.: Am. J. Surg. **131:**748, 1976.)

PHYSICAL ASSESSMENT

The severity of the diaphragmatic defect and the amount of viscera herniated into the thoracic cavity will, of course, determine the clinical manifestations. The newborn infant may be severely ill to the point of requiring resuscitation at birth, or the infant may remain asymptomatic until later in childhood or adult life. Some cases are only discovered through routine chest x-ray examinations. As a rule, the incidence of morbidity and mortality is higher the sooner the symptoms develop.[5,18,28]

When the defect is severe and symptoms are present at birth, a medical-surgical emergency exists. The infant often makes no further respiratory effort other than an initial gasp. Cyanosis quickly develops and resuscitative measures must be carried out. When spontaneous respirations are established, the situation presents itself much like that of respiratory distress syndrome, that is, deep intercostal and sternal retractions. This condition may result in hypoxia, hypercarbia, and severe acidosis. With successive respiratory efforts, air is swallowed and enters the bowel. Distention in the herniated bowel causes a shift of the mediastinum toward the unaffected side; this further compromises pulmonary ventilation since the increased pressure decreases maximum expansion of the uninvolved lung.

In addition to the symptoms of respiratory distress already mentioned, other symptoms are often present to alert the health care team to the possibility of a diaphragmatic hernia. The thorax may bulge, and there may be a scaphoid abdomen. Breath sounds on the affected side are decreased or absent, and bowel sounds may be heard over the chest. There is a dullness to percussion. Heart sounds are also often displaced toward the unaffected side. X-ray studies of the chest are required to confirm the diagnosis. Both posteroanterior and lateral chest x-ray films are indicated. When the defect goes undetected until later in life, the child may present with respiratory distress, vomiting, cramping from strangulation of the bowel, poor physical development, and signs of malnutrition.[4,10,24,28]

PATHOPHYSIOLOGY

Congenital diaphragmatic hernias occur in three basic locations of the diaphragm. These include the anterolateral-retrosternal sinus (sinus of Morgagni or Larrey), the esophageal hiatus, and the most common site, the posterolateral aspect (the foramen of Bochdalek). The defect can be present on either side of the posterolateral aspect, but it occurs about five times more frequently on the left side. The reason for this is twofold. One is that the liver serves to buttress the abdominal contents, and the other is that the pleuroperitoneal canals close first on the right side and then on the left side. The defect rarely occurs bilaterally.[4,13,22,28] Paralysis and eventration of the diaphragm may present a somewhat similar clinical picture. Paralysis occurs most commonly with difficult breech deliveries. Hyperextension of the neck may inflict injury to the brachial plexus and phrenic nerve. Eventration results from an insufficient amount of muscle. Since this chapter deals primarily with diaphragmatic hernia, these entities will not be discussed further.[15,17,20]

Usually, it is the hollow organs that herniate into the thoracic cavity. Their hollowness allows for greater flexibility and thus easier passage through the defect, particularly when the defect is small. On occasion, however, the large organs such as the liver or spleen may be present in the thoracic cavity.[5,24]

In infants who have congenital diaphragmatic hernia, the lungs are often hypoplastic. It is presumed that the lungs' growth is restricted, resulting in hypoplasia caused by the presence of abdominal organs in the thoracic cavity. After repair of the hernia, the lungs usually do not expand to fill the chest cavity immediately. Within a week to months the lungs approach normal capacity. It should be mentioned here, as it will be again, that no attempts should be made to force expansion of a hypoplastic lung since this may cause a rupture of the alveoli, resulting in a tension pneumothorax.[3,13,16,23]

Even after surgical correction of the hernia, inadequate pulmonary ventilation often persists, resulting in severe hypoxia. A study made by Naeye and associates[23] revealed a high incidence of an abnormally increased muscle mass in the pulmonary arteries of hypoplastic lungs of infants having diaphragmatic hernia. This increase in muscle mass causes a persistent pulmonary vascular resistance. Normally, at birth, the first breath brings forth an increase in oxygen in the lungs. The lungs' expansion and increase in PaO_2 reduces pulmonary vascular resistance. At the same time, there is an increase in the systemic vascular resistance caused by the absence of a previous shunt, that is, the placenta, resulting in an increased blood flow from the pulmonary vein to the left atrium. This increased volume in the left atrium causes the closure of the foramen ovale.[23,27] In infants with severe symptoms of diaphragmatic hernia, there is poor pulmonary ventilation, causing less than adequate Pao_2 levels. This ensuing hypoxia causes further pulmonary vascular resistance in addition to the increased pulmonary muscle mass. The consequence of these occurrences is a return to a fetal-type circulation or right-to-left shunting at either the atrial or ductal levels or both.[27] The use of pulmonary vasodilators to combat this effect will be discussed later.

Another commonly associated anomaly is malrotation of the bowel. This is seen in up to 60% of cases. The high frequency of this occurrence is due to the fact that the herniation occurs at the time when the gut returns to the abdomen and normal rotation takes place. This defect can be resolved at the same time the hernia is reduced. One author compares this condition of diaphragmatic hernia to that of intracorporeal omphalocele. Space in the abdominal cavity is limited to accommodate the viscera. Respiratory complications may occur during reduction similar to those occurring following omphalocele reduction. This is primarily caused by elevation of the diaphragm, resulting in respiratory embarrassment and inferior vena caval obstruction.[28]

MEDICAL TREATMENT
Transport or initial admission

Once the diagnosis of diaphragmatic hernia is suspected or confirmed, the initial therapeutic treatment is placement of a nasogastric tube to low intermittent suction or a repogle to low continuous suction. A repogle is preferable since it is a larger tube with more openings in the tip of the catheter to provide for better drainage of the stomach contents. The nasogastric tube or the repogle will help prevent dilatation of the gastrointestinal tract caused by air swallowed by the neonate. The importance of this process is that it prevents further compression of the lungs, which causes impairment of pulmonary function.[11,14,20,32]

If the infant is having any respiratory distress, he should be intubated at this time. Bagging an infant with a diaphragmatic hernia with an AMBU bag and mask could lead to forcing air into the stomach,

thereby dilating the gastrointestinal tract. With an endotracheal tube, the pressure needed to ventilate the infant can be controlled. Early intubation is important; if the infant's condition deteriorates during transport or before reaching the surgical suite, time is not lost trying to intubate him. Intubating an infant is stressful enough when the infant has stable vital signs. When the infant's vital signs have deteriorated and intubation is necessary as a lifesaving intervention, the procedure becomes more stressful. Many times it requires more time to intubate the infant. Once intubated, the amount of pressure being given through the endotracheal tube must be closely monitored. If too much endotracheal pressure is given, both lungs could rupture, leading to further impairment of pulmonary functioning. Therefore the minimum amount of pressure needed to provide the infant with adequate pulmonary ventilation should be used at all times. When using high pressures with the endotracheal tube, the infant should be assessed for any signs of a possible pneumothorax. Since the pulmonary functioning is already somewhat impaired, liberal use of oxygen is recommended.[11,14,20,32]

If the infant is irritable following intubation, dimethyl tubocurarine iodide (Metubine*) can be given to reduce the possibility of extubation and decrease oxygen needs. (See Chapter 28.) The importance of dimethyl tubocurarine iodide is that it places the infant in an unconscious paralytic state in which he will not be struggling and possibly creating a pneumothorax in the unaffected lung. This drug allows complete respiratory control of the infant. Again, the amount of pressure given through the endotracheal tube must be monitored extremely closely.

The infant also requires a glucose solution to maintain normal body nutrient requirements and energy requirements. The physician should start a peripheral IV or, if time allows, place an umbilical arterial catheter. The glucose solution and the rate of admission should meet the infant's needs without fluid overload. In this way the infant not only re-

---

*Dimethyl tubocurarine iodide (Metubine) is presently being used at James Whitcomb Riley Children's Hospital; other institutions may be using other types of medication that produce the same end result, an unconscious coma-type state.

ceives fluids for body metabolism, but the IV also provides an avenue for administration of drugs should they be required. An arterial catheter has the advantage of making it possible to rapidly obtain arterial blood for blood gas analysis, Pao_2, $Paco_2$, pH, and base deficit. The blood gas analysis is important as an assessment of how well the infant is being ventilated and the acid-base balance.[14]

During the transport or on arrival at the hospital, the infant's vital signs (temperature, heart rate, respiratory rate, and blood pressure), color, IV, nasogastric or repogle, Dextrostik, oxygen concentration, and endotracheal tube pressure being used to ventilate the baby need to be closely documented and monitored before surgery. The infant should be in as stable a condition before surgery as possible to improve his chances of survival.

Surgery

Since this chapter is written from a nursing standpoint, we are not concerned with describing the detailed surgical procedure for repair of a diaphragmatic hernia. There are basically two approaches the surgeon can take in repair of the defect: (1) thoracic approach and (2) abdominal approach.[11,14,20,32]

Thoracic approach. Basically, in the thoracic approach the entrance is made through the chest wall. The viscera are replaced into the abdomen, and the defect is sutured closed. A chest tube is placed to underwater seal by the surgeon, and the entrance is sutured closed. The only advantage of this approach is that there is an excellent view of the defect. The disadvantages are that (1) the surgeon will experience problems in reducing the herniated abdominal contents into the small abdominal cavity; (2) the surgeon will not be able to see a malrotation of the bowel should it occur; and (3) placing the herniated viscera into the small abdominal cavity could cause increased intra-abdominal pressure, which could put pressure on the diaphragm and cause some impairment of pulmonary function. The thoracic approach is preferably used on children 1 year of age or older or on children who have had a recurrence of a former repaired diaphragmatic hernia.[11]

Abdominal approach. The abdominal approach is the preferred method of diaphragmatic hernia re-

pair. An abdominal incision is made, the herniated viscera are reduced out of the chest, the diaphragmatic hernia defect is closed, a chest tube is placed to underwater seal, and the abdominal wall is closed. If the abdominal wall is difficult to close because of increased intra-abdominal pressure from the viscera now in the abdominal cavity, a ventral hernia may need to be created. After the abdominal cavity has had several months to expand and the child shows no evidence of respiratory insufficiency, the ventral hernia can be repaired.[11]

In either procedure no attempt should be made to expand the lung on the affected side. Excess pressure could result in rupture of one or both of the infant's lungs.[11,32]

Medical management: postoperative care

Chest tube. The chest tube is placed to underwater seal drainage with a small amount of negative pressure applied. Care should be taken to avoid large amounts of suction being applied since this could lead to rupture of the lung. Accurate measurement of the chest tube drainage should be noted, and replacement of chest tube drainage should be implemented. Replacement of fluid lost is done to prevent a fluid and electrolyte imbalance in the infant. Chest tube drainage is usually replaced milliliter for milliliter with a Plasmanate solution.[11,14,20,32]

Endotracheal tube. After surgery if the affected lung is not hypoplastic, the infant shows no respiratory distress, and the arterial blood gas studies show good lung ventilation, the infant can be extubated and placed in a hood with oxygen. If the infant does not meet the above requirements, he should be maintained on a ventilator. Liberal use of oxygen is recommended. The Pao_2 should be maintained between 100 and 150 to ensure good oxygenation during the infant's critical period, while the infant is a fresh postoperative patient, or while the infant maintains a persistent fetal circulation state (this will be mentioned later). Once the infant's condition improves, his Pao_2 level can be allowed to fall below 100 (50 to 80) to wean him off the ventilator and oxygen therapy. The amount of endotracheal tube pressure must be assessed closely. The minimum amount of pressure needed to provide the infant with adequate pulmonary ventilation should be used at all times. Blood pressure must be closely monitored if PEEP is being used, since this will cause a decrease in venous return to the heart because of the positive pressure in the thoracic cavity.[32]

The infant should be given dimethyl tubocurarine iodide to keep him in a paralytic-coma state so that he cannot struggle or become irritable, which can lead to a possible pneumothorax in the unaffected lung. If a hypoplastic lung expands (as evidenced on chest x-ray films done to monitor the infant's lung status) or the infant's arterial blood gas results show good lung ventilation, the infant should be weaned off the dimethyl tubocurarine iodide. If the infant continues to improve, he should be weaned off the ventilator slowly. Once extubated, the infant should be closely assessed for respiratory status.

Acidosis. The occurrence of acidosis is associated with improper lung ventilation. Respiratory acidosis should be handled by making the proper ventilator changes to correct the acidosis. Metabolic acidosis should be managed through administration of sodium bicarbonate or THAM. Blood pH's need to be monitored closely, especially after ventilator changes or administration of the above-mentioned medications.[11,14,20,32]

Nasogastric or repogle tube. To keep the gastrointestinal tract compressed nasogastric tube to low intermittent suction or repogle to low continuous suction should be maintained after surgery. Expansion of the bowel could cause pressure on the wound site, leading to pressure on the lungs and pulmonary impairment. Any gastric drainage should be replaced as ordered by medical staff so that the infant does not encounter a fluid-electrolyte imbalance from loss of gastric fluids.[11,14,20,32]

Fluids and electrolytes. While the infant is being kept in the NPO state, he must be maintained on IV fluid solutions. The type of fluid should be such that it meets the needs of the infant. The rate of administration should be such that it provides the infant with a sufficient amount of fluid and electrolytes without overloading. If the infant is going to remain NPO for a prolonged period of time, he should be receiving hyperalimentation fluids and possibly Intralipid. (See Chapter 27 and Appendix C.)

Antibiotics. Once the infant has returned from surgery, prophylactic antibiotics should be started. This should be done because the infant has had major surgery. The skin, which is the first line of defense, has been broken. Any drainage from the wound site could provide a medium for bacterial growth. Therefore the infant must be assessed for possible signs and symptoms of infection during this postoperative period.[32]

Persistent fetal circulation. In persistent fetal circulation the infant fails to change from a fetal state of circulation to that of a newborn-adult state of circulation. The major concern is that there is pulmonary hypertension in the lungs, which causes decreased blood flow through the lungs, decreased oxygenation of the blood, and generalized body hypoxia. If the infant maintains a persistent fetal circulation state and proper ventilator settings do not provide for adequate lung ventilation, the infant should be started on tolazoline (Priscoline). (See Appendix A.) This drug helps to reverse the persistent fetal circulation state. At this time, the infant should be maintained on dimethyl tubocurarine iodide to keep him from any voluntary respiratory effort that might be aggravating the persistent fetal circulation state. If the infant's blood pressure decreases and the tolazoline must be maintained, dopamine should be infused to maintain the blood pressure. Once the infant's blood gases are improved, the infant should be gradually weaned off the tolazoline and dopamine. Once the infant is stable after these are discontinued, weaning off the dimethyl-tubocurarine iodide should begin. After this, the infant should be weaned off the ventilator. The medications just mentioned (tolazoline, dopamine, and dimethyl tubocurarine iodide) should only be used in medical settings where the medical health team is properly trained in the use and understanding of these very dangerous drugs.

Correction of the ventral hernia

The purpose of the ventral hernia is to create an area to contain the bowel because of insufficient space in the abdominal cavity. Complete reduction of the diaphragmatic hernia without creation of a ventral hernia could cause an increase in intra-abdominal pressure leading to: ''1) elevation of diaphragms with respiratory embarrassment or 2) inferior vena caval obstruction with cardiovascular embarrassment.''[11] The delay in repair allows the abdominal cavity to gradually expand. At a later date when the infant is more physically mature and has gained weight, the child will be more stable for surgical repair of the ventral hernia.[11]

SUMMARY

As time goes on so does the development of better methods of caring for newborn infants. Much progress has been made in the area of neonatology. Four areas that have been proposed as related to decreasing the mortality rate of infants with diaphragmatic hernia are (1) safer and faster transportation of these infants to the unit by trained personnel, (2) use of medications such as dimethyl tubocurarine iodide (These are muscle relaxants that place the infant in an unconscious coma-type state in which the infant will not be struggling or irritable, causing a possible pneumothorax. In the past measures such as tiptoeing around the infant's bed or quickly quieting down another crying infant to minimize the environmental disturbances or use of sedatives such as chloral hydrate proved ineffective), (3) maintenance of high Pao_2 levels (100 to 150) during the infant's critical period to assure good oxygenation, and (4) better education and training of the personnel working with these infants.

Protocols

Problem □ Transport of initial admission

GOAL: To stabilize the infant

Rationale: To ensure infant is in a stable physiological state prior to transport or surgery to minimize stress

DIAGNOSTIC

1. Perform a quick, generalized assessment of the infant while gathering the necessary equipment.
2. Assess color, note respiratory movements (movement of chest and abdomen, use of accessory muscles, note any grunting or gasping sounds, and so forth), note position of body (on back or side, are limbs flexed or do they appear limp at infant's side).
   Rationale: To provide baseline data for determining changes in the infant's condition

THERAPEUTIC

1. Insert a nasogastric or repogle tube and attach the nasogastric tube to low intermittent suction or repogle tube to low continuous suction immediately.
   Rationale: To decompress the stomach and limit dilatation of the gastrointestinal tract, which could lead to compression of the lungs and impairment of pulmonary functioning

DIAGNOSTIC

1. Assess contents aspirated from stomach (color, amount, odor, and so forth).
   Rationale: To ensure essential baseline data as well as document fluid replacement needs[11,14,20,23]

EDUCATIONAL

1. Provide simple explanations regarding all procedures for parents.
   Rationale: To reduce parental anxiety

GOAL: To promote adequate ventilation
   Rationale: To avoid respiratory acidosis

DIAGNOSTIC

1. Assess respiratory status (note retractions, grunting, hypercapnia).
   Rationale: To note respiratory distress, which requires intubation

THERAPEUTIC

1. Assist physician with intubation or perform the intubation (if properly trained in newborn intubation) with someone assisting).
   Rationale: To provide for adequate ventilation and minimize utilization of limited energy resources
2. If irritability persists following intubation, administer dimethyl tubocurarine iodide according to hospital protocol.
   Rationale: To avoid irritability, which can result in extubation and consume limited energy resources

3. Elevate the head of the infant's bed at least 30 degrees, and turn the infant to the affected side.
   Rationale: To allow for maximal lung expansion[11,14,20,32]

GOAL: To promote fluid and electrolyte balance
Rationale: To avoid seizures, asphyxia, and death, which can result from fluid and electrolyte imbalance

DIAGNOSTIC

1. Assess fluid and electrolyte needs.
   Rationale: To ensure that the type of fluid and rate of administration are appropriate to meet the needs of the individual infant

THERAPEUTIC

1. Start a peripheral IV or place a umbilical arterial catheter (if time available) before transporting or before the infant goes to surgery.
   Rationale: To ensure that an open line is available to administer fluids, electrolytes, and medications if necessary

GOAL: To support physiological functions prior to transplant or surgery
Rationale: To prevent unnecessary stress

DIAGNOSTIC

1. Assess vital signs (temperature, heart rate, respiratory rate, and blood pressure), color, glucose level (Dextrostix), nasogastric or repogle tube function and aspirate, oxygen concentration, and amount of endotracheal tube pressure used to ventilate the infant.
   Rationale: To closely monitor the infant's status prior to transport or surgery and record and report changes

Problem □ Postoperative care

GOAL: To promote adequate ventilation (Infant will return from surgery with a chest tube attached to underwater seal.)
Rationale: To avoid respiratory acidosis

DIAGNOSTIC

1. Assess respiratory-ventilatory status.
   Rationale: To obtain baseline data in order to plan further care

THERAPEUTIC

1. Attach chest tube to negative suction according to physician's orders. Note prescribed amount of negative suction to be used.

2. Place a chest tube clamp at the bedside
   Rationale: To seal this system if a leak occurs

DIAGNOSTIC

1. Inspect chest tube system for leaks. (All connection sites should be taped to assure that they will not separate and create a leak in the system.)
   Rationale: To avoid the collapse of a lung

2. Check chest tube system for fluctuations in the water seal drainage bottle and check chest wall for movements.
   Rationale: To indicate the system is functioning properly

3. Record the amount of chest tube drainage.
   Rationale: To note changes in drainage, which may indicate bleeding or infection

4. Inspect chest tube dressing for any drainage from the wound site.
   Rationale: To indicate bleeding or infection

THERAPEUTIC

1. Suction the endotracheal tube only as necessary to keep the chest tube patent.
   Rationale: To be aware that oversuctioning, when it is unnecessary, serves only to provide additional stress to the infant

2. Lubricate the suction catheter.
   Rationale: To allow for easier insertion of the suctioning of the endotracheal tube

3. Administer a small amount of sodium chloride solution (or whatever the institution suggests) by way of the endotracheal tube.
   Rationale: To assist with the removal of thick mucous secretions.

4. Position the endotracheal tube so that it does not kink.
   Rationale: To provide for maximal ventilator assistance and to prevent fluid collecting from humidity in the ventilator from draining into the infant's endotracheal tube and lungs

GOAL: To maintain endotracheal tube patency until ventilatory assistance is no longer needed
Rationale: To allow time for hypoplastic lung expansion after surgical repair of the hernia

DIAGNOSTIC

1. Inspect the tape holding the endotracheal tube in place frequently.
   Rationale: To assure that the tube is being held in place

THERAPEUTIC

1. Suction the nose and mouth frequently
   Rationale: To check that secretions from the nose and mouth do not loosen the tape holding the endotracheal tube in place
2. Notify the physician immediately if the endotracheal tube becomes untaped or retape the tube if prepared to carry out this procedure.
   Rationale: To avoid unintentional extubation
3. Administer dimethyl-tubocurarine iodide slowly by IV push if ordered by the medical staff.
   Rationale: To be aware that excessive or inadequate amounts of this medication can result in death for the stressed infant

DIAGNOSTIC

1. Take chest x-ray film following retaping of the endotracheal tube.
   Rationale: To ensure its proper position is maintained
2. Monitor breath sounds closely.
   Rationale: To be aware that changes in breath sounds are generally one of the first indicators that an infant's condition is deteriorating
3. Assess all neonates treated with dimethyl-tubocurarine iodide for small movements indicating that the drug is wearing off and needs to be repeated.
   Rationale: To prevent the possibility of extubation and conserve energy resources

GOAL: To prevent respiratory acidosis
Rationale: To ensure adequate ventilation

DIAGNOSTIC

1. Assess for respiratory acidosis. (Measure blood pH; auscultate for cardiac murmurs, equality of breath sounds, and congestion; observe for grunting, abdominal breathing, use of assessory muscles, and retractions.)
   Rationale: To indicate inadequate ventilation

THERAPEUTIC

1. Adjust ventilator setting according to physician's order.
   Rationale: To make sure appropriate ventilator changes are made promptly and medications (sodium bicarbonate or THAM) are administered in proper dosage slowly by IV push

GOAL: To maintain compression of the gastrointestinal tract

Rationale: To avoid pressure on the wound site, which could lead to pressure on the lungs and ventilatory compromise

DIAGNOSTIC

1. Measure and record quantity and description of all gastric drainage.
   Rationale: To ensure replacement of lost fluids

THERAPEUTIC

1. Maintain nasogastric tube to low intermittent suction or repogle tube to low continuous suction.
   Rationale: To maintain compression of the gastrointestinal tract
2. Replace gastric drainage with fluids ordered by medical staff.
   Rationale: To avoid dehydration and fluid and electrolyte imbalance[11,14,20,32]

GOAL: To maintain fluid and electrolyte balance by provision of IV fluids
Rationale: To ensure that infant receives adequate fluids, electrolytes, and energy resources while in the NPO state

DIAGNOSTIC

1. Monitor fluid and electrolyte status (Ca, K, Na, and so forth), gastric drainage (amount, odor), insensible water loss, urine (specific gravity), blood status (Hct, CBC, platelets), weight, and presence of edema.
   Rationale: To establish parameters for fluid replacement

THERAPEUTIC

1. Administer IV fluids as ordered at correct administration rate.
   Rationale: To be aware that fluids replaced too quickly can cause cardiovascular stress
2. Administer hyperalimentation fluids or Intralipid according to orders during prolonged NPO periods. (See Chapter 27 and Appendix C for further information regarding hyperalimentation and Intralipid administration.)
   Rationale: To promote growth and repair

GOAL: To prevent infection
Rationale: To be aware that major surgery has occurred resulting in a break in the skin, which is the infant's first line of defense against infection

DIAGNOSTIC

1. Assess for signs and symptoms of infection (change in behavior, lethargy, and so forth)
   Rationale: To plan further care[32]

2. Note quantity and quality of wound drainage.
   Rationale: To check drainage, which is a medium for bacterial growth and may indicate infection

THERAPEUTIC

1. Administer antibiotics as ordered in correct dose according to medical orders.
   Rationale: To reduce the possibility of infectious stressors
2. Change all dressings using aseptic technique.
   Rationale: To avoid contamination of an open wound, which will result in infection

GOAL: To promote transition circulation (For interventions, see Chapter 25.)
   Rationale: To be aware that persistent fetal circulation is a complication seen in the diaphragmatic hernia patient

GOAL: To provide parental support and education

DIAGNOSTIC

1. Assess parents' knowledge base.
   Rationale: To ensure that data provided to parents is appropriate to their level of knowledge

THERAPEUTIC

1. Include parents whenever possible in care provision.
   Rationale: To provide the parents opportunities to interact with the infant and to feel that they provide a significant part of the infant's care (This interaction will also promote parent-infant bonding.)

EDUCATIONAL

1. Develop a teaching plan with objectives.
2. Utilize written materials.
3. Explain all procedures.
4. Encourage parents to demonstrate care competencies.
5. Provide positive reinforcement.
6. Answer all questions honestly.
   Rationale: To reduce parental anxiety and promote bonding (Parents must feel competent in the care of their neonate before they can take the child home.)

REFERENCES

1. Aladjem, S., Brown, A., and Sureau, C. Clinical perinatology, ed. 2, St. Louis, 1980, The C. V. Mosby Co.
2. Alistair, P.: Neonatology: a practical guide, New York, 1977, Medical Examination Publishing Company Inc., p. 86.
3. Areechon, W.: Hypoplasia of lung wilth congenital diaphragmatic hernia, Br. Med. J. **1:**1933, 1963.
4. Behrman, R., et al.: Neonatal-perinatal medicine: diseases of the fetus and infant, ed. 2, St. Louis, 1977, The C. V. Mosby Co.
5. Blank, E., and Campbell, J.: Congenital posterolateral defect in the right side of the diaphragm, Pediatrics **57**(5): 807, 1976.
6. Boyden, E.: The structure of compressed lung in congenital diaphragmatic hernia, Am. J. Anat. **134:**497, 1972.
7. Collins, D., et al.: A new approach to congenital posterolateral diaphragmatic hernia, J. Pediatr. Surg. **12**(2):149, 1977.
8. Evans, H., and Glass, L.: Perinatal medicine, Baltimore, 1976, Harper & Row, Publishers, Inc.
9. Greenwood, R., et al.: Cardiovascular abnormalities associated with congenital diaphragmatic hernia, Pediatrics **57**(1):92, 1976.
10. Grmoljez, P., and Lewis, J.: Congenital diaphragmatic hernia: Bochdalek type, Am. J. Surg. **132:**744, 1976.
11. Harberg, F., et al.: Congenital anomalies of the diaphragm, Am. J. Surg. **132:**747, 1976.
12. Hislop, A., and Reid, L.: Persistant hypoplasia of the lung after repair of congenital diaphragmatic hernia, Thorax **31:** 450, 1976.
13. Katz, S., et al.: Eventration of the diaphragm with gastric perforation, J. Pediatr. Surg. **9**(3):411, 1974.
14. Kirchner, S., et al.: Delayed radiographic presentation of congenital right diaphragmatic hernia, Pediatr. Radiol. **115:** 155, 1975.
15. Meeker, I. A., Jr., and Kincannon, W. N.: The role of ventral hernia in the correction of diaphragmatic defects in the newborn, Arch. Dis. Child **40:**146, 1965.
16. Moore, K.: The developing human, Philadelphia, 1973, W. B. Saunders Co.
17. Naeye, R., et al.: Unsuspected pulmonary vascular abnormalities associated with diaphragmaric hernia, Pediatrics **58**(6):902, 1976.
18. Osebold, W. R., and Soper, R. T.: Congenital posterolateral diaphragmatic hernia past infancy, Am. J. Surg. **131:** 748, 1976.
19. Rowe, R.: Abnormal pulmonary vasoconstrictions in the newborn, Pediatrics, vol. 59, no. 3, 1977.
20. Schaffer, A., and Avery, M. E.: Diseases of the newborn, ed. 4, Philadelphia, 1977, W. B. Saunders Co.
21. Woolley, M.: Congenital posterolateral diaphragmatic hernia, Surg. Clin. North Am. **56**(2):317, 1976.

BIBLIOGRAPHY

Boix-Ochoa, J., et al.: Acid-base balance and blood gases in prognosis and therapy of congenital diaphragmatic hernia, J. Pediatr. Surg. **9**(1):49, 1974.
Brill, P., et al.: Massive gastric enlargement with delayed presentation of congenital diaphragmatic hernia: report of three cases, J. Pediatr. Surg. **12**(5):667, 1977.
Buckner, D.: Congenital diaphragmatic hernia, Perinatal Care, Summer issue, June, 1977.
Glasson, M., et al.: Congenital left posterolateral diaphragmatic hernia with previously normal chest x-ray, Pediatr. Radiol. **3:**201, 1975.

Lewis, M. A., and Young, D.: Ventilatory problems with congenital diaphragmatic hernia, Anesthesia **24**(4):571, 1969.

Miller, F., Vareno, L. A., and Shocat, S.: Umbilical arteriography for the rapid diagnosis of congenital diaphragmatic hernia in the newborn infant, J. Pediatr. **90**(6):993, 1977.

Priebe, C., and Wichern, W.: Ventral hernia with a skin-covered Silastic sheet for newborn infants with a diaphragmatic hernia, Surgery **82**(2):569, 1977.

Rees, J. R., et al.: Bochdalek's hernia: a review of twenty-one cases, Am. J. Surg. **129**:259, 1975.

Tsuchida, Y., et al.: Prolonged postoperative hypercapnia in congenital diaphragmatic hernia, J. Pediatr. Surg. **4**(3):313, 1969.

Wiseman, N., and MacPherson, R. I.: "Acquired" congenital diaphragmatic hernia, J. Pediatr. Surg. **12**(5):657, 1977.

Wohl, M. E., et al.: The lung following repair of congenital diaphragmatic hernia, J. Pediatr. **90**(3):405, 1977.

Chapter 18

Apnea of the premature infant

Pattiann Yost Schmitt

Abramson[1] defines apnea as "the absence of respiration from any cause." It was noted by Babson and associates[3] that 30% of infants born after less than 30 weeks' gestation and weighing less than 1750 gm at birth exhibited apneic periods. In the same study it was of significant value that nearly all the infants born after less than 30 weeks' gestation displayed apneic spells.[3]

Of the various respiratory distress syndromes, apnea is a common and outstanding symptom. There are various theories that relate probable causes, but not one can fully explain this phenomenon. However, the obvious correlation between apnea, hypoxemia, and neurological damage prompts researchers to study apnea in the neonate in further depth.[27]

This chapter will review the suggested pathophysiology relating to neonatal apnea, the associated causes, and the diagnosis and treatment being currently used by the collaborative health care team. In addition, a protocol of nursing care for the apneic premature infant with supportive scientific rationale will be provided as a foundation for nursing practice.

BREATHING PATTERNS OF THE NEONATE

Respiratory irregularity in breathing patterns of full-term newborns is a common finding.[4,27] Behrman[4] cites several causes of respiratory irregularities that are normal occurrences while the newborn tries to adapt to an extrauterine state. Such causes are gas trapping related to the gradual disappearance of lung fluid, mismatching or both ventilation and perfu-

sion, and intracardiac and pulmonary right-to-left shunting leaving areas of the lung poorly perfused.[27]

According to Behrman,[4] establishment of lung function at birth is directly related to gestational age. Correspondingly, as the weight and age of the infant lower, the respiratory irregularity becomes more pronounced.[27]

The sleeping infant has been observed to first breathe rapidly then slowly. The premature infant has been observed to vary his respirations from regular in rhythm to chaotic and without a definite pattern.[27]

There has been a documented irregular pattern of respiration that has been noted to be a nonpathological condition of healthy premature infants called periodic breathing. Avery[2] has stated criteria under which an infant can be seen to have periodic breathing as follows:

1. Periodic breathing usually occurs in well premature infants more than 24 hours of age.
2. The respiratory pattern is cyclic. Periods of regular breathing for 10 to 15 seconds are followed by periods of no breathing for 10 to 15 seconds.
3. There is no cyanosis, and no change in heart rate is evident.
4. The average respiratory rate is approximately 30 to 40/min.
5. The most striking characteristic is a marked change in frequency of periodic breathing with increase of gestational age. (That is, periodic breathing is more frequent the more immature the baby and becomes dramtically less frequent after 36 weeks' gestational age.)

This pattern of apneic pauses (10 to 20 seconds) followed by rapid respirations that are followed by another apneic pause is not correlated with bradycardia during apneic spells. There are no noted color changes such as circumoral cyanosis.[27,29] Several researchers have investigated this pattern of respiration. Of worth noting is the study by Rigatto and Brady[25] on periodic breathing and apnea in preterm infants; their data confirm the hypothesis that periodic breathing may be due to a depressed respiratory system. Of significance in their study to this protocol is the statistical validity that hypoxia (by whatever cause) precipitated infants to hypoventilate and establish a respiratory acid-base aberration. Through this study it was found that the major defect in this respiratory pattern (periodic breathing) was not a problem with the lungs or peripheral chemoreceptors but a deficiency in the central chemoreceptors (or respiratory center).[25]

It has also been observed that periodic breathing is more common in infants during REM (rapid eye movement) sleep.[2,27] In premature infants 90% of their sleep is REM sleep, while 50% of full-term infants' sleep is known to be REM sleep. Adults have only 20% REM sleep. According to research, REM sleep is a primitive form of sleep related to inadequate development and maturity of the reticular formation.[21]

APNEIC SPELLS IN THE PREMATURE INFANT

Concerned with the possible correlation of frequent apneic spells in the neonatal period and concurrent brain injury, Avery[2] has also described characteristics of the premature infant with apnea.

1. Periods of apnea of more than 20 seconds and/or those accompanied by bradycardia less than 100/min and cyanosis are termed apneic spells.
2. Bradycardia and cyanosis are followed by hypotonia and unresponsiveness, the former occurring in most premature infants after 20 seconds and the latter after 45 seconds; the smaller the infant the shorter the time periods.
3. Avery cites Daily and associates[9] by stating that with prolonged monitoring at least 25% of the premature babies in intensive care demonstrate such spells occurring only in conjunction with periodic breathing.

In a study by Daily and associates,[9] the respiratory patterns of 22 premature infants were observed, and it was found that apnea consisting of 30 seconds or longer occurred in 25% of these 22 infants in the first 10 days of life. Bradycardia (less than 100 beats/min) ensued within 30 seconds or less after the onset of apnea. Also, Daily and associates[9] noted that all apneic episodes occurred during expiration while the premature infant was experiencing periodic breathing. Heart rate falls were most dramatic during these times of apnea, and the more quickly the fall in heart rate, the more vigorous the means of stimulation that was needed to end the apneic episode.

PATHOPHYSIOLOGY

In reviewing the current literature concerning apnea of the premature neonate, it was noted that the pathogenesis of apnea is not clearly defined. Several theories have been studied by researchers to suggest the possible causative relationships, but central to most of the theories is the structure and function of the respiratory center and its complexities.

The "respiratory center" is a group of neurons located bilaterally in the reticular substance of the medulla oblongata and pons in the brain stem.[13,15] According to Guyton,[13] the respiratory center is divided into three major areas:

1. Medullary rhythmicity area
2. Apneustic area
3. Pneumotaxic area

The medullary rhythmicity area (also known as the medullary respiratory center) is located beneath the lower part of the fourth ventricle in the medulla of the brain stem.[13,15] Within this center are neurons that discharge during inspiration and expiration. It is within the medullary respiratory center that the rhythm of respiration is established.[13,15,29] It alone is responsive to carbon dioxide levels in the blood. Increased CO_2 (carbon dioxide) will result in increased respiration, and decreased CO_2 produces decreased respiration.[15] However, the medullary respiratory center is not able to produce a smooth pattern of respiration when functioning singularly.[13,15,29]

The apneustic and pneumotaxic areas are located in the reticular substance of the pons, which is located superior to the medulla. These areas are not primarily concerned with rhythmicity of respiration but are related to the frequency of the respiratory response.[13,15,18,29] The exact functions of these centers are unclear, but it is thought that the apneustic center (which is just above the medulla in the pons) is capable of changing the rhythmicity of respiration on stimulation, resulting in such situations as apnea or periodic breathing.[13,29] The pneumotaxic center (superior to the apneustic area) provides a balance by inhibiting impulses to the apneustic center and is able to change the rate of respiration and the ratio of inspiration to expiration.[13,29]

Jacobsen[15] best describes the functions of the apneustic and pneumotaxic areas as follows " . . . these centers (apneustic and pneumotaxic) play onto the medullary respiratory center to determine the respiratory output. The axons from the cells in the medullary reticular center descend to the appropriate spinal cord levels to innervate the diaphragm and the intercostal and associated muscles of respiration." When these three centers, the spinal cord, and cerebral cortex are intact and integrated physiologically, there is normal rhythmical respiration observed.[13,15]

The maturity and functional status of the central nervous system (CNS), state of oxygenation, and acid-base balance are a few of the influences that will affect the integration and functioning of the respiratory center.[18,29] Obviously, any internal influence (CNS immaturity, pH imbalance, hypoxia) or external influence (temperature fluctuations, pain, vasovagal stimulation) that may interfere with the control of respiration in the CNS may contribute to the development of apnea in premature infants.[18,29] Thus an understanding of the control of respiration is essential to the identification of possible underlying causes of apnea.

Avery[2] proposes that "periodic breathing" is a result of the influence of a system that modulates respiration that is not completely developed and mature in the premature infant. Avery[2] also states that: "Periodic breathing results in apneic spells when this vulnerable system is insulted by any provocative factors discussed . . . (i.e., immaturity, pulmonary insufficiency, primary disease of the CNS, and metabolic aberrations)." Daily and associates[9] showed that "apneic episodes greater than 20 seconds duration are always preceded by periodic breathing in preterm infants, which suggests that in these infants, low O_2 tension may lead to apnea."

Rigatto and Brady[26] support Daily's hypothesis by the findings that suggest "preterm infants breathing periodically hypoventilate" and suggest that "hypoxia may be the primary event leading to periodic breathing."

DIFFERENTIAL DIAGNOSIS

Several factors that must be considered when attempts are made to reveal the cause of apnea of the premature are listed below:

  I. Immaturity of CNS
      A. Prematurity
      B. Congenital syndromes
      C. Biogenic amines
 II. Thermoregulatory fluctuations
III. Vasovagal responses and hyperactive reflexes
 IV. Hypoxia depressing the CNS
      A. Respiratory distress syndrome, hyaline membrane disease
      B. Patent ductus arteriosus
      C. Pulmonary infection (pneumonia)
      D. Airway obstruction (aspiration)
      E. Respiratory acidosis
  V. Metabolic aberrations depressing the CNS
      A. Hypoglycemia
      B. Hypocalcemia
      C. Metabolic acidosis
      D. Sepsis
 VI. Anemia
VII. CNS disorders and diseases
      A. Seizure activity
      B. Hypoxic/ischemic encephalopathy
      C. Cerebral contusion
      D. Intracranial hemorrhage
      E. Passive drug addiction

CNS immaturity

As stated earlier in a study by Babson and associates,[3] it was reported that nearly all neonates born after less than 30 weeks' gestation displayed apneic spells. Of those neonates born after 32 weeks' gestation and weighing less than 1750 gm, 30% exhibited apneic spells. Avery[2] says "extreme immaturity per se is the most common association of severe apnea spells."

Therefore the premature infant born with an immature nervous system and frequently with respiratory problems has a strong tendency to exhibit apnea from inadequate intrauterine gestation. The stress of adaptation to extrauterine life, with the combined inadequacies of immaturity, leads to potential apneic spells.

Along with immaturity of the central nervous system owing to premature birth, a new congenital syndrome characterized by the simultaneous failure of control of ventilation (Ondine's curse) and intestinal motility (Hirschsprung's disease) has been reported by Haddad.[14] In his study, three infant deaths were reported (two of whom were siblings) after rigorous medical interventions were made to reverse the respiratory failure. Postmortem studies of these infants did not reveal anatomical defects, although Haddad postulated that serotonergic neurons were responsible for the new syndrome.[14]

Also of interest when speaking of immaturity of systems and the premature infant is the phenomenon of decreased concentrations of urinary catecholamines, dopamine, norepinephrine, and epinephrine in apneic infants. Kattwinkel[18] relates the clinical findings of infants with decreased urinary catecholamine levels to adults with dysautonomia or animals given an alpha blocking agent. It was apparent through his study of neonatal apnea that there was some part of adrenergic blockade in these infants in that they had difficulty maintaining blood pressure through lack of vasoconstriction, difficulty maintaining cerebral blood flow, and resultant respiratory irregularities during periods of hypoxia.[18]

Hypoxemia

"There happens to be a direct relationship between hypoxemia and periodic breathing or apnea."[21]

Hypoxemia is defined as reduced oxygen in the arterial blood.[13] Consequently, there is a diminished amount of oxygen delivered to the cells of the body.

To fully understand the paradoxical response the premature infant has to hypoxia, it is first necessary to review the normal physiological response of man to hypoxia.

According to Guyton,[13] the goal of respiration is to control and balance the concentrations of oxygen (O_2), carbon dioxide (CO_2), and hydrogen ions (pH) in the body fluids. Accordingly, any change in the concentration of oxygen, carbon dioxide, or hydrogen ions results in a change in respiratory activity.

Carbon dioxide and hydrogen ion changes will be registered by the respiratory center mainly, but changes in oxygen will be almost entirely detected by the peripheral chemoreceptors that will then stimulate the respiratory center.[13] These peripheral chemoreceptors will be the responsive sites in man to a hypoxic state. They are located outside the central nervous system in the large arteries of the thorax and neck. Most of the chemoreceptors are located in the carotid and aortic bodies along with their afferent nerve connectors to the respiratory center. According to Guyton,[13] "The carotid bodies are located bilaterally in the bifurcations of the common carotid arteries, and their afferent nerve fibers pass through Hering's nerve to the glossopharyngeal nerves and then to the medulla. The aortic bodies are located along the arch of the aorta; their afferent nerve fibers pass to the medulla through the vagus nerve."

When changes occur in the arterial concentration of oxygen, the chemoreceptors are stimulated and the rate of afferent nerve impulse transmission from the carotid and aortic bodies is increased to the respiratory center. When the respiratory center is stimulated, there is an increase of alveolar ventilation and a consequent increase in respiratory rate to raise the concentration of available oxygen. When the level of arterial oxygen concentration is increased, the chemoreceptors' detection of a hypoxic state is reversed, and the corresponding stimulation of the afferent pathways to the respiratory center is diminished. Consequently, the respiratory rate will then return to normal rhythm and rate through this feedback mechanism.[13]

Brady and Ceruti[8] studied newborn infants and found a surprising ventilatory response to hypoxia. Initially, the infant would have a brief increase in respiratory rate in response to the hypoxic state followed by periodic breathing, respiratory depression, and occasionally apnea. Infants over 18 days of age in this study showed an increase in ventilatory rate in response to hypoxia, not a decrease as exhibited by the newborn.

This resultant hypoventilatory response to hypoxia by infants periodically breathing was also reported by Rigatto and Brady.[25] However, the statistical data from this study suggest that the major cause of this response was not in the lung at the peripheral chemoreceptor level but at the respiratory center.

The response of the premature infant to hypoxia contrasted to the response of the adult is indeed paradoxical, and the underlying cause of such a phenomenon is still under scrutiny.

In overview, any disorder that would contribute to hypoxemia could be associated with apnea of the premature infant. Such conditions as persistent fetal circulation, patent ductus arteriosus (PDA), respiratory distress syndrome, pneumonia, hyaline membrane disease, or any disorder that would be associated with airway obstruction (aspiration syndrome) are cited to cause hypoxia leading to CNS depression.[18,21,29]

Hypercapnia

It would be only appropriate now to speak to the response of the premature infant to a high arterial carbon dioxide level. Again, a short review of normal physiology is necessitated.

According to Guyton,[13] the respiratory center is stimulated by an increase in the concentration of carbon dioxide or hydrogen ions in the fluids of the medulla. His studies show that increases in arterial levels of carbon dioxide alone can increase the rate of alveolar ventilation by six or seven times. The same response of increased ventilation will occur with increased hydrogen ion concentration (a lowered pH) alone, but it was noted that the carbon dioxide effect on the respiratory center is much stronger.

At a certain threshold of P_{CO_2} breathing is initiated; therefore, P_{CO_2} is considered important to the control and stimulus of respiration.[13,21] As the level of P_{CO_2} increases, the rate of respiration increases.[13,21] Studies have indicated that infants with periodic breathing hypoventilate and consequently have higher P_{CO_2} levels.[4,8,21,26] These infants with periodic breathing need a higher concentration of P_{CO_2} in the arterial blood to initiate breathing from the respiratory center.[21,25] Thus the threshold to stimulate respiration for these infants is higher. As gestational age increases, the response to hypercapnia increases and the frequency of periodic breathing decreases.[2,25] Rigatoo and Brady[25] thus felt that the major defect in the ventilatory response of premature infants was located in the central receptors in the respiratory center.

Metabolic disorders

Although the previous discussion has been related to apnea and the immature responses by the systems of a premature infant, it is also crucial to assess other conditions such as hypoglycemia, hypocal-cemia, and metabolic acidosis that may provoke apneic spells.

Hypoglycemia. Hypoglycemia is a prevalent disorder among preterm infants and especially those with intrauterine growth retardation.[3] Babson[3] states that 5% to 10% of low birth weight infants have hypoglycemia owing to insufficient glycogen and fat stores. This decreased rate of entry of glucose into the bloodstream makes physiological homeostasis increasingly more difficult for the premature infant. Concurrently, an apneic spell itself causes an increased rate of removal of blood glucose causing further problems with hypoglycemia.[3] Consequently, metabolic aberration is thought to depress the respiratory center, thereby decreasing cortical afferent activity to the center.[18] Thus, apnea, cyanosis, and listlessness become apparent clinical symptoms with hypoglycemic states.

Hypocalcemia. Hypocalcemia has also been detected by researchers to be a provocative factor of apnea.[3,18,21,29] Bolognese[16] states that neonatal hypocalcemia can be noted to occur in 26% to 50% of preterm infants. Babson[3] further supports this statement by concluding that 30% of preterm infants weighing less than 2000 gm at birth will have hypocalcemia.

All newborns are born with a degree of hypoparathyroidism caused by the suppressed function of the fetal parathyroid owing to the transferred maternal parathyroid hormone.[3,6] In normal newborns the function of the parathyroid gland improves in time. In the preterm infant this physiological state is compounded by the fact that this neonate has not received the intrauterine calcium accumulation that is normally occurring at term from the mother, thus rendering the infant calcium deficient.[6]

Another factor compounding neonatal hypocalcemia is the normal decreased physiological response of phosphorus excretion by the newborn renal system.[6] Again, this state is eventually reversed in the normal newborn in time, but the preterm infant compounds the hypocalcemic state by having a continual buildup of phosphorus levels in the blood. Without adequate excretion of phosphorus through the kidneys, a hyperphosphoremic state ensues, which causes further depression of serum calcium levels by stressing the subnormal states of the parathyroid gland.[3]

This metabolic aberration could be another provoking factor of apnea since the clinical symptoms are relevant to CNS disturbances such as twitching hypertonia, seizures that may lead to an anoxic state.[3,6]

Acidosis. In reference to metabolic imbalances, acidosis is another factor to consider when assessing the etiology of apnea. Metabolic acidosis is caused most often by a hypoxic state and a resultant lactic acid accumulation from anaerobic metabolism.

Bolognese[6] states: "Fetuses with a premature respiratory acidosis (high P_{CO_2}, near normal base deficit, moderate fall in pH) usually respond very well as neonates. Those with combined respiratory and metabolic acidosis and large base deficits recover much more slowly. The neonate achieves acid-base stability primarily by pulmonary excretion of carbon dioxide. Renal mechanisms for handling hydrogen ions are incompletely developed in the newborn."

With a metabolic acidemia, the pH is lowered enough to cause increased pulmonary vascular resistance, leading to decreased blood flow through the lungs, decreased exchange of O_2 and CO_2 at the alveoli, and a disruption in cell metabolism. Consequently, a pending problem with inadequate O_2-CO_2 exchange causes CNS disruptions and irregularities in the respiratory center.[6,13]

Sepsis

Another factor known to be associated with apneic attack is sepsis. Kattwinkle[18] feels sepsis also depresses the respiratory center by decreasing cortical afferent traffic to the respiratory center just as the preceding metabolic causes did.

According to Kleiman,[20] some clinical signs of neonatal bacterial sepsis include "not doing well," abnormal temperature findings, hypoglycemia, hyperglycemia, bradycardia, cyanosis, and apnea.

Anemia

Anemia can be associated with apneic spells.[2,18,29] Decreased oxygen-carrying capacity of the hemoglobin and decreased total blood volume can contribute to poor cardiovascular system perfusion and resultant respiratory center irregularities.

In the oxygen dissociation curve of normal adult blood, the P_{50} (the oxygen tension at 50% oxygen saturation) is 27 mm Hg.[13] The fetal hemoglobin dissociation curve is shifted to the left of the normal adult curve,[2,29] which means that fetal hemoglobin has a greater affinity for oxygen than does adult hemoglobin.[2,29] Also fetal hemoglobin requires lower O_2 tension to release oxygen to the cells of the body.[2,29] This fetal oxygen dissociation response is of crucial importance, especially in conditions of hypoxia and the possibility that the respiratory center of the infant may be less sensitive to a lowered oxygen level. Thus, prolonged apnea may result.[2,29]

Thermoregulation

In the premature infant, maintenance of a homeostatic temperature is impaired.[2,3,18] Babson[3] cites the large surface area and the paucity of subcutaneous tissues (including decreased metabolic response to cooling and limited ability to sweat and/or shiver) as the contributing causes of deficient thermoregulation.

There are studies supporting that either hyperthermia or hypothermia can cause an increase in metabolic rate and oxygen consumption, resulting in an increase in apneic attacks. Daily and associates[9] report an increased incidence of apnea in premature infants exposed to higher environmental temperatures.

According to Kattwinkle,[18] apnea that is increased by a warm or cool environment is an example of the influence of decreased afferent input by the sensory thermal receptors to the CNS, thus causing a modification in respiratory status.

Perlstein and associates[24] also supported these findings when they studied the responses of premature neonates to sudden increases in incubator air temperature. They also found apnea and higher temperatures to be significantly related.

Babson[3] states that an increase in metabolic rate, an increase in O_2 requirements, an increase in acidosis and hypoxia, a rise in free fatty acids in the blood, and a reduction in glucose are correlates to vasoconstriction and hypothermia.

Obviously, a neutral thermal environment is necessary to minimize the metabolic and oxygen demands of the premature infant and to decrease the chances of apneic attacks.

Vasovagal responses

By citing several investigative studies, Kattwinkle[18] describes abnormal and hyperactive reflexes that have been demonstrated to cause apnea in the early neonatal period. Cardiac arrhythmias and apnea can result from deep suctioning and stimulation of the posterior pharynx. Gasp and apnea, following full lung inflation, are significant findings in the first few days of life.

Laryngeal taste receptors that are innervated through the superior laryngeal nerves can cause apnea in response to various chemical stimuli such as glucose, sterile water, and cow's milk. Of interest is that saline, amniotic fluid, or sheep milk will not produce apnea. Nipple feedings that stimulate the sucking reflex have also been shown to cause bradycardia and apnea.[18]

CNS diseases and disorders

Along with CNS immaturity, CNS depression from inadequate oxygenation or metabolic balance decreases afferent stimulation to the CNS diseases and disorders that, standing alone, can precipitate apneic attacks.

Seizures are cited by Avery[2] as an infrequent but often dramatic occurrence in the neonatal period. The etiology of neonatal seizures is diverse and can be related to many associated factors.[21] Of basic importance is the understanding that the characteristics of the seizure patterns of the neonate depend on the neuroanatomical and neurophysiological development of the CNS.[2] Avery[2] states that, unlike infants, newborns rarely have well-defined, generalized, tonic-clonic seizures and prematures have even less organized spells. The differences between infant, newborn, and premature seizure activity is directly related to the developmental state of the nervous system.[2]

The seizure activity of the premature infant is defined by Avery[2] as "subtle," with such characteristics of tonic horizontal ± jerking of the eyes, repetitive blinking or fluttering of the eyes, drooling, sucking, other oral buccal movements, tonic posturing of limbs, and apnea.

Perinatal complications that could cause subtle seizure activity and apnea in the premature neonate are hypoxic-ischemic encephalopathy of birth, asphyxia, cerebral contusion associated with obstetrical trauma, and intracranial hemorrhage.[21] Metabolic disturbances such as hypoglycemia, hypocalcemia, and hypomagnesemia have been documented as related to seizures. Of worth mentioning are additional hyponatremic and hypernatremic states,

pyridoxine deficiency, hyperbilirubinemia, and amino acid withdrawal. Of the infectious causes of seizure activity, Avery[2] cites bacterial meningitis as the underlying cause in two thirds of the cases. Correspondingly the passive addiction of neonates to narcotics or barbiturates at birth is becoming frequently associated with seizure activity.

DIAGNOSTIC AND THERAPEUTIC MANAGEMENT OF THE PREMATURE INFANT WITH APNEA

At this point, it seems appropriate to reemphasize the fact that respiratory irregularities of the preterm infant are a frequent occurrence.[4,27] Not all brief respiratory pauses constitute an apneic attack, and differentiation between periodic breathing and apnea must occur. However, most researchers state that bradycardia (less than 100 beats/min) and/or cyanosis associated with cessation of breathing for more than 15 seconds should be considered apnea. Therefore, this condition requires simultaneous diagnostic and therapeutic intervention.

Diagnostic management

Management of the apneic premature neonate becomes as varied as the many postulated theoretical bases and the associated causes. Once the first apneic attack has occurred, the neonate needs prompt evaluation for the etiological causes. Early assessment of bradycardia, cyanosis, and hypoxia resulting from an apneic attack must occur.*

Neonatal response to cutaneous stimulation (increased afferent input to CNS) during the apneic period must be critically evaluated.[18,29] An assessment of the thermoregulatory status of the neonate and environment should be instituted in light of decreased afferent input into the CNS.[2,3,6,18,29]

Vasovagal responses to suctioning, stimulation of posterior pharynx, hyperinflation of the lungs, stimulation of sucking reflexes, and responses to chemical stimuli through the laryngeal receptors also need to be considered as hyperactive responses ascending to the CNS.[18]

Of prime consideration should be hypoxic states that depress the CNS. Such hypoxemia can be associated with respiratory distress syndrome, hyaline membrane disease (HMD), pulmonary infection,

---

*See references 2, 3, 6, 18, 21, and 29.

patent ductus arteriosus (PDA), airway obstruction, and/or respiratory or metabolic acidosis.[2-4,18,29]

Concurrently, an evaluation of metabolic homeostasis should be made. Metabolic depression of CNS functioning is related to hypoglycemia, hypocalcemia, sepsis, and metabolic acidosis.[2,3,18,29]

An investigative approach to the hematological system should be made for the assessment of anemia, hypovolemia, and oxygen-carrying capacity as a potential underlying disorder cuasing inadequate CNS perfusion and oxygenation.[2,3,18,29]

Accordingly, seizure activity may be of concern with an apneic neonate. Primary CNS disorders such as hypoxic-ischemic encephalopathy from birth asphyxia, cerebral contusions associated with obstetrical trauma, and intracranial hemorrhage may present from underlying causes initiating apneic attacks.[2,15,18]

After such assessments are made for possible etiological causes, treatment is directed at the underlying disorder.

Therapeutic management

Prevention. In a preventive concern, Kattwinkle[18] feels that all neonates with birth weights under 1800 gm should be placed on apnea monitors for at least 10 days. Kattwinkle cites Daily and associates[9] as his supportive rationale. Daily and associates documented 25% of premature infants will have at least one apneic spell in the first 10 days of life.[18] Monitoring the heart rate only may be sufficient, since bradycardia follows apnea in most cases. Some infants though may have a fixed heart rate during apneic spells; they require apnea monitoring.[3] Daily and associates[9] also documented the clinical need for respiratory monitoring and the initiation of appropriate nursing interventions and consequential aversion of CNS damage.[9] A suggested treatment protocol for apnea in the premature infant follows:[18]

  I. Diagnose and treat precipitating cause (for example, respiratory disease, hypotension, sepsis, anemia, hypoglycemia).
 II. Decrease environmental temperature to low neutral thermal environment.
III. Initiate stimulation.
    A. Cutaneous
    B. Vestibular (oscillating water bed)

  IV. Start low-pressure nasal CPAP.
   V. Administer theophylline.
  VI. Mechanical ventilation (seldom necessary).

Cutaneous stimulation

According to Maiels,[21] 40% of premature infants with apnea will not require therapy, another 55% will respond to cutaneous stimulation, and another 5% to 10% will require further treatment.

Provision of gentle sensory stimulation is often the primary nursing intervention used to stimulate respirations.[29] By rubbing the back, stroking the legs, and repositioning with a slightly extended neck, diffuse cutaneous stimulation can be provided to the respiratory center through afferent pathways. Other measures noted to increase the input of afferent stimulation are oscillating water beds and rocking beds that stimulate the vestibular nerve and proprioreceptors.[15,18,29]

Thermoregulation

In a study by Daily and associates[9] it was noted that the incidence of apnea increased significantly when premature neonates were exposed to higher environmental temperatures. Avery[2] also cites that hypothermic environments can precipitate apneic attacks. Provisions must be made, therefore, to control and stabilize the premature's core temperature and environmental temperature within a neutral thermal zone of 36.3° to 36.5° C.[2,3,18,29]

To minimize metabolic requirements and oxygen consumption, ambient air temperature should be set 1.5° C warmer than the infant's abdominal skin temperature. Recording skin temperature every 15 to 30 minutes in this environment until the premature infant has reached a core thermal temperature of 36.3° to 36.5° C is an important nursing measure.[29]

Thermal control of premature infants is medically managed with isolettes equipped with a servo-control apparatus and with careful observation of ambient and core temperature by all members of the collaborative health team.

Avoidance of vasovagal responses and hyperactive reflexes

In maintenance of the premature infant with apnea, careful avoidance of vasovagal responses and hyperactive reflexes should be observed. As mentioned previously, certain vasovagal and hyperactive reflex actions have been associated with apnea as cited by Kattwinkle.[18] Vigorous catheter suctioning that stimulates the posterior pharynx and nipple feedings stimulating the sucking reflex are associated with bradycardia and apneic spells.[18,29]

Infants who are resuscitated with bag and mask for prolonged apnea must be treated cautiously. Overinflation of the lungs and the use of excessive oxygen concentrations with the AMBU bag subject the premature infant to respiratory alkalosis and acute hypoxia, which will suppress the respiratory drive.[13,18,29]

Lastly, there has been evidence that the trigeminal area of the face that has a sensitivity to heat and cold can cause apnea on stimulation of the trigeminal nerve.[18] Such situations could be caused by a cool mist in an oxygen hood flowing across the face of a premature infant. Oxygen hoods need to be adjusted to a neutral thermal environment just as the isolette to prevent cold or warm stimulation associated with apneic spells.[18]

Hypoxia

After diagnostic measures have been employed to assess the potential hypoxic state associated with an apneic attack, the medical treatment for reversal of a low arterial oxygen concentration should be instituted.

Apnea that has been found to be associated with primary respiratory causes can be managed well with oxygen therapy and proper treatment for the pulmonary disorder involved.[18,29] Increasing the FIO_2 (forced inspired oxygen), AMBU bagging, utilizing continuous positive airway pressure (CPAP), and implementing total ventilatory support are measures cited by many researchers to be effective in alleviating apneic episodes and increasing levels of arterial oxygen.*

Rigatto and Brady[25] studied apnea in premature infants and found hypoxia as the primary event leading to hypoventilation, periodic breathing, and apnea. These findings helped support the thought that hypoxia renders the respiratory control system unstable and unable to reverse its hypoxic state. It was this study that proposed that small and careful

increases in inspired oxygen are warranted to prevent periodic breathing and apnea.[25]

Maiels[21] states, "All premature infants should have a bag and mask available at the bedside." It is important to note here that 100% oxygen is not used on apneic infants; 100% oxygen concentration is closely correlated with retrolental fibroplasia as well as atelectasis.[6] Accordingly, an acute case of hyperoxia will decrease the respiratory stimulus through elimination of the chemoreceptor drive.[13] Bagging should be instituted with oxygen concentrations similar to the levels the infants were breathing before the attack.[3,21,25]

When it becomes impossible to compromise between a minimal FIO_2 and an acceptable Po_2, CPAP (constant positive airway pressure) of 3 to 5 cm of water pressure delivered through the airway with nasal prongs may be instituted by medical management.[27] A decreased functional residual capacity of the lung (decreased lung volume) and an increasing intrapulmonary shunt could be related to the preterm infant with apnea.[27] With successful utilization of CPAP, oxygenation is improved through a functional residual capacity, right-to-left shunting is decreased, and the development of persistent fetal circulation might be prevented.[18,27,29]

Aminophylline therapy

Of recent interest is the medical management of apneic spells with the administration of aminophylline (theophylline). To fully understand the effect theophylline has on the CNS of the premature neonate, a brief review of pharmacological actions is necessary.

Caffeine, theophylline, and theobromine are methylated xanthines. Xanthine is itself dioxypurine and is structurally related to uric acid. The methylated xanthines stimulate the CNS, act on the kidney to produce diuresis, stimulate cardiac muscle, and relax smooth muscles (such as bronchial muscles). Each of the xanthines has a different intensity of action on the previously mentioned structures. Theophylline has specific effects as a respiratory stimulant, whereas caffeine is a powerful CNS stimulant.*

Theophylline is reported to work by inhibiting cellular phosphodiesterases, which are inhibitors of

---

*See references 2, 3, 4, 6, 9, 18, and 26.

*See references 7, 10, 12, 18, 21, 23, and 27.

cyclic AMP activity. Cyclic AMP has the effect of stimulating the respiratory center; with the administration of theophylline and resultant inhibition of phosphodiesterases, cyclic AMP becomes stronger in stimulating the respiratory center.[7,10]

Theophylline therapy can also stimulate other systems of the body, but the observable effects involve the CNS and circulatory systems. Such symptoms as tachycardia, vomiting, restlessness, jitteriness, and seizures are clinical signs of the toxic effects of this alkaloid.[10,21]

Recently, theophylline has been used to treat neonatal apnea of prematurity. Several studies have supported the rationale that theophylline has a definite central stimulating effect. Of significance is a study by Gerhardt and associates[12] that noted a decreased incidence of apneic episodes from 29.7 to 4.4 per day. Dietrich and associates[10] also reported a decrease in the incidence of apneic episodes in the nine premature infants studied, along with increased wakefulness and amount of active (REM) sleep. Peabody and associates[23] documented that serum levels of theophylline of 5 to 15 μg/ml decreased apneic attacks and their adverse effects, including hypoxemia, bradycardia, and iatrogenic hyperoxemia.

All researchers agreed that periodic checks of serum theophylline levels are necessary. (The toxic level occurs at 13 to 14 μg/ml).[10,12,23] Of biochemical interest to this study are the findings by Bory and associates[7] that confirmed the effectiveness of theophylline in the treatment of apnea in the newborn. This case history by Bory and associates concluded that the biotransformation of aminophylline in adults and neonates differs widely. In adults, the major metabolic process involves demethylation oxidation to monomethylxanthines and methyl uric acids from theophylline. Bory and associates[7] found two premature infants' metabolites from aminophylline to be caffeine, owing to a deficiency in N-demethylation and C-oxidation of the drug.

This finding is truly significant in the utilization of theophylline in premature infants who may have potential deficits of N-demethylation and C-oxidation. Therefore the actions of theophylline in premature infants should account for the potential effects contributed by caffeine concentrations in the plasma. Bory and associates[7] suggest that both theophylline and caffeine serum levels be measured while aminophylline is administered to a premature infant.

If apnea continues to ensue with CPAP and theophylline therapy, full ventilatory assistance will be considered with the instillation of a nasotracheal tube and support of a respirator. With total ventilatory support, adequate oxygenation with a low FIO_2 can be attained with constant negative extending pressure (CNEP) by applying this continual negative pressure to the airway. This means of support may open up atelectatic alveoli, thus removing shunting from this cause and distending the patent alveoli creating a larger area for O_2-CO_2 diffusion.[3,27]

Anemia

If clinical and diagnostic findings document the diagnosis of anemia, the usual treatment is blood transfusions.[2,3,29] By increasing the oxygen-carrying capacity of the blood, the transfusion of adult hemoglobin will provide release of oxygen to tissues at higher oxygen tensions.[13,29]

Hypoxia secondary to anemia can be prevented by careful observation of blood loss (that is, frequent serum tests) and frequent evaluation of the hematocrit and hemoglobin results.[3,29]

Metabolic aberrations

Metabolic aberrations such as hypoglycemia and hypocalcemia that are associated with apnea can be easily assessed and corrected to prevent or reverse apneic spells.

After an episode of apnea, immediate assessment of the premature neonate needs to be initiated. Dextrostix should be ascertained as an immediate reflection of the glucose level in the blood. If the Dextrostix shows barely perceptible blue coloration (indicating a level below or around 25 mg/dl), confirm this result by obtaining a serum blood glucose.[29]

Medical management of hypoglycemia from the related causes discussed earlier in differential diagnosis usually involves parenteral administration of 10% to 25% glucose solutions under careful titration and control with infusion pumps. Administration of the hypertonic solution is based on neonatal weight in kilogram per milliliter of glucose infused. Of importance here is to note that reduction of the intravenous glucose solution after the appropriate serum levels have been obtained must be done gradually to prevent a hypoglycemic reaction.[2,3,6,29]

At the time an apneic attack occurs, blood determination of calcium, phosphorus, and sodium should be ascertained. Hypocalcemia, hyperphosphoremia, and hyper- or hyponatremia are known to precipitate apneic attacks in the premature infant.* Treatment of hypocalcemia can be approached parenterally or orally, depending on the symptomatology of the neonate, which may be a continual requirement for several days. Calcium gluconate is administered intravenously, while calcium lactate may be given orally. Gradual discontinuance of this drug is suggested.[2,3,6]

As a preventive measure, high-risk neonates are frequently given calcium gluconate along with the intravenous dextrose solution. Secondary to the subnormal or absence of parathyroid function and decreased calcium levels of the premature neonate, prophylactic calcium may be added to intravenous fluids to lessen the incidence of hypocalcemia-related apneic attacks.[3]

Hyponatremia consisting of a decreased serum sodium can cause damage to the CNS owing to an increase in brain volume with interstitial edema.[2] A neonate with severe respiratory distress syndrome owing to inappropriate secretion of antidiuretic hormone (ADH) has a strong potential to develop hyponatremia and concurrent apneic episodes.[4] Treatment of this state could involve intravenous administration of sodium in milliequivalents equal to 60% times the kilograms of body weight times the milliequivalents of serum sodium deficit below 135 mEq/L.[3]

Conversely, hypernatremic states are also dangerous owing to the shift of water away from the brain (since sodium does not cross into the CNS). Dilatation and rupture of capillaries in the brain occur when pressure differences are detected because of the fluid shift. Treatment includes measures to reduce serum sodium values.[3,6]

Sepsis

Once the diagnosis of a neonatal infection has been made, immediate treatment should begin. According to Kleinman,[20] "the most important aid in establishing the diagnosis of neonatal sepsis is to consider the diagnosis early." Clinical symptomatology and the array of laboratory tests useful in

*See references 2, 3, 4, 14, 18, 21, and 29.

diagnosis are important basic steps to be carried out before the correct therapy can begin. Treatment for suspected bacterial sepsis with antibiotics is relevant to which organism is responsible for the infection. Kanamycin and penicillin or ampicillin are considered by Kleinman to be the most effective broad-spectrum therapy to treat a suspected infectious process and prevent fatality.[20]

If temperature fluctuations become a clinical symptom, measures to attain a neutral thermal zone need to be instituted owing to the sensitivity of the premature infant's thermal receptors to the CNS, increased metabolic demands, and increased oxygen consumption.[2,8,18]

Metabolic acidosis

Metabolic acidosis is an imbalance of excess hydrogen ions potentially caused by cellular hypoxia or energy starvation (hypoglycemia) with production of lactic acid and other glycolytic by-products.[2,13] Newborns and especially premature neonates are vulnerable to an acidemia because of their limited ability to excrete hydrogen ions by the fetal renal system.[2-4] This problem is treated by giving alkali support with sodium bicarbonate to neutralize acids in the blood and those released from new bone formation that the immature kidney is unable to excrete.[2,3,18]

Those infants who remain acidotic have difficulty gaining weight, become lethargic, and develop frequent and severe apneic attacks. Treatment of metabolic acidosis includes supplementing intravenous therapy or oral feedings with adequate amounts of sodium bicarbonate to attain an arterial blood pH of 7.30 to 7.35.[3,6]

Management of CNS disorders

Continuous or frequent seizure activity in a premature infant warrants prompt evaluation of metabolic disorders, CNS disturbances, or meningitis (sepsis).[2,4] Assessment of glucose, calcium, and phosphorus serum levels should be considered when defining an underlying cause of seizure activity. If metabolic homeostasis is achieved but seizure activity continues, determination of a specific etiological diagnosis should be started. If detected, infectious causative agents need prompt attention with antibiotics. Treatment of affected infants with passive addiction to narcotics also necessitates immediate action for the first few days of life. Kattwinkle[18] recommends nalaxone (antagonist) for correction of maternal narcotic overdose.

When considering the etiology of seizure activity in the premature neonate, it becomes necessary to make corollaries between potential hypoxic/ischemic encephalopathy, cerebral contusion, and intracranial hemorrhage from histories of obstetrical trauma and perinatal complications.[18,29] Retrospectively, the most effective form of treatment for such neurological injuries is prevention. Prevention of intrauterine anoxia and hypoxia through careful intrapartal monitoring along with recognition of fetal compromise are the most important preventive therapies.[2,3,18] Prompt attention for the asphyxiated newborn with supportive ventilation, body temperature maintenance, circulatory collapse treatment, and glucose and bicarbonate administration appropriately is essential for proper resuscitation of the compromised fetus.[16]

After the initial insult and assessment of the result and symptomatology, treatment will be concerned with the clinical symptoms. Hypoxic/ischemic encephalopathy and intracranial hemorrhage are treated most often with phenytoin (Dilantin) and phenobarbital to control seizure activity and minimize oxygen demands of the hypoxic cerebral tissue.[2] Treatment of cerebral edema with steroid therapy (dexamethasone) may be indicated in inflammatory reactions to cerebral insult.[2] Optimum oxygen arterial levels are hoped to be maintained, but with increased intracranial pressure and hypoxic tissues of the cerebral area, there is no guarantee that hypoxia of the brain tissue will ever be reversed or capable of receiving adequate oxygenation.[2,4]

COMPLICATIONS OF APNEA

The outstanding complication of apnea in the premature neonate is the high potential for neurological insult.* There may not be one general theory that all researchers can agree on as the etiological basis for apnea in the premature infant, but it can be said that there is universal agreement among researchers that prolonged apneic spells in the neonatal period complicated by hypoxia can be correlated with complications of neurological deficits and damage.[2,18,29]

Not necessarily considered a complication but

---

*See references 2, 4, 8, 9, 18, 21, 25, 26, and 29.

playing an important role in biological and psychosocial environmental stresses of this neonate is the prematurity of birth.[28] Such issues as development of attachment or bonding on the part of the parent and the infant and the separation that occurs with a neonate in a high-risk unit can cause stress within a family unit.[19] Some researchers feel that there are sensitive periods immediately following postpartum that are essential for proper attachment between the newborn and parents, especially between the mother and infant.[17,19,28] Other studies related the influence the newborn has on the mother in caregiving by the type of feedback the infant returns to the caregiver.[19] Premature infants would be severe risks since they are incapable of giving as much feedback as normal newborns.[19]

In a study by Klaus and Kennell,[19] crucial and sensitive periods in which the process of attachment between mother and child may develop were defined as follows:

Planning the pregnancy
Confirming the pregnancy
Fetal movement
Birth
Seeing the baby
Touching the baby
Caretaking

In the event of premature birth that requires separation from the mother for several days or weeks, it could be noted that the actual caretaking of the infant has been transferred to hospital personnel. "Touching the baby may also be a period in jeopardy during the early postpartal period due to fetal-maternal complications."[19]

Along with actual loss of caring for her newborn, maternal reactions to having a premature baby are considered an emotional crisis and involve psychological tasks. Kaplan and Mason[17] define four psychological tasks a mother who gives birth to a premature neonate must complete:

1. Prepare for possible loss (anticipatory grief).
2. Acknowledge and face maternal failure to deliver a full-term infant.
3. Process of relating to the infant.
4. Learn how the premature infant differs from a full-term infant and understand special needs.

Obviously, the resultant mothering behavior of premature infants is a function of each individual mother and her ability to tolerate stress, not only in the hospital environment but later when the high-risk infant will go home.[19]

The use of an apnea monitor to help prevent sudden infant death syndrome (SIDS) is now a common device used in the home environment for up to 1 year.[5] By the signal of the occurrence of a prolonged apneic spell occurring during sleep, parents can have a means to manage and assist the infant with apnea.[5] Concurrently, the parents are faced with the potential of a fatal apneic episode, since the monitor is not a totally perfect mode of treatment. In a study by Black,[5] families believed using the monitor changed their lives significantly, but at the same time they felt that the monitor was an anxiety reducer and well worth the trouble. Community education and awareness concerning life with a child and an apnea monitor could help ease some of the stress.[5]

The prematurity of the neonate, biological and psychological environmental stresses endured by the neonate, mother, and father, as well as separation of infant from the mother with care given by the medical and nursing personnel set up the potential for this premature infant with apnea and a monitor at home to be a vulnerable child. The child is thus at high risk for attachment and later emotional and intellectual development.[27]

PROGNOSIS

Naeye[22] compiled data to define the frequency of the various underlying disorders associated with apnea of the premature neonate. From this study neonates who have repeated apneic episodes lasting longer than 20 seconds have high death rates.

This study has strong prognostic results owing to the sample of 10,965 preterm infants (between 20 and 30 weeks' gestation) and 39,861 term infants (those born after 37 weeks' gestation). Of the preterm infants, 324 had multiple apneic episodes and 125 had a single episode within the first 28 days of life.[22] Of the term infants, 114 had multiple apneic episodes, and 182 had a single recorded episode. Of interest to this study is that of the 324 preterm infants with multiple apnea spells, 58% died in the first month of life. Also, 18% of the 125 preterm infants with a single spell of apnea died.[22]

Naeye[22] found amniotic fluid infection resulting in neonatal pneumonia as the underlying cause of death in 30% of the preterm infants with multiple apneic spells. The next relevant finding of 30% was also related to this group of preterm infants with multiple attacks of hypoxia-related disorders such as abruptio placentae, erythroblastosis fetalis, placenta previa, large placental infarcts, and umbilical cord compression.

Another striking feature of this study concerns the preterm infants with a single episode of apnea. Of these preterm infants, 50% died. All of these were infected infants. In this same group of preterm infants with a single episode of apnea and a hypoxia-related disorder, there was no incidence of perinatal death in noninfected infants.[22]

Such findings direct the necessity to diagnose and treat the underlying disorders of apneic infants. If congenital pneumonia from amniotic fluid infection is present, the risk of perinatal death of the premature infant with apnea is extremely high.[22]

It is obvious that there need to be more investigations on the outcome of early detection and treatment of such congenital infections. Naeye[22] states that congenital pneumonia is oftentimes misdiagnosed or unrecognized in the presence of atelectasis, hyaline membrane disease, and pulmonary hemorrhage.

Another prognosticator associated with fetal mortality is the utilization of a clinical appraisal method (Apgar scoring) at birth. Drage[11] cites Apgar in that the "one-minute Apgar score has proven its value as a predictor of neonatal survival and future neurological damage, but the five-minute scoring appears to have greater value for prognosticating neurologic damage at one year of age." Apgar was cited by Drage[11] to state that infants demonstrating a first Apgar score of 1 have a neonatal death rate inversely proportional to the score of 1.

Drage[11] found neonatal mortality to be 49% with 5-minute Apgar scores of 0 or 1. By correlating low Apgar scores with neurological sequelae, delayed neurological development, motor disorders, and seizures, Drage was able to make significant predictions concerning neonatal mortality and morbidity.

The final question of prognostication is of the determination of a potential quantitative relationship. Further studies need to be done to investigate the variables of severity of insult and the degree of brain damage.

Protocol

Problem □ Premature neonate with periods of apnea lasting longer than 20 seconds and with corresponding bradycardia (less than 100 beats/min), cyanosis, and hypotonia[2]

GOAL: To provide nursing care to the premature infant with apnea by identifying and treating the etiology and underlying causes of apnea

Rationale: To attain early identification of provocative factors and to treat underlying disorders that are associated with apnea in the premature infant that are highly correlated with neurological deficit and damage[2]

DIAGNOSTIC

1. Continually assess the irregular respiratory pattern of the neonate noting the frequency of occurrence, duration in seconds of cessation of respiration, corresponding heart rate changes, cyanosis, and hypotonia of extremities.

   Rationale: To differentiate between apnea and periodic breathing (Respiratory irregularities of the preterm infant are a frequent occurrence.[4,27] Not all respiratory pauses constitute apnea.)

2. Assess the apneic neonate's response to cutaneous stimulation during pauses of respiration.

   Rationale: To understand that 40% of premature infants with apnea will not require therapy and another 55% will respond to cutaneous stimulation[21]

3. Assess the neonate's response to situations producing vasovagal stimulation or causing hyperactive reflexes.

   Rationale: To stimulate certain laryngeal reflexes and posterior pharynx nervous innervation can result in bradycardia and apnea in the premature neonate[18,29]

4. Frequently evaluate the thermoregulatory status of the neonate and his environment.

   Rationale: To prevent hyperthermia or hypothermia, which can precipitate apneic attacks by decreasing the afferent input to the CNS[18]

5. Frequently assess arterial oxygen concentration (PO_2), arterial carbon dioxide concentration (PCO_2), and the hydrogen ion concentration, (pH).

   Rationale: To be aware that there appears to be a direct relationship between hypoxemia and periodic breathing and apnea[2,18,21,26,29]

6. Assess the percentage of oxygen concentration utilized to reverse hypoxic states and the amount used during assisted ventilation procedures.

   Rationale: To use 100% FIO_2 with an apneic infant during bagging is contraindicated (One hundred percent oxygen concentration used in premature assisted ventilation causes retrolental fibroplasia and atelectasis.[13,21] Hyperoxia will decrease the respiratory stimulus through elimination of the chemoreceptor drive, thus leaving the respiratory control system unable to respond.[13,21,26] Careful small increases in inspired oxygen concentration are warranted to prevent periodic breathing and apnea.[25]

7. Assess the minimal level of FIO_2 the premature infant with multiple apneic attacks can tolerate to maintain an acceptable PO_2 in the arterial blood.

   Rationale: To be aware that if it becomes impossible to compromise between a minimal FIO_2 and an acceptable PO_2 (that is, requiring more than 60% FIO_2 to maintain a PO_2 above 45 mm Hg), constant positive airway pressure (CPAP) may be necessary to promote adequate oxygenation in the hypoxic neonate[3,18,27,29]

8. When CPAP is instituted, continual assessments of oxygen concentration utilized, amount of water pressure in centimeters utilized, and whether warmed and humidified oxygen mixture is utilized should be observed. Also the safety pop-off valve should be evaluated.

Rationale: To check for safety hazards of a mechanical device and risk to the premature infant of hyperoxemia, overdistention of alveoli, and drying of airway passages[3] (Oxygen concentration that was used before CPAP should be used to initiate CPAP. Air-oxygen mixture should be warmed and humidified if more than 40% is delivered or baby is intubated. Safety (pop-off) valve should be set at 20 to 30 cm H_2O.[3,27]

9. Observe signs and symptoms of pneumothorax with thorough chest assessment.

    Rationale: To check for excessive positive pressure causing overdistention of distal air sacs that rupture and allow air into the pleural spaces[3,27]

10. Frequently assess the therapeutic levels of theophylline (aminophylline) when used as medical management for multiple apneic attacks.

    Rationale: To check for toxic levels, which occur at 13 to 14 mEq/ml and contribute to such symptoms as tachycardia, vomiting, restlessness, jitteriness, and seizures[21] (Theophylline is a methylated xanthine that stimulates the CNS, acts on the kidney to produce diuresis, stimulates cardiac muscle, and relaxes smooth muscle.[23] Serum levels of 5 to 15 μg/ml have been shown to decrease apneic attacks.)

11. Be aware of concurrent diagnoses that are associated with hypoxemia and apnea of the premature infant.

    Rationale: To be aware that reversal of pulmonary disorders or treatment of symptomatology often resolves the problem with apneic spells[18,22,29] (Disorders that are cited to cause hypoxia leading to CNS depression are patent ductus arteriosus, hyaline membrane disease, pneumonia, and airway obstruction [aspiration pneumonia].)

12. Evaluate the hematocrit and hemoglobin of the premature neonate.

    Rationale: To be aware that anemia can be associated with apneic spells from decreased blood volume and decreased oxygen-carrying capacity, thus creating a hypoxic event[2,18,29]

13. Frequently assess metabolic homeostasis (serum calcium, glucose, and phosphorus levels).

    Rationale: To be aware that metabolic aberrations such as hypoglycemia, hypocalcemia, and hyperphosphatemia are prevalent among preterm infants with immature systems and are strongly associated with apnea by depressing the respiratory center and thereby decreasing afferent activity effectiveness at the center[2,3,18,21,29]

14. Assess acid-base homeostasis and the aberration of metabolic acidosis.

    Rationale: To be aware that metabolic acidosis is caused most often by a hypoxic state with resultant anaerobic metabolic processes that cause an accumulation of lactic acid and inadequate O_2-CO_2 exchange at the cellular level[13]

15. Assess clinical symptomatology of the premature neonate with acidemia (that is, decreased weight gain, lethargy, frequent apneic attacks).

    Rationale: To be aware that newborns and especially premature newborns are vulnerable to acidemia because of their limited ability to excrete hydrogen ion by their immature renal systems[2]

16. Detect early the premature infant with clinical signs or diagnostic signs of sepsis.

    Rationale: To be aware that sepsis of the premature infant is another associated cause of apneic attacks[2,3,20,29] and depresses the respiratory center by decreasing the cortical afferent traffic[18]

17. Consider other etiological conditions that prompt seizure activity and/or apneic spells.

    Rationale: To be aware of other conditions that may prompt seizure activity and/or apneic spells, such as passive addiction to narcotics at birth, potential hypoxic/ischemic encephalopathy, cerebral contusion, intracranial hemorrhage, and history of obstetrical trauma or perinatal complications[2,4,15,18]

THERAPEUTIC

1. Place premature infant on heart rate monitor and, if available, apnea monitor.
   a. Use of heart rate monitor:

(1) Electrodes—place "stick-on" electrodes on dry, clean skin on the anterior chest (right upper, left lower sternal, and left leg if ground leg required).

(2) Alarm settings—place heart rate upper and lower limits between 80 and 90 beats/min and 180 and 200 beats/min.[3]

b. Use of apnea monitor:

(1) Electrodes (except mattress type)—may be placed in same area as anterior heart electrodes or slightly farther apart to detect movement of chest wall.

(2) Alarm settings—settings by respirations per minute (that is, 20/min) or duration of apnea (10- to 15-second interval) may be used.

c. Nursing interventions when alarm signals:

(1) Check the infant for apneic episode.

(2) Rule out false alarm if infant shows good respiration and good color.

(3) Check for lead failure, faulty placement, or poor alarm settings.[3]

Rationale: To be aware that at least 25% of all premature infants will have at least one apneic spell in the first 10 days of life[9] (Monitoring heart rate may alone be sufficient if bradycardia follows the apneic attack.[3] Monitoring for respiratory irregularities with sound equipment can elicit appropriate nursing measures and avert consequential CNS damage.[9])

2. Provide gentle sensory stimulation to infant during apneic pause.

a. Rub the back.

b. Stroke the legs.

c. Reposition with a slightly, extended neck.

d. Use oscillating water beds; rocking beds.

Rationale: To provide gentle stimulation is often the primary nursing intervention used to initiate respirations[29] (Diffuse cutaneous stimulation can provide the respiratory center with impulses through the afferent pathways. Water and rocking beds are measures to increase afferent input by stimulating the vestibular nerve and proprioreceptors.[15,18,29]

3. Avoid certain procedures that cause vaso-vagal stimulation and initiate a hyperactive reflexive response as much as possible. Avoid:

a. Vigorous catheter suctioning that stimulates the posterior pharynx

b. Nipple feedings stimulating the sucking reflex

c. Overinflation of lungs during assisted ventilation

d. Utilizing too high a concentration of FIO_2 in ventilatory assistance

e. Instillation of chemical stimulants to laryngeal nerves (such as glucose, sterile water, cow's milk)

f. Cool or warm stimulation of trigeminal nerve area of face when administering FIO_2 and humidity under an oxygen hood

Rationale: To avoid stimulation of these vasovagal responses and hyperactive reflexes of the premature infant, which cause resultant bradycardia and apnea[18]

4. Ensure that environmental temperature is about 1.5° C warmer than the infant's abdominal skin temperature (36.3° to 36.5° C) by recording the skin temperature and ambient temperature readings every hour[29]

Rationale: To provide a neutral thermal zone (36.3° to 36.5°), which will minimize metabolic requirements and oxygen consumption, thereby increasing the afferent pathways to the CNS from the thermal receptors[15,18,29]

5. Assist the very small premature infant with a servo-control apparatus, keeping the isolette away from windows and perhaps utilizing an internal shield.

Rationale: To be aware that temperature homeostasis is impaired in the premature infant because of his large surface area, the paucity of subcutaneous fat ("brown fat"), lessened muscular activity, decreased metabolic response to cooling, and limited ability to sweat or shiver[3] (Servo-control is an automatic sensing device used in the modern incubator for maintaining a premature infant's temperature with a thermister control attached to the infant.[3,29])

6. Ensure that optimal oxygenation is occurring between neonate and environment:
   a. Frequently check the isolette O_2 concentration.
   b. Frequently assess the infant's blood oxygen levels.
   c. Have bag and mask available at the bedside of an apneic infant.
   d. Note if clinical symptoms of hypoxia are evident: cyanosis, irregular respirations, or hypotonia.
   e. Control thermal status of neonate.
   f. Support adequate hydration by assessment of intake and output, weights, and serum osmolality.

   Rationale: To be aware that hypoxia has been stated to depress the CNS and respiratory center. (Ensuring adequate oxygenation will decrease the frequency of respiratory irregularity. Homeostasis is necessary to decrease the metabolic requirements and oxygen consumption. Situations such as hyperthermia, hypothermia, and dehydration increase the chance for a hypoxic response.[2,3,9,29]

7. Provide assisted ventilation during apneic attacks related to underlying hypoxic states.
   a. Do gentle hand bagging to avoid hyperinflation with FIO_2 concentration the same or slightly higher than present FIO_2.
   b. Bagging should be applied briefly to relieve cyanosis and improve tone.

   Rationale: To relieve hypoxia and initiate respirations and to prevent assisted hyperventilation that would reduce CO_2 and remove the direct stimulus to breathe spontaneously (Careful manipulation of equipment, evaluation of the FIO_2 concentration, and prevention of overinflation of the premature infant's lungs are imperative to prevent hyperoxic states.[6,18,21,29])

8. Provide safe nursing care for the neonate who is started on CPAP.
   a. Monitor O_2 levels of FIO_2, amount of centimeters of H_2O pressure used in CPAP, humidification of oxygen, and setting of safety (pop-off) valve.
   b. Monitor blood pressure frequently, especially with increases in centimeters of H_2O pressure (increased CPAP).
   c. Sigh or inflate neonate's lungs every 30 minutes.
   d. Complete a chest assessment of both lung fields for full aeration.
   e. Note gastric distention and place orogastric tube for decompression if necessary.
   f. Respond as a member of the collaborative health team to the life-threatening situation of tension pneumothorax.
   g. Emergency equipment should be closely available (that is, needles for aspiration, chest tube insertion tray).

   Rationale: To prevent pneumothorax (CPAP inhibits alveolar collapse by applying constant positive pressure to the infant's airway. It can be delivered by a head chamber, a mask, nasal prongs, or by intubation. CPAP without intubation is the mode of preference because of its greater safety factor.[2,27] During increases of pressure of CPAP, blood pressure should be watched closely for hypotension owing to impedance of venous return. Sigh or full lung inflation should be accomplished every 30 minutes to prevent hypercapnia from Pco_2 accumulation. Pneumothorax indicates a medical emergency.[2,3,27])

9. Administer theophylline carefully.
   a. Closely monitor parenteral infusion utilizing a mechanical infusion pump.
   b. Observe for signs of toxicity (increased heart rate, vomiting, restlessness, seizures).
   c. Note the frequency and duration of apneic spells and any adverse effects of apnea (cyanosis and hypotonia).

   Rationale: To stimulate other parts of the body (usually involved are the CNS and circulatory systems)[23] (It is used to treat premature infants with apnea because of its central stimulation.[21] Researchers have reported decreases in the incidence of apneic episodes and adverse effects of apneic attacks.[10,12,23])

10. When medical management institutes transfusion therapy for a Hct <45% with fresh whole blood, the perinatal nurse must be attentive to the following:

    a. Transfusion rate (10 ml Hgb to ↑ Hct 5%)[3]

    b. Signs of transfusion reaction (that is, fever, rash, chills)

    c. Signs of volume overload (that is, rales on inspiration during pulmonary assessment, ↑ heart rate, ↑ blood pressure, and respiratory distress)

    d. Prevention of any further blood loss (Make records accounting for all blood drawn.)

    e. Reevaluation of Hgb/Hct levels

    Rationale: To be aware that administration of blood will increase the oxygen-carrying capacity of the blood and the transfusion of adult hemoglobin will provide release of oxygen to fetal tissues at higher oxygen tensions[2,3,6,13,29]

11. Utilize Dextrostix when apnea occurs in the premature infant.

    a. If Dextrostix shows a barely perceptible blue color or no color indicating a level around or below 25 mg/dl, confirm this finding with a serum blood glucose.[29]

    Rationale: To be aware that hypoglycemia (blood glucose below 20 mg/dl) in low birth weight infants is due to insufficient glycogen and fat stores[3] and apneic spells cause an increased rate of removal of blood glucose causing further problems with homeostasis and compounded hypoglycemia[4,13]

12. Through medical management, regain glucose homeostasis with proper parenteral administration.

    a. Administer a 10% to 25% glucose solution under careful titration, using safety precaution of infusion pumps.

    b. Correlate glucose infusion to neonatal weight (kg/ml of glucose infused).

    c. Reduce parenteral infusion rate gradually after normal glucose levels are attained.

    Rationale: To be aware that glucose is a necessary step in energy metabolism at the intracellular level[2,13] and that available levels of blood glucose are necessary in order to be utilized by tissues (especially the CNS) for energy requirements and metabolic life[13] (Intravenous hyperalimentation with a high glucose content may result in hyperglycemia, increased serum osmolality with resulting diuresis and dehydration, and risk of septicemia from bacteria that was not prevented from entering the fetal system by filters.[2] [Bacteria proliferates in the high glucose composition].[2,13,20] Measures must be taken to gradually wean the neonate from the hypertonic solution to prevent hyperinsulinism and hypoglycemia.[13])

13. Immediately evaluate calcium and phosphorus status of apneic infant. If necessary, administer parenteral or oral calcium.

    Rationale: To be aware that hypocalcemia in the premature infant with apnea is related to a maturational delay in the responsiveness of the fetal renal tubule to parathyroid (Hyperphosphatemia occurs because of a decreased response of phosphorus excretion by the fetal renal system. In the preterm infant, hypocalcemia is compounded by the fact that the neonate has not received the intrauterine calcium accumulation normally occurring at term.[2,3,4])

14. Treat the acidotic premature infant who has apneic spells.

    a. Give alkali support with sodium bicarbonate.

    b. Administer either parenterally or orally.

    c. Observe arterial blood pH to normal level of 7.30 to 7.35.

    Rationale: To be aware that metabolic acidosis is an imbalance of excess hydrogen ions potentially caused by cellular hypoxia or energy starvation (hypoglycemia) with production of lactic acid[2,13] (Giving alkali support with sodium bicarbonate will neutralize those acids in the blood and those acids released by new bone formation that the immature kidney is unable to excrete.[2,3,18] A pH of 7.30 to 7.35 is necessary for decreased pulmonary resistance, leading to increased blood flow into the lung, increased O_2-CO_2 exchange at the alveoli, and restoration of aerobic cell metabolism for optimal oxygenation of the CNS and its tissues.[6,13]

15. Treat the premature neonate with apnea and concurrent bacterial sepsis.
    a. Detect clinical signs of sepsis early.
    b. Institute immediate parenteral antibiotic therapy.
    c. Observe for irregularities and fluctuations of the neonate's core temperature.
    d. Knowledge of the therapeutic and toxic levels of the antibiotic administered and the system of metabolizing the drug and its excretion is necessary.
    Rationale: To aim treatment at the causative agent with antibiotic therapy (Cultures to detect which organism is responsible must be carried out so appropriate therapy may be administered. Temperature fluctuations need close observation and control so as not to further tax the metabolically compromised neonatal system. Awareness of metabolism and excretion of the antibiotics employed and the therapeutic and toxic levels are safe nursing measures when administering any antibiotic to an immature biological system such as the premature neonate.[2,18,20])

16. Treat resultant symptomatology (seizures and frequent apneic spells) of premature infants with history of obstetrical trauma and/or perinatal complications.
    a. Medical management may include anticonvulsant therapy to those infants with seizure activity.
    b. Medical management may involve the support of a premature withdrawal from passive narcotic addiction.
    c. Medical management may include antiinflammatory drugs for cerebral edema.
    d. Continually assess duration of apnea, frequency, and adverse effects.
    e. Frequently evaluate arterial blood gases, serum electrolytes, hematological values, thermal control, acid-base balance, and sepsis.

Rationale: To be aware that after the insult of CNS disorders and diseases such as hypoxic-ischemic encephalopathy, cerebral contusion, and intracranial hemorrhage, treatment will be concerned with the alleviation of clinical symptomatology[2,18,29]

EDUCATIONAL (family unit)

1. Minimize the emotional stress of the parents of a critically ill neonate or a "well" premature infant by being attentive to the following responsibilities as a perinatal nurse in the collaborative health care team:
   a. If the antepartum period has prognostic signs that may be indicative of a high-risk birth, it is crucial that the parents be prepared for the potential problems and special care the infant may receive.
   b. If the neonate requires intensive care, explain the purposes of the equipment that will be used by the infant to the parents before entering the high-risk area.
   c. Keep the parents well informed of the neonate's progress and prognosis in the high-risk area. Encourage the parents to ask questions to facilitate understanding and help in the coping process.
   d. Encourage the parents to visit the high-risk area as often as possible to touch and see their ill infant.
   Rationale: To facilitate and strengthen the parent-infant ties during the hospitalization of the critically ill neonate (Some researchers feel that there are sensitive periods such as during the postpartum period that are essential for proper attachment between newborns and parents.[19])

2. When the neonate is able to tolerate such activities, encourage the mother to hold, touch, and feed her ill infant with anticipatory guidance from the perinatal nurse and tender concern for the mothering process.
   a. Give the mother a comfortable chair or rocker to sit in.
   b. Note how the infant is held. (The contact of the mother's chest or abdomen with the infant's trunk is known as "cuddling."[19])
   c. Note how the mother is attentive to infant. ("Is the mother's face in such a position

that her eyes and those of the infant meet fully in the same vertical plane?''[19])

d. Note how the mother holds the bottle to feed the infant. (The bottle should be perpendicular to the baby's mouth and milk should fill the tip of the nipple.)[19]

e. Give positive emotional support and encouragement.

Rationale: To allay anxiety in the mother of inadequacies in caring for her newborn.[28] (When the mother's holding and feeding behavior included such actions as holding the baby away from her body during feeding, poor positioning of bottle, and lack of milk in the nipple of the bottle, it was felt by Klaus and Kennel[19] that these mothers [that were separated from their newborns owing to critical illness] had incomplete attachment or diminished maternal affection. This concept is supported by the high incidence of premature infants who are later diagnosed as ''failure-to-thrive'' from no organic disease and are consequently known as ''vulnerable children.''[19,28]

3. Provide support systems and encouragement for the parents who take their children home with an apnea monitor. Provide educational basis for use and troubleshooting and also provide insight on the impact of apnea monitors on family life.

Rationale: To be aware that the parents of an infant who goes home with an apnea monitor will have a significant, but temporary, impact on their personal and social lives (Immediately issues of sudden infant death, operation of the equipment, and full-time responsibility for appropriate interventions if apnea occurs confront the parents.[5] The educational basis for coping with the shortcomings of a mechanical device and how to overcome the problems it may pose are important areas to cover with the parents before returning home.[15] Parents need to feel that asking relatives or friends to help during the time of apnea monitoring the high-risk baby in the family is appropriate and considered a strong source of support and alleviation of anxiety.[5] There is evidence

that this special child presents a vulnerable child's syndrome because of the specialized care, increased anxiety level, and change of life-style that occurs.[5,18,28])

4. Render the support of the public health nurse in the family's neighborhood as a strong support system and source for information.

Rationale: To help the family deal more effectively with the change of life-style and to assess the situation for potential threats to the child at risk

EDUCATIONAL (nursing staff)

1. Ongoing in-service training and staff development programs must be offered by the institution to assure quality care of the high-risk neonate.

Rationale: To be able to identify the possible etiology and implement safe and therapeutic care with special emphasis on prevention and maintenance of the family unit.

REFERENCES

1. Abramson, H., editor: Resuscitation of the newborn infant and related emergency procedures in the perinatal center special care nursery, ed. 3, St. Louis, 1973, The C. V. Mosby Co.
2. Avery, G. B.: Neonatology-pathophysiology and management of the newborn, Philadelphia; 1975, J. B. Lippincott Co.
3. Babson, S. G., Pernoel, M. L., and Benda, G. I.: Diagnosis and management of the fetus and neonate at risk, ed. 4, St. Louis, 1980, The C. V. Mosby Co.
4. Behrman, R. E.: Neonatal-perinatal medicine: diseases of the fetus and infant, ed. 2, St. Louis, 1977, The C. V. Mosby Co.
5. Black, L.: Impact of the apnea monitor on family life, Pediatrics 62(5):681, 1978.
6. Bolognese, R. J., and Schwarz, R. H.: Perinatal medicine: management of the high risk fetus and neonate, Baltimore, 1977, The Williams & Wilkins Co.
7. Bory, C., et al.: The biotransformation of theophylline to caffeine in premature newborns, Lancet 2:1204, 1978.
8. Brady, J. P., and Ceruti, E.: Chemoreceptor reflexes in newborn infants: effects of varying degrees of hypoxia on heart rate and ventilation in a warm environment, J. Physiol. 184:631, 1966.
9. Daily, W. J., et al.: Apnea in premature infants: monitoring, incidence, heart rate changes, and an effect of environmental temperature, Pediatrics 43(4):510, 1969.
10. Dietrich, J., et al.: Alterations in state in apneic preterm infants receiving theophylline, Clin. Pharmacol. Ther. 24:474, 1978.
11. Drage, J. S., and Berendes, H.: Apgar scores and outcome of the newborn, Pediatr. Clin. North Am. 13:635, 1966.
12. Gerhardt, T., et al.: Aminophylline therapy for idiopathic

apnea in premature infants: effects on lung function, Pediatrics **62**(5):801, 1978.

13. Guyton, A. C.: Textbook of medical physiology, ed. 4, Philadelphia, 1971, W. B. Saunders Co.

14. Haddad, G., et al.: Congenital failure of automatic control of ventilation, gastrointestinal motility and heart rate, N. Engl. J. Med. **57**(6):517, 1978.

15. Jacobson, S., et al.: Introduction to the neurosciences, Philadelphia, 1972, W. B. Saunders Co.

16. Kant, W. P.: Resuscitation comes first, Emerg. Med. **9**:30, 1977.

17. Kaplan, D., and Mason, E.: Maternal reactions to premature birth viewed as an acute emotional disorder, Am. J. Orthopsychiatr. **30**:539, 1960, as cited by Klaus, M., and Kennell, J.: Mothers separated from their newborn infants. In Schwartz, J., and Schwartz, L. L., editors: Vulnerable infants, New York, 1977, McGraw-Hill Book Co., p. 113.

18. Kattwinkle, J.: Neonatal apnea: pathogenesis and therapy, J. Pediatr. **90**(3):342, 1975.

19. Klaus, M., and Kennell, J. H.: Mothers separated from their newborn infants. In Schwartz, J., and Schwartz, L. L., editors: Vulnerable infants, New York, 1977, McGraw-Hill Book Co., p. 113

20. Kleinman, M.: Infections in the newborn. In Schreiner, R., editor: Management of neonatal problems, Indiana University School of Medicine, Department of Pediatrics, Section of Neonatal-Perinatal Medicine, 1979.

21. Maiels, J.: Apnea. In Schreiner, R., editor: Management of neonatal problems, Indiana University School of Medicine, Department of Pediatrics, Section of Neonatal-Perinatal Medicine, 1979.

22. Naeye, R.: Neonatal apnea: underlying disorders, Pediatrics **63**(1):8, 1979.

23. Peabody, J., et al.: Transcutaneous oxygen monitoring in aminophylline-treated apneic infants, Pediatrics **62**(5):698, 1978.

24. Perlstein, P., et al.: Apnea in premature infants and incubator-air-temperature changes, N. Engl. J. Med. **282**:461, 1970.

25. Rigatto, H., and Brady, J.: Periodic breathing and apnea in preterm infants. 1. Evidence for hypoventilation possibly due to central respiratory depression, Pediatrics **50**(2):202, 1972.

26. Rigatto, H., and Brady, J.: Periodic breathing and apnea in preterm infants. II. Hypoxia as a primary event, Pediatrics **50**(2):219, 1972.

27. Scarpelli, E., et al.: Pulmonary disease of the fetus and newborn, Philadelphia, 1978, Lea & Febiger.

28. Schwartz, J., and Schwartz, L.: Vulnerable infants—a psychosocial dilemma, New York, 1977, McGraw-Hill Book Co.

29. Sham, B., and Messerly, A.: Apnea in the premature infant, Nurs. Clin. North Am. **13**(1):29, 1978.

Chapter 19

Care of the asphyxiated newborn

Pattiann Yost Schmitt

The neonatal period, especially the first 24 hours of life, is the time of highest risk and greatest mortality occurring in childhood.[25] Perinatal asphyxia, a complex mixture of hypoxemia, hypercarbia, and circulatory insufficiency caused by many perinatal pathologies, is continuing to be a high, correlated cause of perinatal death and lifelong disabilities.* However, with prompt and skillful management, asphyxiated neonates need not suffer such sequelae. Through the development and recognition of neonatal resuscitation as an emergency situation, health care delivery to neonates at risk has shown evidence of decreased mortality and morbidity.†

The purpose of the chapter is to review and support the current perinatal nursing practice of providing collaborative health care to maternal-fetal units designated at risk for perinatal asphyxia.

PHYSIOLOGY
Developmental anatomy and physiology of the fetal lung

At birth, immediate changes involving pulmonary and cardiovascular systems occur within the neonate.[3,30] The fetal lung and fetal circulation must make transitions to extrauterine life. Since these physiological changes are so critical in the adaptation by the fetus to the first few minutes of life, the development of these systems in utero must be understood.[1,3,5,10,44]

Four weeks after conception when the embryo is 3 mm in length, the lung begins development in the caudal end of the primitive pharyngeal floor where the laryngotracheal groove appears.[3,30,41,43,47] This groove splits into two parts during the fourth week. The part at the cranial end of the laryngotracheal tube becomes the trachea and larynx, and the other portion located at the caudal end of the laryngotracheal tube becomes the lung bud.[30,41,43,47]

From 26 to 28 days of age, the lung bud divides into two bronchopulmonary buds that differentiate into the right and left bronchi and lungs.[30,47] These first 5 weeks of lung development are included under the first phase of lung development called the embryonic period.[47]

Continuing through a series of asymmetrical dichotomous branchings, the conducting airways are developed.[30,41,43,47] Between the sixth and seventh week, 10 principal branches on the right bronchi and 8 branches on the left bronchi are formed.[41] Between the tenth and fourteenth week, 75% of bronchial branching will occur so that by the sixteenth week bronchial branching is complete. At this point the developing lung has a glandular appearance with the conducting airways established and lined with columnar epithelium. This period is known as the pseudoglandular period (5 to 17 weeks).[30,47]

The canalicular period (13 to 25 weeks) is characterized by the proliferation and attenuation of mesenchyma, which permits the blood capillaries to invade into the future air spaces. The columnar epithelium that lined the areas in the pseudoglandular period now becomes irregular and thinned with capillaries protruding into the epithelium.[30,47] Toward the end of this period various types of alveolar lining epithelium (type I and type II) can be seen that lead to more areas of close approximation of the capillary lumen to airway surfaces. Thus the

---

*See references 1-7, 9, 15, 20, 23, 25, 36, and 39.
†See references 1, 5, 6, 9, 20, 23, and 36.

terminal generations of the airways are lined with flattened epithelium. The lumina of the bronchi and bronchioles enlarge, and with the vascularization of this lung tissue each terminal bronchiole develops two or more respiratory bronchioles, which in turn divide into sacculations called alveolar ducts. At this stage of lung development, extrauterine survival is not realistic.[30,44,47]

The terminal sac period (24 weeks to birth) is the time of development when the alveolar ducts differentiate into clusters of thin-walled terminal air sacs or the primitive alveoli.[30,47] Preparation for extrauterine life proceeds rapidly. Undifferentiated cells are maturing for potential air-blood interface, and the capacity for surfactant production is well underway by the type II alveolar pneumocytes.* Concurrently, lymphatic capillaries are actively developing.[41] According to Stalhman and Gray,[41] at 26 weeks the production of surfactant (a lipoprotein substance capable of lowering the surface tension at the air-alveolar interface to maintain patency and facilitate expansion at end expiration) may be present in abundance with mature-appearing type II alveolar cells.[41] "The compliance of this lung would still not approach that of a mature infant, despite the ability to produce surfactant, because of the large amount of residual connective tissue present. This would be a great disadvantage to the poor chest wall stability of the infant who is liveborn at this gestational age."[41] In accordance with the disadvantages of birth at 26 weeks' gestation, absence or deficiency of surfactant can contribute highly to the causes of respiratory distress in the premature infant.[30,41,43,47]

The final phase of lung development is known as the alveolar period (late fetal period to 8 years).[30,47] As the lining of the terminal air sacs become extremely thin, the human adult pulmonary alveoli are formed. The mature neonate has a considerable number of alveoli present at birth. The number of alveoli doubled at term from the number found at 24 to 27 weeks' gestation in a study by Emery and Mithal.[16] They also noted that at 8 years of age there was another doubling of the number of alveoli present at birth. The lungs at birth are filled with liquid from the amniotic cavity, tracheal glands, and the liquid secreted by the lung itself.[10,30,43,47] The fetus

is able to make respiratory movements in utero that are rapid, shallow, and promote material into the lungs.[10] However, the fetus can make deep respiratory movements that will cause aspiration of amniotic cavity contents into the lungs when subjected to severe stress such as asphyxia.[10,21] Thus the end result of the birth process involves aeration of the lungs by the replacement of intra-alveolar fluid by air.[21,30]

Developmental anatomy and physiology of the fetal circulation

"The cardiovascular system is the first system to function in the embryo."[30] During the embryonic phase, cardiac development has been detected at the end of the third week (18 or 19 days) in the cardiogenic area of the lateral mesoderm germ layer of the trilaminar embryo.[11,30] Blood vessels first appear in the extraembryonic mesoderm of the yolk sac, connecting stalk, and chorion early in the third week.[11,30] By the end of the third week, paired heart tubes form in the mesenchymal cells in the cardiogenic area and begin to fuse into the primitive heart tube. The paired heart tubes and the blood vessels in the embryo, connecting stalk, chorion, and yolk sac link up to form the primitive cardiovascular system by day 21, with circulation started by the end of the third week.[11,30]

Fetal circulation is markedly different from that of the live neonate.[3] In utero, oxygenated blood returns to the fetus from the placental intervillous system by the umbilical vein. A portion of this oxygenated blood goes directly into the inferior vena cava (IVC) and through the ductus venosus, while the remainder flows through the liver before returning to the IVC. As the blood passes from the IVC into the right atrium (RA), a major portion of the blood is deflected directly across the RA through the foramen ovale by an anatomical structure called the crista dividens. The blood that passes through the foramen ovale into the left atrium mixes with a small amount of venous blood from the lungs via the pulmonary veins. This mixture of well-oxygenated blood then enters the left ventricle through the mitral valve and is ejected through the ascending aorta to the cerebral arteries and upper extremities. Concurrently, the remainder of the IVC flow that was not deflected through the foramen ovale enters the large flow of venous blood from the superior vena cava returning

---

*See references 3, 30, 41, 43, and 47.

from the upper body. The blood in the RA that does not cross the atrial septal defect, enters the right ventricle and is pumped through the pulmonary artery toward the lung. In the fetus the pulmonary vessels in the lung are tightly constricted; therefore little blood enters the lungs, and the majority is shunted through the ductus arteriosus (DA) into the descending aorta. The delivery of well-oxygenated blood during intrauterine life is directed to the heart and brain rather than the kidney and gut.[3,30] Pulmonary blood flow in the fetus is low and is noted to receive only 10% to 20% of the right ventricular output. The placenta is the organ during fetal life that handles the process of oxygenation and elimination of waste products from metabolism of the blood by incorporating the principle of simple diffusion across the placental membrane.[3,6,30]

THE FIRST BREATH

The minutes immediately after delivery are critical.[1,3,5,10] Important and crucial changes are occurring in the neonate. The fetal alveoli and bronchi are filled with fluid during intrauterine life. The lung secretes liquid and contributes to the fluid within the amniotic cavity.[10] According to Chernick,[10] chemical analysis of the lung liquid supports that it is formed in the lung. It has a lower pH, protein, and sodium bicarbonate levels than amniotic fluid. Also this lung liquid has a higher osmolality and sodium and chloride levels than amniotic fluid. This analysis refutes the theory postulated by some researchers that lung liquid was only a simple ultrafiltrate of plasma.

In 1941, Potter and Bohlender[33] proved that liquid was secreted by the lung when they described an infant with an anomalous lobe that was not connected to the trachea but was distended with liquid. This lobe proved that liquid was secreted into the lobe and it could not have been aspirated amniotic fluid.[10]

The rate of formation of this lung fluid has been studied by animal researchers. Most recent studies by Platyker and associates[32] utilized a fetal sheep preparation in which tracheal fluid was collected in a latex balloon. Rate of flow was measured at 3 ml/kg/hr. They observed that advancing gestational age did not seem to affect the rate of flow of lung fluid but was markedly reduced by the administration of catecholamines to the fetus. Correlations

were made to suggest that intrauterine stress might reduce the rate of production of lung fluid.[10,32]

Lung liquid must be removed rapidly within minutes after birth to facilitate an adequate air-liquid interface for gas exchange. Much of the fluid is expressed from the fetus by thoracic compression during the passage through the vaginal canal and is replaced by air owing to elastic recoil of the thorax.[3,10,41] According to Chernick,[10] "a volume of fluid equivalent to one-third of the functional residual capacity is squeezed out of the nose and mouth during vaginal delivery: this effect is absent during cesarean sections." The remaining two thirds is absorbed by the pulmonary circulation and lymphatics after respirations are established.* This tendency is secondary to the increased pulmonary blood flow at the alveolar level at birth and the tendency of the lung liquid (that is of low colloid osmotic pressure) to move into the bloodstream where protein content is four times greater.[10,43] Subsequently, the time required to clear the lung of fluid is stated to be variable from 6 to 24 hours after birth.[10]

The healthy infant takes his first breath within 15 to 20 seconds after delivery.[21] The first breath depends on elicitation of the respiratory center. The state of arousal of the respiratory center is dependent on peripheral chemoreceptors and biochemical drives such as high P_{CO_2} and/or low pH and low P_{O_2}.[3,21,48] The new surroundings (cold, bright delivery room; noise; lights; cutaneous stimulation) also give rise to an intense shower of afferent sensory impulses to the respiratory center.[21] When there are no breaths, there are no exchanges of gas, and the biochemical stimuli (increased P_{CO_2} levels, decreased P_{O_2} levels, and decreased pH) will be increasing. Sooner or later, efferent impulses will be sent to the diaphragm from higher centers. This diaphragmatic contraction will create a negative intrathoracic pressure that will suck in air through the airways into the lungs to increase intrathoracic volume. Thus the first breath of life is accomplished.[21]

Initially, a large amount of pressure is required to open the normal alveolus owing to the viscosity of the fluid in the airways, the forces of surface tension, and tissue resistive forces.[3,10,29,34] The first breath has a tidal volume of 12 to 67 ml, which

*See references 3, 5, 10, 21, 41, and 43.

leaves a residual volume and establishes the functional residual capacity.[21] According to Chernick,[10] lung liquid is 100 times more viscid than air and requires a pressure of 58 cm H_2O to make liquid flow at a rate of 0.7 ml/sec. Karlberg and associates[22] measured the volume and pressure changes in 11 spontaneously breathing babies during their first breath. Five of these showed a pattern of lung expansion, suggesting that there was an opening pressure with the baby producing a negative intrathoracic pressure of up to 50 cm H_2O before any air entered the lung. Five other infants, however, did not show this phenomenon and expanded their lungs without any apparent respiratory effort. It was postulated that this was achieved by passive recoil of the thorax after the compression effect of passage through the birth canal.[10,21]

Milner and Saunders[29] repeated the studies of Karlberg and associates in view of their clinical observations that most babies managed to expand their lungs without a large intrathoracic pressure change. After studying 17 healthy term babies, 5 babies expanded their lungs with less than 20 cm H_2O. The characteristic opening pressure pattern described by Karlberg and associates was seen in only one infant, which later made Milner and Saunders conclude that opening pressures greater than 10 cm H_2O were rarely seen in term infants.[29] This was quite a contrasting view in the literature in relation to the pressure of the first breath.

Once the first breath has been accomplished, the alveolus may be fully inflated on successive breaths with only a small pressure increase.[3,10,29,34] This phenomenon occurs because surfactant, the lipoprotein secreted by type II alveolar cells, causes the pressure curve for deflation to be much different from that of inflation, therefore allowing the alveolus to remain open at pressures well below the critical opening pressures.[1,3,6,10,21]

When the lungs inflate at birth, a marked decrease in pulmonary vascular resistance occurs. Accordingly, the pulmonary blood flow will increase from 10% of the total flow in utero to essentially the entire output from the right ventricle.[3,10] There is a small portion of blood flow from the right ventricle that is not ejected to the lungs and continues to be shunted into the systemic circulation through the foramen ovale or ductus arteriosus.[3,6,11]

According to McMurphy and associates,[28] the ductus arteriosus begins to close 5 to 15 minutes after the onset of breathing secondary to an increase in oxygenation and oxygen tension, bradykinin, serotonin, and acetylcholine, which in effect cause contraction of this fetal vessel.[3,11,23,27] However, hypoxia or asphyxia may cause the neonate to revert to fetal circulation within the first few weeks of life.[3,23,27] According to Stahlman,[41] factors such as asphyxia, shock, or repeated reflex blood flow redistribution have more of an adverse effect on extrauterine pulmonary function than lung maturation.

PATHOPHYSIOLOGY OF ASPHYXIA

To properly resuscitate and care for an asphyxiated infant, it is important to understand the pathophysiology involved. There are several studies that have investigated asphyxia, but the limitations of these data have been attributed to the utilization of animals in the experiments in which there are significant differences between degrees of maturation and rates of development.[23] Consequently, one should have a conscious awareness when relating animal data to human neonates.[23]

The studies of Dawes and associates[12] with rhesus monkeys have shown the "natural history of asphyxia to be qualitatively similar for all animal species." They assessed the survival competence in newborns of various animal species by measuring the time from asphyxiation at birth to the last gasp. The events and physiological changes that occurred during asphyxiation of the rhesus monkey fetus at birth are highly comparative to the human newborn. By tying the umbilical cords while the heads were secured in saline-filled rubber bags, the rhesus monkeys were asphyxiated for a time interval of 10 minutes. They observed rapid gasps that occurred shortly after the asphyxiating event associated with movement of the arms and legs in a thrashing motion that gradually began to decrease by 1 minute. The next 0.5 to 1 minute was characterized by cessation of respirations and was called "primary apnea." It has been found in studies that spontaneous respirations can be induced by appropriate sensory stimuli during the period of primary apnea.[3,5,21,28,34]

For 4 or 5 minutes following the onset of primary apnea, the monkeys displayed spontaneous deep gasping and decreasing respiratory effort, a decline in heart rate from 180 beats/min to 80 to 100 beats/min, and a persistent fall in arterial blood pres-

ciates[26] noted marked coloration throughout the basal ganglia and especially the cortex, indicating a breakdown of the blood-brain barrier to albumin. The dye was seen primarily inside the neurons. Lou and associates[26] postulated that the breakdown of the blood-brain barrier is most likely caused by maximal vasodilatation of cerebral vessels and a moderate arterial hypertension rather than being directly caused by tissue hypoxia. "The breakdown of the blood-brain barrier and edema may further aggravate circulatory disturbances in severe and prolonged asphyxia."[26] Consequently, the passage of albumin from the blood to the neurons will enhance the transport of bilirubin (albumin-bound) to the neurons. Thus, asphyxiating insults can raise suspicion of kernicterus in the small, asphyxiated neonate.[26]

The source of aerobic metabolism is ATP and P-creatine, and when these brain energy sources fall, the important energy-dependent processes such as ion transport and neuronal activity become markedly decreased or activity may cease.[3,15,23] Within minutes of the anoxic insult, changes in the central nervous system can be observed by severe slowing or cessation of electrical activity on the EEG and development of coma clinically.[15]

Blood glucose levels in the fetus are half the maternal values.[3,5,23] Immediately after birth, hepatic glycogen is mobilized to support a stable source of glucose for the brain in response to the birthing process. Consequential to increased sympathetic stimulation of the maternal unit, the neonate's glucose levels are normally elevated at birth but will fall within the first few hours of life.[3,4,7] This fall in energy reserve can be associated with early central nervous system changes such as hypotonia, lethargy, hypothermia, and respiratory irregularities.[3,4,7,23]

When anaerobic degradation is utilized by the neonate, several substrates may be metabolized. Myocardial glycogen reserves that are stored locally during fetal life or carbohydrates from liver glycogen stores are the most available substrate.[12] Brain tissue metabolizes glucose as its primary energy source, but glycerol, free fatty acids, and ketone bodies (beta-hydroxybutyrate, acetoacetate) may be used as metabolic substrates,[3,12,15,23] although Klaus and Fanaroff[23] state that hypoxic or glycogen-depleted neonates probably will be unable to utilize glycerol, free fatty acids, or ketone bodies owing to the high oxygen requirements for utilization.

The inherent ability of the neonate to deal with an asphyxiating event better than an adult has been researched.[12,14,15] Animal studies revealed that some newborn animals who have an immature brain have a lower metabolic rate than an adult member of the same species. Owing to this lower energy metabolism, animals were able to increase the rate of anaerobic metabolism and utilize the energy more efficiently. Thus, resuscitation was successful within recoverable periods of hypoxia. Sustained hypoxia, however, followed in death.[12,14,15]

Another factor that contributed to adaptability in these studies was a complete circulatory system. This would enable redistribution of lactate and hydrogen ion to other tissues that are being perfused.[12,14,15,23] Concurrent administration of sodium bicarbonate and glucose benefited the asphyxiated animal when CO_2 was eliminated by areas of perfusion and pH levels began to rise.[13,14,23]

Asphyxiated neonates respond not only with pulmonary decompensations and metabolic aberrations, but they also show evidence of circulatory changes.* The asphyxiated neonates who have trouble expanding their lungs and maintaining respirations have consequential falls in PO_2 and pH and rises in PCO_2, causing a metabolic and respiratory acidosis. Hypoxia and acidosis cause vasoconstriction of the arterioles of the lung creating a high pulmonary vascular resistance. This high pressure makes blood flow through the pulmonary system small and creates a large shunt (right-to-left) through the ductus arteriosus. Retrograde from the high pulmonary vascular resistance is the right ventricle and right atria, which consequentially creates high pressure in an effort to push blood through the constricted arterioles of the pulmonary bed. The blood return to the left atria from the pulmonary bed is low creating a low intra-atrial pressure. When the right atrial pressure exceeds the left atrial pressure, the foramen ovale opens and blood flows through it right-to-left. This shunting of blood through the ductus arteriosus and foramen ovale is a return to fetal-like circulation. One exception to fetal circulation, however, is not involved. There is no oxygenated blood in the inferior vena cava from the umbilical vein of the

---

*See references 1, 3, 5, 7, 11, 23, and 36.

placenta after birth. The venous blood shunted across the foramen ovale goes to the brain by the way of the ascending aorta. The descending aorta carries even less oxygenated blood to the viscera owing to the mixture of venous blood from the ductus arteriosus.[1,3,11,23]

Assisted ventilation of the asphyxiated neonate in a fetal circulatory pattern is very difficult. Pulmonary vascular resistance is high, hydrogen ion is accumulating, myocardial glycogen stores are becoming decreased, and consequentially blood flow to other organs of the body is limited. Acidemia continues to surmount as anaerobic metabolism becomes the primary source of energy production. Concentration gradients across cell membranes begin to leak essential ions. Shocklike symptoms begin to develop and, if not reversed, myocardial failure and brain damage ensue.[1,3,11,23]

Resuscitation of these infants should begin immediately to oxygenate recoverable hypoxic cells of the myocardium and brain by providing lung expansion.[3,23] To be most effective in resuscitating an asphyxiated neonate, the infant should be identified in the antepartum, intrapartum, or postpartum period as a neonate at high risk for a hypoxic insult or asphyxiating event.

MANAGEMENT OF THE MATERNAL-FETAL HIGH-RISK PATIENT
Antepartum

So that the collaborative health team can provide proper intrapartum and postpartum management, the maternal-fetal unit that is threatened as a "re-productive-risk" must be identified.*

According to Butnarescu and associates,[9] "most individuals have the potential for healthy reproduction, but pregnancy carries with it the danger of risk because of our inability to predict or control unknown or unexpected variables." A "reproductive risk" can be described as being psychosocial, genetic, biophysical, or economic in nature.[9] It has been recognized in many studies that there are comparable and contrasting relationships between risk factors existing before and during pregnancy and subsequent risk to fetal outcome.[9,31] These risk factors have degrees of severity and magnitude that range from minimal risk to maximum death of

mother and/or fetus that creates damage to the family and society.[9,31] Butnarescu and associates[9] concur that reproductive risk occurs on a continuum that may span more than one generation. This risk is costly to the maternal-fetal unit, the family, and society in relation to the expenditure of human and material resources. Consequently, the threatened maternal-fetal unit must be understood and managed as a unit at risk within the family structure and within society. By using such weapons as education, research, and accessible health care services, sequelae from reproductive risk can be reduced through early assessment, diagnosis, and treatment of risk conditions.*

Early detection of the maternal-fetal high-risk unit is the best preventive health care that can be delivered.* Nurses need to continue to take responsibility for the efforts used to recognize and treat reproductive risk in its earliest stages of development. Since the nurse is often the patient's first contact with the perinatal health care system, initial identification of the high-risk patient by the nurse would be optimal at the first prenatal visit. Throughout the country, obstetricians have been developing tools that will help predict relationships between a numerical score and perinatal death.[3,4,23,31] These scoring systems can be used to grade pregnancies according to risk. One such tool is developed by Morrison and Olsen.[31] They used an antepartum risk scoring tool as a component of the prenatal records for all pregnancies. Reviewing 16,733 deliveries, they found 19% of the pregnant population to be scored as high risk. This same group had a perinatal mortality rate of 69/1000 births compared to the low-risk group that had a perinatal mortality incidence of 7/1000. The high-risk group accounted for 70% of the total perinatal deaths. They recommended the use of a screening tool as a method of identifying and recording statistical trends and not a "dictation for the final management of the pregnancy."[31]

Identified maternal factors adapted from Schreiner[36] that have been associated with asphyxia at birth and known to adversely affect the perinatal outcome follow:

Maternal disease (renal, pulmonary, cardiac, hematological, endocrine, infectious, collagen)

---

*See references 3-5, 7, 9, 19, 23, and 31.

*See references 3-5, 7, 9, 19, 23, and 31.

Diabetes mellitus

Anemia (hemoglobin less than 10%)

Maternal malnutrition

Maternal drugs (magnesium, ethyl alcohol, barbiturates, narcotics)

History of previous perinatal morbidity or mortality

Less than 16 or greater than 35 years of age

Nonpregnant weight less than 100 pounds or greater than 200 pounds

Surgery in pregnancy

Poor prenatal care

Prolonged rupture of membranes (greater than 24 hours)

Abruptio placentae, placenta previa, or other antepartum hemorrhage

Blood type or group isoimmunization

Low urinary estriol

Toxemia of pregnancy, hypertension

These factors can be recognized during a prenatal visit and promote advance preparation for possible respiratory support of the threatened fetus.[39]

Assessment of specific historical problems by a thorough prenatal nursing assessment is extremely important. Many of the assessed risks will be associated with subsequent problems either during the remaining prenatal period or during labor and/or the neonatal period.[7] Because of the interrelated association of these problems, the development of a plan of care that can be implemented throughout the antepartum, intrapartum, and postpartum periods must be instituted by the collaborative efforts of the members of the health care team.[4,7,9,23]

In developing such a plan, a reliable informant to facilitate the formation of a data base is necessary.[9] This can be accomplished through a complete prenatal nursing assessment or by the use of the questionnaire method for risk scoring.[9,31] It must also be stated that the task of designating a patient as low risk or high risk must incorporate a psychosocial as well as a medical assessment.[4,7,9,18] Pregnancy may have a profound effect on the behavior of a patient; therefore, in an effort to deliver "holistic" health care, the effect of the pregnancy on the patient's emotions and relationships (that is, family) must be taken into consideration.[4,7,9,18,24]

A clinical assessment (physical examination) and collection of biochemical data are also essential components in developing a data base.[7,9] A thorough physical examination of all systems including the breasts, abdomen, and pelvis should be performed on the first prenatal visit. Measurements of maternal vital signs and fetal vital signs along with maternal weight must also be done on every routine visit. Important assessments concerning fetal movements, lie, and presentation must also be documented at each visit.[4,7,9]

Recently, biochemical diagnosis and evaluation of the maternal-fetal unit has become an important component in the assessment of maternal-fetal well-being.[9] Blood studies that are done on the initial visit and some that are done serially give the health team increasing amounts of data on which to plan appropriate health care. Some of these include blood type studies for maternal grouping and Rh factor, serology for diagnosis and early treatment of syphilis, hematocrit and hemoglobin for differentiation of anemias, white blood count profiles for detection of infection and blood abnormalities, antibody studies for sensitization to isoantigens, rubella titers for presence of rubella antibodies, and serum glucose levels to detect hypoglycemia or hyperglycemia. Urine studies can also be beneficial in the formation of a data base. Presence of bacteria, protein, glucose, and estriols is noted. Cervical and vaginal smears and cultures to detect the presence of gonorrhea are essential for correct treatment. Accordingly a Papanicolau smear for diagnosis of cervical cancer is also in order.[3,4,9,19]

Amniotic fluid studies have been of recent value in supporting a high-risk data base. Detection of the lecithin/sphingomyelin ratios for fetal lung maturity is an important analysis that can be made from amniotic fluid aspirates. Creatinine determinations for assessment of fetal renal function can also be performed. Detection of fat cells in the amniotic fluid is another helpful index of maturity. Conversely, amniotic fluid can also be used to detect fetal well-being through the abnormal presence of bilirubin and meconium indicating fetal distress.[3,4,9,19]

Clinical ultrasonography has come of age and usefulness in the assessment of the high-risk pregnancy. Confirmation of pregnancy, gestational size, and fetal maturity by the biparietal diameter of the fetal head has made antenatal assessments increasingly valid. Sonar has also been demonstrable in the detection of intrauterine growth retardation.[9,19]

The more recent data concerning oxytocin challenge testing and nonstress testing have confirmed the relationship of respiratory function of the fetus and potential placental insufficiency with uterine contractions in high-risk maternal-fetal units. Thus, assessments concerning the process of birthing can be made prior to actual labor.[9,19,35]

From these subjective and objective data the process of formulating a problem list begins.[7,9] Inclusion of historical medical and psychosocial data is an important component of the problem list, although some of the historical problems cannot be resolved. However, the problems that may develop from these identified risks may be resolved with prompt medical attention. The problem list then becomes an active portion of the records, revised continually to assess the high-risk pregnancy.[7,9]

The role of the perinatal nurse in the atenatal clinical setting is one of education, support, and communication. The high-risk population of maternal-fetal units that is associated with higher mortality and morbidity rates is often associated with poverty, lack of education, and teenage pregnancy.[3,4,7,9,18] Middle-class patients will generally seek adequate prenatal care. They are able to maintain an adequate level of health and nutrition and can afford adequate maternity care. Thus, reproductive risk factors are usually identified early in the prenatal course of a middle-class high-risk patient, which statistically reduces the chance of perinatal mortality and morbidity through early recognition and proper management.[3,4,7,9,19]

The incidence of perinatal death continues. The health care team can increase fetal salvage and improve maternal health by recognizing that a great number of high-risk pregnancies are being kept from adequate prenatal care. Barriers such as impersonalized health care, lack of transportation and babysitting services, and language and cultural barriers keep the group most in need of maternity care from receiving it.[19]

Other methods need to be utilized to bring this group of women to adequate prenatal care. Patient teaching and special group services for pregnant teenagers are examples of personalizing health care. Individual counseling sessions with the social worker to help identify environmental, emotional, and physical strengths and weakness can be instituted. Financial assistance can be investigated also. Family planning services have been active in delivering education concerning birthing, child care, and reproductive controls. Whenever possible, the emphasis on family-centered care should be reiterated.[18,19]

Communication between the perinatal nurse and patient is an important element of prenatal care. Allowing time for questions, explaining routine and special antepartal high-risk testing, and supporting the patient through the months of close observation are vital roles of the nurse in a high-risk situation.[9,18,19,24]

Intrapartum

For many years, obstetricians have worked toward reducing mortality and morbidity with the birthing process.[3] Recently, the attitude to reexamine the factors that play a role in survival and look at the total picture of gestation, antepartal and intrapartal, has been emphasized.[3,4,7,9,23] The hazards of fetal distress during parturition have received increasing amounts of study, research, and innovations.[35,42] The results of this work are such recent techniques in the management of labor and assessment of fetal well-being as electronic monitoring of uterine activity and fetal heart rate and fetal scalp blood sampling.*

In the past, labor was assessed in terms of duration.[3] Normal parturition times were set up for primiparas amd multiparas and the three stages of labor. However, with the dawning of electronic surveillance and fetal scalp blood determinations of pH, it has been documented that labor may compromise the fetus if it is only a few contractions in length.[3,35,42] Therefore, Avery[3] states, ''normal labor is better defined as that degree of labor that does not encroach significantly on the fetal margin of reserve.''

Labor consists of a series of repetitive stresses to the fetus that may be strong enough in magnitude to threaten its quality of life or life itself.[3] Each uterine contraction is a forceful mechanical stress to the unborn fetus, where the energy may be applied most generally to the fetal vertex or on some part of the fetal body in malpresentations. The compression of the fetal head during uterine contractions can cause molding of the head, caput succedaneum, and even intracranial hemorrhage.[3]

Umbilical cord compression may occur when the

---

*See references 1, 3-5, 7, 9, 23, 35, and 42.

cord is found around the body or near the vaginal outlet.[3,7,9] Uterine contractions can be associated with varying degrees of cord compression.[3] Also, a more subtle effect of uterine contractions on the fetus can be documented as the impedance of intervillous space blood flow by each contraction.[3,7,9] This phenomenon occurs when intramyometrial pressure rises with a uterine contraction. Under pressure increases from the contracting uterus, the venous outflow from the intervillous space is shut off, producing congestion and a decrease in transfer of carbon dioxide and waste products between mother and fetus. As the intramyometrial pressure rises higher as in the peak of a contraction, the arterial inflow is also shut off so that the intervillous space between the placenta and uterine wall is closed to the maternal side. Oxygen exchange at this point of increased myometrial contraction is drastically altered. For seconds to minutes, the unborn fetus must respond to a physiological asphyxiation with each strong uterine contraction that is associated with a decrease in oxygen transfer and an increase in the buildup of carbon dioxide and waste products.[3]

In retrospect, it is known that the unborn fetus responds physiologically to asphyxiation with an immediate accumulation of Pco_2 and concomitant fall in pH yielding a respiratory acidosis. Continued hypoxia will deprive the fetus of sufficient levels of oxygen to carry out aerobic metabolism. Consequently, glucose can be oxidized only to pyruvate and lactate (anaerobic metabolism), which is known as an energy expensive and inefficient metabolic process. Free organic acids accumulate, causing an increase in hydrogen ion concentration and a further fall in pH constituting a metabolic acidosis.[1,3,5,7]

The transient falls in fetal or uterine perfusion generally cause a mild respiratory acidosis, but prolonged hypoxia to the fetus causes a combined acidosis that will persist some time after the insult is removed.[7]

Data concerning the fetal acid-base balance during labor are obtained through samples of capillary blood from the fetal scalp.* The fetal capillary pH is lower than that of adults, ranging from 7.25 to 7.35 during the first stage of labor, although it has been documented that higher pH values are found in

*See references 1, 3, 5, 7, 10, and 23.

neonates delivered by cesarean section or those fetuses not yet subjected to labor.[7] The gradual decline in fetal pH determinations is noted to be during the second stage of labor owing to the increased activity of the uterus and expulsive efforts by the mother. The combination of these two events just prior to birth causes a reduction in the arterial and venous flow in the intervillous space and a resultant hypoxia and hypercapnia.[3,7,23]

According to Bolognese and Schwarz,[7] "interpretation of fetal blood pH levels has not been completely uniform, but most authors consider values less than 7.20 to be suggestive of significant asphyxia and those between 7.20 and 7.24 preacidotic." Fetuses with a respiratory acidosis (high Pco_2, near normal base deficit, moderate fall in pH) usually respond well as neonates. Those with combined respiratory and metabolic acidosis and large base deficits recover much more slowly. Therefore the mildly acidotic neonate is able to achieve acid-base balance with pulmonary excretion of carbon dioxide, but the renal mechanisms for handling hydrogen ion excess in a combined acidosis are incompletely developed in the newborn and less adequate in the premature.[1,3,5,7,23]

Bolognese and Schwartz[7] made quite an extensive review of the current literature concerning the ability to predict Apgar scores by using fetal capillary pH levels. The prediction ability is about 80%, with false normal pH values occurring in 6% to 20%. The explanation for the false normal values in the presence of low Apgar scores is secondary to depression from sedatives or anesthetics, which produce poor respiratory efforts and flaccidity at birth. Also the occurrence of prematurity, fetal infection, or meconium aspiration could be attributed to a false normal value as a result of a hypoxic insult just prior to birth.[7]

Before the advent of electronic surveillance monitoring, fetal heart rate (FHR) was evaluated intermittently with a stethoscope between contractions. This method was incomplete because of the inability to evaluate fetal heart beats during contractions. With the introduction of fetal heart rate monitoring, a reliable recording of the instantaneous fetal heart rate during labor is assessed. Advances in understanding the fetal cardiovascular responses to stress have also been made with this continuous monitoring system.[7] The baseline FHR is a demonstration of a balance between parasympathetic and sympathetic influences from the autonomic nervous system observed on the monitor as minute-to-minute slowing down and speeding up of the FHR.[3] The measurement of the beat-to-beat variability of FHR is an essential assessment of fetal well-being that needs to be made by the perinatal nurse.[1,3,5,7,23]

The fetal cardiac response to stress is different from that of adult responses. The normal adult response to hypercapnia, hypoxia, and acidosis is an increased heart rate secondary to sympathetic nervous system stimulation.[3,9] In the fetus a small amount of hypoxia will elicit a transient increase in heart rate as proved by Dawes and associates[13,14] in the rhesus monkeys, but prolonged hypercapnia, hypoxia, and acidosis will cause parasympathetic stimulation with resultant bradycardia. This physiological concept is observable on the FHR monitor by the initial increase in heart rate in response to stress with a following decrease in the FHR.[9] The fetal cardiac response is also affected by uterine contractions, intervillous perfusion of the placenta, head compression, and cord compression. These causes of inadequate oxygenation of the fetus display characteristic patterns of the FHR in relation to the uterine contractions. Interpretation of monitor records could be a protocol of its own and is not the primary purpose of the plan of care in this chapter; however, detection of the patterns associated with perinatal asphyxia will be mentioned for detection of the maternal-fetal unit at risk during the intrapartum period. These patterns include decreased variability, fetal tachycardia (early), fetal bradycardia (late), late decelerations, and variable decelerations.*

The role of the perinatal nurse during the intrapartum period is one of support, communication, and anticipation. Nursing care of the mother being monitored during labor includes recognition and treatment of FHR patterns and assessment of the physical and psychological condition of responses of the patient to monitoring.[9] If possible, attention should be given to all patients during the antepartal period to provide an accurate description of anticipated monitoring procedures and policies.[42] During labor, it is necessary to explain the rationale for and procedures associated with intrapartum monitoring.

---

*See references 3, 4, 7, 9, 23, 35, and 42.

''Explanations should be brief and as nontechnical as possible yet cover the areas of concern to most patients. The opportunity to ask questions if the information is unclear should be actively and repeatedly offered.''[42]

As a member of the collaborative health team, the perinatal nurse who practices in labor and delivery has the responsibility of forming a data base concerning her patient. Subjective data (historical problems, complications of this pregnancy, and reproductive health history) and objective data (physical examination, measurements of maternal and fetal vital statistics, and biochemical analysis) must be gathered by the perinatal nurse to formulate a plan of management individualized for each patient. Identification of maternal factors associated with perinatal asphyxia during the intrapartum period must be recognized and brought to the attention of the health team.[3,6,9] The following is a list of intrapartum factors associated with asphyxia at birth[36]:

Cephalopelvic disproportion
Sedative or analgesic drugs
Prolonged labor (first stage greater than 24 hours, second stage greater than 2 hours)
Precipitous labor (less than 3 hours)
Difficult delivery
Maternal hypotension
Cord compression (nuchal cord, cord knot, compression by head in breech delivery)
Prolapsed umbilical cord
Cesarean section
Breech or other abnormal presentations
Forceps delivery other than low elective

Delivery and resuscitation

Fetal asphyxia may be caused by maternal factors as listed on pp. 312 and 313 and intrapartum factors as listed above. Such factors are multiple births, polyhydramnios, oligohydramnios, immature lecithin/sphingomyelin ratios, premature birth, postterm delivery, large or small for gestational age, abnormal heart rate or rhythm, meconium-stained fluid, and fetal acidosis (pH less than 7.20).[36] There are also various congenital anomalies that may prevent or impede lung expansion such as choanal atresia, hypoplastic lungs, diaphragmatic hernias, hydrothorax, or ascites.[5] The effect of birth trauma is difficult to evaluate from the effect of asphyxia, although precipitous labors and difficult forceps deliveries have been associated with perinatal birth asphyxia.[5]

The nurses and physicians who practice emergency health care in the perinatal focus of labor and delivery must be prepared to deliver prompt and adequate treatment to the asphyxiated neonate immediately after birth, whether it is expected or not.* These members of the health care team need to be trained in methods of resuscitation for the neonate and mother.[5] Understanding the normal cardiopulmonary events that take place with the onset of respiration is essential knowledge to have when dealing with a normal delivery and with the birth of a neonate who fails to breathe secondary to fetal central nervous system depression.[5]

Emergency resuscitation that is effective and prompt is the result of trained personnel and carefully checked equipment that was present and functioning prior to the delivery.† According to Kanto,[20] the minimum requirements for equipment include resuscitation "bag with premature and newborn masks, a laryngoscope with blades of proper size, endotracheal tubes, blood pressure monitoring equipment, a thermal source, a bulb syringe or DeLee trap, stethoscope, suction apparatus, IV setups for scalp vein and umbilical procedures, a stylet and adapter, and a pharyngeal airway. Immediate access to oxygen, epinephrine diluted 1:10,000, sodium bicarbonate, Narcan, and a volume expander—albumin." According to Sheldon,[39] the essential equipment can be conceptually thought of under three basic areas as follows:

Location (out of mother's view if possible)
  Heat: radiant warmer
  Oxygen: plus a portable tank if nursery is some distance away
  Good light: a procedure spotlight may be helpful
  Suction: wall, bulb, and DeLee trap
Ventilation
  Source of positive pressure ventilation with pure oxygen
  Masks, term and preterm sizes
  Endotracheal tubes (2.5, 3.0, and 3.5 mm), adapters to fit bag
  Laryngoscope and blades (at least two sizes), spare parts
  Stylets, scissors, tape, tape measures

Source of positive end-expiratory pressure (Gregory system or Carden valve and manometer)
Drug administration
  Syringes, including one 60 ml, several of each
  Needles, straight and butterfly
  Stopcocks, catheters
  Umbilical catheterization tray

Sheldon[39] emphasizes that the most common complicating feature in delivery room asphyxia is hypothermia. Whenever people are bending over the newborn interrupting the radiant heat source from above, the neonate is exposed to the chilling cold of the delivery room and resultant acidosis. At times, it becomes necessary to remind colleagues of this fact.

The clinical management of the neonate is a controversial issue depending on which author is read. The most controversy is found in the area of mode of delivery of the neonate and the selection of procedures to initiate and maintain respiratory efforts of the newborn through adequate ventilation, although most authors agree that quick assessment of respiratory status helps the practitioner decide the type and extent of resuscitation.[1]

Most infants need no special and extraordinary procedures at birth other than being kept in the head-down position at all times during the delivery while the cord is clamped and expeditious pharyngeal suctioning if there is vaginal mucus or blood in the neonate's mouth.*

As soon as the head is delivered, the removal of excessive thick mucus from the nose and mouth with a bulb syringe should be accomplished by the obstetrician.[1] It is especially important to note the color, consistency, and presence of meconium in the amniotic fluid just prior to birth. On the delivery of the head of a neonate who is meconium stained or bathed in meconium-stained fluid, the removal of the meconium, mucus, or blood clots from the infant's mouth with a bulb syringe is an important procedure to perform prior to the delivery of the rest of the body.[1-4,7,20] Performing suctioning prior to the delivery of the chest prevents aspiration of the amniotic contents in the oropharynx into the bronchi with the first gasp of respiration.[1]

To keep the pharyngeal contents out of the trachea with the first breath, it is mandatory that the infant

*See references 1-7, 9, 15, 20, and 23.
†See references 1-7, 9, 15, 20, 23, and 36.

*See references 1-4, 20, 25, 39, and 44.

Table 19-1. The Apgar scoring system*

Sign	0	1	2
Heart rate	Absent	Slow (below 100)	Over 100
Respiratory effort	Absent	Weak cry; hypoventilation	Good; strong cry
Muscle tone	Limp	Some flexion of extremities	Active motion; extremities well flexed
Reflex irritability (response to stimulation of sole of foot)	No response	Grimace	Cry
Color	Blue; pale	Body pink; extremities blue	Completely pink

*Adapted from Apgar, V.: Anesth. Analg. **32**:260, 1953.

be kept in a head-down position during and immediately after delivery. This will prevent the first gasp from drawing foreign material into the bronchi in a head-up position.[1-3] One contraindication to keeping the head-down position immediately after birth is subdural hemorrhage caused by the trauma of birth.[1]

Immediately on receiving the baby after delivery, the perinatal nurse begins to make assessments about the first gasp and first cry as well as the onset of sustained respirations.[1,2] In 1953, Virginia Apgar[2] introduced a scoring method to assess and evaluate the noenate at birth according to the first gasp, first cry, and onset of sustained respirations. Evaluations of heart rate, muscle tone, reflex irritability, and color are also made by this scoring method. In evaluating the use of the Apgar score in over 27,000 infants, it can be demonstrated that perinatal mortality is inversely proportional to the score the infant received at 1 minute of life. The score was able to reflect the handicaps of those infants unable to respond actively to birth and resuscitative efforts such as premature infants, infants delivered by cesarean sections, and neonates subjected to obstetrical and anesthetic risks.[1,2] Therefore the Apgar score has proved to be a valuable prognosticator of neonatal survival and neurological sequelae.[1,2] The 5-minute score has a stronger predictability of neurological damage at 1 year of age than does the 1-minute score.[1,2]

To evaluate the neonate according to the Apgar scoring method (Table 19-1), the five variables—heart rate, respiratory rate and effort, muscle tone, reflex irritability, and color—should be separately evaluated and then given a score of 0, 1, or 2. The scores of each variable are then added, and the Apgar score is given for 1 minute and 5 minutes of life.[1,2,6]

The heart rate should be evaluated with a stethoscope and the person auscultating the heart rate should indicate the heartbeats by a motion or tapping of the forefinger. Sometimes pulse rate may be obtained from the pulsations of the umbilical stump, which are palpable for 10 minutes or longer after birth. The recommended method is chest auscultation and evaluation of the normal newborn pulse, which varies between 100 and 170 beats/min. Maternal drugs, hyperthermia, or moderate asphyxia may result in tachycardia. A bradycardia, or pulse rate less than 100 beats/min, may indicate primary apnea or secondary apnea. If initiation of stimulation does not increase the heart rate or respiratory effort, secondary apnea is recognized and assisted ventilation is necessitated.*

The respiratory effort is evaluated at birth. Usually respiratory effort is initiated in the first 30 seconds of life and begins to have a regular rhythm by 90 seconds. If the baby is born with acidosis, difficulty maintaining respirations or evidence of persistent apnea will be noted. Correction of this hypoventilatory status as soon as possible is of prime importance secondary to the increase in Pco_2 levels during hypoventilation and increasing acidosis.*

The muscle tone may be decreased secondary to maternal drugs, anesthesia, asphyxia, central nervous system damage, severe prematurity, and rare diseases such as congenital myasthenia gravis.[1,2,5] Evaluation of muscle tone is made through ob-

*See references 1, 2, 6, 7, 13 and 15.

serving the neonate's extremities for spontaneous flexion and extension during the first few minutes of life.[1,2,6,7]

Reflex irritability of the neonate can be noted in response to cutaneous stimulation, painful stimulation (vitamin K injection), grimacing, and crying. If stimulation such as suctioning the nose or oropharynx causes crying, a score of 2 is given. If only a grimace is elicited, a score of 1 is given. No response to suctioning with a catheter or bulb syringe scores 0.[1,2,6,7]

The color of the neonate can be evaluated according to the body and the peripheral extremities since many newborns have acrocyanosis well after the Apgar scores have been given, although central cyanosis, which exhibits a blue cast all over the neonate's body, is indicative of low cardiac output, cardiac disease, or pulmonary disease. This is especially valid if the neonate continues to be cyanotic after ventilation with oxygen.[1,2,6,7]

The Apgar scoring method has been used as a guide for resuscitation methods. A score of 0 to 3 indicates severe distress and necessitates immediate resuscitation. Neonates with Apgar scores of 4 to 7 are considered in moderate distress and may need resuscitative efforts. A score of 7 to 10 requires observation and close surveilance to prevent delayed respiratory depression secondary to drugs, anesthetics, and central nervous system anomalies.[1-5,36]

The normal neonate that requires no resuscitative responses by the perinatal staff should be suctioned again, remain under observation, and have a quick head-to-toe physical examination performed. The moderately depressed neonate will generally respond to gentle stimulation such as rubbing the chest, slapping the soles of the feet, or blowing oxygen over the face. The oropharynx should be suctioned well and the infant examined for possible upper airway obstruction. If no evidence of obstruction is found, provision of cutaneous stimulation is in order to initiate breathing. Similarly, the moderately depressed neonate responds like the group of monkeys who experienced primary apnea in the studies of Dawes and associates.[1-5,13-15]

If the moderately depressed neonate fails to initiate respirations with stimulation, ventilatory assistance with a bag and mask is in order. According to Berman and Saunders,[6] there are several devices that can be used for positive pressure ventilation.

Table 19-2. Average blood pressures of normal newborns*

Weight	Age	
	1 hour	12 hours
Over 3000 gm		
Systole	70	66
Diastole	44	41
Mean	53	50
200-300 gm		
Systole	59	59
Diastole	32	35
Mean	43	42
1000-2000 gm		
Systole	49	50
Diastole	26	30
Mean	35	38

*Adapted from Kitterman, J. A., et al.: Pediatrics **44:**959, 1969.

Most importantly, a pop-off valve and manometer should be part of the system for safety and more accurate compliance determination. Most infants will need 25 to 30 cm H_2O pressure to expand the lungs! The infant who has not taken a spontaneous breath may require up to 50 cm H_2O pressure to inflate unexpanded alveoli.[36] In most cases, however, after the first two or three breaths, only 20 cm H_2O pressure is needed for ventilation and aeration.[36] Assisted ventilatory rates should not exceed 40/min so that sufficient time for expiration is allowed. When bag and mask are used, there is a tendency to inflate the stomach with air. Insertion of a nasogastric tube will keep the stomach decompressed and give more room for pulmonary expansion.[4,6,36]

If bradycardia develops during heart rate evaluation, laryngoscopy should be performed, the cords visualized, foreign material suctioned out, and/or the trachea intubated. Consequently, ventilation can be achieved via the endotracheal tube and bag. The moderately depressed neonate's blood pressure should be measured, and a volume expander should be given if necessary. Table 19-2 lists the average blood pressures of normal newborns according to weight and time after delivery.[6]

Severely depressed neonates will require immediate resuscitation. If evaluation of respirations is poor or absent and the heart rate is less than

100 beats/min, laryngoscopy should be performed, foreign material removed from oropharynx and trachea, and an endotracheal tube should be inserted.[1-6,20,36] These infants are often in shock, are pale, and have weak pulses.[36]

When the heart rate is absent or less than 100 beats/min and does not increase after 1 minute of assisted ventilation, cardiac massage is begun in coordinated efforts with the ventilatory assistance. "Two fingers are applied just above the heart to the left of the lower sternal border and sufficient pressure is applied for 1 to 2 cm of depression."[36] Cardiac massage should be performed with ventilation in a 3:1 ratio. It is essential to be observant of this coordination so as not to inflate the lungs during compression of the chest. The result could be subsequent barotrauma. With well-coordinated and performed efforts, cardiopulmonary resuscitation of the neonate will provide sufficient cardiac output to prevent anoxic cerebral damage.[1,5,6,36] During this active performance of resuscitation, massage should be stopped at intervals to reevaluate the heart rate and rhythm.[36]

Arterial blood gases are important parameters to assess during resuscitation of a severely depressed neonate.* An umbilical arterial catheter can be inserted and directed just above the abdominal aorta bifurcation at the vertebral level of L3-4.[3,4,6,23,36] The arterial blood sample will help evaluate acid-base status and level of oxygenation. It is a well-known fact that resuscitation efforts in the presence of severe acidosis are ineffective.†

The severely depressed neonate at this time may respond to resuscitation with an increased heart rate and spontaneous respirations, although no change in cardiopulmonary status is a more likely occurrence owing to the severe metabolic processes that have evolved during the asphyxiating event. Interventions with medicinal therapeutic agents is the next required resuscitative measure.[1]

In most cases, drugs will not be necessary to resuscitate a distressed neonate. However, when ventilation with oxygen and cardiac massage are ineffectual, administration of drugs is necessary. Table 19-3 lists the drugs most commonly used in

resuscitation, their indications for use, routes of administration, and dosages.[36]

When drugs are administered, they usually are given via the umbilical vein catheter. Hypotension is noted by pallor, poor capillary refill, mottling of the skin, and a low measurement on blood pressure recordings. Asphyxia and acute blood loss during the intrapartum period are causes of hypotension. Accordingly, shock also presents clinically as hypotension. The neonate should receive volume expanders such as whole blood or a 5% protein solution at 10 to 20 ml/kg over 5 minutes.*

Severely stressed infants also have difficulty maintaining their serum glucose levels. Intravenous solutions such as D_5W, $D_{10}W$, or $D_{25}W$ may be administered to correct the hypoglycemic response of the neonate to asphyxiation.†

If there is a maternal history of respiratory depressant drugs such as barbiturates or anesthetic agents, naloxone (Narcan) should be administered at 0.01 mg/kg to reverse the central respiratory depression and resultant hypoventilation.[1,3,36]

Nearly all severely asphyxiated neonates will have a mixed respiratory and metabolic acidosis.‡ Respiratory acidosis can be intervened with by assisted ventilation, and the hypoventilation is reversed causing increased Po_2 levels and removal of Pco_2. Metabolic acidemia can be caused by and perpetuated by hypotension and hypoxia. Before metabolic aberrations can be corrected, the causes must be reversed. However, in the case of severe, prolonged asphyxia, administration of alkali buffers is indicated to neutralize excess hydrogen ions. One to 2 mEq/kg of sodium bicarbonate diluted to 0.3 to 0.5 mEq/ml with sterile water is given by slow infusion (over 5 minutes) through the umbilical vein catheter above the level of the umbilicus. Infusion of sodium bicarbonate too quickly will cause serious hyperosmolar damage by causing a fluid shift that may be related to intracranial hemorrhage.§ Also, it must be evident that there is an open system for removal of excess CO_2 by the lungs through adequate ventilation. Sodium bicarbonate is degradated

---

*See references 1, 3, 5, 20, 23, and 36.
†See references 1, 3, 5, 12, 14, 15, 20, 23, 36, and 39.

*See references 1, 3-6, 20, 23, and 36.
†See references 1, 3-6, 20, 23, and 36.
‡See references 1, 3-6, 20, 23, and 36.
§See references 1, 3, 5, 6, 15, and 36.

Table 19-3. Indications and dosages of drugs commonly used in neonatal resuscitation*

Drug	Indication	Route of administration	Dose
Whole blood or 5% protein solution	History of blood loss, shock, hypotension	IV	10-20 ml/kg
$D_{25}W$	Asphyxia	IV	4 ml/kg over 5 minutes
Naloxone	Maternal narcotic administration and neonatal depression	IV	0.01 mg/kg
$NaHCO_3$, 0.88 or 1 mEq/ml	Severe metabolic acidemia or severe asphyxia not responsive to routine resuscitation	IV	1-2 mEq/kg over 5 minutes; dilute 1:2 with sterile water
Epinephrine 1:10,000	Cardiac arrest, severe bradycardia not responsive to routine resuscitation	IV (while performing cardiac massage) or intracardiac injection	0.1-0.3 ml/kg of 1:10,000 solution
Calcium gluconate, 10%	Severe bradycardia	IV	1 ml/kg slowly
$CaCl_2$, 10%	Severe bradycardia	IV	0.1 ml/kg slowly
Atropine	Sinus bradycardia	IV or IM	0.03 mg/kg
Isoproterenol	Bradycardia, hypotension	IV infusion	4 mg/250 ml D_5W
THAM	Metabolic acidemia	IV infusion	Titrate against the heart rate
Narcan	Respiratory depression caused by barbiturates	IV or SL	0.005 mg/kg—2 ml IM (pediatric strength); 0.1 ml/mg of adult Narcan sublingually

*Adapted from Schreiner, R.: Neonatology for the pediatrician, Indianapolis, 1978, Section of Neonatal-Perinatal Medicine, Department of Pediatrics, James Whitcomb Riley Hospital for Children; and Berman, L., and Saunders, B.: Perinatol. Neonatol., p. 22, January/February, 1980.

further to CO_2 and H_2O in the oxidation-reduction equation.[3,6] Infusion of sodium bicarbonate can therefore actually cause further decreases in pH and a more serious acidemia without adequate removal of the CO_2 by the pulmonary system.[1,3,6,15] Some have advocated the utilization of pure alkali (THAM) when adequate pulmonary exchange is jeopardized by neonatal respiratory distress syndromes,[1,3] although it stands with difficulty in administration and has serious complications when inappropriately utilized as does sodium bicarbonate. Consequently, the administration of alkali therapy should be done precisely based on acid-base arterial determinations.

Indications for the use of epinephrine, atropine, and isoproterenol are cardiac arrest, bradycardia, or shock that is unresponsive to routine resuscitation.[1,3,6,15,36] Calcium gluconate and calcium chloride are administered under the presence of severe bradycardia and possible depletion of myocardial stores of calcium responsible for adequate contractility.[3,12,15,36]

As seen with the moderately depressed neonate,

the need for intervention frequently cannot wait for assigning Apgar scores. There are times when the urgency of the situation can be evaluated more quickly by assessing the heart rate and respiratory response. The time frame of 60 seconds to assign the first score and select a method of resuscitation based on this score is oftentimes too long. The time right after delivery is precious, especially when the asphyxiation process has occurred in utero. If the neonate is born with secondary apnea owing to uterine asphyxiation, 60 seconds of inadequate resuscitative efforts may prove to be fatal.[36]

The severely depressed neonate will require immediate resuscitative efforts. Oftentimes the perinatal health care team is anxiously awaiting the birth of this anticipated newborn from the earlier communication about the factors associated with perinatal asphyxia during the antepartum and intrapartum period.[9] There are times, however, when the birth of a severely depressed neonate is unexpected, and evaluation and resuscitative efforts must be made immediately.[36] Without the interventions of the prepared perinatal health team, asphyxia in the compromised neonate may result in death or permanent central nervous system damage. As evidence of this fact is that asphyxia is one of the leading causes of mortality and morbidity in the newborn.*

SPECIAL CARE OF THE ASPHYXIATED NEONATE AND HIGH-RISK FAMILY

Care for the asphyxiated neonate does not end with resuscitation. Once the neonate has been stabilized in the delivery room and transferred to the newborn special care unit or to a regional center, continued close observations of the clinical, biochemical, and respiratory status must be instituted by the perinatal health care team. Appropriate measurements of vital functions and metabolism are crucial to detect adverse responses to stress and to prevent further complicating sequelae.[36]

Again, the level of promptness and efficiency of well-educated perinatal health care members is essential in the functioning of an intensive care unit.† According to Schreiner,[36] ''Only with structured programs which train personnel and maintain proficiency in both acute and convalescent management of neonatal asphyxia can the ultimate goal of eliminating preventable causes of psychomotor retardation be achieved.''

The nursing management of the neonate with asphyxia admitted to the special care unit is a process of assessment, intervention, and evaluation.[9] A problem list that identifies the areas of focus and need can be developed from the subjective data base collected on admission and from biochemical and physical objective findings.[9]

The initial care of this infant should include a maternal and newborn history, physical assessment of the newborn, gestational age assessment, and collection of vital signs.[4,7,9]

Continuing physical care of the neonate, once stabilized in special care, includes the maintenance of a neutral thermal environment, continuous monitoring of vital signs, and detection of respiratory patterns such as apnea, periodic breathing, dyspnea, retractions, grunting, or nasal flaring. Detection of blood sugar levels with Dextrostix as a screening device, determination of hematocrit and hemoglobin, and analysis of arterial blood gases are impor-

tant laboratory indices to be done on admission and give an indication of current status.*

If positive pressure ventilation has been used during resuscitative efforts and the abdomen is distended, the placement of a nasogastric or orogastric tube should be instituted so as not to compromise the respiratory effort.†

Maintenance of fluid volume in the asphyxiated neonate is another area of prime concern. Insertion of a peripheral IV will provide adequate hydration and allow caloric intake.[4,5,7]

The neonate may arrive in the special care unit with an umbilical catheter in place or the catheter may be inserted after the admission. Above all, proper aseptic technique when inserting the catheter and during its installation is necessary.

Reduction of risk for nosocomial infections should be practiced by all members of the health care team with strict handwashing and protection of invasive sites.

Observation of the clinical signs and symptoms of sepsis, hyperbilirubinemia, and necrotizing enterocolitis, which are common problems, is an anticipatory role of the perinatal nurse caring for a stressed neonate.

Administration of medicinal therapeutics whether parenterally or intravenously should be done safely, aseptically, and within the therapeutic range for weight and age of the neonate. Complications and contraindications of medicinal agents should be uppermost in the mind of the perinatal nurse.[1]

Careful attention to skin care, oral hygiene, and positioning are other nursing measures to be considered in the care of the high-risk neonate.

The incidence of child abuse is high in neonates who are born prematurely and experience a prolonged separation time from the mother.[9,18,24,37] The perinatal nurse has a role in establishing a firm maternal-paternal-infant bond that will provide for family interactions. Observations of visits, touching the newborn, eye-to-eye contact, talking to the baby, participating in the infant's care, and phone calls made concerning the infant are sound reactions by the parents that will encourage and promote family bonding.[9,18,24,37]

Psychosocial care of the high-risk family should

---

*See references 1-7, 9, 15, 20, 23, 25, and 36.
†See references 1, 4, 5, 7, 9, 20, and 23.

*See references 1, 3-5, 7, 9, 20, 23, and 25.
*See references 3-5, 7, 9, 20, and 23.

also include measures to keep contact with the family if they are unable to visit with phone calls, letters, and snapshots. This will help the mother who is unable to come to visit the baby "formulate a realistic concept about her newborn."[9]

Answering questions as honestly and truthfully as possible is a role the perinatal nurse must incorporate to build the trust of the parents who are in crisis and stress. Utilizing members of the immediate family such as grandparents, the nurse will be able to give the high-risk family support systems outside the health care system to help them survive their crisis situation.[9,18]

The newborn in intensive care, despite the loud noises, continued light, and continual auditory stimulation, can develop a sensory deprivation from being overshowered with the wrong kind of stimuli. It must be remembered that ordinary stimuli such as gentle touch, stroking the back, talking softly with eye-to-eye contact as well as visual stimulation of colors, wall decorations, and mobiles are experiences a normal baby would experience.[50] "The longer the infant does not have his senses stimulated, the more difficult it is to elicit them later," stated Butnarescu.[9]

According to Yura and Walsh,[50] the need to love and be loved takes priority immediately at birth. "The infant needs to be warm, to feel protected, nursed at intervals to feel nurtured, held firmly to be accepted, and stroked, talked to, and cuddled to feel attached." Tender loving care by the mother, maternal figure, or caretaker is highly significant in fulfilling the newborn's need for support through acceptance of human contact.

"What each human being becomes depends in great measure on his early relationship among humans. Deprivations in these human exchanges can culminate in varying degrees of illness. For the infant tactile stimulation is basic to the development of healthy emotional and affectional relationships."[50]

COMPLICATIONS AND PROGNOSIS OF ASPHYXIA

At this point, it is evident that a severe asphyxiating insult can cause many complications for the neonate. Many of the organ systems of the neonate are adversely affected by the hypoxemia. The cardiovascular system has effects that range from bradycardia to heart failure.[3] Severe hypoxia has even shown evidence of ECG changes and cardiac isoenzyme elevations indicating myocardial ischemia, injury, and infarction.[3,12,15] Also, after a hypoxic episode when the neonate has returned to a fetal circulatory pattern, it may not be possible for the infant to reverse the pattern to adult circulation, consequently leading to increasing hypoxemia to other systems and deteriorating acid-base balance.[1,3,11,21]

Most importantly the central nervous system is affected by an asphyxiating insult. Eventually brain cells deteriorate from breakdown of ionic gradients across cell membranes and the accumulation of lactate. Mitochondrial swelling results in release of proteases of lysosomes and cell destruction begins. How long a brain cell can be hypoxic and not lose its capacity for survival is unknown. Clinical signs of such hypoxic events within the CNS of a neonate are irregularity in respirations and periodic breathing analogous to Cheyne-Stokes respiration patterns in adults; such signs are indicative of bilateral hemispherical disturbance.[3] Pupillary response to light may or may not be present depending on gestational age and intactness of the third cranial nerve.[3] Spontaneous eye roving movements are present with hypoxic-ischemic insults. Only in babies with severe anoxia could there be signs of brain stem disturbances such as fixed dilated pupils and eye movements absent and not elicitable by doll's eye phenomenon.[3]

Most commonly, one may think of seizure activity when considering hypoxia and ischemia of the CNS. However, if seizure activity occurs before the first 24 hours of life and in the delivery room, such problems as hyponatremia, hypoglycemia, and a developmental abnormality of the brain should be considered.[3,20]

At approximately 24 hours of age the infant becomes less depressed, and seizures are evidenced associated with this change in level of consciousness.[3] These types of seizures are subtle and multifocal clonic types. Of consideration in prognostic outlook is the infant who has sustained prolonged ischemia and has impressive patterns of motor weakness. Full-term infants will display weaknesses in the hip and shoulder areas, while preterm infants will have bilateral lower limb weakness.[3]

In severe cases of hypoxic-ischemic insult, there

will be evidence of stupor or coma. Clinically, the infant will have a full anterior fontanelle signifying cerebral edema and/or intraventricular hemorrhage.[3] Those infants who survive such an insult and have gradual improvement of CNS function will be faced with a variable neurological sequelae influenced by the amount of hypoxia endured, the duration of the ischemic insult, and the rapidity of reversal of clinical symptomatology.[3,27,38,46]

The quality of survival after severe birth asphyxia was studied by Thomson, Searle, and Russell[46] with 31 children who survived severe birth asphyxia (defined by a 1-minute Apgar score of 0 or a 5-minute score of less than 4). The children investigated were 5 to 10 years of age at the time of the study. Neurological and psychological assessment was made and compared to a control group. Twenty-nine (93%) of the asphyxiated group had no serious neurological or mental handicap. Two were slightly disabled and mentally retarded. Thomson and associates[46] concluded ''that the quality of life enjoyed by the large majority of the survivors was such as to justify a positive approach to the resuscitation of very severely asphyxiated neonates.''

Scott[38] also investigated the outcome of very severe birth asphyxia and associated any later handicap with factors leading to prolonged partial intrapartum asphyxia, while acute periods of more complete asphyxia were not necessarily harmful. At a period of 3 to 7 years later, he found 75% of his 48 newborns asphyxiated at birth to be apparently normal.

Obviously, the recommendations of McManus and associates[27] concerning the identification of the high-risk pregnancy, fetal monitoring, appropriate resuscitation at delivery, and early transfer of compromised infants to neonatal intensive care units are valid improvements in the prevention of cerebral palsy.

The kidney is another vital organ of the neonate that may be adversely affected by an asphyxiating insult. Inadequate oxygenation of the organ itself or a decreased cardiac output to the glomerulus will cause prerenal azotemia and possible renal shutdown with acute tubular necrosis. Without the kidneys to filter metabolic wastes from the blood, the neonate will continue to circulate toxic substances that will alter homeostasis significantly.[1,3,7,9,20]

Concurrently, the gastrointestinal tract is also affected by hypoxemia. Being the organ whose blood supply is shunted away first when hypoxia occurs, it is highly vulnerable to infarction from anoxia. When such an event occurs, a malabsorption pattern results. The severest form is known as necrotizing enterocolitis, and it carries a high morbidity and mortality rate alone.[1,3,7,9,20]

The systems just mentioned have been affected in one way or another by hypoxemia that has resulted from some type of hypoxic-ischemic insult in utero, during the birthing process, or while establishing adaptation to extrauterine life. It would be optimal for the nurse to consider iatrogenic causes of hypoxia and institute actions to prevent further insult. Some of these are umbilical artery and vein catheters that may occlude vessels, thus preventing blood flow to an organ or extremity, or the potential embolus formation that can occur and be shed throughout the body when invasive techniques are utilized. The amount of oxygen therapy (FIO_2) the neonate is receiving should be monitored closely, not only for evidence of inadequate amounts of oxygen delivered but also for an assessment of the excessiveness of oxygen.

Retrolental fibroplasia is a condition in which the retinal vessels constrict in the presence of increased oxygen tension. The result of such prolonged constriction is eventually obliteration and adherence of the vessel walls that show eventual degenerative changes. There are several stages of involvement that may resolve in a reversal of constricted vessels; a mild myopia; or a complete obliteration, retinal detachment, and resultant blindness.[3]

Another complication that has not been studied well is the long-term effect of being involved with invasive techniques, intensive care therapy, and probable intubation over several days. The response of the adult in ICU settings is made evident by the patient's emotions and verbal or nonverbal behaviors. The constant stimulation of sounds, monitors, nurses, physicians, pain, and touching that is not always loving may have deleterious long-term effects that have not been studied well.

Furthermore, much can be said about the psychological and sociological trauma that is occurring by the fact that mother and infant are separated and that she has produced a high-risk infant.[18,24,37] Klaus and Kennell[24] have studied this stressful situation in premature birthing experiences, anticipatory grief reactions, and bonding difficulties. Another view of the stressful situation and its outcome is the concept of ''vulnerable child syndrome'' as a psychological sequela of early infancy health crisis. This situation in effect has set the stage for stressful family life and the child for neglect or abuse.[37]

The complications of asphyxia are as many and varied as all the biological, genetic, psychological, and social elements involved. The role of the perinatal nurse in caring for the asphyxiated infant or the neonate at high risk for asphyxia will be one of anticipation, prevention, recognition, collaboration, interventions, and evaluation. The plan of care will be individualized for each high-risk situation that has a different set of elements than the last asphyxiated neonate for which the nurse cared. This neonate is a new life with unique characteristics who will try to adapt to the extrauterine world despite the risks we have identified. In the focus of perinatal health care will be physicians and nurses anxiously awaiting the arrival of the high-risk neonate and carefully assessing the process of extrauterine adaptation.

Protocols

Problem □ Identification of the maternal and fetal factors associated with asphyxiated neonates in the antepartal period

GOAL: To recognize early the high-risk maternal-fetal unit
  Rationale: To detect high-risk infants early so that their progress in labor and delivery can be monitored and resuscitation can be started at birth (Early detection and management will decrease the risk of poor fetal outcome.[3])

DIAGNOSTIC
1. Gather data concerning the pregnancy through the utilization of a nursing history and physical assessment.
   Rationale: To identify high-risk patients would be optimal health care[9]
2. Utilize a questionnaire screening tool or patient interview method (or both) as an assessment of specific historical psychosocial, genetic, biophysical, and economic problems; assessments of the reproductive health history; and an assessment of the status of the current pregnancy.
   Rationale: To identify risks during the remaining prenatal period, during labor, and/or during the neonatal period[1,7]

3. Perform a clinical evaluation of the patient including all systems, measurements of maternal and fetal vital signs, measurements of fundal height, maternal weight, and evaluation of fetal movement, lie, and presentation whenever possible.
   Rationale: To evaluate maternal systems and vital statistics in relation to the growing fetus (Evaluation of fetal gestation and maternal characteristics must be correlated. ''Early detection of the potential for, or existence of problems associated with, reproductive risk is the best insurance for the prevention of extensive damage to or death of the pregnant woman and her unborn or newborn child.''[9]
4. Assess the patient's level of communication and learning, along with assessments involved with psychosocial attitudes (that is, self, family, the pregnancy, attire, verbal and nonverbal communications, body language).
   Rationale: To identify areas of psychosocial risk (Inclusion of psychosocial, communication, and learning capacities should be noted. Indications of psychosocial risk may be apparent at any point in pregnancy.[9,18]

5. Focus on the relevance of routine laboratory studies and their outcomes when collecting objective data on the first prenatal visit. These studies should include: *blood type studies* for maternal blood group and Rh factor, *serology* for a diagnostic basis for detection of syphilis, *hematocrit* and *hemoglobin* for differentiation of anemias, *white blood count* and *differential* for detection of infection and blood abnormalities, *antibody studies* for sensitization to isoantigens, *rubella titers* for the presence of antibody formation, *serum glucose* for detection of hypoglycemia or hyperglycemia, and *urine studies* for the presence of glucose, protein, bacteria, and ketones. Also included are the *Papanicolau smear* for diagnosis of cervical carcinoma and *vaginal smears* and *cultures* for the presence of gonnorrhea.*

   Rationale: To broaden the scope of objective assessments in the antepartal period through use of technological innovations (Interpretation of the results and their significance to the plan of care is viewed as an essential tool by perinatal medicine and nursing.[9])

6. Assess the biochemical results and evaluations of special antepartal procedures used to help diagnose and manage certain diseases and disorders in high-risk pregnancies including *amniotic fluid studies* for detection of fetal lung and renal maturity, presence of fat cells through cytological examination of the fluid, and presence of bilirubin or meconium in the fluid during fetal distress, *clinical ultrasonography* for establishing fetal maturity and gestational assessments of size, and *oxytocin challenge testing* and *nonstress testing* to measure the respiratory function of the uteroplacental unit prior to the onset of labor.*

   Rationale: To provide "useful adjuncts to nurses in planning and providing care to pregnant families at reproductive risk"[9] (The nurse will find that much of the clinical assessment activity is within the limits of nursing practice, and utilization of biochemical analysis will help broaden and support her assessments as much as give a direction and focus of planning care.[9])

7. Identify those patients who have subjective and objective data bases as reproductive risks. Especially for the purpose of this protocol, identify those patients who have maternal factors associated with perinatal asphyxiation (see list on pp. 312 and 313).

   Rationale: To identify reproductive risk as being a psychosocial, genetic, biophysical, or economic entity[9] (It has been recognized in many studies that there are comparable and contrasting relationships existing before and during pregnancy that are a risk to fetal outcome.*)

THERAPEUTIC

1. Bring the nursing assessments made that may constitute a reproductive risk to the attention of the other members of the perinatal health care team.

   Rationale: To become a collaborative member of the perinatal health care team in planning for the care of a high-risk patient, directiveness in nursing assessments and "efforts will be made that will contribute to the reduction of reproductive risk and move prospective parents, their children, and society toward the goal of reproductive health."[9]

2. Promote optimal maternal-fetal unit processes by encouraging the high-risk mother to take measures that will provide her with adequate rest at night and during the day.

   Rationale: To encourage optimal maternal health, nutrition and rest, physically and psychologically for proper differentiation and development of the growing fetus

3. Encourage the intake of a nutritionally sound diet (high-protein, high-vitamin, and high-mineral) during pregnancy.

   Rationale: To foster fetal growth and maintenance[4] (The mother's health and that of her offspring depend in large measure on the quality rather than the quantity of her food intake. Faulty maternal nutrition, including vitamin and mineral lack, has an adverse effect on fertility, embryogenesis, and fetal growth.[4])

4. Support the compliance of the high-risk maternal unit to ingest daily mineral and vitamin supplementations during pregnancy.

*See references 1, 3-5, 7, 9, and 23.

*See references 1, 3-5, 7, 9, and 23.

Rationale: To point out to the patient that nutritional supplementation is not a replacement for sound nutrition in pregnancy but an adjunctive measure to daily nutritional requirements for the differentiation, development, and growth of the fetus[4,7]

5. Utilize resources such as dietitians in the antepartal period for patient counseling when evidence of poor nutrition is noted. Accordingly, referrals to community health agencies concerning lack of economic resources for a high-protein diet may be instituted.

Rationale: To identify high-risk patients having need of special dietary counseling, including women with anemia, chronic metabolic disorders (diabetes mellitus, thyroid, cardiovascular, and renal disorders), weight 10% under or 20% over the recommended weight at onset of pregnancy, history of previous complicated pregnancies (abortions, toxemia, premature rupture of placenta, and low birth weight infants), socioeconomic difficulties (adolescents, poor), and obstetrical complications such as hyperemesis gravidarum (A good pregnancy diet is not a simple task for these women. Lack of knowledge, money, or motivation are some reasons why these women have difficulty attaining a high-protein, high-mineral, and high-vitamin diet.[4,7])

6. Administer therapeutic agents to the high-risk maternal-fetal unit when the diagnosed disorder necessitates medicinal interventions (for example, administration of iron sulfate and folic acid in iron deficiency anemias).

Rationale: To institute medicinal intervention in the antepartal period for those patients who have been identified to have maternal factors associated with asphyxia in the perinatal period (Comprehension of the therapeutic agent utilized and possible complications that may occur to mother or fetus during the course of its utilization is an important function of the perinatal nurse dealing with a high-risk pregnancy.)

7. Facilitate compliance of future antepartal visits by making appointments, counseling sessions, and other perinatal assessments convenient and accessible for the high-risk patient.

Rationale: To ensure positive reproductive outcome (The relationship between antepartal care, continuity, and positive reproductive outcome has been studied by many researchers.[3,4,7,9] Inadequate assessments, diagnosis, and treatment of risk conditions has been proved to lead to poor reproductive outcome. Facilitating the best antepartal assessments, diagnosis, and treatments through early recognition and continuity of patient care is a key role in the function of a perinatal nurse.[9])

8. Provide emotional support and understanding of the high-risk maternal-fetal unit during this time of uncertainty, fear, and stress.

Rationale: To promote good psychological adaptation (The high-risk pregnancy presents a risk to the health or the normal development of the child and mother. In addition, the emotional effects of the risk pregnancy, the stress of additional medical procedures, and the potential loss of the child may drastically affect the psychological development of the family itself.[18])

EDUCATIONAL

1. Promote patient and family education of the "high-risk" pregnancy by having opportunities to discuss routine care during the antepartum period, infant care, the process of labor and delivery, and specific counseling about the patient's risk situation and family changes at her level of understanding.

Rationale: To help families make satisfactory adjustments to the stresses created by a high-risk pregnancy through education[18]

2. Help the high-risk mother who is having difficulty with her nutritional status bring a dietary recall of what she eats every day to her next visit for evaluation.

Rationale: To make the mother feel more involved with her own care and foster compliance[18]

3. Counsel and help reinforce education concerning future reproductive risks for the involved family when genetic factors, maternal age, or biophysical factors could create potential poor fetal outcome.

Rationale: To reach patients who would benefit most from specialized antenatal care prior to the conception of the reproductive risk or in its earliest stages of development[9,19]

Problem □ Maternal-fetal unit presents in the intrapartum period with factors associated with perinatal asphyxia

GOAL: To detect the asphyxiated fetus in utero early

Rationale: To avoid brain damage by identifying fetal hypoxia and fetal hypotension early[27,38,46] and to detect early and manage properly fetal distress in utero, thus decreasing the risk of fetal mortality and morbidity*

DIAGNOSTIC

1. Gather subjective and objective data through utilization of nursing history, physical examination, measurements, and biochemical analysis of the maternal-fetal unit requiring intrapartum nursing care.

   Rationale: To afford patients optimal health care delivery through identification of high-risk patients[9] ("Early detection of the potential for, or existence of problems associated with, reproductive risk is the best insurance for the prevention of extensive damage to or death of the pregnant woman and her unborn or newborn child."[9])

2. Assess the patient's level of communication and learning, along with assessments involving psychosocial attitudes (that is, self, family, the pregnancy, labor and delivery, verbal and nonverbal communications, and body language).

   Rationale: To identify level of understanding and psychosocial attitudes (Indications of psychosocial risk may be apparent at any point in pregnancy.[9,18])

3. Assess the status of labor of the patient through clinical assessments of uterine contractions, their timing, duration, and frequency; assessments of cervical dilatation and effacement; and assessments of maternal and fetal vital statistics (that is, temperature, heart rate, blood pressure, respiratory rate of mother, fetal heart rate of the fetus with a stethoscope).

Rationale: To promote a decrease in reproductive risk and to facilitate specific nursing responsibilities in the planning of care for intrapartum patients through keeping current with the recent technological advances and keeping clinical assessment skills sharpened[9]

4. Note the color, consistency, and odor of the amniotic fluid.

   Rationale: To detect whether amniotic fluid is stained, thick, or foul-smelling, indicating meconium staining, which necessitates fetal heart rate monitoring and scalp blood sampling to determine the presence of asphyxia[7]

5. Institute continuous fetal heart rate monitoring to evaluate the labor process.

   Rationale: To detect baseline features that would necessitate intervention (According to Avery,[3] "Normal labor is defined as that degree of labor that does not encroach significantly on the fetal margin of reserve." Mild to moderate variable decelerations are generally of no consequence to the fetus except when they are accompanied by a rising baseline, loss of variability, or falling pH. Baseline features such as absent variability, tachycardia, bradycardia, and periodic features such as late decelerations and variable decelerations [rebound accelerations] are considered ominous signs and require immediate intervention.*

6. Assess fetal blood sampling when indicated.

   Rationale: To obtain data concerning the fetal acid-base balance during labor through samples of capillary blood from the fetal scalp† (According to Bolognese and Schwarz,[7] "interpretation of fetal blood pH levels has not been completely uniform, but most authors consider values less than 7.20 to be suggestive of significant asphyxia and those between 7.20 and 7.24 preacidotic.")

7. Identify those patients who have subjective and objective criteria evidenced to be considered a reproductive risk. Especially for the purpose of this protocol identify those ma-

---

*See references 1, 3-5, 7, 9, 18, and 23.

*See references 1, 3-5, 7, 9, 23, 35, and 42.
†See references 1, 3, 5, 7, 10, and 23.

ternal-fetal units who have factors associated with perinatal asphyxiation (see list on p. 316).

Rationale: To detect early and manage consequences of fetal distress in the intrapartum period, thus decreasing the risk of poor fetal outcome*

THERAPEUTIC

1. Bring to the attention of the other members of the perinatal health care team (that is, obstetrician, pediatrician, nursery nurses) the nursing assessments made that may constitute a reproductive risk.

   Rationale: To ensure directiveness in nursing assessments and "efforts will be made that will contribute to the reduction of reproductive risk and move prospective parents, their children, and society toward the goal of reproductive health"[9]

2. Promote measures that improve uterine blood flow.

   a. Avoid supine position.

      Rationale: To ensure that blood flow through the abdominal aorta and inferior vena cava does not become obstructed by the uterus and result in supine hypotension from inadequate blood return to the right heart and consequential diminished cardiac output[3,7]

   b. Reduce uterine contractions.

      Rationale: To be aware that the use of uterotonic agents (oxytocin) is associated with an increased incidence of late decelerations and careful control and use of these agents can stimulate effective uterine contractility[3-5,7,9,24]

   c. Maintain maternal-fetal hydration.

      Rationale: To be aware that the sympathetic blockade accompanying epidural anesthesia may result in diminished uterine blood flow (Epidural anesthesia and concomitant use of oxytocin has been noted to cause late decelerations. Maintaining hydrated patients in the lateral position will help combat the sympathetic loss of tone in lower maternal extremities and hypotension.[3,7,9])

   d. Detect and correct maternal hypotension through intravenous therapy.

      Rationale: To prevent risk of maternal hypotension to the fetus by correcting for the effects of epidural or spinal anesthesia by ensuring that the patient is properly hydrated prior to receiving the anesthetics[4,5,7,9]

3. Promote measures that will improve umbilical blood flow.

   a. Change maternal position by moving her from side to side, to Trendelenburg position, or even to knee-chest position.

      Rationale: To attempt to relieve severe variable decelerations by changes in maternal position to increase uterine blood flow and fetal oxygenation[3,7,9]

   b. Give support to the mother who requires maneuvers to alter the anatomical relationship of the fetus, umbilical cord, and uterine wall.

      Rationale: To alleviate severe variable decelerations manipulations of the fetal position to increase uterine blood flow through the umbilical cord and ensure adequate oxygenation may be required[3,7,9]

   c. Elevate the vertex when mother is in the Trendelenburg position.

      Rationale: To place the mother in the Trendelenburg position before the vertex is elevated, thus minimizing the chances for cord prolapse and subsequent variable decelerations[7]

4. Enhance the maternal levels of oxygen (3 to 4 liters).

   Rationale: To bring about a small rise in Po_2 levels in the fetus and support adequate tissue oxygenation*

5. Alert pediatrician and special care nursery of the presence of meconium-stained amniotic fluid and persistent fetal distress signs in a high-risk pregnancy.

   Rationale: To be certain that adequately trained personnel and the necessary resuscitation equipment are ready in the delivery room[7]

---

*See references 1, 3-5, 7, 9, and 23.

---

*See references 1, 3-5, 7, 9, and 23.

EDUCATIONAL

1. Deliver patient education appropriate to the level of understanding and learning concerning the rationale and procedures that are associated with intrapartum monitoring.

   Rationale: To decrease the patient's level of anxiety and fear, promote opportunities to ask questions, and develop a relationship through communication with the perinatal nurse[42]

2. Prepare the high-risk patient and family for cesarean section when surgical intervention is the medical treatment indicated in severe fetal distress.

   Rationale: To allay fear, guilt, and difficulty in bonding to the infant along with other physical and psychological stresses[18]

3. Provide in-service and staff development programs for the labor and delivery room nurses concerning the management of fetal distress and asphyxiation.

   Rationale: To keep perinatal health care personnel informed of the continual developments of new techniques, thus helping to improve the quality of perinatal health care (Frequent reinforcement of clinical skill and technical assessments by the perinatal nurse in a learning situation will help substantiate and support the nurse's role as a collaborative member of the health team.)

Problem □ Birth of an asphyxiated neonate

GOAL: To provide initial resuscitative care; to evaluate the asphyxiated neonate; and to utilize approaches of resuscitation according to the guidelines of a mildly depressed, moderately depressed, or severely depressed neonate

Rationale: To be aware that asphyxia is considered to be a major cause of perinatal mortality and morbidity[3,36]

DIAGNOSTIC

1. Assess risk factors associated with perinatal asphyxia during the antepartum and the intrapartum period (see lists on pp. 312 and 313 and p. 316).

   Rationale: To implement therapeutic prevention and management in the care of the high-risk pregnancy by early assessment, diagnosis, and treatment of the known risk conditions on the part of the perinatal health care team[9]

2. Assess fetal factors associated with asphyxia at birth[36]:
   a. Multiple births
   b. Polyhydramnios
   c. Oligohydramnios
   d. Immature L/S ratio
   e. Premature delivery (less than 38 weeks)
   f. Postterm delivery (greater than 42 weeks)
   g. Increased rate of growth (LGA)
   h. Decreased rate of growth (SGA)
   i. Meconium-stained amniotic fluid
   j. Abnormal heart rate or rhythm
   h. Fetal acidosis (fetal scalp capillary blood pH less than 7.20)

   Rationale: To deliver prompt and adequate treatment to the neonate at risk for asphyxiation[9,36]

3. Be aware of the mode of delivery when anticipating an asphyxial insult.

   Rationale: To be aware of the fact that precipitous labors, difficult forceps deliveries, and cesarean sections are associated with perinatal asphyxiation more frequently than a normal vaginal delivery[5]

4. Assess medicinal agents that may have been used during the intrapartum period that may cause difficulty in breathing for the neonate.

   Rationale: To be aware that respiratory depressants such as barbiturates, narcotics, and anesthetic agents are known to cause central nervous system depression of the newborn and create a potential asphyxial episode[1,3,5,6,36]

5. Evaluate emergency apparatus and personnel to be present at the birth of an asphyxiated neonate (see list on p. 317).

   Rationale: To ensure that the members of the perinatal health care team who practice in the labor and delivery area and nursery areas are trained and educated in methods of resuscitation for the neonate and mother[5] (Emergency resuscitation that is effective and prompt is the result of trained personnel and carefully checked equipment that was present and functioning prior to the delivery.*)

---

*See references 1-7, 9, 15, 20, 23, and 36.

6. Assess the amniotic fluid at the time of delivery.

   Rationale: To be ready to initiate resuscitation at the delivery of the meconium-stained infant's head (Obstetricians will suction the nose and oropharynx free of the amniotic fluid contents then continue to deliver the shoulders and the body. The meconium-stained neonate will require special resuscitative efforts such as visualization of the cords and tracheal aspiration.[1,3,5,6,20])

7. A quick assessment of respiratory effort and heart rate should be made upon delivery.

   Rationale: To help the practitioner decide the type and extent of resuscitation[1]

8. Evaluate the neonatal status at 60 seconds of life:

   a. Assess heart rate with the stethoscope.

   Rationale: To be aware that the normal newborn pulse varies between 100 and 170 beats/min; that maternal drugs, hyperthermia, or a moderate asphyxia may result in tachycardia; and that a bradycardia or pulse rate less than 100 beats/min may indicate primary or secondary apnea*

   b. Evaluate the respiratory effort.

   Rationale: To be aware that assessments of the first gasp and the first cry and maintenance of sustained respiratory excursions are important aspects to evaluate at birth; that usual respiratory effort is initiated in the first 30 seconds of life and regularity begins by 90 seconds; and that a baby born with acidosis will have difficulty maintaining respirations or will evidence apnea*

   c. Assess muscle tone through observation of spontaneous muscular movements of the extremities.

   Rationale: To be aware that muscle tone will be decreased secondary to maternal drugs, anesthesia, asphyxia, central nervous system damage, and severe prematurity and that evaluation of muscle tone as flaccid, some flexion, or active motion is characteristic of the Apgar scoring method[1,2,6,7]

   d. Assess reflex irritability to stimulation.

   Rationale: To note reflex irritability of the neonate in response to cutaneous stimulation, painful stimulation (vitamin K injection), grimacing, and crying (If stimulation such as suctioning the nose or oropharynx causes crying, a score of 2 is given. If only a grimace is elicited, a score of 1 is given; when no response is elicited, the score is 0.[1,2,6,7])

   e. Assess color.

   Rationale: To evaluate the neonate according to central cyanosis, bluish gray cast of the whole body, or by peripheral cyanosis, bluish gray cast of the hands and feet (Evaluation of color should be reexamined after oxygen therapy.[1,2,6,7])

9. Determine the Apgar score at 1 minute and 5 minutes (Table 19-1).

   Rationale: To assess and evaluate the neonate at birth (The five variables of heart rate, respiratory rate and effort, muscle tone, reflex irritability, and color are separately evaluated and given a score of 0, 1, or 2. Then the scores of each variable are added and an Apgar score for 1 minute and 5 minutes of life is given to the neonate.[1,2,6])

10. Observe for signs and symptoms of respiratory distress in the immediate newborn period such as nasal flaring, grunting, substernal retractions, cyanosis, diminished breath sounds, and rales and rhonchi on auscultation.

    Rationale: To continue close surveillance even under the most favorable circumstances (that is, Apgar scores between 7 and 10) since delayed respiratory depression may occur secondary to drugs, anesthetic agents, congenital defects in the central nervous system, inadequate develment of lung alveoli, and other anatomical defects[36]

11. Assess patency of the airway when signs of respiratory distress are evident following birth.

---

*See references 1, 2, 6, 7, 13, and 15.

Rationale: To suction the oropharynx and nose again if the neonate appears to be in distress, to examine for upper airway obstruction (that is, mucus, meconium, blood), and to visualize the cords and trachea if the oropharynx is clear and neonate is distressed[1,3,5]

12. Interpret data and biochemical analysis relating to respiratory function and aberrations.

Rationale: To be aware that respiratory distress will be manifested by increasing P_{CO_2}, falling P_{O_2}, decreasing pH, and base deficit confirming acidosis[1,3,5,15,48]

13. Interpret data and biochemical analysis of metabolic parameters to detect metabolic aberrations (that is, serum glucose, calcium, bicarbonate, chloride, potassium, sodium, lactate levels).

Rationale: To be aware that repeated asphyxial episodes in utero and after birth deplete the cardiac glycogen stores and the ability of the neonate to withstand delivery and establish respirations[12] (To maintain some cardiac output, the asphyxiated neonate depends on its production of energy by anaerobic glycolysis of the glycogen supply in the cardiac muscle, which results in high tissue lactate buildup and causes a resultant fall in the pH of the blood. Asphyxiation causes a reduction in the available energy for maintenance of normal ionic concentration gradients, which causes the cell to leak potassium and other intracellular ions. Sodium is thought to reenter to the cell with water to buffer the lactate buildup within the cell. Hypoxia can have severe effects on normal metabolic processes of the neonate.[1,3,15])

14. Assess effective ventilatory assistance when the moderately or severely depressed neonate necessitates resuscitation with bag and mask or requires intubation.

Rationale: To note bilateral expansion of the infant's chest during assisted ventilation (Auscultation of both sides of the chest should be performed to detect breath sounds as well as the area over the stomach to check placement of the endotracheal tube. If the endotracheal tube is improperly placed, the stomach will distend with air that will be heard with a stethoscope. If breath sounds are audible on one side of the infant's chest but not the other, the endotracheal tube needs to be pulled back slightly and breath sounds reevaluated.[6,36])

15. Assess clinical signs relating to pneumothorax such as increasing tachypnea, rapid development of cyanosis, increased anteroposterior diameter of the chest, shift of apical cardiac impulse, hyperresonance to chest percussion, abdominal distention from a depressed diaphragm, and falling blood pressure.[4]

Rationale: To be aware that pneumothorax can be caused by rupture of the distal air sacs and escape of air into the interstitial spaces and by positive pressure ventilation when the distal air sacs are overdistended through resuscitative efforts that are too vigorous[4]

16. Assess radiological examination when resuscitative efforts have been prolonged and difficult.

Rationale: To note by means of radiological examinations conditions such as pneumothorax, congenital anomalies, diaphragmatic hernias, and other severe forms of respiratory distress[44]

17. Observe for clinical signs of deterioration and shock (that is, respiratory distress, diminished breath sounds, retractions, bradycardia or asystole, hypotension, weak pulse, pallor, and mottling of skin).

Rationale: To recognize the severe complications of asphyxia is a major responsibility of nurses in delivering quality health care (When these symptoms are noted, the infant's life and future well-being are in jeopardy. Anticipatory care to prevent such sequelae is optimal health care delivery.[9])

THERAPEUTIC

1. On delivery of the infant's head, the obstetrician may suction the nose and oropharynx.

Rationale: To remove secretions quickly so as not to interrupt the process of delivery (Some obstetricians feel the neonate should be suctioned at the delivery of the head because some infants take the first gasp as the body is being delivered before being placed in the head-down position. Those not in favor of suctioning prior to complete delivery claim that the act of suctioning may stimulate the neonate to breathe before being delivered.[1])

2. Special attention should be given to suctioning the nose and oropharynx when the baby is meconium stained or delivered through meconium-stained fluid.

   Rationale: To prevent aspiration of material that could obstruct the bronchi by removal of thick meconium or blood clots prior to the first gasp[1]

3. Initial care of the neonate should include:
   a. Maintain head-down position.

      Rationale: To keep the pharyngeal contents out of the trachea with the first breath (It is imperative that the infant be kept in the head-down position during and immediately after delivery. One sharp breath in the head-up position may draw enough force to pull material in the oropharynx into the tracheobronchial tree.[1,3,5,6,20])

   b. Suction upper airway with bulb or DeLee catheter.

      Rationale: To prevent or reduce the incidence of severe aspiration[1]

   c. Place under radiant heater and dry with a warm towel.

      Rationale: To provide a neutral thermal environment and decrease the response of the neonate to cold stress[1,3,5,6,23]

4. Provide cutaneous stimulation by blowing oxygen over the face, rubbing the chest, drying the body, and slapping the soles of the feet when there is air exchange and spontaneous respirations with a heart rate greater than 100 beats/min.

   Rationale: To elicit response in minimally depressed neonates or those with Apgar scores of 7 to 10 by gentle stimulation and maintenance of spontaneous respirations through stimulation of the central nervous system from the efferent stimuli of cutaneous touch, rubbing, and cold[15]

5. Administer oxygen by blow-by or by bag and mask when neonate's heart rate is greater than 100 beats/min but respiratory effort is poor.

   Rationale: To help the mildly to moderately asphyxiated neonate reverse the hypoxic event, which may be due to a uterine insult or depression from maternal drugs or anesthesia[4]

6. Administer naloxone (Narcan) (Table 19-3) in the presence of maternal respiratory depressants.

   Rationale: To counteract narcotic drugs in the depressed neonate in the presence of maternal depressant drugs[1]

7. Remove airway obstructions, visualize the cords and trachea, and institute suctioning of the larynx when a meconium-stained infant is delivered or in a moderately depressed neonate (Apgar score of 4 to 6) who fails to respond to cutaneous stimulation or has a heart rate greater than 100 beats/min with irregular and poor respirations.

   Rationale: To visualize the cords for meconium-stained fluid below, at, or above the vocal cords by laryngoscopy (Prompt suctioning will reduce meconium aspiration into the lungs and decrease the risk of asphyxiation. Berman[6] states, "Meconium was found in the trachea of 56% of those with meconium staining and was aspirated from the airway of all patients who later became symptomatic. Several of these had meconium in the airway, even though none was found in the mouth or larynx.")

8. If meconium is visualized at or below the cords, immediate intubation and suctioning are necessitated.

   Rationale: To remove meconium-stained fluid, mucus, or blood at or below the cords before the first gasp to prevent further aspiration and increased severity associated with meconium aspiration syndrome[1,3,5,6,23]

9. Avoid utilization of positive pressure ventilation until oropharynx and trachea are cleared of meconium or amniotic fluid contents.

Rationale: To be aware that positive pressure ventilation will force the contents of the oropharynx and trachea down into the bronchi of the lungs causing aspiration and increasing perinatal risk*

10. If there is no evidence of spontaneous respirations after intubation and assisted ventilation and bradycardia ensues, treatment of the neonate will involve procedures to resuscitate the severely depressed neonate (Apgar score of 0 to 3) beginning with external cardiac massage (see Fig. 4-10).

    Rationale: To improve the systemic circulation and carry oxygenated blood to acidotic tissues by compressing the midsternum with two fingers at a ratio of three compressions to one ventilation or 100 to 200 times/min[1,4,20]

11. Administer alkali slowly by intravenous infusion of sodium bicarbonate or THAM, (Table 19-3) according to quantitated acid-base studies.

    Rationale: To prevent hyperosmolar problems[20,36] (Prolonged respiratory acidosis will cause a concurrent metabolic acidosis. If there is proper removal of CO_2 through adequate ventilation, administration of sodium bicarbonate will help balance and neutralize excess hydrogen ion. If there is difficulty in achieving full alveolar expansion secondary to prematurity or hyaline membrane disease, a pure alkali such as THAM should be considered.)

12. Make measurements of the neonate's blood pressure (Table 19-2).

    Rationale: To be aware that hypotension may be due to asphyxia or acute blood loss as in abruptio placentae and that in the presence of inadequate response to ventilatory assistance and ensuing bradycardia, cardiovascular collapse and shock may occur[1,3,36]

13. Administer whole blood or volume expanders intravenously (Table 19-3).

    Rationale: To be aware that whole blood will increase the circulatory blood volume and oxygen-carrying capacity of the systemic circulation and that plasma or 5% protein solutions will cause expansion of the intravascular space through increased colloid pressure creating increased cardiac output and blood pressure*

14. Administer intravenous glucose (Table 19-3).

    Rationale: To help reestablish metabolic processes that are jeopardized during asphyxia[14] (Stressed infants have an impaired ability to maintain glucose homeostasis.[36] The fetal stores of glycogen in the cardiac muscle could be well depleted prior to birth owing to intrauterine hypoxic insults.[14])

15. Administer epinephrine intravenously (Table 19-3).

    Rationale: To increase heart rate and cardiac output (As a sympathomimetic amine, which has the property to stimulate the central nervous system, epinephrine will cause stimulation of the respiratory system also.[1])

16. Administer calcium chloride or calcium gluconate intravenously (Table 19-3).

    Rationale: To correct severe bradycardia that persists despite all other resuscitative efforts (Calcium is involved with proper contractility and depolarization of cardiac cells. Stress or inadequate fetal stores owing to prematurity can deplete calcium stores.[12])

17. When heart rate and respiratory status are stable, transfer infant to special care nursery or transport to a level III nursery in the region.

    Rationale: To provide the infant with additional observation, support, and interventions that may be necessary to provide for growth and development at the optimal level possible for that infant

18. Take special precautions to prevent iatrogenic problems such as:

    a. Emboli in umbilical artery catheters; watch for blanching of the feet, cool extremities, or cyanosis of toes and check catheter size.

---

*See references 1, 3-5, 7, 20, and 23.

*See references 1, 3, 5-7, 20, and 23.

b. Do not allow irrigation of umbilical catheters if they seem to be clotted off.

c. Maintain sterile field during insertion by physician.

d. Monitor neonatal vital signs: blood pressure, heart rate, respirations, temperature, and pulses.

Rationale: To be aware that umbilical catheters are associated with a 5% to 10% complication rate of hemorrhage, infection, sclerosis, necrosis, air embolism, and perforation (Mortality or morbidity rates of the high-risk neonate are already high at birth. Introduction of new technology and its complicating consequences further increases the insult. Prevention of all possible complications and awareness of the presenting symptoms are major roles of the perinatal nurse.[9,36])

EDUCATIONAL

1. Provide in-service education and staff development programs for labor and delivery and nursery personnel who would be responsible for prompt and accurate resuscitative practices with the infant at high risk.

   Rationale: To provide prompt and therapeutic resuscitation and to promote and maintain a high level of quality care to the high-risk infant[1,9,20]

2. Provide emotional and physical support to the mother and her family.

   Rationale: To help the patient and her family cope with stresses (The patient and her family are the central issues in the management of a high-risk pregnancy. Education, support, and assistance in maintaining the family integrity are appropriate areas of nursing interventions. Care of the high-risk neonate and high-risk family need not focus only on the medical interventions but on emotional and psychological support for all members of the family.[18,37] The care of the high-risk family after delivery is very important. If the pregnancy ends with the birth of a well child, the parents may need help adjusting from a risk state. If a stillbirth occurs or the child is born disabled, nursing care is essential for helping parents get through an emotionally difficult time by helping the family

share and by listening. Parents will feel less emotionally isolated if they are supported by the health care team as they work through their grief reaction.[18,45,50])

REFERENCES

1. Abramson, H.: Resuscitation of the newborn infant, ed. 3, St. Louis, 1973, The C. V. Mosby Co.
2. Apgar, V.: A proposal for a new method of evaluation of the newborn infant, Anesth. Analg. **32**:260, 1953.
3. Avery, G. B.: Neonatology: pathophysiology and management of the newborn, Philadelphia, 1975, J. B. Lippincott Co.
4. Babson, S. G., Pernoll, M. L., and Benda, G. I.: Diagnosis and management of the fetus and neonate at risk, ed. 4, St. Louis, 1980, The C. V. Mosby Co.
5. Behrman, R.: Neonatal-perinatal medicine, ed. 2, St. Louis, 1977, The C. V. Mosby Co.
6. Berman, L. S., and Saunders, B. S.: Newborn resuscitation, Perinatol. Neonatol. **4**(1):22, 1980.
7. Bolognese, R., and Schwarz, R.: Perinatal medicine—management of the high-risk fetus and neonate, Baltimore, 1977, The Williams & Wilkins Co.
8. Braly, P., and Freeman, R.: The significance of fetal heart rate reactivity with a positive oxytocin challenge test, Obstet. Gynecol. **50**(6):689, 1977.
9. Butnarescu, G., et al.: Perinatal nursing. Vol. 2: reproductive risk, New York, 1980, John Wiley & Sons, Inc.
10. Chernick, V.: Mechanics of the first inspiration, Semin. Perinatol. **4**:347, 1977.
11. Crelin, E.: Development of the lower respiratory system, Clin. Symp. **27**(4), 1975.
12. Dawes, G. S., et al.: The importance of cardiac glycogen for the maintenance of life in foetal lambs and newborn animals during anoxia, J. Physiol. **146**:516, 1959.
13. Dawes, G. S., et al.: The treatment of asphyxiated mature foetal lambs and rhesus monkeys with intravenous glucose and sodium carbonate, J. Physiol. **169**:167, 1963.
14. Dawes, G. S., et al.: The effect of alkali and glucose infusion on permanent brain damage in rhesus monkeys asphyxiated at birth, J. Physiol. **65**:801, 1964.
15. Dorand, R.: Neonatal asphyxia—an approach to physiology and management, Pediatr. Clin. North Am. **24**(3):455, 1977.
16. Emery, J. L., and Mithal, A.: The number of alveoli in the terminal respiratory unit of man during late uterine life and childhood, Arch. Dis. Child. **160**:35, 1960.
17. Hutchison, A., and Russell, G.: Effective pulmonary capillary blood flow in infants with birth asphyxia, Acta Paediatr. Scand. **65**:669, 1976.
18. Johnson, S. H.: High-risk parenting: nursing assessment and strategies for the family at risk, Philadelphia, 1979, J. B. Lippincott Co.
19. Jones, M. B.: Antepartum assessment in high-risk pregnancy, J. Obstet. Gynecol. Nurs. **4**:23, 1975.
20. Kanto, W. P.: Resuscitation comes first, Emergency Med. p. 31, October, 1977.
21. Karlberg, P.: The first breaths of life. In Gluck, L., editor:

Modern perinatal medicine, Chicago, 1974, Year Book Medical Publishers, Inc., p. 391.

22. Karlberg, P., et al.: Pulmonary ventilation and mechanics of breathing in the first minutes of life, including the onset of respiration, Acta Paediatr. Scand. **51:**121, 1962.

23. Klaus, M., and Fanaroff, M. B.: Care of the high-risk neonate, ed. 2, Philadelphia, 1979, W. B. Saunders Co.

24. Klaus, M., and Kennell, J.: Maternal infant bonding, St. Louis, 1976, The C. V. Mosby Co.

25. Koch, J.: Code pink: a system for neonatal resuscitation, J. Obstet. Gynecol. Nurs. p. 49, September/October, 1978.

26. Lou, H. C., et al.: Pressure passive cerebral blood flow and breakdown of the blood-brain barrier in experimental fetal asphyxia, Acta Paediatr. Scand. **68:**57, 1979.

27. McManus, F., et al.: Is cerebral palsy a preventable disease? Obstet. Gynecol. **50**(1):71, 1977.

28. McMurphy, D. M., et al.: Developmental changes in constriction of the ductus arteriosus: responses to oxygen to vasoactive agents on the isolated ductus arteriosus of the fetal lamb, Pediatr. Res. **6:**231, 1972.

29. Milner, A. D., and Saunders, R. A.: Pressure and volume changes during the first breath of human neonates, Arch. Dis. Child. **52:**918, 1977.

30. Moore, K.: Before we are born: basic embryology and birth defects, Philadelphia, 1977, W. B. Saunders Co.

31. Morrison, I., and Olsen, J.: Perinatal risk and antepartum risk scoring, Obstet. Gynecol. **53**(3):362, 1979.

32. Platyker, A. C. G., et al.: Surfactant in the lung and tracheal fluid of fetal lamb and acceleration of its appearance by dexamethasone, Pediatrics **56:**544, 1975.

33. Potter, E. L., and Bohlender, G. P.: Intrauterine respirations in relation to development of fetal lung, Am. J. Obstet. Gynecol. **42:**14, 1941.

34. Saunders, R. A., and Milner, A. D.: Pulmonary pressure/volume relationships during the last phase of delivery and the first postnatal breaths in human subjects, J. Pediatr. **93**(4):667, 1978.

35. Schifrin, B., et al.: Routine fetal heart rate monitoring in the antepartum period, Obstet. Gynecol. **54**(1):21, 1979.

36. Schreiner, R. L.: Resuscitation of the newborn. In Schreiner,

R.: Neonatology for the pediatrician, Indianapolis, 1978, Section of Neonatal-Perinatal Medicine Department of Pediatrics, The James Whitcomb Riley Hospital for Children.

37. Schwartz, J. L., and Schwartz, L. H.: Vulnerable infants—a psychosocial dilemma, New York, 1977, McGraw-Hill Book Co.

38. Scott, H.: Outcome of very severe birth asphyxia, Arch. Dis. Child. **51:**712, 1976.

39. Sheldon, R.: Management of perinatal asphyxia and shock, Pediatr. Ann. p. 17, April, 1977.

40. Shelley, H. J.: Blood sugars and tissue carbohydrates in foetal and infant lambs and rhesus monkeys. J. Physiol. **53:**527, 1960.

41. Stahlman, M. T., and Gray, M. E.: Anatomical development and maturation of the lungs, Clin. Perinatol. **5**(2):181, 1978.

42. Starkman, M.: Fetal monitoring—psychologic consequences and management recommendations, Obstet. Gynecol. **50**(4):500, 1977.

43. Strang, L. B.: Growth and development of the lung: fetal and postnatal, Annu. Rev. Physiol. **39:**253, 1976.

44. Storer, J. S.: Respiratory problems unique to the newborn, Respir. Care **20**(12):1146, 1975.

45. Sundeen, S., et al.: Nurse-client interaction—implementing the nursing process, St. Louis, 1976, The C. V. Mosby Co.

46. Thomson, A. J., Searle, M., and Russell, G.: Quality of survival after severe birth asphyxia, Arch. Dis. Child. **57:**620, 1976.

47. Thurlbeck, W.: Postnatal growth and development of the lung, Am. Rev. Respir. Dis. **III:**803, 1975.

48. Tunell, R., Copher, D., and Persson, B.: The pulmonary gas exchange and blood gas changes in connection with birth. In Stetson, J. B. and Swyer, P. R., editors: Neonatal intensive care, St. Louis, 1976, Warren H. Green, Inc., p. 89.

49. Wesenberg, R.: The newborn chest, New York, 1973, Harper & Row, Publishers, Inc.

50. Yura, H., and Walsh, M.: Human needs and the nursing process, New York, 1978, Appleton-Century-Crofts.

Chapter 20

Neonatal infections

Patricia J. Blake

Immunology contains fascinating and challenging concepts descriptive of maternal-fetal-neonatal relationships. This chapter deals only with the current concepts of pathogenesis, microbiology, diagnosis, and management of infections in the fetus and newborn and their interrelations with maternal morbidity. Protocols of nursing management for nurse practitioners in the high-risk newborn area are proposed.

IMMUNOCOMPETENCE OF THE FETUS

It is only in recent years that the human neonate has been found to be immunocompetent. The idea that the newborn is ''immunologically null'' was based on the following observations: (1) passively acquired antibodies had diminished antibody/antigen reactions; (2) newborn serum contained few plasma cells in the lymphoid system; and (3) the infection rate during the first few weeks of life increased.[11]

Today it has been proved that fetal lymphocytes are able to recognize foreign cell antigen in mixed lymphocyte reactions (MLR) in the liver as early as 10 weeks' gestation (before the thymus is completely developed). MLR reactive lymphocytes have been found in the fetal thymus as early as 12 weeks' gestation and a response to mitogen phytohemagglutinin (PHA) as early as 13 weeks' gestation. These thymic cells induced by PHA are not cytotoxic, while lymphocytes in fetal peripheral blood are able to both proliferate and exhibit cytotoxicity when stimulated with PHA. It appears that the normal fetus develops a functional cellular immune system by the end of the first trimester.

Normally, only small amounts of fetally produced immunoglobulins are present. This is generally thought to be due to a relative lack of antigenic stimulation in utero. On the other hand, it is well known that the human fetus is able to mount a significant humoral response that is proven in the increased quantitative values of fetal IgM and traces of IgD and IgE. These are diagnostic to congenital infections contracted in utero.[10] IgM and IgG have been measured in culture of the human spleen.

INFECTIONS OF THE FETUS

Pregnant women are potential hosts to the infectious stressors in their environment. Such infections are generally localized and have no effect on the developing fetus. However, some organisms may enter the maternal bloodstream and lead to fetal infections. Transplacental spread following maternal septicemia is the usual route by which the fetus becomes infected. Other portals of entry are from adjacent areas such as the genitalia and peritoneum. Advanced technology of an intrusive nature, such as monitors and intrauterine transfusions, has also been responsible for some infections.

Adjacent maternal tissue

Infectious agents in the genital tract may invade the amniotic fluid prior to the rupture of membranes and produce a fetal infection. The actual pathway by which the infection invades the fetus is not clearly understood. A few hypothesize that there are microscopical defects in the fetal membranes that allow organisms to penetrate. Another hypothetical pathway is descent through the fallopian tubes in women with salpingitis or peritonitis.

Modern technology

Invasive diagnostic and therapeutic procedures for fetal disorders are a potential pathway for infectious organisms. Fetal monitoring devices have caused abscesses, osteomyelitis, and streptococcal sepsis at the site of fetal attachment. Intrauterine transfusions have led to isolated cases of fetal cytomegalovirus infections.

Maternal septicemia

In the absence of ruptured fetal membranes invasion of the fetus by microorganisms is generally by the transplacental route following invasion of the maternal bloodstream. Lymphocytes and neutrophils can carry the microorganisms in the blood. They can also become attached to erythrocytes or be independent of any cellular components.

If there is an invasion of the maternal bloodstream by microorganisms or their products, four consequences are possible: (1) placental infection without fetal infection, (2) fetal infection without placental infection, (3) absence of placental and fetal infection, (4) infection of the placenta and fetus.

Placental infection without fetal infection can, and frequently does, remain localized in the placenta (focal villositis). The reasons for the lack of spread are unknown, but it has been noted in cases related to maternal tuberculosis, rubella, syphilis, malaria, cytomegalovirus, and coccidioidomycosis.

Following placental infections fetal defenses may include the placental macrophage, villose trophoblasts, and local immune factors such as lymphokines and antibodies.

Fetal infections without placental infections are theoretically possible when the organisms traverse the chorionic villi directly via placental leaks, diapedesis, and pinocytosis. However, clinically this is difficult to substantiate, since most generally there are other areas demonstrating placentitis.

Invasion of the maternal bloodstream by microorganisms is not uncommon, and yet there are, relatively speaking, few cases of fetal and placental infection. Mechanisms for protection of the placenta and fetus from bloodborne microorganisms are not clearly understood. Most probably protection is provided by the efficient maternal reticuloendothelial system and circulating leukocytes that clear the microbes from the bloodstream.

Bacterial invasion of pregnant women may affect the fetus in other indirect ways. High fever, anoxia, toxins, and metabolic derangements during maternal infections can have significant effects on the pregnancy and developing fetus. Among known bacterial diseases responsible for these results are typhoid fever, pneumonia, gram-negative sepsis, urinary tract infections, varicella, variola, rubeola, and rubella. Abortion, stillbirth, and premature delivery as well as low birth weight infants may follow as a consequence.

Infections of the placenta and the fetus may be disseminated via direct extension of placental infection to the fetal membranes followed by secondary infections of amniotic fluid and subsequently aspiration by the fetus and/or as the result of emboli of necrotic chorionic tissue. The consequences of hematogenous transplacental spread are varied. One effect is the death and resorption of the embryo. This usually occurs before the woman knows she is pregnant and is, therefore, difficult to substantiate. Abortion and/or stillbirth of the fetus is another consequence. Intrauterine death may occur owing to fulminating infections, and/or organogenesis may be halted by the infections to such a degree that functions necessary for viability are interrupted.

The exact mechanisms of premature expulsion of the fetus from the uterus are not clearly understood. The mystery remains as to "whether fetal death caused or resulted from expulsion of the fetus."[9] There are numerous conditions that could affect the outcome of intrauterine infections including virulence, stage of pregnancy, tissue tropism of the organisms, placental damage, and morbidity of the maternal illness. Among known organisms causing this outcome are smallpox, *Salmonella typhi,* and *Vibrio* fetus. Influenza and vaccinia as causative agents are still a controversial issue.[9]

Another consequence may be a normal or abnormal premature or term infant. Premature birth may follow any fetal infection regardless of the causative agent. Agents frequently implicated include cytomegalovirus, herpes simplex, rubeola, smallpox, hepatitis, and *Vibrio* fetus. *Salmonella typhosa, Mycobacterium tuberculosis, Treponema pallidum,* and a few protozoan agents are sometimes found.

"Small-for-date" infants may also be the result of

intrauterine infections. However, this must be distinguished from other causes of low birth weight. Usually the differentiation lies in the finding of decreased numbers of morphologically normal cells in the infant of an infectious process. Other low birth weight infants have normal numbers of parenchymal cells but less amounts of cytoplasm. Rubella and cytomegalovirus are the two agents for which causal relationships have been evidenced.

Finally, developmental anomalies may be the result of intrauterine infections. Once again rubella and cytomegalovirus are the substantiated causative agents. It appears that the mode of action of viruses lies in their ability to cause cell death, alteration in cell growth, or chromosomal damage. There is some evidence that coxsackieviruses B_3 and B_4 are associated with congenital heart disease. These and other congenital infections rarely are manifest in the neonatal period and will be discussed later.

It remains difficult to distinguish whether the infant acquired the infection in utero, during the delivery process, or postnatally. One possible criterion is the onset of clinical symptoms and signs in relationship to the minimum incubation period of the disease (that is, 3 days for enteroviruses, 10 days for varicella and rubella). If infection occurs during these time limits, it was most likely an intrauterine infection.

IMMUNE RESPONSE OF THE NEONATE

At birth the T- and B-cell system has developed a degree of functional integrity in the newborn. However, little data are available on the functional interaction of T- and B-cell immunity.

Humoral and perhaps cellular factors derived from maternal sources provide the neonate with his unique immune responses. Maternal antibodies, which also have a suppression effect on neonatal antibody formation, provide some protection if the antibodies can effectively cross the placental barriers, such as diphtheria. However, some antibodies such as tetanus are not as effectively transferred across the placenta to the infant.[6]

Passive immunity by maternal IgG antibodies confers limited protection against many organisms including measles, rubella, streptococci, meningococci, and *Hemophilus influenzae*. Vaccina, varicella, pertussis, tetanus, and diphtheria do not sus-

tain high titers of antibody, and unless the mother was recently immunized or infected, maternal antibodies provide only partial protection.

Antibodies against gram-negative organisms such as *Escherichia coli* and *Salmonella* are of the IgM class and do not cross the placenta. Some IgG antibodies that do cross the placenta are protection against somatic antigens of gram-negative organisms. IgM is thought, however, to be the major defense against gram-negative organisms. Recently work is under investigation regarding the necessity of complement for full expression of IgM as opsonins[6-8] to *E. coli*.

During the neonatal period, levels of IgG decrease sharply. IgM levels, on the other hand, rise rapidly during 4 to 7 days of life probably owing to colonization of the intestinal tract, skin, and respiratory tract. IgA is found in sera from 5 to 23 days and has been detected in several sites: saliva, tears, and urine of neonates. IgD is essentially considered absent in cord blood but has been noted on occasion. Little, if any, IgE crosses the placenta. However, a skin test can become positive about 21 days of age. Elevation of serum IgE before 1 year of age is highly correlated with atopic disease in the first 2 years of life.[6]

T-cells and their products such as lymphokines are active areas of research. Structurally the neonate is capable of antigenic stimulation to response. Developmental immaturity of inflammatory components rather than T-cell deficiency has provided the basis for most discussions on immune cellular responses.[6]

COMMON INFECTIONS OF THE NEONATE
Bacterial

Staphylococcal. Pneumonia caused by staphylococcal organisms has the same signs and symptoms as any other type of pneumonia; increased respiratory rate and generalized signs in the lungs. Complications are respiratory distress, pneumothorax and emphysema.[3,11] It is most often seen with septicemia. However, other staphylococcal infection occurs in paronychia, breast, umbilicus, and as osteomyelitis and pemphigus.

Escherichia coli. *E. coli* and *Pseudomonas* flourish in warm moist environments. They are not susceptible to wide-spectrum antimicrobial therapy. The naked premature infant in an incubator with increased humidity and air contaminated by feces is a prime victim for these organisms and subsequent septicemia and meningitis.

Septicemia. Septicemia in infants occurs within the first 30 days of life, involving the bloodstream and meninges.[2] The organisms are usually gram negative. Predisposing factors are prematurity, premature rupture of the membranes, and other obstetrical complications of labor and delivery. The infant is vaguely unwell with a high heart rate, moderate temperature, lethargy, anorexia, jaundice, and purpura.

Meningitis. Along with symptoms similar to septicemia are later problems of vomiting, high-pitched cry, convulsions, and bulging or tensed anterior fontanelle.[3] Causative agents are generally gram-negative bacteria and *E. coli*. Intrathecal as well as other parenteral therapy is used.

Pseudomonas. *Pseudomonas* is normal in small amounts in the gastrointestinal tract. At times pink macular eruptions are found on the buttocks and trunk.[3] These become papules and contain the bacilli. Marked vasculitis is present in all the lesions and may be responsible for a high mortality rate associated with this disease.

Streptococcal (beta hemolytic). Beta-hemolytic streptococcal infections are clinically similar to *E. coli* infections, but the CNS fluid smear shows gram-positive cocci in streptococcal meningitis. The most virulent streptococcal infection is, of course, beta hemolytic.[3]

Candida. White plaques difficult to scrape with a tongue blade or oral mucosa on the tongue are indicative of *Candida*. It can also be noted as a fire red, scaly eruption on the perineum. For oral candidiasis oral nystatin may be used and special nipple precautions taken, but isolation of the infant is not necessary. Nystatin ointment is applied to the perineal rash at each diaper change.[3,8]

Viral

Cytomegaloviruses (CMV) are a common cause of recognized congenital infections.[2] Most mothers are asymptomatic and harbor the virus in the cervix and urine. Congenital infection is documented by recovery of the virus from the nasopharynx and urine. Large inclusion cells are generally present in the urine of infected children as well as IgM levels of 22 mg/dl. Specific IgM antibodies are also present. Damage is to the brain by direct tissue destruction and calcification. Chorioretinitis is also a result of direct infection. The virus is shed for many months by the infant to other members of the family. Isolation procedures are necessary. Antiviral therapy has been used, generally with disappointing results.[5]

Herpes simplex virus. Herpes simplex has two strains that infect man: Type I generally is seen as oral blisters of fever and the common cold. Type II produces cervicitis and vaginitis and is accepted, generally, as venereally transmitted.[2] The infant born with HSV II appears normal until about 3 weeks of age. Then symptoms appear as (1) vesicular lesions of the skin and throat and possibly conjunctivitis; (2) central nervous symptoms, resulting from increased cells, pressure, and protein in the spinal fluid; and (3) systemic disease. Local infection carries a good prognosis for about 50% of the infants. The others progress to systemic disease, and 90% of these are fatal. Diagnosis is confirmed by levels of IgM above 22 mg/dl and IgM antibody to HSV.

The virus can also be isolated from the lesions. Chemotherapy using adenine arabinoside is under study. No other therapy is known. Cesarean sections are recommended for delivery if the mother has vaginal lesions. Congenital HSV may produce a syndrome of microcephaly, cerebral calcification, chorioretinitis, and mental retardation.

Rubella. Rubella is associated primarily with infections during the first trimester of pregnancy. Severe congenital malformations may occur: deafness, congenital heart disease, microcephaly, hepatosplenomegaly, mental retardation, and death.[2]

Antibody titers determined by hemagglutination inhibition are the most useful laboratory test. After a rash appears, complement fixation antibody increases. Infected newborns will have an IgM of 22 mg/dl and antibody specific to rubella.

The virus can be isolated from the nasopharynx. Infants are infectious, and contact with pregnant women is to be avoided. Vaccines are available; therefore, rubella is preventable. This fact deserves the wide dissemination of vaccine provided in the past several years.

Varicella. Varicella in the first 4 months of pregnancy may result in CNS damage, encephalitis, hypoplasia of extremities, cataracts, and scarring of the skin.[2] If contracted in the last few days before delivery, the disease may be fatal to the infant. Varicella immune globulin (VIG) vaccine should be administered as soon as birth occurs. Antibody tests are available to confirm diagnosis and/or immunity.

Others. Other common viral diseases having deleterious results from morbidity to mortality include coxackievirus, echovirus, mumps virus, and viral hepatitis.

Spriochetal

Syphilis. The diagnosis of syphilis in the mother is very important. Routine serological tests should be done. Syphilis may result in severe fetal damage.[2,5,8] It is acquired from the mother via the vascular route. Leutic infection may cause abortion, stillbirth, and death. The spirochete does not cross the placenta in the first trimester; therefore, embryogenesis is not directly affected. The infant may be small for gestational age and may have secondary syphilis: mucocutaneous lesions, osteochondritis, and hepatosplenomegaly. Infants should show elevated IgM and have fluorescent treponemal antibody tests, which will be positive in active disease.

In the absence of specific gamma M, FTA test, a positive VDRL, normal radiographs of bones, and an asymptomatic infant, the physician may (1) follow the infant clinically with serological tests every 6 to 8 weeks, (2) treat the infant with aqueous penicillin (50,000 to 100,000 units/kg/day) in two divided doses every 12 hours for 10 to 14 days or one dose of benzathine penicillin G (50,000 units/kg).[5,8]

DISCUSSION AND SUMMARY

Perinatal infections (bacterial, viral, spirochetal) can cause birth defects, fetal and newborn disease, or death. Infectious diseases may occur in sporadic incidences or in waves of microendemic or endemic cases. Because of the newborn's inability at the time to respond to infection in a classical fashion, early diagnosis is often difficult. Clinical presentation in the newborn may differ greatly from the picture of older children and adults.

Prevention prior to parturition is, of course, the ideal. Transplacental infections, although rare, generally end in fetal death and/or abnormalities. Success in therapy for the newborn depends on early diagnosis and appropriate therapy.

Nurses are vital members of the team caring for the septic infant. They are available for continuous assessment of the infant through observation, palpation, and auscultation. Nurses provide the link between physicians, parents, infants, technicians, and other team members. Their competency, knowledge, and interpersonal relationships can provide the infant and parents with the highest quality of care available.

Protocols

Clinical signs and symptoms of infection in the neonate may be "nonspecific, minimal, and vague and may mimic other pathologic conditions."[8] Among conditions easily identifiable and to be ruled out are hypoglycemia, hypocalcemia, respiratory distress, blood group incompatibilities, drug withdrawal, CNS pathology, and gastrointestinal obstruction. When infection is suspected, a diagnostic workup is begun immediately.[8]

Problem □ Care of the septic newborn

GOAL: To diagnose the causative agent
  Rationale: To detect the causative agent early, allowing specific rather than general therapy to be initiated
DIAGNOSTIC
  1. Review maternal history.
    Rationale: To assess the history of pregnancy, early labor, and labor for exposures to infectious agents and/or conditions with high correlations to neonatal sepsis

a. Premature rupture of membranes (24 hours +), foul odor, maternal fever
b. Prolonged and difficult labor with or without signs of fetal distress
c. Postdelivery problems requiring prolonged resuscitative procedures, intubation and ventilation, umbilical and arterial venous cannulation, and surgical procedures
   Rationale: To be aware that opportunistic disease is closely correlated with intrusive procedures
d. Physical findings suspicious of sepsis, that is, hyperthermia irritability, vomiting, anorexia, diarrhea, abdominal distention, cyanosis, apnea, jaundice, lethargy
   Rationale: To note early signs and symptoms of sepsis during routine procedures and assessments

THERAPEUTIC
1. Inform physician of any historical data relevant to pregnancy and labor, such as exposure to or acquired infections during pregnancy, premature rupture of membranes, prolonged labor, prolapsed cord.
   Rationale: To ensure prompt attention, which can either be preventive or indicative of need for increased assessments
2. Care for the mother and neonate using precautionary nursing care regarding isolation.
   Rationale: To be aware that preventive measures for isolation are indicated for other mothers and infants
3. Monitor all the infant's vital signs.
   Rationale: To provide early determination of infant's status regarding sepsis

EDUCATIONAL
1. Provide emotional support for the mother and the father. This is accomplished by establishing relationships with a consistent person for feedback and communication, allowing touch as much as possible with their infant, and repetition of information.
   Rationale: To enhance the precautionary procedures and decrease some of the anxiety
2. Personnel should be trained by staff development in the care of high-risk septic infants. Advanced educational preparation is recommended.
   Rationale: To increase quality nursing care of infant

Problem □ Data needed to pinpoint diagnosis

GOAL: To gather data necessary to initiate therapy to enhance the ability of infant to cope effectively with sepsis
Rationale: To rule out causes of sepsis in order to use specific therapeutic measures to overcome infectious process

DIAGNOSTIC
1. A blood survey should be done.
   Rationale: To assess sepsis early and effectively
   a. White blood count
      Rationale: To note decrease to 5000 or less in bacterial sepsis or 25,000
   b. Differential count
      Rationale: To note increased bands in bacterial sepsis and immature forms of polymorphonuclear leukocytes (Caution should be used here because immature infants may present with some data.)
   c. Hematocrit, hemoglobin
      Rationale: To note that some strains hemolyze RBC's and decrease values
   d. Platelet count
      Rationale: To note decrease in gram-negative infection with intravascular coagulopathy or normal values
   e. Bilirubin
      Rationale: To indicate hemolysis if no other coexisting pathology[7]
   f. Gram's stain of spinal fluid
      Rationale: To indicate bacteria on positive stain
   g. Urinalysis
      Rationale: To detect urinary infections by white blood cells, casts, and bacteria
   h. Chest x-ray
      Rationale: To note presence of pneumonic infiltrates on radiographs
   i. Serum immunoglobulins, especially IgM
      Rationale: To note that increases in cord blood, 20 mg/dl, usually indicate intrauterine sepsis and/or maternal-fetal transfusion: serial blood samplings indicated (If fetus is exposed to intrauterine infection for short period, IgM levels may be low.[4,8])

j. TORCH test

Rationale: To rule out toxoplasmosis, syphilis, rubella, cytomegalovirus, and herpes simplex

k. Cultures and sensitivities of the following as indicated by clinical picture: nose and throat, urine, spinal fluid, blood, umbilical cord, rectal

Rationale: To show type of organisms that may be causative agents of sepsis as well as choice of specific antimicrobial therapy (blood, spinal fluid, and urine most important[8])

l. Differential laboratory tests to rule out disease with similar signs and symptoms: blood glucose, electrolytes, blood types and factors, serology, viral diseases.

Rationale: To note that overlying symptoms approximate diseases such as hypoglycemia, hypocalemia, blood incompatibilities, syphilis, cytomegalic inclusion disease[4,8]

THERAPEUTIC

1. Promote full and accurate collection of specimens for laboratory tests, that is, use of proper aseptic technique, controls or need for limited fasting and/or fluids, proper storage of blood, feces, and urine before delivery to laboratory.

a. Blood, urine, spinal fluid

Rationale: To ensure against contamination, which will lead to inaccurate diagnosis and treatment

2. Support of infant during examinations both physiologically and emotionally through control of environment, proper positioning, touch, and verbalization.

Rationale: To ensure infant's well-being (the infant's physiological well-being is soon depleted with repeated blood drawings, limited fluids [IV's indicated], and intrusive procedures. The emotional trauma of no sleep and/or interrupted sleep periods, pain, and cool air may be detrimental to emotional well-being.)

EDUCATIONAL

1. All personnel new to high-risk nurseries need added skills and insights. This need is most beneficially and efficiently filled by unit staff development. For nurses with more experience, in-depth understanding of physiological reactions and interactions may be acquired by continuing education. Grand rounds for staff development (interdisciplinary) and literature should be kept current.

Rationale: To ensure that a diagnosis is not misdirected if specimens are contaminated or collected inaccurately

2. Parents must become involved with this valuable diagnostic process. Relevant signs and symptoms to note are awareness of tests and their purpose.

Rationale: To help parents arrive at a realistic perception of the event and allow expressions of feelings, that is, guilt, anxiety

Problem □ Diagnosed septic infant

GOAL: To maintain and support infant in physiological and emotional defense to sepsis

Rationale: To give physiological and emotional support so that an infant can mount a self-defense to sepsis

DIAGNOSTIC

1. Continuous serial assessments including physical assessments, neurological checks, vital signs, and laboratory tests, that is, WBC cultures and sensitivity, urinalysis, urine specific gravity, liver function (fractionated bilirubins).

Rationale: To apprise the physician and nurse of the infant's progress

2. There should be continuous collaboration between physician and nurse.

Rationale: To effect the best care and therapy of the septic infant

THERAPEUTIC

1. Place in isolette.

Rationale: To serve the purpose of isolation of a susceptible infant from the environment as well as other infants from the affected one

2. Temperature control. Isolettes/incubators provide warmth, overhead warmers.

Rationale: To be aware that the septic infant frequently responds to sepsis with a hypothermic reaction (especially low birth weight, preterm neonate); term infants may run a low-grade temperature[3,8]

3. Adequate hydration should be maintained through accurate reporting of intake and output, urine specific gravity, skin turgor, and blood pressure.

   Rationale: To be aware that a well-hydrated infant is less vulnerable to electrolyte complications (acidosis-alkalosis-calcemia problems) and skin/mucous membrane breakdown

4. Assess blood gases: amount of FlO_2 titrated to maintain infant's arterial Po_2 50 to 100 ml dyspnea oxygen therapy assist in lung inflation, gas exchange, and further pulmonary complications.

   Rationale: To check for minimal acceptable levels of O_2 to maintain adequate cerebral oxygenation

5. Assess kidney function: urine specific gravity, accurate intake/output, sugar, protein, liver function, fractionated bilirubin.

   Rationale: To determine effect of drug therapy on kidney and liver as the drugs are absorbed, detoxified, and excreted (Immaturity of infant's kidneys and liver make drug reactions somewhat unpredictable in newborns.[8])

6. Assess central nervous system complications: seizures (tremors, muscular twitching), apnea, pupilary reactions, vomiting, irritability, high-pitched cry.

   Rationale: To check for increased intercranial pressure, which will be reflected in the preceding physiological changes

7. Provide metabolic support with parenteral fluids, hyperalimentation, or oral feedings as infant's condition indicates.

   Rationale: To maintain energy needs as well as restorative needs and to replace losses through skin and gastrointestinal and urinary tracts (Caloric requirements for growth increase during infection, while energy is used for mobilizing the body's defenses.)

8. Administer drugs as indicated.

   Rationale: To be aware that vigorous broad-spectrum antimicrobial therapy is indicated in septic infant (Advantages and disadvantages of drugs are carefully considered. Neonate's reactions are somewhat different from adult reactions and, therefore, often unpredictable. Most hazard stems from gram-negative organisms.)

   a. Use of parenteral drugs as indicated.

      Rationale: To discourage use of oral antibiotics in neonate because of ineffective ingestion and absorption[3,8]

   b. Initial use of a combination of penicillin and an aminoglycoside is recommended.

      Rationale: To treat for broad-spectrum and gram-negative organisms, which are the most frequent causative agents of newborn sepsis (Carbenicillin and ampicillin are active in vitro against streptococci, *Listeria monocytogenes,* enterococci, and many *E. coli* strains. Aminoglycosides, kanamycin, and gentamicin are effective against coliform diseases and staphylococci. Kanamycin is preferred for coliform, while *E. coli* is resistant. Kanamycin is not effective against *Pseudomonas* but carbenicillin is. Gentamycin should be reserved for bacteria resistant to kanamycin.[4,5] In newborns the following drugs should be avoided: sulfisoxazole and novobiocin, which are associated with cases of kernicterus; tetracycline, which is deposited in bones and teeth; cephalothin, which may cause a positive Coombs' reaction; and chloramphenicol, which is extremely toxic [gray spinal syndrome]. Careful use of chloramphenicol is indicated in *Salmonella* infections.)

   c. Provide organism-specific drug therapy as ordered.

      Rationale: To be aware that once culture and sensitivity reports are received, the drugs of choice will be the ones that are bactericidal and have the least adverse side effects[4,5]

EDUCATIONAL

1. Nurses: education on administration of drug therapy including choice of drugs, dosage, routes of administration, effectiveness, and adverse effects is imperative. The can be done by unit staff development and/or CEU programs.

Rationale: To provide the nurse with knowledge of safe and therapeutic administration
of essential medications for infant with
sepsis

2. Parents: educate parents on early side effects
of drugs to be noted as appropriate, that is,
nausea, vomiting, diarrhea.

Rationale: To allow parent's insights into
treatments, assessments, and plan of care
(Parents can help in some assessments, that
is, feeding behavior, irritability, temperature, color, stools, and so forth. It also helps
parents to tolerate therapies and emotionally
support infant with touch and verbalization.

Problem □ Shock, adrenal insufficiency, intravascular coagulopathy, congestive heart failure, and hyponatremia

GOAL: To detect any early signs or symptoms of extreme complications of severe neonatal infections
Rationale: To prevent fulminating and fatal complications to infectious diseases of the neonate
THERAPEUTIC

1. Continuous assessment of vital signs and laboratory tests such as RBC, hematocrit, platelets, Gram's stains, urinalysis, including a
screen for cytomegalic inclusion bodies, specific gravity, liver function, and bilirubin).
Rationale: To detect complications early,
make diagnosis, and begin therapy

2. Assist with therapy.
a. Intravascular coagulopathy, prothrombin,
fibrinogen, factors V and VIII, fresh whole
blood, heparin (use is controversial).[8]
Rationale: To provide blood element re-
placements when defect is in clotting
factors[4,8]
b. Shock—plasma expanders and fresh whole
blood may be used.

Rationale: To maintain volume and oxygenation of vital organs

c. Hydrocortisone may be used if infant remains in profound shock.
Rationale: To treat septicemia (although
evidence does not point to insufficient
secretion of adrenal steroids during septicemia, autopsy has revealed adrenal
hemorrhage.[4,8])

d. Electrolytes should be monitored by serial
blood chemistries every 24 hours.
Rationale: To avoid metabolic acidosis and
hypoglycemia, which can result from
shock[4]

REFERENCES

1. Blake, P., and Perez, R.: Applied immunological concepts, New York, 1978, Appleton-Century-Crofts.
2. Bolognese, R. L., and Schwarz, R. H.: Perinatal medicine, Baltimore, 1977, The Williams & Wilkins Co.
3. Brown, R. J. K., and Valman, H. B.: Practical neonatal pediatrics, ed. 3, London, 1975, Blackwell Scientific Pub-lications.
4. Gotoff, S. P.: Infections. In Behrman, R. E., editor: Neo-natal-perinatal medicine: diseases of the fetus and infant, ed. 2, St. Louis, 1977, The C. V. Mosby Co.
5. McCracken, G. H., Jr., and Nelson, J. D.: Antimicrobial therapy for newborns: practical application of pharmacology to clinical usage, New York, 1977, Grune & Stratton, Inc.
6. Miller, M.: Host defense in the human neonate: monograph in neonatology. New York, 1978, Grune & Stratton, Inc.
7. Nejedla, A.: The development of immunological factors in infants with hyperbilirubinemia, Pediatrics **45**:102, 1970.
8. Pierog, S., and Ferrara, A.: Approach to the medical care of the sick newborn, ed. 2, St. Louis, 1976, The C. V. Mosby Co.
9. Remington, J. S., and Klein, J. O., editors: Infectious dis-eases of the fetus and newborn infant, Philadelphia, 1976, W. B. Saunders Co.
10. Stevenson, D. D., et al.: Development of IgE in newborn human infants, J. Allergy Clin. Immunol. **48**:61, 1971.
11. Stiehm, E. R., and Fulginiti, V. A.: Immunologic disorders in infants and children, Philadelphia, 1973, W. B. Saunders Co.

Chapter 21

Disseminated intravascular coagulation

Marlys Connallon

Disseminated intravascular coagulation (DIC) is a pathological syndrome in response to an underlying disease process that results in the inappropriate activation of the clotting process. DIC is characterized by the intravascular consumption of platelets and plasma clotting factors, especially factors II, V, VIII, and fibrinogen. This widespread coagulation within the circulation results in the deposition of fibrin thrombi in small vessels and the production of the hemorrhagic state when the level of platelets and clotting factors drops to values insufficient to maintain hemostasis. The accumulation of fibrin in the microcirculation produces mechanical injury to the red cells, leading to erythrocyte fragmentation and microangiopathic anemia.*

Owing to the formation of fibrin, the fibrinolytic process is stimulated to dissolve the fibrin clots. Fibrin degradation products are the end product of clot lysis and have an anticoagulant effect. All of this results in the three problems of hemorrhage, ischemia, and anemia.[8,10,32]

Because large amounts of platelets, fibrinogen, and clotting factors are consumed, DIC has also been called "consumptive coagulopathy" or acute defibrination syndrome.[27] "In 1962, Aballi and Lamerens[1] introduced 'secondary hemorrhagic disease of the newborn,' to emphasize that not all bleeding in the neonate was a result of vitamin K deficiency."[34] They found that hemorrhage occurred commonly in premature low birth weight infants and also in infants who were anoxic, acidotic, or septic.[34]

The literature reports a wide range in the incidence of DIC, depending on the method of reporting and the diagnostic criteria used for DIC. Hathaway[18] reported in a survey at the University of Colorado Medical Center that approximately 1% of all nursery admissions have significant hemorrhagic complications; also, approximately 40% of the deaths have associated hemorrhage or thrombosis described at autopsy. This would appear to be fairly consistent with the survey by Patel[35] who describes necrotizing enterocolitis as occurring in 3% to 8% of all premature infants in intensive care centers, of which the hematological abnormalities include thrombocytopenia, neutropenia, and DIC. Because of the secondary nature of the syndrome, DIC has a higher incidence in high-risk newborns. Hathaway[19] reports that in an observation period of 8 months, 11 of 19 sick newborn infants were shown to have either laboratory and/or pathological evidence of DIC. Three of the affected infants had severe viral disease (rubella, cytomegalic inclusion virus, and herpes simplex). Seven of the infants had severe idiopathic respiratory distress syndrome (IRDS), and one infant (the product of a severely toxemic mother) had transient respiratory distress.

Whaun and Oski[41] reported that in the pediatric age group they studied, 60% of all DIC occurred in newborns; 79% of the affected infants were septic, usually from gram-negative infections.

Because of the immature coagulation system, the newborn and especially the premature infant are at risk of developing DIC from a variety of stimuli, or underlying disease processes, common to premature and sick term infants. Because DIC is secondary to

---

*See references 2, 3, 8, 10, 18, 22, and 32 to 34.

the underlying disease, the clinical manifestations and outcomes are variable.

The physiological deficiencies of procoagulants and anticoagulants lead to the paradoxical situation of both excessive bleeding and thrombotic tendencies in the infant. The pathological intermediaries of the disorders common to the neonate, hypoxia, acidosis, hypotension, and hypothermia, exaggerate these thrombohemorrhagic tendencies.[17]

The process of DIC may be triggered by intrauterine or maternal factors, intrapartal factors, and neonatal factors. By being aware of these factors, which may trigger DIC, the perinatal nurse can be alert for the often rapid onset and variable clinical signs and symptoms of DIC. Many of the triggering mechanisms can be prevented from occurring through careful monitoring of the neonate during the antepartum, intrapartum, and newborn period and thereby initiating appropriate nursing intervention. Medical management is primarily aimed at treatment and correction of the underlying disease process. Alternate therapy forms, such as heparin therapy, exchange transfusions, and plasmapheresis, have been tried with varying degrees of reported effectiveness.

NORMAL HEMOSTASIS

The normal hemostatic mechanism is composed of three lines of defense, the extravascular, vascular, and intravascular phenomena. Both the physical effect of the surrounding tissue (for example, skin, muscle, elastic tissue) in tending to close and seal the defect in the injured blood vessel and the biochemical effects of substances released from the injured tissues (thromboplastin) and the reaction with plasma and platelet factors act to produce the extravascular phenomena of hemostasis. In addition, tissue thromboplastin, which is present in both the intravascular and extravascular compartments, can activate the clotting mechanism.[6]

In the vascular process the damaged blood vessel constricts almost instantaneously. This vasoconstriction is important in the early control of hemorrhage following injury to a vessel. This reflex is believed to be enhanced by the release of serotonin. Serotonin is released from platelets, which adhere to the margins of the injury or defect in the wall of the vessel. Serotonin promotes a local, direct, biochemically stimulated narrowing of the torn blood

vessel and of intact vessels in the immediate area. When the injured blood vessel is contracted, blood flow is diverted so that the intraluminal pressure is reduced to promote the formation of an effective platelet plug.[6,25]

Platelets are 1- to 2-μ particles formed by disintegration of large megakaryocytes, a type of white blood cell produced in the bone marrow. Platelets normally have a thin membrane that is negatively charged on the outside; the endothelial walls of the vessels throughout the circulation are also normally negatively charged so that the platelets are repelled from the walls. However, when a vessel ruptures, the damaged endothelium loses its negative charge, allowing the platelets to stick at the point of rupture. Likewise, platelets can stick to foreign bodies in the circulation as well as clots that have already formed.[16]

When the platelets stick to the exposed basement membrane and subendothelial collagen within the lumen of the injured blood vessel, they undergo swelling, degranulation, and release of adenosine diphosphate, vasoactive amines (serotonin), phospholipids, and other thrombogenic substances. In turn, adenosine diphosphate mediates the aggregation of platelets into an occlusive plug; the catecholamines (serotonin) maintain vascular contraction; and platelet phospholipid (PF3) catalyzes two steps in the coagulation sequence.[6]

It is the intravascular or coagulation process that transforms the plug into a permanent or definitive seal.[6,25] Within the intravascular phenomena a hemostatic balance is normally maintained between the coagulation process and the fibrinolytic and anticoagulation processes. Fibrinolysis and anticoagulation prevent the inappropriate onset of intravascular coagulation and the excessive consumption of clotting factors. They restrain and limit the autocatalytic reactions of coagulation, and they allow for the eventual repair of the vascular defect by lysis of the fibrin clot and reestablishment of luminal continuity.[6]

NORMAL COAGULATION

The study of coagulation has been greatly facilitated by the use of a standard nomenclature for the coagulation factors developed by the international committee formed in 1954. This committee approved a method of double labeling a given factor

Table 21-1. The blood clotting factors

Factor Roman numeral	Preferred name	Synonym	Definition
I	Fibrinogen		A protein that, when modified by thrombin, forms the clot (fibrin)
II	Prothrombin		An alpha globulin that, when acted on by thromboplastin, accelerin, and calcium, is converted to thrombin
III	Thromboplastin		An unidentified substance or substances present in tissues to promote prothrombin conversion to thrombin
IV	Calcium		A substance that is necessary in the first and second stages of coagulation
V	Proaccelerin	Labile factor, Ac globulin	A plasma factor that participates in the first and second stages of coagulation
VI	Accelerin	Serum Ac globulin	Active form of factor V
VII	Proconvertin	Stable factor, SPCA	A plasma factor required for conversion of prothrombin to thrombin
VIII	Antihemophilic factor (AHF)	Antihemophilic globulin (AHG), antihemophilic factor A	A thromboplastic precursor deficiency that is required for classic hemophilia; found in the beta globulin fraction
IX	Plasma thromboplastin component (PTC)	Christmas factor, antihemophilic factor B, autoprothrombin II	A factor that participates in thromboplastin formation
X	Stuart factor	Stuart-Prower factor, Prower factor, autoprothrombin C	Participates in thromboplastin formation and prothrombin conversion
XI	Plasma thromboplastin antecedent (PTA)	Antihemophilic factor C	Reacts with activated Hageman factor and forms thromboplastic substance
XII	Hageman factor	Glass or contact factor	A factor concerned with initiation of clotting in vitro; becomes activated by contact with rough surface; deficiency unaccompanied by clinical manifestations
XIII	Fibrin-stabilizing factor	Fibrinase	A serum factor responsible for the stabilization of the fibrin clot

Modified from Lynch, M. J., et al.: Medical laboratory technology and clinical pathology, ed. 2, Philadelphia, 1969, W. B. Saunders Co.; O'Brian, B. S., and Woods, S.: Am. J. Nurs. **78:**1878, 1978; and Oski, F. A., and Naiman, J. L.: In Schaller, A. J. editor: Major problems in clinical pediatrics, ed. 2, vol. IV, Philadelphia, 1972, W. B. Saunders Co.

with a Roman numeral and a descriptive term. The list of currently accepted factors extends through factor XIII.[25,34,40] Table 21-1 lists these clotting factors.

According to current concepts, two major pathways exist to activate the coagulation system or clotting cascade: the intrinsic and the extrinsic pathways. Fig. 21-1 depicts the entire sequence of the clotting cascade. Blood clotting factors are present in an inactive form, which if stimulated becomes an active form. It is postulated that this "cascade" of enzyme actions permits a very great amount of material to be changed.[25]

The intrinsic pathway, occurring within the vascular lumen, is "triggered off by the activation of Factor XII (Hageman factor) and Factor XI (PTA) through surface contact, collagen, or other negatively charged substances. This complex, in the presence of calcium, then activates Factor IX (PTC). Activated Factor IX interacts with Factor VIII (AHG), platelet plospholipid, and calcium to form a complex which activates Factor X (Stuart Factor)."[10,33,34]

"In the extrinsic system, tissue thromboplastin, along with Factor VII (proconvertin) and calcium, forms a complex, which also activates Factor

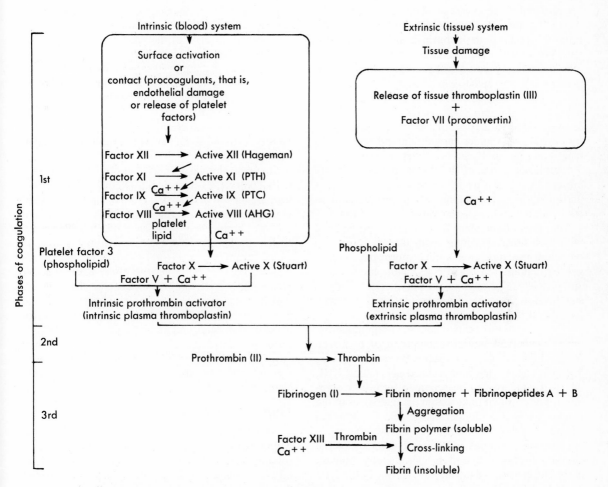

Fig. 21-1. Clotting cascade. (Modified from Lynch, M. J., et al.: Laboratory technology and clinical pathology, ed. 2, Philadelphia, 1969, W. B. Saunders Co.; O'Brien, B. S., and Woods, S.: Am. J. Nurs. **78:**1878, 1978; and Oski, F. A., and Naiman, J. L. In Schaller, A. J., editor: Major problems in clinical pediatrics, ed. 2, vol. IV, Philadelphia, 1972, W. B. Saunders Co.)

X."[33,34] Many tissues, particularly blood vessel walls, lung, and brain, contain a lipid-protein complex (tissue thromboplastin), which in the presence of proconvertin (factor VII) is capable of directly activating factor X (Stuart factor). The extrinsic pathway initiates clotting of extravasated blood, and because endothelium also contains tissue thromboplastin, it may operate intravascularly as well.[6] From this point, both the intrinsic and extrinsic systems proceed in a similar fashion.[33,34]

In the second phase of coagulation, factor II (prothrombin) is activated to thrombin by a complex that includes activated factor X, factor V (proaccelerin), platelet phospholipid, and calcium. Thrombin acts as an enzyme to activate the fibrinogen molecule, forming fibrinopeptides and fibrin monomers, which means a single molecule of activated fibrin.

Fibrinogen is one of the plasma proteins usually present in the plasma in a concentration of about 0.3%. Fibrinogen is a long, axially oriented molecule with a weight of approximately 330,000.[10]

The fibrin monomers automatically polymerize with each other into long fibrin threads forming a reticulum that precipitates out to form the familiar gel that entraps red blood cells, white blood cells, and platelets to form clot. The polymerized fibrin is stabilized as insoluble fibrin by means of activated factor XIII.[16]

The bonds in this gel that hold the fibrin monomer units together are initially composed of hydrogen bonds, and this gel can readily be dissociated by high salt concentration or reduced pH. Factor XIII, which is converted to an activated form by thrombin, forms covalent links within the interstices of the clot so that it is no longer dissociable.[10] Thrombin has other actions, as well: it can directly aggregate human platelets; it has an autocatalytic effect on the clotting mechanism; and it can directly convert plasminogen into plasmin, the active fibrinolytic agent.[10]

Thrombin is a potent enzyme. Its unchecked presence in the plasma would be a disaster. Deykin[10] states, "In 10 ml. of blood sufficient thrombin exists—if prothrombin were to be completely converted to thrombin—to clot 2500 ml. of plasma in 15 secs." Fortunately, there are efficient mechanisms that limit the unimpeded evolution of thrombin. Several mechanisms limit the conversion of prothrombin to thrombin. The liver has a critical function in the removal of particulate tissue thromboplastin and of activated Factors IX, X, and XI. Rapid blood flow is also important in that it dilutes the concentration of activated clotting intermediates, thereby retarding the rate of conversion of prothrombin to thrombin.[10]

Furthermore, in blood there is a series of inactivators that progressively impede the procoagulant activity of each of the precursors of prothrombin.[10,33,34] The rate of inactivation of an activated clotting intermediate by these circulating inhibitors is relatively slow, and whether or not they have an important role in vivo has not been demonstrated.[10]

In addition to these anticoagulation functions, the liver synthesizes all clotting factors, except possibly factors VIII and XIII, for which the site of biosynthesis is unknown.[6]

Once the clot has formed, the fibrin threads gradually contract, expressing plasma out of the clot but keeping the red blood cells, platelets, and other solid elements. The plasma that is extruded from the clot has no fibrinogen in it because this has been converted to fibrin. This plasma, without fibrin, is called serum.[16]

After the clot is formed, to effect permanent repair of the blood vessel the clot becomes organized, which means there is an ingrowth of fibrous cells to form connective tissue. The process continues for several days, and endothelial cells simultaneously grow over the vascular surface of the clot to form a new, smooth lining on the inside of the vessel, thereby restoring the integrity of the negatively charged lining.[16]

FIBRINOLYTIC SYSTEM

Normally, when fibrin is deposited on vessel walls or in tissues, it is slowly broken down into soluble fibrin split products (FSP) by plasmin. Plasmin is a potent proteolytic and nonspecific enzyme that splits arginine and lysine bonds. Although plasmin has a high affinity for insoluble fibrin, it can also attack fibrinogen and factors V and VIII. Plasminogen is the inactive precursor of plasmin that is normally found in plasma. It is activated into plasmin by a variety of factors present in plasma, urine, and tissue. Like the coagulation system, the fibrinolytic system is normally held in check by a variety of inhibitors. Normal blood contains inhibitors of plasminogen activators and plasmin. Thus, both the

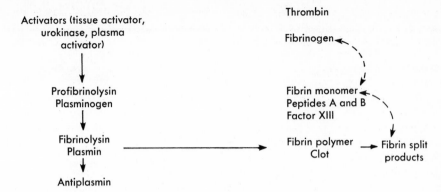

Fig. 21-2. Fibrinolytic system. The dashed lines represent possible fibrin monomer complex formation. (Modified from Lynch, M. J., et al.: Laboratory technology and clinical pathology, ed. 2, Philadelphia, 1969, W. B. Saunders Co.; O'Brian, B. S., and Woods, S.: Am. J. Nurs. **78:**1878, 1978; and Oski, F. A., and Naiman, J. L. In Schaller, A. J., editor: Major problems in clinical pediatrics, ed. 2, vol. IV, Philadelphia, 1972, W. B. Saunders Co.)

coagulation system and the fibrinolytic system are held in a state of dynamic equilibrium that can be easily disturbed by a variety of stimuli.[10,33,34] Fig. 21-2 outlines the fibrinolytic activity of plasmin.

This delicate balance between activation and inhibition of plasmin is of particular interest in the neonate, since adaptation to extrauterine life requires maturation of the coagulation as well as the fibrinolytic systems. The next section will discuss the ontogenesis of human hemostasis, which like other physiological functions occurs in an orderly fashion.

ONTOGENESIS OF HUMAN HEMOSTASIS

From the study of previable fetuses obtained from therapeutic abortions, the normal development of human hemostasis has been determined. Bleyer, Hakami, and Shepard[6] present an excellent and comprehensive review of this process. This developmental sequence is summarized in Table 21-2.[6]

According to Bleyer, Hakami, and Shepard,[6] "Vascular contraction in response to injury develops during embryogenesis (by 8 weeks), although blood vessels may not achieve optimal structural strength until term." This early vasoconstrictive response is considered by Bleyer, Hakami, and Shepard[6] to be the most primitive, which also oc-

curs in nearly all forms of life possessing a circulatory system.

In their studies, Bleyer and his colleagues[6] found platelets in all specimens more than 80 mm crown-rump length (11 weeks' gestational age). Cells resembling mature platelets were found, as well as slightly larger rounded platelets that stained less intensely and contained fewer granules. The latter cells were observed in only fetuses of 10 to 12 weeks' gestation. Platelet clumps were frequent in blood smears of fetuses 90 to 120 mm crown-rump length, suggesting that platelets are capable of adhering to each other by 12 to 15 weeks' gestational age. Megakaryocytes were seen in the hematopoietic tissue of the liver and spleen at 10 weeks' gestational age, and electron microscopy of the cells revealed dense granules similar to those found in the mature platelet. By 30 weeks, megakaryocytic activity in the bone marrow is fully instituted, and the blood platelet count approaches adult values. These findings are similar to those of other authors.[14,18,20,34]

In addition, recent studies have demonstrated that a number of platelet functions are poorly developed at birth and may be particularly deficient in the premature infant. Platelet factor 3 release and in vitro platelet aggregation to ADP, epinephrine, collagen,

Table 21-2. Development of human hemostasis*

Characteristics	Fetal	Preterm infant	Term infant	Age at which adult levels attained
Vascular				
Vasoconstriction	Present at end of embryonic period	Present	Present	Optimal at term
Capillary fragility	Increased	Increased	Normal	Close to term
Bleeding time	Prolonged	Normal	Normal	Prenatally
Whole blood clotting time (WBCT)	11 wk	Increased	Decreased or normal	Close to term
Prothrombin time (PT) (N 12-14 sec)	Prolonged at 15-20 wk	Increased (12-21 sec)	Increased (13-20 sec)	3-4 days
Partial thromboplastin time (PTT) (N35-45 sec)		Increased (70-145 sec)	Increased (45-70 sec)	2-9 mo
Thrombin time (TT) (N 1:8-10 sec)		Increased (11-17 sec)	Increased (10-16 sec)	1-3 days
Platelets				
Count	Circulate at 10-11 wk	Normal	Normal	Prenatally
Function	Adherence at 12-15 wk	↓ Adherence	↓ Adherence ↓ Clot retraction ↓ Platelet factor 3 release	?
Clotting factors				
I (fibrinogen)	Synthesized as early as 5 wk 50% level reached by 15 wk	↓ (60%-90%)	↓ (60%-90%)	2-4 days
II (prothrombin)		↓ (20%-80%)	↓ (25%-65%)	2-12 mo
V (proaccelerin)		↓ (50%-85%)	Normal (80%-200%)	Prenatally
VII (proconvertin)		↓ (20%-45%)	↓ (20%-70%)	2-12 mo
VIII (antihemophilic factor)		↓ (20%-80%)	Normal (70%-150%)	Prenatally
IX (Christmas)		↓ 10%-25%)	↓ (20%-60%)	3-9 mo
X (Stuart)		↓ (10%-45%)	↓ (20%-55%)	2-12 mo
XI (plasma thromboplastian antecedent)		↓ (5%-20%)	↓ 15%-70%)	1-2 mo
XII (Hageman)		?	↓ (25%-70%)	9-14 days
XIII (fibrin-stabilizing factor)		Normal (100%)	Normal (100%)	Prenatally
Thrombotest (for vitamin K–dependent factors II, VII, IX, X)	First registers at 10 wk	↓ (30%-50%)	↓ (40%-68%)	2-12 mo

*Adapted from Bleyer, W. A., Hakami, N., and Shepard, T. H.: J. Pediatr. **79:**838, 1977.

and thrombin are impaired in most premature and many term infants.[14,18,20]

Because of these platelet functional characteristics, the newborn and particularly the premature infant may have an increased susceptibility to intracranial bleeding and other hemorrhagic manifestations.[20] However, this mild platelet function is only transiently seen in the neonatal period (1 to 2 weeks), and this impairment is of questionable clinical significance, since the bleeding time (an in vivo measure of platelet function) is normal.[14]

Bleyer, Hakami, and Shepard[6] summarize their findings by stating, "During early fetal life, platelets derived from hepatic and splenic megakaryocytes appear in the circulation [by 11 weeks], and assume microscopic identity with adult platelets [by 12 weeks], and become capable of forming aggregates [by 12 to 15 weeks]. Platelet number approximates adult values by 30 weeks' gestation, but maturation of platelet function is delayed until term or later.''

Clottable and fibrinolytic proteins appear in the plasma between 10 and 11 weeks' gestation. Blood from embryos and fetuses less than this age does not clot.[6] Prior to this stage, the whole blood clotting time (WBCT) is infinite, and thereafter the WBCT promptly assumes rates comparable to and frequently shorter than adult levels. This stage corresponds to completion of hepatic histogenesis and vascularization of the spleen and presumably to the release of clotting factors from these organs. Thereafter, individual clotting factors reach adult levels at varying rates.

Factors VIII, V, XIII, and fibrinogen reach adult levels in utero. Clotting activities of the vitamin K–dependent factors (IX, X, VII, II) and the contact factors (XII, XI) rise slowly, being low at birth and attaining adult levels during the first year of postnatal life.[6]

Fibrinogen is synthesized by the liver as early as 5 weeks' gestation and reaches substantial plasma levels by 15 weeks. In the early 1950's Burstein and associates postulated the existence of a special fetal fibrinogen.[6] Fibrinogen from newborns differs qualitatively from adult fibrinogen. It coagulates more slowly on the addition of excess thrombin (prolonged thrombin time), particularly at alkaline pH, and it forms a fibrin clot characterized by less optical density, diminished compressibility, increased tensile strength, and a higher resistance to fibrinolysis. Although newborn and adult fibrinogen have the same molecular weight, size, shape, immunological properties, and amino acid composition, a difference in electrical charge can be demonstrated by column chromatography. The latter finding can be localized to three peptides on two-dimensional paper chromatography and may reflect differences in amino acid sequence.[6]

The concept of a ''fetal fibrinogen'' is attractive, particularly in analogy with embryonic and fetal hemoglobins. However, as Bleyer, Hakami, and Shepard[6] state, ''Slow conversion of fibrinogen to the fibrin polymer [prolonged thrombin time] may also be due to circulating antithrombin substances [e.g., heparin] or antipolymerization agents [e.g., fibrin split products].'' Several investigators have found heparin-like substances and fibrin degradation products in the blood of newborn infants. Recently, Muller, Van Doorm, and Hemker[31] reported on the basis of their studies that, ''contrary to current beliefs, the newborn has no vitamin K deficiency, but is 'anticoagulated' by heparin or a heparin-like substance.'' They propose that this heparin-like substance is produced in organs that are readily perfused before birth but will have an active circulation afterwards (that is, the lungs). This substance may serve to prevent thrombosis in these organs.[31]

Fibrinolytic activity is detectable by 10 to 11 weeks' gestational age and remains quite active throughout gestation. The term infant shows marked fibrinolytic activy that decreases to adult levels in a few days.[18] Plasminogen is decreased in the neonate and fetus but reaches adult levels by 6 months of life. The increased fibrinolytic activity is believed to be related to high activator levels in the fetus. The antiplasmin levels are normal. In spite of the elevated fibrinolytic activity, fibrin-fibrinogen degradation or fibrin split products (FSP) are not significantly elevated in normal infants.

Although the clot lysis time tends to increase during early fetal life, simultaneous comparison of clot lysis time and WBCT at various gestational ages suggests that the rate of fibrinolysis is linearly proportional to the rate of clotting. In other words, its subsequent development appears to parallel hemostasis, balancing throughout gestation the tendency to clot formation.[6] This parallel development prevents inappropriate intravascular clotting, dissolves clots, repairs thrombosed vessels, and thereby ensures free blood flow through the microvasculature, for example, within the fetoplacental circuit.[6] The studies by Markarian and associates[28] emphasize that age is an important factor when comparing fibrinolytic activity in the neonatal period. The lesser degree of fibrinolytic activity (longer fibrinoly. times) in premature infants as compared to full-term infants exemplifies the role of immaturity.[28]

Despite the deficiencies of many of the clotting factors, the whole blood of the newborn clots more quickly than adult whole blood, as measured by Lee-White clotting time and thromboelastograph.[34] This hypercoagulability has been related to a deficiency of naturally occurring anticoagulants or protease inhibitors, the most potent of which is an alpha-2-globulin designated antithrombin III (AT-III). The lowest levels of AT-III are observed in infants who develop RDS.[18,33]

This has been consistent with the findings of Suzuki, Wake, and Yoshiaki,[38] whose results indicate that the low level of plasmin inhibitors works synergistically with the high value of activator. They suggest the low level of antithrombin II could be the reason for coagulation disorders, such as disseminated intravascular coagulation, in preterm infants. Other naturally occurring anticoagulants, such as antiactivated XI and antiactivated X, are also low in the newborn.[17,33]

ETIOLOGIES OF DISSEMINATED INTRAVASCULAR COAGULATION

Because the hemostatic system of the term infant, and particularly the preterm infant, is immature, the newborn is susceptible to coagulation disorders from a variety of stimuli.

Disseminated intravascular coagulation was first described as the generalized Shwartzman reaction (GSR), which is produced in young rabbits by two properly spaced intravenous injections of bacterial endotoxin. Although the first (preparatory) injection triggers some intravascular clotting, the activated coagulation factors and fibrin are rapidly cleard by the reticuloendothelial system. As a result, fibrin thrombi do not persist in small blood vessels. However, as a result of the first injection, the reticuloendothelial system is damaged or functionally altered so that the second (provocative) injection of endotoxin results in significant intravascular coagulation with depletion of platelets; prothrombin; and factors V, VIII, and fibrinogen; and widespread formation of fibrin thrombi in small blood vessels.[2]

As such, DIC is not a disease entity per se but a complication of an underlying disease that triggers overstimulatin of the normal coagulation process.[32] Three types of injury may activate the coagulation system to initiate this disorder: (1) injury to the endothelial cell by exposing underlying collagen activates factor XII (Hageman factor) and, subsequently, the intrinsic clotting system; (2) tissue injury produces thromboplastin, which activates the extrinsic clotting system; and (3) red cell, leuko-

cyte, or platelet injury results in overproduction of phospholipid, which is needed for the proper functioning of both the intrinsic and extrinsic clotting systems.[5,8]

The activation of factor XII (Hageman factor) is thought to occur in viremia; heat stroke; gram-negative endotoxemia, especially meningococcemia; gram-positive septicemia; and hyperacute renal allograft rejection. The consequences of factor XII activation are not only initiation of blood coagulation but activation of three other plasma pathways: the kallikrein, fibrinolytic, and complement systems. The activation of prekallikrein to kallikrein results in the formation of bradykinin, a potent vasodepressor, which may be in part responsible for hypotension in septicemia.[8,10] Furthermore, bacterial endotoxin itself, through a neurotoxic mechanism, results in the decreased perfusion of the splanchnic bed. As a result of these two mechanisms, blood flow through the liver may be profoundly impaired, drastically reducing the efficiency of hepatic clearance and of dilution of the activated clotting intermediates.[10] Poor liver and spleen perfusion impairs the function of the reticuloendothelial system, which phagocytizes activation products of the clotting system. This impairment contributes to the development of DIC.[26]

The activation of the fibrinolytic system through factor XII activation is accomplished by the conversion of plasminogen to plasmin by activation of a proactivator. Finally, activation of factor XII can initiate the complement system, at least in the fluid phase.

When thromboplastic substances are released, factor XII (Hageman factor) is not affected and the blood pressure remains normal. High concentrations of thromboplastin occur in tumors, as well as in leukemic leukocytes, and may be a consequence of massive breakdown of tumor cells.[8] Thromboplastin may also be passed transplacentally to the fetus of a toxemic mother.[38] Massive tissue thromboplastin release is encountered in abruptio placentae, dead fetus syndrome, amniotic fluid embolism, and in patients with massive blunt trauma. The high risk of postoperative thromboembolism is also linked by some investigators to the intraoperative release of tissue thromboplastin.[26]

Platelet breakdown can be caused by antibody-antigen complex interactions, as encountered with mismatched blood transfusions, severe anaphylactoid reactions, or the acute rejection of transplanted kidneys. Metabolic acidosis may cause intravascular platelet breakdown, thus explaining consumption coagulopathy in nonseptic shock conditions.[26] Examples of DIC initiated by ruptured erythrocytes are malaria, microangiopathic hemolytic anemia, mismatched plasma, and blood transfusion.[26]

PATHOPHYSIOLOGY OF DIC

The outcome of any of these events will be the formation of activated factor X, which converts prothrombin to thrombin in the circulating blood and results in the formation of fibrin.[8] Thrombin also initiates a massive aggregation of platelets, which then further activates the clotting system. These platelet-rich microemboli, especially in the lung microvasculature, will present early before any classical symptoms of DIC may be present. Hypoxia, dyspnea, and tachypnea associated with any of the disease entities in the list below should be suspect of a beginning process of DIC.[26]

Events triggering DIC in the newborn*

A. Maternal conditions
   1. Preeclampsia/eclampsia
   2. Abruptio placentae
   3. Dead twin fetus
   4. Severe Rh sensitization
   5. Infant of diabetic mother
   6. Third trimester bleeding/spontaneous labor
B. Intrapartal conditions
   1. Fetal distress—hypoxia and acidosis
      a. Birth asphyxia
      b. Hemorrhagic shock
      c. Meconium aspiration
      d. Amniotic fluid embolism
      e. Breech delivery
   2. Placental abnormalities
      a. Abruption
      b. Chorioangioma
      c. Infarction (postmature, SGA)
   3. Traumatic delivery
C. Neonatal conditions
   1. Sepsis (both bacterial and viral)
      a. Intrauterine
      b. Extrauterine

*Modified from references 2 to 4, 7, 11, 14, 18, 20 to 22, 24, 26, 29, 30, 33 to 36, 39, and 41.

2. Prematurity
3. Hypoxia and acidosis
   a. Respiratory distress syndrome
   b. Pulmonary hemorrhage
   c. Severe organ necrosis (NEC)
4. Stasis
   a. Polycythemia
   b. Renal vein thrombosis/indwelling catheters
   c. Giant hemangiomas
   d. Cold injury
5. Hypoglycemia
6. Erythroblastosis fetalis
7. Mismatched blood transfusions

Thrombin participates in various feedback reactions, resulting in the release of platelet contents, making phospholipids more available, and increasing the activity of factors V and VIII. This activation then converts the platelet-rich microthrombi to fibrin-rich microthrombi. The process is estimated by experimental studies to occur in 20 to 30 minutes.[26] These factors (V and VIII) become unstable after thrombin alteration and rapidly lose their activity. Finally, thrombin directly or indirectly converts plasminogen to plasmin, the enzyme of the fibrinolytic system. Thus thrombin causes consumption of fibrinogen, platelets, plasminogen, and factors II, V, and VIII.[3,8]

Thrombin is neutralized by antithrombin III and gradually depletes this protein. In secondary fibrinolysis, most of the plasmin activity occurs within the fibrin clots. The fibrin degradation products (FDP) produced by plasmin are critical to the occurrence of the hemorrhagic diathesis in DIC as well as useful in the diagnosis of DIC.[8]

The digestion of fibrinogen or fibrin by plasmin yields fragment X, a clottable derivative. Fragment X is degraded further to fragment Y and fragment D. Fragment Y directly inhibits the clotting action of thrombin on fibrinogen, while fragment D is responsible for disordered fibrin polymerization. The end result is a competition between massive coagulation and fibrinolysis.[8,10] Not only is there the paradoxical interaction of hemorrhage and thrombosis, but the accumulation of fibrin in the microcirculation produces mechanical injury to the red cells, leading to erythrocyte fragmentation and a hemolytic anemia.

Because of this complex pathophysiological process, three major problems result: (1) a tendency

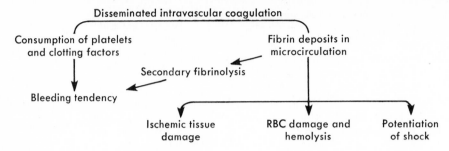

Fig. 21-3. Development of clinical disease from DIC. (From Hematology by Williams, W. J., et al. Copyright © 1972 McGraw-Hill Book Co. Used with the permission of McGraw-Hill Book Co.)

toward generalized bleeding, because clotting factors and platelets are depleted and the fibrinolytic process is stimulated; (2) ischemia of organs and tissues from vascular occulsion by emboli; and (3) anemia secondary to red cell fragmentation on the fibrin strands (generally seen only in chronic forms of DIC).[32]

DIC may be triggered in the newborn by maternal conditions, intrapartal conditions, or neonatal conditions. The list on p. 355 outlines these triggering events.[21] In general, gram-negative sepsis, acidosis, hypoxia, hypoglycemia, and hypotension appear to be the most common initiating events during the first days of life.[12,13] Coagulation disturbances are seen in many of the sickest infants with respiratory distress syndrome.[3]

The end result may be hemorrhage (for example, intracranial hemorrhage), shock, and organ ischemia or necrosis (as with renal cortical necrosis, necrotizing enterocolitis, or diffuse thromboembolic disease).[3] Fig. 21-3 presents the clinical outcomes of DIC. As a result of thrombi present in the brain, kidneys, skin, and gastrointestinal tract, the patient may manifest coma, anuria, azotemia, skin necrosis, and intestinal ulceration.[27]

SIGNS AND SYMPTOMS OF DIC IN THE NEWBORN

The clinical manifestations of DIC in the newborn are variable, depending on the underlying disease process and, in part, on the severity of the coagulation disturbance.[20,33,34] Hemorrhage, in the form of prolonged oozing from venipuncture sites or the umbilical stump, is the most common manifestation. Other hemorrhagic manifestations may include petechiae, scattered purpura, ecchymosis, or severe pulmonary, cerebral, gastrointestinal, and intraventricular hemorrhages and general diathesis. Thrombotic manifestations may present with thrombosis of peripheral or central vessels with tissue necrosis and gangrene.[33,34] Thrombosis with infarction is primarily a consequence in disorders characterized by massive release of particulate thromboplastin into the circulation, for example, in amniotic fluid embolism where fibrin deposition is predominant.[10]

On physical examination, normal infants may have petechiae over the presenting part secondary to venous congestion or trauma of delivery. These petechiae appear shortly after birth, gradually disappear, and are not associated with bleeding. Generalized petechiae, small superficial ecchymoses, and mucosal bleeding suggest a platelet abnormality, most commonly thrombocytopenia. Larger ecchymoses and some forms of localized bleeding (cephalohematomas, umbilical cord bleeding, gastrointestinal bleeding) usually are associated with a generalized coagulation disturbance owing to vitamin K deficiency, DIC, or liver disease.[14] Any of these hemorrhagic or thrombotic phenomena associated with the presence of the previously described triggering events are highly suggestive of DIC in the newborn.

LABORATORY FINDINGS IN DIC

Knowledge of the basic coagulation scheme provides the foundation to understand the factors evaluated by the various laboratory tests of hemostasis. The prothrombin time (PT) is a test of the extrinsic clotting cascade (factors VII, X, V, II, and fibrino-

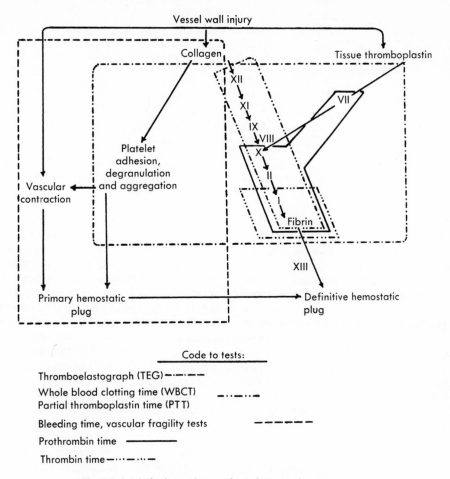

Fig. 21-4. Methods used to evaluate hemostatic components.

gen).[14] Thus a prolonged one-stage prothrombin time represents deficiencies of VII, X, and II.[18] Since the partial thromboplastin time (PTT) is a measure of the intrinsic system, a prolonged PTT represents low factors of XII, XI, and IX.[18] Fig. 21-4 presents the components evaluated by each test within the basic coagulation scheme.[6]

Individual clotting factors are estimated by the degree to which study plasma corrects the coagulation of plasma known to be deficient in that factor. The level of factor XIII is judged by the solubility of the fibrin clot in urea or weak acids. Only fibrinogen (I) is measured directly by the amount of fibrin formed per unit volume of plasma. Fibrinolytic

activity is interpolated from the rapidity with which serum dissolves fibrin clots.[6]

A major problem in assessing coagulation disorders in the newborn has been that the techniques were designed to evaluate hemostasis in the child and adult. Bleyer, Hakami, and Shepard[6] suggest that expressing values as percentages of adult control subjects does not signify normal levels for that period of development. Clotting factor activity in the perinatal period is deficient relative to adult standards but may be perfectly adequate for the newborn. Table 21-3 demonstrates the normal values of coagulation tests for individuals in the perinatal period.[19,34] In addition, the coagulation

Table 21-3. Coagulation tests*

Subject	Activated PTT (sec)	Prothrombin time (sec)	Thrombin time (sec)	Whole blood clotting time	Platelets
Normal adult or child	44 (37-50)	13 (12-14)	10	Normal	200,000-450,000
Term pregnancy	44	13	10	Decreased	290,000
Fetus, early, 10-15 weeks	—	—	—	Decreased	Present
Preterm, 27-31 weeks	—	23	—	—	275,000 ± 60,000
Preterm, 32-36 weeks	70	17 (12-21)	14 (11-17)	—	220,000-190,000
Term (appropriate for gestational age)	55 ± 10	16 (13-20)	12 (10-16)	Slight decrease	190,000

*Modified from Hathaway, W. E., Mull, M. M., and Pechet, G. S.: Pediatrics **43**:233, 1969; and Oski, F. A., and Naiman, J. L. In Schaller, A. J., editor: Major problems in clinical pediatrics, ed. 2, vol. IV, Philadelphia, 1972, W. B. Saunders Co.

tests have other important limitations. The volume of blood required restricts the number and accuracy of studies that can be performed on an individual infant. Bleyer, Hakami, and Shephard[6] state that the anticoagulant volume is rarely adjusted to the hematocrit; therefore the more variable and frequently higher hematocrit in the newborn results in increased variability and dilution of clotting factor activity. Finally, since the test reagents are derived from adult sources, they fail to distinguish factors unique to the newborn, such as fetal clotting proteins or fetal fibrinolysins.[6]

Two other important variables must be considered when collecting venous blood for neonatal coagulation studies: (1) The ratio of blood to anticoagulant (3.8% sodium citrate) should be 19:1. The usual ratio used for adults (9:1) may give spurious results in neonates with hematocrits over 60%. (2) Blood should not be drawn from heparinized catheters, since minute amounts of this anticoagulant can prolong the PTT.[14]

Given these intervening variables and the physiological alterations commonly seen, the laboratory diagnosis of DIC in the neonatal period may be difficult. Fortunately, many of the factors that are normally consumed in DIC, such as platelets, factors V, VII, and fibrinogen, are present in normal or near normal adult values in the neonate, so that deviations from these values are of great diagnostic significance.

The diagnosis of clinically significant DIC is suggested by moderate to severe thrombocytopenia (levels less than 100,000 should be considered abnormal, even in very small premature infants)[14] and prolonged PT, PTT, and thrombin time unresponsive to parenterally administered vitamin K beyond the newborn range.* Confirmatory laboratory signs include low fibrinogen and low factor V and VIII levels.[18,20] Oski[33] believes that decreased levels of factor V and fibrinogen are most common in the sickest of infants and may, therefore, reflect impaired hepatic synthesis of this factor and fibrinogen in a sick, immature infant and do not establish the presence of DIC. Elevated levels of fibrin degradation products occur invariably in older infants, children, and adults with DIC but may not always be present in the newborn.[17,29,32-34,41] This may be a result of a relative deficiency of plasminogen and plasminogen activators during the newborn period.[33] Leukocytes frequently show toxic granulation, and the white blood cell count may be elevated with a predominance of immature forms.[34] The presence of a hemolytic anemia with red cell fragmentation (microangiopathic hemolytic anemia) may be visible in the peripheral smear.* As fibrin deposits form in the vascular tree, red cells become ensnared in the fibrin meshwork and undergo shear deformation. The cells emerge with aberrant shape and size and have been termed "helmet cells" or schistocytes.[10] The microangiopathic process that produces the hemolytic anemia is accompanied by a significant degree of hyperbilirubinemia and reticulocytosis.[20] Fibrin deposits in the blood vessels stimulate the fibrinolytic mechanism, resulting in a shortened euglobulin lysis time and the detection of fibrin

*See references 2, 14, 20, 22, 33, and 34.
*See references 2, 10, 14, 20, 22, 33, 34, and 41.

Table 21-4. Differential features of bleeding disorders in the neonate*

Features	DIC	Vitamin K deficiency
Uniformity of clotting defect	Variable	Constant
Capillary fragility	Usually abnormal	Normal
Bleeding time	Often prolonged	Normal
Clotting time	Variable	Prolonged
One-stage prothrombin	Moderately prolonged	Very prolonged (5% or less)
Partial thromboplastin time	Prolonged	Prolonged
Thrombin time	Usually prolonged	Normal for age
Fibrin degradation products	May be present	Not present
Factor V	Decreased	Normal
Fibrinogen	Often decreased	Normal
Platelets	Often decreased	Normal
Red cell fragmentation	Usually present	Not present
Response to vitamin K	Diminished or absent	Spectacular
Associated disease	Severe, may include sepsis, hypoxia, acidosis, or obstetrical accident	Usually trivial (trauma may be precipitating factor)
Previous history	Above illnesses, vitamin K given	No vitamin K given or mother receiving barbiturates or anticonvulsants

*Modified from Hathaway, W. E.: Pediatr. Clin. North. Am. **17:**929, 1970; and Oski, F. A., and Naiman, J. L. In Schaller, A. J., editor: Major problems in clinical pediatrics, ed. 2, vol. IV, Philadelphia, 1972, W. B. Saunders Co.

degradation products in the blood and urine of the infants.[20] All of these laboratory findings in the presence of bacterial septicemia or other known predisposing disorders are indicative of DIC in the neonate.[20,21] Table 21-4 presents differential features of bleeding disorders in the neonate.[17,34]

TREATMENT OF THE INFANT WITH DIC

The objectives in treating the infant with DIC are (1) control of the underlying disorder, (2) termination of the intravascular coagulation process, and (3) control of bleeding.* It is generally agreed that successful management depends on the ability to correct the condition that initiated the process. If the underlying condition is brought under control, intravascular coagulation will cease. Thus, management may include the administration of appropriate antibiotics, correction of abnormalities of pH and electrolytes, maintenance of adequate oxygenation and blood pressure, exchange transfusion for Rh problem, or surgery or irradiation for hemangiomas.[21,34]

Within the literature there is little consensus regarding what form of specific therapy to employ or what therapy is effective. There is disagreement

*See references 8, 14, 20, 21, and 32 to 34.

over the effectiveness of heparin therapy as well as whether heparin should be given before or after replacement therapy. Experience with heparin therapy in the neonate is limited because of insufficient controlled studies. Some authors have found that although heparin may improve the coagulation abnormalities, there is no improvement in the survival rate.[9,34] Other authors agree that heparin is less effective in treating the neonate with DIC than the adult with DIC.[3,15,19] A possible explanation is the markedly prolonged clearance of heparin from the circulation in newborns, which could intensify the second or fibrinolytic phase of DIC.[3,15] Another possibility relates to estrogen. Gross and Melhorn[15] state that in pregnant rabbits the generalized Shwartzman reaction occurs following a single endotoxin dose; therefore, they suggest that in the susceptible neonate with recent and prolonged estrogen exposure, the triggering action may be enhanced, thereby interfering with the heparin effect.[15]

The rationale for the use of heparin to treat DIC is that it blocks the consumption of coagulation factors.[29] Heparin is the most potent, reliable antagonist of thrombin.[8] Heparin is a conjugated polysaccharide that is secreted into the circulatory system continually by the mast cells located in the pericapillary connective tissue throughout the body. These cells appear to be typical basophils, one of the types of white blood cells.[16] Although heparin inhibits more than 20 different enzymes in vitro, its only known function in vivo is activation of lipoprotein lipase and anticoagulant activity.[8] Heparin inhibits various stages of the coagulation system in concert with its plasma cofactor, antithrombin III.[8,16] The primary action of heparin is the inhibition of thrombin, but the inhibition of the activation of facotr IX by XI and factor VIII by IX has also been shown.[8,34] Heparin can be demonstrated to have a direct effect on fibrinogen level or turnover.[8] Heparinase, a liver enzyme, metabolizes heparin to an inactive form, which is then excreted via the kidneys.[32]

Heparin therapy is recommended to be used in (1) infants who have a diagnosis of sepsis (bacterial or viral) with multiple system involvement, hypotension, or generalized bleeding; (2) infants with generalized bleeding after delivery in high-risk pregnancies (intrauterine asphyxia, toxemia, abruptio placentae, or placenta previa); or (3) those who have definite thrombotic complications. These infants (except those with definite localized thrombosis) should have laboratory evidence of a consumption coagulation as demonstrated by low platelets, fibrinogen, and factors V and VIII before heparin is used.[17]

It is generally agreed that the initial intravenous ''push'' dose is 100 units/kg and then a maintenance dose of 600 units/kg/day. The maintenance dose may be given continuously or given as 100 units/kg at 4-hour intervals.[17,20,32,33] The dose of heparin should be adjusted in keeping with the monitoring test.[33] The aim is to maintain the whole blood clotting time in the range of 20 to 30 minutes or the activated partial thromboplastin time in a range of 60 to 70 seconds.[34]

Although the partial thromboplastin time (PTT) is a more accurate test of heparin anticoagulation than the clotting time, it is unreliable in DIC. A prolonged PTT during therapy cannot distinguish between the effects of heparin and the clotting factor depletion or anticoagulant effects of the fibrin degradation products associated with DIC. The very low insensitivity of the whole blood clotting time to either low factor levels or moderately high fibrin degradation product titers makes this test (WBCT) a more appropriate control for heparin.[8]

The effectiveness of heparin therapy can be judged by repeated platelet counts. If the consumption process has been halted, the platelet count should remain stable and then, after a variable period often 2 to 3 days, begin to rise and eventually reach above normal levels.[34] Heparin therapy should be continued until the process of DIC has been halted.[8,33,34] If the desired therapeutic effect (that is, cessation of bleeding or improvement in the patient) is not obtained, repeat coagulation studies should be done just prior to the next dose of heparin.[17] Effective treatment should be reflected by a return toward normal of factors II, V, VIII, fibrinogen, and platelets.[33] Therefore the indications for discontinuing heparin therapy are (1) a sustained increase in platelet count and a significant reduction toward normal of the PTT and PT screening tests and (2) evidence of control or clear improvement in the underlying disease process that is presumed to have initiated the intravascular coagulation.[20]

When the process is believed halted, heparin is discontinued. Then 4 to 5 hours after the last dose, the platelet count, prothrombin, partial thromboplastin, and thrombin times are determined. If the tests are in the normal range, they should be repeated in 6 to 8 hours. If the tests continue to remain normal, it can be assumed that the process of consumption is over.[34]

The second controversy exists over the use of replacement therapy. Some authors maintain that replacement therapy should be administered *only* after heparin therapy has been achieved.[2,27,33,34] Oski and Naiman[34] state, ''Replacement prior to that time will merely provide more fuel for the process of DIC and increase the deposition of fibrin.'' In contrast to this approach, Glader and Buchanan[14] administer fresh platelet concentrates (1 unit/5 kg body weight every 12 to 24 hours) and fresh frozen plasma (10 to 15 ml/kg of body weight every 12 to 24 hours) without the concomitant use of heparin and report they frequently see clinical improvement following this conservative approach. Whaun and Oski[41] suggest that a well-controlled study is required to evaluate the role of heparin and exchange transfusion in the treatment of DIC in the neonate.

In those infants who continue to bleed after platelet and plasma transfusions, other forms of therapy such as exchange transfusion may be considered. A two-volume exchange transfusion with fresh heparinized blood or blood stored less than 72 hours in citrate-phosphate-dextrose (CPD) may be used to control the bleeding by providing clotting factors and platelets, thereby terminating the clotting process.[14,15,33,34] In addition, exchange transfusion may remove fibrin degradation products and some of the toxic factors causing DIC.[3,14,15] Finally, adult red blood cells have a lower oxygen affinity than neonatal red blood cells, and this may reduce tissue damage caused by hypoxia.[3,14] This property is not without its dangers. Adamkin[3] reports two infants near term who received exchange transfusions for hyperbilirubinemia and subsequently developed retrolental fibroplasia in the absence of environmental hyperoxia and clinical respiratory distress. The etiological role of this increased oxygen availability to the retinal vessels following exchange transfusion must be considered. The exchange transfusion may need to be repeated every 12 hours if coagulation does not return to normal. The maintenance of the partial thromboplastin time at less than twice the normal value appears to be a convenient guide to management.[33]

The blood components commonly used in treating the bleeding infant are platelets, fresh frozen plasma, and fresh whole blood. A unit of platelets equals that number of platelets obtained from 1 unit of blood. Platelets are suspended in plasma, approximately 1 unit of platelets in 15 to 30 ml of plasma. The administration of 1 unit of platelets to a neonate generally elevates the platelet count to well over $100,000/\mu l$. Subsequently, the platelet count should decline slowly over 8 to 10 days. Failure of a neonate to sustain a platelet increase indicates platelet destruction (sepsis, DIC, antiplatelet antibody).[14]

Fresh frozen plasma contains adequate concentrations of all clotting factors; 10 to 15 ml/kg given every 12 hours provides adequate hemostasis for most causes of bleeding owing to lack of clotting factors.[14] Rather than a simple plasma transfusion, other researchers[37] have found plasmapheresis or exchange of fresh frozen plasma therapy, used in patients with meningococcemia and DIC, to be more effective than heparin therapy alone. This procedure requires the expertise of a plasmapheresis team. Whenever coagulation factors and platelets are given at the same time in the neonate, the volume of platelet concentrate (largely plasma) needs to be included in calculating plasma therapy.[14]

Fresh whole blood must be used for exchange transfusions rather than banked whole blood or packed red blood cells. Banked whole blood more that 12 hours old contains few platelets and decreased quantities of labile clotting factors (V and VIII). Packed red blood cells are devoid of platelets as well as significant amounts of clotting protein.[8,14]

The secondary fibrinolytic response that frequently accompanies intravascular coagulation is probably beneficial because of the lysis of the fibrin thrombi. Excessive fibrinolysis leading to defibrination as a primary event is extremely rare and almost is never seen in children.[2] Abilgaard[2] states, ''Although both primary and secondary fibrinolysis can be blocked effectively with epsilon amino caproic acid (EACA), it is doubtful that this or similar agents are indicated in the treatment of intravascular clotting, unless there is evidence that fibrinolysis has become prominent.''

Corticosteroid therapy is of recognized value in several conditions associated with DIC, particularly if intravascular clotting is blocked by heparin prior to or at the time of steroid administration. A study by Thomas and Good has shown that the generalized Shwartzman reaction can be elicited by a single dose of endotoxin in rabbits treated with cortisone.[2] However, more recently Corrigan and Jordan[9] were unable to show that cortisone treatment prepared rabbits for the Shwartzman reaction, despite using large doses of both cortisone and endotoxin. Furthermore, their studies indicated that no significant depletion of fibrinogen occurred in cortisone-treated rabbits given a single dose of endotoxin.

COMPLICATIONS OF DIC

The complications from DIC are generally related to the fibrin deposition and emboli that produce tissue ischemia and necrosis, the depletion of clotting factors leading to hemorrhage and shock, and a microangiopathic hemolytic anemia that can produce hyperbilirubinemia.[4,18] The outcomes of these processes are many and varied.

Fibrin thrombi are more frequently found in the kidney than any other organ and are present in two thirds of patients with DIC. Fibrin deposition in the glomerular capillaries leads to bilateral renal cortical necrosis and progressive azotemia and anuria, and if intervention is not effective, death will occur.[2] Peritoneal dialysis may be required in those with progressive azotemia until such time as renal function returns.[4] Fibrin thrombi can also be demonstrated in the adrenal glands, brain, heart, lungs, and testes in another one quarter to one half of the patients.[8] As a result of thrombi present in the brain, skin, and gastrointestinal tract, the patient may manifest coma, skin necrosis, and intestinal ulceration.[27] Hemorrhage may be seen as hematuria or blood from body orifices, as well as pulmonary, cerebral, or intraventricular, hemorrhages.[21]

No long-term studies have been found by this author to determine the eventual outcomes for those infants who have survived such devastating assaults. It can be presumed that the potential exists for extensive brain damage, such as by being manifested by seizure disorders, mental retardation, learning disability, cerebral palsy, sensory disability, acute and chronic respiratory distress, and impairment.

In many of the disease processes associated with DIC, the process becomes a vicious cycle. For example, necrotizing enterocolitis (NEC) can trigger DIC. The thrombi from the DIC process can further the necrosis of the intestines and thus contribute to the progression of NEC.

DIC is highly associated with septicemia and shock. Corrigan and Jordan[9] report that disseminated intravascular coagulation was diagnosed in 96% of 26 children with septic shock. Of the 24 children who received heparin in addition to standard therapy, 58% died in shock. These authors[9] suggest that improvement in the hypotension probably has a major role in abolishing disseminated intravascular coagulation.

PROGNOSIS FOR THE INFANT WITH DIC

The mortality rate in all age groups regardless of cause is generally agreed to be 60% to 66%.[9,34,35,41] As discussed earlier, heparin therapy has not always showed improvement in survival statistics.[9,34,41] DIC associated with septic shock or necrotizing enterocolitis (NEC) appears to be the most devastating. Tissue thromboplastin, which is released in these conditions, creates added problems in the management of DIC. In the study reported by Patel,[35] two thirds of infants with NEC who died had DIC; only one sixth of the survivors had DIC. Patel suggests that the onset of DIC may occur prior to the onset of NEC and becomes more severe as the disease progresses.[35] Prognosis depends partially on

the effectiveness in correcting the underlying triggering event. Diffuse hemorrhage involving brain, lungs, adrenal glands, kidneys, pericardium, and myocardium is a manifestation of terminal coagulopathy.[35]

To improve survival rates, the progression of DIC must be halted before the onset of hemorrhage and shock.

RESPONSE OF OBSTETRICAL AND NEONATAL PERSONNEL TO THE INFANT WITH DIC IN THE DELIVERY ROOM AND NURSERY

At present, the best method of success remains as appreciation of the conditions associated with DIC in the newborn, their prompt recognition, and early treatment. Frequent platelet counts, hemoglobin determinations, and examination of peripheral smears for signs of red cell fragmentation provide a useful surveillance system for the early detection of DIC.[34] These should be employed in all infants born after difficult deliveries, in those born after complicated pregnancies, in those with congenital abnormalities that may predispose to infections, and in those infants with problems of acidosis or hypoxia.[21,34]

The ideal intervention would be the prevention of DIC. Primary prevention is aimed at those triggering events over which the obstetrical and perinatal personnel have some control. In the mother, a condition associated with DIC in the infant is severe Rh sensitization.[21] The routine administration of anti-D gamma globulin to Rh-negative women within 48 hours after each delivery or abortion will eliminate Rh isoimmune hemolytic disease.[22] In a fetus with known Rh incompatibility, intrauterine exchange transfusion may be indicated to correct this triggering event in infants or mothers who have not received immunization for Rh incompatibility.

During labor and delivery, fetal distress with hypoxia and acidosis may occur. All high-risk pregnancies and all women who receive oxytocin should be monitored during labor. Early signs of fetal distress detected by fetal heart rate (FHR) monitoring include late deceleration (Type II dip), loss of baseline variability, and increasing baseline rate. The late deceleration pattern is often noted in pregnancies that are complicated by diabetes, toxemia, hypertension, Rh disease, maternal hypotension in the supine position, and hypertonicity of the uterus caused by excessive oxytocin.[22] There are also conditions known to trigger DIC in the newborn. If late deceleration patterns occur with evidence of fetal acidosis (pH below 7.2 in two or more specimens) and hypoxia, as determined by fetal blood sampling, and this is not corrected by the administration of oxygen to the mother and change in her position, prompt delivery by cesarean section may be indicated.[22]

DIC is highly associated with sepsis in the newborn. The incidence of sepsis with DIC ranges from 79% to 96%.[9,41] Sepsis with DIC in the newborn is frequently associated with certain congenital malformations, such as tracheoesophageal fistula, meconium peritonitis, and ileal atresia, as well as with prematurity and obstetrical complications. In the study reported by Whaun and Oski,[41] 72% of the newborns with DIC were either premature or their mothers had complicated pregnancies or difficult deliveries, such as prolonged rupture of the membranes, abruptio placentae, maternal diabetes, polyhydramnios, and difficult delivery with fetal anoxia.[41] As can be readily discerned from this list, all infants within the neonatal intensive care unit are at risk of developing DIC. DIC is a syndrome occurring in "sick" infants.[14]

Recognition of DIC in the neonate depends not only on laboratory surveillance but on information obtained through a complete history, including familial bleeding problems, maternal illnesses (especially infections), drug administration (maternal and neonatal), and documentation that vitamin K was given at birth.[14] It is important that this information accompany the infant to the nursery so that nursery personnel may be alert for the potential for DIC in the newborn.

In those newborns considered at high risk of developing DIC, as well as in the infant diagnosed with DIC, the nurse should be alert for signs of bleeding and vascular occlusion. Petechiae, ecchymosis, and prolonged bleeding or oozing from the umbilical stump may occur, or massive bleeding may develop, particularly at the site of any lesion. Bleeding may also be subtle. The nurse should check all stools for guiac, urine for occult or gross blood, gastric drainage for blood, and decreasing arterial pressure. Evidence of thrombosis presents as symptoms of those associated with the system involved: renal system involvement may cause

hematuria; CNS involvement may cause changes in activity level or muscular tonus, apneic spells, irritability, convulsions, and bulging of the fontanelle; integument involvement may present with acrocyanosis leading to gangrene.[32]

Once DIC has been diagnosed in the neonate, therapy is generally directed at resolving the underlying disease process to remove the stimulus for clot formation. If the infant is septic, nursing care will be aimed at assisting in obtaining blood, urine, and spinal cultures; hematological evaluation; and chest x-ray films. An intravenous line will need to be started for the initiation of antibiotic therapy. In addition, supportive therapy, including monitoring the circulatory status via a continuous arterial pressure determination, oxygenation, acid-base balance, electrolytes, glucose, bilirubin, platelet count, and maintaining a normal thermal and respiratory state, may be indicated.

Infants with DIC need to be protected from unnecessary bleeding and should not receive intramuscular injections. Prolonged pressure or pressure dressings should be applied over bleeding sites.[32] Blood studies should be obtained when appropriate from existing intravenous or arterial lines instead of heel or finger sticks. However, for coagulation studies, it is important not to draw blood from a heparinized line.[32]

In the heparinized infant who requires surgical corrective procedures to correct the triggering event of DIC, it may be necessary to neutralize the heparin in the infant's plasma prior to performing the surgery. This may be done with protamine sulfate.[2]

Whether heparin therapy is employed or not, most authorities agree that replacement therapy is required to replace depleted clotting factors. The infant's blood type should be determined prior to the need to administer blood components. This could be determined prior to the infant arriving in the nursery if the infant is known to be at risk of developing DIC. It is the nurse's responsibility to determine that this has been done and that the blood components used are compatible with the infant's blood type.

The placenta has been advocated as a source of blood supply for the infant. In addition to delayed clamping of the cord with the infant lower than the placenta, following every high-risk delivery, placental blood should be drawn into a preheparinized

20-ml syringe and 20-gauge needle after prepping the umbilical cord with povidone-iodine (Betadine) solution. This gives a heparinized concentration similar to the heparin concentration of a unit of heparinized blood from the blood bank.

SUMMARY AND DISCUSSION

In summary, all infants of high-risk pregnancies and infants who develop complications postnatally and require intensive care treatment are at risk for developing DIC. DIC is a syndrome associated with "sick" infants, most commonly asphyxia and sepsis. Immediate and vigorous intervention aimed at these underlying disease processes is essential to prevent or halt the occurrence of DIC in the newborn. Therapeutic measures include the alleviation of fetal distress, treatment of infection, maintenance of circulatory support via external cardiac massage and intravenous replacement fluids, provision for ventilatory and gas-exchange support, and heparin therapy.

Heparin therapy is the most controversial area in the literature. Whether the physician decides to use heparin or not, treatment always involves therapy aimed at the underlying disease process that initiated the abnormal clotting response. Depending on the infant's condition, replacement therapy may be indicated to replace depleted clotting factors and the hemolyzed red blood cells to alleviate the anemia.

Even with vigorous treatment, including heparin therapy, mortality rates for infants with DIC are high, ranging up to 66%. Those infants who survive frequently have renal and central nervous system sequelae requiring long-term care and follow-up. The best care is the early recognition and treatment of those events known to initiate DIC. A successful outcome for the infant can only be possible if DIC is recognized early in the course of its progression.

Protocols

Problem ☐ Possible development of DIC in the high-risk infant

GOAL: To recognize possible "triggering" event and/or fetal distress early and intervene to prevent DIC

Rationale: To decrease the risk of poor fetal outcome owing to DIC

DIAGNOSTIC

1. Obtain a complete prenatal history, including the events leading up to admission to labor and delivery.

   Rationale: To assess history for any possible underlying disease process (such as Rh incompatibility, recent maternal infection, prolonged rupture of the membranes with foul-smelling amniotic fluid, or signs of fetal distress with meconium staining of the amniotic fluid) that may cause anticipated problems for this fetus

2. Institute continuous fetal monitoring.

   Rationale: To note changes in fetal heart rate pattern in relation to uterine contractions (such as decreased baseline variability and late decelerations), which are indicators of fetal distress (Fetal distress and hypoxia are associated with the development of DIC in the infant.)

3. Fetal blood sampling should be done when indicated.

   Rationale: To provide a highly effective means to screen for fetal distress in the high-risk pregnancy along with fetal heart rate monitoring

4. Monitor maternal circulatory and acid-base status.

   Rationale: To be aware that maternal hypotension and acidosis are transmitted to the fetus resulting in fetal distress

THERAPEUTIC

1. Inform the physician of any fetal heart rate abnormalities noted.

   Rationale: To institute prompt medical management

2. Administer oxygen (3 to 4 L/min) to the mother and place her in the left lateral position if signs of fetal distress are noted (as assessed by

FHR monitor, fetal blood sampling, or meconium in amniotic fluid).

Rationale: To increase Pao₂ levels and decrease acidosis in the fetus

3. Perform fetal blood sampling in a sterile manner.

Rationale: To minimize chances of infection in the fetus or the mother

4. Support maternal circulation and acid-base balance.

Rationale: To note that maternal hypotension will cause uterine hypoperfusion with resultant hypoxemia of the fetus and fetal distress and that maternal acidosis may likewise cause fetal distress

5. Avoid potentially depressant drugs (anesthetics, narcotics) as much as possible.

Rationale: To avoid the depressant effect, which is more prolonged in the fetus than the mother, being transmitted to the fetus (The depressant effect adds to other problems of the distressed infant and potentiates the possible development of DIC.)

6. Prepare for emergency cesarean section if indicated.

Rationale: To prevent further stress to an already compromised fetus

7. Notify nursery of possible high-risk infant.

Rationale: To have nursery personnel and equipment prepared for a possibly distressed infant who is at risk for developing DIC

EDUCATIONAL

1. Provide in-service education programs for labor room personnel concerning the management of high-risk pregnant women whose labor may be complicated by a potential "triggering" event of DIC.

2. Provide patient with an explanation of all procedures and medical treatments appropriate to her level of understanding.

Rationale: To decrease the patient's anxiety, which will enable her to cope with the situation and will potentially decrease her level of catecholamine secretion, which has an adverse effect on the fetus

Problem □ Infant delivered who is at risk for DIC

GOAL: To prevent the development of DIC

Rationale: To prevent mortality and morbidity in the neonate

DIAGNOSTIC

1. Note color, consistency, odor, and amount of amniotic fluid.

Rationale: To assess for possible causes of fetal distress (such as infection, meconium staining, or congenital abnormalities, which predispose to the development of fetal distress)

2. Evaluate infant's Apgar score at 1 and 5 minutes of life.

Rationale: To provide a quick reliable assessment of the infant's condition at birth and to alert personnel of anticipated problems

3. Observe for signs of respiratory distress, such as nasal flaring, grunting, substernal retractions, pallor, acrocyanosis, tachypnea (≥60/min) or tachycardia (≥160/min).

Rationale: To recognize asphyxia or respiratory distress early for the successful resuscitation and future well-being of the infant

4. Assess the appearance and size of the placenta.

Rationale: To obtain evidence of the adequacy of perfusion to the infant in utero, which may indicate potential problems for the infant

5. Closely monitor the infant's vital signs, including blood pressure.

Rationale: To provide information concerning cardiopulmonary status and early recognition of respiratory distress, thermal stress, or hypovolemic shock

6. Document the administration of vitamin K after doing so.

Rationale: To distinguish vitamin K deficiency and to prevent it

7. Assess for the presence of petechiae, ecchymosis, cephalohematoma, and prolonged bleeding or oozing from the umbilical stump.

Rationale: To recognize the signs of bleeding and to halt the progression of DIC

THERAPEUTIC

1. Have personnel in the delivery room who are experienced in resuscitation of the high-risk infant.

   Rationale: To provide high-quality care to the infant to ensure a successful outcome

2. Initiate prompt resuscitation to include airway control, oxygenation, and circulatory support (closed chest massage) if indicated.

   Rationale: To prevent the sequelae of asphyxia, which includes DIC

3. Provide for cardiovascular support, if indicated, by delayed clamping of the cord with the baby held below the level of the uterus (×45 seconds) or draw placental blood into a heparinized syringe to be used for volume expansion.

   Rationale: To prevent shock and circulatory collapse and the subsequent development of DIC (Placental blood is a perfect match for the infant if no blood incompatibilities are the cause of the infant's distress.)

4. Place the infant immediately under a radiant warmer and dry the infant.

   Rationale: To minimize heat loss and additional stress to the infnat

5. Monitor arterial blood gases, when indicated.

   Rationale: To assess effectiveness of resuscitation and evaluate the infant's present cardiopulmonary status

6. If infant's condition permits, allow the mother and father (if present) to touch and see their infant.

   Rationale: To provide psychological support to parents and to enhance parental contact and involvement with their infant

7. When the infant's heart rate and respiratory status are stable, transfer the infant to an intermediate or neonatal intensive care unit, depending on the infant's condition.

   Rationale: To provide the infant with additional observation, support, and intervention that may be necessary to promote the optimal well-being for this infant

EDUCATIONAL

1. Keep mother and family informed of what is being done for their infant. Ensure that the mother knows where her baby is being transferred and how she or her family may contact the neonatalogist. Ensure that a member of the transport team has contacted the mother prior to the transport of her infant.

2. Personnel who are giving care to these infants are training in neonatal physiology and immediate management of the high-risk neonate.

   Rationale: To provide immediate quality care to ensure a successful outcome for the infant

Problem □ Infant with DIC

GOAL: To correct the underlying disease process, which triggered the coagulation defect and to halt the progression of DIC

Rationale: To ensure optimal physiological well-being and intact survival of the infant

DIAGNOSTIC

1. The following laboratory work should be done:

   a. Serum electrolytes

   b. Cultures: blood (not from umbilical catheters), urine, and CSF

   c. Dextrostix q hr × 4, followed by q hr × 24 hr, and if stable, as necessary thereafter; serum glucose levels should be drawn immediately if Dextrostix is less than 45 mg%.

   d. Type and cross-match blood

   e. CBC with differential and platelet count, reticulocyte count, peripheral smear

   f. Coagulation studies: WBCT, PT, PTT, TT, fibrinogen levels, presence of fibrin degradation products

   Rationale: To assess physiological parameters for abnormalities, which may indicate an underlying disease process having the potential for DIC or the coagulation complications of DIC

2. A chest x-ray film should be taken.

   Rationale: To determine the presence of underlying disease processes, such as pneumonia or early hemorrhage from the coagulation disturbance

3. Monitor the arterial blood gases.

   Rationale: To determine the oxygenation and acid-base status, which may be contributory to the process of DIC

4. Continuously assess by observation, auscultation, palpation, and percussion of:
   a. Respiratory status: apnea, tachypnea, cyanosis, respiratory distress, rales, rhonchi, adventitious sounds, grunting, flaring, retractions, generalized, decreased, or unequal breath sounds; or the presence of bowel sounds in the chest
   b. Cardiac and circulatory status: tachycardia, bradycardia, blood pressure via the Doppler method or via an arterial transducer, strength and uniformity of peripheral pulses, cyanosis, heart murmurs, pallor, hepatosplenomegaly
   c. Renal function: Presence of ambiguous sex assignment as with adrenal insufficiency leading to shock, proteinuria, hematuria, glycosuria, output, specific gravity, osmolarity, and edema
   d. Central nervous system status: lethargy, irritability, seizures, jitteriness
   e. Metabolic function and balance: temperature, hypo-hyperglycemia, glycosuria, hyperbilirubinemia
   f. Gastrointestinal function: abdominal distention, presence of bowel sounds, diarrhea, poor feeding, vomiting, presence of blood in gastric or stool specimens
   Rationale: To assess physiological and physical parameters that may change owing to underlying disease process or other complications of the hemorrhagic and thrombotic processes of DIC
5. Obtain a complete prenatal and intrapartum history of the mother and infant.
   Rationale: To obtain the data base as to the events of the pregnancy and previous pregnancies, labor, and delivery, which may provide clues to the underlying disease process and anticipated problems for this infant
6. Document all parental visiting, telephone calls, and education.
   Rationale: To assess parental coping responses to their critically ill infant, as well as to provide information essential in planning parent education and in the follow-up evaluation of the parent-infant unit

THERAPEUTIC
1. Promote maintenance of and/or improvement of respiratory status:
   a. Postural drainage, percussion, and suctioning as necessary depending on the assessment of lung involvement on x-ray examination and auscultation
   Rationale: To prevent stasis of secretions and the development of atelectasis and infection (Movement out of the bronchi is facilitated by the use of gravity, hand pressure, and vibration applied to the thoracic wall and the removal of secretions by suctioning.)
   b. Oxygen therapy and/or ventilatory assistance depending on the patient's condition
   Rationale: To promote lung inflation and gas exchange to maintain Pao$_2$ between 45 and 70 mm Hg
   c. Provide a warmed (32° to 35° C) humidified environment for the infant to breathe by humidity added to the isolette and/or bubbling the oxygen supply through warm, sterile, distilled water.
   Rationale: To liquify secretions and to prevent heat loss through the respiratory tract
   d. Provide adequate hydration.
   Rationale: To promote thin pulmonary secretions, which can easily be removed from the bronchial tree.
   e. Observe for signs and symptoms indicative of respiratory infection, pulmonary infarction, or hemorrhage.
   Rationale: To be aware that infections are frequently the underlying process associated with DIC, and hemorrhage and thrombosis leading to infarction are the outcomes of DIC
2. Assessment of kidney function by measuring:
   a. Urinary output (1.5 to 3.0 ml/kg/hr)
   b. Urine specific gravity (1.005 to 1.010)
   c. Edema
   d. Hematuria, proteinuria, and/or glycosuria
   Rationale: To assess for possible changes in kidney function, which may reflect circulatory impairment, hypotension, or hypoxia leading to renal impairment (These changes may contribute to the progression of the coagulation defects.)

3. Observe for CNS complications, such as signs of intracranial hemorrhage and/or increased intracranial pressure or seizures.
   Rationale: To be aware that CNS complications are associated with DIC as well as contributing to the development of DIC
4. Observe for gastrointestinal complications, such as necrotizing enterocolitis (NEC) with ulcerations and bleeding, by assessing gastric secretions and stool for occult bleeding, presence of watery diarrhea, abdominal distention, poor feeding, and gastric retention with bilious drainage.
   Rationale: To be aware that NEC is highly associated with the development of DIC, as well as being a complication of DIC owing to thrombosis of the mesenteric vessels with resultant intestinal necrosis
5. Provide metabolic support by:
   a. Maintain adequate fluid, electrolyte, and caloric requirements, usually parenterally in the sick infant with DIC.
      Rationale: To meet the resting metabolic needs, provide sufficient energy for physical activity and the increased metabolic needs created by the underlying disease process (that is, sepsis), and meet the energy needs for growth
   b. Promote the acid-base balance by correction of volume deficits, hemoglobin deficits, abnormal cardiac output, or respiratory failure.
      Rationale: To be aware that metabolic acidosis means inadequate oxygenation and perfusion and it usually accompanies and aggravates the process of DIC
6. Maintain the infant in a neutral thermal environment.
   Rationale: To decrease oxygen consumption and prevent further stress to the compromised infant with DIC
7. Administer drugs, as indicated, which may include:
   a. Antibiotics
      Rationale: To treat sepsis, which is the most frequent cause of DIC
   b. Heparin

Rationale: To halt the coagulation process and depletion of the clotting factors
   c. Blood components (fresh frozen plasma, fresh platelet concentrates, fresh heparinized blood, or fresh whole blood in CPD)
      Rationale: To replace depleted clotting factors and RBC's
8. Promote the emotional and development needs of the infant and his family.
   Rationale: To develop a sense of trust in the infant and facilitate the bonding process between the family and their infant, so that future well-being and development of the newborn will be enhanced
9. Maintain follow-up evaluation of the infant with assessment of psychological and physiological growth and development.
   Rationale: To provide early intervention for any assessed deficits

EDUCATIONAL
1. Family unit:
   a. Allow the family time to express their feelings concerning the infant's condition and prognosis.
      Rationale: To meet the parents' needs for information and emotional support and to allow the parents to develop appropriate coping mechanisms
   b. Maintain open communication and daily contact with the family concerning the infant's condition, treatments, and prognosis. Reinforce the physician's explanations.
      Rationale: To allow the family to develop a realistic perception of the events and to assist the family in making informed decisions concerning the care of their infant
   c. Encourage the family to visit, touch, and assist in the care of their infant. Be available to assist the family when they visit and explain the equipment used in the care of their infant and how they can assist in the care.
      Rationale: To facilitate the parent-infant bonding process and to promote a sense of well-being needed by their infant
   d. Begin discharge planning at the time of admission, based on the expected outcome, the needs of the family, and the resources available to them.

Rationale: To assist the family in meeting their needs, including time to work through their grief response

2. Nursing staff: In-service education must be provided to the nursing staff concerning early recognition of DIC and its complications, as well as the necessary nursing care needs of the infant with DIC.

Rationale: To assure a successful outcome for the infant with DIC through rapid early recognition of the coagulation disorder and intensive aggressive care to halt the underlying disease process and depletion of the clotting factors (The nursing staff is in the best position for this early recognition and needs to have the necessary information if a successful outcome is the goal for infants with DIC.)

REFERENCES

1. Aballi, A. J., and Lamerens, S. D.: Coagulation changes in the neonatal period and in early infancy, Pediatr. Clin. North Am. **9:**785, 1962.
2. Abildgaard, C. F.: Recognition and treatment of intravascular coagulation, J. Pediatr. **74:**163, 1968.
3. Adamkin, D. H.: New uses for exchange transfusion, Pediatr. Clin. North Am. **24:**599, 1977.
4. Belman, A. B.: Renal vein thrombosis in infancy and childhood, Clin. Pediatr. **15:**1033, 1976.
5. Birch, C. R.: Disseminated intravascular coagulation, Nurs. Times **74:**15, 1978.
6. Bleyer, W. A., Hakami, N., and Shepard, T. H.: The development of hemostasis in the human fetus and newborn infant, J. Pediatr. **79:**838, 1977.
7. Cohen, I. J.: Cold injury in early infancy, relationship between mortality and disseminated intravascular coagulation, Isr. J. Med. Sci. **13:**405, 1977.
8. Connan, R. W., Minna, J. D., and Robbey, S. J.: Disseminated intravascular coagulation: a problem in critical-care medicine, Heart Lung **3:**789, 1974.
9. Corrigan, J. J., and Jordan, C. M.: Heparin therapy in septicemia with disseminated intravascular coagulation, N. Engl. J. Med. **283:**778, 1970.
10. Deykin, D.: The clinical challenge of disseminated intravascular coagulation, N. Engl. J. Med. **283:**636, 1970.
11. Du, J. N. H., Briggs, J. N., and Young, G.: Disseminated intravascular coagulopathy in hyaline membrane disease, massive thrombosis following umbilical artery catheterization, Pediatrics **45:**287, 1970.
12. Eagle, M.: Septicaemia proceeding to disseminated intravascular coagulation, Nurs. Times **74:**17, 1978.
13. Favara, B. E., Franciosi, R. A:, and Butterfield, L. J.: Disseminated intravascular and cardiac thrombosis of the neonate, Am. J. Dis. Child. **127:**197, 1974.
14. Glader, B. E., and Buchanan, G. R.: The bleeding neonate, Pediatrics **58:**548, 1976.

15. Gross, S., and Melborn, D. K.: Exchange transfusion with citrated whole blood for disseminated intravascular coagulation, J. Pediatr. **78:**415, 1971.
16. Guyton, A. C.: Function of the human body, Philadelphia, 1969, W. B. Saunders Co. p. 108.
17. Hathaway, W. E.: Coagulation problems in the newborn infant, Pediatr. Clin. North Am. **17:**929, 1970.
18. Hathaway, W. E.: Coagulation, hemostasis, and thrombosis in the fetus and newborn. In Hematology in the perinatal patient, Marco Island, Fla., 1973, Mead Johnson Symposium on Perinatal and Developmental Medicine (No. 4), December 2-6, 1973.
19. Hathaway, W. E., Mull, M. M., and Pechet, G. S.: Disseminated intravascular coagulation in the newborn, Pediatrics **43:**233, 1969.
20. Honig, G. R., and Hruby, M. A.: Disorders of the blood and hematopoietic system. In Behrman, R. E., editor: Neonatal-perinatal medicine: diseases of the fetus and infant, ed. 2, St. Louis, 1977, The C. V. Mosby Co., p. 379.
21. Keener, P. A.: DIC flow sheet, Indianapolis, 1975, Community Hospital of Indianapolis, Inc.
22. Korones, S. B.: High-risk newborn infants, ed. 3, St. Louis, 1981, The C. V. Mosby Co.
23. Larcan, A., et al.: Acute renal failure and disseminated intravascular coagulation during puerperal fever, Semaine des Hopitaux de Paris **54:**595, 1978.
24. Leissring, J. C., and Vorlicky, L. N.: Disseminated intravascular coagulation in the neonate, Am. J. Dis. Child. **115:**100, 1968.
25. Lynch, M. J., et al.: Medical laboratory technology and clinical pathology, ed. 2, Philadelphia, 1969, W. B. Saunders Co., p. 718.
26. Mammen, E. F.: Blood coagulation and pulmonary function, Int. Anesth. Clin. **15:**91, 1977.
27. Marder, V. J., and Sherry, S.: Fibrinogenesis. In Frohlich, E. D., editor: Pathophysiology: altered regulatory mechanisms in disease, Philadelphia, 1972, J. B. Lippincott Co., p. 547.
28. Markarian, M., et al.: Fibrinolytic activity in premature infants, Am. J. Dis. Child. **113:**312, 1967.
29. Miller, D. R., Hanshaw, J. B., O'Leary, D. S., and Hnilicka, J. V.: Fatal disseminated herpes simplex virus infection and hemorrhage in the neonate, J. Pediatr. **76:**409, 1970.
30. Moore, C. M., McAdams, A. J., and Sutherland, J.: Intrauterine disseminated intravascular coagulation: a syndrome of multiple pregnancy with a dead twin fetus, J. Pediatr. **74:**523, 1969.
31. Muller, A. D., Van Doorm, J. M., and Hemker, H. C.: Heparin-like inhibitor of blood coagulation in normal newborn, Nature **267:**616, 1977.
32. O'Brian, B. S., and Woods, S.: The paradox of DIC, Am. J. Nurs. **78:**1878, 1978.
33. Oski, F. A.: Hematological problems. In Avery, G. B., editor: Neonatology: pathophysiology and management of the newborn, Philadelphia, 1975, J. B. Lippincott Co., p. 404.
34. Oski, F. A., and Naiman, J. L.: Hematological problems in the newborn. In. Schaller, A. J., editor: Major problems in clinical pediatrics, ed. 2, vol. IV, Philadelphia, 1972, W. B. Saunders Co., p. 236.

35. Patel, C. C.: Hematologic abnormalities in acute necrotizing enterocolitis, Pediatr. Clin. North Am. **24:**579, 1977.
36. Purohit, D. M., Levkoff, A. H., and Pai, S.: Management of multifetal gestation, Pediatr. Clin. North Am. **24:**481, 1977.
37. Scharfman, W. B., Tillotson, J. R., Taft, E. G., and Wright, E.: Plasmapheresis for meningococcemia with disseminated intravascular coagulation, N. Engl. J. Med. **300:** 1277, 1979.
38. Suzuki, S., Wake, N., and Yoshiaki, K.: New neonatal problems of blood coagulation and fibrinolysis. I: the change of plasmin inhibitor levels in the newborn infant, J. Perinat. Med. **4:**213, 1976.

39. Symchych, P. S., Krauss, A. N., and Winchester, P.: Endocarditis following intracardiac placement of umbilical venous catheters in neonates, J. Pediatr. **90:**287, 1977.
40. Tilkian, S. M., Conover, M. B., and Tilkian, A. G.: Clinical implications of laboratory tests, ed. 2, St. Louis, 1979, The C. V. Mosby Co., p. 188.
41. Whaun, J. M., and Oski, F. A.: Experience with disseminated intravascular coagulation in a children's hospital, Can. Med. Assoc. J. **107:**963, 1972.

Chapter 22

Neonatal thrombocytopenia

Diane Irene Gorgal

In the newborn period there is an increased susceptibility to bleeding complications. This susceptibility is due to the physiological quantity of coagulation factors, functional deficits in coagulation, and an increased incidence of sepsis and birth trauma.[21] Thrombocytopenia is one of the bleeding disorders associated with neonatal hemorrhage. Thrombocytopenia is defined as a platelet count less than 100,000/mm.[3]

Hathaway[22] found that in 158 newborns admitted to an intensive care unit 51% had at least one platelet count less than 150,000/mm³; 31% had counts less than 100,000/mm³; and 15% had counts less than 50,000/mm³. The clinical manifestations of thrombocytopenia, such as petechiae, are apparent when the platelet count reaches 50,000/mm³.

Thrombocytopenia is often an acquired disease of a sick newborn. Perinatal nurses utilizing their assessment skills can recognize the clinical manifestations as well as the factors associated with thrombocytopenia. Early detection of thrombocytopenia will lead to earlier management of hemorrhagic and neurological sequelae.

BLOOD COAGULATION

Blood coagulation is dependent on the functioning of two hematological systems: platelet-vessel interaction and plasma protein coagulation factors. The plasma protein coagulation system consists of sequential reactions of clotting factors. The formation of fibrin and the subsequent development of the cross-linked fibrin clot are essential for hemostasis. The role this system plays in coagulation will not be discussed in this chapter.

The platelet-vessel interaction process is the first physiological response to an injured blood vessel. A loose primary clot is formed by the platelets. Together with the coagulation factors a definitive hemostatic plug is formed.

PLATELETS

Platelets or thrombocytes arise from the megakaryocytes formed from the stem cells in the bone marrow.[3] Platelet production is under humoral regulation by the substance thrombopoietin. The site of thrombopoietin production has not been determined.[3,13] The normal adult platelet count is 250,000 to 350,000/mm³.[6,18]

Platelets, as the name suggests, are disk-shaped anuclear cells with a distinct membrane. They are 2 to 4 μ in diameter with a number of cytoplasmic inclusions or dense bodies. These inclusions are sites for serotonin deposits, adenosine diphosphate (ADP) storage, and other substances. These substances are utilized in the process of forming the lost primary plug.

The mean life span of a circulating platelet is 9.9 $\pm$ 0.6 days.[13] Twenty percent of all platelets are in the splenic pool. Eighty percent of the platelets are circulating in the blood and liver.[6] Platelets are removed from the circulation by the spleen and the reticuloendothelial system. Splenomegaly enlarges the splenic platelet pool, thereby decreasing the platelet count.[6]

Platelets respond in three ways to an injured blood vessel: The first response is the initial adhesion to collagen. The second response is the alteration in morphological structure. The third response is the

371

surface-induced release.[13,22] The initial adhesion of platelets begins when the endothelial collagen is exposed in the ruptured blood vessel. Metabolic and structural alterations occur in the platelet as they adhere to the exposed collagen. The following substances are released from the platelet dense bodies to initiate the extrinsic clotting system and ensure the formation of a hemostatic plug: ADP, platelet factor III and IV, serotonin, and tissue factor. Adenosine diphosphate (ADP) is released in two distinct waves, which leads to the aggregation of platelets. Platelet factor III and platelet factor IV are released. Serotonin release is essential for the contractibility of the injured blood vessel wall. Thromboxane A_2 tissue factor is released from the injured tissue and initiates the extrinsic clotting system. These mechanisms arrest bleeding at the capillary level.[3]

The aggregation of platelets is dependent on the ADP released from the platelet as well as calcium and one or more plasma proteins including fibrinogen.[26-28] The first aggregation wave is induced by epinephrine and ADP, which directly affect the platelet intercellular transmission. This phase is irreversible. The second wave of aggregation is produced by ADP and epinephrine and is accompanied by the development of platelet factor III and serotonin.[26,27] Platelet factor III is a lipoprotein involved in the development of the intrinsic prothrombin activator.[24] Medications, especially acetyl salicylic acid, cause a release defect during the second wave of aggregation, thereby prolonging bleeding time.[6,8,9] Fig. 22-1 is a schematic diagram of platelet-vessel interaction.[22]

Platelets, antigen, and antibodies are categorized in the PL platelet antigen series. The nomenclature proposed by Carby and Shulman[9] uses the abbreviation PL to refer to platelet antigen. Each of the antigenic systems on the platelets are identified by a superscript consisting of a capital letter and an allele, which is indicated by a number next to the superscript. Antiplatelets refer to the corresponding isoantibodies. Ninety-eight percent of the population are PL^{A1} positive.[21,35,41] PL^{A1} incompatibility is the most common cause of over half of all the isoimmune thrombocytopenia purpura cases.[21] Other platelet antigen antibodies are: PL^{E1}, which occurs in 99% of the population, PL^{E2}, which occurs in 5% of the population, and antiplatelet PL^{A2}, which occurs in 26% of the population.[12,35]

FETAL AND NEONATAL COAGULATION

Platelets appear in the fetal circulation around 11 weeks' gestation. Megakaryocytes are found in the fetal yolk sac between 5 and 6 weeks' gestation. The fetal liver is the second site for hematopoiesis. The bone marrow functions as the third site for hematopoiesis in the fetus after the third month of gestation. Bleyer found that at this time fetal blood clots can be

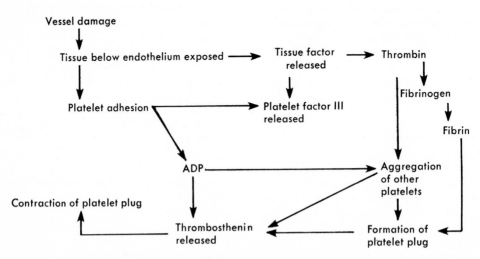

Fig. 22-1. Perinatal coagulation following vessel damage.

formed.[5] Platelets assume microscopical identity with adult platelets by 12 weeks' gestation.

Newborn term infants' platelet counts are in the same range as the platelet counts for older children and adults.[20] Term infant platelet counts range from 190,000 ± 94,000[21] to 251,000 ± 68,000[21] to 300,000.[36] Foley[11] studied umbilical cord artery and vein blood samples from 80 uncomplicated deliveries. Maternal hemostasis mechanisms were hyperactive at the time of delivery, whereas coagulation activity in the infant was less active. The mean maternal platelet count was 160,000/mm³, and mean platelet count in the infant was 233,000/mm³ at birth. Platelet counts differed from artery to vein. The mean umbilical vein platelet count was 233,000/mm³, whereas the mean umbilical artery count was 205,000/mm³. Foley[11] speculated that stored platelets were released from the placenta at the time of placental separation.

Platelet counts in the full-term infant with hypoxia are lower. Chadd[7] studied the effect of hypoxia on the platelet count of 24 infants. The mean platelet count in the hypoxic group was 133,500/mm³. The control group had a mean platelet count of 161,900/mm³.

Platelet counts do not differ significantly in varying gestational ages. Sells[40] assigned 106 infants into five gestational age categories to determine their platelet counts. The gestational age groups under study were: 40 to 42 weeks, 37 to 39 weeks, 34 to 36 weeks, 31 to 33 weeks, and 27 to 30 weeks. Sells found no significant difference between each gestational age group and that of adult platelet counts. Aballi and Lamerens[1] found that only 14% to 15%

of normal preterm infants had platelet counts between 100,000/mm³ and 150,000/mm³.

Research studies indicate that the adult levels of circulating platelets are found in fetuses of 27 weeks' gestation or greater. Thus perinatal nurses should be aware that altered platelet counts in the newborn indicate a pathophysiological process.

PLATELET FUNCTION AND ACTIVITY

Although the platelet count is normal in the infant, the platelet function is altered.*

Null and Hathaway[33] measured the platelet functions of 64 infants of various gestational ages. Three significant changes in the platelet functioning were noted in the infants. Clot retraction of the loose hemostasis plug was grossly defective; platelet aggregation with ADP, collagen, and thrombin was prolonged; and platelet factor III activity was decreased in the infants. These alterations did not prolong the bleeding time (BT) in any of the infants.

Additional platelet functions have been reported to be abnormal. These include abnormal platelet retention, abnormal release of platelet factor 3 and platelet adenine nucleotides,[18,20,21] and abnormal release of serotonin.[22]

These alterations of platelet functioning appear to be a transient physiological function that lasts 3 to 4 weeks after birth. By 1 month of age in the newborn, platelet activity and function have reached adult levels.[18,22,35]

Table 22-1 summarizes the platelet-vessel interaction functioning in the fetus and newborn.

---

*See references 5, 10, 15, 18, 21, 22, 32, and 35.

Table 22-1. Vascular-platelet interactions in fetus and newborn*

Vascular-platelet interactions	Normal adult values	27 to 31 weeks' gestation	32 to 36 weeks' gestation	Term	Term infant 1 to 2 months
Capillary fragility	N	Increased	N	N	N
Platelet count (10³/mm³)	300 ± 500	275 ± 60	290 ± 70	310 ± 68	280 ± 56
Platelet aggregation with ADP, epinephrine, collagen	N	Abn	Abn	Abn	N
Platelet factor 3	N	Abn	Abn	Abn	N
Platelet factor 4	N	NA	NA	N	N
Bleeding time (min)	4.0 ± 1.5	NA	4 ± 1.5	4 ± 1.5	N

N, normal; Abn, abnormal; NA, not available.
*Values obtained from compilation of data by Hathaway, W. E., and Honnar, J.: Perinatal coagulation, New York, 1973, Grune & Stratton, Inc.; and Gross, S. J., and Stuart, M. J.: Clin. Perinatol. **4**(2):259, 1977.

PATHOPHYSIOLOGY OF THROMBOCYTOPENIA

Thrombocytopenia, a platelet count of less than 100,000/mm^3, is an acquired disease most often seen in a sick newborn.[22] The eight most common etiologies of thrombocytopenia are[22,35]:

1. Immune disorders
   a. Isoimmune
   b. Autoimmune
2. Infections
   a. Bacterial
   b. Viral
   c. Protozoal
3. Maternal antenatal medications
4. Disseminated intravascular coagulation (DIC)
5. Exchange transfusions
6. Excessive peripheral utilization
   a. Hemangiomas
   b. Hyperviscosity syndrome
7. Inherited (chronic) thrombocytopenia
   a. Wiskott-Aldrich syndrome
   b. May-Hegglin disorder
8. Bone marrow abnormalities

Isoimmune and autoimmune thrombocytopenia are destructive disorders of the platelets. The platelets are destroyed by antiplatelet antibodies. The source of the antiplatelet antibody production is the mother.[23]

In isoimmune thrombocytopenia the platelets from the fetal circulation, which are antigenically different from the mother, enter the maternal circulation via the placenta.[23,37] The most common specific platelet antigen incompatibility is PL^{A1}, which causes 50% of all thrombocytopenias.[23] The isoimmune antibody is an IgG immunoglobulin that crosses the placenta.[12] The maternal antiplatelet antibodies enter the infant's circulation and coat the platelets.[12] The platelet destruction is confined to the infant's platelets and is similar to Rh sensitization. The occurrence of isoimmune thrombocytopenia is 1 out of 5000 live births.[15,31] McIntosh[30] states that isoimmune thrombocytopenia is an inherited autosomal dominant trait that frequently recurs in families. Sitarz, Driscole, and Wolff[41] state that the greatest risk to these infants is intracranial bleeding during birth or after birth.

Clinical manifestations in these infants are generalized petechiae and purpura.[23,31,35,41] The platelet count is below 100,000/mm^3 in the infant. Maternal platelet counts are in the normal range for isoimmune thrombocytopenia.[23,31,35,42] Treatment by transfusing with donor platelets would be ineffective because of the circulating antiplatelet antibodies circulating in the infants' blood. Ninety-eight percent of the general population have platelet antigen PL^{A1}; therefore, maternal platelets would be effective in improving the infants' platelet count. Transfusion of maternal platelets is necessary for a period of 6 to 8 weeks because the infants' platelet count will spontaneously recover at that time.[6]

Autoimmune thrombocytopenia is directed toward all platelets, maternal and infant. This disorder occurs when maternal antibodies are produced on an autoimmune basis and passively transfer across the placenta to cause neonatal thrombocytopenia.

Territo and Finklestein[42] studied mothers with platelet counts below 100,000/mm^3 at birth. Of the infants born of mothers in this group, 79% had thrombocytopenia, whereas 27% of all infants born of mothers with platelet counts above 100,000/mm^3 had thrombocytopenia.

The duration of this disease in the newborn period is from 1 to 2 weeks.[42] Territo and Finklestein[42] state that autoimmune thrombocytopenia is a transient disease in the newborn. Jones[24] states that the time of maximum risk to the infant is between 2 and 4 days after birth when the platelet count reaches the lowest level.

Clinical manifestations are bleeding shortly after birth, petechiae, and purpuric spots on the infant.[23,35] Bleeding sites include epistaxis, melena, hematuria, and oozing from the umbilical cord and puncture wounds.[35] The platelet count is below 100,000/mm^3 in both the infant and mother.[15,22,23,42]

Territo and Finklestein[42] report a 6% to 17% perinatal mortality rate associated with autoimmune thrombocytopenia. The treatment is to prevent hemorrhage and the risk of intracranial bleeding.[41]

Infections are associated with thrombocytopenia. Common infections include cytomegalovirus (CMV), disseminated herpes simplex, toxoplasmosis, syphilis, and rubella.[22,35] Infections cause thrombocytopenia in three ways: (1) Causative infection or its metabolites may inhibit the production of megakaryocyte platelets. (2) A platelet-antibody reaction could occur with the infectious agent, which would increase platelet sequestration. (3)

DIC is associated with infections, thereby causing a decrease in circulating platelets. (4) Platelet sequestration is influenced by reticuloendothelial hyperplasia, which is associated with infections.[39]

Neonatal thrombocytopenia associated with congenital rubella is caused by a decrease of megakaryocytes in the bone marrow. Petechiae, purpura, and hepatosplenomegaly are the clinical manifestations. Thrombocytopenia occurs within the first 24 hours and usually spontaneously resolves itself by 4 to 6 weeks.[10,22] Exchange transfusion or platelet transfusions may be necessary to correct the low platelet count.

Other clinical signs are related to the disease entities themselves. Cytomegalovirus and toxoplasmosis present with listlessness, twitching, and microcephaly. Disseminated herpes simplex infection is usually fatal.[2,10]

Diagnostic findings include (1) moderate to severe hemolytic anemia, (2) decreased hemoglobin, and (3) increased nucleated red blood cells in blood sugar.[35]

Drugs can produce idiosyncratic effects in the mother that cause maternal as well as neonatal thrombocytopenia. One of the mechanisms is an immune reaction in which antibodies are formed against a drug haptene complex.[41] Drugs that produce an immune thrombocytopenia are sulfonamides, quinidine, and quinine.[5,41] Acetylsalicylic acid,[8,9,18] promethazine hydrochloride,[16] alphaprodine, and meperidine[18] also cause thrombocytopenia in the newborn. Clinical evidence of thrombocytopenia has not been noted in those infants whose mothers received promethazine, alphaprodine, and meperidine.[18]

Medications have been demonstrated to delay the secondary wave of platelet aggregation in the newborn.[25,26] The release of endogenous adenosine diphosphate in response to collagen and epinephrine is prolonged by the interference from medications.

Corby and Shulman[9] studied platelet aggregation in the newborn associated with antenatal medications. Group one took no systemic medications 1 week prior to their estimated date of confinement. Group two received meperidine (Demerol) and promethazine hydrochloride (Phenergan) with no acetylsalicylic acid, and group three received acetylsalicylic acid (aspirin) during the week prior to their estimated date of confinement. Group three was the only group that showed a prolonged aggregation time. The acetylsalicylic acid (aspirin) prolonged aggregation time to 4 minutes in the newborn.

Champion and associates[8] showed alterations in platelet aggregation and bleeding time in patients on 10 grains of aspirin. Three other medications, diphenhydramine (Benadryl), triprolidine hydrochloride combined with pseudoephedrine (Actifed), and glyceryl guaiacolate, showed no alterations in platelet aggregation or bleeding time.

Other medications and pharmacological agents have been associated with thrombocytopenia. Intralipids[22] and phototherapy[29,35] have been associated with low platelet counts. Chlorpromazine and imipramine inhibit the second wave of collagen-epinephrine–induced platelet aggregation.[25,26]

The platelet count is used to distinguish between the two types of drug-induced thrombocytopenia. In the immune drug-induced thrombocytopenia the platelet count is below 100,000/mm^3 in the mother and infant. If only the infant's platelets are less than 100,000/mm^3, thrombocytopenia is not an immune drug response.[22,35]

Neonatal thrombocytopenia associated with exchange transfusions is a transient asymptomatic condition. The platelet count will decrease a few days after the procedure, probably owing to shorter survival time in transfused platelets.[41] The thrombocytopenia occurs between the end of the transfused platelets' life and the production of new platelets by the newborn.

Disseminated intravascular coagulation is associated with a low platelet count in sick infants. This disorder depletes platelets as well as coagulation factors. Thrombocytopenia associated with this disorder was discussed in Chapter 21.

Excessive peripheral utilization of platelets can cause thrombocytopenia. Such conditions as polycythemia, hyperviscosity syndrome, and giant hemangioma deplete the circulating platelets.[22] Orenstein[34] noted a case of a 2880 gm full-term infant with what was believed to be a large occipital mass and probably an encephalocele. The infant had gastrointestinal bleeding and a falling platelet count. The hemangiomas trap platelets producing a fall in the platelet count. Nine days after birth the infant's hemangioma was removed surgically and platelets were administered. The infant's platelet count improved.

Inherited or chronic thrombocytopenia is a rare condition that seldom results in a clinical bleeding episode during the neonatal period. Wiskott-Aldrich syndrome is a sex-linked recessive disorder. The clinical manifestations include petechiae and an atopic dermatitis that appear at about 6 months of age.[4] May-Hegglin disorder has not been described in the newborn period.[35]

Bone marrow abnormalities affect the megakaryocyte production, thereby producing a thrombocytopenia in the infant.[19] Conditions that produce hypoplastic thrombocytopenia include congenital anomalies, disorders such as bilateral absence of the radii (TAR), Fanconi's pancytopenia, and Down's syndrome.[22,35]

The causes of thrombocytopenia vary from immune reaction to drug induced to sepsis related. Perinatal nurses through their assessment skills of observation and palpation can identify conditions that are associated with thrombocytopenia in the newborn.

CLINICAL MANIFESTATIONS

Thrombocytopenia is not always associated with clinical manifestations. Medications and exchange transfusions can lower the platelet count, but the infant demonstrates no clinical signs.[9,22]

The common clinical manifestations of thrombocytopenia include*:
1. Petechiae, generalized pinpoint hemorrhagic lesions that do not disappear when pressure is applied to them[3] (In adults the platelet count must fall below 20,000 to 30,000/mm³ before petechiae are present.[20]
2. Purpura, a condition in which hemorrhages occur in the skin, mucous membranes, serous membranes, and elsewhere
3. Oozing from the umbilical cord and puncture wounds
4. Bruising over the presenting part
5. Ecchymosis with large cephalohematomas, extravasation of blood into the subcutaneous tissues discoloring the skin

As thrombocytopenia becomes more severe and/ or widespread, the following clinical manifestations may also be observed in the newborn.
1. Epistaxis (nosebleed)
2. Hematemesis (blood in vomitus)

---

*See references 5, 6, 10, 13 to 16, 20 to 22, 30, 35, and 36.

3. Hematuria (blood found in urine)
4. Melena (the passage of stool colored black by altered blood)

Hepatosplenomegaly is not a clinical manifestation of thrombocytopenia. It is associated with conditions such as infections that cause thrombocytopenia. Hepatosplenomegaly is utilized as a differentiating condition to diagnose the etiology of the thrombocytopenia.

DIAGNOSTIC APPROACH

The maternal history and physical examination are important considerations in diagnosing and treating neonatal thrombocytopenia. Once a maternal data base is collected, a newborn physical examination and laboratory findings will provide a data base for management of thrombocytopenia.

Maternal history should include[6,18]:
1. Infections during pregnancy
2. History of easy bruising or bleeding
3. Medications taken during pregnancy
4. Collagen-vascular diseases
5. Previous surgeries, especially splenectomy
6. Obstetrical complications
7. History of bleeding complications in the mother's family
8. Findings obtained from a physical examination of the mother
9. Neonatal history from previous children, especially problems with prolonged bleeding or bruising
10. Laboratory studies such as complete blood count, blood type, and coagulation studies

A newborn history should include information on:
1. Antenatal medications and complications
2. Intrapartal history
3. Time of vitamin K administration
4. Type and amount of birth trauma

This information combined with a physical examination of the infant will be used as the data base for the perinatal nurse to plan intervention for the infant's and family's care.

Physical examination of the newborn provides necessary information to differentiate the cause of thrombocytopenia as well as to identify the possibility of neonatal thrombocytopenia. Congenital anomalies such as those found with congenital rubella syndrome (congenital heart defects, cataracts, and microcephaly) are associated with thrombocytopenia. Hemangiomas and absence of radii and trisomy syndromes are associated with thrombocytopenia.[23,43]

The following laboratory studies provide information on coagulation and platelet functions*:

1. Platelet count to count the number of platelets by phase optic or electron microscopy
2. Bleeding time (BT) to test the formation of the platelet plug; a measure of the interaction between platelets and injured vascular endothelium
3. Peripheral blood smear to provide information on morphology and proportion of large platelets (Normal—two to three clumps of platelets can be identified under microscopy on high power; more than 15% larger than 2.5 μ in diameter suggests an increase in platelet turnover.)
4. Platelet factor III to be measured by prothrombin consumption test, thromboplastin generation test, and thromboplastin activity[13]
5. Examination of bone marrow used to evaluate platelet production, the number of megakaryocytes, their size, and number of nuclei per cell; bone marrow evaluation useful to exclude underlying infiltrative disorders such as leukemia
6. Serology test for platelet antigens and isoantibodies, available at only a few laboratories

The perinatal nurse should be knowledgeable about the different types of coagulation studies. Infants with thrombocytopenia may have a range of blood studies drawn to determine the etiology of the thrombocytopenia. The most common laboratory test will be the platelet count.

Oski and Haiman[35] outlined an approach to the diagnosis of thrombocytopenia that categorizes the newborn's physical conditions relating to thrombocytopenia.

MOTHER

1. History and physical—clinical manifestation of thrombocytopenia
2. Platelet count

Low

1. Maternal ITP, SLE
2. Drug purpura
3. Inherited

Normal

_____

*See references 3, 5, 6, 13 to 15, 18, 22, and 35.

INFANT
Normal

1. Isoimmune
2. Medications
3. Inherited
4. Early congenital aplastic anemia

Hepatosplenomegaly

1. Infections
2. Congenital leukemia
3. Associated with Rh erythroblastosis
4. Blood transfusion

Congenital anomalies

1. Giant hemangioma
2. Rubella syndrome
3. Absent radii
4. Trisomy syndromes

TREATMENT FOR THROMBOCYTOPENIA

Treatment therapy is dependent on the cause or associated cause of the thrombocytopenia purpura.

For infants with isoimmune thrombocytopenia, Oski and Haiman[35] outlined the blood exchange transfusion criteria as:

1. Thrombocytopenia below 30,000/mm^3 and below 10,000/mm^3 several hours after birth
2. High reticulocytosis
3. Amegakaryocytosis
4. Early jaundice
5. Signs of melena or hematuria
6. Ecchymosis
7. Hematomas

Hathaway, Mahasandana, and Makowski[23] recommend that fresh blood from any normal donor can be used for the exchange transfusion. This should be followed by maternal platelets washed with normal plasma to remove isoantibodies.

Splenectomies have been performed with good results.[35] Oski and Haiman recommend that the risk of overwhelming infection is high in the infant; therefore, a splenectomy should not be performed.

Grosfeld, Noffis, Holes, and Newton[17] recommend splenectomy in severe cases with intracranial hemorrhage. Splenectomy is not an elective procedure in the newborn because of postsplenectony infections.[17]

McIntosh and O'Brien[30] state that pooled blood bank platelets from random donors are unlikely to be compatible with infant's platelets. If random donors' platelets were given, the platelets would be destroyed by the circulating maternal antiplatelet antibodies. Until platelet typing is readily available, the use of maternal platelets has been advocated.

Pearson, Shulman, Marder, and Cone[37] have advocated the use of prednisone in the prenatal period. Prednisone, 2 mg/kg daily in divided doses, is recommended for infants with severe thrombocytopenia with platelet counts less than 25,000/mm³ and clinical bleeding.[37]

Autoimmune thrombocytopenia or idiopathic thrombocytopenia purpura is acquired by the neonate from the mother. This condition can be treated prenatally by administering prednisone to the symptomatic mother.[2,22] The initial dose is 60 to 80 mg/day of prednisone, gradually reducing the dose over several weeks. The optimal dosage for the mother is the level that improves the platelet count and maintains adequate hemostasis.[22] Maternal splenectomy is a form of treatment only in life-threatening situations.[22]

The neonate delivered of a mother with autoimmune or idiopathic thrombocytopenia usually has a mild transient disorder. Infants who do not present with bleeding diathesis do not require special treatment. Infants with serious life-threatening hemorrhage are treated with blood exchange transfusions. Platelet concentrations are given after the exchange transfusion.[23,35]

The mode of birth for infants whose mothers have autoimmune or idiopathic thrombocytopenia is determined by the maternal platelet count. Territo and Finklestein[42] showed that 79% of all infants born of mothers whose platelet counts were less than 100,000/mm³ had neonatal thrombocytopenia. Sitarz, Driscole, and Wolff[41] state that the greatest risk to the infant from hemorrhage is intracranial hemorrhage owing to birth trauma. Mennuti, Schwarz, and Gill[31] state that all mothers will platelet counts below 100,000/mm³ should have cesarean sections. Jones, Asher, and Rutherford[24] state that the greatest risk to the infant is about 2 to 4 days after birth. The issue of vaginal birth vs cesarean birth to minimize birth trauma, especially intracranial trauma and hemorrhage, is still controversial.

Blood and blood products are used to manage thrombocytopenia owing to a causative agent. The perinatal nurse should be knowledgeable about the storage and administration of blood and platelets.

There are three basic modes of platelet administration: whole blood, platelet-rich plasma, or platelet concentrate.[42] A unit of platelets is defined as the number of platelets obtained from 1 unit of blood.[18]

Murry and Gardner[32] found that the optimal storage temperature for platelets is 20° to 22° C or room temperature. If platelets are exposed to temperatures of 4° C, as the temperature in blood refrigerators, the shape of the platelet is altered from a disk to a sphere.[32] Platelets treated with the anticoagulant solution acid citrate dextrose (ACD) will reduce the aggregation time, and the shape of platelets will be altered.

To maintain platelet viability, platelets should not be stored at 4° C or kept in the administration container greater than 72 hours. Platelet-rich plasma and platelet concentration should be administered to the infant within 6 hours from the platelet bag.[44]

If fresh whole blood is given to the infant, it should be administered within 12 hours. After 12 hours, very few platelets and clotting factors V and VIII are left in fresh whole blood. Red blood cells contain no platelets.[44]

Thrombocytopenia treatment and management include treatment of the underlying disease. Therefore antibiotics may be used for infants with associated infections.[22,35]

COMPLICATIONS

The complications from thrombocytopenia purpura can be as severe as intracranial hemorrhage and central nervous system sequelae.[22,25] Laros and Sweet[25] reported a mortality rate of 21% in infants whose mothers had idiopathic thrombocytopenia. Hathaway and Hannar[22] state that 20% to 25% of the infants with thrombocytopenia have severe bleeding that can lead to central nervous system hemorrhage. Territo and Finklestein[42] report a 6% to 17% perinatal mortality rate associated with autoimmune thrombocytopenia.

The role of platelets in the development of intraventricular hemorrhage has not been explained.[43] The infant who develops intraventricular hemorrhage presents with clinical features of sudden collapse, pallor, hypotension, poor peripheral circulation, and hypotonia. The precise site of the hemorrhage has been proposed as the terminal vein in the subependymal zone.[43] Turner[43] has found that by using replacement of coagulation factors as well as platelets it is possible to reduce the incidence of intraventricular hemorrhage.

CONCLUSION

The pathophysiological role of coagulation defects as a factor in perinatal morbidity is not well explained. The high risk of intraventricular hemorrhage in these infants suggests that acute observation of the early clinical signs of thrombocytopenia is essential. The perinatal nurse and all nurses should include in their assessments information relating to bleeding disorders. Significant improvement in perinatal care of the thrombocytopenic infant will follow with platelet typing and successful antenatal and intrapartal care.

Protocols

Problem □ **Delivery of newborn of mother with signs and symptoms of thrombocytopenia**

GOAL: To identify maternal risk factors that are associated with thrombocytopenia

Rationale: To detect and manage thrombocytopenia early, thereby decreasing risk of hemorrhage and neurological sequelae in postnatal period

DIAGNOSTIC

1. Review maternal data base, history, and physical condition at the time of admission for factors that predispose the infant to thrombocytopenia.

   Rationale: To be aware that neonatal thrombocytopenia may be suspected with the mother has a positive maternal history and/or physical examination indicates thrombocytopenia

2. Draw maternal blood studies for diagnosis of thrombocytopenia during labor. The following laboratory tests should be drawn:
   a. Platelet count
   b. Type and cross match
   c. DIC workup
   d. PL^{A1} antigen type (not available in all hospitals)
   e. Platelet antibody type (not available in all hospitals)

   Rationale: To be aware that maternal platelet counts of less than 50,000/mm^3 indicate that a cesarean birth could be the method of choice for delivery to prevent cerebral trauma

3. Observe the fetal presenting part for prolonged bleeding after the completion of fetal blood sampling; the presenting part should be observed through the endoscope, which is inserted through the cervix, for at least one contraction.

   Rationale: To be aware that the greatest risk to the infant with thrombocytopenia is intracranial bleeding, which may occur during the birth process

4. Assess the physical condition of the newborn at the time of birth. A complete physical examination should include assessment of all systems. The following findings are significant:
   a. Congenital anomalies such as bilaterally absent radii (TAA) and Down's syndrome
   b. Birth trauma to the head
   c. Bleeding or oozing of blood from fetal scalp electrode site, clamped umbilical cord, or other puncture sites
   d. Skin disorders such as petechiae, purpura, and hemangiomas

   Rationale: To check for physical signs and symptoms of thrombocytopenia, which may be present at the time of birth, and hasten treating this disorder

5. An Apgar score must be evaluated at 1 and 5 minutes.

   Rationale: To provide a systematic appraisal of the infant's condition at birth

THERAPEUTIC

1. Have personnel in the delivery room who are trained in the immediate management of the high-risk infant, such as a perinatal nurse and pediatrician.

   Rationale: To be aware that 79% of infants born of mothers with thrombocytopenia have thrombocytopenia

2. Dry infant completely and place in prewarmed infant warmer.

   Rationale: To provide a neutral thermal environment, thereby preventing any added stress to the newborn

3. Administer 0.5 to 1.0 mg vitamin K IM.

   Rationale: To replace vitamin K and decrease hemorrhage owing to decreased vitamin K

4. Chart physical findings of infant, such as birth trauma, cephalohematoma, petechiae, bruises, and anomalies.

   Rationale: To provide baseline data for observing signs of bleeding

5. When heart rate, respiratory status, and bleeding manifestation are stable, transfer to an intermediate care nursery or a neonatal intensive care unit depending on infant's condition.

   Rationale: To provide the infant with ventilation support, assessment of neurological damage from intraventricular hemorrhage, and nursing and medical care not provided in the normal newborn or special care nursery

6. The intermediate care nursery is the nursery of choice with infants needing:

   a. Observation for signs of bleeding

   b. Assessment of physical condition

   Rationale: To provide the infant with support and interventions that may be necessary to manage hemorrhagic complications

7. Encourage maternal-infant attachment by:

   a. Allowing the mother and significant other to view their infant before the infant is transferred

   b. Allowing the mother and significant other to touch the infant before the infant is transported to another hospital or transferred to the newborn unit.

   c. Refering to protocol on high-risk parenting

   Rationale: To realize that separation of the mother and her infant can prolong the maternal-infant attachment, which could influence future caregiving

EDUCATIONAL

1. In-services should be provided to the labor and delivery staff as well as the newborn staff on bleeding disorders of the newborn. In-service topics could include:

   a. Physical assessment of the newborn for signs of bleeding

   b. Maternal assessment for factors that predispose the infant to bleeding disorders

   c. Coagulation studies

   d. Treatment of maternal thrombocytopenia

   Rationale: To ensure that labor and delivery staff as well as the nursery staff are knowledgeable about high-risk deliveries so that optimal care for the mother and her infant is provided

Problem □ Infant with signs and symptoms associated with thrombocytopenia

GOAL: To maintain hemostasis of the newborn's coagulation system

   Rationale: To promote physical well-being in the infant

DIAGNOSTIC

1. Obtain a complete antepartal and intrapartal history of the mother and infant. Maternal history should include:

   a. Prenatal infections

   b. Medications taken before and during pregnancy

   c. Family history of bleeding disorders

   d. Previous surgeries such as splenectomy and how the mother tolerated the surgery

   e. Obstetrical course, prenatal complications, and laboratory values

   f. Intrapartal history, including length of labor, fetal distress, amount of bleeding, type of delivery, type and amount of analgesia and anesthesia

   g. Mother's physical condition, including bleeding from mucous membranes and gastrointestinal system, bruising, and skin integrity

   h. Neonatal history should include:

   (1) Physical examination of all systems

   (2) Assessment of physical anomalies

   (3) Time and amount of vitamin K given to the infant

(4) Assessment of birth trauma, head injuries

(5) Apgar score

(6) Gestational age

Rationale: To obtain a data base on probable etiology of condition and treatment given to the infant in the delivery room

2. Continuous assessment should be made of the newborn's physical condition including:

a. Assessment of skin conditions:

(1) Petechiae: generalized pinpoint hemorrhagic lesions that do not disappear when pressure is applied to them

(2) Purpura: a condition in which hemorrhages occur in the skin, mucous membranes, serous membranes, and elsewhere

(3) Ecchymoses: extravasation of blood into the subcutaneous tissues discoloring the skin

(4) Bruising: over presenting part as well well as generalized bruising

(5) Bleeding: oozing from umbilical cord or puncture sites such as heel and finger from Dextrostix sticks

(6) Jaundice: yellow pigmentation of the skin from RBC breakdown

b. Assessment of gastrointestinal/genitourinary function

(1) Hematuria: blood in the urine

(2) Hematemesis: blood in vomitus

(3) Melena: the passage of stools colored black by altered blood

c. Assessment of spleen and liver functioning for normal size and location

d. Assessment of cardiac/respiratory status for changes in normal heart sounds and breath sounds and quantity and quality of respirations

e. Assessment of hematological and coagulation functioning from laboratory values:

	28 weeks	34 weeks	40 weeks
Hemoglobin (gm/100)	14.5	15.0	16.8
Hematocrit (0/0)	45	47	53
Platelets (1000's/mm³)	275 ± 60	290 ± 70	310 ± 68
Partial thromboplastin time	117 sec	113 sec	71 sec
Prothrombin time	21 sec	18 sec	16 sec
Fibrinogen		23/mg/dl	
Red blood cells (mm³)	4.0	4.4	5.25

Rationale: To recognize signs and symptoms of hematological changes and complications that may indicate a change in the infant's condition

3. Assess infant for signs of potential CNS dysfunction:

a. Crying—for strength and type

b. Sucking—for strength and coordination

c. Tone—for hypotonia

d. Limb movements—for jerking movements and symmetrical movements

e. Eye movements—for setting-sun appearance and nystagmus

f. Cardiorespiratory changes—for color changes, hypotension, poor peripheral circulation, apnea, bradycardia

4. Assess for CNS complications by:

a. Measuring the infant's head circumference on admission and daily

b. Checking deep tendon reflexes

c. Transilluminating the head with a flashlight with two "D" cells and a tight-fitting rubber cone over the front of the flashlight (A 2-cm halo in the frontal region or a 1-cm halo in the occipital region is suggestive of an abnormality.)

Rationale: To be aware that intracranial hemorrhage is a serious complication of thrombocytopenia

5. Observe infants under phototherapy or receiving Intralipid for signs of bleeding.

Rationale: To be aware that low platelet counts have been reported to be associated with phototherapy and Intralipid

6. Observe for blood transfusion complication such as fever, shock, tachycardia, and convulsions when administering blood products.

Rationale: To be aware that a blood incompatibility may result during blood transfusion

7. The following blood work should be drawn on admission to the nursery. The blood-drawing sites include heel stick or umbilical arterial line. Heel sticks are contraindicated when the infant has an umbilical arterial line.
   a. Hemoglobin: preterm, 1500 to 1750 gm; term, 12 to 24 hours
   b. Hematocrit (Refer to diagnostic No. 2e.)
   c. Reticulocytes: preterm, 8.0 ± 3.5; term, 4.0 ± 1.5
   d. Red blood cell count
   e. Serum electrolytes including:
      (1) Sodium mEq/L: preterm, 139.6; term, 145.0
      (2) Potassium: preterm, 5.6; term, 6.3
      (3) Calcium: preterm, 9.2; term, 7.8
      (4) Chloride: preterm, 108.2; term, 63.0
      (5) Glucose
   f. White count with differential leukocytes: preterm, 6800 to 14,000; term, 6700 to 14,700
   g. Coagulation studies including:
      (1) Platelet count
      (2) PT (Refer to diagnostic No. 2e.)
      (3) PTT (Refer to diagnostic No. 2e.)
      (4) Fibrinogen
   h. Blood cultures
   i. Blood gases for infants with respiratory distress symptoms (Possible sites for drawing blood gases include radial, brachial, dorsal pedal, and umbilical arteries and capillary "heel sticks." Heel sticks are contraindicated when the infant has an umbilical arterial line.)
   Rationale: To obtain baseline laboratory data

8. Draw blood for platelet count and hematocrit throughout the hospitalization when the infant has:
   a. Signs of bleeding or oozing from puncture sites
   b. Prolonged bleeding from a puncture wound: preterm; 1 to 8 minutes (normal); full term; 1 to 5 minutes (normal)
   c. Clinical manifestations of thrombocytopenia: petechiae, purpura
   Rationale: To be aware that the newborn's coagulation system is affected by changes in health status with infections as well as medications

THERAPEUTIC

1. Hematest all stools, urine, and nasogastric secretions.
   Rationale: To be aware that hemorrhagic complications of thrombocytopenia can extend to the gastrointestinal system

2. Maintain infant in a neutral thermal environment throughout procedures by:
   a. Placing an overhead warmer over the infant and working area
   b. Keeping the infant in an isolette or under a radiant warmer
   Rationale: To decrease additional stress on the sick infant by maintaining metabolic and caloric energy balance during procedures

3. Administer maternal platelets or donor platelets when indicated by:
   a. Checking expiration time and date
   b. Checking donor number
   c. Checking patient identification
   d. Storing platelets at room temperature
   e. Administering platelets from the bag within 6 hours
   Rationale: To maintain viability of platelets and safely administer platelets to improve platelet level

4. Administer packed red blood cells as a transfusion or an exchange transfusion when indicated.
   Rationale: To maintain hemostasis and eliminate antiplatelet antibodies in infant's circulation

5. Place firm, continuous pressure for 15 minutes over all puncture sites after drawing blood or doing heel sticks.
   Rationale: To minimize the chance of hemorrhage from the puncture site

6. Administer ordered medications to infant, which may include:
   a. Antibiotics
      Rationale: To treat the underlying cause of thrombocytopenia
   b. Corticosteroids

Rationale: To be aware that corticosteroids may have an ameliorating effect on isoimmune thrombocytopenia for unknown reasons

7. Handle the infant gently during all procedures, turn the infant frequently, and keep all equipment wires and parts off the infant's body.

Rationale: To minimize bleeding or bruising from rough handling and pressure

EDUCATIONAL

1. Establish in-service continuing education programs for all nursery personnel covering the pathophysiology, assessment, and management of bleeding disorders of the newborn.

Rationale: To provide nursery staff with current information and assessment knowledge about thrombocytopenia

2. Encourage parents and family to participate in the care of their newborn by such activities as feeding the infant and discussing infant care.

Rationale: To encourage parent-infant bonding and the development of parenting skills

REFERENCES

1. Aballi, A. J., and Lamerens, S. D.: Coagulation changes in the neonatal period and in early infancy, Pediatr. Clin. North Am. **9:**785, 1962.
2. Ayromlooi, J.: A new approach to the management of immunologic thrombocytopenic purpura in pregnancy, Am. J. Obstet. Gynecol. **130**(2):235, 1978.
3. Beck, W. S., editor: Hematology, ed. 2, Cambridge, 1977, Massachusetts Institute of Technology.
4. Blake, P. J., and Perez, R. C.: Applied immunologic concepts, New York, 1978, Appleton-Century-Crofts.
5. Bleyer, W. A., Hakami, W., and Shepard, T. H.: The development of hemostasis in the human fetus and newborn infant, J. Pediatr. **79**(5):838, 1971.
6. Boxer, G. J.: Platelets, Hematology lecture, sophomore medical student class, Indiana University, April 27, 1979.
7. Chadd, N. A., Elwood, P. P., and Gray, O. P.: Coagulation defects in hypoxic full term newborn infants, Br. Med. J. **4:**516, 1971.
8. Champion, L. A., Schwartz, A. D., Luddy, R. E., and Schendler, S.: The effects of four commonly used drugs on platelet function, J. Pediatr. **89**(4):653, 1976.
9. Corby, D. G., and Shulman, I.: The effects of antenatal drug administration on aggregation of platelets of newborn infants, J. Pediatr. **79**(2):307, 1971.
10. Evans, N., and Glass, L.: Perinatal medicine, New York, 1976, Harper & Row, Publishers, Inc.
11. Foley, N. E., and Clayton, J. K.: Haemostatic mechanisms in maternal umbilical vein and umbilical artery blood at the time of delivery, Br. J. Obstet. Gynaecol. **84**(2):81, 1977.
12. Fredman, S. O., and Gold, P.: Clinical immunology, ed. 2, New York, 1976, Harper & Row, Publishers, Inc.
13. Gilchrist, G. S.: Platelet disorders, Pediatr. Clin. North Am. **19**(4):1047, 1972.
14. Gill, F. M.: Thrombocytopenia in the newborn, Pediatr. Ann. **4:**71, 1974.
15. Glader, B. E., and Buchanan, S. R.: Care of the critically ill child: the bleeding neonate, Pediatrics **58**(4):548, 1976.
16. Goodwin, J. W., Godden, J. O., and Chance, G. W.: Perinatal medicine, Baltimore, 1976, The Williams & Wilkins Co.
17. Grosfeld, J. L., Noffis, D., Holes, E. T., and Newton, W. A.: The role of splenectomy in neonatal idiopathic thrombocytopenia purpura, J. Pediatr. Surg. **5**(2):166, 1970.
18. Gross, S. J., and Stuart, M. J.: Hemostasis in the premature infant, Clin. Perinatol. **4**(2):259, 1977.
19. Guyton, A.: Textbook of medical physiology, ed. 4, Philadelphia, 1971, W. B. Saunders Co.
20. Hathaway, W. E.: Coagulation problems in the newborn infant, Pediatr. Clin. North Am. **17:**129, 1970.
21. Hathaway, W. E.: The bleeding newborn, Clin. Perinatol. **2**(1):83, 1975.
22. Hathaway, W. E., and Honnar, J.: Perinatal coagulation, New York, 1973, Grune & Stratton, Inc.
23. Hathaway, W. E., Mahasandana, C., and Makowski, E. L.: Cord blood coagulation studies in infants of high-risk pregnant women, Am. J. Obstet. Gynecol. **121**(1):51, 1975.
24. Jones, R. W., Asher, M. I., Rutherford, C. J., and Munro, H. M.: Autoimmune (idiopathic) thrombocytopenia purpura in pregnancy and newborn, Br. J. Obstet. Gynaecol. **84:**679, 1977.
25. Laros, R. K., and Sweet, R. I.: Management of idiopathic thrombocytopenia purpura during pregnancy, Am. J. Obstet. Gynecol. **122**(2):182, 1975.
26. Marcus, A. J.: Platelet function: part I, N. Engl. J. Med. **280**(22):1213, 1969.
27. Marcus, A. J.: Platelet function: part II, N. Engl. J. Med. **280**(23):1278, 1969.
28. Marcus, A. J.: Platelet function: part III, N. Engl. J. Med. **280**(24):1330, 1969.
29. Maurer, H. N., and Fratkin, N. F.: Effects of phototherapy on platelet counts in low–birth weight infants and on platelet production and life span in rabbits, Pediatrics **57:**506, 1976.
30. McIntosh, S., and O'Brien, T.: Neonatal isoimmune purpura: response to platelet infusions, J. Pediatr. **83:**1020, 1973.
31. Mennuti, M., Schwarz, R. H., and Gill, F.: Obstetrical management of isoimmune thrombocytopenia, Am. J. Obstet. Gynecol. **124:**565, 1976.
32. Murry, S., and Gardner, F. H.: Effect of storage temperature on maintenance of platelet viability—deleterious effect of refrigerated storage, N. Engl. J. Med. **280**(2):1094, 1969.
33. Null, H. M., and Hathaway, W. E.: Altered platelet function in newborns, Pediatr. Res. **4:**229, 1970.
34. Orenstein, D. F., et al.: Hemangioma thrombocytopenia syndrome, Am. J. Dis. Child. **131:**680, 1977.
35. Oski, F., and Haiman, J. L.: Major problems in clinical pediatrics: hematologic problems in clinical pediatrics, ed. 2, Philadelphia, 1972, W. B. Saunders Co.

36. Pearson, H. A., Shulman, N. R., Marder, V. J., and Cone, T. E.: Isoimmune neonatal thrombocytopenia purpura: clinical and therapeutic considerations, Blood **13**(2):154, 1964.
37. Pillitteri, A.: Nursing care of the growing family: a child health text, Boston, 1977, Little, Brown & Co.
38. Platelets for transfusion, Lancet **1**(7740):25, 1972.
39. Schaffer, A. J., and Avery, M. E.: Disease of the newborn, ed. 4, Philadelphia, 1977, W. B. Saunders Co.
40. Sell, E. J., and Cooregan, J. J.: Platelet counts, fibrinogen concentrations and factor V and factor VIII in healthy infants according to gestational age, J. Pediatr. **82**(6):1028, 1973.
41. Sitarz, A. L., Driscole, J. M., and Wolff, J. A.: Management of isoimmune neonatal thrombocytopenia, Am. J. Obstet. Gynecol. **124**:39, 1976.
42. Territo, M., and Finklestein, J.: Management of autoimmune thrombocytopenia in pregnancy and in the neonate, Obstet. Gynecol. **41**:579, 1973.
43. Turner, T. L.: Neonatal coagulation defects, Clin. Endocrinol. Metabol. **5**(1):89, 1976.
44. The use of blood, Chicago, 1971, Abbott Laboratories.
45. Vain, N. E., and Bedros, A. A.: Treatment of isoimmune thrombocytopenia of the newborn with transfusion of maternal platelets, Pediatrics **63**(1):107, 1979.

Chapter 23

Neonatal seizures

Elizabeth Gale

In the neonatal period, seizures are one of the most common symptoms of disease, injury, malformation, or functional disturbance of the central nervous system.[9,15] It is imperative that all nursery personnel—nurses and aides—understand the difference between a seizure that may occur in the older child and one that may occur in the neonate. The nurse must be able to recognize a neonatal seizure, understand and know what the probable causes are, know what diagnostic evaluations to include and what to look for in these evaluations, know what is the most likely treatment, and know what the nurses' responsibilities of care for a neonate who is at risk of seizure are.

RECOGNITION

The type of seizure that occurs in the neonate differs considerably from that seen in older infants, and the type that occurs in premature infants differs from that seen in full-term neonates. Unlike older infants, neonates rarely have well-organized generalized tonic-clonic seizures. Premature infants have even less well-organized seizures than neonates.

Since neonatal seizures may take varied and subtle forms, their recognition requires a high index of suspicion on the part of an alert nursery staff, particularly the nurses and aides who spend considerably more time observing the infant than the physicians. Volpe[17] listed five types of seizure activity observed in the neonate. These are subtle, multifocal clonic, focal clonic, tonic, and myoclonic.

The most frequent type of seizure seen in the neonate is classified as subtle. It is called subtle be-

cause its clinical manifestations are readily overlooked. Such manifestations may consist of tonic posturing of a limb, tonic posturing of the whole body, repetitive blinking, drooling, sucking or sudden chewing, facial twitching, unusual cry, limpness, or apnea.[4,15,17] Apnea as a manifestation of seizure is almost always accompanied by one of the other subtle manifestations. Subtle seizures, in general, are most common in the premature infant.*

Multifocal clonic seizures are manifested by clonic movements of one limb that migrate to another part of the body in a nonordered fashion; that is, right arm jerking may be accompanied or followed by left leg jerking.[4,6,14,17]

Focal clonic seizures are typically well localized and are not usually accompanied by unconsciousness. In the neonate, focal clonic seizures are more commonly a manifestation of bilateral cerebral disturbance—that is, a metabolic encephalopathy—than of focal disease.

Tonic seizures, when generalized, may appear like decerebrate posturing of older patients, but accompanying stertorous breathing, eye twitching, or clonic movements stamp them as seizures.[17]

Myoclonic seizures are usually synchronous and take the form of single or multiple jerks or flexion of upper and/or lower extremities.[17]

Nurses need to be able to distinguish between jitteriness and seizure activity. Jitteriness may be defined as "a movement disorder with qualities primarily of tremulousness but occasionally also of clonics."[17] The distinction of jitteriness from seizures is usually readily made if the following points

---

*See references 1, 4, 9, 14, 16, and 17.

are remembered: jitteriness is not accompanied by abnormalities of gaze or extraocular movement, whereas seizures usually are; jitteriness is exquisitely stimulus-sensitive, and seizures are not; and the dominant movement in jitteriness is tremor (that is, the alternating movements are rhythmic, of equal rate and amplitude), whereas the dominant movement in seizures is clonic jerking (that is, the movements have a fast and slow component).[1,9,16,17]

ETIOLOGY

As stated before, a seizure in a neonate is a symptom, not a disease. Seizures in the neonate usually occur within the first 48 hours but have been known to occur later. The literature suggests that most seizure activity is of the subtle type and may be overlooked initially by nurses and physicians.*

Neonatal seizures can be classified into different categories. These include perinatal complications, metabolic disturbances, infections, and developmental anomalies. Perinatal complications include birth trauma and anoxia. Birth trauma usually results in vascular bleeding, that is, subarachnoid and subdural bleeding and thrombosis.

Anoxia or ischemic encephalopathy is most often secondary to birth asphyxia. Again, anoxia often leads to vascular bleeding, that is, periventricular hemorrhage and periventricular and intraventricular bleeding.†

Metabolic disturbances are the next most frequent cause of neonatal seizures. Hypocalcemia is the most frequent cause of metabolic neonatal seizures.[14,15,17] Hypocalcemia is diagnosed by the finding of a serum calcium concentration below 7 mg/dl.[1,4,15] Hypocalcemia has two major causes in the neonate. The first occurs in the first 2 or 3 days of life and is seen most often in low birth weight infants and frequently follows obstetrical trauma. Hypocalcemia rarely occurs alone. It usually is accompanied by hypomagnesemia and/or increased serum levels of phosphorus (greater than 8 mg/dl). When the serum calcium levels are less than 7 mg/dl and the serum phosphorus levels are greater than 8 mg/dl, tetany results. The second is late onset tetany. This is rarely seen in the neonate today but in the past was caused by feeding the

neonate cow's milk or a formula low in calcium and high in phosphorus. Hypocalcemia may also be caused by maternal hyperparathyroidism or neonatal hypoparathyroidism.[1,4,9,15]

Hypoglycemia may be of the transient type or persistent type. Transient hypoglycemia may occur in the infant of a diabetic or prediabetic mother, or it may be associated with low birth weight infants, septicemia, meningitis, intracranial hemorrhage, or other evidence of central nervous system disturbance. Persistent hypoglycemia may be produced by islet cell tumors, galactosemia, glycogen storage disease, and idiopathic hypoglycemia.[1,9,14] The initial diagnosis of hypoglycemia can be achieved with a Dextrostix. However, a "true" diagnosis can only be achieved by doing two serum glucose levels. A serum glucose level less than 30 mg/dl is indicative of hypoglycemia.[4]

Hyponatremia and hypernatremia are other causes of neonatal seizures. Hyponatremia in a neonate may present with lethargy, irritability, convulsions, tremors, or other signs of seizure activity. It may result from water retention owing to the increased excretion of antidiuretic hormone during meningitis or sepsis or to the increased loss of sodium with diarrhea or sweating. Hyponatremia may also occur as a complication of inaccurate parenteral fluid administration to the infant or the mother during labor. Determination of the etiology is important because hyponatremia secondary to excessive water retention should be treated with fluid restriction, but excess sodium loss requires sodium replacement.

Hypernatremia in the neonate has resulted from accidental substitution of salt for sugar in formula feedings and from the administration of a high-sodium formula or parenteral fluids to infants whose kidneys cannot adequately conserve water. Seizures may occur secondary to venous thrombosis or to petechialization of the brain. Seizures most commonly occur during rehydration, when the slow equilibration of sodium across the cell membrane leads to a marked flow of water into the brain, resulting in intracellular edema and decreased potassium.[1,4]

Pyridoxine deficiency is a rare cause of seizures that may occur in utero or in the first hours of life. Pyridoxine deficiency is secondary to a lack of exogenous vitamin B_6; it produces seizures at several weeks of life and is associated with abnormal

---

*See references 3, 4, 6, 14, 16, and 17.
†See references 1, 3, 4, 6, 9, and 14 to 17.

Table 23-1. Pharmacological agents used to treat neonatal seizures of nonmetabolic etiology*

Drug	Indications	Dose/route	Contraindications	Untoward effects	Toxic effects
Phenobarbital	Control of neonatal seizures	Varies, commonly 10 mg/kg/day IV or PO	Severe renal or hepatic dysfunction, hypersensitivity to barbiturates	Excitement, drowsiness, dermatitis, nausea, vomiting	Lethargy; respiratory, circulatory, and renal depression
Phenytoin	Control of nonmetabolic neonatal seizures unresponsive to phenobarbital; used in conjunction with phenobarbital	Varies, initially 10 mg/kg/day; therapeutic range, 5-15 mcg/ml; monitor levels 2, 4, 6 and 12 hr after initial dose and 1 hr prior to dose for 2 days	Seizures of metabolic etiology, hyperbilirubinemia (Bilirubin displaces phenytoin from protein; this may result in phenytoin toxicity.)	Hypotension, morbiliform (measles like) rash; rare, paralytic reactions, vomiting, and blood dyscrasia	Hypotension
Diazepam	Short-term control of neonatal seizures rapidly; not recommended for neonates because of its short-term activity	Variable, usually 0.1 to 0.3 mg/kg slowly IV until seizure stops	Desired long-term control, hyperbilirubinemia	CNS depression, phlebitis, circulatory collapse, respiratory depression, pallor	CNS depression
Paregoric	Drug of choice to use on narcotic withdrawal infants	0.05 ml/kg or 2 gtts every 4 hr	Unknown	Addiction, constipation	Sleepiness, constipation

*Modified from Bergersen, B. L.: Pharmacology in nursing, ed. 14, St. Louis, 1979, The C. V. Mosby Co.; Jalling, B.: Acta Paediatr. Scand. **64:**514, 1975; and Jalling, B., Borius, L. O., Kallberg, N., and Agurell, S.: Eur. J. Clin. Pharmacol. **6:**234, 1973.

tryptophan metabolism. Pyridoxine dependency, an endogenous disease, has no associated chemical abnormalities. Patients with dependency require continued administration of pyridoxine to prevent the recurrence of seizures and cerebral damage.[4]

Drug withdrawal is another metabolic classification that can cause seizures. The seizure activity is usually of the myoclonic type. The neonate is usually lethargic, yawns frequently, may or may not present with rhinorrhea, and startles easily. The drug of choice for treatment is paregoric. However, diazepam and phenobarbital are also used.[5,11]

Less common, yet important, metabolic disorders of which seizures may be the initial symptom in the first month of life are phenylketonuria (PKU) and maple syrup urine disease. Another metabolic disorder associated with seizures in the newborn is kernicterus, in which seizures may occur late in the course of the disease.[4]

The third cause of neonatal seizures is infections. Septicemia, bacterial and fungal meningitis, encephalitis commonly caused by herpes simplex virus, cytomegalic inclusion disease, toxoplasmosis, and coxsackievirus B are the most common types.

The fourth category is developmental anomalies, which includes porencephalic cysts, agenesis of corpus callosum, hydranencephaly, and other cerebral malformations.

DIAGNOSTIC EVALUATION

Diagnostic evaluation must begin with a carefully taken history (concerning both mother and baby) and physical examination. The most immediate laboratory tests should be directed toward the most dangerous, but readily treatable, diseases; thus lumbar puncture and blood sugar determination are first. Serum blood levels of sodium, calcium, phosphorus, and magnesium should be done. Most physicians will order an EEG, but all the EEG will show is whether the neonate is or is not experiencing seizures.*

---

*See references 1, 3, 5, 6, 9, and 14.

In addition, the following subjective data should be included: a complete maternal family history with emphasis given to complications occurring during pregnancy as well as medications taken. Labor and delivery records should also be reviewed.

THERAPEUTIC MANAGEMENT

The object of care is to treat the underlying disease. The cause of seizures should be established prior to therapy if possible, since provision of pharmacological therapy may alter important symptoms. Phenobarbital alone can mask hypocalcemia, a known cause. Supportive care should include oxygen, fluids, and measures to maintain temperature. Pharmacological management of seizures requires rapid achievement of therapeutic blood levels and maintenance of desired levels to avoid cerebral damage.

Table 23-1 reflects selected characteristics of the pharmacological management of seizures of nonmetabolic etiology,[20] and the list below shows those of metabolic etiology.

Metabolic etiology of neonatal seizures and treatment

Etiology	Treatment
Hypocalcemia	10% calcium gluconate, 2 ml/kg diluted with water IV (do not mix with sodium bicarbonate)
Hypomagnesemia	50% magnesium sulfate, 0.2 ml/kg IM
Hypoglycemia	50% dextrose
Hyponatremia	Sodium chloride
Pyridoxine	Vitamin B_6
Phenylketonuria	Diet
Maple syrup urine disease	Diet
Infections	Organism-specific antibiotics

Protocol

Problem □ Identify, monitor, and manage neonatal seizures

GOAL: To prevent complications and promote family-infant attachment

DIAGNOSTIC

1. Complete prenatal, labor and delivery, and postnatal history:
   a. If infant is transferred to a special care nursery, the referring hospital should make sure the baby's records are complete and a copy is sent along with him.
   b. If records are inadequate or missing, the physician and/or nurse should contact the referring hospital for missing data.
2. Complete physical examination.
3. Check temperature, pulse, respirations, and blood pressure.
   Rationale: To establish baseline data or note abnormalities and because some drugs cause hypotension and need a baseline blood pressure
4. Use Dextrostix.
5. Check admitting CBC with electrolytes.
6. Observe infant's movements.
7. Distinguish between jitteriness and/or seizure activity.
8. Notify physician of suspected seizure activity.
9. Keep seizure record at bedside. Record the data, time, length of seizure, activity, description of seizure activity, and patient's status pre- and postseizure. Recognizable seizure activity includes the following:
   a. Tonic-clonic movement
   b. Tonic extension of limb or body
   c. Myoclonic jerk
   d. Clonic movement of one extremity
   e. Limpness
   f. Apnea or transient alteration of respiratory rate
   g. Tremors
   h. Vasomotor changes (pallor, mottling)
   i. Irregular eye movements (blinking, nystagmus, jerking, sudden opening)
   j. Facial twitching
   k. Chewing, sucking
   l. Abnormal cry
10. Laboratory work should be performed.
    a. Urinalysis
    b. CBC
    c. Fractionated bilirubin
    d. Electrolytes (serum)
    e. Calcium (serum)
    f. Dextrostix or serum glucose
    g. Alkaline phosphatose
    h. <p
    i. Blood culture if temperature increases
11. Use monitors with alarms:
    a. Cardiac
    b. Apnea
12. Perform transillumination of skull.

THERAPEUTIC

1. Maintain open airway.
2. Monitor vital signs—temperature, pulse, respirations, and blood pressure every 2 hours.
3. Give medications on time.
4. Give oxygen if necessary.
5. AMBU bag at bedside.
6. NPO.
7. Maintain patent IV.
8. Monitor respiration, heart rate, and blood pressure with apnea, cardiac, and blood pressure monitors.
9. Monitor oxygen if conditions warrant it.
10. Continue to monitor and record any seizure activity.
11. Note patient's level of consciousness.
12. Provide sufficient nutrients to meet caloric needs.
13. Feed in upright position and observe for the following:
    a. Vomiting
    b. Abdominal distention
    c. Infant's interest in feeding, ability to suck, and if infant tires easily
14. Keep upright ½ hour after all feedings.
15. Maintain infant's temperature between 36° and 37° C.

16. Provide for the developmental needs of the infant.
    a. Place bright-colored toys in crib or isolette.
    b. Talk gently and quietly while caring for infant.
    c. Encourage parents to visit.

EDUCATIONAL

1. Help parents understand the nature of the disease.
2. Help parents understand the treatment involved.
3. Help parents understand and accept their emotional reactions to their baby's disease.
4. Elicit areas of concern or needs for knowledge from parents concerning their baby.
5. Help parents understand the need for and function of equipment.
6. Identify for parents personnel caring for their baby.
7. Orient the parents to the unit and hospital.
8. Help parents understand the need for parenting activities.
9. Help parents understand the long-term effects of the disease process.
10. Help parents understand the long-term effects of the pharmacological agents involved.
11. Instruct parents on the whys, whens, and hows of giving the pharmacological agents.
12. Familiarize parents with resource personnel and services available.

REFERENCES

1. Avery, G. B., editor: Neonatology: pathophysiology and management of the newborn, Philadelphia, 1975, J. B. Lippincott Co.
2. Bergersen, B. L.: Pharmacology in nursing, ed. 14, St. Louis, 1979, The C. V. Mosby Co.
3. Boros, S. J., and Nystrom, J.: Neonatal seizures: quality of survival, Minnesota Med. **60:**99, 1977.
4. Freeman, J. M.: Neonatal seizures—diagnosis and management, J. Pediatr. **77:**701, 1970.
5. Herzlinger, R. A., Kandall, S. R., and Vaughan, H. G., Jr.: Neonatal seizures associated with narcotic withdrawal, J. Pediatr. **91:**638, 1977.
6. Hopkins, J. J.: Seizures in the first week of life: a study of aetiological factors, Med. J. Aust. **2:**647, 1972.
7. Jalling, B.: Plasma concentrations of phenobarbital in the treatment of seizures in newborns, Acta Paediatr. Scand. **64:**514, 1975.
8. Jalling, B., Borius, L. O., Kallberg, N., and Agurell, S.: Disappearance from the newborn of circulating prenatally administered phenobarbital, Eur. J. Clin. Pharmacol. **6:**234, 1973.
9. Klaus, M. H., and Fanaroff, A. A.: Care of the high-risk neonate, Philadelphia, 1973, W. B. Saunders Co.
10. Lambrosos, C. T.: Treatment of status epilepticus with diazepam, Neurology **16:**629, 1966.
11. Neuman, L. L., and Cohen, S. N.: The neonatal narcotic withdrawal syndrome: a therapeutic challenge, Clin. Perinatol. **2:**99, 1975.
12. Painter, M. J., Pippenger, C., MacDonald, H., and Pitlick, W.: Phenobarbital and diphenylhydantoin levels in neonates with seizures, J. Pediatr. **92:**315, 1978.
13. Pitlick, W., Painter, M., and Pippenger, C.: Phenobarbital pharmacokinetics in neonates, Clin. Pharmacol. Ther. **23:**346, 1978.
14. Rose, A. L., and Lombroso, C. T.: Neonatal seizure states: a study of clinical, pathological, and electroencephalographic features in 137 full-term babies with a long-term follow-up, Pediatrics **45:**404, 1970.
15. Schwartz, J. F.: Neonatal convulsions: pathogenesis, diagnotic evaluation, treatment, and prognosis, Clin. Pediatr. **4:**595, 1965.
16. Seay, A. R., and Bray, P.: Significance of seizures in infants weighing less than 2,500 grams, Arch. Neurol. **34:**381, 1977.
17. Volpe, J.: Neonatal seizures, N. Engl. J. Med. **289:**413, 1973.

Chapter 24

Congenital hydrocephalus

Lorraine Dayton and Rosanne Harrigan Perez

Hydrocephalus, or excessive accumulation of cerebrospinal fluid (CSF) in the ventricles of the brain with consequent enlargement of the cranium, occurs in about 1 in 2000 fetuses, accounting for about 12% of all severe malformations found at birth.[13,28] Hydrocephalus is due to inadequate absorption of CSF, with a corresponding increase of fluid under pressure within the intracranial cavity, or to obstruction within the ventricular system.[22] Hydrocephalus is a pathological condition with many variations. The amount of CSF, however, is always increased and the CSF pathways are always dilated.[4]

Hydrocephalus is the most common cause of an excessive rate of head growth in the neonatal period. Developmental malformations (aqueductal stenosis, the Arnold-Chiari malformation, the Dandy-Walker syndrome, and other dysplastic lesions) may account for the majority of cases.[19] Hydrocephalus is not of itself a disease, rather it is the end result of a number of disease processes that produce an accumulation of CSF.[17] Normally, there is a delicate balance between the rate of formation and the absorption of CSF. The entire volume is absorbed and replaced every 12 to 24 hours. In hydrocephalus this balance is disturbed.[5]

PATHOPHYSIOLOGY OF HYDROCEPHALUS

CSF is formed in all ventricles by the choroid plexus and by filtration from capillaries; it flows out of the fourth ventricle into the subarachnoid space and reenters the blood via the arachnoic villi that project into the major aural sinuses.[10] It then flows along the tissue spaces of the sheaths of all the cranial and spinal nerves and is taken up by the vascular system. Normally the amount absorbed equals the amount secreted.[22] Interference with this pathway at any point may produce an increase in CSF pressure, enlargement of the ventricles at the expense of the surrounding brain, and enlargement of the cranium.[10]

There are two types of hydrocephalus—communicating and noncommunicating—which may be either congenital or acquired. In communicating hydrocephalus, the CSF can flow through the ventricular system around the spinal cord, but it is not reabsorbed from the cerebral subarachnoid space. In noncommunicating hydrocephalus the circulation of fluid is blocked somewhere within the ventricular system.[4] Congenital hydrocephalus is most frequently of the obstructive or noncommunicating type.[5]

The cerebral aqueduct is the most common site of intraventricular obstruction of CSF flow, evidently because it is the longest and narrowest passage and, perhaps, also because there is no choroid plexus in it. In congenital obstruction, the lumen of the aqueduct is either absent or greatly malformed and replaced by multiple tenuous channels in irregular disposition. Stenosis of the aqueduct results in dilatation of the lateral and third ventricles, while the fourth ventricle and cerebellum are of normal size or are compressed by the expansion of the hemispheres in the supratentorial compartment. The onset of hydrocephalus depends on the nature of the disease process and on the degree to which the aqueduct is obstructed. Congenital atresia induces progressive hydrocephalus in utero or shortly after birth.[16]

Stenosis of the aqueduct occurs as a familial, sex-linked trait affecting males only but being transmitted by unaffected females. This disease accounts for only a small fraction of all cases of aqueductal obstruction.[16] The most common is Bickers-Adams-Edwards syndrome.[11] Congenital atresia or stenosis of the aqueduct also may occur as the only cerebral lesion, or it may coexist with other deformities, most often with the Arnold-Chiari malformation or with hydranencephaly.[16]

A large number of teratogenic agents are known to induce hydrocephalus in experimental animals, but a precise mode of action has been defined for only a few. Congenital stenosis of the aqueduct was induced in rats born to mothers fed with a diet deficient in vitamin B_{12} or folic acid. Stenosis of the aqueduct is also induced in rats by subcutaneous injection of trypan blue into the mothers during early gestation.[16] With prenatal zinc deficiency experiments, congenital hydrocephalus was frequently encountered.[1] Fetal infection with myxovirus localizes selectively in the ependyma, inducing necrosis of ependymal cells and subsequent congenital stenosis of the aqueduct in the absence of residual inflammatory changes. Congenital stenosis of the aqueduct has also been observed as a hereditary trait in mice. These data show that a variety of nutritional, infectious, or hereditary factors can induce aqueductal stenosis during fetal life, but they do not allow for definite conclusions as to the etiological factors operative in man.[16]

Aqueductal stenosis is by far the most common isolated congenital defect producing hydrocephalus. The two other most common causes of congenital hydrocephalus are Arnold-Chiari malformation and the Dandy-Walker syndrome. In the Arnold-Chiari malformation, usually associated with myelomeningocele, the displacement of the medulla and cerebellar tonsils into the cervical spinal canal usually prevents the normal flow of fluid from the fourth ventricle into the subarachnoid space. In the Dandy-Walker syndrome, there is a cystic expansion of the fourth ventricle that may be secondary to failure of development of the normal ventricular foramina of Luschka and Dagendie.[10]

Other less frequent congenital causes of hydrocephalus include glial webs at the junction of the aqueduct and fourth ventricle, arachnoid cysts in the posterior fossa, and aneurysm of the great vein of Galen. Vein of Galen aneurysms are the result of abnormal communications of the vein with one or more cerebral arteries. Enlargement of the vein resulting from the abnormally high intravascular pressure produces hydrocephalus by obstructing the underlying posterior third ventricle and the proximal portion of the aqueduct.[10]

There is also a small group of infants who have idiopathic hydrocephalus at birth in which the infant has no history of infection, contact with teratogenic agents, or any obvious anatomical anomaly.[31] In all forms of congenital hydrocephalus, the occurrence of impressive ventricular dilatation prior to the development of rapid head growth and signs of increased intracranial pressure must relate to the developmental state of the cerebrum in the neonatal period. The most relevant features are the paucity of myelin and relative excess of water in the cerebral white matter. In hydrocephalus the white matter is encroached on and the gray matter relatively spared. Apparently in the human newborn less force is required to compress the cerebral white matter than to overcome the restrictions of the dura and skull.[29]

The central spinal canal in hydrocephalus is not an adynamic space, rather it is an active space that responds to hydrodynamic events in the brain's ventricular system.[19] Structural changes in the brain consist of flattening and tears in the ependymal lining, vacuolation in the periventricular white matter, and increase in the periventricular water content, the latter with no apparent loss in the cellular elements of the brain.[8]

The recognition of hydrocephalus dates back to ancient times, but no insights were obtained into the pathogenesis of the disease until the physiology of flow of CSF was understood.[16] What is most important is that infantile hydrocephalus, whether congenital in origin or acquired, does not become manifest and is not ordinarily diagnosed in the majority of affected infants until some time after birth.

PRENATAL DIAGNOSIS OF HYDROCEPHALUS

Since the treatment of hydrocephalus is usually straightforward, early diagnosis is the key to success. In vertex presentations, abdominal palpation reveals a broad, firm mass above the symphysis; the thickness of the abdominal wall usually prevents detection of the thin, elastic, hydrocephalic cranium. The high head forces the body of the infant upward with the result that the fetal heart is often loudest above the umbilicus, a circumstance not infrequently leading to suspicion of a breech presentation. Vaginally, the broader dome of the head feels tense, but more careful palpation may reveal the very large fontanelles, the wide suture lines, and the indentable, thin cranium characteristic of hydrocephalus. Since the distended cranium is too large to enter the pelvis, breech presentations are fairly common, occurring in about one third of such cases. Whatever the presentation, gross cephalopelvic disproportion is the rule and serious dystocia the usual consequence.[28]

There is a high association of gross fetal abnormalities, especially hydrocephalus, in hydramnios, the accumulation of amniotic fluid in excess of 2000 ml. Marked hydramnios may cause severe maternal distress because of pressure of the grossly enlarged uterus on the diaphragm, the venous return from the lower extremities, or the gastrointestinal tract. Premature labor frequently intervenes.[26]

With advances in technology, the possibility for greater fetal diagnostic capability is becoming significant. Recent refinement in ultrasonic encephalography make possible intrauterine detection of ventricular enlargement and more precise diagnosis of hydrocephalus. This advance may increase the early diagnosis of obstructive hydrocephalus and deepen the obstetrical management dilemma because in many instances fetuses found to have hydrocephalus at or near birth are delivered via destructive craniotomy.[12]

A diagnosis of fetal hydrocephalus has been made even before viability; the diagnosis was made by a discrepancy between the sonographic fetal head size, the uterine size by both clinical and sonographic examination, and x-ray films. This report demonstrates the importance of correlating clinical history and findings with the ultrasonic scan. In this case the parents elected early termination of the pregnancy.[15] Certainly the ultimate decision for management of perinatal hydrocephalus should be derived with full parental participation. In some circumstances, cesarean section may be indicated to maximize the opportunity for survival through subsequent early operative treatment. However, should circumstances dictate a vaginal delivery with cere-

bral decompression, useful information for counseling may be obtained if the aqueductal area is not destroyed.[12]

LABOR AND DELIVERY OF HYDROCEPHALIC FETUS

The delivery of a hydrocephalic fetus has usually been performed either by deflating the head during the labor transvaginally or by performing a cesarean section. Most often, the size of the hydrocephalic head must be reduced to allow passage of the head through the birth canal. With a cephalic presentation, as soon as the cervix is dilated somewhat (3 cm or so) the huge ventricles may be tapped transvaginally with a needle. With cesarean section, it is also desirable at times to remove CSF just before delivery of the fetal head to circumvent the need for a very large uterine incision. With a breech presentation, labor is allowed to progress, and the breech and trunk are delivered. With the head over the inlet and the face toward the mother's back, the needle is inserted transvaginally just below the anterior vaginal wall and into the aftercoming head through the widened suture line. If this transvaginal maneuver should fail, fluid may be withdrawn through a needle inserted transabdominally into the fetal head. The transabdominal approach to removal of CSF might also be used in case of a cephalic presentation before trying to stimulate labor with oxytocin.[28] Comparing this technique with transvaginal craniotomy, it is thought that the former presently has the great advantage of preventing the danger of uterine rupture during labor, since the latter cannot be performed before cervical dilatation has reached 4 to 5 cm.[12]

RADIOGRAPHICAL DIAGNOSIS OF HYDROCEPHALUS
Prenatal

In vertex presentations, roentgenography provides confirmation of hydrocephalus in the demonstration of a large globular head with a thin, sometimes scarcely visible, cranial outline. Hydrocephalus is somewhat more difficult to diagnose with a breech presentation, since the radiographical outline of a normal fetal head often appears enlarged to a degree suggestive of hydrocephalus. This is the consequence of the large fetal head lying more anterior and the divergence of x-rays inherent in diagnostic x-ray machines. Therefore in breech presentations, the diagnosis may not be considered until it is found that the head cannot be extracted. The mistake may be avoided by particular attention to the following criteria: (1) the face of the hydrocephalic infant is very small in relation to the large head; (2) the hydrocephalic cranium tends to be globular, whereas the normal head is ovoid; and (3) the shadow of the hydrocephalic cranium is often very thin or scarcely visible.[28] The difficulties inherent in radiological diagnosis may be avoided by the use of sonography. The marked difference between the size of the hydrocephalic head and the thorax is apparent in sonograms.

Neonatal

A ventriculogram, commonly called a "bubble study," is one of the most important tests that may be done to establish a diagnosis and cause of congenital hydrocephalus. X-ray films are taken with the baby in various positions. The air bubble, which rises as the baby's head is lowered, should reach the sacral subarachnoid space by the time the child is in a head-down position. If, for example, the bubble does not enter the fourth ventricle, one can assume that there is a block at the level of the aqueduct of Sylvius and that the baby has noncommunicating hydrocephalus.[4]

SIGNS AND SYMPTOMS OF HYDROCEPHALUS

Although enlargement of the head secondary to hydrocephalus may be apparent at or prior to birth, head circumference is often normal at birth even when there is CSF obstruction on a congenital basis. However, the anterior fontanelle in these infants is frequently very large, and palpation reveals increased tension.[10] Not infrequently, the head circumference exceeds 50 cm and sometimes reaches 80 cm. The volume of CSF is usually between 500 and 1500 ml, but as much as 5 liters may accumulate.[28]

In communicating hydrocephalus the increase in the size of the infant's head is due to an excessive amount of CSF. The fluid that is not absorbed in the subarachnoid space accumulates, compressing the brain and distending the cranial cavity. The sutures fail to close and the bones of the skull become thin. There is an excess of spinal fluid outside the brain. The convolutions of the brain are flattened

and atrophied. Usually, however, the pressure of the fluid does not enlarge the head as much as in noncommunicating hydrocephalus because the brain atrophies, and this increases the space the fluid may fill without enlargement of the skull. The fontanelles are tense and widened. The infant tends to be irritable and anorexic. In noncommunicating hydrocephalus, after birth an increase in the size of the head is noticeable. The fontanelles widen instead of narrowing and are tense. The infant becomes increasingly helpless and less able to raise his head. The neck muscles are underdeveloped from lack of use. Affect and normal response may be diminished.[22] Neurological signs include spasticity of legs and, to a lesser extent, of arms, ataxia, tremor, imbalance, and clumsiness of fine movements. Intellectual impairment is closely related to the degree of physical disability.[16]

The traditional clinical criteria, that is, split cranial sutures, bulging anterior fontanelle, and abnormally rapid head growth, may develop after a major degree of ventricular dilatation has already occurred.[29] Using ventriculography, Lorber[20,21] studied 172 infants with meningomyelocele or encephalocele, regardless of clinical impression of hydrocephalus, and found 55 infants with head circumference below the tenth percentile who had ventricular dilatation. There was an 80% incidence of hydrocephalus in the absence of clinical signs of increased intracranial pressure or enlarged head circumference. Schonenberg examined the skull x-ray films of infants with proven hydrocephalus and noted that 12 of 39 showed normal sutures.[30] These studies indicate that enlarging head circumference may be a late and insensitive indicator of hydrocephalus in certain infants.[30]

Nystagmus or convergent strabismus may be present. The eyes seem to be pushed downward and protrude slightly; this represented the typical "setting-sun" position with the sclera visible above the iris. This is caused by downward pressure on the orbit. Pressure on the sixth cranial nerve may cause internal rotation of the eyes.[19] The upper lids are retracted by the taut skin over the bulging forehead. The scalp is shiny and the veins are dilated.[18] The bridge of the nose may also be flat and broad in addition to the forehead having a bulging appearance.[6]

The infant's cry is shrill and high pitched, and the baby is irritable and restless.[6] As the head continues to enlarge, the baby will be lethargic and may vomit frequently. Convulsions may occur, and these infants have little resistance to infection.[22] If the hydrocephalus remains untreated, the chronic distention of the cerebral hemispheres inevitably induces tissue damage and hemispherical atrophy. The brunt of the atrophy is borne by the white matter.[16] Many complications, both prenatally and neonatally, may develop from the developing hydrocephalus.

COMPLICATIONS OF CONGENITAL HYDROCEPHALUS
Prenatal

Rupture of the uterus is probably the greatest prenatal danger and is the outcome of most untreated cases during labor and delivery. Hydrocephalus prediagnoses to rupture not only because of obvious disproportion but also because the great transverse diameter of the cranium overdistends the lower uterine segment. Rupture may occur before complete dilatation of the cervix.[28]

Neonatal

Many patients with hydrocephalus owe their survival to the development of commercially available implantable devices, but unfortunately the quality of life for these patients is frequently impaired and interrupted by failures of their shunt system.[7] The high frequency and the seriousness of complications resulting from any form of shunt treatment makes this otherwise excellent method of treatment of hydrocephalus an extremely hazardous procedure.[21] A major complication of shunt therapy for hydrocephalus is shunt dependence, which may be unavoidable as it is necessary to divert the CSF to prevent symptomatic elevation of intracranial pressure. This is the result of loss of all absorptive and compensatory mechanisms for handling CSF other than diversion via the shunt.[25] Blockages and infections of the shunt system frequently may threaten life, vision, and intelligence. Early shunting is particularly dangerous.[21] Infection is probably the greatest and most frustrating problem encountered. In addition to the usual signs and symptoms of central nervous system infection, swelling, redness, and tenderness along the shunt tract may develop. Infection is combatted with massive doses of antibiotics intravenously or directly into the ventricles. If infection persists, the shunt must be removed and

ventricular pressure kept at a normal level by temporary, external ventricular drainage. Once the ventricular system is free of infection, a new shunt can be inserted. Often, long-term antibiotic coverage is necessary after the baby's discharge.[3]

PROGNOSIS OF THE HYDROCEPHALIC INFANT

The prognosis for the infant with hydrocephalus treated by a shunting procedure is dependent on several factors including the degree of damage to the brain already present at the time of shunting, the presence of other malformations of the brain, and the amount of success in keeping the shunt functional.[10] If effective treatment is begun early, the baby's head may be relatively normal in size and his intellectual and motor development unimpaired. The outcome of treatment depends on the time it is begun, the success of the shunting procedures, good follow-up care, and the child's innate intellectual and motor abilities.[4] Since shunts have only been in use since the 1950's, long-term statistics are not available. However, with steady improvement in materials and techniques, life expectancy should gradually increase.[3]

When moderate hydrocephalus is treated, the cortex can rapidly reconstitute its normal thickness, and there may be no neurological or intellectual deficits. Only when the cortical mantle is less than 0.5 cm in thickness is it correlated with poor intellectual outcome.[2] Factors responsible for the poor prognosis in infants with extreme hydrocephalus manifested at birth include severity of the neural malformation itself, the potentially irreversible pressure effects of abnormal ventricular distention, the high rate of infection, and the greater chance of intracranial birth injury to the large head. Weller and Shulman have postulated that progressive hydrocephalus with a rising CSF pressure may result in failure of brain growth and mental retardation unless ventricular drainage is instituted prior to the time neural damage is irreversible.[24]

The long-range prognosis of congenital hydrocephalic infants is conflicting in the literature to say the least. Lawrence and Coates found that the hydrocephalus apparently had arrested spontaneously in 18 of 182 unoperated patients (46%) who were alive over a 20-year period.[24] Of the survivors with arrested hydrocephalus, 73% were educable and 38% had IQ scores in the normal range.[24] Yashon reported spontaneous arrest of hydrocephalus and survival without surgical treatment in 31 of 58 patients (53%), and 10 of the living patients seemed to be functioning at nearly normal levels.[24] With current methods of surgical treatment by ventricular diversion through one-way valves, infantile hydrocephalus can be relieved with an extended survival of 60% to 80%, with 50% to 84% of the survivors having good intelligence. In contrast, among the 34 patients with overt hydrocephalus at birth treated by similar surgical procedures at the Indiana University Medical Center, only 44% have survived and one third have normal intelligence.[24] The surgical results in extremely hydrocephalic infants with myelomeningoceles closely parallel the findings of Lorber[20,21] in 36 similar cases with 14 survivors, 3 of whom have normal intelligence. Virtually all of the cases treated nonsurgically died early or later in childhood.[24]

Attempts to correlate frontal mantle thickness and future intellectual potential have had mixed results. Some authors conclude that no good correlation exists, citing examples of superior intellectual development despite extreme hydrocephalus and a mantle 3 mm thick. Other workers have found a near normal distribution of intelligence in patients with hydrocephalus whose frontal mantles measure more than 2.8 cm in thickness.[25]

Indeed, the obstetrical experience with infants born obviously hydrocephalic has been notably poor. In a 20-year review to 1952, Feeney and Barry found that only 10 of 93 live-born hydrocephalic infants survived long enough for corrective surgery. Nearly half to two thirds of the affected fetuses in these surveys were stillborn.[24] The further prognosis for these infants is unpredictable.

TREATMENT OF THE HYDROCEPHALIC INFANT IN THE NURSERY

If it is decided that the infant is to be treated, two methods have been described regularly in the literature. Hydrocephalus is most commonly treated with a shunting procedure, the purpose of which is to reduce the volume of the ventricular system to normal and completely restore the attenuated cortical mantle.[9] Shunting of CSF from the ventricular system is into the bloodstream, peritoneum, or pleural space.[10] The most common shunts are the ventriculoatrial and the ventriculoperitoneal. Ventricular shunts are necessary in treating noncommunicating hydrocephalus and may be used for communicating hydrocephalus. Lumbar shunts are rarely done now as they may cause spinal nerve root compression with resultant loss of function.[4] Most important, ventricular shunting operations should be performed on infants with overt hydrocephalus manifested at birth to afford them a chance for survival and psychomotor development.[24]

In suitable cases, intermittent cranial compression by means of an elastic bandage or a helmet with an inflatable innerlining may be effective.[9] Compressive cranial wrapping has been used in America as an alternative to the shunt procedure for the treatment of mild to moderate hydrocephalus. Compressive cranial wrapping can stop hydrocephalus within 6 months if applied from an early stage without the risks of septicemia, subacute ventriculitis, and pulmonary thromboses common with shunting procedures. Animal experiments suggest that in neonatal hydrocephalus the skull expands because the sutures are lax and unable to resist the slightly raised intracranial pressure. If the bones of the cranial vault are supported by external pressure, the ventricular CSF pressure rises slightly to the point at which it may open a stenosis or increase transventricular absorption of CSF. In addition, the increased pressure may reduce production of CSF by the choroid plexuses. The use of an elastic cap has the advantages of simplicity, ease of application, and reproducibility of pressure from one application to the next. Also, the tension can be readily varied to maintain head growth at the norm by varying the number of layers.[27]

Occasionally positive results in treating hydrocephalus have been achieved by using acetazolamide (Diamox) and more recently by using isosorbide (Hydronol). These medications reduce intercranial pressure in infants whose hydrocephalus is considered too advanced for surgical therapy. Infants with more residual brain mass tend to respond better, suggesting that a shift of extraventricular intracerebral fluid is more critical than changes in the large ventricular fluid pool. In England, Lorber-Sheffield used isosorbide treatment on 60 hydrocephalic infants, which resulted in success in 52%, partial success in 15%, and failure in 33%.[20,21] It is not yet possible to present or compare long-term results. It is evident that severe cases of hydrocephalus, in which the cerebral mantle is less than 15 mm, are not likely to respond well to isosorbide. Isosorbide does not eliminate the need for surgery. Nevertheless, it provides a means of reducing the number who would otherwise become shunt dependent for life and who constantly run the risk of dying from the complications of shunt therapy.[20]

Some infants are not candidates for any of the above therapies because of the severity of the condition or the wishes of the parents not to have any active measures taken. In these cases, only supportive medical and nursing treatment is employed. The routine nursing care consists of frequently turning the patient to prevent respiratory complications and decubitus ulcers from developing. Tincture of benzoin or a silicone spray applied to sides of the head where the bones appear most prominent tends to keep the skin from breaking down. The tendency to vomit is typical of these patients, and every consideration should be given to measures that will decrease this tendency such as time of feeding and holding for feeding; despite their huge heads, these infants can be held for feeding with their head supported on an adult-sized pillow.[23]

If surgery is the treatment of choice, postoperatively, in addition to receiving routine care, the infant should be observed for signs of intracranial pressure, which would indicate that the valve is not functioning. If an infant is unusually irritable, the intracranial pressure may be rising. the infant off the operative site also makes for more comfort, and this position helps prevent skin breakdown over the valve, especially for babies with enlarged, heavy heads. In addition, the infant is kept flat for 2 to 4 days to prevent formation of a subdural hematoma, which could result from a too rapid loss of fluid.[3]

Nursing staff must keep an exact record of the number and amount of voidings, since the voidings are bound to increase in number; this, together with excessive loss of spinal fluid, results

in extra loss of sodium chloride. Salt must be added to the diet to make up for this loss.[23] Normal diet can be resumed as soon after surgery as the infant can tolerate it. The infant usually can be put back on the formula on the first postoperative day and should be fed slowly and carefully to prevent aspiration.[3] The symptoms of dehydration to be watched for specifically are sunken fontanelles and poor skin turgor.[23]

Whatever the treatment of choice, the baby's head circumference should be measured daily. In the interest of accuracy, it is better if the same person does the measurement each time, using the same tape measure.[5]

Nurses do not find it difficult to understand the anxiety and apprehension parents feel if this condition is present in their infant, but they may feel quite helpless in trying to give them support. The nurse's acceptance of the infant with tender care and concern for the infant's welfare helps convey warmth of feeling. The nurse's matter-of-fact acceptance of the infant's handicap, as well as the treatment of the infant as a baby with normal needs, helps put the situation on a more realistic basis. Arrangements should be made to give much of the normal, daily care at times when parents are able to be present. They need to learn how to hold and handle the baby in as normal a manner as possible. Undoubtedly, they need much encouragement. A mother should be encouraged to help with her infant's care when there are others present to give her support. She can be encouraged to feel the valve in the shunting device, for example, if the infant has been treated, and to develop an understanding of its function.[5]

Every infant has the need and the right to be picked up, loved, and held in a loving, comforting manner. When any infant has suffered a painful or uncomfortable experience, the need for emotional support becomes much greater.[5]

CONCLUSION

Marked hydrocephalus of prenatal origin occurs in approximately 0.2% of all deliveries.[11] The ultimate decision for management of perinatal hydrocephalus should be derived with full parental participation. In some circumstances, cesarean section may be indicated to maximize the opportunity for survival through subsequent early operative treatment. However, circumstances may dictate a vaginal delivery with cerebral decompression, with subsequent demise of the infant; counseling information for the parents as to the cause of the hydrocephalus must be investigated in an orderly fashion. Whatever the outcome, births of this type are a terrible tragedy for all concerned; the hopes and the dreams of 9 months or perhaps a lifetime may lie shattered. This is a situation in which the nurse will be called on to exercise nursing skill to the utmost, not only during labor but also after the delivery, and particularly if there is an obvious abnormality or if fetal demise occurs.

Protocols

Problem □ Presence of sequelae that may be indicative of fetal hydrocephalus

GOAL: To recognize signs and symptoms of fetal hydrocephalus early
Rationale: To decrease the risk of maternal complications and/or poor fetal outcome

DIAGNOSTIC

1. Review family and maternal history.
   Rationale: To assess history for any possible causes of hydrocephalus, including either exposure to teratogenic agents or previous family history of the disorder
2. Serial determination of fundal heights and relationship of these measurements to appropriate fundal heights for estimated gestation are necessary.
   Rationale: To be aware that there is a high association of gross fetal abnormalities, especially hydrocephalus, with hydramnios, which manifests itself as larger than normal fundal heights
3. Frequent abdominal palpations for determination of fetal position and presence of enlarged fetal head should be done.
   Rationale: To ckeck for large fetal head, which may be too large to enter pelvis, thus making breech presentations very common
4. Frequent determination of position of fetal heart tones should be done.
   Rationale: To be aware that a large, high fetal heart is often loudest above the umbilicus in both vertex and breech presentations
5. Perform sonographic examination when indicated.
   Rationale: To detect the marked difference between the size of the fetal head and the thorax
6. Perform roentgenographic examination when sonography is unavailable.
   Rationale: To check for demonstration of a large globular head with a thin, sometimes scarcely visible cranial outline, which provides confirmation of fetal hydrocephalus
7. Observe mother closely for signs of premature labor and/or premature rupture of the fetal membranes.
   Rationale: To be aware that premature labor and/or premature rupture of the fetal membranes is common because of the overdistention of the uterus

THERAPEUTIC

1. Inform a physician of any abnormalities noted in diagnostic procedures.
   Rationale: To initiate prompt medical management if indicated either by further assessments or termination of the pregnancy
2. Notify nursery of possible hydrocephalic infant.
   Rationale: To have nursery personnel and equipment prepared for a possibly distressed infant
3. Restriction of activities or bed rest for comfort of the mother may be indicated.
   Rationale: To be aware that abdominal pain, dyspnea, and/or difficulty in ambulation may be present because of the enlarged uterus

4. Removal of some of the amniotic fluid may be indicated if the hydramnios is marked.
   Rationale: To treat symptomatic hydramnios

EDUCATIONAL

1. Provide in-service educational programs for the prenatal nursing personnal concerning the diagnosis and management of women whose pregnancies may be complicated by fetal hydrocephalus.
   Rationale: To be aware that nurses are the ones who are responsible for direct patient care, and therefore they are in the position of detecting early warning signs of the presence of congenital hydrocephalus and/or maternal complications

2. Provide patient with an explanation, appropriate to her educational level, of all procedures and medical treatments.
   Rationale: To decrease the patient's anxiety level, thereby enabling her to better cope with the situation at hand

3. Provide the parents with possible long-term sequelae of the birth of an infant with congenital hydrocephalus.
   Rationale: To ensure that the ultimate decision for management of perinatal hydrocephalus, with the most important aspect being the method of termination of pregnancy, should be derived with full parental participation

Problem □ Labor and delivery of infant with congenital hydrocephalus

GOAL: To minimize both infant morbidity or mortality and maternal complications during labor and delivery
Rationale: To provide optimal outcome for both mother and infant

DIAGNOSTIC

1. Observe mother closely for signs of uterine dysfunction such as lack of progress of cervical dilatation or fetal distress.
   Rationale: To be aware that overdistention of the uterus may result in uterine atony

2. Observe for signs of prolapsed cord such as fetal distress.
   Rationale: To be aware that the incidence of prolapsed cord is greatly increased over the general population owing to the increased

rate of breech presentations and the added disproportion of fetal head to thorax

3. Observe for signs of placental abruption such as vaginal bleeding, hypertonic uterus, uterine tenderness, absence of fetal heart tones, and evidence of maternal hypovolemia.[28]
   Rationale: To be aware that placental abruption is more common in these patients following the rupture of membranes because of the escape of massive quantities of amniotic fluid and the decreased pressure in the uterus beneath the placenta[28]

4. Observe for signs of cephalopelvic disproportion such as failure of the labor to progress and fetal distress.
   Rationale: To be aware that abnormal presentations with failure of the huge head of the hydrocephalic infant to pass through the birth canal are common

5. Observe for signs of uterine rupture such as sharp, shooting pain in the abdomen and cessation of uterine contractions.[28]
   Rationale: To be aware that when the disproportion between the head and the pelvis is so pronounced that engagement and descent do not occur, the lower uterine segment becomes increasingly stretched, and the danger of rupture becomes imminent[28]

6. Institute continuous fetal heart monitoring.
   Rationale: To determine any stress factors that may endanger fetal or infant survival rate (Changes in fetal heart rate pattern are indicators of fetal distress.)

THERAPEUTIC

1. Inform the physician of any abnormalities noted in labor patterns or fetal heart rates.
   Rationale: To ensure prompt medical management if indicated either by further assessment or delivery

2. Have personnel in the labor and delivery rooms who are trained in immediate management of the high-risk pregnancy.
   Rationale: To provide high-quality care to the mother and infant

3. Notify the nursery of the possible admission of a hydrocephalic infant.
   Rationale: To have nursery personnel and equipment prepared for a possibly distressed infant

4. Perform cesarean section when cephalopelvic disproportion or fetal distress is present.

   Rationale: To maximize the opportunity for infant survival and to minimize the possibility of maternal complications

5. Remove CSF prior to delivery when indicated either by transabdominal or transvaginal method.

   Rationale: To circumvent the need for a very large uterine incision during cesarean section; to lessen the possibility of uterine rupture during labor owing to the presence of a huge fetal head, and to reduce the size of the hydrocephalic head; allowing passage of the head through the birth canal

6. Based on an assessment of the infant's condition, initiation of emergency care may be deemed necessary.

   Rationale: To support and/or maintain adequate cardiopulmonary functioning and to correct associated metabolic disturbances that might occur in such infants

7. When heart rate and respiratory status are stable, transfer the infant to a neonatal intensive care unit.

   Rationale: To provide the infant with additional observation, support, and interventions that may be necessary to provide for growth and development at the optimal level possible for that infant

EDUCATIONAL

1. Personnel who are giving care to this high-risk family unit must be trained in physiology and immediate management of the high-risk unit.

   Rationale: To provide immediate quality care to the high-risk mother and infant

2. Provide emotional and physical support to the mother and her family.

   Rationale: To keep the mother and family informed of what is being done for their infant, which helps to decrease their anxiety levels and reduces the chances of their fantasizing unrealistic situations or appearance of the infant

Problem □ Mother delivering an infant with congenital hydrocephalus

GOAL: To maintain optimal physiological functioning and emotional support to the postpartum mother of a hydrocephalic infant

Rationale: To promote optimal well-being of the mother

DIAGNOSTIC

1. Observe mother for signs and symptoms of postpartum hemorrhage.

   Rationale: To be aware that hemorrhage may be the result of the uterine atony caused by overdistention[28]

2. Observe the mother for signs of infection, most notably fever.

   Rationale: To be aware that premature rupture of membranes, prolonged labor, and cesarean section all predispose this mother to infection

3. Observe family unit for dysfunction in adaptation to the hydrocephalic infant.

   Rationale: To be aware that births of this type are a terrible tragedy for all concerned and that a state of emotional shock may prevail, in which disbelief, noncomprehension and sometimes denial prevail

THERAPEUTIC

1. Allow time for the family unit to express their feelings about the condition of the infant and the prognosis.

   Rationale: To help the parents explore their feelings and methods of coping with the family crisis

2. Inform the parents of the possibility of bearing a subsequent infant with hydrocephalus (genetic counseling).

   Rationale: To be aware that it has been estimated that 2% of all cases of uncomplicated hydrocephalus are X-linked (The empirical risk in these sporadic cases has been calculated to be 0.5% to 1.0%. In the X-linked form, if there have been other affected brothers and/or male maternal relatives, a 25% recurrence risk exists for each subsequent pregnancy, and a 50% risk exists that any subsequent male will be affected. In the autosomal recessive form, the chance for the mother to be a carrier of the gene is small, but the recurrence risk may be as high as 25% in all future pregnancies.[12])

EDUCATIONAL

1. Education must be provided to the nursing staff caring for high-risk families in crisis by in-service education programs, provision of current pertinent literature, and/or on-the-job training.

   Rationale: To provide the nurse with the tools necessary for early recognition and prompt treatment of the family unit during this period of crisis

2. Educate each parent as to how to recognize and cope with the crisis mechanisms in play in the other parent and in other family members.

   Rationale: To recognize that crisis mechanisms are operating will go a long way in helping the family understand one another's reactions and making them better prepared to cope with the situation at hand

Problem □ Presence of an infant with congenital hydrocephalus

GOAL: To recognize signs or symptoms of congenital hydrocephalus early, to maintain optimal physiological functioning of the infant, and to enhance the infant's ability to cope effectively with the pathophysiological processes of hydrocephalus
Rationale: To promote optimal physical well-being of the infant

DIAGNOSTIC

1. Ventriculogram

   Rationale: To determine the presence of obstruction in the ventricular system as the cause of hydrocephalus

2. Observe the infant for signs or symptoms of increasing hydrocephalus including:
   a. Enlargement of the head circumference
   b. Widening of sutures
   c. Fontanelles wide and tense
   d. Anorexia
   e. Irritability
   f. "Setting-sun" eyes
   g. Lethargy
   h. Shrill and high-pitched cry
   i. Bradycardia
   j. Apnea
   k. Convulsions

   Rationale: To recognize early signs and symptoms that may lead to the diagnosis of hydrocephalus

3. Obtain a complete prenatal and intrapartum history of mother and infant.

   Rationale: To obtain a data base as to the infant's condition, possible cause of the disorder, and treatments received prior to admission to the nursery

4. Continuously assess by observation, auscultation, palpation, and percussion:
   a. Respiratory status
   b. Cardiac function
   c. Renal function
   d. Central nervous system function
   e. Metabolic balance
   f. Gastrointestinal tract function

   Rationale: To recognize early complications or other congenital malformations that may further compromise the sick infant

5. Complete neurological examination of the infant.

   Rationale: To determine the physiological adaption to the extrauterine environment

6. If surgical treatment is used, observe infant for signs of increased intracranial pressure such as unusual irritability, vomiting, tense fontanelles, lethargy, bradycardia, and apnea.

   Rationale: To indicate that the valve in the shunt system is not functioning

7. If surgical treatment is used, observe the infant for signs of dehydration such as sunken fontanelles and poor skin turgor.

   Rationale: To be aware that the excessive loss of spinal fluid through the shunting system results in extra loss of sodium chloride, which could result in dehydration

8. If surgical treatment is used, observe the infant for signs of infection such as fever, irritability, redness along shunt or suture line, and vomiting.

   Rationale: To be aware that bacteria may be easily introduced into the sterile ventricular system during surgery, and the infant's debilitated condition may further enhance the susceptibility to develop an infection

THERAPEUTIC

1. Surgical shunting procedure.

   Rationale: To remove CSF from the ventricular system where it can be reabsorbed by the bloodstream, peritoneum, or pleural space will relieve intracranial pressure and in turn prevent further damage of brain tissue and maintain optimal survival for the infant

2. Compression cranial wrapping.

Rationale: To open a stenosis or increase transventricular absorption of CSF along with reducing production of CSF by the choroid plexuses[27]

3. Administer drugs such as acetazolamide (Diamox) and isosorbide when appropriate.

Rationale: To use hyperosmotic agents that "pull" CSF fluid from the ventricular system to reduce intracranial pressure in infants whose hydrocephalus is considered too advanced for other methods of therapy and as temporary treatment until surgical treatment can be completed

4. Frequently turn the infant.

Rationale: To prevent decubitus ulcers from developing over areas where constant pressure occurs since the infant often cannot turn the huge head

5. Position infant on side or abdomen.

Rationale: To avoid aspiration of vomitus since the infant is often unable to move the huge head and tends to vomit frequently because of increased intracranial pressure

6. Feed small, frequent feedings.

Rationale: To avoid overdistending the stomach (The rapid loss of fluid postoperatively will increase the infant's fluid requirement, and the healing of the surgical incision requires a greater protein intake.)

7. Measure head circumference daily.

Rationale: To check for enlarging head circumference, which is a cardinal sign of increasing hydrocephalus in neonates.

8. Pickup and hold the infant as much as possible. Placing the large head on an adult pillow may aid in this.

Rationale: To be aware that every infant has the need and the right to be picked up, loved, and held in a loving, comforting manner (A human infant must have caring human contact to survive and grow.)

9. Reemphasize and repeat physician's explanation of the cause, present condition, treatment, and probable prognosis of the infant.

Rationale: To help the family unit arrive at a realistic perception of the infant and the events around the crisis situation

10. Encourage the family unit to visit, touch, and assist in the care of the infant when appropriate. Be available to assist the family unit when they visit, and help the family unit keep in touch with the infant until his discharge.

Rationale: To facilitate early, parent-child contact to provide an optimal environment for promotion of parent-infant bonding

EDUCATIONAL

1. Education must be provided to the nursing staff caring for sick infants by in-service education programs, provision of current pertinent literature, and/or on-the-job training.

Rationale: To provide the nurse with the tools necessary for early recognition and prompt treatment of complications in these infants and to facilitate the nurse's recognition of the needs of the family unit during this period of crisis

2. Educate parents as to possible prognosis of the infant.

Rationale: To give the parents an appropriate data base for decision as to placement of the infant either at home, medical foster care, or in an institution

3. Educate parents as to possible complications of hydrocephalus.

Rationale: To give the parents an appropriate data base for early recognition of complications so that medical treatment can be promptly sought

REFERENCES

1. Adeloye, A., and Warkany, J.: Experimental congenital hydrocephalus, Child's Brain **11**:325, 1976.
2. Behrman, R. E., editor: Neonatal-perinatal medicine, ed. 2, St. Louis, 1977, The C. V. Mosby Co.
3. Braney, M. L.: The child with hydrocephalus, Am. J. Nurs. **73**(5):828, 1973.
4. Brenner, W. E., Bruce, R. D., and Hendricks, C. H.: The characteristics and perils of breech presentations, Am. J. Obstet. Gynecol. **118**:118, 1974.
5. Broadribb, V.: Foundations of pediatric nursing, ed. 2, Philadelphia, 1973, J. B. Lippincott Co.
6. Clausen, J. P., et al.: Maternity nursing today, New York, 1973, McGraw-Hill Book Co.
7. Dawson, B. H., Dervin, E., and Heywood, O. B.: The problems of design and implantation of shunt systems for

the treatment of hydrocephalus, Dev. Med. Child Neurol. **17**(Suppl. 35):78, 1977.

8. Drapkin, A. J., and Sahar, N.: Experimental hydrocephalus: cerebrospinal fluid dynamics and ventricular distensibility during early states, Child's Brain **4**(5):278, 1978.
9. Epstein, F. J., Hockwald, G. M., Wold, A., and Ransohoff, J.: Avoidance of shunt dependency in hydrocephalus, Dev. Med. Child Neurol. **17**(Suppl. 35):71, 1975.
10. Evans, H. E., and Glass, L.: Perinatal medicine, New York, 1976, Harper & Row, Publishers, Inc.
11. Faivre, J., Lemaree, B., Bredagne, J., and Pecker, J.: X-linked hydrocephalus, with aqueductal stenosis, mental retardation, and adduction-flexion deformity of the thumbs, Child's Brain **11**:226, 1976.
12. Ferry, P. C., and Pernoll, M. L.: Rational management of perinatal hydrocephalus, Am. J. Obstet. Gynecol. **126**(2):151, 1976.
13. Fitzpatrick, E., Reeder, S. R., and Mastroianni, L.: Maternity nursing, ed. 12, Philadelphia, 1972, J. B. Lippincott Co.
14. Fowler, G. W., Sukoff, M., Hamilton, A., and Williams, J. P.: Communicating hydrocephalus in children with genetic inborn errors of metabolism, Child's Brain **1**:251, 1975.
15. Freeman, R. K., McQuoun, D. S., Secrist, L. J., and Larson, E. J.: The diagnosis of fetal hydrocephalus before viability, Obstet. Gynecol. **11**(1):109, 1977.
16. Friede, R. L.: Developmental neuropathology, New York, 1975, Springer-Verlag New York, Inc.
17. Guidetti, B., Giuffre, R., Palma, L., and Fontana, M.: Hydrocephalus in infancy and childhood, Child's Brain **2**:209, 1976.
18. Konobkin, F.: The relationship between head circumference and the development of communicating hydrocephalus in infants following intraventricular hemorrhage, **56**(1):74, 1975.
19. Kuuamura, K., Malone, D. G., and Raimondi, A. J.: The central (spinal) canal in congenital murine hydrocephalus: morphological and physiological aspects, Child's Brain **4**(4):216, 1978.
20. Lorber, J.: Isosorbide in the medical treatment of infantile hydrocephalus, J. Neurosurg. **39**(6):702, 1973.
21. Lorber, J.: Isosorbide in treatment of infantile hydrocephalus, Arch. Dis. Child. **50**(5):431, 1975.
22. Marlow, D. R.: Textbook of pediatric nursing, ed. 3, Philadelphia, 1969, W. B. Saunders Co.
23. Marsh, J. B., and Dickens, M.: Armstrong and Browder's nursing care of children, ed. 3, Philadelphia, 1970, F. A. Davis Co.
24. Mealey, J., Gilmor, R. L., and Bubb, M. P.: The prognosis of hydrocephalus overt at birth, J. Neurosurg. **39**(3):348, 1973.
25. Naidich, T. P., et al.: Evaluation of pediatric hydrocephalus by computed tomography, Radiology **119**(2):337, 1976.

26. Page, E. W., Villee, C. A., and Villee, D. B.: Human reproduction—the care content of obstetrics, gynecology and perinatal medicine, ed. 2, Philadelphia, 1976, W. B. Saunders Co.
27. Porter, F. N.: Hydrocephalus treated by compressive head wrapping, Arch. Dis. Child. **50**(10):817, 1975.
28. Pritchard, J. A., and MacDonald, P. C.: William's obstetrics, ed. 15, New York, 1976, Appleton-Century-Crofts.
29. Volpe, J. J., Pasternak, J. F., and Allan, V. C.: Ventricular dilation preceding rapid head growth following neonatal intracranial hemorrhage, Am. J. Dis. Child. **131**:1212, 1977.
30. Weller, R. O., and Williams, B. N.: Cerebral biopsy and assessment of brain damage in hydrocephalus, Arch. Dis. Child. **50**(10):763, 1975.
31. Young, D., and Weller, B. F.: Baby surgery: nursing management and care, Baltimore, 1971, University Park Press.

BIBLIOGRAPHY

Borno, R. P., et al.: Vaginal delivery of a hydrocephalic fetus after transabdominal encephalocentesis, Am. J. Obstet. Gynecol. **128**(8):917, 1977.
Braun, F. K. T., Jones, L., and Smith, D. W.: Breech presentation as an indicator of fetal abnormality, J. Pediatr. **86:**419, 1975.
Dickason, E. J., and Schult, M. O., editors: Maternal and infant care, New York, 1975, McGraw-Hill Book Co.
Epstein, F., Wold, A., and Hochwald, G. M.: Intracranial pressure during compressive head wrapping in treatment of neonatal hydrocephalus, Pediatrics **7:**786, 1974.
Gardner, W. J.: Hydrodynamic factors in Dandy-Walker and Arnold-Chiari malformations, Child's Brain **3**(4):200, 1977.
Hoffman, H. J., Hendrick, E. B., and Humphreys, R. P.: Manifestations and management of Arnold-Chiari malformation in patients with myelomeningocele, Child's Brain **1:** 255, 1975.
Jansen, J.: Sex-linked hydrocephalus, Dev. Med. Child Neurol. **17:**633, 1975.
Reuck, J., and Thienpont, L.: Fetal Chiari's type III malformation, Child's Brain **2:**85, 1976.
Udvarhelyi, G. P., and Epstein, M. N.: The so-called Dandy-Walker syndrome: analysis of 12 operated cases, Child's Brain **1:**158, 1975.
Wasserman, E., and Slobody, L. B.: Survey of clinical pediatrics, ed. 6, New York, 1974, McGraw-Hill Book Co.
Welch, L.: The principles of physiology of the cerebrospinal fluid in relation to hydrocephalus including normal pressure hydrocephalus, Adv. Neurol. **13:**247, 1975.
Willson, M. A.: Multidisciplinary problems of myelomeningocele and hydrocephalus, Phys. Ther. **45**(12):1139, 1965.

Chapter 25

Persistent fetal circulation

Nancy S. Edwards and Carol Millay

Since the original description of persistent fetal circulation (PFC) by Gersony and associates[13] in 1969, the literature related to this syndrome has increased considerably. Acknowledging the many articles that have been written and the studies that have been conducted in an effort to determine more precisely the etiology, pathophysiology, and most effective treatment of PFC, this chapter is yet another attempt at clarifying a recognized pathological condition of the newborn and presenting appropriate treatment measures.

Herrera[17] notes the various terms that have been devised in an attempt to describe and identify this entity more accurately, such as "persistent pulmonary vascular obstruction," "persistence of the fetal cardiopulmonary circulatory pathway," "persistent pulmonary hypertension," and "persistent transitional circulation." Based on the discussion of different terminology by Behrman,[1] "persistence of the fetal circulation" (PFC) will be used in this chapter.

PHYSIOLOGY

To understand PFC, one must first understand the anatomical structure of the fetal circulation. During fetal life the lungs are basically nonfunctional. The liver also functions only partially. Because of this (decreased use of the lungs and liver), the fetal heart must pump large quantities of blood through the placenta. Therefore the fetal circulation is especially designed to operate in a considerably different manner from that of the adult. Oxygenated blood from the placenta, as illustrated in Fig. 25-1, returns to the fetal heart via the umbilical vein and ductus venosus, thereby bypassing the liver. The oxy-

genated blood then enters the inferior vena cava and travels up to the heart. Once it reaches the heart, the blood enters the right atrium and is shunted through the foramen ovale to the left atrium. Oxygenated blood from the placenta is then pumped to the rest of the fetal body, especially the head and forelimbs.[16]

Blood also enters the right atrium from the superior vena cava. This blood is mainly deoxygenated and is directed downward through the tricuspid valve into the right ventricle. The deoxygenated blood is then pumped from the right ventricle into the pulmonary artery. Once in the pulmonary artery the blood either travels through the lungs or shunts through the patent ductus arteriosus into the descending aorta. From here the blood flows through the two umbilical arteries into the placenta where it becomes oxygenated.[16] Because the lungs are collapsed and filled with fluid, the pulmonary vascular resistance is high, causing the majority of blood to shunt through the ductus arteriosus.

The transition from fetal to extrauterine circulatory pattern begins with the onset of pulmonary ventilation and the exclusion of placental circulation. Expansion of the lungs with air and the increase in pulmonary alveolar, arterial, and venous oxygen content result in a sharp drop in the pulmonary vascular resistance and an increase in pulmonary perfusion.[27]

At birth the circulatory system must make two primary changes. The first involves the placenta (Fig. 25-2). Blood flow through the placenta is literally cut off, causing an increase in systemic vascular resistance. This increase in systemic vascular resistance causes an increase in aortic pressure and an

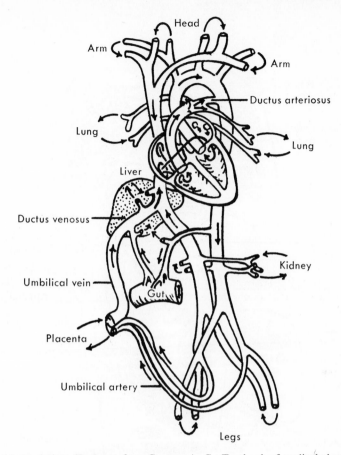

Fig. 25-1. Fetal circulation. (Redrawn from Guyton, A. C.: Textbook of medical physiology, ed. 4, Philadelphia, 1977, W. B. Saunders Co.)

increase in the pressures in the left ventricle and left atrium.

The secondary primary change occurs in the pulmonary vascular system. Expansion of the lungs results in a decrease in pulmonary vascular resistance. In fetal life the lungs are collapsed and filled with fluid, resulting in compression of the blood vessels. With expansion of the lungs at birth, these vessels are no longer compressed and the resistance to blood flow is decreased. Also during fetal life the lungs are hypoxic and hypercapnic, which causes vasoconstriction of the pulmonary blood vessels, but vasodilatation takes place when the lungs are expanded with air, therefore eliminating the hypoxia and hypercapnia. These changes reduce the resistance of blood through the lungs, which reduces the pulmonary arterial pressure. The pressures in the right ventricle and right atrium are also reduced.[27]

At birth the vascular system also has two secondary changes. These changes involve the closure of the foramen ovale and the closure of the ductus arteriosus. The high left atrial pressure and the low right atrial pressure that occur secondary to the primary changes cause the blood to flow backward from the left atrium into the right atrium. Fortunately, there is a small valve that lies over the foramen ovale on the left side of the atrial septum. This

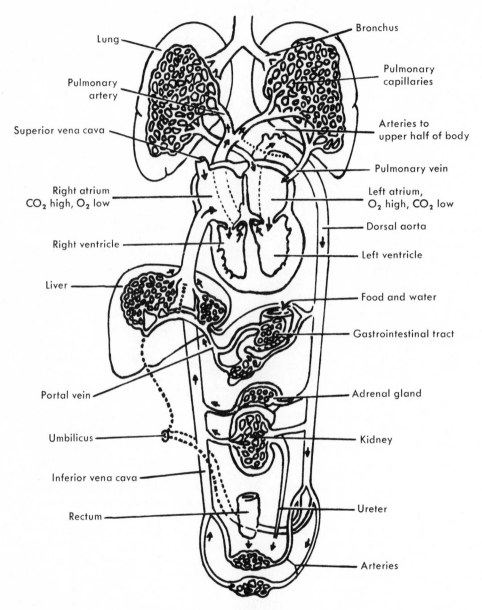

Fig. 25-2. Newborn circulation. (Redrawn from Arey, L. B.: Developmental anatomy, ed. 7, Philadelphia, 1974, W. B. Saunders Co.)

valve closes over the foramen ovale, thereby preventing further backflow. The valve becomes adherent and forms a permanent closure over the foramen ovale in two thirds of all persons within a few months to a few years. However, even if permanent closure does not occur, the left atrial pressure throughout life remains greater than the right atrial pressure, and the back pressure keeps the valve closed.

In relation to the ductus arteriosus, similar effects occur. The increased systemic resistance increases the aortic pressure, while the decreased pulmonary resistance reduces the pulmonary arterial pressure. As a result, the blood flows backward through the ductus arteriosus from the aorta to the pulmonary artery. The ductus arteriosus is thought to close by one of two ways or possibly both in conjunction: The first is called functional closure. The muscular wall of the ductus arteriosus constricts to stop blood flow and it becomes occluded with fibrous tissue that grows in the lumen. The second, the anatomical closure of the ductus arteriosus, is not completely understood. It is thought that the increase in oxygenation of the blood causes it to constrict.[27]

PATHOPHYSIOLOGY

To repeat, "within a few minutes of birth, there is [normally] a dramatic fall in pulmonary vascular resistance which leads to increased pulmonary blood flow . . . [followed by] a further less rapid reduction in pulmonary vascular resistance over the next six to eight weeks of life."[37] However, this decrease in pulmonary vascular resistance does not occur in PFC. Rather, pulmonary vasospasm causes a persistently elevated pulmonary vascular resistance. With pulmonary hypertension equal to or greater than systemic pressure, there is right-to-left shunting of blood through the ductus arteriosus and/or the foramen ovale.*

As noted by Rudolph,[2] the hypoxemia and acidosis resulting from the extrapulmonary shunt cause constriction of the pulmonary vasculature, which then increases the shunt. One can readily appreciate the perpetual problem thus generated (Figs. 25-3 and 25-4).

Several explanations have been advanced for the persistent pulmonary hypertension in these infants such as an excessive increase in the smooth muscle of the pulmonary arteries—the hypertrophy being caused by sustained fetal pulmonary arteriolar vasoconstriction as a result of chronic intrauterine hypoxia, fetal hypertension, and intrauterine partial constriction of the ductus arteriosus.[9,20,37] Behrman[1] (in connection with this suggestion), states that although the "small pulmonary arteries are constricted and may be hypertrophied . . . there is no injury to intimal layers."

Further, Levin and associates[21] note that one possibility suggestive of a disease of pulmonary vessels as an etiology is an increased amount of circulating pulmonary vasoconstrictor during intrauterine or postnatal life.

Herrera[17] reports that Melmon and associates and Heymann and associates "postulate a defect of the kininogen-bradykinin system that normally would produce a decrease in pulmonary vascular resistance and constriction of the ductus."

PFC may be produced by indomethacin given to the mother, which inhibits the synthesis of prostaglandin, resulting in constriction of the ductus and pulmonary hypertension.[17] Similarly, Hymann and Rudolph suggest the same problem resulting from salicylates, which would cause inhibition of prostaglandin synthesis.[17]

The role of perinatal asphyxia in the development of pulmonary vasoconstriction has been implicated by many investigators.* This is plausible owing to the documentation that pulmonary vasoconstriction occurs in the presence of hypoxia and acidosis.[9]

A review of the literature reveals various attempts to classify the syndrome of PFC. Aside from the central pathology of pulmonary hypertension with right-to-left shunting of blood, the clinical picture of these infants may vary according to these classifications.

Gersony[12] reports that abnormal right-to-left shunting, owing "to a persistent elevation of pulmonary vascular resistance," occurs in several diseases, specifically hyperviscosity, atypical respiratory distress syndrome, hypoglycemia, and from idiopathic causes, and suggests identification of the specific disease within the syndrome.

Herrera[17] divides the syndrome into (1) the primary or idiopathic type and (2) the secondary type,

---

*See references 5, 9, 12, 24, and 35 to 37.

*See references 1, 7, 11, 24, 33, and 35.

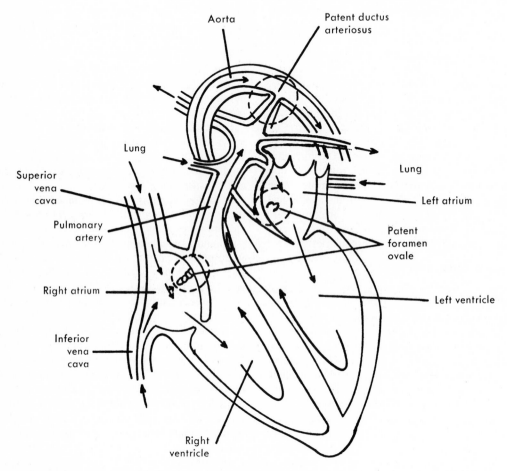

Fig. 25-3. Persistent fetal circulation. (Redrawn from Guyton, A. C.: Textbook of medical physiology, ed. 4, Philadelphia, 1977, W. B. Saunders Co.)

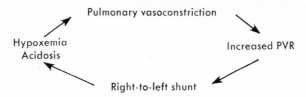

Fig. 25-4. Schematic representation of PFC cycle.

which is associated with respiratory distress syndrome, neonatal asphyxia, polycythemia, hypoglycemia, meconium aspiration syndrome, and transient tachypnea of the newborn.

Radford[30] chooses to classify PFC according to increasing severity as follows:

Type 1: Cyanosis + tachypnea
Type 2: Cyanosis + tachypnea + myocardial ischemia on ECG ± cardiac failure ± cardiac murmur
Type 3: Cyanosis + tachypnea + cardiac involvement + acidosis ± hypotension

Rowe[33] suggests an acute type with two forms. The simple form consists of vasoconstriction with normal myocardial function. This would include idiopathic PFC and PFC secondary to birth asphyxia, pneumothroax, aspiration, polycythemia, diaphragmatic hernia, or pulmonary infection. In the complex form one finds pulmonary vasoconstriction with myocardial dysfunction. The second major type presented is the chronic form in which there is usually normal myocardial function, and it is "characterized by persistent severe hypoxia secondary to chronic pulmonary vasoconstriction."[33]

Consequently, a right-to-left extrapulmonary shunt owing to pulmonary hypertension may exist alone or in combination with any one of a variety of conditions that may produce hypoxia. Some of these disorders are polycythemia, hypoglycemia, aspiration syndromes, pneumonia, transient tachypnea of the newborn, and diaphragmatic hernia.[9,37]

CLINICAL PICTURE

The clinical picture of the infant with PFC presented in the literature is variable and appears to be dependent on the severity of the condition. The most frequently cited presentation is an infant at or near term with varying degrees of cyanosis owing to the hypoxemia[9,12,19,21] who may be tachypneic,[19,21,34,37] grunting,[37] or retracting[19,37] with these signs appearing within 24 hours after birth.[9,12,19]

According to Schaeffer and Avery,[34] there is usually an absence of severe retractions and grunting. Gersony[12] reports varying degrees of respiratory distress, while Emmanouilides and Baylen[9] report that severe respiratory distress is usually not present. In addition, hypoxemia[19,37] and acidemia[21,37] are also reported.

Most any picture may be seen on the chest x-ray film, but it usually shows clear lung fields.[35] There may be normal or decreased pulmonary vascularity and, at times, pulmonary overexpansion with flattening of the diaphragm, suggesting small airway disease.[9]

Heart size may be normal, or mild to moderate cardiomegaly may be noted.[12,34,35,37] Emmanouilides and Baylen[9] report that whereas cardiomegaly is always present and moderate or severe hepatomegaly may be present in those infants with myocardial dysfunction, neither is usually evident in infants with normal myocardial function. Infants with PFC may also have a systolic murmur.[9,34]

Electrocardiogram changes may be evident with right axis deviation[37] and nonspecific ST and T wave changes.[9]

An echocardiographic study by Riggs and associates[31] revealed an increased right ventricular pre-ejection period/right ventricular ejection time (RPEP/RVET) consistent with the elevated pulmonary artery pressure and pulmonary vascular resistance of PFC, and an elevated left ventricular preejection period/left ventricular ejection time (LPEP/LVET), suggesting left ventricular dysfunction.

There is reason to suspect PFC when the Po_2 value of a blood sample from the right radial or brachial artery is significantly higher than the Po_2 value from a sample simultaneously obtained from the descending aorta through an umbilical arterial catheter.[9,17,21] This may be indicative of a veno-arterial shunt at the ductal level.

The necessity and difficulty in distinguishing PFC from cyanotic congenital heart disease is frequently cited in the literature.[1,9,17,30] Cardiac catheterization may be necessary to make a final diagnosis.[11,17]

Although the literature relating to PFC does not always specify the infant's sex, there is suggestion of a male predominance.[30] One report estimates the incidence of PFC as 1 in 1454 births.[30]

The prognosis for these infants depends on the severity of the condition and the period of time elapsed before diagnosis and intervention. PFC is potentially fatal,[30] with an overall mortality rate of about 50%[17]; however, with "early recognition and vigorous treatment, the survival rate increases significantly."[37]

MANAGEMENT

Therapeutic measures are directed toward (1) correcting the complications of increased pulmonary vascular resistance such as right-to-left shunting of blood through the ductus arteriosus and/or foramen ovale, hypoxia, inadequate pulmonary blood flow, inadequate oxygenation, respiratory distress, metabolic acidosis, a labile cardiorespiratory system, and death; (2) promoting neonatal circulation by ventilatory support, decreasing pulmonary vascular resistance, and increasing oxygenation; and (3) promoting growth and development by dealing with the lack of the infant's response to parents during the acute phase, the limitations on physical stimulation/contact during the acute phase, and the parents' lack of understanding regarding the infant's condition.

Initially, a thorough evaluation of the infant needs to be undertaken; if present, hypothermia, hypoglycemia, polycythemia, hypocalcemia, or any other associated disorder must be promptly treated.[21,30] These conditions may be contributing to the elevated pulmonary vascular resistance.[17,37] Most importantly, cyanotic congenital heart disease must be ruled out.[18]

Supportive therapy includes intravenous fluids, oxygen administration, and correction of acid-base imbalances.[10,28,33]

Although cyanosis oftentimes does not respond to oxygen, the administration of 100% FIO_2 has been advocated by several investigators. Levin and associates[21] report that demonstration of right-to-left shunting through the ductus arteriosus by obtaining simultaneous temporal and abdominal aortic Po_2's is more easily recognized "when the infant is breathing 100% oxygen." In addition, to distinguish between PFC and cyanotic congenital heart disease, Peckham and Fox[28] use hyperventilation with 100% FIO_2 because they have found this will usually raise the Po_2 in infants with PFC to above 100 mm Hg, whereas most infants with cyanotic congenital heart disease will have little, if any, response. Also, the labile nature of the Po_2 in these infants justifies an increased FIO_2.

In more severe cases, mechanical ventilation and additional pharmacological agents may be necessary. Therefore these infants should be transferred to a tertiary neonatal intensive care unit where physicians and nurses familiar with this type of intensive care are available.

Levin and associates[21] found it necessary to utilize mechanical ventilation on some of the infants in their study because of severe hypoxemia. They note that "CPAP alone is probably not effective, because pulmonary hypoperfusion and not atelectasis is the primary problem."[21] Mechanical ventilation with high pressures and rates has been employed to keep the Pco_2 between 25 and 30 mm Hg.[28] "Hyperventilation was associated with a simultaneous decrease in pulmonary artery pressure, an increase in pO_2 and improvement in pulmonary mechanics."[28] Two explanations are offered by these authors for the relationship between decreased Pco_2 and decreased pulmonary artery pressure: (1) "hyperventilation produced improved oxygenation and correction of acidosis in prealveolar arterioles which resulted in decreased pulmonary vascular resistance" and (2) "hyperventilation may stabilize the airways of overdistended alveoli [often found in infants with PFC] thereby improving both ventilation and perfusion." Tudehope[37] notes the use of hyperventilation but warns of possible cerebral hypoperfusion when the CO_2 tension is markedly reduced.

In addition to hyperventilation, the use of nondepolarizing muscle relaxants such as curare or dimethyltubocurarine may be used. According to Tudehope,[37] "Curare has been suggested since this results in release of histamine, which is a pulmonary vasodilator, [and it] also increases chest wall compliance and eliminates struggling.'' Levin and associates[21] cite a ''dramatic increase in pO_2'' with the use of curare for the same reasons. The amount of curare used by these investigators was 1 mg intravenously, although the total number of doses was not specified. Other institutions use dimethyltubocurarine (Metubine) (see boxed material below).

Another pharmacological agent that has been used to increase pulmonary vasodilatation is tolazoline (Priscoline), an alpha-adrenergic blocking agent (see boxed material on p. 413). The efficacy of this drug is questionable. Both positive and negative reports are found in the literature.

According to Grover and associates as reported by Herrera,[17] the ''injection of Tolazoline directly into the pulmonary artery of eight patients with VSD met with improvement in the pulmonary hypertension.''

Korones and Eyal[19] report a dramatic increase in the Po_2 of five infants with severe hypoxemia following intravenous tolazoline. Goetzman and associates[14] similarly report that in 8 of 10 patients without apparent lung disease, there was a ''marked improvement in PaO_2'' following administration of intravenous tolazoline. Moodie and associates[25] agree with the positive results obtained when infants with severe pulmonary disease and pulmonary hypoperfusion are managed with tolazoline. The use of this drug to treat persistent pulmonary hypertension associated with severe hypoxemia in an infant with diaphragmatic hernia resulted in improvement in the infant.[21]

Despite the positive results of the aforementioned studies, some infants showed no response.[9] A variable response in Po_2 and pulmonary artery pressure following the administration of tolazoline was found in the study by Peckham and Fox,[28] and in some patients there was an actual increase in the pulmonary artery pressure.

A PROTOCOL FOR THE USE OF DIMETHYLTUBOCURARINE (METUBINE) IN THE NEWBORN INTENSIVE CARE UNIT*

INTRODUCTION

Nondepolarizing muscle relaxants such as *d*-tubocurarine, pancuronium, and dimethyltubocurarine have been used safely as adjuncts to surgical anesthesia and in the management of tetanus neonatorum. These agents are useful in the newborn intensive care unit to aid in the ventilatory management of those infants already on respirators and yet demonstrating evidence of inadequate ventilation owing to such factors as the infant's own uncoordinated breathing efforts or the high resistive forces of the thorax.

DRUG

d-Tubocurarine has three significant side effects: histamine release (bronchospasm, skin flush, hypotension), vagal inhibition (tachycardia), and sympathetic blockade (hypotension). Dimethyltubocurarine (Metubine) is the only currently available nondepolarizer that is not associated with any of the above side effects in clinically useful doses.

INDICATIONS

1. Improvement of alveolar ventilation when mechanical ventilation is being limited by the patient's uncoordinated breathing efforts
2. Reduction of oxygen consumption by eliminating the work of breathing when persistent hypoxemia is secondary to limited oxygen transport
3. Reduction of the peak transthoracic pressure in the patient prone to the development of barotrauma or those with recalcitrant manifestations of barotrauma

CONTRAINDICATIONS

There are no absolute contraindications. Physicians, nursing staff, and respiratory therapy personnel must have a thorough awareness of the total dependence of the curarized infant on continuous assisted ventilation and the need for effective pulmonary physiotherapy. However, in some patients (for example, pneumothorax, PIE) vigorous percussion may not be indicated.

*Modified from James Whitcomb Riley Children's Hospital, Indianapolis, Ind.

Continued.

A PROTOCOL FOR THE USE OF DIMETHYLTUBOCURARINE (METUBINE) IN THE NEWBORN INTENSIVE CARE UNIT—cont'd

DOSAGE

Neonates have a wide range of sensitivity to non-depolarizing muscle relaxants; therefore, dosage must be individualized. Younger infants may show an even greater variability.

Initial dose of dimethyltubocurarine. 0.5 mg/kg IV push is used in both preterm and term infants. (Although standard texts suggest one tenth this dose, we have found it inadequate for the degree of paralysis desired.) Respiratory paralysis should occur within 3 minutes; if not, initial dose should be repeated.

Subsequent doses. If spontaneous respiratory effort and/or movement requires repeat medication in less than 2 to 3 hours, the dosage may need to be increased. If more than 4 hours elapse between the need for subsequent doses, the dosage should be reduced.

REVERSAL

Pharmacological reversal of neuromuscular block should rarely be required in the newborn ICU. In those occasional instances where it is not desirable to continue mechanical ventilatory support until the effects of the neuromuscular block have worn off, atropine, 0.02 mg/kg, and neostigmine, 0.05 mg/kg, injected simultaneously will reverse a residual block when other causes of a prolonged block are not present (see below). The maximum dose of atropine and neostigmine is 0.03 and 0.08 mg/kg, respectively.

PROLONGED BLOCK

Neuromuscular blockage may be prolonged by several factors:

1. Certain antibiotics (including kanamycin, colistin, viomycin, streptomycin, neomycin, polymyxin, lincomycin, and clindamycin)
2. Most general anesthetics (particularly halothane, enflurane, and diethyl ether)
3. Acidosis
4. Hypo- or hyperthermia
5. Overdosage
6. Hypocalcemia
7. Hypokalemia
8. Decreased renal excretion

ROUTINE ORDERS SUGGESTED

1. Apnea monitor (backup for ventilator alarm)
2. Suction as necessary
3. Initial dose given by physician
4. Nurse to notify physician when infant shows return of spontaneous respiratory efforts
5. Respiratory therapist to be informed that patient is on dimethyltubocurarine
6. Nasogastric tube to straight drainage
7. Credé bladder as needed
8. Arterial blood gases determined 15 minutes after initial dose

CAUTIONS

1. Sometimes mechanical ventilatory support must be *increased* after curarization, for example, increased peak pressure and/or rate. This indicates that minute ventilation prior to paralysis was being accomplished primarily by the baby and not the ventilator. If this possibility is not anticipated, there can be a sudden deterioration in the child's condition after dimethyltubocurarine is administered.
2. Chest physiotherapy and suctioning are performed *only* on a prn basis owing to observations that those babies with significant barotrauma and/or shunting often deteriorate during and after such manipulation.
3. Curarinized babies generally become very edematous, so careful control of fluid balance is necessary.
4. Although dimethyltubocurarine does not have the degree of histamine-like side effects observed with *d*-tubocurare, that is, hypotension and cutaneous vasodilatation, some babies will still exhibit a drop in blood pressure, so the medication should always be given slowly with appropriate monitoring of systemic pressures.

GUIDELINES FOR THE USE OF TOLAZOLINE*

I. Indications
   A. Tolazoline is a competitive α-adrenergic blocking agent, shown to be clinically effective in reversing hypoxia secondary to primary or secondary pulmonary hypertension.
   B. To further evaluate the efficacy, uniformity in dosage and monitoring is mandatory. For this reason the following protocol has been devised.
   C. Clinical criteria for use
      1. $Po_2 < 60$ on $FIO_2 = 100\%$
      2. Appropriate mechanical ventilation, that is, $Pco_2 = 25$ to 35 mm Hg in infants >2000 gm; $Pco_2 = 35$ to 40 in infants <2000 gm.
      3. Respiratory paralysis should be tried prior to, and independent of, the initial dose of tolazoline.

II. Restrictions
   A. Approval of neonatal faculty or fellow must be obtained.
   B. Vigorous attempts to correct metabolic or respiratory acidosis must be made prior to drug administration.
   C. Hypovolemia and/or hypotension should be corrected prior to loading dose.
   D. Dopamine therapy should not be started until attempts at plasma expansion have proven unsuccessful and the neonatal faculty or fellow consulted.
   E. Tolazoline should *not* be used in the presence of congenital cardiac disease.

III. Monitoring
   A. Laboratory
      1. Baseline—may be admission laboratory work or immediately after tolazoline infusion.
         a. ECG and echocardiogram.
         b. CBC, platelet count, BUN, electrolytes, creatinine, SGOT, alkaline phosphatase, and calcium.
         c. Routine—daily Hct, platelet count, electrolytes, and creatinine
         d. At end of therapy: ECG, echocardiogram, SGOT, and alkaline phosphatase.

   B. Nursing
      1. Blood pressure
         a. Preferably by transducer.
         b. Record before and after loading dose, hourly during first 4 hours, then every 4 hours.
      2. Accurate intake and output.
      3. Nasogastric tube to intermittent suction.
      4. Urine specific gravity, Hemastix, and Diastix q 4 hr.
      5. Hematest all gastric aspirate and stools.
      6. Weigh daily immediately after dose of paralyzing agent.
      7. Record all data on flow sheet, particularly information regarding the initial bolus.

IV. Methods
   A. Loading dose
      1. 1 to 2 mg/kg in D_5W or $D_{10}W$ over 15 minutes.
      2. Administration should be via vein that drains into the superior vena cava (scalp or upper extremity).
   B. Maintenance
      1. 1 to 2 mg/kg/hr by continuous infusion (D_5W or $D_{10}W$ with electrolytes by pump).
      2. Volume of diluent may be regulated in accordance with the fluid requirements of the infant.
      3. Weaning is done as tolerated by patient when $FIO_2 \leq 60\%$.
      4. Indications for, and results of, tolazoline infusion (including side effects and complications) should be documented in the physician's progress notes.
   C. Response
      1. Definition: Rise in Po_2 by 25 mm Hg during the first 4 hours of infusion. Current evidence suggests that a delayed response may occur as late as 4 hours.
      2. The drug should be discontinued if no response occurs by 4 hours or clinical complications occur (that is, severe hypotension or bleeding).

*Modified from James Whitcomb Riley Children's Hospital, Indianapolis, Ind.

When tolazoline is used, it is administered via an arm or scalp vein. Goetzman and associates[14] administered the drug in the amount of 2 mg/kg over 10 minutes in a scalp vein. This was followed by a continuous intravenous infusion of 1 to 2 mg/kg/hr. The scalp vein was "chosen to provide the highest initial exposure of tolazoline to the lungs by avoiding the right to left shunting of inferior vena caval blood across the foramen ovale." The same dosage was used by Peckham and Fox,[28] but the drug was administered by continuous intrapulmonary artery infusion rather than via peripheral infusion.

Herrera[17] warns that extreme caution should be used when administering tolazoline. In the study conducted by Stevenson and associates,[36] an 82% complication rate was associated with tolazoline administration. A review of the literature reveals a number of known or possible side effects of tolazoline. These include thrombocytopenia, gastrointestinal bleeding, hematuria, renal failure, pulmonary hemorrhage, hypotension, and shock.[14,17,36] It has been necessary to use dopamine to maintain blood pressure when rapid volume expansion did not correct the hypotension.[36]

A recent study by Lock and associates[22] suggests that prostaglandin I_2 (Prostacyclin) may be a useful pharmacological agent to effect the desired pulmonary vasodilatation. In referring to the report by Rudolph and associates, these investigators state that tolazoline "is not a specific pulmonary vasodilator in either man or in hypoxic lambs [whereas] prostaglandin I_2, a normal constituent of neonatal pulmonary vessels, perferentially dilates the pulmonary [as opposed to the systemic] circulation in hypoxic neonatal lambs."[22] Following a course of prostaglandin I_2 administered directly into the pulmonary artery of a term infant with severe and refractory hypoxemia secondary to pulmonary vasoconstriction, the pulmonary arterial pressure decreased to two thirds the aortic pressure and no further respiratory support was required.

The labile nature of infants with PFC is noted by Tudehope,[37] that is, "the pulmonary arterial vasculature of the newborn is highly labile and readily reverts to the fetal state of vasoconstriction." Likewise, Peckham and Fox[28] report pulmonary pressure changes both related to adjustments in the FIO_2 or ventilator as well as "when there were no specific changes in therapy." In studying the effect of routine care on the Po_2 of newborn infants, Dangman

and associates[6] report a variation of ± 15 mm Hg in infants at rest. A decrease in Po_2 by as much as 50 mm Hg was cited during crying, and routine care such as physical examination and taking vital signs resulted in a decrease in Po_2 as high as 30 mm Hg.

Coupling this Po_2 variability in newborn infants with the lability of the cardiorespiratory system of infants with PFC, the considerations that are necessary in the physical care of these infants are obvious. Only those procedures that are absolutely necessary to enhance the infant's recovery should be carried out; that is, "minimal stress" should be employed. Agitation of the infant should be avoided as much as possible. Close observation and monitoring are imperative; however, monitoring should be carried out by continuous methods, arterial blood gases should be followed by an arterial catheter and/or a continuous transcutaneous Po_2 monitor, routine weighing of the infant is deferred until the infant has stabilized, Dextrosticks should be kept to a minimum unless hypoglycemia is suspected, suctioning is on a prn basis, and percussion and postural drainage are avoided unless absolutely necessary.

Martin and associates[23] report improved oxygenation in preterm infants when placed in a prone position. Similar improvement in oxygenation may be noted in infants with PFC, and it is, therefore, worthwhile trying.

Further, the Po_2 variability in newborns also is an indication for keeping infants with PFC who are 36 weeks' gestational age or greater in a slightly hyperoxic range. The risk of retrolental fibroplasia in infants of this gestational age is less than the risk of the pathophysiology of PFC.

Another important area of management involves the family unit. Brazelton[3] states that "the periods of pregnancy, birth and early infancy are critically important times for parents and infant to learn about each other [and] the kind of nurturance parents provide will influence the quality of a baby's attachment to them, which in turn will influence the child's capacity to nurture his or her own offspring, as well as the child's capacity to relate to society in general."

According to Robson,[32] eye-to-eye contact and the social smile in the early months of development "generally foster positive maternal feelings. . . ." Also, Hersh and Levin[18] discuss the positive reaction of a mother to behaviors in her newborn infant. Referring to Swedish research, it is indicated that early mother-child contact in the hospital is very important. When first-time mothers were allowed to hold their naked infants 1 hour after birth, they showed more affection to their infants several days later. Reference is made to another Swedish study in which newborns were given to their mothers 15 to 20 minutes after birth. In a follow-up study, a display of more affection was observed from these mothers than from those mothers who were routinely separated from their infants. Responses from the infants included more smiling and less crying.[32]

The father's reaction to being present at the delivery and holding the infant soon after birth also seems to be more positive.[18] Dr. Ross D. Parke of the University of Illinois, Urbana-Champaign, is quoted by Hersh and Levin[18]: "There are very few differences between mother-child and father-child interactions."

Recognizing the critical importance of interaction among the members of the family unit soon after birth, questions regarding the necessary disruption during this time when an infant is ill and requires care in an intensive care unit become of paramount importance. What is the effect on the infant and parents when anticipated responses to one another are thwarted? What effect does the limitation on physical stimulation/contact during the acute phase of the illness have on the parents and infant? How can normal growth and development be promoted? What is the parents' level of understanding regarding their infant's condition? What are their feelings? These are all questions that must be addressed if an intact family unit is to be enhanced.

Acknowledging the relationship between parents' response to their sick infant and their individual ability to cope with stress and the support systems available to them, the birth of a sick infant is nonetheless a crisis event. Their plans and expectations are suddenly interrupted.[15]

Specifically, an infant with PFC will usually be transferred to a neonatal intensive care unit. Consequently, the problem now facing the parents is separation from their newborn infant. Prior to transport, the parents should be given the opportunity to see and touch their infant; they should be given the phone number of the nursery and encouraged to call and visit frequently any time during the day or night, and the importance of their involvement with their baby should be stressed.[8]

Once in the newborn intensive care unit, the infant may be intubated; given dimethyltubocurarine, tolazoline, and other intravenous fluids; and be put on a "minimal stress" regime. The interference with the infant's spontaneity and the restrictions on the parents' desired spontaneous behavior toward their infant present an additional stressful situation.[4,15] At this time, the parents need explanations at their level of understanding relating to the environment of the nursery, the condition of their baby, and the purpose of the treatment approaches. Questions should be encouraged and answered realistically, and the feelings and reactions of the parents must be dealt with.[15]

Even during this critical period, despite the limitations and restrictions, a planned program of psychological stimulation for the infant can be instituted as reported by Brown and Hepler.[4] Parents participation is an important aspect of this program.

As the infant progresses and restrictions related to physical involvement are lifted, more direct involvement of the parents in the care of their baby should be encouraged. They should be urged to talk to and touch their baby, and means of soothing and comforting their infant should be suggested.[36] Appropriate infant stimulation techniques to promote normal growth and development should be shared with the parents.

Kaplan and Mason have outlined developmental tasks that parents must accomplish if they are to be able to relate to their infant to any meaningful degree[15]:

1. Preparation for the fact that their infant may die
2. Acceptance that a normal, full-term infant was not produced
3. Resumption of interaction with the infant who was born
4. Comprehension of the infant's problems, and emotional acceptance of and commitment to the care of their child

SUMMARY

PFC remains a challenging entity of the newborn. It is hoped that with early recognition, diagnosis, and intervention involving a comprehensive management approach, the infant will be afforded the opportunity to develop to the fullest emotional and physical potential.

Protocols

Problem □ Persistent pulmonary vasoconstriction

GOAL: To correct the complications of increased pulmonary vascular resistance (that is, right-to-left shunting of blood through the ductus arteriosus and foramen ovale, hypoxia, inadequate pulmonary blood flow, inadequate oxygenation, respiratory distress, metabolic acidosis, labile cardio-respiratory system, and death)

DIAGNOSTIC

1. A physical examination should be performed.
2. A chest x-ray examination should be done.
3. Cardiac catheterization may be necessary.
4. An electrocardiogram should be taken.
5. An echocardiogram should be taken.
   Rationale: To rule out cyanotic congenital heart disease or lung disease and to evaluate for signs indicative of PFC*
6. Blood cultures should be taken.
   Rationale: To detect possible infection[9]
7. Labwork (hematocrit, glucose, calcium) should be done to rule out associated disorders.
8. Evaluation of vital signs (to detect hypotension and/or hypothermia) should be done.
   Rationale: To be aware that these conditions may be contributing to increased pulmonary vascular resistance[17,37]
9. Arterial blood gases (simultaneously obtained from right radial or brachial and umbilical arterial catheter) should be analyzed.
   Rationale: To be aware that there is reason to suspect PFC when the Po_2 value of a blood sample from the right radial or brachial artery is significantly higher than the Po_2 value from a sample simultaneously obtained from the descending aorta through an umbilical arterial catheter[9,17,21,33]
10. Review maternal history and Apgar scores.
    Rationale: To be aware that the role of perinatal asphyxia in the development of pulmonary vasoconstriction is implicated by several investigators†

11. Determine onset of cyanosis and respiratory distress.
    Rationale: To be aware that symptoms usually present within 24 hours of life if PFC[9,12,19,37]

THERAPEUTIC

1. Correct any metabolic or cardiovascular abnormalities present.
   Rationale: To be aware that these conditions may be contributing to increased pulmonary vascular resistance[17,37]
2. Administer 100% FIO_2.
   Rationale: To be aware that demonstration of right-to-left shunting through ductus arteriosus in arterial blood gases is more easily recognized when infant is breathing 100% oxygen[21]; that response of Po_2 to 100% FIO_2 assists in distinguishing PFC from cyanotic congenital heart disease[28]; and that fluctuations in Po_2 both at rest and when disturbed warrant a slightly hyperoxic range[35]
3. Obtain arterial blood gases (within 10 minutes of any change in FIO_2 or ventilatory settings or every 2 hours otherwise through either arterial catheter or continuous Po_2 monitor).
   Rationale: Common sense
4. "Minimal stress" (that is, quiet environment: avoid agitating infant; Dextrosticks limited to once per shift unless hypoglycemia suspected; no percussion, postural drainage, or suctioning unless absolutely necessary; routine weighing deferred).
5. Post sign on infant's bed that he is on "minimal stress" so that all personnel will be aware of this.
6. Monitor by continuous methods.
7. No heelsticks (trauma may interfere with accurate assessment of color of feet if umbilical arterial catheter in place) should be done.
   Rationale: To be aware that the pulmonary arterial vasculature of the newborn is highly labile and readily reverts to the fetal state of vasoconstriction[37] and that pulmonary pressure changes are observed even with no changes in FIO_2 or ventilator settings[37]

---

*See references 9, 11, 12, 31, 35, and 37.
†See references 1, 7, 11, 24, 33, and 35.

8. Assess femoral pulses if umbilical arterial catheter in place.

   Rationale: To prevent potential problems associated with umbilical arterial catheters, which interfere with proper circulation

9. Proper maintenance of intravenous fluids should be carried out.

   Rationale: Common sense

10. Accurate intake and output should be recorded.

    Rationale: Common sense

Problem □ Lack of transition to normal circulation after birth

GOAL: To promote neonatal circulation by instituting ventilatory support, decreasing pulmonary vascular resistance, and increasing oxygenation

DIAGNOSTIC

1. Evaluate arterial blood gases.

   Rationale: To be aware that there is reason to suspect PFC when the Po_2 value of a blood sample from the right radial or brachial artery is significantly higher than the Po_2 value from a sample simultaneously obtained from the descending aorta through an umbilical arterial catheter[9,17,21,33]

2. Observe closely

   Rationale: Common sense

3. Assess labwork (hematocrit, creatinine, platelet count, electrolytes, SGOT, alkaline phosphatase).

   Rationale: See tolazoline protocol, p. 413.

4. Electrocardiogram should be taken.

5. Echocardiogram should be taken.

   Rationale: See tolazoline protocol, p. 413.

6. Assess respiratory effort.

   Rationale: To be aware that spontaneous respiratory effort may indicate need for increased dosage of dimethyltubocurarine (see dimethyltubocurarine protocol, pp. 411 and 412)

7. Assess need for increased ventilatory support.

   Rationale: To be aware that mechanical ventilatory support may need to be increased after curarization, indicating that minute ventilation prior to paralysis was being accomplished primarily by infant and not the ventilator (see dimethyltubocurarine protocol, pp. 411 and 412)

THERAPEUTIC

1. Administer intravenous tolazoline.

   Rationale: To increase pulmonary vasodilatation, thereby decreasing the pulmonary vascular resistance[14,17,19]

2. Institute mechanical ventilation.

   Rationale: To correct severe hypoxemia[21]

3. Maintain alkalotic state.

   Rationale: To be aware that hyperventilation is associated with a simultaneous decrease in pulmonary artery pressure, an increase in Po_2, and improvement in pulmonary mechanics[28]

4. Maintain hyperoxic range.

   Rationale: To be aware that demonstration of right-to-left shunting through ductus arteriosus in arterial blood gases is more easily recognized when infant is breathing 100% oxygen[21]; that response of Po_2 to 100% FIO_2 assists in distinguishing PFC from congenital heart disease[28]; and that fluctuations in Po_2 both at rest and when disturbed warrant a slightly hyperoxic range[35]

5. Administer dimethyltubocurarine (or curare).

   Rationale: To obtain desired result of release of histamine, a pulmonary vasodilator, and to increase chest wall compliance and eliminate struggling[37]

6. Draw blood for arterial blood gases.

   Rationale: Common sense

7. Observe for spontaneous respiratory efforts or other spontaneous movements

   Rationale: To be aware that spontaneous respiratory effort may indicate need for increased dosage of dimethyltubocurarine (see dimethyltubocurarine protocol, pp. 411 and 412)

8. Closely observe IV sites for signs of infiltration.

   Rationale: Common sense

9. Suction mouth every 2 hours.

   Rationale: To be aware that excessive oral secretions are produced in curarinized infants

10. Use Credé bladder prn.

11. Place infant on apnea monitor.

12. Accurately record intake and output.

13. Use nasogastric tube to straight drainage.

14. If weight absolutely necessary, do so only after dimethyltubocurarine dose administered.
    Rationale: See dimethyltubocurarine protocol, pp. 411 and 412
15. Hematest gastric aspirates, urine, and stools.
    Rationale: To check for gastric bleeding owing to the histaminic action of tolazoline on gastric secretion[14]
16. Administer antacid prn if gastrointestinal bleeding occurs.
    Rationale: To buffer gastric acidity, thereby reducing gastric irritation
17. Do urine specific gravity and Diastix every 4 hours.
    Rationale: See tolazoline protocol, p. 413
18. Accurately record medications and infant's condition.
    Rationale: Common sense

Problem □ Interruption of normal adaptation of new family unit

GOAL: To promote growth and development by dealing with lack of response of infant to parents during acute phase, limitations on physical stimulation/contact during acute phase, and lack of parents' understanding of infant's condition

DIAGNOSTIC
1. Evaluate infant regarding growth and development.
   Rationale: To determine needs before beginning a planned program[4]
2. Determine infant's level of response.
   Rationale: To set realistic goals for infant
3. Assess parents' experience with well and ill children.
   Rationale: To be aware that learning is an evolving process in which each step must be mastered before the next step can be learned[29]
4. Assess parents' degree of involvement with infant.
   Rationale: To be aware that parents often have ambivalent feelings toward their sick infant and this ambivalence has to be worked through if parents are to relate to the infant[15]
5. Determine family's need for professional resources (that is, financial, emotional, and so forth).

Rationale: To be aware that the crisis of giving birth to a sick infant can deplete the family financially, emotionally, and physically
6. Follow-up after discharge from hospital.
   Rationale: To continue assessment of infant and parents

THERAPEUTIC
1. Acquaint parents with staff involved in infant's care.
   Rationale: Common sense
2. Allow parents to express feelings and offer support.
   Rationale: To provide opportunity for parents to deal with their own feelings so they can be more open to infant[15]
3. Assist with and reinforce signs of positive adaptation and involvement with infant.
   Rationale: To be aware that behaviors that are positively reinforced tend to be repeated
4. Make appropriate referrals for family as deemed necessary.
5. Initiate Infant Stimulation Program[26] below progressing as infant's condition permits).
   Rationale: To foster normal growth and development

Infant stimulation program*

Coordination — infant's ability to see things, hold things, and reach for things
1. Behavior — infant's hands sometimes open with fingers extended instead of always held tightly fisted
   Activities
   a. Play with infant's hands — hold them, pat them, run your finger across the palm and fingers.
   b. Place infant's blanket in his hand — have him touch and feel it or give him small, soft stuffed animal to touch.
   c. When washing infant's hands, firmly rub the washcloth over the palms.
   d. Hold a finger or small object out to infant, moving it closer to the palms of his hands.
2. Behavior — infant's eyes follow bright red toy that moves from left to right in front of his face
   Activities
   a. Hold small penlight about 12 inches above infant's face — slowly move it from the left

---

*Adapted from The Nisonger Center: Infant stimulation program, Columbus, Ohio, 1978.

to the right side of his face; if eyes do not follow, try again, moving it more slowly.

b. Shake a brightly colored, noise-making toy (for example, a rattle) while moving it from right to left in front of the infant's face so he will follow it with his eyes.

3. Behavior—infant turns head to follow moving rattle
   Activities
   a. Hold squeaky toy 8 to 12 inches above infant's head—squeak it and move it to his left side so he must turn his head to see it; do the same on the right side.
   b. While standing over infant and talking to him as he lies in crib, move slowly from his right side to his left side; he should watch you with his eyes.

Locomotion—infant's ability to move about
1. Behavior—infant lifts head up when lying on abdomen
   Activities
   a. Lay infant on his abdomen and shake a bright colored toy in front of his face and raise it; talk to him, getting him to raise his head.
   b. Lay infant on his abdomen on your lap and hold him so his head is slightly lower than the rest of his body (for just a second), he should lift his head.
2. Behavior—infant rolls over part way when on his back and his head is turned to one side
   Activities
   a. Turn infant's head to the right and gently push his left shoulder toward his right side; as he begins to learn how to roll, decrease the amount of push.
   b. Do same thing to infant's left side; place a brightly colored toy on his left side so he will want to roll over to look at it.
   c. Leave infant propped on his side with a sturdy pillow behind his back—place some colorful toys within reach for him to look at.
3. Behavior—infant straightens leg when someone pushes the bottom of his foot
   Activities
   a. While infant lies on his back, move his legs in a bicycling motion, stopping to push his knees toward his chest; this should cause him to straighten his legs.
   b. Place the infant close to the bottom of crib so when he stretches his legs out, he will push on crib.

Cognition—infant's growth in intellectual abilities such as reasoning and knowing how things work
1. Behavior—infant feels objects with his fingers
   Activities
   a. Make a "touching" board out of different materials like velvet, aluminum foil, pieces of carpet, and burlap; place the board so the infant can reach it and place his hand on the materials so he can feel them.
   b. Provide a toy like a small stuffed animal to play with; place animal in the infant's hand and rub it against other parts of his body so he can feel it.
   c. Dress the infant in clothing with different textures.

Receptive language—infant's ability to understand what is said to him
Ideas and activities
   1. Sing softly to the infant and gently rock him when he cries.
   2. Talk to the infant in a calm, soothing voice when he is upset.
   3. When the infant is awake, talk quietly to him while looking into his face, thereby encouraging him to watch you as you talk to him.
Behavior 1—stops crying when familiar person speaks quietly to him
Behavior 2—blinks or stops moving when a rattle is shaken near him
Expressive language—infant describes his growth in the ability to make other people understand what he needs or says
Ideas and activities
   1. Encourage infant to vocalize (cry and make sounds); this permits him to develop the vocal and respiratory coordination for breath control that is necessary for speech to develop.
Behavior 1—infant cries when hungry, wet, or tired
Behavior 2—infant makes noises in his throat, gurgles, coos, sighs, grunts, squeals and blows bubbles
Socialization—infant describes his growth in ability to understand that he is a person among others as well as to learn how to take care of himself
1. Behavior—infant stops crying when he is picked up
   Activities
   a. When infant cries, pick him up; as you hold him, talk to him using his name frequently and tickle and gently stroke him.
   b. Hum or sing softly to the infant when you are holding him or when you are near him; hold or position him so he can see your face as you sing to him.

2. Behavior—infant looks at the face of the person holding him—the person's eyes, mouth, and hair
   Activities
   a. Hold infant on your lap as he faces you; talk or sing to him and gently rock him from side to side as you talk or sing to him.
   b. While infant is lying face up in his crib, bring your face close to his face and touch noses, kiss his cheek, or otherwise touch him; repeat this frequently, talking softly to him as you do it.
   c. Take infant's hand and touch your face with it, talk to him while you do this naming the parts of your face as his hand touches them.

EDUCATIONAL

1. Encourage and answer questions related to infant, his condition, therapeutic measures, and so forth.
   Rationale: To provide information parents need can positively influence how they will view their infant and meet his special needs[15]
2. Provide information related to nursery routine—visiting policies, phone policies, and so forth.
   Rationale: Common sense
3. Stress importance of parents' involvement in infant's care.
   Rationale: To be aware that parents feel guilty about the illness and incompetent to care for their infant: one of the most important goals is to return infant to his parents; positive input and support from staff can bolster self-confidence[15]
4. Instruct parents regarding Infant Stimulation Program.
   Rationale: To foster normal growth and development
5. Fill in gaps of knowledge related to normal infant care and growth and development.
6. Advise as to follow-up after discharge from hospital.

REFERENCES

1. Behrman, R. E.: Persistence of the fetal circulation, J. Pediatr. **89**(4):636, 1976.
2. Bolognese, R. J., and Schwarz, R. H.: Perinatal medicine: management of the high-risk fetus and neonate, Baltimore, 1977, The Williams & Wilkins Co.
3. Brazelton, T. B.: Reaching out to new parents, Child. Today **7**(4):27, 1978.
4. Brown, J., and Hepler, R.: Stimulation—a corollary to physical care, Am. J. Nurs. **76**(4):578, 1976.
5. Bucciarelli, R. L., Egan, E. A., Gessner, I. H., and Eitzman, D. T.: Persistence of fetal cardiopulmonary circulation: one manifestation of transient tachypnea of the newborn, Pediatrics **58**(2):192, 1976.
6. Dangman, B. C., et al.: The variability of Po_2 in newborn infants in response to routine care (abstract), Pediatr. Res. **10**:422, 1976.
7. Drummond, W. H., and Bissonnette, J. M.: Persistence of the fetal circulation (PFC): development of an animal model (abstract), Pediatr. Res. **10**:423, 1976.
8. Eager, M.: Long-distance nurturing of the family bond, Matern. Child Nurs. J. **2**(5):293, 1977.
9. Emmanouilides, G. C., and Baylen, B. G.: Neonatal cardiopulmonary distress without congenital heart disease, Curr. Probl. Pediatr. **9**(7):4, 1979.
10. Field, T. M.: Effects of early separation, interactive deficits, and experimental manipulation on infant-mother face-to-face interaction, Child Dev. **48**(3):761, 1977.
11. Fox, W. W., et al.: Pulmonary hypertension in the perinatal aspiration syndrome, Pediatrics **59**(2):205, 1977.
12. Gersony, W.: Persistence of the fetal circulation: a commentary, J. Pediatr. **82**(6):1103, 1973.
13. Gersony, W. M., Duc, G. V., and Sinclair, J. C.: P.F.C. syndrome, Circulation **40**(Suppl. 3):111, 1969.
14. Goetzman, B. W., et al.: Neonatal hypoxia and pulmonary vasospasm: response to tolazoline, J. Pediatr. **89**(4):617, 1976.
15. Goldson, E.: Parents' reactions to the birth of a sick infant, Child. Today **8**(4):13, 1979.
16. Guyton, A.: Textbook of medical physiology, ed. 5, Philadelphia, 1976, W. B. Saunders Co.
17. Herrera, A.: Persistent fetal circulation, Perinatol. Neonatol. September/October, p. 50, 1979.
18. Hersh, S. P., and Levin, K.: How love begins between parent and child, Child. Today **7**(2):2, 1978.
19. Korones, S. B., and Eyal, F. G.: Successful treatment of "persistent fetal circulation" with tolazoline, Pediatr. Res. **9**:367, 1975.
20. Levin, D., Hyman, A., Heymann, M., and Rudolph, A.: Fetal hypertension and the development of increased pulmonary vascular smooth muscle: a possible mechanism for persistent pulmonary hypertension of the newborn infant, J. Pediatr. **92**(2):265, 1978.
21. Levin, D. L., et al.: Persistent pulmonary hypertension of the newborn infant, J. Pediatr. **89**(4):626, 1976.
22. Lock, J., et al.: Use of prostacyclin in persistent fetal circulation, Lancet **1**(8130):1343, 1979.
23. Martin, R. J., Herrell, N., Rubin, D., and Fanaroff, A.: Effect of supine and prone positions on arterial oxygen tension in the preterm infant, Pediatrics **63**(4):528, 1979.
24. Merten, D., Goetzman, B., and Wennberg, R.: Persistent fetal circulation: an evolving clinical and radiographic concept of pulmonary hypertension of the newborn, Pediatr. Radiol. **6**:74, 1977.
25. Moodie, D. S., et al: Tolazoline as adjuvant therapy for ill neonates with pulmonary hypoperfusion, Chest **74**(5):604, 1978.

26. The Nisonger Center: Infant stimulation program, Columbus, Ohio, 1978.
27. Moore, K. L.: Before we are born: basic embryology and birth defects, Philadelphia, 1974, W. B. Saunders Co.
28. Peckham, G. J., and Fox, W. W.: Physiologic factors affecting pulmonary artery pressure in infants with persistent pulmonary hypertension, J. Pediatr. **93**(6):1005, 1978.
29. Pohl, M. L.: The teaching function of the nursing practitioner, ed. 2, Dubuque, Iowa, 1973, Wm. C. Brown Co.
30. Radford, D.: Persistent fetal circulation: two cases with myocardial dysfunction and severe acidosis, Med. J. Aust. **1**:27, 1979.
31. Riggs, T., et al.: Persistence of fetal circulation syndrome: an echocardiographic study, J. Pediatr. **91**(4):626, 1977.
32. Robson, K. S.: The role of eye-to-eye contact in maternal-infant attachment, Child Fam. **15**(2):119, 1976.
33. Rowe, R. D.: Abnormal pulmonary vasoconstriction in the newborn, Pediatrics **59**(3):318, 1977.
34. Schaffer, A. J., and Avery, M. E.: Diseases of the newborn, ed. 4, Philadelphia, 1977, W. B. Saunders Co.
35. Silverstein, E., et al.: Persistence of the fetal circulation: radiologic considerations, Am. J. Roentgenol. **128**:781, 1977.
36. Stevenson, D., et al.: Refractory hypoxemia associated with neonatal pulmonary disease: the use and limitations of tolazoline, J. Pediatr. **95**(4):595, 1979.

BIBLIOGRAPHY

Bucciarelli, R. L., et al.: Transient tricuspid insufficiency of the newborn: a form of myocardial dysfunction in stressed newborns, Pediatrics **59**(3):330, 1977.

Erdman, D.: Parent-to-parent support: the best for those with sick newborns, Matern. Child Nurs. J. **2**(5):291, 1977.

Levy, R. J., et al.: Persistent pulmonary hypertension in a newborn with congenital diaphragmatic hernia: successful management with tolazoline, Pediatrics **60**(5):740, 1977.

Riemenschneider, R. A., Nielsen, H. C., Ruttenberg, H. D., and Jaffe, R. B.: Disturbances of the transitional circulation: Spectrum of pulmonary hypertension and myocardial dysfunction, J. Pediatr. **89**(4):622, 1976.

Schreiner, R.: PFC. Unreleased videotape, 1980.

Zamansky, H., and Strobel, K.: Care of the critically ill newborn, Am. J. Nurs. **76**(4):566, 1976.

Chapter 26

Congenital heart disease

Carol Leykauf

INCIDENCE

Congenital malformations of the cardiovascular system are among the most frequently occurring clinically significant anomalies in the neonate. A serious form of congenital heart disease occurs in 1 of every 125 live births (8 per 1000) and accounts for about 50% of the deaths caused by congenital defects in the first year of life.[4,10]

ETIOLOGY

Congenital heart disease is a result of developmental errors in the heart or great vessels, which occur between the second and seventh weeks of gestation.[3]

The etiology of most congenital heart defects is not known. However, several factors are associated with a higher than normal incidence of the disease. These include *environmental factors* such as (1) maternal infections—rubella, mumps, chickenpox, or influenza during the first trimester of pregnancy; (2) maternal age over 40 years; (3) diabetic women; (4) women taking prescribed and/or over-the-counter drugs; (5) women exposed to radiation; and (6) noxious influences such as maternal alcoholism—"fetal alcohol syndrome"—vitamin deficiency, and anoxia. The incidence of some cardiac defects seems higher in neonates living at high altitudes and low oxygen pressures than those born at sea level.[3,4,11]

Several *genetic factors* are also implicated in congenital heart defects. There is increased risk of congenital heart disease in the neonate who (1) has a chromosomal aberration such as Down's syndrome (trisomy 21), (2) has parents with congenital heart disease, or (3) has siblings with a heart defect. The incidence of cardiovascular malformation in the offspring of patients who have been treated for congenital heart disease is less than 3%. Generally, parents can be supported in a decision to have additional children when one child has congenital heart disease, since the recurrence rate is about 2%. However, if two siblings are affected, it is probable that the recurrence rate is higher.[3,4]

FETAL CIRCULATION AND ITS ADJUSTMENTS TO NEONATAL CIRCULATION

Although a detailed presentation of fetal circulation will not be included, certain basic hemodynamic concepts are important to an understanding of congenital heart disease and require discussion.

Prior to birth, the nonaerated, developing lungs have a high pulmonary vascular resistance and cannot accept all the systemic venous return. Therefore, part of the systemic venous blood entering the right atrium is shunted through the foramen ovale into the left atrium. The remaining venous return passes into the right ventricle, where part of it is shunted through the ductus arteriosus into the aorta. These two right-to-left shunts protect the fetal lungs from receiving more blood than they can accommodate.[10]

With the first breath at birth, pulmonary arteriolar resistance drops, probably caused in minor part by the expansion of the lungs but mostly by the increased Po_2. The pulmonary vasodilator effect of oxygen is paralleled by its constrictive effect on the ductus. The pulmonary flow thus increases after birth, with the ductus closure shutting off the runoff from the pulmonary artery and the pulmonary vascular bed opening up to receive the increased amount of blood. As a result, pressures in the right ventricle and the pulmonary artery drop rapidly. At the same time, resistance and hence pressure in the systemic circuit rise, because of cutting the cord, a cold environment, and a transient drop in pH.[3]

The preceding pressure relationships are important in the shunting of blood through abnormal cardiac communications. Septal defects are frequently overlooked in the neonatal period because there are equal pressures between the right and left heart (no shunt, no murmur). However, at about 6 weeks of age when pressure differentials approach adult levels, sufficient blood will flow through the defect to cause a murmur.

CONGENITAL HEART MALFORMATIONS

For the following discussion, the congenital malformations will be classified based on two clinical features: the presence or absence of cyanosis and the degree of pulmonary vascularity (increased, normal, or decreased).

Acyanotic lesions are the most commonly detected cardiac anomalies, but resources differ regarding the most frequently identified acyanotic lesion. Some state that ventricular septal defects are most common, while other longitudinal studies show that atrial septal defects or patent ductus arteriosus is the most frequently occurring lesion.[3,8]

Acyanotic heart defects with increased pulmonary vascularity

The combination of increased pulmonary vascular marking and acyanosis indicates the presence of a cardiac defect that permits the passage of blood from a higher pressure, left-sided cardiac chamber to a lower pressure, right-sided cardiac chamber. Although only oxygenated blood enters the systemic circulation, this is at the expense of an overworked left atrium and ventricle.[8]

The degree of left-to-right shunting and severity of symptoms depend on three factors: pressure gradient between left and right sides of the heart, compliance of left and right ventricles, and the size of the defect. The greater the systemic vascular resistance, the greater the degree of left-to-right shunting. Any condition that increases the resistance to left ventricular outflow, such as aortic stenosis or systemic hypertension, will increase left-to-right shunting. Conversely, the greater the pulmonary vascular resistance, the lesser the degree of left-to-right shunting. Any condition that increases the resistance to right ventricular outflow, such as pulmonary stenosis or pulmonary hypertension, will decrease left-to-right shunting. There is also a lesser degree of left-to-right shunting in the neonate owing to decreased compliance of the right ventricle. As this chamber becomes thinner walled and more compliant, there is a greater degree of left-to-right shunting because the right ventricle accepts an increased volume of blood. There will be a greater degree of left-to-right shunting with large defects. Thus there will be a greater number of clinical findings and a greater severity of those found.

Patent ductus arteriosus (increased pulmonary flow under high pressure). Patent ductus arteriosus comprises 10% of all congenital heart disease, excluding premature infants. It occurs about twice as frequently in females as in males. It frequently occurs as an isolated anomaly but may occur with other congenital heart defects.

The ductus arteriosus is a blood channel that links the descending aorta to the pulmonary artery at its bifurcation during fetal life. It begins to close during the first day of life in a term infant, with complete closure occurring within 2 to 3 weeks.[5] Closure is dependent on the ability to utilize oxygen effective and inhibition of prostaglandins.

Hemodynamics. When the ductus remains open after birth, the higher aortic pressure causes blood to flow from the aorta, through the ductus, into the pulmonary artery. In extreme cases one half to two thirds of the left ventricular output may be shunted through the ductus, and the oxygenated blood recirculates through the pulmonary circulation.[4] The effect of this altered circulation is increased work load on the left ventricle; the volume of blood that the heart must pump to meet the requirements of the peripheral tissues is increased. Left ventricular hypertrophy develops as a compensatory mechanism. Right ventricular hypertrophy may develop in a complicated left-to-right shunt as a result of chronically increased pulmonary flow causing irreversible pulmonary vascular damage and pulmonary hypertension.[9]

Clinical manifestations. When the volume of blood flowing through the ductus is large, growth may be retarded because of poor tissue oxygenation owing to decreased systemic blood flow. Because of increased pulmonary blood flow, dyspnea and congestive heart failure may develop. However, unless the defect is very large or is associated with other cardiac lesions, these symptoms usually do not occur until after the third month of life. When the pulmonary vascular resistance approximates the adult pressure gradient, the lungs are able to handle a larger volume of blood flow, and thus a greater degree of left-to-right shunting takes place. There is an increased incidence of respiratory infections and episodes of pneumonia.[3,8]

There is a characteristic "machinery murmur" that is continuous throughout systole and diastole. This murmur is usually loud in intensity and maximal at the upper left sternal border.[3] Another common feature is a widened pulse pressure. The systolic pressure rises because the increased left ventricular stroke volume causes a rapid rise in the aortic pressure. The low diastolic pressure is a result of the continuous shunting of blood through the aortopulmonary communication.[11] Radial pulses are difficult to palpate in newborns or small infants. Therefore bounding radial arterial pulses in this age group may suggest patent ductus.[8]

Chest x-ray findings show increased pulmonary vascular markings, aortic and pulmonary artery dilation, and cardiomegaly of the left atrium and left ventricle.[3]

Cardiac catheterization is usually not necessary to confirm the diagnosis because of the characteristic auscultatory and radiological findings. However, it may be recommended to exclude associated lesions.

Treatment. Surgical intervention involves surgical division or ligation of the patent vessels. It is felt that diversion of the ductus is more satisfactory than ligation because of complete assurance against recanalization and subsequent development of bacterial endocarditis.[3]

Although the cardiopulmonary bypass is not necessary and the correction itself takes only about 15 minutes, it is a stressful surgery for a premature infant versus a term infant or when performed at the optimal age of 1 to 3 years. There has been research into nonsurgical means of closing the ductus and reports of successful ductal closure in pre-mature infants who were treated with oral administration of indomethacin. Indomethacin is one of several substances known to inhibit the synthesis of prostaglandins, which presents closure of the ductus arteriosus. Therefore, inhibiting the synthesis of prostaglandins by giving indomethacin will aid in closing the ductus or in reducing the size of the ductus and the amount of left-to-right shunting.[6]

Ventricular septal defect (increased pulmonary flow under high pressure). Isolated anomalies of the ventricular septum are among the most common cardiac malformations. They are frequently associated with other defects such as patent ductus arteriosis, atrial septal defect, coarctation of the aorta, pulmonic stenosis, and transposition of the great vessels.

A ventricular septal defect is an abnormal opening between the right and left ventricle. Defects in the lower muscular portion of the interventricular septum are usually small and may close spontaneously. A significant number (estimated by some to be 50% to 80%) close during the first year of life.[4] Defects in the upper membranous portion of the septum tend to be large and cause a greater degree of shunting not only because of their size but also because blood flowing through the defect enters the pulmonary artery almost directly.

Hemodynamics. After birth the pulmonary vascular resistance is decreasing, and thus the pressure in the left ventricle becomes higher than in the right ventricle. Oxygenated blood is shunted from the left ventricle, through the ventricular septal defect, to the right ventricle, and into the pulmonary artery. The left ventricle recirculates increased pulmonary flow through the ventricular septal defect as well as trying to maintain adequate cardiac output in the face of decreased systemic circulation. Because of this increased cardiac work load and gradual left ventricular hypertrophy, left-sided heart failure may occur.[8]

A large left-to-right shunt may significantly overload the pulmonary circulation and thus place a great work load on the right ventricle. Furthermore, increased flow may eventually make the pulmonary vasculature fibrotic and less elastic with subsequent pulmonary hypertension developing. Right ventricular hypertrophy may occur when pulmonary hypertension exists. A marked increase in pulmonary vascular resistance may limit the magnitude of a left-to-right shunt or may result in a bidirectional shunt.[4] When pulmonary vascular resistance exceeds systemic vascular resistance, the left-to-right shunt is replaced by a right-to-left shunt (Eisenmenger's complex).[5]

Clinical manifestations. When the volume of blood being shunted through the septal defect is large, physical development may be retarded; systemic circulation is deprived of a significant amount of the blood intended for tissues of the body. Development usually falls below the third percentile line on a standard development chart.[3] Dyspnea, exercise intolerance, easy fatigability, and recurrent respiratory tract infections and pneumonia are almost invariably present; in addition, episodes of congestive heart failure occur after pulmonary vascular resistance falls, and adult pressure gradient is reached at 3 to 6 months.[3]

A harsh pansystolic murmur, heard best at the lower left sternal border, is the classic auscultatory finding in patients with a ventricular septal defect. A systolic ejection murmur, heard best at the upper left sternal border, indicates increased pulmonary flow. A diastolic murmur, which is heard at the apex, indicates a left-to-right shunt of considerable magnitude as increased pulmonary venous return flows across the mitral valve.[4]

Chest x-ray findings show increased pulmonary vascular markings, aortic and pulmonary artery dilatation, and cardiomegaly of the left atrium and left ventricle.[3]

Cardiac catheterization shows that blood from the right ventricle has a higher oxygen content than that from the right atrium. Pulmonary artery pressure approximates the pressure level in the aorta. When there is a large defect, communication becomes less and less restrictive, culminating in equilibrium of systolic pressure in two ventricles.[5] Passage of the cardiac catheter across the defect into the left ventricle furnishes indisputable evidence for the presence of a ventricular septal defect.[4]

Treatment. Because of the risk of subacute bacterial endocarditis, prevention of infection with prophylactic antibiotics is essential for any surgical intervention.

When medical management for congestive heart failure is not therapeutically successful or development of pulmonary hypertension is suspected at cardiac catheterization, surgical intervention is urgently indicated.

Palliative (closed heart surgery) pulmonary artery banding may be done to prevent increased pulmonary flow. An artificial pulmonary stenosis is created by placing a thin tape of synthetic material around the main pulmonary artery immediately above the pulmonic valve; the subsequent increase in pulmonary vascular resistance will decrease left-to-right shunting.[3]

Corrective (open heart surgery) closure of the defect with insertion of a synthetic patch is usually done at 3 to 4 years of age. Only the smallest defects, probably those that should not have been operated on in the first place, should be closed by direct suture. All others should be patched.[3] Some medical centers are doing corrective repair during the first year of life because it is felt that initial repair prevents potential complications of palliative surgery. The pulmonary artery band may be too loose (congestive heart failure), too tight (cyanosis), or may permanently damage the pulmonary valve.[7] Deep hypothermia during open heart surgery is a new technique that enables surgeons to correct cardiac defects in infants under 1 year of age. To achieve hypothermia, the infant is surface cooled to about 25° C by applying ice packs to the trunk, upper portion of the limbs, and crown of the head. Further cooling to 20° C is done by the heat exchanger on the cardiopulmonary bypass machine; the resultant circulatory arrest allows proper visualization in a bloodless and relaxed heart. Deep hypothermia allows tissue survival under relatively anoxic conditions for about 40 to 45 minutes. If the surgical procedure takes longer than 45 minutes, cardiopulmonary bypass is initiated for about 5 minutes to perfuse the infant's body, and then surgery can be continued under total circulatory arrest for another 40 to 45 minutes.[2]

Atrial septal defect (increased pulmonary flow under low pressure). Anomalies of the atrial septum comprise approximately 10% of all patients who have congenital heart disease. The defect is more common in females.

An atrial septal defect is an abnormal opening between the right and left atria. Depending on the phase of arrested embryological development, the lesion may be one of three types: (1) sinus venosus defects, in which the superior portion of the atrial septum fails to form; (2) ostium primum defects, in which there is inadequate development of the endocardial cushions; and (3) ostium secundum defects, in which the foramen ovale fails to close.[11] Since the ostium secundum defects are the most common, the following discussion will explain the hemodynamics, clinical manifestations, and treatment of those defects.

Hemodynamics. After birth the pulmonary vascular resistance decreases, and thus the pressure in the left atrium becomes higher than in the right atrium. Oxygenated blood is shunted from the left atrium, through the atrial septal defect, to the right atrium, right ventricle, and into the pulmonary artery. The major hemodynamic abnormality is volume overload of the right ventricle; increased pulmonary blood flow results in right ventricular hypertrophy, which may lead to right-sided heart failure.[4]

It should be noted that the pressure difference between the atria is not the sole determinant of the direction or degree of shunting in atrial septal defect. At birth there is little or no shunting in either direction because the distensibility (compliance) of the two ventricles is the same. Occasionally, transient neonatal cyanosis may be detected because of a right-to-left shunt resulting from decreased compliance of the right ventricle. During the newborn period the relatively thick-walled neonatal right ventricle becomes thinner and begins to offer less resistance to filling than the left ventricle; normally, it is thicker and less compliant than the right ventricle because of having to overcome high systemic vascular resistance.[5] Despite the increased left-to-right shunting with increased compliance, congestive heart failure in infancy is not usually caused by atrial septal defect because the right ventricle can accommodate larger volumes of blood than the left ventricle.[8]

Clinical manifestations. Retardation of growth, especially weight, characterizes the symptomatic infant with atrial septal defect.[5] Dyspnea, exercise intolerance, easy fatigability, and recurrent respiratory tract infectious are present in varying degrees. Subacute bacterial endocarditis is rare because of the absence of jet lesions or turbulence owing to the low velocity of flow across the interatrial communication.[5]

A systolic ejection murmur, heard best at the second interspace along the left sternal border, represents increased ventricular flow through the pulmonic valve to the pulmonary artery. A diastolic murmur, which is heard at the apex, indicates left-to-right shunt of considerable magnitude as increased pulmonary venous return flows across the tricuspid valve.[4] It should be mentioned that murmurs may not be noted in the neonatal period because of the relatively small left-to-right shunt occurring through the defect in infancy.

Chest x-ray findings show increased pulmonary vascularity, pulmonary artery dilatation, and cardiomegaly of the right atrium and right ventricle. The left ventricle and aorta are smaller than usual, owing to the decreased amount of blood they carry.[4]

Cardiac catheterization shows that blood from the right atrium has a higher oxygen content than that from the superior vena cava. The pressures in the right side of the heart are frequently normal but may show moderate right ventricular and pulmonary hypertension. The catheter frequently enters the left atrium from the right atrium, but the passage of the catheter through the atrial septum does not by itself indicate the presence of an atrial septal defect—it may simply demonstrate an anatomically, but not necessarily functionally, patent foramen ovale.[3]

Treatment. Prevention of infection and vigorous antibiotic treatment of upper respiratory infections as well as pneumonia are essential.

Corrective (open heart surgery) closure of the defect with insertion of a synthetic patch is usually done between 4 and 10 years of age. Closure involves the same principles as discussed under ventricular septal defect.

Acyanotic heart defects with normal pulmonary vascularity

Coarctation of the aorta and aortic stenosis are termed obstructive lesions because they obstruct the blood flow from the heart. The usual response to this obstruction is myocardial hypertrophy, since the ventricles and atria must push against the obstruction to create adequate cardiac output.[8]

Coarctation of the aorta. A coarctation of the aorta is a relatively common anomaly composing 5% to 10% of congenital heart disease. Sex ratio is approximately 2:1, with males predominating.[3] There is a strong tendnecy for coarctation of the aorta to be associated with other cardiac malformations such as aortic stenosis, patent ductus arteriosus, ventricular septal defect, atrial septal defect, and transposition of the great arteries.[5]

A coarctation of the aorta is a localized narrowing of the aortic lumen. Depending on its relation to the ductus arteriosus, there are two types of this anomaly: (1) preductal (infantile type)—narrowing proximal to the ductus arteriosus and left subclavian artery and (2) postductal (adult type)—narrowing distal to the ductus arteriosus and left subclavian artery; 98% occur just below the origin of the left subclavian artery.[4]

Hemodynamics. The principal physiological problem is the maintenance of adequate blood flow and pressure in the lower half of the body. This is effected by way of three adaptive mechanisms: The first is the elevation of the systolic pressure in the proximal arota. The second is vasoconstriction in the arterioles to maintain a high diastolic pressure. The third is the bypassing of the aortic constriction by development of collateral circulation.[3]

Coarctation is particularly likely to produce significant symptoms during early infancy and young adulthood. Infants may develop severe congestive heart failure because of the interaction of three mechanisms: First, with the postnatal increase in left ventricular output as well as the increase in resistance at the coarctation level when the ductus closes, the left ventricular work increases. Second, if there is little collateral network and the narrowing is severe, the left ventricular work increases. Third, a contributing factor is the presence of associated anomalies such as left-to-right shunts through septal defects.[3]

Clinical manifestations. Since most of these children are well developed and asymptomatic, coarctation of the aorta may not be diagnosed until a routine physical examination reveals hypertension or a murmur. A hypertensive state may result in epistaxis, dizziness, headaches, or possibly intracranial hemorrhage. Left ventricular failure may occur secondary to the hypertensive state. Deficient circulation to the legs may be manifested by cold feet as well as arterial spasm with subsequent painful cramping of the legs and loss of function, especially on exertion.

The classic sign of coarctation of the aorta is the inequality in pulsations and blood pressures between the upper and lower extremities. Normally, the systolic blood pressure in the legs should be 20 to 40 mm Hg higher than that in the arms because of peripheral resistance. In coarctation of the aorta the blood pressure in the legs is much lower than that obtained in the arms. If a difference of more than 40 mm Hg between the right and left arms is found, there may be coarctation proximal to the left subclavian artery. On simultaneous palpation, the femoral, popliteal, posterior tibial, and dorsalis pedis pulsations are weak and delayed or absent compared with the bounding pulses of the arms and carotid vessels.[4] It is important to note that femoral pulses may vary in the infant. As long as the ductus is patent, the femoral pulses are readily palpable. As soon as the ductus closes, the femoral pulses disappear and heart failure may ensue; the infant is irritable, has feeding problems, dyspnea, tachypnea, tachycardia, diaphoresis, and circumoral cyanosis.

The common murmur is systolic in time (90% of the patients), ejection in nature, and maximal over the base of the heart; it radiates down the sternum to the apex and to the interscapular area and frequently is loudest in the back. The murmur may be produced by the coarctation, by tortuous collateral vessels, by abnormalities of the aortic valve, or by associated structural anomalies of the heart such as septal defects.[4]

Chest x-ray fiindings may show left ventricular enlargement or massive cardiomegaly if congestive heart failure develops. There is a dilated ascending aorta proximal to the coarctation. Notching of the lower rib margin may be evident in an older child as collateral intercostal arteries erode the bone.

Treatment. The treatment of infants with coarctation of the aorta and congestive heart failure should be attempted first by medical means such as digitalis and diuretics. Excluding the systolic murmur and the hypertension of the arms, clinical manifestations of this anomaly may disappear within days, with few, if any, relapses. If there is no response to medical management, the infant should be catheterized to determine whether there are co-existing malformations; there is a high incidence of this situation in those who do not respond to medical treatment.[3]

It should be noted that the presence of a patent ductus arteriosus may be hemodynamically beneficial. When severe coarctation in a young infant is complicated by a closing ductus that results in limited systemic circulation, prostaglandin E_1 may be used as an emergency measure to prevent ductal closure.[8]

If the child is asymptomatic, surgery is deferred until the late preschool to early school age period; the aortic lumen approximates adult size and hypertension is less fixed than waiting much longer than 10 years of age.

Corrective surgery involves surgical resection of the coarcted portion of the aorta with end-to-end anastomosis of the proximal and distal segments. If narrowing is so extensive that primary anastomosis is not practical, a synthetic graft may be inserted.[3] It is usually done as a closed-heart procedure because collateral circulation is well developed. If diagnostic measures indicate otherwise, the cardiopulmonary bypass will be utilized to prevent decreased blood supply to the lower extremities by cross clamping during the operative procedure.

Aortic stenosis. Congenital aortic stenosis accounts for about 5% of all cardiac malformations; it is more common in males, with a sex ratio of approximately $4:1$.[5] Ventricular and atrial septal defects, patent ductus arteriosus, and coarctation of the aorta can occur as associated anomalies.[3]

Congenital aortic stenosis may be divided anatomically into valvular, subvalvular, and supravalvular. In the valvular type, representing about 75% of all cases, the cusps are most frequently bicuspid; there appears to be hypoplasia of one of the three cusps and fusion with the remaining cusp.

Hemodynamics. The psychological stress of aortic stenosis is imposed on the left ventricle. The problem is to maintain an adequate blood flow and pressure in the systemic circulation through a narrowing of the left ventricular valve. Since the size of the orifice is seriously reduced, the left ventricular diastolic volume and end diastolic pressure increase so as to increase the left ventricular peak systolic pressure. Left ventricular

hypertrophy develops as this ventricle attempts to maintain the necessary systolic pressure. The increased oxygen requirement of the hypertrophied left ventricle is not met by a proportionate increase in the coronary blood flow; there is a shortening of diastolic filling time and a squeezing effect on the coronary arteries by the high left ventricular systolic pressure. The myocardial ischemia that results may be followed by fatal cardiac arrhythmias, causing sudden death.[3]

Congestive heart failure is uncommon in early childhood but represents a serious problem in the neonate with isolated severe aortic stenosis. The obstructed thick-walled left ventricle, with decreased compliance and small cavity size, has difficulty in accepting the sudden postnatal increment in blood volume. Temporary patency of the ductus diverts right ventricular blood into the arota and delays onset of symptoms, but when the ductus closes, the entire right ventricular output enters the pulmonary circulation and left heart.[5] These infants (two thirds of them less than 3 months old) often are critically ill with left-sided and right-sided heart failure. Unlike those with simple coarctation, they do not continue to do well with conservative treatment; the reason may be the effect of aortic stenosis on coronary perfusion.[3]

Clinical manifestations. Because the hypertrophied left ventricle is capable of increasing its cardiac output with little or no increase in filling pressure, the child may be completely asymptomatic. Physical development is usually excellent. However, there is evidence that mild aortic stenosis may become severe during the adolescent growth spurt, paralleling the increase in resting output, the effect of the jet stream on the aortic valve, and the advent of strenuous athletic activities.[3] Fatigue and dyspnea on exertion may be present with severe obstruction to left ventricular outflow. Significant symptoms are angina and syncope, which usually accompany vigorous exercise but may occur during minimal effort or at rest. Although both are rare (less than 10%) in children, their presence indicates myocardial and cerebral ischemia, which predispose to sudden death.[3] Because of this factor, competitive athletics and activities requiring sustained exertion without the opportunity for rest are inadvisable.[9]

A harsh systolic ejection murmur is audible maximally in the aortic area and radiates to the neck and down the left sternal border toward the apex.[4] A murmur may not be heard in congestive heart failure because of decreased cardiac output. In slightly less than half of the cases the murmur was discovered before the child was 1 year old; in a third of them the child was between 1 and 4 years old, and in the remainder the child was between 5 and 8 years of age.[3]

Chest x-ray findings may reveal signs of slight left ventricular enlargement; marked enlargement is seldom present except in infants with severe obstruction and heart failure.[5] The ascending aorta is frequently prominent because of poststenotic dilatation.

Left cardiac catheterization reveals left ventricular hypertension with an increased end diastolic pressure and systolic pressure gradient across the stenotic valve.

Treatment. Aortic valvular stenosis is usually treated by an aortic commissurotomy (valvotomy), which is a palliative procedure to mobilize fused commissures of the valve orifice. The surgery carries the risk of aortic insufficiency if the commissures are incised too widely. Furthermore, significant stenosis may remain or recur. Valve replacement may then be necessary for satisfactory hemodynamics.

Aortic valvular surgery is indicated in those children experiencing recurrent angina, syncope, and congestive heart failure as well as those with gross left ventricular hypertrophy and systolic pressure gradient greater than 50 mm Hg. The optimal age for surgery is between 5 and 15 years of age.[3]

Cyanotic heart defects

Cyanosis, a bluish discoloration of the skin and mucous membranes, results when there is greater than 5 gm of reduced hemoglobin in the capillary blood. (Normally, capillary blood contains about 2.5 gm hemoglobin, which has dissociated from oxygen.) Peripheral cyanosis results from reduced blood flow in the peripheral circulation, which can be caused by low cardiac output; it involves specific body parts, such as the hands and feet, and it is milder in degree. Central cyanosis results from arterial unsaturation, which can be of either pulmonary (impaired ventilation or diffusion) or cardiac (intracardiac or extracardiac right-to-left shunting and mixing) origin; it is more generalized

and more severe in degree. Normally, blood in the pulmonary veins, left side of the heart, and systemic arteries is more than 95% saturated with oxygen. If there is less than 91% saturation, there is arterial unsaturation.[3] When arterial saturation is less than 75%, a significant degree of cyanosis is present.

Cyanosis is associated with several other clinical manifestations that result from decreased tissue oxygenation. Dyspnea on exertion occurs because the heart is not meeting the metabolic demands for oxygen. Any event that increases metabolic demands, such as crying, feeding, or fever, will cause increased shortness of breath and increased cyanosis. Clubbing can be described as a widening and thickening of the ends of the fingers and toes accompanied by convex fingernails. Full-blown clubbing has been seen in children as young as 2 to 3 weeks old; however, it usually does not appear until the child is 1 or 2 years old.[3] Polycythemia is a compensatory mechanism in which the bone marrow is stimulated to produce more red blood cells in an effort to increase the oxygen-carrying capacity. However, not only do iron stores need to keep pace with hemoglobin needs of the increased red cell volume, but the increased red cells can result in an increase in systemic resistance (increased blood viscosity), a decrease in cardiac output, and an ultimate decrease in oxygen delivery to the tissues.[3] Interference with growth and development at the organ and cullular level is another effect of arterial unsaturation.

There are some significant complications in cyanotic heart disease. Cerebral thromboses are more common in the presence of extreme polycythemia and may be precipitated by dehydration and iron deficiency anemia. They occur more frequently in patients under the age of 2 years. Conversely, patients with brain abscesses are usually over the age of 2 years. It is possible that infected emboli from the systemic reservoir are carried across the ventricular defect and propelled directly through the carotid arteries up to the brain. It is also feasible that cerebral thrombi, inherent in the polycythemia of these patients, may become secondarily infected during a transient episode of bacteremia.[3]

In most infants and children with cyanotic heart disease an anomaly is present that allows some of the systemic venous blood to bypass the lungs and directly enter the systemic arterial circulation. These anomalies may be divided into those with increased pulmonary vascularity (such as transposition of the great vessels) and those with decreased pulmonary vascularity (such as tetralogy of Fallot). The former condition allows admixture of systemic and pulmonary venous returns, and the later condition results in obstruction to pulmonary blood flow.

Complete transposition of the great vessels (increased pulmonary vascularity). Complete transposition is one of the most common forms of serious heart disease in infants, with the incidence ranging from 9.5% to 19% depending on the selected population.[3] Sex ratio is 2 to 4:1 with males predominating.[5]

Transposition of the great vessels refers to a change in the anatomical relationship of the pulmonary artery and the aorta; the aorta arises from the right ventricle and the pulmonary artery from the left ventricle. However, the great veins are not similarly transposed.

Hemodynamics. Blood originating in the right atrium enters the right ventricle, aorta, systemic capillary bed, and systemic venous bed and returns to the right atrium via the cavae, never having left the systemic circulation. Similarly, blood originating in the left atrium enters the left ventricle, pulmonary artery, pulmonary capillary bed, and pulmonary venous bed and returns to the left atrium via the pulmonary veins, never having left the pulmonary circulation. Thus blood in the systemic circulation recirculates within its own system, and blood in the pulmonary circulation recirculates within its own system. Blood from the systemic venous bed must somehow enter the pulmonary circulation to be oxygenated, and oxygenated blood from the pulmonary circulation must somehow return to the systemic bed. This interchange is accomplished when the two independent circulations are joined by an atrial septal defect, ventricular septal defect, or patent ductus arteriosus, singly or in combination.[5] The degree of mixing is determined by the pressure differences between the ventricles, resistance to left ventricular (pulmonary vascular resistance) and right ventricular outflow, and the size of the communication between the two systems.

It should be noted that the type of coexisting defect can be hemodynamically significant. If a patent ductus arteriosus is the only communication between the two circulations, cyanosis and arterial unsaturation become profound when this fetal structure follows normal neonatal closure. Although a ventricular septal defect may permit adequate arterial oxygen saturation, the increased pulmonary flow with this high-pressure/high-flow communication leads to pulmonary venous congestion and congestive heart failure. Furthermore, early severe pulmonary vascular disease prevails in transposition with high-pressure/high-flow communication. This hemodynamic sequela causes a decrease in both pulmonary flow and intercirculatory mixing; consequently, systemic arterial oxygen saturation decreases.[5] The only situation in which a ventricular septal defect would be better than an atrial septal defect is if there is moderate pulmonary stenosis to regulate the pulmonary blood flow; ventricular septal defect with coexisting pulmonary stenosis permits a satisfactory systemic arterial oxygen saturation without excessive volume overload of the left heart.[5] Since an atrial septal defect permits increased pulmonary flow with a lower pressure in the pulmonary circuit, it provides adequate intercirculatory mixing without pulmonary overload; serious pulmonary vascular disease usually does not occur until later.

Clinical manifestations. In addition to cyanosis and clubbing, the infant may experience paroxysmal dyspneic attacks during the first months of life. However, these are more commonly encountered with tetralogy of Fallot. Although there is dyspnea on exertion, squatting is also seen more frequently with tetralogy of Fallot.

Normal or high birth weight may create an initial impression of good health, but the illusion rapidly fades. Growth retardation is almost invariable after the first few months and is generally appreciable in infants surviving their first year.[5]

The character of the murmur depends on the associated lesion; a systolic murmur is heard if a ventricular septal defect is present.

Chest x-ray findings reveal increased pulmonary vascularity and marked cardiomegaly.

Cardiac catheterization reveals that oxygen saturation values from the pulmonary artery are higher than from the aorta. Atrial pressures may be normal, but they may be increased with patent ductus arteriosus or ventricular septal defect. Right and left ventricular pressures are initially equal, but after the neonatal period is there is no ventricular septal defect or pulmonary stenosis, right ventricular pressure is greater than that in the left ventricle.[3]

Treatment. Most infants with transposition of the great vessels will die in infancy unless a palliative procedure is performed. At the time of diagnostic cardiac catheterization, an atrial septostomy is done. This procedure involves the passage of a balloon-tipped catheter into the right atrium and across the interatrial septum into the left atrium; the balloon is then inflated to a diameter of 1 to 1.5 cm and is abruptly withdrawn into the right atrium to tear the atrial septum. It is repeated (5 to 10 times) until there is no resistance to withdrawal of the balloon across the interatrial septum. After an adequate septostomy, mixing of the blood occurs at the atrial level, significant elevation of arterial oxygen saturation occurs (75% to 85%), and tachypnea is relieved because of reduction of pulmonary venous pressure.[4] If this procedure does not maintain adequate oxygen saturation (less than 65%) or if it is not feasible because of thickening of the atrial septum (after age 2 to 3 months), an atrial septectomy is done. In this Blalock-Hanlon procedure the surgical creation of an atrial septal defect allows blood in the pulmonary and systemic circulations to intermix. This procedure may be accompanied by volume overload of the left heart unless pulmonary flow is regulated by obstruction to left ventricular outflow. Therefore a pulmonary artery band is done to minimize congestive heart failure and to protect the pulmonary vasculature. Conversely, a systemic-pulmonary artery shunt (such as Blalock-Taussig) may be done with severe coexisting pulmonary stenosis to minimize serious hypoxia.[3]

Intra-atrial correction should not be postponed indefinitely in infancy beyond the age of 1 year because irreversible pulmonary vascular disease is possible as young as 2 to 3 years. In this procedure an atrial baffle of Dacron or pericardium is developed that directs systemic venous blood to the mitral valve and left ventricle; pulmonary venous blood flows through the tricuspid valve to the right ventricle. Thus systemic venous blood is ejected by the left ventricle to the lungs for oxygenation, and arterialized pulmonary venous blood is pumped by the right ventricle into the aorta.[4]

Tetralogy of Fallot (decreased pulmonary vascularity). Tetralogy of Fallot accounts for at least 15% of all patients more than 2 years of age who have congenital heart disease. It is the most common single lesion in patients with cyanotic disease who live beyond infancy.[3]

Anatomically, the tetralogy of Fallot consists of a ventricular septal defect; pulmonary stenosis that may be infundibular (muscle below the valve), valvular, supravalvular, or combined, causing obstruction to flow into the pulmonary artery; right ventricular hypertrophy because the right ventricular pressure is at systemic levels owing to obstruction and equalization of pressure across the ventricular septal defect; and dextroposition of the aorta so that it overrides the ventricular septal defect. The degree of right-to-left shunting is determined by the severity of the pulmonary stenosis and the size of the ventricular septal defect.

Hemodynamics. Systemic venous return to the right atrium and right ventricle is normal. When the right ventricle contracts, the outflow of blood is resisted by the pulmonary stenosis and blood is shunted across the ventricular septal defect in the aorta.[4]

There are two hemodynamic handicaps. First, because of the right-to-left shunt, central cyanosis of varying degree is present in most patients. Second, because of the pulmonary obstruction, which cannot be met with a right ventricular pressure appreciably higher than the systemic arterial pressure (owing to the presence of a ventricular defect), the pulmonary blood flow is limited, and exertional dyspnea is prominent. The presence of the ventricular septal defect thus places a limit (that of the systemic arterial pressure) on the pressure exerted by the right ventricle. Although these patients may be extremely limited in their activities, cardiac failure is almost never seen during childhood because the right ventricle is protected from doing too much pressure work.[3]

Clinical manifestations. Cyanosis may not be present at birth. Apparently, as long as the ductus arteriosus remains patent, sufficient blood passes through the lungs to prevent cyanosis.[4] As it closes, 75% of the patients become cyanotic by 1 year of age. The time of appearance and the severity of the cyanosis depend on the severity of the pulmonary stenosis and the development of collateral circulation.[5] Clubbing of the fingers and toes usually accompanies cyanosis.

A characteristic of this defect is the hypoxic episode or "tetrad spell." These episodes consist of uncontrollable crying followed by paroxysms of dyspnea, gasping respirations, increasing cyanosis, unconsciousness, and possible seizures. Their onset may not be caused by any environmental factor; yet, they may be precipitated by crying, feeding (especially breakfast), or a bowel movement. One of the postulated mechanisms is that a vulnerable respiratory control center, which is especially sensitive after prolonged sleep, reacts to a sudden increase in cardiac output provoked by the aforementioned stressors. The increased systemic venous return in the presence of pulmonary stenosis increases the right-to-left shunt. The resultant arterial hypoxia, metabolic acidosis, and increased Pco_2 further stimulate the respiratory center to maintain continuing hyperpnea.[5] The disappearance of the systolic murmur, caused by obstruction of the right ventricular outflow tract, suggests that the spells may be associated with spasm of the right ventricular outflow tract.[3] The duration of the spell is a few minutes to several hours; the frequency is every 2 to 3 months or several in one day. These spells usually start at 3 to 6 months of age, have their peak incidence at 1 to 2 years, and disappear before 5 years of age.[3]

As they begin to walk, these toddlers discover dyspnea on exertion is relieved by assuming a characteristic squatting position. The arterial oxygen saturation is increased so that the child is able to resume physical activity within a few minutes. Squatting decreases venous return of markedly unsaturated blood from the legs so that a smaller volume of highly unsaturated venous blood reaches the heart. Increased systemic vascular resistance via squatting decreases right-to-left shunting of unsaturated blood.[5]

Birth weight is lower than normal and growth retardation is present.

A loud systolic murmur may be more pansystolic at the lower left sternal border (ventricular septal defect) and ejection at the upper left sternal border (pulmonary stenosis). An inaudible murmur occurs when severe pulmonary stenosis decreases pulmonary flow.

The chest x-ray film reveals a relatively small heart of right ventricular contour and a poorly vascularized lung field ("boot-shaped"). Any cardiac enlargement shown on the x-ray film almost exclusively involves the right ventricle and the right atrium.[3]

Cardiac catheterization reveals decreased oxygen saturation values of the left ventricle as compared with the left atrium (systemic arterial unsaturation). There is systolic hypertension in the right ventricle (systemic pressure level) and a sudden fall of pressure as the catheter enters the pulmonary artery. The passage of the catheter across the ventricular septum into the aorta is the only direct way of proving the presence of a ventricular septal defect.[3]

Treatment. Although the majority of patients require surgical treatment, astute medical management is necessary before operation. The prevention or prompt treatment of dehydration is important to avoid hemoconcentration and possible thrombotic episodes.[3] Antibiotic therapy is essential, especially with surgical procedures, to prevent bacterial endocarditis. Iron therapy as well as oral propranolol may decrease the frequency and severity of paroxysmal dyspneic attacks.

Anastomotic procedures. Taussig observed that the prognosis was better when the ductus arteriosus was patent.[3] She and Blalock devised a procedure whereby an artificial ductus is created by anastomosis of the end of the left subclavian artery to the side of the pulmonary artery. Pulmonary blood flow may also be increased by side-to-side anastomosis of the pulmonary artery to the ascending aorta (Waterston) or the descending aorta.[3] Although the Blalock-Taussig technique was previously avoided in infants less than 6 months of age because of small subclavian arteries, modification of the shunt technique assures adequate patency in the small infant. Furthermore, left-sided heart failure and pulmonary hypertension are less frequent after the Blalock-Taussig technique than after aortopulmonary shunts. Total correction is technically less complicated after a Blalock-Taussig shunt.

Although the Blalock-Taussig shunt will decrease cyanosis, dyspnea, and "tetrad spells", the affected arm will have decreased function (no pulses or blood pressure) and be underdeveloped. Collateral circulation delivers blood flow to the arm.

Corrective procedure. To prevent complications of palliative surgery and growth retardation (emotionally and intellectually as well as physically), many centers are doing one-stage correction using deep hyperthermia.

While the patient's circulation is temporarily maintained on the cardiopulmonary bypass machine, the right ventricle is opened, the obstruction to right outflow is relieved, and the ventricular septal defect is closed. In addition, the right ventricular outflow tract is enlarged with a patch (similar to ventricular septal defect) if a significant pressure gradient persists between the right ventricle and pulmonary artery. Although this produces pulmonary valve incompetence, pulmonary regurgitation is preferable to pulmonary stenosis. A previously established systemic-pulmonary shunt must be closed prior to cardiotomy.[3] Corrective repair is usually done between the ages of 3 and 5, but, as already mentioned, it is sometimes performed during the first 2 years of life.

Protocols

Problem □ Congestive heart failure

GOALS:

1. To assist in measures to improve myocardial function
2. To assist in measures to promote elimination of retained sodium and water
3. To decrease tissue oxygen demands and cardiac work load
4. To provide adequate oxygenation and nutrition to body tissues

Rationale: To minimize or alleviate disease conditions (anemia, respiratory infections) and circumstances (physiological/psychological work) that could contribute to the development of congestive heart failure

DIAGNOSTIC

1. Closely monitor all vital signs.

   Rationale: To check *temperature*—hyperthermia (a sign of infection) or hypothermia (loss of heat to ambient air); *heart rate*—tachycardia, 160 beats/min (compensatory mechanism by the sympathetic nervous system to maintain adequate stroke volume and tissue perfusion), or bradycardia, 120 beats/min (cardiac toxicity of digitalis owing to excessive vagal stimulation); and *respiratory rate*—tachypnea, 60 breaths/min (stimulation of carotid reflexes and the respiratory center in response to decreased arterial oxygen saturation) (Respirations are carefully monitored during a resting state, since fast, labored breathing greatly increases cardiac demands.)

2. Assess respiration.

   a. Cyanosis is a sign of low arterial oxygen saturation, decreased blood volume, or stasis in the systemic circulation. It may be generalized or confined to specific body parts such as the hands, feet, circumoral area, mucous membranes, or nail beds. The degree varies from dusky, to mild, to moderate, to severe.

   b. Dyspnea is shortness of breath that is caused by a decrease in distensibility of the lungs.

   c. Orthopnea is dyspnea of recumbency when increased venous return to right heart increases pulmonary congestion.

   d. Retractions are present when additional respiratory muscles are utilized when there is decreased distensibility of the lungs.

   e. Nasal flaring is an attempt to widen the airway during inspiration because of air hunger.

   f. Grunting is an attempt to retain air in the lungs during expiration to increase arterial oxygen level.

   g. Diaphoresis is caused by stimulation of the sympathetic nervous system.

   h. Cough is caused by pulmonary congestion and/or muscosal swelling and irritation.

   i. Rales are caused by air flowing through moisture in the tracheobronchial tree.

   j. Rhonchi are caused by obstruction to air flow from swelling of the bronchial mucosa.

Rationale: To assess signs and symptoms of pulmonary congestion (As the left ventricle fails, blood volume and pressure increase in the left atrium, pulmonary veins, and lungs. Eventually the pulmonary capillary pressure exceeds the plasma osmotic pressure, causing fluid transudation from capillaries into surrounding interstitial spaces.)

3. Assess cardiac function.
   a. S_3 heart sounds indicate vibrations against the ventricle walls as blood flow is abruptly stopped when the dilated ventricles can no longer accommodate the volume.
   b. S_4 heart sounds indicated atrial contraction in response to ventricular resistance during filling of the ventricles.
   Rationale: To assess signs and symptoms of cardiac compensation vs decompensation (Increased blood volume causes the ventricles to dilate; ventricular dilatation results in extra heart sounds, S_3 and/or S_4).

4. Assess for systemic congestion.
   a. Edema forms as sodium and water retention cause systemic vascular pressure to rise. Edema is usually generalized and too difficult to detect in infants; periorbital edema may develop in recumbent positions.
   b. Hepatomegaly occurs from pooling of blood in the portal circulation and transudation of fluid into the hepatic tissues. With hepatomegaly, the liver edge will be felt 3 cm or more below the costal margin.
   c. Coolness and/or cyanosis of the extremities occurs when venous congestion reduces peripheral blood flow, thus redistributing blood from the skin to more vital organs.
   Rationale: To assess signs and symptoms of systemic congestion (Venous blood returning to the right heart encounters resistance from residual blood in those chambers. There is an increase in systemic hydrostatic pressure and fluid transudation into the interstitial spaces.)

5. Assess the general condition of the infant.
   a. Activity level—some infants are continuously restless, even during sleep; others are very lethargic and never awaken on their own for feeding.

   b. Posturing—in cardiac disease there is decreased muscle tone, and the arms become flaccid with the exertion of eating.
   c. Cry—in cardiac disease the cry is weak and muffled or loud and breathless, and there is a lack of movement of the arms and legs when crying (severe distress).
   Rationale: To further assess for the presence of cardiac disease

6. Assess feeding behavior.
   a. The infant may be anorexic, indicating venous congestion of the gastrointestinal tract.
   b. The infant may become increasingly pale or cyanotic when feeding.
   c. The infant may become increasingly diaphoretic when feeding.
   d. The infant may show poor sucking from lack of energy or be unable to close the mouth around the nipple because of dyspnea.
   e. The infant may have difficulty in coordinating sucking, swallowing, and breathing and may pull away from the nipple to take a breath.
   f. The infant may feed slowly, with pauses to rest, and may become exhausted and take less than formula quota.
   Rationale: To detect feeding difficulty, which is often the first sign of congestive heart failure

7. Monitor intake and output (use 24-hour urine collector or weigh diapers, 1 gm = 1 ml) and daily weight.
   Rationale: To detect fluid and sodium retention owing to the R-A-A cycle via sympathetic nervous system stimulation (Decreased cardiac output decreases blood flow to the kidneys and decreases glomerular filtration rate. Renin is released by the kidneys, which produce angiotensin which stimulates the adrenal cortex to secrete aldosterone. This affects tubular reabsorption of sodium. Sodium retention results, and increased osmotic pressure stimulates hypothalamic osmoreceptors to increase ADH production. This stimulates the posterior pituitary to secrete antidiuretic hormone, which affects tubular reabsorption of water.

Intake and output and daily weights are diagnostic tools used to evaluate the effect of diuretic therapy.)

8. Monitor for side effects of medications.
   a. Digitalis—the earliest manifestation of digitalis toxicity is vomiting, usually with anorexia and nausea, caused by stimulation of the emetic control center in the medulla. Cardiac arrhythmias might occur; premature ventricular contractions can progress to ventricular tachycardia and fibrillation; and prolonged AV conduction time (increased P-R interval on ECG) can progress to complete heart block.
   b. Diuretics—hypokalemia, which may occur with furosemide and the thiazides, enhances the effects of digitalis, increasing the risk of digitalis toxicity. If fluid retention is accompanied by loss of sodium, diuretics would cause additional sodium loss, resulting in hyponatremia. Decreased urinary output may indicate dehydration.

   Rationale: To identify and alleviate untoward effects

THERAPEUTIC

1. Decrease cardiac demands.
   a. Provide physical rest
      (1) Complete bath and linen change should be done only when necessary.
      (2) Care giving activities should be organized to provide for periods of uninterrupted sleep.
      (3) Feeding schedule should accommodate the infant's sleep and wake patterns.
   b. Provide emotional rest.
      (1) Encourage parents to participate in care, such as feeding, bathing, positioning, and providing social/tactile stimulation.
      (2) Encourage parents to stay with their infant to provide holding, rocking, and cuddling, which fosters growth and developmental gaining of a sense of trust.
   c. Preserve body temperature. Preservation of body temperature is important when infant is receiving cool, humidified oxygen and in infants who tend to be diaphoretic and lose heat via evaporation.

Rationale: To provide physical/emotional rest and conserve energy, which will decrease the metabolic needs of the tissues for oxygen and thus decrease cardiac work load

2. Reduce respiratory distress.
   a. Positioning—semi-Fowler's position facilitates breathing by decreasing the pressure of the viscera on the diaphragm and thus increasing lung volume for better expansion.
   b. Oxygen therapy is given to increase the oxygen tension of alveolar air when there is congested circulation through the alveolar-capillary membrane and subsequently to increase blood oxygenation to the tissues. Cool humidification is important to prevent the formation of thick secretions and the drying effect of oxygen on the mucous membranes.

   Rationale: To decrease the work of the respiratory muscles as well as cardiac work load

3. Improve myocardial function by using digitalis glycosides.
   a. Prevent toxicity.
      (1) Use correct preparation—in pediatrics digoxin (Lanoxin) is used almost exclusively because of its more rapid onset and decreased risk of toxicity as a result of a shorter half-life.
      (2) Calculate the dosage carefully; compare calculations with another nurse before giving the drug. Measure the dosage with a tuberculin syringe for greater accuracy (narrow margin of safety between therapeutic and toxic doses).
      (3) Count apical pulse prior to giving the drug and withhold dose if pulse is lower than 100 beats/min in infants. Since the peak action is in 6 to 8 hours, the PM reading is significant after an AM dose.

      Rationale: To be aware that digitalis increases the force of contraction, decreases the heart rate and slows the conduction of impulses through the atrioventricular node, and finally enhances diuresis by increased renal perfusion

(The beneficial effects are increased cardiac output, decreased heart size, decreased venous pressure, and relief of dyspnea.)

4. Promote fluid loss.
   a. Diuretics interfere with renal tubular reabsorption of sodium and water; they are divided into groups based on their chemistry and exact sites of action in the renal tubule. Furosemide is an example of a rapid-acting diuretic—diuresis begins 5 minutes after intravenous injection. Thiazides are examples of maintenance diuretics—diuresis begins 1 hour after oral administration. Prevent hypokalemia.
      (1) Encourage foods high in potassium such as bananas, oranges, whole grains, legumes, and leafy vegetables.
      (2) Give potassium elixir mixed with fruit juice to disguise the bitter taste and to prevent intestinal irritation.
      (3) Give spironolactone (Aldactone), which minimizes potassium loss.
   b. A low sodium diet assists with adequate diuresis to decrease cardiac work load. (Low sodium formulas are available.) Because of dyspnea on exertion, sucking becomes an exhausting activity, and the infant is unable to consume adequate caloric intake. Minimize the respiratory effort of feeding.
      (1) Small frequent feedings are scheduled after 2 to 3 hours of sleep.
      (2) Feed as soon as the infant appears hungry, such as when sucking on his fists rather than when crying for a long period of time.
      (3) Hold in semiupright position.
      (4) Use soft nipple that does not flow too fast.
      (5) Thicken the formula with pureed foods so that the nipple hole can be enlarged to facilitate the flow of formula.
      (6) Allow brief rest periods when the infant pulls away from the nipple.
   c. Fluid restriction may not be appropriate for an infant who is having feeding difficulty or necessary if diuretics and sodium restriction provide adequate diuresis.

Rationale: To decrease circulatory blood volume and increase the effectiveness of digitalis on the heart

EDUCATIONAL

1. Explain to the parents the infant's need for rest, both physical and emotional, and how they can help maintain that rest by comforting baby when upset, feeding when hungry, changing when wet, and not waking him when asleep.
   Rationale: To help parents feel a sense of confidence in themselves as parents and a sense of trust in the health team, which will subsequently motivate them to aid in the optimal implementation of the therapeutic care
2. Explain to the parents the important considerations regarding the administration of digoxin (Lanoxin).
   a. They should know the action and side effects.
      (1) Repeating a vomited dose may result in overdose. Furthermore, vomiting may indicate toxicity.
      (2) Taking radial pulse by palpation may reveal cardiac arrhythmia.
   b. They should know about dividing the maintenance dose during the day; giving the drug every 12 hours maintains therapeutic blood levels.
   c. They should practice measuring the correct dosage and giving it to the infant.
   Rationale: To ensure maximum effectiveness of the drug and to prevent serious complications (If parents understand why this drug is therapeutically important and potentially dangerous, they will be motivated to aid in the optimal implementation of the therapeutic plan.)
3. Explain to the parents normal behavior of infants with cardiac defects during feeding that might alarm them. Also, share the helpful feeding hints in therapeutic plan 4b with the parents.
   Rationale: To ensure parents understand that infants with congestive heart failure may tire or become cyanotic before completion of the feeding (This can be frightening for parents and implies that they are less than adequate as parents, particularly when weight gain is less than optimal.)

4. Explain to the parents the early signs of congestive heart failure such as anorexia, fatigue, weight gain, dyspnea, and decreased activity tolerance so they can be adequately prepared to seek medical attention if necessary.

   Rationale: To ensure that the parents will be adequately prepared on the infant's discharge (Knowing the early signs will make going home less frightening.)

Problem □ Paroxysmal dyspneic attack

GOALS:
1. To avoid postulated stress situations that predispose to cardiopulmonary distress
2. To identify the signs of the hypoxic episode and implement nursing therapies that will relieve arterial unsaturation, hyperpnea, increased cyanosis, and possibly metabolic acidosis
3. To provide emotional support for the parents

Rationale: To minimize the possibility of serious sequelae to the hypoxic episode, such as seizures, hemiparesis, or even death

DIAGNOSTIC
1. Closely monitor all vital signs.

   Rationale: To check *temperature*—hyperthermia (a sign of infection; fever as well as infection increases the metabolic demands of the body for oxygen) or hypothermia (loss of heat to ambient air, increases the metabolic demand of the body for oxygen, and causes increased cyanosis owing to vasoconstriction and reduced blood flow); *heart rate*—tachycardia, 160 beats/min (compensatory mechanism to try to deliver more oxygen to the tissues in arterial oxygen saturation), or bradycardia, 120 beats/min (cardiac toxicity of propranolol owing to excessive beta-adrenergic inhibition); and *respiratory rate*—tachypnea, 60 breaths/min (stimulation of carotid reflexes and the respiratory center in response to decreased arterial oxygen saturation)
2. Assess respiration.
   a. Cyanosis is a bluish discoloration of the skin and mucous membranes that results when there is greater than 5 gm of reduced hemoglobin in the capillary blood. The darker the skin pigmentation, the greater

the amount of deoxygenated hemoglobin must be present for cyanosis to be evident. *Peripheral* cyanosis results from reduced blood flow in the peripheral circulation, which can be caused by low cardiac output; it involves specific body parts, such as the hands and feet, and is milder in degree. *Central* cyanosis results from arterial unsaturation owing to shunting of unoxygenated blood directly into the systemic circulation; it is more generalized and is more severe in degree. Any event that increases metabolism and thus causes a demand for additional oxygen will result in a more severe degree of cyanosis. Ironically, one author[1] feels that although cyanosis increases with the attack, paroxysmal dyspneic attacks are more of a problem in patients with initially milder cyanosis.

   b. Dyspnea is shortness of breath that occurs from increased pulmonary resistance as the lungs are unable to oxygenate adequate supplies of blood, resulting in "air hunger." Dyspnea becomes very intense with progression of the "tetrad" spell.

   Rationale: To assess signs and symptoms of arterial unsaturation (As deoxygenated blood is trying to enter the pulmonary circuit in spite of the pulmonary stenosis, it encounters even greater resistance to right ventricular outflow tract obstruction if a spasm of the pulmonary valve occurs).
3. Assess cardiac function.

   Rationale: To assess the changes of cardiopulmonary blood flow that occur with arterial unsaturation and/or during the paroxysmal dyspneic attack (The disappearance of the systolic murmur, caused by obstruction of the right ventricular outflow tract, suggests that the spells may be associated with spasm of the right ventricular outflow tract.)
4. Monitor intake and output.

   Rationale: To detect whether the patient becomes dehydrated (too hypoxic to drink during intense dyspnea, leading to decreased intake and output) as this will cause hemoconcentration of the blood, which will increase cardiac work load (A situation of the heart not meeting the demands of the body for oxygen [arterial unsaturation] already exists in cyanotic heart disease.)

5. Monitor the CBC.

Rationale: To watch for iron deficiency anemia (The hematocrit reflects the volume of red cells, and the hemoglobin reflects iron stores. In infancy iron deficiency is common, and the cyanotic infant may show an elevated hematocrit value but have an improper hemoglobin value. Such an infant would have iron deficiency anemia. "Tetrad" spells may be precipitated by iron deficiency anemia. Normal hematocrit should be three times that of hemoglobin which is 10 to 14 gm/dl during first year of life.)

6. Monitor the arterial blood gases.

Rationale: To watch for the development of metabolic acidosis, which could occur during a hypoxic episode (Under reduced arterial oxygen saturation, pyruvic acid is anaerobically converted to lactic acid. Laboratory findings of metabolic acidosis include lowered plasma pH below 7.35, diminished plasma bicarbonate concentration below 20 mEq/L, and carbon dioxide combining power that is lowered.)

7. Monitor for side effects to medications.

   a. Propranolol (Inderal)—nausea, vomiting, and diarrhea are gastrointestinal effects. Bradycardia and bronchospasm are cardiopulmonary effects.

   b. Morphine—nausea, vomiting, and constipation are gastrointestinal effects. Marked respiratory depression and bradycardia are cardiopulmonary effects.

   Rationale: To identify and alleviate untoward effects

THERAPEUTIC

1. Decrease cardiac demands.

   Rationale: To decrease the metabolic needs of the tissues for oxygen and thus decrease cardiac work load

2. Reduce respiratory distress.

   a. Positioning—infants often breathe easier in the knee-chest position, which decreases venous return and reduces the work load of the right heart.

   b. Oxygen therapy is given to increase the oxygen tension of alveolar air when there is intracardiac mixing and arterial unsaturation. Ultimate degree of increase in blood oxygenation to the tissues is via corrective surgery.

   Rationale: To decrease the work of the respiratory muscles as well as cardiac work load

3. Assist in providing emergency treatment during the acute attack.

   a. Knee-chest position is assumed to decrease venous return and prevent increase in right-to-left shunting, which would increase arterial unsaturation.

   b. Oxygen is administered.

   c. Morphine is given to slow respirations, which tends to break the vicious cycle, decreases venous return, which prevents increase in right-to-left shunting (improves arterial saturation); and relieves anxiety.

   d. Propranolol (beta-adrenergic blocking agent) is given to lower heart rate and myocardial contractility (decreases oxygen requirements of the myocardium) and to counteract infundibular spasm.

   e. Sodium bicarbonate is given to correct metabolic acidosis.

   Rationale: To prevent progression of the following events: profound arterial unsaturation, hyperpnea, increased cyanosis, possibly metabolic acidosis, seizures, hemiparesis, or even death

4. Minimize possible precipitators of the attack, especially in the morning.

   a. Crying—anticipate the infant's needs. Feed the infant every few hours to prevent excessive hunger, change the diapers frequently to avoid irritation, and schedule periods of holding and rocking to give extra security.

   b. Feeding—feed as soon as the infant appears hungry and feed slowly with rest periods to avoid overexertion.

   c. Defecation—avoid constipation and straining. Holding the breath and straining increase intrathoracic pressure and decrease venous return; when breath is released, there is a sudden increase of venous return, placing an increased demand on the heart.

Rationale: To be aware that any event that increases the metabolic demands for oxygen, such as crying and feeding, or gives increased blood flow to the right heart, such as the Valsalva maneuver, may increase cardiac work load and thus precipitate a paroxysmal dyspneic attack

EDUCATIONAL

1. Explain to the parents the infant's need for rest, both physical and emotional, and how they can support this comfort.

   Rationale: To ensure that the parents will feel a sense of confidence in themselves as parents and a sense of trust in the health team and will be subsequently motivated to aid in the optimal implementation of therapeutic care

2. Explain to the parents the important considerations regarding the administration of propranolol.

   a. They should know the action and side effects.

   b. They should know about dividing the maintenance dose during the day to maintain therapeutic blood levels.

   c. They should practice measuring the correct dosage and giving it to the infant.

   Rationale: To ensure that propranolol is administered properly for maximum effectiveness and to prevent serious complications by early detection of side effects (If parents understand why this drug is therapeutically important and potentially dangerous, they will be motivated to aid in the optimal implementation of the therapeutic plan.)

3. Explain the possible precipitators of a paroxysmal dyspneic attack, and yet emphasize that sometimes the attacks occur without any known environmental cause.

   Rationale: To prevent frustration and anxiety for the parents because it is not possible to totally eliminate these factors that may not even precipitate attacks

4. Offer suggestions regarding what to do during and after the paroxysmal attack. During and after the attack the infant needs to rest and attain a position of comfort, usually sidelying with knees flexed (knee chest) and head/chest elevated. Keep infant warm to prevent increased metabolism and vasoconstriction.

   Rationale: To lessen parent's anxiety by giving them some control (Effective learning of how to care for their infant [sense of confidence in themselves as parents] requires active participation.)

5. Give emotional support to the parents.

   Rationale: To ensure that parents will be able to cope with their anxiety (Parental anxiety fosters anxiety [increased cardiac work load] in the infant. High levels of anxiety can interfere with their understanding the infant's heart condition and, consequently, optimal therapeutic care.)

REFERENCES

1. Kawabori, I.: Cyanotic congenital heart defects with decreased pulmonary blood flow, Pediatr. Clin. North Am. **25:**761, 1978.
2. King, O. M.: Care of the cardiac surgical patient, St. Louis, 1975, The C. V. Mosby Co.
3. Nadas, A. S., and Tyler, D. C.: Pediatric cardiology, Philadelphia, 1972, W. B. Saunders Co. p. 296.
4. Nelson, W. E.: Textbook of pediatrics, Philadelphia, 1975, W. B. Saunders Co., p. 1019.
5. Perloff, T. J.: The clinical recognition of congenital heart disease, Philadelphia, 1978, W. B. Saunders Co., p. 525.
6. Rudolph, A. M., and Heymann, M. A.: Medical treatment of the ductus arteriosus, Hosp. Pract. **12:**64, 1977.
7. Sade, R. M., and Castaneda, A. R.: Recent advances in cardiac surgery in the young infant, Surg. Clin. North Am. **56**(2):451, 1976.
8. Scipien, G., et al.: Comprehensive pediatric nursing, New York, 1979, McGraw-Hill Book Co., p. 656.
9. Stevenson, J. G.: Acyanotic lesions with normal pulmonary blood flow, Pediatr. Clin. North Am. **25:**739, 1978.
10. Tyson, K. R. T.: Congenital heart disease in infants, Clin. Symp. **27**(3):2, 1975.
11. Whaley, L. F., and Wong, D. L.: Nursing care of infants and children, St. Louis, 1979, The C. V. Mosby Co., p. 1311.

Chapter 27

The family of the high-risk newborn

Pamela K. Manuel Lemons

The delivery of a premature or sick newborn creates a crisis for the entire family. In the case of the premature infant the stress begins with the onset of labor. In many cases obvious signs of early labor are at first ignored; the thought of delivery at this point in pregnancy is so preposterous that it is quickly dismissed, and the symptoms are instead attributed to the "flu" or "overdoing."

At term a mother is ready to discharge her fetus. She has attached a face and a name (maybe several) to her infant, and she is impatient to actually see the infant and terminate the pregnancy. She goes to the hospital at the expected time, the events follow an expected sequence, and she is carried along by the feeling that everything is normal and will end in success. Contrast this setting to a mother in premature labor. The atmosphere of the hospital is one of emergency rather than routine. There is great concern for her safety as well as that of her infant as is evidenced by the frequent examinations and fetal and maternal monitoring. The mother is often told that she will receive no anesthesia because of the infant's condition, which further heightens her anxiety. But even at this late point a mother may deny that her infant's delivery is imminent.

After birth, the parents of a premature infant have a heightened concern about whether their baby is normal and if he will live. They see their baby for a few brief moments before he is whisked away to the ICU, and their most vivid recollection is of how weak, small, and blue he seemed. The mother is then typically placed on a maternity ward where she feels lost and adrift from all the mother-baby couples. She expects at any moment someone will tell her the baby has died. The staff avoids talking to her because they are not sure of how to respond. They know the mother needs support, but they don't know how to give it without either raising her hopes falsely or adding to her anxiety by pessimism. The parents then usually turn to the premature nursery for solace but only meet with further frustration. They are often not even able to see their infant well, obscured as he is by the isolette, tubes, and equipment. Rarely do they feel comfortable touching the baby for fear of hurting him. The baby they see is hardly one that inspires hope and pride—certainly not the robust, healthy infant they had imagined and longed for. If anyone comes to visit them and their baby, they offer only sympathy for the "tiny, pitiful thing." Is it any wonder parents feel guilt and failure when eyeing their offspring and often visit for only brief periods?

When the parents leave the hospital without their infant, it is the affirmation of their worst fears. They have failed, and failed miserably, in their parental role. Now they must somehow come to terms with that guilt as well as coping with the fact that their child may well die or, if he does survive, be left with residual damage. What an overwhelming task.

CRISIS THEORY

According to Bibring,[1] even under "normal" conditions pregnancy can be considered a developmental crisis. Failure of the pregnant woman to resolve the crisis of pregnancy leads to the personality disorganization that is the hallmark of any person who is not able to mobilize his resources when faced with an acute problem.[4] Sadness, increasing anxiety, acute depression and a feeling of helplessness mirror the individual's inability to cope and lead to further regressive behavior.[6] Therefore, when pregnancy is considered to be a "normal" developmental crisis, we would anticipate the woman expending a great deal of time and energy working through resolutions of the problem since the solution is unique in terms of the woman's life experience. It is not unusual for women to manifest neurotic behavior, resulting from the anxiety produced by going through the crisis of pregnancy, that at other points during their lifetime would be indicative of pathology.[2]

DEVELOPMENTAL TASKS OF PREGNANCY

Rubin[12] describes four broad areas of psychosocial development that occur during a normal pregnancy:
1. The mother seeks safe passage for herself and her child during pregnancy, labor, and delivery.
2. The child is accepted by significant others.
3. Binding in occurs (refers to the process of incorporating the child into the mother's self-concept).
4. Giving of oneself occurs.

In describing these developmental tasks Rubin emphasizes the fact that the mother often vacillates between acceptance and rejection of the pregnancy. It is generally very late in pregnancy that the woman becomes firmly affiliated with the fetus and begins to look forward to the birth with happy anticipation. The woman's wish to terminate the pregnancy seems to correspond well with that time in pregnancy when the infant's chance for survival is maximal—in the final 4 weeks. A family loses much when these maternal tasks are interrupted by a preterm delivery. At a time in pregnancy when a woman should be actively engaged in adapting to her changing role and body image, she is plunged into the crisis of dealing with an unexpected and often devastating event. Interruption of the "work" of pregnancy may enhance the anxiety and guilt the mother experiences and may actively interfere with her ability to "attach" to her newly born infant.[10]

The psychological preparation for a new child during pregnancy normally involves the wish for the "ideal" or "perfect" child and conversely the dread of a damaged child. In the process of childbearing

when the mother bears a normal child, the discrepancy between the "perfect" child and her own infant are worked out as a healthy mother-child relationship is developed. However, in the case of the premature or sick newborn the discrepancy between the desired child and the actual outcome is so great that the mother may be unable to establish a relationship at all. Thus this simultaneous loss of the idealized child and adaptation to the "defective" child make a demand that is most likely overwhelming, and the reaction to this situation is to grieve for the lost child.[9]

GRIEF AND GRIEVING

> Grief fills the room up of my absent child,
> Lies in his bed, walks up and down with me,
> Puts on his pretty looks, repeats his words,
> Remembers me of all his gracious parts,
> Stuffs out his vacant garments with his form,
> Then have I reason to be fond of grief.

William Shakespeare
King John, 1596

A person's ability to "grieve" as a response to loss is learned gradually in the normal course of growth and development. This task is closely related to the person's ability to establish meaningful object relationships[14] and reflects a healthy person's sadness at the withdrawal of this source of gratification. Thus, when a family uproots and moves on to a bigger home, better job, and so forth, it is only natural that they experience a sense of sadness for the tiny cottage they leave behind. The "loss" of the old house will eventually become submerged as the excitement of the new house and new friends grows, and the family will have successfully resolved their grieving process. It is important to remember though that resolution of grieving takes time and cannot be rushed. Indeed there are several intervening variables that can act to impede the whole process: (1) unsound intervention, (2) failure to provide optimum conditions for healing, and (3) the individual resources that are not up to the task.[5]

According to Engel,[5] the "successful" grieving process has three phases:
1. *Shock and disbelief:* The event of loss evokes a strong denial reaction in the individual—"Oh no, it can't be, it can't be happening." This reaction is accompanied by a stunned, numbed feeling during

which the person refuses to think about the loss. He may go about his daily business in "robot" fashion, or he may be totally immobilized by grief. This phase may last for moments or days and alternates with periods of overwhelming sadness as the reality begins to penetrate through the defense of denial.

2. *Developing awareness:* Depending on the individual, this stage may take some time to appear. Awareness of the loss suffered becomes acute, and anguish accompanies this realization. Anger may be expressed toward those people who were close to the dead person. Certain individuals may feel they were somehow responsible for the death and actually inflict physical harm on themselves. These expressions of anger are probably a result of the bereaved's frustration at being deserted by the one beloved.

Crying is an essential element of this phase and is the "work" of the mourner. While displays of grieving differ from culture to culture, the need for crying is universally felt and seems to involve the realization of the loss and the regression to a more vulnerable and childlike status. Because of his regression to the status of a child, the mourner is usually comforted and supported by his meaningful others, which gives him the strength to cope with the tragedy. Tears are thought to be so necessary a part of grieving that "tearless" sorrow is thought to be an ominous sign and may predispose the mourner to some type of pathological grief. The need to openly express grief is said well by Shakespeare (*Macbeth*, 1605): "Give sorrow words: the grief that does not speak whispers the o'erfraught heart and bids it break."

3. *Restitution:* During the third phase of grieving the mourner becomes able to cope with reality and recover from the event. The funeral rituals that are a part of every culture help the person initiate the recovery process by drawing the entire family together, forming a strong support system for the mourner to rely on. The actual funeral rites and burial reemphasize the unequivocal loss of the loved one and make denial very difficult if not impossible to maintain. In addition, the mourner usually finds some solace in religious and spiritual beliefs, which may even lead him to the expectation that he will be united with the loved one after his own death.

Although the burial of the loved one signifies the finalization of the loss, the bereaved continues his work of mourning. As the reality of death becomes ingrained, the resolution of the loss may go as far as a year. This process at first will be characterized by a preoccupation with the deceased, an inability to think of anything else. He thinks about and talks about the deceased incessantly until he has built him into the most perfect person imaginable. During this idolization process any negative or hostile feelings about the deceased are repressed. At the same time the mourner will often take on characteristics (consciously or unconsciously) of the deceased. As the dependence on the lost one decreases, he will be able to give up some of the characteristics and mannerisms he has adopted. He will be able to think of things he did not like about the deceased and build a memory that includes these negative (as well as positive) qualities. He will lose some of the preoccupation of thought he had for the deceased and will be able to concentrate his energies and thoughts on other things. Probably the best indication that grieving has been successfully resolved is the loved one's ability to "remember comfortably and realistically both the pleasures and disappointments of the lost relationship."[5]

Parents who have undergone the trauma of a premature birth are often not able to move through the final resolution of the grieving process but are frequently fixated at the stage of "developing awareness." Attempts to withdraw investment from the desired "healthy" child are interfered with by the existing child's need for attention and love. The parents may feel that they are the cause of the child's prematurity and search themselves endlessly for an answer to the question "why?". Feelings of self-doubt and inadequacy may plague the parents almost as if the "defective" child reflects their own flaws and imperfections[7] and actively interferes with the attachment process.

DEVELOPMENTAL TASKS ASSOCIATED WITH A PRETERM DELIVERY

Kaplan and Mason[9] were the first authors to endorse the theory that a family moved through a series of tasks when dealing with the crisis of a preterm delivery. Knowledge of these tasks allows the health care professional to anticipate maternal and paternal behavior and reactions and provides a framework for helping the family cope with their stress.

1. *Anticipating grief:* The parents must realize that their child may die. This involves withdrawal from the relationship already established before the child was born so that the parents simultaneously hope the child will survive and yet prepare for his death. If this very first step is to successfully resolved, it is imperative that the parents interact with their infant—touch him, be involved with him, attach to him in some way. When we discourage parents to bond to their infants in the mistaken notion that we are doing them a favor, we do instead a great disservice and probably greatly prolong thier grieving if the infant does die.

The parents reaction at this time follows the previously described mourning reactions: feeling of loss, intense longing for the desired child, resentment toward fate's cruel blow, and incapacitating sorrow.[13]

2. *Maternal failure:* The mother must admit that she has failed to produce a full-term infant. The feeling of failure and guilt described earlier is part of the depression and crying that accompany this stage and is a sign that the parents are struggling to cope. These reactions are healthy and usually are observable until the baby stabilizes and the chance for survival improves. Anger is a frequent accompaniment of this stage and may be aimed at the health care facility and those professional people who are actively working to "salvage" the baby. Realization that this anger is founded in the family's *own* sense of failure and guilt will allow the nursing and medical staff to accept that anger as a normal reaction to a very stressful situation and will allow the staff to "depersonalize" the verbal barbs that are often hurled under such conditions.

3. *Relating to the infant:* This stage involves the parents resuming their investment of energy into the process of getting to know their infant. The parents had heretofore been preparing for a loss, but now they are given hope that the outcome will be good and they start to believe that the baby will survive. At this point it seems very appropriate to explore methods of infant feeding with the family. The initial decision of whether to breast or bottle feed usually takes place before the infant is born. The sudden arrival of a small, sick infant may seem to take the decision out of their hands since many parents do not even realize that it is possible to nurse a premature infant. To persuade a mother lying on the delivery room table to take medication to dry up her milk seems totally inappropriate. The stress the family is under already is monumental; to further add to their anxiety and fear by pushing the issue is unreasonable. Taking away the hope the mother may have had of breast-feeding her infant must add to the feeling that the infant will surely die. In a few hours when the condition of the infant warrants and the family has had some time to adapt to their situation, the topic can be discussed.

Breast-feeding should be presented in a positive light but not in such a way that the parents feel criminal if they decide to bottle feed. The data that support breast milk for the premature infant should be discussed as well as what is required of the mother to establish and maintain lactation. If the family decides to formula feed, caretaking should be fostered in other capacities. Those families that indicate an interest in breast-feeding should be provided with written information on the subject and should be placed in close contact with some person who will be able to assist them with pumping and collection techniques. A 30-minute videotape with a 14-page study guide, designed to reinforce the information presented, is available through NICER Productions at the Indiana University School of Nursing. The film is entitled *Breast Milk And The Sick Newborn* and provides the mother with a working knowledge of various expression techniques and optimal collection and storage procedures for the safe handling of human milk.

It is impossible to overemphasize the feeling of failure the mother is laden with after a premature delivery. She feels as if she let her baby down by not carrying him to term. She searches over and over in her mind to find some reason that she went into labor and blames herself for initiating contractions. Her feelings of inadequacy and inferiority are strengthened by her inability to take care of her infant like a normal mother. This situation is certainly a setup for disturbance of maternal attachment. Prolonged separation and lengthy hospitalization compound the problem. Unchecked, this initial disturbance can be carried far beyond infancy and results in either maternal overprotectiveness and overindulgence or, conversely, in open hostility toward her child.[8] It is not unusual to find a premature child 5 years later as a battered child. Anything the health care professional can do to negate the mother's feeling of guilt and failure will help to prevent disturbances from occurring. It was common a number of years ago to "isolate" parents from becoming involved with infants whose chances for survival were slim in the mistaken notion that we were protecting them from a very painful experience. It is now recognized that those parents who are denied the opportunity to interact with their infants may have tremendous feelings of guilt from withdrawing their support from the infant before his or her death and will often proceed to have a greatly prolonged and potentially pathological course of mourning.[11]

4. *Relating to the premature infant:* In this fourth and final step the parents must come to understand the uniqueness of the premature infant and how his needs and growth differ from a full-term infant. This is done over those long weeks of hospitalization as the parents are educated by the medical and nursing staff, by reading books on child care, and by talking to other parents of premature infants. It is important that the parents see their child's differences as being temporary—that the child will not necessarily require special handling for an indefinite length of time. In a case where outcome appears good, the infant is discharged often somewhere near 40 weeks' gestation and acts appropriate for a newborn.

Satisfactory completion of these four tasks—(1) anticipatory grief, (2) maternal failure, (3) relating to the infant, and (4) relating to the premature infant—is usually a clinical impression of the family interaction. Success is mirrored by the family's ability to provide adequate care and a loving environment, seeing their infant as potentially normal, and taking pride and satisfaction in fulfilling their role.

CONCLUSION

There are many factors that are operative in making the family that produces a preterm or sick newborn infant "at risk." A working knowledge of crisis theory, the developmental tasks of pregnancy, grief and grieving, and the developmental tasks associated with a preterm birth are necessary if the health care professional is to intervene in a manner that is most beneficial to the parents. The realization that the impact of a single statement can be carried by the parents for a lifetime necessitates that any interaction be undertaken with utmost care and considers where that particular family is in relation to their crisis event. Survival of the high-risk infant at the expense of his family's intactness is a tragic and preventable outcome.

Protocols

Problem □ Unexpected termination of pregnancy with delivery of an infant at risk

GOAL: To understand and support a family in crisis
   Rationale: To provide the family with a base on which they can begin to build a relationship with their child and increase their ability to cope with the eventual outcome of this devastating event
DIAGNOSTIC
   1. Explore with the family past and present coping mechanisms used in times of stress.
      Rationale: To detect whether behaviors that were beneficial in the past will or will not be appropriate for this particular situation
   2. Identify the support system that operates in this family. (Is the father normally the strongest in a crisis situation? Grandparents? Significant others?)

   Rationale: To encourage the family to rely on a person who has been supportive in a past crisis, which may increase their ability to cope
   3. Review the role each member plays in the family under normal circumstances and how these roles have now been altered.
      Rationale: To be aware that it is common for role designation to change within a family when a crisis occurs and for family members to deviate from previously accepted roles
   4. Discuss the family's perceptions of this crisis event.
      Rationale: To be aware that each family's response to this situation is unique and should not be "stereotyped" by the hospital staff's

previous experiences with other families in similar circumstances

5. Evaluate those factors that would increase the family's stress during the crisis; that is, are there other events happening spontaneously that compound the problem, such as loss of income because of wage earner's inability to work, absence of medical insurance, or illness of other family members.

   Rationale: To be aware that if the stress on a family becomes overwhelming, they will be unable to mobilize their coping mechanisms

THERAPEUTIC

1. Validate what the parents' perception of their infant's condition is by asking them to repeat to you what they have been previously told about their baby.

   Rationale: To understand that it is very confusing for a family to be told a different story by each member of the health care team and may add to their anxiety

2. Speak in simple terms. Make explanations short and concise. Repeat information several times.

   Rationale: To be aware that people reacting to a crisis are unable to understand lengthy and complex explanations

3. Avoid use of qualifiers (that is, *very* ill, *many* survive, *most* have complications) and statistics.

   Rationale: To be aware that parents may attach undue importance to these terms and may be either overly optimistic or pessimistic according to their interpretation

4. Continuously validate with the parents their interpretation of the infant's problem/condition by having them restate it in their own words.

   Rationale: To ensure that what you have said to the family is what they *heard* you say

5. Find an adequate support system for the family if they are unable to find one of their own. (Refer to social service, financial aid, minister of religious preference if indicated, and so forth.

   Rationale: To furnish the family in crisis with specific direction in locating alternate means of support

EDUCATIONAL

1. Help the family to gain an *intellectual* understanding of this crisis by explanation of premature labor, fetal growth and development, and transport of a high-risk infant.

   Rationale: To lessen the parent's anxiety and fear and therefore increase their ability to cope with the situation

2. Find the family new methods of coping with this very unique situation.

   Rationale: To be aware that coping mechanisms that may have been useful in the past may not work for the parents

Problem □ Premature delivery interrupted the tasks of pregnancy that must now be completed postnatally

GOAL: To aid the completion of the developmental tasks of pregnancy

Rationale: To be aware that failure to complete the tasks of pregnancy may enhance the mother's guilt and anxiety over producing a preterm infant and therefore adversely affect her ability to attach to her infant

DIAGNOSTIC

1. Evaluate the mother's expectations of this pregnancy.
   a. Was the pregnancy planned?
   b. Did she have prenatal care?
   c. Which baby is this for the mother? First, second, and so forth?
   d. What did she think the baby would be like?
   e. Did she have a mental picture of the baby?
   f. Did she look forward to having a new baby?

   Rationale: To contrast the behavior of this mother with that described by Rubin will give the health care professional some idea of where this mother lies on the continuum of completion of the developmental tasks of pregnancy

2. Determine the mother's support system.
   a. Is she married, single, or cohabiting in a single home?
   b. Does she have housing for herself and her infant?
   c. Is she financially dependent or independent?

Rationale: To be aware that lack of a support system may indicate the mother was not yet to that point in her pregnancy where she actually accepted the infant would indeed be born

3. Assess what this pregnancy meant to the mother in terms of her life-style and future goals.

   Rationale: To be aware that the reorganization of her schedule and previous activities may have negative connotations for this mother

4. Determine what the mother's perceptions of labor were, whether she considered it a positive or negative experience.

   Rationale: To be aware that a labor associated with high anxiety and/or unanticipated trauma may alter the mother's feeling toward her newborn infant

5. Explore the mother's prenatal expectations of this baby.

   Rationale: To be aware that the discrepancy between the "anticipated" child and the child the mother bore is apt to be tremendous and presents the mother with further stress to cope with

6. Assess the mother's readiness to assume a maternal role and actually begin caretaking activities.

   Rationale: To ensure that the mother has completed the work of pregnancy, which is necessary before she can be expected to assume the work of motherhood

THERAPEUTIC

1. Provide an environment for the mother that will encourage and enhance her attachment to her infant. Attachment can be hastened by many "mothering" activities: seeing the baby, touching or caressing the baby, holding the baby, feeding or nursing the baby, verbally interacting with the baby, and so forth.

   Rationale: To be aware that mothers who are denied the experience of caring for their newborn infants may have difficulties establishing a relationship—difficulties that can extend well beyond the newborn period

2. Communicate all information about caretaking skills and needs of the preterm infant in a friendly and nonthreatening manner.

Rationale: To ensure that the mother who has failed to produce a full-term infant and is laden with guilt and self-doubt is constantly reassured of her ability to adequately care for her infant

3. Provide as many opportunities as possible for the mother to get to know her infant by placing her in a situation where she can successfully interact with her infant (taking temperature, mouth care, feeding, bathing, stimulation programs, and so forth). Comments like "she sure calms down when she hears your voice" or "he always seems to eat better when his mommy feeds him" will bolster the mother's confidence when handling her infant.

   Rationale: To be aware that a new mother is often insecure when learning to care for her infant and is greatly intimidated by the nurses' ability to handle "her" baby with ease

4. Assist the mother in adapting her perception of the "ideal" or anticipated infant to her own small, preterm infant through discussing the premature infant's characteristics and needs as they relate to the full-term baby, stressing that special care and handling will only be required for a relatively short period of time. Verbally reassure the mother that it is normal for mothers of premature infants to feel sad and depressed when they care for a baby that does not match their visual image of what their baby would look like.

   Rationale: To be aware that the discrepancy between the expected outcome of pregnancy and the actual outcome is often so great that the mother/family actually grieved for the "normal" baby that was lost when this "less than perfect" infant was born.

5. Adequately prepare the mother/family before seeing the baby for the first time by describing his appearance and the purpose of the equipment being used to assist him. Self-developing pictures of the infant that are sent via the father to the mother from the referral hospital are helpful until the mother is able to visit and see the infant for herself.

Rationale: To be aware that the mother's fantasized fears of what her infant looks like are often frightening and interfere with her attachment process.

6. Explain to the mother that the ambivalence she may have felt for her pregnancy/infant prenatally is a normal feeling and part of each woman's preparation for a major role change.

   Rationale: To be aware that the infant who is delivered early in the third trimester of pregnancy may be born before true affiliation and acceptance have occurred

7. Encourage the mother to use whatever person she has as her main support to help her through this crisis by allowing that person to accompany the mother when visiting and including that person when discussing the infant's condition and care.

   Rationale: To be aware that in times of crisis people often regress to a dependent and childlike state and need strong support and help in resuming their adult role and coping with the stressful situation

EDUCATIONAL

1. Provide the mother/family with written material, audiovisual aids, and demonstrations of the special caregiving skills that are needed for the preterm infant. Content areas should include:
   a. Feeding techniques—initiating and supporting lactation if applicable
   b. Temperature regulation
   c. Need for verbal, visual, and tactile stimulation

   Rationale: To teach new psychomotor activities using a variety of methods and chosing one that is the easiest for the learner

2. The Brazelton *Neonatal Behavioral Assessment Scale*[3] could be taught to the mother to illustrate her infant's ability to interact and to "cue" the mother to her own particular infant's needs.

   Rationale: To make the mother aware that each infant is individual and reacts to a situation in a unique manner

3. Establish a parent group that meets weekly at a regular time to allow parents to discuss their feelings, needs, and fears in an open and nonthreatening environment. These sessions should be managed by a person skilled in communication methods and knowledgeable about the care of preterm infants.

   Rationale: To provide the opportunity for parents in similar circumstances to gain strength and reassurance from each other and benefit from appropriate role models that are offered

Problem □ It is necessary for the parents to simultaneously hope for their infant's survival while preparing themselves for the fact that he may well die

GOAL: To help the family through their process of grief and grieving

   Rationale: To be aware that the loss of an object of love will be accompanied by feelings of grief

DIAGNOSTIC

1. Assess the stage of grieving the family is at as described by Engel.
   a. Shock and disbelief
      (1) Statements of "I can't believe it" or "It can't be true"
      (2) Flat affect
      (3) Unusual behavior
      (4) Denial that anything is wrong with the infant
      (5) Inability to think clearly to do normal everyday activities
      (6) Inability to eat or sleep
   b. Developing awareness
      (1) Anger
      (2) Verbal insults
      (3) Preoccupation with infant
      (4) Crying, sadness, depression
   c. Restitution
      (1) Family begins to show reality orientation and recover from event
      (2) Resumption of normal activities

   Rationale: To be aware that a person undergoing a loss will normally progress thru certain stages of grieving

2. Observe for maladaptive reactions to the birth of the infant.
   a. Overindulgence in alcohol or drugs
   b. Psychosomatic illness
   c. Aggressive behavior
   d. Neurotic and psychotic states

Rationale: To be aware of deviations from the expected behavior patterns seen in the grieving person, which may indicate pathology and a need for prompt intervention

3. Assess the parents' perception of the cause of their infant's prematurity.

Rationale: To be aware that guilt and self-blame will frequently accompany the parents' grief at having produced an infant at risk

THERAPEUTIC

1. Communicate to the family that they will likely experience a grief reaction similar to that of Engels' stages of grieving.

Rationale: To reassure the family by letting them know that other families have shared their feeling of loss

2. Provide an environment that is private where the family can openly vent their feelings.

Rationale: To ensure that the fears and sorrow of the grieving parent can be expressed

3. Recognize that the behaviors that express grief vary from culture to culture and allow the family the freedom to grieve in their own fashion.

Rationale: To be aware that deviations from the anticipated pattern of grieving do not always indicate that the behavior is pathological

4. Allow parents to use whatever coping mechanisms they find useful in dealing with their situation.

Rationale: To be aware that anger, frustration, and hostility are normal by-products of grief

5. Support the grieving family at whatever phase they present until they are able to actively move to the next plateau.

Rationale: To realize that when the individual's resources are such that he can face the situation, he will move automatically to the next stage (The process of grieving is *not* time limited and varies greatly with each person.)

EDUCATIONAL

1. In-service training sessions should be provided for all nursing personnel. The following topics should be discussed to assist the staff in dealing with grieving families:

a. Normal grieving process
b. Communication skills
c. Techniques for intervention—appropriate coping mechanisms
d. Techniques to deal with parental hostility and anger
e. Discussion on staffs' feelings on death

Rationale: To provide quality care to families who are grieving by ensuring that the nursing staff has an adequate understanding of the grieving process

2. Utilize available resources such as films, written material, and contact with other families in similar situations to assist families to grieve in a healthy fashion.

Rationale: To assist the parents in their grieving process by providing a role model

REFERENCES

1. Bibring, G. L.: Some considerations of the psychological processes in pregnancy, Psychoanal. Study Child **14:**113, 1959.
2. Bibring, G. L., et. al.: A study of the psychological processes in pregnancy and of the earliest mother-child relationship. I: some propositions and comments, Psychoanal. Study Child **16:**9, 1961.
3. Brazleton, T. B.: Neonatal behavioral assessment scale, Philadelphia, 1973, J. B. Lippincott Co.
4. Caplan, G.: Theory and practice of mental health consultation, New York, 1970, Basic Books Inc, Publishers.
5. Engel, G. L.: Grief and grieving, Am. J. Nurs. **64:**93, 1964.
6. Fisk, S. L.: Crisis and motivation: a theoretical model, Arch. Phys. Med. Rehabil. **48:**592, 1967.
7. Goodman, L.: Continuing treatment of parents with congenitally defective infants, Soc. Work **9:**92, 1964.
8. Green, M., and Solnit, A. J.: Reactions to the threatened loss of a child: a vulnerable child syndrome, Pediatrics **34:**58, 1964.
9. Kaplan, D., and Mason, E.: Maternal reaction to premature birth viewed as an acute emotional disorder. In Parod, H., editor: Crisis intervention, New York, 1965, Family Service Association of America.
10. Klaus, M. H., and Kennell, J. H.: Mothers separated from their newborn infants, Pediatr. Clin. North Am. **17**(4):1015, 1970.
11. Klaus, M. H., and Kennell, J. H.: Maternal-infant bonding, St. Louis, 1976, The C. V. Mosby Co.
12. Rubin, R.: Maternal tasks in pregnancy, Matern. Child Nurs. J. **4:**143, 1975.
13. Solnit, A. J., and Stark, M. H.: Mourning and the birth of a defective child, Psychoanal. Study Child **16:**523, 1961.
14. Thaler, O.: Grief and depression, Nurs. Forum **5:**9, 1966.

BIBLIOGRAPHY

Brazleton, T. B.: The parent-infant attachment, Clin. Obstet. Gynecol. **19:**373, 1976.

Kubler-Ross, E.: On death and dying, New York, 1969, MacMillan, Inc.

Perez, R. C., and Burks, R.: Transporting high-risk infants, J. Emerg. Nurs. **4:**14, 1978.

Schoenberg, B., et al., editors: Loss and grief: psychological management in medical practice, New York, 1970, Columbia University Press.

Taylor, P. M., and Hall, B. L.: Parent-infant bonding: problems and opportunities in a perinatal center, Semin. Perinatol. **3**(1): 73, 1979.

Ujhily, G. B.: Grief and depression, Nurs. Forum, **5**(2):23, 1966.

Volkan, V.: Typical findings in pathological grief, Psychiatr. Q. **44:**231, 1970.

SECTION FIVE

PERINATAL PROCEDURES

Chapter 28

Neonatal procedures

Richard L. Schreiner and Dennis C. Stevens

RESUSCITATION OF THE NEWBORN

It is mandatory that every nurse and physician involved in the delivery room be competent in neonatal resuscitation. There should be at least one person—physician, nurse, anesthetist, or respiratory therapist—at each delivery who is capable of resuscitating an asphyxiated infant. Likewise, every delivery room should be properly equipped to provide the total support required during such a crisis. Only when this complement of equipment and trained personnel is routinely available in every delivery room will the incidence of neonatal deaths and long-term central nervous system disabilities owing to acute asphyxia be maximally reduced.

Equipment

A prerequisite to good resuscitation is good equipment. The following list is a suggested minimum for resuscitation equipment.

Overhead radiant heater
Light source
Heated, humidified oxygen
Suction
Sterile suction catheters
Suction bulb
Sterile umbilical vessel catheterization tray
3.5 and 5 Fr umbilical catheters
Medications
Intubation equipment (see list on p. 455)

Responsibility for the upkeep and periodic inspection of the resuscitation equipment should be designated to a specific individual.

Evaluation of the infant

For many years, the Apgar score (Table 28-1) has been used as a guide in selecting the resuscitative method required for any particular infant. A score of 0 to 3 indicates severe distress and the need for immediate vigorous resuscitative measures. Infants with Apgar scores of 4 to 7 are in moderate distress and *might* require vigorous resuscitation. If the score is 7 to 10, observation is usually all that is required. However, continued close surveillance is very important even under the most favorable circumstances since delayed respiratory depression may occur owing to drugs, anesthetic agents, and a variety of anatomical defects.

The need for intervention frequently cannot wait for assigning Apgar scores. The urgency of the situation can be assessed more rapidly by evaluating two parameters of cardiopulmonary function: (1) respiration and (2) heart rate.

Technique

Maintaining adequate temperature control is best done by immediate drying of the infant followed by placement of the infant under a radiant warmer. In addition, it is critical, especially in very low birth weight infants, to avoid all currents of air from air conditioners, and resuscitation should not be performed near cold objects such as cold windows. Whenever possible, it is preferable to increase the room temperature immediately before the delivery of a very low birth weight infant since even with drying and care of the infant under a radiant warmer, it is frequently difficult to maintain a normal body temperature when the room is cold.

Table 28-1. Apgar score

Sign	0	1	2
Heart rate	Absent	Below 100	Over 100
Respiratory effort	Absent	Slow, irregular	Good, crying
Muscle tone	Flaccid	Some flexion of extremities	Action, motion
Reflex irritability	No response	Grimace	Vigorous cry
Color	Blue, pale	Body pink, extremities blue	Completely pink

The most important aspects of resuscitation in the newborn are oxygenation and ventilation. Most infants who require resuscitation can be resuscitated adequately with oxygenation and ventilation. In addition, when an infant is not responding to such support, the most frequent reason is that oxygenation and ventilation are not being carried out appropriately. Therefore, whenever an infant is not responding to resuscitation, as demonstrated by relief of cyanosis and an increased heart rate, the first thing that should enter the resuscitator's mind is that some error is being made. For example, the infant may not be receiving 100% oxygen, either because the resuscitation bag will not deliver 100% oxygen or possibly because the oxygen tube has been accidentally disconnected from the source of oxygen. The resuscitation bag may have a pressure pop-off valve so that no more than 40 cm H_2O of inspiratory pressure can be maintained. The endotracheal tube may be misplaced, either into the esophagus or down the right main stem bronchus. These are the most common mistakes made in the delivery room and account for most of the situations when an infant fails to respond to resuscitative measures. Oxygenation and ventilation are the keys to resuscitation, not the use of drugs. Although drugs may be indicated, they are the least important aspect of resuscitation.

There is considerable controversy concerning when an infant should be intubated. Infants can usually be ventilated and oxygenated adequately with bag and mask ventilation. Unsuccessful prolonged attempts at intubation, which result in cyanosis and bradycardia of the infant, must be avoided. When ventilating with a bag and mask, it is important to avoid overextension or flexion

of the head, either of which may result in occlusion of the trachea. In addition, a tight seal of the mask over the infant's nose and mouth must be maintained.

On delivery of the infant's head in a vertex presentation, bulb suction of the nose and oropharynx should be performed. If there is meconium in the amniotic fluid or the infant is meconium stained, thorough suctioning of the nose, mouth, and pharynx with a bulb and/or a DeLee mucus trap should be carried out before delivering the shoulders, if time permits. This suctioning should be rapid and not interfere with expeditious delivery of the child.

When respirations are spontaneous with no apparent obstruction of air exchange and the heart rate is greater than 100 beats/min, close observation is all that is required. If respiratory efforts are inadequate or labored but the heart rate is greater than 100 beats/min, additional measures may be indicated. The nose and oropharynx should be gently suctioned with a soft catheter, and warm humidified oxygen should be given by mask. The heart rate must be monitored continuously since a falling rate may necessitate more aggressive intervention.

If these procedures do not result in an improvement in respiratory effort or if the heart rate deteriorates, bag and mask ventilation with supplemental oxygenation should be initiated. The infant who has not breathed spontaneously may require high initial ventilatory pressures (greater than or equal to 50 cm H_2O) to inflate unexpanded alveoli. In most cases, after two or three breaths the delivery pressure need not exceed 20 cm H_2O. The effectiveness of positive pressure ventilation must be evaluated constantly by observing chest expansion, by auscultation of air exchange, and by monitoring the clinical course. When bag and mask ventilation is used, the tendency to inflate the stomach can be minimized by insertion of a nasogastric tube and/or by gentle abdominal pressure.

If resuscitation by bag and mask does not ventilate the child adequately, the clinical course deteriorates, or the infant is profoundly depressed (that is, absent respiratory rate and a heart rate of less than 100 beats/min), endotracheal intubation should be performed. These severely affected infants are often in shock as reflected by their pallor and weak pulses.

When the heart rate is less than 100 beats/min and does not respond to 60 seconds of assisted ventilation, external cardiac massage should be initiated by an assistant. Two fingers are applied just above the heart to the left of the lower sternal border, and sufficient pressure is applied for 1 to 2 cm depression. The massage rate should be approximately 100 to 120/min. The assisted respiratory rate should be 40 to 60/min. Massage should be stopped periodically to assess spontaneous cardiac activity or improvement in heart rate.

Intubation

Endotracheal intubation by either the oral or nasal route should always be performed under controlled conditions. With the exception of the infant at risk for meconium aspiration (who should have the cords visualized and meconium suctioned before the first breath) and the infant with a diaphragmatic hernia, the airway can usually be maintained and respiration supported with a resuscitation bag and mask. As with any procedure in the neonate, intubation should never further jeopardize the infant's clinical status.

Procedure

1. All equipment as listed below should be available prior to starting the procedure.
   a. Laryngoscope with a straight blade: size 0 for premature and newborn infants and size 1 for larger neonates and older infants
   b. Endotracheal tubes: sizes ranging from 2.5 mm internal diameter for small premature infants (less than 1000 gm) to 3.5 mm tubes for full-term infants (Cole tubes are available for emergency orotracheal intubation.)
   c. McGill forceps for nasotracheal intubation and a stylet for orotracheal intubation
   d. Resuscitation bag, mask (sizes for very small premature infants, larger premature infants, and full-term infants), and oxygen
   e. Sterile suctioning equipment and gloves (for suctioning)
   f. Xylocaine jelly to lubricate the tube
   g. Tape and benzoin to anchor the tube
2. The infant's heart rate should be monitored by an assistant tapping out the rate with his finger.
3. Body temperature should be maintained by placing the infant under a warmer.
4. Oxygenation should be maintained before and after the procedure with O_2 and a resuscitation bag with mask. During the procedure O_2 should be administered over the face.
5. The nasopharynx should be gently suctioned and the gastric contents aspirated.
6. The infant should receive 100% O_2 by bag and mask for several breaths prior to intubation.
7. The infant is intubated.
   a. The laryngoscope is held between the thumb and index finger of the left hand (Fig. 28-1). After insertion of the blade, the third and fourth fingers are used to elevate the chin, and the fifth finger is used to apply pressure over the hyoid bone to bring the larynx more directly into view.
   b. The infant is positioned supine *without* hyperextension of the neck.
   c. The laryngoscope blade is inserted through the right side of the mouth (Fig. 28-2). The larynx is visualized by gentle elevation and sweeping of the blade to the left to remove the tongue from the field of vision. The tip of the blade is inserted into the vallecula.
   d. With elevation of the tip of the blade the vocal cords are visualized. The orotracheal tube is introduced through the right corner of the mouth and passed through the cords (Fig. 28-3). The barrel of the laryngoscope blade is used only for visualization, not as a guide for the tube. In nasotracheal intubation the tube is passed through the nares into the pharynx prior to visualization of the cords (Fig. 28-4). On visualization of the cords the tip of the tube is grasped with the McGill forceps and advanced (Fig. 28-5).
   e. The tube should be positioned with the 2 cm mark at the vocal cords in a 1 kg infant and up to 3 cm in a full-term infant.
   f. Check the lettering at the mouth or nares as an indicator of position.
   g. Bag the infant and auscultate breath sounds bilaterally. With unilateral breath sounds the tube has probably passed into a main

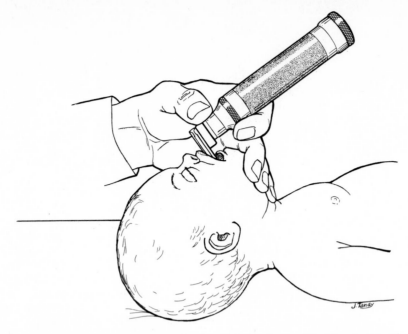

Fig. 28-1. Laryngoscope is held between thumb and index finger of left hand. (Modified from Schreiner, R. L., editor: Care of the newborn, New York, 1981, Raven Press.)

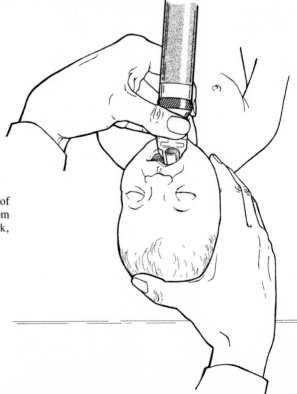

Fig. 28-2. Laryngoscope is inserted into right-hand side of mouth, and tongue pushed toward left. (Modified from Schreiner, R. L., editor: Care of the newborn, New York, 1981, Raven Press.)

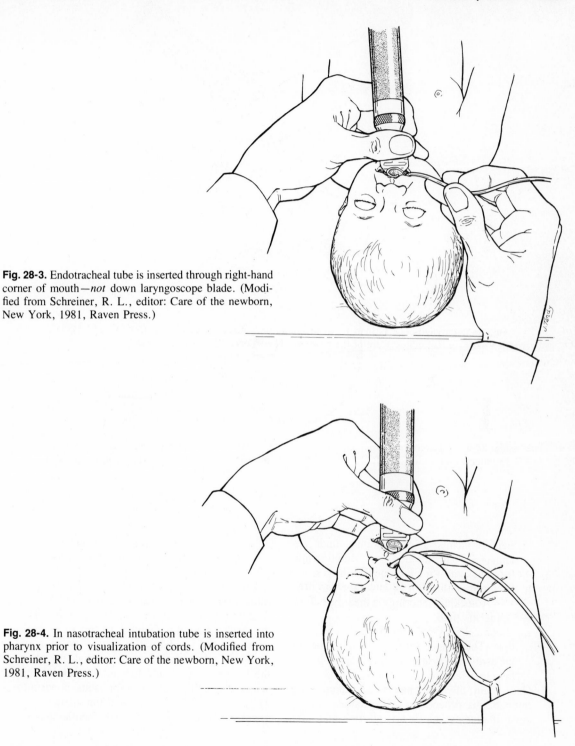

Fig. 28-3. Endotracheal tube is inserted through right-hand corner of mouth—*not* down laryngoscope blade. (Modified from Schreiner, R. L., editor: Care of the newborn, New York, 1981, Raven Press.)

Fig. 28-4. In nasotracheal intubation tube is inserted into pharynx prior to visualization of cords. (Modified from Schreiner, R. L., editor: Care of the newborn, New York, 1981, Raven Press.)

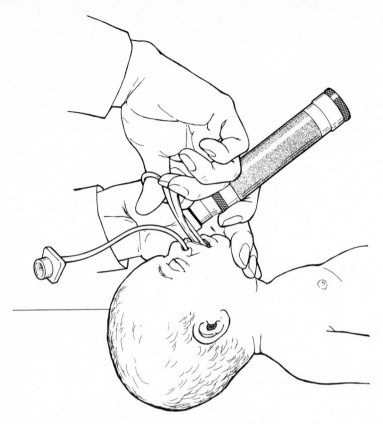

Fig. 28-5. In nasotracheal intubation tube is grasped with McGill forceps and gently advanced. (Modified from Schreiner, R. L., editor: Care of the newborn, New York, 1981, Raven Press.)

stem bronchus. If the breath sounds are unilateral, pull the tube back slowly while listening until they are equal.

h. Secure the tube with ½-inch tape and benzoin. Check the lettering on the tube before taping the tube.

i. Order a chest x-ray film to check tube position. The proper location of the tube on the x-ray film is above the carina but below the clavicles.

8. Once again, the infant needs close monitoring through this procedure. All attempts should cease if bradycardia (heart rate less than 100 beats/min) or cyanosis occurs. The infant should be stabilized with bag and mask ventilation prior to repeat attempts.

Procedural pitfalls. A few recurrent errors in the intubation procedure account for most failures. A common error is the tendency to hyperextend the neck. Although helpful in the older child or adult, in the newborn the resting position of the head is preferred. Next is the tendency to insert the laryngoscope blade too far. Usually in this instance the orifice of the esophagus is visualized. This opening is horizontal and the glistening white vocal cords are not visualized. Gentle withdrawal and elevation of the tip of the blade will usually allow visualization of the cords.

Another common procedural error in intubation is malposition of the tube, either in a main stem bronchus or in the esophagus. As a result, atelectasis, deterioration of blood gases, and worsening clinical condition may be observed. Careful auscultation prior to anchoring the tube and close attention to prevention of tube slippage may prevent such problems.

The kitten as a teaching model for neonatal intubation. Teaching endotracheal intubation is difficult. Rubber models are fairly accurate anatomically, but they are very inflexible. Also, of course, there are no secretions. Stillborn infants and cadavers also lack secretions, have no movement of the mouth or cords, and may not be readily or predictably available. Only a limited number of people can be taught to intubate anesthetized patients in the operating room and there is always the possibility of trauma to the patient. Unfortunately, most nurses, physicians, and respiratory therapists learn their intubation skills in emergency situations.

We have found the anesthetized kitten to be a very effective, realistic teaching model for endotracheal intubation. Animals are readily available year round. They are especially well suited for those who intubate newborn infants because the kitten larynx is very similar in size and anatomy. The epiglottis is slightly larger and broader than the infant's, and the kitten's teeth make it slightly more difficult to insert the laryngoscope blade.

Kittens approximately 4 months old are used so that a size 0 laryngoscope blade (the size for neonates) may be used. A size 1 blade is needed for cats. The kittens are anesthetized with approximately 40 mg ketamine injected into the triceps muscle. Ketamine is a safe general anesthetic that leaves the laryngeal reflexes intact. It takes effect in less than 5 minutes and usually lasts at least 30 minutes. The animals are usually awake within 60 minutes.

To prevent any movement of the animal's extremities, the kitten is wrapped in a towel with the head exposed. The mouth is easily opened to insert the blade between the teeth. A stylet in the tube may be useful, especially for beginners, to help

guide the tube (2.5 or 3.0 mm) between the cords.

A kitten's vocal cords are very sensitive, and laryngospasm is readily induced when the endotracheal tube is inserted. Younger, smaller kittens tend to have less spasm of the larynx than older animals.

The main difference between kitten intubation and emergency intubation in the human is the intubator's anxiety level in the human situation. The intact laryngeal reflexes, vocal cord spasm, and presence of secretions in the live kitten provide an authentic, effective teaching model for endotracheal intubation.

Drug therapy. If a spontaneous heart rate of greater than 100 beats/min is not sustained after 3 minutes of adequate ventilation and external cardiac massage, drugs are required. In most cases drugs are not required to stabilize the patient with acute asphyxia, and they never replace ventilation and oxygen therapy. Caffeine and other so-called respiratory stimulants should never be used for acute cardiopulmonary support. They are ineffective and their side effects may further endanger the patient's already precarious status. When drugs are necessary, they are usually administered by an umbilical vein catheter passed into the inferior vena cava, if possible. Table 28-2 lists the drugs, indications for use, routes of administration, and the order in which they are usually given.

Hypotension may be recognized by pallor, mottling of the skin, and poor capillary filling as well as measured by low blood pressure and weak pulses. The child who is hypotensive because of acute blood loss should receive either whole blood or other volume expanders such as plasma or a 5% protein solution. This is given in a dose of 10 to 20 ml/kg over 5 minutes.

It is important to remember that hypotension in the newborn is frequently caused by hypoxia. Therefore one's approach should also include the immediate treatment of hypoxia with ventilation and oxygenation. When ventilation and oxygenation do not immediately improve the hypotension, one usually must presume that hypovolemia might be present. This is especially true when there is evidence of bleeding such as with placenta previa and abruptio placentae. In these situations when an infant is hypotensive, plasma expanders are indi-

Table 28-2. Drugs in resuscitation

Drug	Indication	Route of administration	Dose
Whole blood or 5% protein solution	History of blood loss, shock, hypotension	IV	10-20 ml/kg
$D_{10-25}W$	Hypoglycemia	IV	2-4 ml/kg over 5 minutes
Naloxone	Maternal narcotic administration and neonatal depression	IV	0.01 mg/kg
$NaHCO_3$ (0.88 or 1 mEq/ml)	Severe metabolic acidemia or severe asphyxia not responsive to routine resuscitation	IV	1-2 mEq/kg over 5 minutes; dilute 1:2 with sterile water
Epinephrine 1:10,000	Cardiac arrest, severe bradycardia not responsive to routine resuscitation	IV (while performing cardiac massage) or intracardiac injection	0.1-0.3 ml/kg of 1:10,000 solution
Ca gluconate, 10%	Severe bradycardia	IV	1 ml/kg slowly
$CaCl_2$, 10%	Severe bradycardia	IV	0.1 ml/kg slowly

cated. Whole blood is preferable, but frequently not available; however, in an emergency situation whole blood may be obtained from either the mother or from the placenta. It is most important in these situations to avoid overheparinization of the blood, and it is mandatory to maintain absolute sterility. If blood is obtained from the placenta in a heparinized syringe, it should be discarded if not used after 30 to 60 minutes.

Although plasma expanders are indicated for hypotension in the delivery room, one must be careful to avoid overadministration. This may result in fluid overload, with congestive heart failure and pulmonary edema. In addition, the overuse of plasma expanders may alter cerebral blood flow, especially in the neonate whose autoregulatory mechanisms are probably impaired, and might possibly predispose to intracranial hemorrhage. Therefore, if hypotension in the neonate does not respond to ventilation, oxygenation, and plasma expanders (10 to 20 ml/kg), considerable thought should be given before repeating the dose of plasma expanders.

Stressed infants have an impaired ability to maintain glucose homeostasis. To avoid this complication, a 10% glucose solution is started intravenously. In the severely depressed baby it may be necessary to administer 2 to 4 ml/kg of 10% to 25% dextrose in water by slow push infusion.

When narcotic analgesics given to the mother might be contributing to the respiratory embarrassment, naloxone is indicated. Naloxone is preferred over nalorphine because of the latter's potential respiratory depressant effects.

Nearly all asphyxiated infants have both respiratory and metabolic acidosis. The principal treatment of acidosis in the neonate is prevention and treatment of the cause, that is, asphyxia. Thus, respiratory acidosis (low pH and increased Pco_2) is treated with ventilation and oxygenation. Metabolic acidosis (low pH and normal or low Pco_2) should also initially be treated with oxygenation and ventilation. The key to resuscitation and treatment of asphyxia in the newborn is oxygenation and ventilation, not the liberal use of alkali (sodium bicarbonate) solutions. If resuscitation is being carried out appropriately with proper ventilation and oxygenation and the infant is still not responding to resuscitation or if the blood gas shows a significant metabolic acidosis (base deficit greater than 10 mEq/L), sodium bicarbonate may be administered. In cases of severe or prolonged asphyxia, 2 to 3 mEq/kg of sodium bicarbonate diluted to 0.3 to 0.5 mEq/ml with sterile water is given by slow infusion, that is, over 5 mintues. Faster infusion rates or the use of more concentrated solutions may result in serious hyperosmolar damage. Subsequent bicarbonate therapy should be administered more precisely based on quantitative blood acid-base studies.

The indicators for aqueous epinephrine are cardiac arrest and severe bradycardia not responsive to routine resuscitation. It should be administered either intravenously or by the intracardiac route.

When given IV, and perfusion is poor; it may be necessary to initiate cardiac massage to hasten the pharmacological effect. The dose is 0.1 to 0.3 ml/kg of a 1:10,000 dilution given after the bicarbonate injection. Calcium gluconate or calcium chloride may be necessary in cases where severe bradycardia persists despite the previous therapeutic measures.

Management of the meconium-stained infant

The meconium-stained child with respiratory distress presents a special problem in resuscitation. A brief guide to the emergency care of this disorder is presented in the following list.

1. Before delivering the shoulders, thoroughly suction the nose, mouth, and pharynx.
2. Immediately after delivery of the infant, repeat suctioning of the upper airway, dry rapidly, and place the infant under radiant warmer.
3. If the baby is depressed or shows signs of respiratory difficulty, aspirate the trachea with mouth-to–endotracheal tube suction.
4. Repeat suction until the trachea is clear of meconium (less than or equal to 60 seconds).
5. Ventilate and oxygenate.
6. Aspirate meconium from the stomach.

When confronted with a cyanotic, apneic, or flaccid newborn infant, our first inclination is to provide ventilatory assistance. This tendency must be modified when aspiration is suspected, since ventilation without clearing the airway might result in death. Whenever the amniotic fluid is meconium stained, the infant should have rapid but careful suctioning of the mouth and nose on delivery of the head.

Immediately after delivery the upper airway should be aspirated again; if there is any indication of respiratory distress or depression or if meconium, especially thick meconium, was present in the pharynx, suctioning of the trachea should be performed under direct laryngoscopy. This can be accomplished by means of a DeLee catheter or, more easily, via mouth-to–endotracheal tube suction and should be repeated until the aspirate is clear. Since the child may well be deteriorating during this important initial step, the entire procedure should take no more than 60 seconds. Only

after the meconium has been cleared from the trachea should ventilation and oxygenation by bag and mask or by endotracheal tube with 100% O_2 begin. Aspirating the stomach of all babies who are meconium stained is also important to minimize the risk of repeated aspiration of regurgitated material.

Umbilical vein catheterization

Umbilical vein catheterization is used for rapid accessibility to the vascular system during resuscitation of the newborn in the delivery room. *Cardiopulmonary resuscitation, especially pulmonary resuscitation (oxygen and ventilation), is the most important aspect of resuscitation in the newborn.* The use of an intravenous line (umbilical venous catheter) should be used only after appropriate cardiopulmonary resuscitation has been instituted. Umbilical vein catheterization is never the first step in resuscitation of the newborn.

Umbilical venous catheterization is relatively easy to perform but carries with it significant major complications, especially when performed by inexperienced personnel. The procedure should be done under sterile conditions. The heart rate should be monitored during the entire procedure. The umbilical area should be carefully prepared with soap. If an iodine preparation is used, it should be removed carefully with alcohol to avoid skin irritation. Hemostasis can be maintained with a loop of umbilical tape at the junction of the cord and the skin or by placing a purse-string suture at the junction of the cord and the skin. The cord should be cut approximately 1 cm from its base.

The umbilical vein is a large vessel with very thin walls. The catheter, which has been flushed with heparinized saline, is then placed in the lumen of the umbilical vein and advanced 4 to 5 cm by gentle pressure. If the catheter is pushed further than 4 to 5 cm, it will do one of two things: (1) it may enter, via the ductus venosus, the inferior vena cava at approximately 10 cm or (2) the catheter may enter into a portal branch into the liver. If resistance is met at 5 or 6 cm, this indicates that the catheter is probably obstructed within the liver. It is best to get x-ray films to document the placement of the catheter, but in a resuscitation this is not possible. Therefore we recommend inserting the catheter approximately 4 to 5 cm and suturing it. This will avoid the possibility of injecting sclerosing solutions into the liver.

Tighten a purse-string suture around the base of the cord. This suture will prevent bleeding from the other noncatheterized vessels. Then, using the same suture material, secure the catheter. The catheter should then be connected to a three-way stopcock and the infusion fluids. Tape the umbilical catheter to the skin after application of benzoin.

Because of the high complication rate of umbilical venous catheters, the principal indications are (1) exchange transfusion and (2) emergency access to the vascular system for resuscitation of the newborn. Complications with umbilical venous catheters include hemorrhage, infection, injection of sclerosing substances into the liver resulting in hepatic necrosis, air embolism, vessel perforation, and possible electrical hazards. Strict technique of insertion and maintenance of catheters must be followed to minimize the complications. Catheters should be removed as soon as possible after resuscitative efforts have been completed.

Conclusion

Care of the resuscitated infant does not end after emergency resuscitation. Continued close monitoring of temperature, respiratory rate, heart rate, blood pressure, glucose, Po_2, Pco_2, hematocrit, and so forth is required in every infant severely depressed at birth. Appropriate attention to the stability of vital functions and metabolism is essential for early recognition and correction of the many sequelae that can occur after periods of significant stress. Only with structured programs that train personnel and maintain their proficiency in both acute and convalescent management of neonatal asphyxia can the ultimate goal of eliminating preventable causes of psychomotor retardation be achieved.

BLOOD CULTURES

The collection of blood cultures imposes relatively little risk to the patient. Virtually all sick neonates should have a blood culture obtained. Numerous sources and techniques for obtaining blood cultures have been advocated. Limited sampling sites, in addition to a relatively small blood volume in the premature infant, limit the availability of samples. The peripheral venous stick is probably the most popular method of obtaining cultures but is also the most difficult for those inexperienced with newborn infants. Alternatively, a sample may be drawn through the umbilical arterial or venous catheter *immediately* after insertion. This, however, carries with it a higher incidence of false positive results because of the greater likelihood of contamination during catheterization. Another method is to obtain the culture at the same time as the initial blood gas sample. The area may be prepped as outlined, the puncture performed with a butterfly needle, and the initial 1 ml sample set for culture. Afterwards, a heparinized tuberculin syringe may be used to obtain the blood gas.

Procedure

1. The puncture site should be double prepped, first with an iodine-containing solution and then with alcohol.
2. Draw a 1 ml sample.
3. The needle that has penetrated the skin is changed. The tops of two culture bottles are prepped in a fashion similar to the skin and half of the sample is placed in each bottle. One bottle is vented to air for the aerobic culture; the anaerobic atmosphere of the second bottle is maintained.
4. Clotted and citrated samples are unsuitable.

INTRAVENOUS FLUIDS

Registered nurses caring for newborn infants should be capable of placing a peripheral IV needle. All premature infants less than 1500 gm or less than 32 weeks' gestation should have a peripheral IV started immediately after birth for at least the first 24 hours. In addition, peripheral IV's are indicated for administration of intravenous fluids to infants not capable of taking adequate fluids via the gastric route, for administration of intravenous antibiotics to infants with sepsis or meningitis, and for treatment of symptomatic hypoglycemia in the newborn.

Materials

Very few materials are needed for the placement of a peripheral IV. The materials include (1) a 27-, 25-, or 23-gauge butterfly infusion set; (2) ½-inch tape; (3) a plastic medicine cup; (4) a bottle of IV fluids; (5) a fluid chamber; and (6) a continuous infusion pump.

Procedure

In the newborn the scalp veins are the easiest veins to use for the placement of IV's. The advantages of the scalp veins are the accessibility of the vessels, the ease of identifying an infiltrated IV, and the minimum restraints needed.

Arteries and veins can usually be differentiated on the scalp because the arteries are more tortuous than the veins, and the arteries fill from below, whereas the veins fill from above. If an artery is accidentally entered, it will usually be obvious by the blanching that occurs in the area when the fluid is infused. Should this occur, it is best to discontinue the IV and begin again.

The area should be shaved clean with an adequate area around the needle site for taping. The tubing of the butterfly needle should be flushed with IV solution (Fig. 28-6).

The needle should be inserted through the skin 0.5 to 1 cm distal to the vein and advanced slowly and superficially toward the vessel until blood appears in the tubing, indicating that the vessel has been entered (Fig. 28-7).

At this point the needle should be flushed with 1 to 2 ml of IV solution (Fig. 28-8). If infiltration occurs, the IV should be discontinued and the process repeated in another site. If infiltration does not occur, the butterfly wings should be taped (Fig. 28-9). After the butterfly wings are taped, it is also

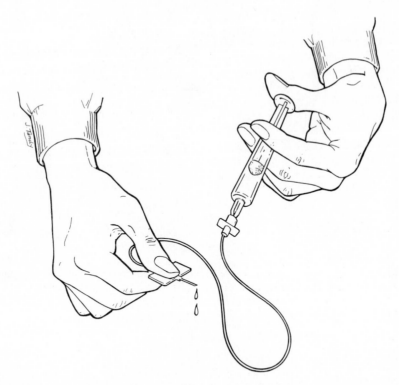

Fig. 28-6. Flushing needle and tubing. (Modified from Schreiner, R. L., editor: Care of the newborn, New York, 1981, Raven Press.)

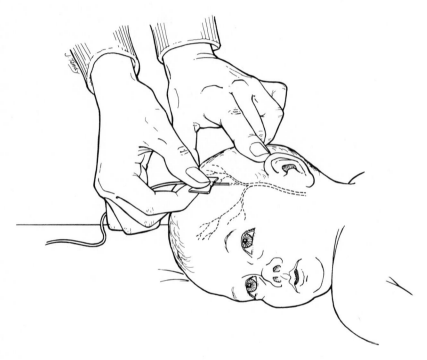

Fig. 28-7. Enter skin slightly distal to desired vein. (Modified from Schreiner, R. L., editor: Care of the newborn, New York, 1981, Raven Press.)

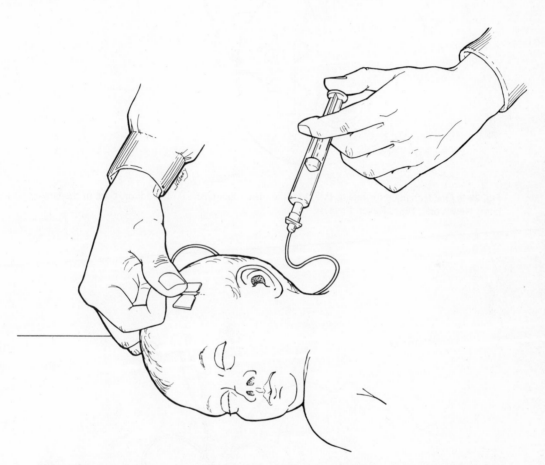

Fig. 28-8. Flush needle to confirm proper placement as demonstrated by lack of blanching or infiltration. (Modified from Schreiner, R. L., editor: Care of the newborn, New York, 1981, Raven Press.)

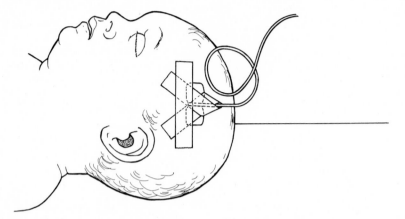

Fig. 28-9. One technique for taping IV. (Modified from Schreiner, R. L., editor: Care of the newborn, New York, 1981, Raven Press.)

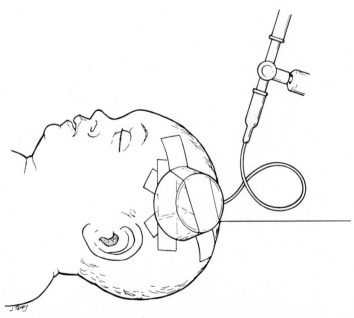

Fig. 28-10. Plastic medicine cup protects needle from accidental dislodgement. (Modified from Schreiner, R. L., editor: Care of the newborn, New York, 1981, Raven Press.)

helpful to tape the tubing of the butterfly set into a loop on the scalp so that it is not accidentally pulled. A small medicine cup can be taped over the butterfly wings, needle, and tape to protect the IV from accidental dislodgement (Fig. 28-10). The IV fluid set is then connected to the tubing of the butterfly set and the IV pump started.

An important complication of peripheral IV's is injection of sclerosing agents into the subcutaneous space. In premature and newborn infants, this can result in necrosis and sloughing of the skin. Because of this, any infiltrated IV must be removed and a new IV started. All intravenous systems increase the chance of infection. Meticulous attention should be paid to sterility during insertion of the needle and to the maintenance of the IV site, tubing, and solution.

Teaching the placement of IV needles

Although the technique of intravenous needle placement is easy to demonstrate on live infants, it is difficult for nurses at community hospitals to acquire the necessary skills unless there is a sick infant requiring intravenous needle placement and an instructor readily available for teaching purposes. Because of the difficulty in instructing students, nurses, and physicians in the proper technique of inserting a peripheral IV in an infant, Indiana University has developed a teaching simulator so that students may see the technique demonstrated, practice the technique, and be tested before going to the bedside. The infant scalp IV model (Medical Plastics Laboratory, Gatesville, Texas) consists of an infant head (Fig. 28-11) with a visible venous pattern. Using the simulator, the student may go through the entire procedure including successful placement of the IV needle as demonstrated by the appearance of blood in the IV tubing.

LUMBAR PUNCTURE

Lumbar puncture (LP) is part of the complete workup of any newborn suspected of sepsis. Any infant with symptoms suggestive of meningitis (seizures, intractable vomiting, and so forth) should have an LP performed.

The equipment required for an LP is simple and

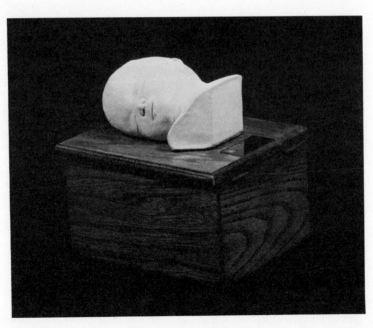

Fig. 28-11. Baby "Ivy" scalp IV simulator. (Medical Plastics Laboratory, Gatesville, Texas.)

should be readily available in any community hospital: (1) 70% alcohol, iodophore solution (Betadine), and 4-inch × 4-inch gauze pads; (2) sterile gloves and two sterile towels; (3) 22- to 25-gauge 1½-inch spinal needle with stylet; and (4) three sterile tubes. This equipment may be available as a locally packaged or commercially produced pediatric LP tray.

Procedure

1. An experienced assistant is needed to immobilize the infant in the lateral decubitus or sitting position (Figs. 28-12 and 28-13). The infant should be held so that the spine is maximally arched in the cephalad-caudad (horizontal) axis but straight in the vertical axis. Care must be taken so that breathing is not compromised. The assistant's hands should be held over the shoulders and lower buttocks, not around the neck and lower legs. *The assistant must pay close attention to the infant's clinical status during the entire procedure!*

2. The L3-4 intervertebral space is located. This is usually between the posterosuperior portion of the iliac crests (Fig. 28-14). In the event of a difficult or traumatic tap, it may be beneficial to move one interspace cephalad.

3. Scrub hands and put on gloves.

4. The infant's back is scrubbed, first with an iodophore solution and then with alcohol. The area of the puncture should be the first area cleansed, with the remainder of the back scrubbed in a concentric circular pattern (Fig. 28-15). The infant's back is draped with sterile towels.

5. The needle is directed toward the umbilicus, but perpendicular to the spine (Fig. 28-16).

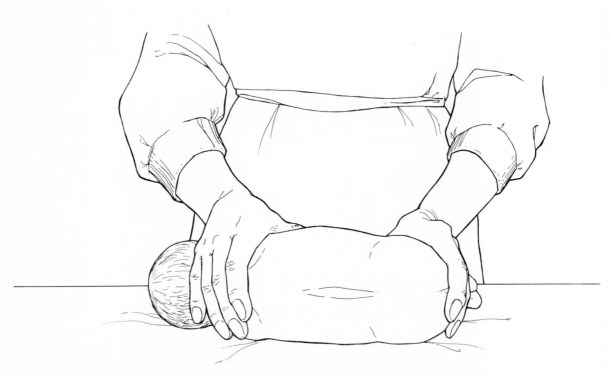

Fig. 28-12. Lateral decubitus position for performing lumbar puncture. Infant's back should be maximally arched yet parallel to table surface. (Modified from Schreiner, R. L., editor: Care of the newborn, New York, 1981, Raven Press.)

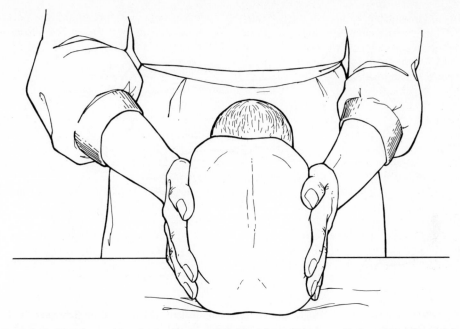

Fig. 28-13. Upright position for lumbar tap. (Modified from Schreiner, R. L., editor: Care of the newborn, New York, 1981, Raven Press.)

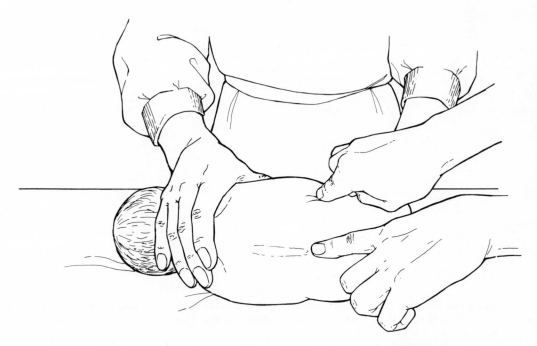

Fig. 28-14. L3-4 interspace is located between iliac crests. (Modified from Schreiner, R. L., editor: Care of the newborn, New York, 1981, Raven Press.)

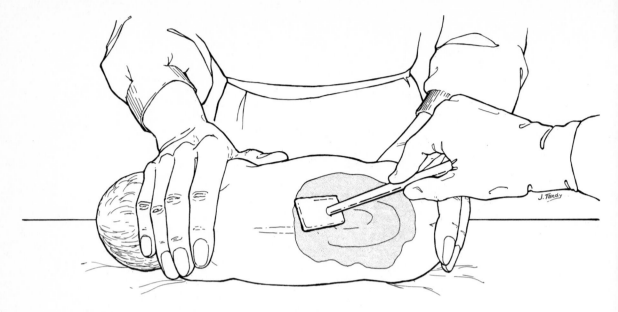

Fig. 28-15. Site is prepped using a circular scrubbing pattern. (Modified from Schreiner, R. L., editor: Care of the newborn, New York, 1981, Raven Press.)

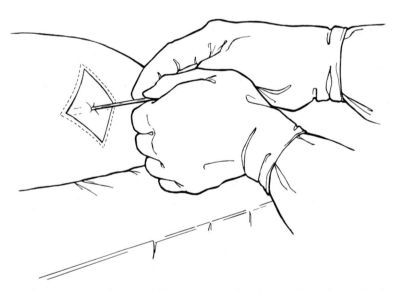

Fig. 28-16. Needle is aimed toward umbilicus but perpendicular to lateral plane of back. (Modified from Schreiner, R. L., editor: Care of the newborn, New York, 1981, Raven Press.)

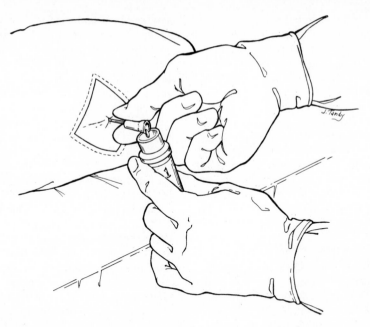

Fig. 28-17. Cerebrospinal fluid is collected in three numbered sterile test tubes. (Modified from Schreiner, R. L., editor: Care of the newborn, New York, 1981, Raven Press.)

6. The needle is advanced 1 to 1.5 cm until decreased resistance is felt; however, this may not be felt in the newborn. The stylet is removed to visualize CSF. It may take 10 to 15 seconds for the CSF to appear if the infant is at rest. If no fluid is obtained, the stylet is replaced and the needle is once again advanced slowly. If the spinal canal is traversed and contact made with bone, bleeding from the anterior venous plexus usually occurs.

7. One half milliliter CSF is allowed to drip into each of three sterile tubes (Fig. 28-17). These are then sent for analysis as follows:
   a. Tube No. 1—glucose and protein
   b. Tube No. 2—culture, sensitivity, Gram's stain
   c. Tube No. 3—RBC and WBC count and differential

A serum glucose should be done prior to the LP for comparison with CSF glucose.

8. Replace the stylet and withdraw the needle.

Procedural pitfalls

It is essential to have the infant well immobilized and positioned with the spine straight in the vertical axis. In addition, the back of the infant should be arched into the fetal position to maximally widen the interspinous spaces. The needle should be inserted directly into the interspace, without lateral deviation. Last, and most important, the needle should be advanced slowly. The most common cause of a traumatic LP is overadvancement of the needle with penetration of the venous plexus on the anterior side of the spinal canal.

Complications

Brain stem herniation is uncommon in the neonate because of the open fontanelles. There are a few reported cases of spinal epidermoid tumors developing years after an LP in infants and children in whom an open needle (without a stylet) was apparently used. Theoretically, these are the result of a core of epidermis being displaced into the spinal canal by the open end of the needle. Last, and most common, is the traumatic LP, which is of little consequence to the patient but confuses the interpretation of CSF results.

Teaching the procedure

A commercially available infant lumbar puncture simulator (Medical Plastics Laboratory, Gatesville, Texas) has been developed at Indiana University. The model consists of a simulated full-term size infant with the anatomical landmarks required for performing a lumbar puncture. The actual procedure may be practiced with the model. A successful attempt is demonstrated by obtaining clear cerebrospinal fluid.

TREATMENT OF A PNEUMOTHORAX

There are a number of methods to treat a pneumothorax. In *term* infants who are in only mild respiratory distress, 100% inspired oxygen concentration may be used for a *few* (1 to 3) *hours*. The pneumothorax is resolved by the principle of nitrogen washout. It is important to emphasize that this treatment should *never* be used in premature infants, and it should never be used as the sole means of therapy in infants with moderate to severe respiratory distress.

A 23-gauge scalp vein needle may be used to aspirate the pneumothorax in emergencies. The needle is connected to a stopcock and a 20-ml syringe and is inserted over the superior edge of the third or fourth rib in the anterior axillary line (Fig. 28-18). As the needle is advanced into the chest, negative pressure should be applied to the plunger of the syringe. This technique can be used to relieve a pneumothorax until a chest tube can be inserted. Needles inserted into the chest are not innocuous and can cause trauma to the underlying lung, with the formation of an iatrogenic pneumothorax. In addition, hemorrhage can occur if one does not

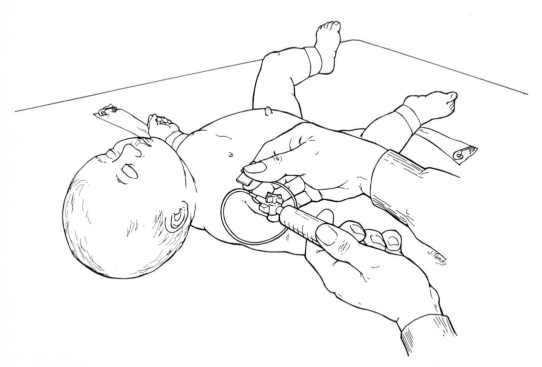

Fig. 28-18. Technique of aspirating a pneumothorax with a stopcock, syringe, and scalp vein needle inserted lateral to nipple. (Modified from Schreiner, R. L., editor: Care of the newborn, New York, 1981, Raven Press.)

avoid the intercostal blood supply that runs along the inferior margin of each rib.

Chest tubes

No. 8 to 10 Fr tubes are used for chest tubes. Additional equipment includes sterile instruments, infant size underwater seal drainage system, sterile connector, suture on a curved needle, plastic tubing, tape, and a surgical light.

Sterile technique is essential. This means that the person performing the procedure observes proper handwashing and wears a sterile gown, cap, mask, and gloves. Those persons assisting are similarly prepared and any observers wear a cap and a mask.

Adequate lighting is essential. The infant's heart rate should be audibly monitored. Adequate oxygen-ation, ventilation, and warmth must be provided. The infant's extremities should be restrained (Fig. 28-19), with arms positioned away from the chest. The anterior chest wall on the side in which the tube is to be inserted should be carefully prepared with surgical soap.

After infiltration with 1% xylocaine, an incision of approximately 0.3 to 0.4 cm is made in the third or fourth intercostal space in the anterior axillary line. A purse-string suture is then placed around the incision. Care should be taken not to traumatize the areola or breast tissue.

The tip of the tube (No. 8 to 10 Fr) should be grasped with a small curved hemostat (Fig. 28-20). An extra hole should be cut in the tube *on the radiopaque stripe* approximately 2 to 4 cm from the tip of the tube. This will provide a hole in both the

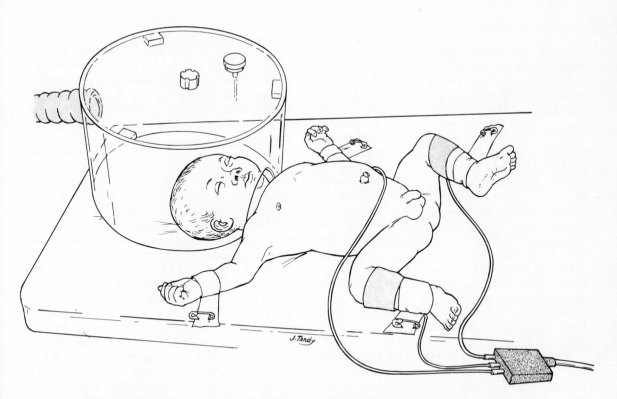

Fig. 28-19. Infant properly restrained, in oxygen, and monitored. (Modified from Schreiner, R. L., editor: Care of the newborn, New York, 1981, Raven Press.)

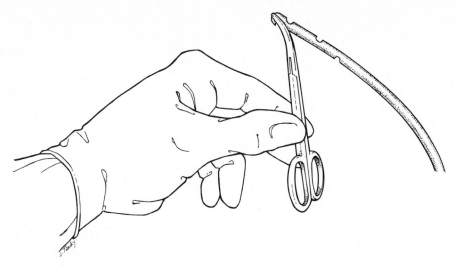

Fig. 28-20. Technique of grasping tip of chest tube. (Modified from Schreiner, R. L., editor: Care of the newborn, New York, 1981, Raven Press.)

posterior and anterior aspects of the hemithorax if the tip of the tube locates posteriorly.

The hemostat is then placed through the incision, point down, perpendicular to the plane of the chest and advanced into the pleural cavity (Fig. 28-21) through the interspace superior to the level at which the skin incision was made (Fig. 28-22). A fair amount of force is required to accomplish this, even in small premature babies.

Once the pleural cavity is entered, the hemostat blades are separated and the tube is advanced between them into the chest so that the last hole is approximately 1.5 cm past the skin incision. The purse-string suture is then tightened and tied. This prevents leakage of air around the incision. Just before anchoring the chest tube in place with the suture, the last hole in the catheter should be rechecked to verify that it is inside the chest. Finally, the ends of the suture are tied around the chest tube itself to prevent the tube from being accidentally dislodged (Fig. 28-23).

The tube is carefully secured with benzoin and tape after an antibiotic ointment is applied to the incision area. The tube is then connected to the underwater seal drainage bottle and the water level observed for fluctuation with respiration. If this is absent, the chest tube may be obstructed or improperly placed. A common aberrant placement is location of the tube in the subcutaneous tissue rather than in the intrapleural space. A tube inserted into the pleural cavity slides easily as though lubricated. Any resistance should suggest an abnormal position.

A chest x-ray film is obtained to determine tube placement and verify its effectiveness in evacuating the pneumothorax. A lateral chest x-ray film may be helpful to determine whether the tip of the tube is placed anteriorly or posteriorly.

If the infant is on a ventilator or if the pneumothorax persists despite proper tube placement, the chest tube should be connected to a continuous suction of about 5 to 15 cm of water. If negative pressure is applied to the chest tube and continuous bubbling results, one of two things is possible. Most likely there is a leak in the system; for example, one hole of the chest tube may be outside the chest or there may be a loose connection within the chest tube system. In a small number of cases, even a large chest tube is inadequate because of a large tear in the visceral pleura. In these cases, surgical intervention may be required to oversew the perforation.

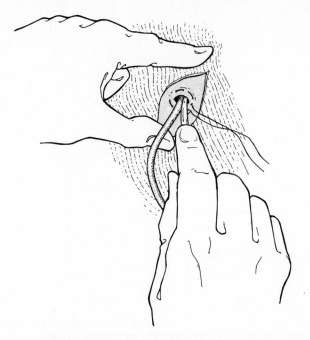

Fig. 28-21. Pressure is applied on hemostat perpendicular to plane of chest. (Modified from Schreiner, R. L., editor: Care of the newborn, New York, 1981, Raven Press.)

Fig. 28-22. Tube should be tunneled under skin so that it enters chest in intercostal space above its point of entry in skin. (Modified from Schreiner, R. L., editor: Care of the newborn, New York, 1981, Raven Press.)

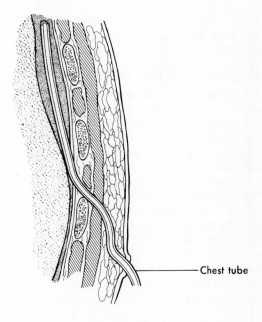

Chest tube

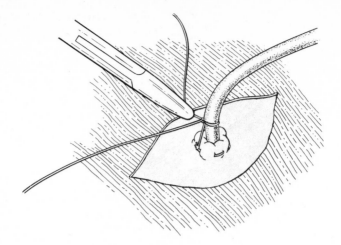

Fig. 28-23. Technique of securing chest tube with sutures. (Modified from Schreiner, R. L., editor: Care of the newborn, New York, 1981, Raven Press.)

Complications

One of the most important complications of chest tube placement is perforation of the lung. The diagnosis of a perforated lung should be suspected when a pneumothorax does not resolve despite proper placement of the chest tube. These infants usually show continuous vigorous bubbling in the chest tube bottle. Trocars should never be used for the placement of chest tubes in neonates because they have been frequently associated with lung perforation.

Teaching chest tube insertion

Teaching nurses and physicians the technique of aspiration of a pneumothorax and chest tube placement is difficult because of the urgency of the situation. Therefore we have used the cat as an animal model for training purposes. Others have used the rabbit model with equal success.

The cats are sedated with intramuscular ketamine hydrochloride (40 to 60 mg in the deltoid muscle) and all four extremities are restrained. After the chest is shaved, surgical soap is applied, and a sterile drape placed. We have found it necessary to place the tube in the middle to anterior axillary line in the sixth to ninth intercostal space in the cat, since failure to penetrate the intercostal mus-

cle often results when attempts are made more anteriorly or superiorly.

We have found the cat model excellent for teaching nurses, house officers, and community physicians the proper technique of chest tube placement. It allows the instructor time to answer questions and carefully discuss the procedure in progress, which is obviously not possible during an emergency with an infant.

Care and maintenance of chest tubes

Each hour the nurse should note the presence of fluctuation or bubbling in the chest tube bottle or tubing. Generally a chest tube placed for a pneumothorax will drain very little fluid, while a chest tube placed postoperatively will have more drainage. With small tubes in small infants, the intrapleural pressure may not be adequate to cause fluctuations in the drainage system, but fluctuation will be noted in the tubing at the chest wall. The presence of fluctuation in the bottle or the tubing indicates that the holes of the chest tube are patent and within the intrapleural space. The presence of bubbling in the chest tube drainage bottle indicates that the chest tube is, in fact, removing air from the intrapleural space. A chest tube may be fluctuating; that is, the holes of the tube are patent and in the intrapleural space, but the tube is not draining the pneumothorax. This may occur when the pneumothorax has accumulated anteriorly, since the infant is in the supine position, and the chest tube has been placed posteriorly. Or the pneumothorax may be accumulated in the subpulmonic area, whereas the chest tube holes may be in the apical area. Therefore it is helpful to turn the infant frequently and note the change in bubbling within the chest tube bottle.

In general, a chest tube placed for the treatment of a pneumothorax should never be clamped, unless it is in preparation for removal. Even brief periods of clamping can result in rapid respiratory decompensation if the pleural leak is still present.

Pleur-Evac (Krale, Division of Deknatel, Inc., Queens Village, New York) drainage systems are frequently used in the newborn intensive care unit. The water in the blue ("suction control chamber") area is connected to the suction. The depth of the water determines the centimeters of water suction. Bubbling in this area does *not* indicate drainage of air from the chest. The pink area ("water seal chamber") of the Pleur-Evac is connected to the baby. Bubbling in this area reflects drainage of air from the chest. Fluctuation in the system means that the hole of the chest tube is patent in the intrapleural space. However, if suction is applied to the system, the suction will cause the water level in the pink area to fluctuate, even if the chest tube is plugged.

Chest tube removal

The chest tube should be left in place until bubbling has not been observed for at least 24 hours. If the infant is on a ventilator, chest tubes are usually left in place for longer periods of time.

The tube should be clamped, the baby's clinical condition closely monitored, and an x-ray film obtained shortly thereafter to identify a possible recurrence. If the lung remains inflated, the tube may be removed 12 to 24 hours after clamping. The tube should be withdrawn rapidly and aseptically. Pressure should be applied to the incision with gauze coated with an appropriate antibiotic ointment or petroleum jelly to prevent entrance of air through the chest tube incision. The gauze should then be taped in place.

SUPRAPUBIC BLADDER ASPIRATION IN THE NEONATE

The reliability of urinalysis and urine cultures in infants is no better than the technique of specimen collection. True clean catch urine samples are impossible to obtain in the neonatal period. Urethral catheterization is also unreliable because of contamination from urethral and preputial colonization and is potentially dangerous because of the possibility of introducing organisms into the bladder. Since the introduction of suprapubic bladder aspiration, it has been proven an efficacious and safe method for urine collection. Any neonate or infant who is evaluated for septicemia should have a suprapubic bladder aspiration for urinalysis and culture.

A listing of the potential complications of suprapubic bladder aspiration in order of frequency is shown below.

Microscopic hematuria
Gross hematuria
Bowel perforation
Abdominal wall hematoma
Perforation of abdominal organs

Most complications of suprapubic bladder aspiration are due to performing the procedure on children in whom it is contraindicated. The most evident, yet most common, mistake is performing this procedure on an infant with an empty bladder. A dry diaper for 1 to 3 hours prior to the procedure is required. Secondly, dehydration is a contraindication to suprapubic bladder aspiration. Other major contraindications to suprapubic bladder aspiration are abdominal distention, organomegaly, genitourinary and abdominal anomalies, and hemorrhagic disorders.

Procedure

1. The infant is checked to see that his diaper (or urine collection bag) has been dry for the preceding hour.
2. An assistant is essential to restrain the infant.
3. Palpate the bladder. In neonates this may not be possible. Scrub the suprapubic area with an antiseptic solution (Fig. 28-24).
4. The assistant may help to prevent the infant from voiding by pinching the proximal penile urethra in the male.

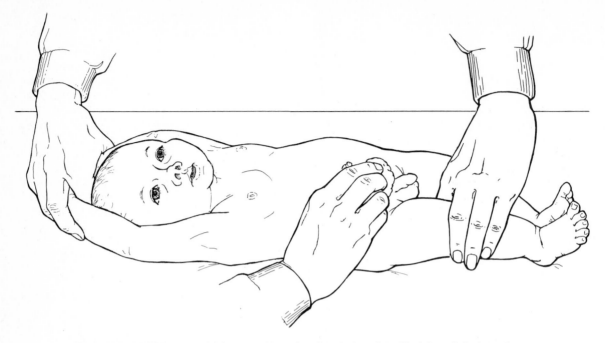

Fig. 28-24. Scrubbing suprapubic area with antiseptic solution. (Modified from Schreiner, R. L., editor: Care of the newborn, New York, 1981, Raven Press.)

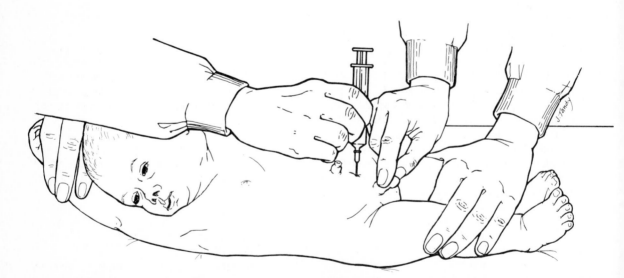

Fig. 28-25. Aim needle perpendicular to table or angled slightly toward head. (Modified from Schreiner, R. L., editor: Care of the newborn, New York, 1981, Raven Press.)

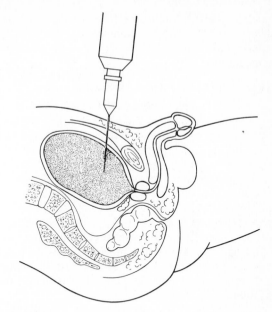

Fig. 28-26. Sagittal view of abdomen showing insertion of needle into bladder. (Modified from Schreiner, R. L., editor: Care of the newborn, New York, 1981, Raven Press.)

5. Aspiration is performed with a suitable needle and syringe (for example, 3 cm, 21-gauge needle on a 3- to 10-ml syringe).
6. The puncture is performed 1 to 1.5 cm above the symphysis pubis in the midline (Fig. 28-25). (There is often a skin crease in this location.) The needle is inserted perpendicular to the table or at slight angle aimed toward the head to a distance of 1 to 2 cm until a slight decrease in resistance is felt when the bladder is penetrated (Fig. 28-26).
7. The needle is withdrawn after the urine is aspirated, and gentle pressure is held over the puncture site until bleeding is stopped.
8. If no urine is obtained, the needle should be withdrawn. Aimless probing and repeated attempts are dangerous.
9. The syringe with urine may be capped and sent on ice to the laboratory for urinalysis and bacteriological studies.

The three most common mistakes resulting in failure to get urine are (1) performance of the procedure in an infant with an empty bladder, (2) insertion of the needle too close to the symphysis pubis (The bladder is an abdominal organ in the neonate and aspiration too close to the symphysis will frequently result in missing the bladder.), and (3) aiming the needle toward the pubis rather than perpendicular to the table or at a slight angle toward the head.

Teaching the technique of suprapubic bladder aspiration

A teaching simulator to demonstrate and practice the proper technique of suprapubic bladder aspiration has been developed. The model (Medical Plastics Laboratory, Gatesville, Texas) consists of a simulated infant with a ''bladder'' that may be filled or emptied with ''urine.'' Both an empty and filled bladder may be simulated. In addition, if the ''student'' inserts the needle too close to the pubis or at an improper angle such that the needle is directed toward the pubis rather than toward the head, the attempt will be unsuccessful; that is, urine will not be obtained.

TECHNIQUES OF OBTAINING ARTERIAL BLOOD

Arterial blood gas analysis is extremely important in neonatal respiratory care. Possible sites of blood sampling include: (1) umbilical arteries; (2) radial, brachial, temporal, dorsal pedal, and posterior tibial arteries; and (3) capillaries ("arterialized"). The femoral arteries are not recommended for obtaining arterial blood because of the potential for vascular compromise to the leg.

Umbilical artery catheterization

Umbilical artery catheterization is a useful procedure in the care of infants requiring frequent arterial blood gas or blood pressure assessment. Additionally, medications and parenteral fluids may be infused by this route; however, special precautions must be taken since bolus infusion of medications has been associated with higher incidence of complications. In spite of their usefulness, umbilical artery catheters must not be used without serious deliberation because of potential complications.

Equipment. All equipment should be assembled prior to catheterization to be sure of its availability and working condition. Supplies and equipment are as follows:

1. Line fluids usually consisting of D_5W or $D_{10}W$ with electrolytes
2. IV fluid chamber
3. IV tubing
4. Infusion pump
5. A 0.22 μ filter
6. Short length of IV tubing
7. Three-way stopcock
8. No. 3.5 or 5 Fr umbilical artery catheter
9. A 3-0 silk suture on an atraumatic needle
10. Flush solution, 10 ml
11. Surgical cap, mask, gown, and gloves
12. Surgical equipment (small clamps, curved Iris forceps without teeth, needle holder)

Procedure for catheterization

1. The infant should be placed under a radiant warmer and all four extremities restrained (Fig. 28-27). The skin temperature should be maintained at 96.5° F by a servo-control mechanism. Oxygen should be administered as needed and the "beep" on the cardiac monitor readily heard.
2. The umbilicus is carefully scrubbed for 5 minutes with a bactericidal solution. Remember to clean off the solution after the procedure to avoid skin irritation.
3. The operator should wear a surgical cap and mask, perform a 5-minute scrub, and put on a surgical gown and gloves, using aseptic technique.
4. The umbilicus is draped in a sterile fashion; the head is left exposed for clinical observation.
5. To provide hemostasis and to anchor the line after placement, a 3-0 silk purse-string suture is placed at the junction of the skin and the cord (Fig. 28-28). Alternatively, a loop of umbilical tape may be used in the same position. The cord is then cut 3 to 4 mm from the skin and the vessels identified. The vein is the largest vessel with a relatively thin wall and large lumen. Two arteries with relatively thicker walls and smaller lumina are usually present.
6. The cord is grasped with two curved hemostats near the selected artery. This provides clear visualization and stabilization of the vessel. Using a curved Iris forceps without teeth, the arterial lumen is gently dilated (Fig. 28-29).
7. A previously prepared No. 3.5 or 5 Fr umbilical artery catheter may then be introduced. The catheter is prepared by cutting off a portion of the larger tapered end and inserting either an 18-gauge stub adapter for the 5 Fr catheter or a 20-gauge stub adapter for the 3.5 Fr catheter. This should then be attached to the three-way stopcock and the air cleared from the line by flushing with a saline solution.
8. During insertion of the catheter, the cord should be retracted cephalad and the catheter advanced with *slow, constant* pressure toward the feet (Fig. 28-30). Resistance is occasionally felt at 1 to 2 cm. This is the junction of the artery and the fascial plane. The resistance may be overcome by *gentle* sustained pressure and rotation of the catheter between the thumb and forefinger. If the catheter passes 4 to 5 cm and meets resistance, this generally indicates that a false passage through the vessel wall has occurred. Occasionally, one may bypass the perforation by attempting catheterization with a No. 5 Fr catheter. If this catheter enters a false passage, further attempts with that vessel are usually unsuccessful.
9. If low placement (L-3 to L-4) is desired, the catheter may be advanced 7 to 8 cm in a small 2-pound premature infant or 12 to 13 cm in a

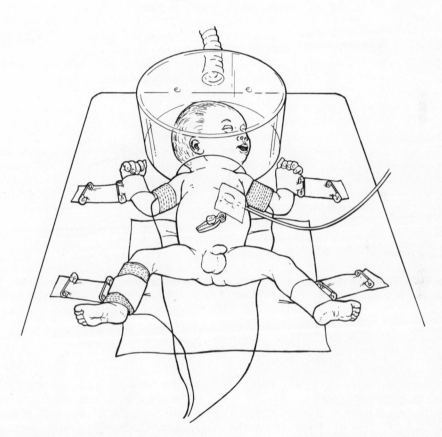

Fig. 28-27. Proper restraint of infant with oxygen administered continuously and cardiac and temperature monitors in place. (Modified from Schreiner, R. L., editor: Care of the newborn, New York, 1981, Raven Press.)

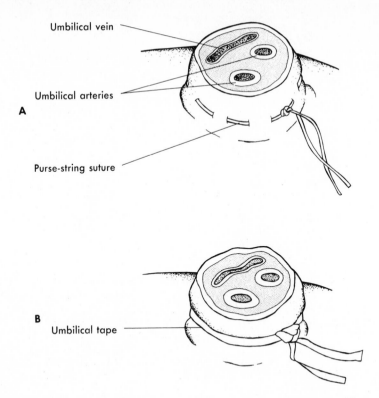

Umbilical vein

Umbilical arteries

A

Purse-string suture

B

Umbilical tape

Fig. 28-28. Technique of preventing bleeding with purse-string suture, **A,** or umbilical tape, **B.** (Modified from Schreiner, R. L., editor: Care of the newborn, New York, 1981, Raven Press.)

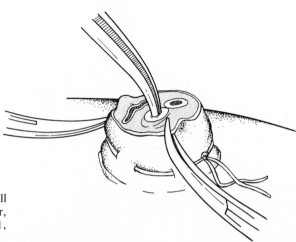

Fig. 28-29. Dilating umbilical arterial lumen with small Iris forceps without teeth. (Modified from Schreiner, R. L., editor: Care of the newborn, New York, 1981, Raven Press.)

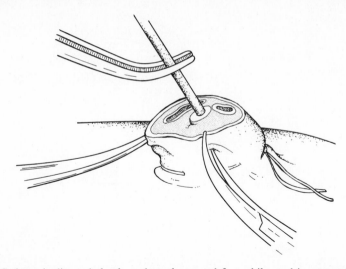

Fig. 28-30. Catheter is directed slowly and gently toward feet while cord is retracted in cephalad direction with small clamp. (Modified from Schreiner, R. L., editor: Care of the newborn, New York, 1981, Raven Press.)

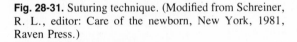

Fig. 28-31. Suturing technique. (Modified from Schreiner, R. L., editor: Care of the newborn, New York, 1981, Raven Press.)

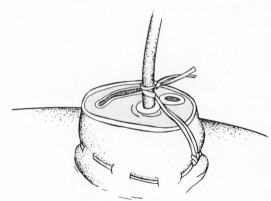

full-term infant. Once sterile technique is broken, the line can no longer be advanced. Therefore it is preferable to position the catheter too high and withdraw as necessary according to the abdominal x-ray film. After positioning, the catheter should be secured with the previously placed suture (Fig. 28-31). Benzoin is applied to the skin, and the catheter is taped to the abdominal wall as illustrated in Fig. 28-32. An x-ray film is obtained and the catheter repositioned at the lower border of the L-3 vertebra if a low position is desired.

Some clinicians prefer a high position (above the diaphragm). There is no convincing evidence to support either a high or low position. X-ray films of an arterial catheter will show the catheter proceeding from the umbilical artery down toward the pelvis, then making an acute turn into the internal iliac artery and toward the head to the bifurcation of the aorta, and then up the aorta slightly to the left of the vertebral column (Fig. 28-33). An umbilical venous catheter will proceed directly cephalad and generally to the right of the spine.

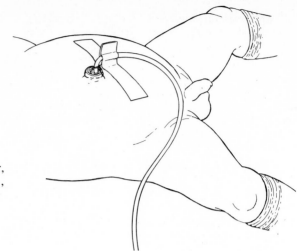

Fig. 28-32. Taping technique. (Modified from Schreiner, R. L., editor: Care of the newborn, New York, 1981, Raven Press.)

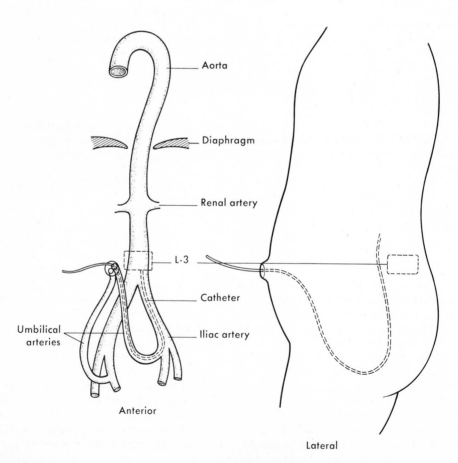

Aorta

Diaphragm

Renal artery

L-3

Catheter

Umbilical arteries

Iliac artery

Anterior

Lateral

Fig. 28-33. If a low position is desired, catheter tip is positioned below third lumbar vertebra. (Modified from Schreiner, R. L., editor: Care of the newborn, New York, 1981, Raven Press.)

Catheterization failure. It has been shown that most umbilical artery catheterization failures result from the catheter perforating the intima of the artery approximately 1 cm below the umbilical stump where the artery curves toward the feet. In this instance, the catheter can be advanced 4 to 6 cm and resistance is then met. The following three maneuvers may be used to prevent vessel perforation:

1. The catheter should be advanced *extremely slowly* and steadily—not with intermittent jabs. The catheter should not be forced through the obstruction at 1 cm.
2. Because the artery curves toward the feet, the umbilical stump should be held with a curved clamp and pulled toward the head so that the catheter is inserted in as straight a fashion as possible (Fig. 28-30).
3. A No. 5 Fr catheter is more blunt than a 3.5 Fr; therefore, if catheterization with a 3.5 Fr is unsuccessful, it is recommended that a 5 Fr catheter be utilized in the other artery.

Catheter care

1. If a low placement is desired, the catheter should be withdrawn to the lower edge of L-3. No catheter should be advanced once sterile technique has been broken.
2. If the catheter becomes plugged, fails to function properly, or blanching or discoloration of the buttocks, heels, or toes is noted, the catheter should be *removed at once. Never flush an obstructed arterial line.*
3. To avoid confusion between bruising and emboli, preexisting bruising of the lower extremities (secondary to breech presentation, and so forth) should be outlined and heelsticks prohibited.
4. When the catheter is to be removed, it should be withdrawn slowly to 3 cm and left 5 to 10 minutes without infusion to allow the artery to spasm and prevent bleeding. The stump should be observed for oozing for 10 minutes after catheter removal.
5. Sterile technique must always be utilized when working with an arterial line. For blood gas analysis, the line should be cleared by withdrawing 0.6 ml of fluid back into a sterile 1-ml syringe. This is set aside for reinfusion. Three-tenths milliliter of blood may then be withdrawn into a sterile, heparinized syringe for

blood gas analysis. The fluid in the first syringe is then reinfused and the line flushed with 0.3 ml of isotonic saline or other electrolyte flush solution. Each time a new syringe is attached to the stopcock, aspirate initially to evacuate trapped air usually present. Tapping the syringe and stopcock will cause the air to rise to the top of the syringe. A syringe should be left attached to the stopcock to maintain sterility.

6. An accurate record of fluid infused and blood removed should be kept on all infants with umbilical artery catheters.
7. A disposable 0.22 μ filter should be included in all systems to prevent infusion of air or particulate matter.

Catheter complications. Although the incidence of major complications is low in most centers where this procedure is in common use, umbilical catheters are not without risk. The incidence of major complications reported varies with the expertise of the physician or nurse inserting the catheter and the personnel caring for it. These complications include hemorrhage, infection, thromboembolic phenomenon (especially to kidneys and gut, legs and spinal cord), vasospasm, air embolism, vessel perforation, electrical hazards, peritoneal perforation, lost catheters, hypertension, and possible effects of plasticizers. It is most important that meticulous technique for the insertion and maintenance of catheters be followed to minimize the risk of these potential complications.

The infant must be watched closely for evidence of vasospasm or embolic phenomenon. We have found it helpful to prohibit heelsticks to avoid confusion of preexisting bruising with embolism or spasm. Whenever the buttocks, heels, or toes become cyanotic or blanched, remove the catheter. Catheters should be removed as soon as frequent arterial blood sampling is no longer required. All catheter sites should be observed for bleeding, particularly after insertion and removal.

Teaching simulator. A commercially available (Medical Plastics Laboratory, Gatesville, Texas) simulator makes it relatively easy to demonstrate and practice the technique of both umbilical artery and umbilical vein catherization. The neonatal umbilical vessel catheterization simulator (Fig. 28-34) consists of a term-sized rubber-skinned doll stuffed

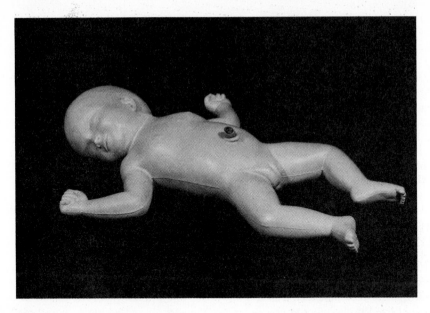

Fig. 28-34. Baby "Umbi" neonatal umbilical artery and vein catheterization simulator. (Medical Plastics Laboratory, Gatesville, Texas.)

with polyurethane foam and having a vinyl multi-tubular "umbilical cord" attached to the hidden blood supply. The "umbilical arteries" are specially designed vinyl vessels with thick walls and small lumina; the "umbilical vein" is a large vein with thin walls similar to that in the infant. Each cord extends into the "abdomen" and blood source and may repeatedly be pulled out and cut, providing a fresh surface for each trainee.

Radial artery puncture

One of the most frequently used methods for obtaining arterial samples from neonates is the radial artery puncture. Before attempting this procedure, it is important to be aware of the anatomy of the wrist (Fig. 28-35). Only the radial artery is used for arterial puncture to preserve the collateral circulation to the hand via the ulnar artery. Note that the median nerve lies in the midline, and the ulnar nerve lies near the ulnar artery. These areas should be avoided when performing punctures.

A heparinized tuberculin syringe is prepared for the procedure. All heparin and air should be ejected from the syringe. The amount of heparin remaining in the neck of the syringe and the hub of the needle is adequate to anticoagulate the sample. Excess heparin may result in inaccurate pH and Pco_2 determinations owing to dilution of the blood sample.

Palpate the pulsation of the radial artery just proximal to the transverse wrist creases (Fig. 28-36). Grasp the infant's wrist and hand in your left hand (if right-handed). Cleanse the area with alcohol. Subcutaneous lidocaine may be administered before doing the radial artery puncture to decrease the pain to the infant. With a heparinized tuberculin syringe and a 25- or 26-gauge needle, penetrate the skin at approximately a 30- to 45-degree angle (Fig. 28-37). While pulling on the plunger of the syringe, push the needle slightly deeper until the radial artery is punctured or until resistance (that is, bone) is met (Fig. 28-38). It is necessary to provide continuous suction on the plunger of the syringe. One can be assured that the radial artery is punctured when blood appears in the hub of the needle. There is some controversy as to whether the needle should be bevel up or bevel down when performing a radial

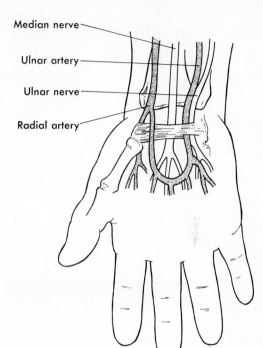

Fig. 28-35. Anatomy of nerves and arteries of wrist (palm up). (Modified from Schreiner, R. L.: Respir. Care vol. 22, 1977.)

Median nerve

Ulnar artery

Ulnar nerve

Radial artery

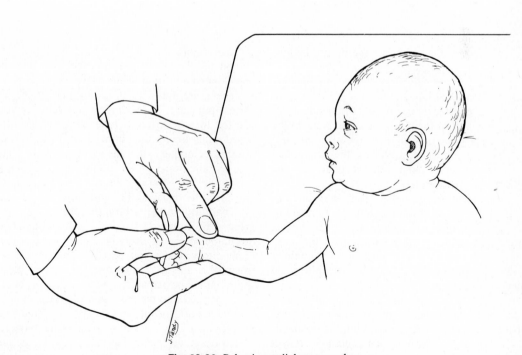

Fig. 28-36. Palpating radial artery pulse.

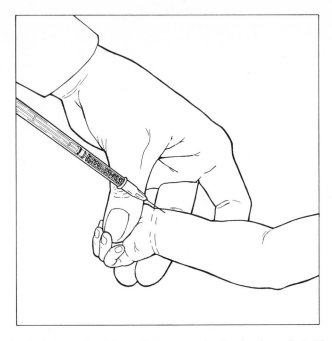

Fig. 28-37. Needle is inserted at 30- to 45-degree angle. Suction is applied. Blood enters syringe when needle enters arterial lumen.

artery puncture in the newborn. We do not believe that this makes any difference because the artery is so small that only a small part of the needle opening is within the arterial lumen.

If resistance is met while pushing the needle deeper, slowly withdraw the needle, staying beneath the skin, and repeat the procedure. After a 0.3 ml sample of blood is obtained, withdraw the needle and apply pressure for 5 minutes or longer to stop the bleeding.

The complications of radial artery puncture include infection, blood loss, arterial laceration, hematoma formation and nerve damage. However, with application of the proper technique, the complication rate should be extremely low. Complications usually arise because of failure to follow the proper technique.

One of the most important complications of any peripheral arterial puncture in the newborn is that the baby may start crying before blood is obtained. The Po_2 and Pco_2 may not then accurately reflect the baby's blood gases before crying; therefore, if

it takes more than a short time to obtain arterial blood and the infant is crying, the procedure should be stopped and tried again later.

There are other methods of performing radial artery puncture. A 25-gauge scalp vein needle connected to a heparinized tuberculin syringe may be used rather than a straight needle. The added benefit of this technique is that the syringe may be changed so that additional blood samples may be obtained. An additional helpful technique is to transilluminate the wrist to visualize the radial artery.

Teaching radial artery puncture. A simulator (Fig. 28-39) may be used to teach and practice the technique of radial artery puncture (Medical Plastics Laboratory, Gatesville, Texas). The simulator consists of a soft arm composed of latex rubber and soft vinyl. The palpable styloid process of the radius incorporated into the simulator provides an anatomical landmark for locating the artery. A radial pulse is provided by a lever in the rear of the model. The intensity of the pulse may be varied so the novice can see the pulsation. As the trainee becomes more

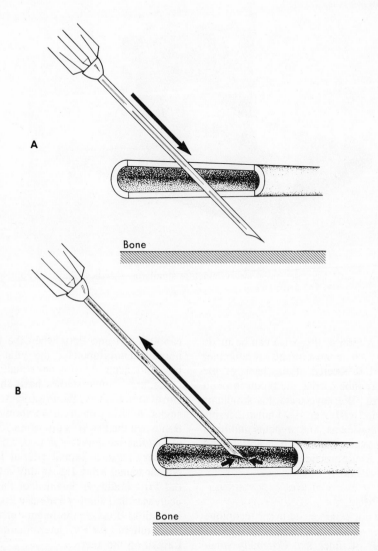

Fig. 28-38. If needle traverses artery, **A,** blood may be obtained when needle is slowly withdrawn, **B.** (Modified from Schreiner, R. L., editor: Care of the newborn, New York, 1981, Raven Press.)

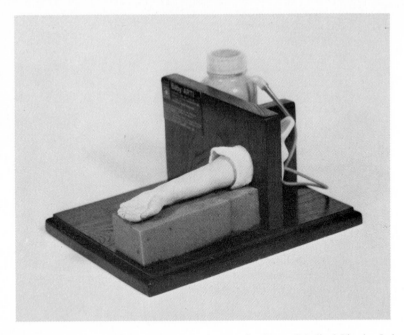

Fig. 28-39. Baby ''Arti'' neonatal radial artery puncture simulator. (Medical Plastics Laboratory, Gatesville, Texas.)

familiar with the procedure, the pulse can be made barely detectable as it is in most infants. A container of simulated blood is located at the back of the model, and a rubber tube carries the blood through the arm to the wrist. We have used this simulator for over 5 years with well over 1000 nurses, respiratory therapists, physicians, and students and have found it extremely successful in demonstrating and allowing the students to practice the technique before going to the bedside.

"Capillary" sticks

Many nurses are not experienced in the technique of arterial puncture. In addition, there is an obvious limit to the number of times that extremely small vessels can be successfully aspirated by a needle. Because of the limitations of these blood sampling techniques, capillary or ''arterialized'' blood has been used. Such samples are usually obtained from the heel. Many investigators have compared the pH, Pco_2 and Po_2 of capillary and arterial samples and have shown a good correlation of the arterial and

capillary pH and Pco_2 when the blood pressure is normal. Unfortunately, the vital measurement of oxygen tension (Po_2) is not equally reliable by both procedures. Some studies have shown a very poor correlation between the Po_2 by arterial and capillary sticks, whereas others have shown a good correlation when the Po_2 is below 60 to 70 mm Hg. Almost all studies have shown a poor correlation between capillary (heelstick) and arterial Po_2 if the Po_2 is greater than 70 mm Hg. In this case, either an arterial Po_2 should be obtained or the FIO_2 should be decreased and another capillary Po_2 obtained. Capillary sticks done on the fingers or toes are probably more reliable for Po_2 determination than those performed on the heel.

A sterile 3-mm lancet is used; a scalpel blade should never be used. Wrap the infant's foot with a warm, but not hot, towel or diaper for 3 minutes. Cleanse the heel with alcohol. Puncture the skin with a single stab on a lateral portion of the foot, just anterior to the heel. Never slash at the heel. Discard the first drop of blood and then allow free flow of blood into a heparinized capillary tube. Place the tip of the tube as near the puncture site as possible to avoid exposing the blood to environmental oxygen. Avoid collecting air in the tube. Avoid excessive squeezing of the foot, since considerable tissue damage may result, and the Po_2 may be artificially lowered. Collect 0.3 ml of blood in the capillary tube and then aspirate the blood into a heparinized tuberculin syringe. Apply a dry pressure dressing to the pressure site until bleeding ceases.

Improperly done, heelsticks can cause lacerations, blood loss, infections, and chronic scarring. The frequency of such complications is low when performed by trained personnel. *The most important potential complication of heelstick blood gases is obtaining false information that may result in the infant being exposed to improper amounts of supplemental oxygen.* Heelstick blood gases should not be used during the first 24 hours of life, when the infant is hypotensive, if there is evidence of peripheral vasoconstriction, or when there is marked bruising of the heel. Additionally, when the capillary Pao_2 is greater than 70 mm Hg, an arterial Pao_2 must be obtained or the FIO_2 decreased and the arterial Po_2 repeated.

APPENDICES

Appendix A

Guidelines for intravenous fat infusions (Intralipid)*

Intralipid, available from Cutter, is a fat emulsion for intravenous infusion in parenteral nutrition. Since the emulsion is isotonic, a central catheter is not required. In the outline that follows, the guidelines for utilization are set forth.

I. Intralipid is available in 10% or 20% concentration. Only the 10% emulsion will be used.
   A. Contents
      1. Soybean oil, 10%
      2. Egg yolk phospholipids, 1.2%
      3. Glycerol, 2.25%
      4. NaOH to adjust the pH to 5.5 to 9.0
   B. Fat distribution
      1. Linoleic acid, the only essential fatty acid, 54%
      2. Oleic acid, 26%
      3. Palmitic acid, 9%
      4. Lineolenic acid, 8%
   C. Caloric value = 1.1 cal/ml (10% emulsion)
   D. Osmolarity = 280 mOsm/L
II. Indications
   A. Calories: The use of Intralipid should be restricted to those patients who are expected to have a long-term energy requirement that cannot be met by alimentary tract feedings. The iso-osmolarity allows the fluid to be given via the peripheral route. Therefore, in cases of infants requiring peripheral vein nutrition, Intralipid may be used to increase the number of calories being provided the patient. Intralipid should make up no more than 40% of the total caloric intake of the patient. Carbohydrate and a source of amino

acid should comprise the remaining 60% or more of the caloric input.
   B. Provision of essential fatty acids (linoleic acid): Those infants who are on long-term total parenteral nutrition without administration of fat may develop essential fatty acid deficiency. At least 8% to 10% of caloric input should probably be supplied by Intralipid for such infants.
III. Contraindications
   A. Abnormal fat metabolism: Pathological hyperlipemia, lipoid nephrosis, acute pancreatitis.
   B. Intralipid may not be mixed with any other solution within the container. Filters may not be used.
   C. No Intralipid preparation may be used if the emulsion appears to be breaking down or "oiling out" on the surface.
   D. Caution should be exercised in the administration of Intralipid to those patients with severe liver damage, pulmonary disease, anemia, coagulopathy, or any infant in whom there is a risk of fat embolism.
   E. Neonates with jaundice should probably not receive Intralipid because of the risk of competition for bilirubin-albumin binding sites.
   F. Premature and small-for-gestational-age infants may have decreased ability to clear the plamsa of fat.
IV. Administration
   A. Dosage: The maximum dose is 4 g/kg/day or 40 cal/kg/day. The initial rate should be 0.1 ml/min for the first 15 minutes to ascertain the presence of idiosyncratic or allergic reactions. The rate may then be increased to administer 1 gm/kg/day (10 ml/kg/day) on the first day, 2 gm/kg/day (20 ml/kg/day) on the second day, 3 gm/kg/day (30 ml/kg/day) on the third day, and maximally 4 gm/kg/day (40 ml/kg/day) on the fourth and subsequent days. The total daily dose

---

*Modified from Ballantine, T., et al.: Guidelines for intravenous fat infusions, James Whitcomb Riley Children's Hospital, September, 1976.

should be administered at a constant rate over a 24-hour period. It should never be given in less than a 4-hour period or faster than 10 ml/kg/ 4 hr.

B. Route: Intralipid should be infused separately from any other intravenously administered solution. It may be infused into the same peripheral vein simultaneously as carbohydrate–amino acid solutions by means of a Y connector or stopcock located near the infusion site. No solutions or additives may be put into the fat emulsion bottle. Likewise, Intralipid may not be added to other infusate bottles. Intralipids should not usually be given through a central alimentation line. For those patients on long-term total parenteral nutrition (with a central line), a peripheral IV may be started and 20 to 30 ml of Intralipid/kg of body weight given twice weekly.

C. Monitoring

1. Hyperlipemia: The nurse should obtain a capillary tube of blood once a shift (q 8 h) and centrifuge the tube. If the serum is cloudy (graded on a 1 to 4 scale), the nurse may stop intravenous Intralipid (but not the amino acid–glucose mixture) and should notify the physician immediately. All spun hematocrit tubes should be saved and dated on a sheet at the baby's bedside for evaluation by the physician.

2. Weekly CBC with platelet count and liver function tests (SGOT, SGPT, bilirubin) should be obtained.

3. Weekly evaluation of serum triglycerides, cholesterol, and free fatty acids should be performed. If the triglyceride level is greater than 300 mg/dl or the free fatty acid is greater than 1000 μM/L, the attending physician should be consulted.

V. Complications

A. Acute

1. The immediate and early adverse reactions occur in less than 1% of patients. They include dyspnea, cyanosis, allergic reactions, hypercoagulability, fever, flushing, and thrombocytopenia in some neonates.

B. Delayed

1. Hepatomegaly, splenomegaly, thrombocytopenia, anemia, leukopenia and abnormalities of liver function tests have been found.

2. Deposition of a brown pigment in the reticuloendothelial system has been described. Its significance is unknown.

3. Free fatty acids may compete with bilirubin-albumin binding and increase the risk of kernicterus.

4. Animals and adult volunteers have transiently decreased pulmonary diffusion capacities following rapid infusion of intravenous fat. Thus infants with pulmonary disease might develop further compromise of pulmonary function if Intralipid is infused at a rate exceeding the infant's ability to metabolize it.

BIBLIOGRAPHY

Borreson, H. C., and Knutrud, O.: Intravenous feeding in pediatric surgery by peripheral veins, Infusiontherapie 2(Suppl): 23, 1973.

Chaptal, J., et al.: Study on lipid and nitrogen parenteral alimentation in the child and in dehydrated infants, Ann. Pediatr. **11**:441, 1964.

Coran, A. G.: Total intravenous feedings of infants and children without the use of a central venous catheter, Ann. Surg. **179**: 445, 1974.

Heo, M. T., et al.: Total intravenous nutrition: experience with fat emulsions and hypertonic glucose, Arch. Surg. **106**:792, 1973.

Jeejeebhoy K. N., et al.: Total parenteral nutrition at home for 23 months, without complication, and with good rehabilitation: a study of technical and metabolic features, Gastroenterol. **65**:811, 1973.

Jeejeebhoy, K. N., et al.: Total parenteral nutrition nutrient needs and technical tips, Part I, Mod. Med. Can. **29**:73, 1974.

O'Neill, J. A., et al.: Variations in intravenous nutrition in the management of catabolic states in infants and children, J. Pediatr. Surg. **9**:889, 1974.

Wilmore, D. W., Moylan, J. A., and Helmkamp, G. M.: Clinical evaluation of a 10% intravenous fat emulsion for parenteral nutrition in thermally injured patients, Ann. Surg. **178**:503, 1973.

Winters R. W., and Hasselmeyer, E. G., editors: Intravenous nutrition in high-risk infants, New York, 1975, John Wiley & Sons, Inc.

Guidelines for the use of peripheral alimentation*

The provision of nutrition for infants in whom gastric feedings is insufficient, or must be withheld, is a significant problem. The use of peripheral alimentation may provide near-optimum nutrition on a short-term basis without the complexities and the potentially serious complications of centrally administered alimentation fluids. The purpose here is to provide guidelines for the administration of peripheral alimentation fluid to patients.

DESCRIPTION

The peripheral alimentation fluid is usually prepared daily by the pharmacy staff on the physician's prescription. The prepared solution is intended for infusion via a peripheral vein within 24 hours of its preparation. The composition of the solution can be varied to provide for the individual requirements and tolerances of different patients. In general, it is desirable to provide 2.4 to 3 gm protein/kg/day, with the remainder of calories supplied by carbohydrates and/or fats. The specific requirements for the various vitamins, minerals, and trace elements are not completely known. The values here suggested are reflections of oral requirements, suggested central alimentation fluid supplementation, or limitations of admixture incompatibilities (for example, calcium).

INDICATIONS

At present there are two indications for the use of peripheral alimentation fluid:

1. In the low birth weight infant in whom adequate oral intake cannot promptly be accomplished, whether because of severe immaturity or underlying illness (for example, severe RDS)
2. In the infant in whom feedings must be withheld for a prolonged period (for example, necrotizing enterocolitis)

CONTRAINDICATIONS

There are very few contraindications to the use of peripheral alimentation with amino acid and glucose solution. If an intravenous fat emulsion (Intralipid) is used, please refer to the Appendix A for the specific contraindications of intravenous fat infusions.

ADMINISTRATION

Route. Peripheral alimentation fluid is intended for the use of peripheral venous administration via a scalp vein needle or intracatheter. The use of the umbilical arterial catheter is to be discouraged; however, under certain circumstances (for example, <1 kg infant) it may be necessary to use this route. This must be first approved by the neonatal fellow and/or attending neonatologist.

Dosage. The peripheral alimentation fluid should be individualized for the patient. The following are only recommended guidelines:

1. Start at a dextrose concentration that is presently being tolerated by the patient.
2. Start at an infusion rate that meets the fluid requirements of the patient.
3. The infusion rate or the glucose concentration may be increased daily.
4. Avoid large fluctuations in the infusion rate by use of a constant infusion pump and by restarting IV promptly.

*Modified from: Guidelines for the use of peripheral alimentation, James Whitcomb Riley Children's Hospital.

Table B-1. To prepare 2% FreAmine, 250 ml

	Dextrose			
	5%	**7.5%**	**10%**	**12.5%**
FreAmine II	60.0 ml	60.0 ml	60.0 ml	60.0 ml
$D_{50}W$	25.0 ml	37.5 ml	50.0 ml	62.5 ml
Na lactate (5 mEq/ml)			1.25 ml	
KCl (2 mEq/ml)			0.5 ml	
Ca gluconate (10%)			3.0 ml	
Potassium phosphate (2 mEq/ml)			2.0 ml	
Mg sulfate (8.12 mEq/2 ml)			0.25 ml	
Multivitamins for infusion			0.5 ml	
Folvite (5000 μg/ml)			0.0125 ml	
Sterile water: qs ad 250 ml				
Calories/milliliter	0.24	0.33	0.41	0.50
At infusion rate of 120 ml/kg/day				
Cal/kg/day	28.8	39.6	49.2	60.0
Gm protein/kg/day	2.4	2.4	2.4	2.4
Gm glucose/kg/day	6.0	9.0	12.0	15.0
At infusion rate of 150 ml/kg/day				
Cal/kg/day	36.0	49.5	61.5	75.0
Gm protein/kg/day	3.0	3.0	3.0	3.0
Gm glucose/kg/day	7.5	11.25	15.0	18.75
At infusion rate of 180 ml/kg/day				
Cal/kg/day	43.0	59.4	73.8	90.0
Gm protein/kg/day	3.6	3.6	3.6	3.6
Gm glucose/kg/day	9.0	13.5	18.0	22.5

5. If the patient is on peripheral alimentation for for more than 1 week, the following should be given by intramuscular injection weekly:
   a. Phytonadione (Aquamephyton), 1 mg/wk, IM
   b. Vitamin B_{12}, 100 μg/wk, IM
6. As feedings are tolerated, the peripheral alimentation fluid infusion can be slowly decreased. Do not abruptly discontinue the peripheral alimentation fluid.
7. A new prescription must be sent to the pharmacy daily in the early morning.
8. See Tables B-1 and B-2.

Use of Intralipid. An intravenous fat emulsion to provide additional calories and essential fatty acids is available, provided specific contraindications to its use are not present. It can provide an additional 30 to 40 calories/kg/day and thus may account for 30% to 40% of the total calories. As the Intralipid infusion is increased, the alimentation fluid rate may need to be decreased to avoid overhydration. Before using Intralipid refer to Appendix A.

Table B-2. The standard peripheral alimentation solution provides the following concentration of nutrients per kilogram of body weight at the given infusion rate

	Infusion rate		
Nutrients	**120 ml/ kg/day**	**150 ml/ kg/day**	**180 ml/ kg/day**
Na (mEq)	3.3	4.1	4.9
K (mEq)	2.4	3.0	3.6
Ca (mEq)	0.6	0.8	1.0
Mg (mEq)	0.5	0.6	0.7
PO_3 (mEq)	2.5	3.1	3.7
Folic acid (μg)	29.8	37.2	44.6
Ascorbic acid (μg)	24.0	30.0	36.0
Vitamin A (IU)	480.0	600.0	720.0
Vitamin D (IU)	48.0	60.0	72.0
Thiamine (mg)	2.4	3.0	3.6
Riboflavin (mg)	0.5	0.6	0.7
Pyridoxine (mg)	0.7	0.9	1.1
Niacinamide (mg)	4.8	6.0	7.2
Vitamin E (IU)	0.24	0.3	0.35

Monitoring. The following are the recommended laboratory tests that should be routinely monitored on all patients on peripheral alimentation fluids.

	First week	After first week
Urinary specific gravity and glucose	q shift	q day
Serum electrolytes, total protein, calcium, BUN, glucose, and hematocrit	2 to 3 ×/week	q week
Blood acid-base (pH and Pco_2 or total CO_2)	q day	q week
Liver function	q week	q week

Additional tests may be required if intravenous fat infusions are used. Daily weight and weekly length and head circumference measurements should be obtained and plotted on growth charts.

COMPLICATIONS

Among the possible complications are the following:

1. Phlebitis
2. Infection
3. Hyper- or hypoglycemia
4. Electrolyte disturbances
5. Hyperchloremic metabolic acidosis
6. Azotemia
7. Glucosuria
8. Eosinophilia
9. Necrosis at infusion site

BIBLIOGRAPHY

Ballantine, T., et al.: Guidelines for intravenous fat infusions, James Whitcomb Riley Children's Hospital, September, 1976.

Benda, G. I., and Babson, S. G.: Peripheral intravenous alimentation of the small premature infant, J. Pediatr. **79:**494, 1971.

Bryan, M. H., et al.: Supplemental intravenous alimentation in low birth weight infants, J. Pediatr. **82:**940, 1973.

Cashore, W. J., Sedaghatian, M. R., and Usher, R. H.: Nutritional supplements with intravenously administered lipid, protein hydrolysate, and glucose in small premature infants, Pediatrics **56:**8, 1975.

Coran, A. G.: The long-term total intravenous feeding of infants using peripheral veins, J. Pediatr. Surg. **8:**801, 1973.

Fomon, S. J., editor: Infant nutrition, Philadelphia, 1974, W. B. Saunders Co.

Fox, J. A., and Krasna, I. H.: Total intravenous nutrition by peripheral vein in neonatal surgical patients, Pediatrics **52:**14, 1973.

Heird, W. C., and Driscoll, J. M., Jr.: Newer methods for feeding low birth weight infants, Pediatr. Clin. North Am. **2:**309, 1975.

Pildes, R. S., Ramamurthy, R. S., Cordero, G. V., and Wong, P. W. K.: Intravenous supplementation of L-amino acids and dextrose in low birth weight infants, J. Pediatr. **82:**945, 1973.

Index